London: Underground

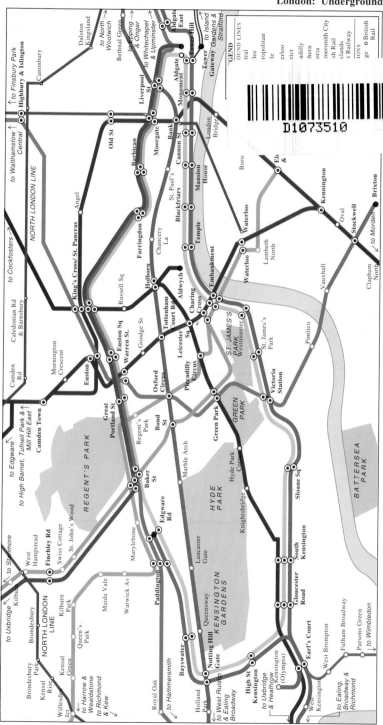

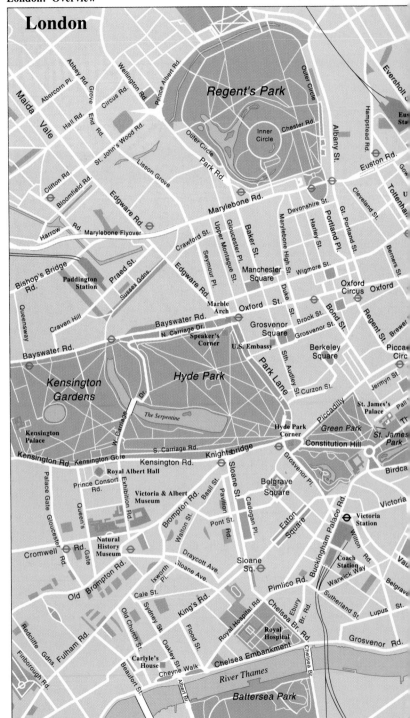

London

Regent's Park

Maida Vale

Abbey Rd Grove

Abercorn Pl.

Wellington Rd.

Circus Rd.

Prince Albert Rd.

Hall Rd.

End Rd.

Outer Circle

Inner Circle

Chester Rd.

Albany St.

Hampstead Rd.

Eus Sta

St. John's Wood Rd.

Lisson Grove

Park Rd.

Euston Rd.

Gow

Clifton Rd.

Bloomfield Rd.

Edgware Rd

Marylebone Rd.

Devonshire St.

Cleveland St.

Tottenhai

Harrow   Rd.

Marylebone Flyover

Crawford St.

Gloucester Pl.

Upper Montague St.

Baker St.

Marylebone High St.

Harley St.

Portland Pl.

Gt. Portland St.

U

Berners St.

Bishop's Bridge Rd.

Paddington Station

Praed St.

Sussex Gdns.

Edgware Rd.

Seymour Pl.

Manchester Square

Wigmore St.

Oxford Circus

Oxford

Queensway

Craven Hill

Bayswater Rd.

N. Carriage Dr.

Marble Arch

Speaker's Corner

Oxford   St.

Duke   St.

Grosvenor Square

Brook St.

Grosvenor St.

Bond St.

Regent St.

Brewer

Bayswater Rd.

U.S. Embassy

Sth. Audley St.

Park Lane

Curzon St.

Berkeley Square

Picca Circ

Kensington Gardens

Hyde Park

The Serpentine

Dr.

N. Carriage

Piccadilly

Hyde Park Corner

Green Park

St. James's Palace

Jermyn St.

Pall

Tr

Kensington Palace

Kensington Rd.

Kensington Gore

S. Carriage Rd.

Kensington Rd.

Knightsbridge

Constitution Hill

St. James Park

Birdca

Palace Gate

Gloucester Rd.

Queen's Gate

Prince Consort Rd.

Exhibition Rd.

Royal Albert Hall

Victoria & Albert Museum

Brompton Rd.

Walton St.

Basil St.

Sloane St.

Pavilion

Pont St.

Cadogan Pl.

Belgrave Square

Eaton Square

Buckingham Palace Rd.

Grosvenor Pl.

Wilton Rd.

Victoria

Victoria Station

Cromwell   Rd.

Natural History Museum

Old   Brompton Rd.

Ixworth Pl.

Draycott Ave.

Sloane Ave.

Sloane Sq.

Coach Station

Warwick Way

Vau

Belgrave

Redcliffe Gdns.

Fulham Rd.

Old Church St.

Sydney St.

Cale St.

King's Rd.

Flood St.

Oakley St.

Royal Hospital Rd.

Pimlico Rd.

Chelsea Br. Rd.

Ebury Br. Rd.

Sutherland St.

Lupus St.

Grosvenor   Rd.

Finborough Rd.

Beaufort St.

Carlyle's House

Cheyne Walk

Albert Br.

Chelsea Embankment

Chelsea Br.

River Thames

Royal Hospital

Battersea Park

King's Cross Station

Pentonville Rd.

City Rd.

St. Pancras Station

King's Cross Rd.

Gray's Inn Rd.

Rosebery Ave.

St. John's St.

Lever St.

Goswell Rd.

Bath St.

East Road

Hoxton St.

Old St.

Kingsland Rd.

City Rd.

Gt. Eastern St.

Shoreditch High St.

Commercial St.

Judd St.

Coram's Fields

Woburn Pl.

Guilford St.

Southampton Row

Farringdon Rd.

Theobalds Rd.

Clerkenwell Rd.

Aldersgate

Moorgate

Barbican Centre

Liverpool St. Station

Charterhouse St.

Smithfield Market

London Wall

Bishopsgate

Houndsditch

ish um

New Oxford St.

Holborn

High

Kingsway

Drury La.

Chancery La.

Fetter La.

Holborn Viaduct

Old Bailey

Newgate St.

St. Paul's

Cheapside

Bank of England

Cornhill

Gracechurch St.

Leadenhall St.

Fenchurch St.

Law Courts

Aldwych

Fleet St.

Queen Victoria St.

Cannon St.

St. Eastcheap

The Tower

Strand

Victoria Embankment

Blackfriars Br.

Blackfriars Station

Southwark Br.

Cannon St. Station

London Br.

Upper Thames St.

Tower Hill

National Gallery

Charing Cross Stn.

Waterloo Br.

National Theatre

Royal Festival Hall

Stamford St.

Southwark St.

River Thames

Todley St.

Tower Br.

ar e

Whitehall

York Rd.

The Cut

Waterloo Station

Waterloo Rd.

Blackfriars Rd.

Union St.

St. Thomas St.

London Bridge Station

Borough High St.

Long La.

Bridge Rd.

Abbey St.

Westminster Br.

Houses of Parliament

Westminster Br. Rd.

Borough Rd.

London Rd.

Tabard St.

Great Dover St.

Harper Rd.

Tower

Willow Walk

Millbank

Lambeth Br.

Lambeth Rd.

Lambeth Palace Rd.

Kennington Rd.

Imperial War Museum

New Kent Rd.

Rodney Pl.

Flint St.

East St.

Old Kent Rd.

erry Rd.

ate llery

Albert Embankment

Black Prince Rd.

Kennington Park Rd.

Crampton St.

Walworth Rd.

Portland St.

Thurlow St.

Vauxhall Br.

Kennington La.

Manor Pl.

Braganza St.

Albany Rd.

Vauxhall Station

Kennington Oval

N

| 0 | 1/2 mile |
| 0 | 1/2 kilometer |

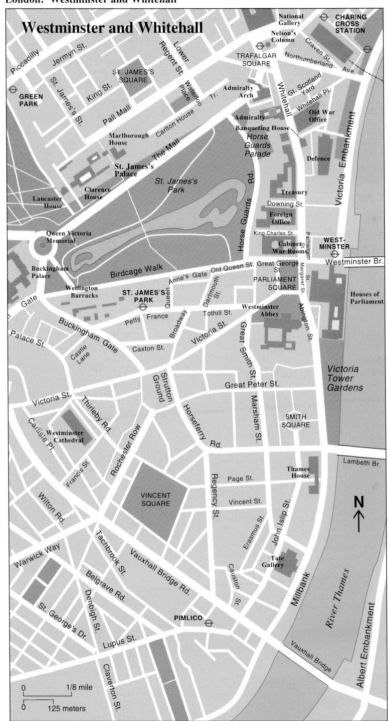

Westminster and Whitehall

National Gallery
CHARING CROSS STATION
Nelson's Column
Craven St.
TRAFALGAR SQUARE
Northumberland Ave.
Piccadilly
Jermyn St.
Lower Regent St.
Waterloo Place
Admiralty Arch
Whitehall
Gt. Scotland Yard
Whitehall Pl.
ST. JAMES'S SQUARE
King St.
St. James's St.
GREEN PARK
Pall Mall
Carlton House Tr.
Admiralty
Old War Office
Banqueting House
Horse Guards Parade
Marlborough House
The Mall
Defence
St. James's Palace
St. James's Park
Horse Guards Rd.
Treasury
Clarence House
Downing St.
Lancaster House
Foreign Office
King Charles St.
WEST-MINSTER
Queen Victoria Memorial
Cabinet War Rooms
Westminster Br.
Buckingham Palace
Birdcage Walk
Anne's Gate
Old Queen St.
Great George St.
Parliament St.
Margaret St.
Wellington Barracks
ST. JAMES'S PARK
PARLIAMENT SQUARE
Gate
Dartmouth St.
Broadway
Tothill St.
Westminster Abbey
Abingdon St.
Houses of Parliament
Buckingham Gate
Petty France
Victoria St.
Caxton St.
Great Smith St.
Palace St.
Castle Lane
Victoria Tower Gardens
Victoria St.
Thirleby Rd.
Stratton Ground
Great Peter St.
Marsham St.
Carlisle Pl.
Westminster Cathedral
Horseferry Rd.
SMITH SQUARE
Francis St.
Rochester Row
VINCENT SQUARE
Page St.
Thames House
Lambeth Br.
Wilton Rd.
Regency St.
Vincent St.
Erasmus St.
John Islip St.
Tate Gallery
Warwick Way
Tachbrook St.
Vauxhall Bridge Rd.
Belgrave Rd.
Causton St.
Millbank
River Thames
St. George's Dr.
Denbigh St.
PIMLICO
Albert Embankment
Lupus St.
Claverton St.
Vauxhall Bridge
Victoria Embankment

N
↑

0   1/8 mile
0   125 meters

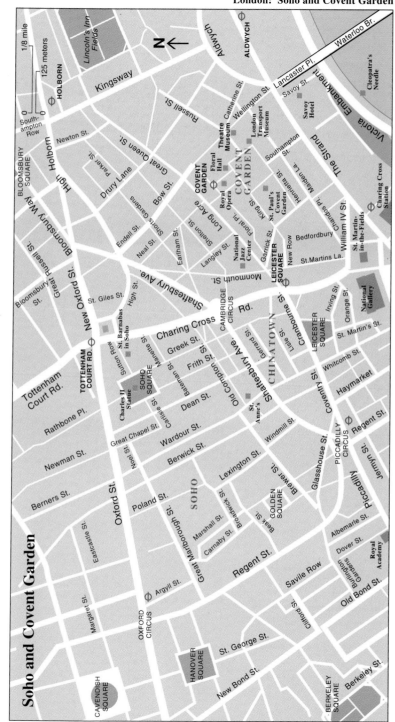

London: Soho and Covent Garden

Soho and Covent Garden

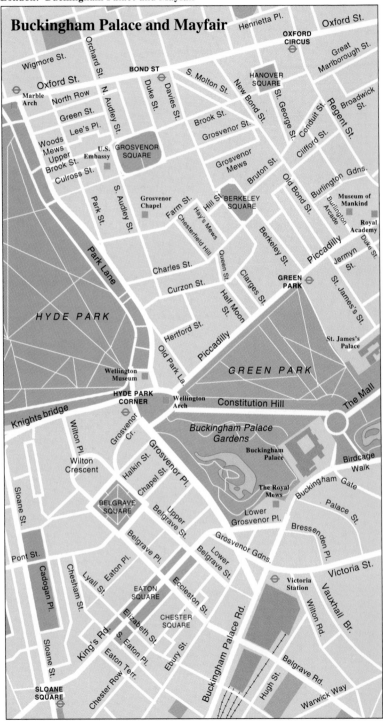

Buckingham Palace and Mayfair

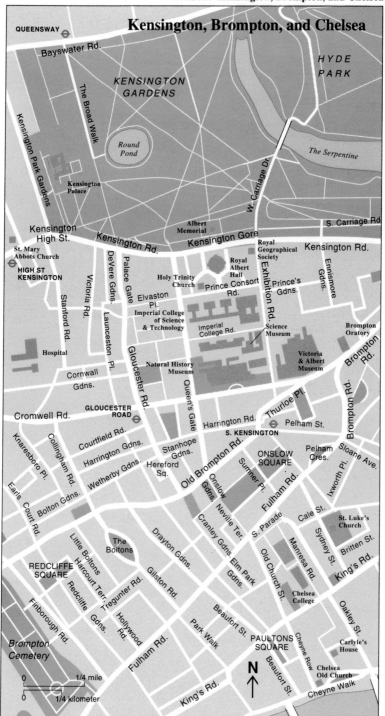

Kensington, Brompton, and Chelsea

The City

Let's Go
LONDON

is the best book for anyone traveling on a budget. Here's why:

▧ No other guidebook has as many budget listings.

In London, we list over 2,500 budget travel bargains. We tell you the cheapest way to get around, and where to get an inexpensive and satisfying meal once you've arrived. We give hundreds of money-saving tips that anyone can use, plus invaluable advice on discounts and deals for students, children, families, and senior travelers.

▧ Let's Go researchers have to make it on their own.

Our Harvard-Radcliffe researcher-writers travel on budgets as tight as your own—no expense accounts, no free hotel rooms.

▧ Let's Go is completely revised each year.

We don't just update the prices, we go back to the place. If a charming café has become an overpriced tourist trap, we'll replace the listing with a new and better one.

▧ No other guidebook includes all this:

Honest, engaging coverage of the city and beyond; up-to-the-minute prices, directions, addresses, phone numbers, and opening hours; in-depth essays on local culture, history, and politics; comprehensive listings on transportation between and within regions and cities; straight advice on work and study, budget accommodations, sights, nightlife, and food; detailed maps; and much more.

▧ Let's Go is for anyone who wants to see London on a budget.

Books by Let's Go, Inc.

EUROPE

Let's Go: Europe

Let's Go: Austria & Switzerland

Let's Go: Britain & Ireland

Let's Go: Eastern Europe

Let's Go: France

Let's Go: Germany

Let's Go: Greece & Turkey

Let's Go: Ireland

Let's Go: Italy

Let's Go: London

Let's Go: Paris

Let's Go: Rome

Let's Go: Spain & Portugal

NORTH & CENTRAL AMERICA

Let's Go: USA & Canada

Let's Go: Alaska & The Pacific Northwest

Let's Go: California

Let's Go: New York City

Let's Go: Washington, D.C.

Let's Go: Mexico

MIDDLE EAST & ASIA

Let's Go: Israel & Egypt

Let's Go: Thailand

Let's Go

The Budget Guide to

LONDON

1995

Julie E. Cooper
Editor

Written by
Let's Go, Inc.
A subsidiary of
Harvard Student Agencies, Inc.

St. Martin's Press ■ **New York**

HELPING LET'S GO

If you have suggestions or corrections, or just want to share your discoveries, drop us a line. We read every piece of correspondence, whether a 10-page e-mail letter, a velveteen Elvis postcard, or, as in one case, a collage. All suggestions are passed along to our researcher-writers. Please note that mail received after May 5, 1995 will probably be too late for the 1996 book, but will be retained for the following edition.
Address mail to:

> **Let's Go: London**
> **Let's Go, Inc.**
> **I Story Street**
> **Cambridge, MA 02138**
> **USA**

Or send e-mail (please include in the subject header the titles of the *Let's Go* guides you discuss in your message) to:
> **letsgo@delphi.com**

In addition to the invaluable travel advice our readers share with us, many are kind enough to offer their services as researchers or editors. Unfortunately, the charter of Let's Go, Inc. and Harvard Student Agencies, Inc. enables us to employ only currently enrolled Harvard students.

About Let's Go

Back in 1960, a few students at Harvard University got together to produce a 20-page pamphlet offering a collection of tips on budget travel in Europe. For three years, Harvard Student Agencies, a student-run nonprofit corporation, had been doing a brisk business booking charter flights to Europe; this modest, mimeographed packet was offered to passengers as an extra. The following year, students traveling to Europe researched the first full-fledged edition of *Let's Go: Europe*, a pocket-sized book featuring advice on shoestring travel, irreverent write-ups of sights, and a decidedly youthful slant.

Throughout the 60s, the guides reflected the times: one section of the 1968 *Let's Go: Europe* talked about "Street Singing in Europe on No Dollars a Day." During the 70s, *Let's Go* gradually became a large-scale operation, adding regional European guides and expanding coverage into North Africa and Asia. The '80s saw the arrival of *Let's Go: USA & Canada* and *Let's Go: Mexico*, as well as regional North American guides; in the '90s we introduced five in-depth city guides to Paris, London, Rome, New York City, and Washington, DC. And as the budget travel world expands, so do we; the first edition of *Let's Go: Thailand* hit the shelves last year, and this year's edition adds coverage of Malaysia, Singapore, Tokyo, and Hong Kong.

This year we're proud to announce the birth of *Let's Go: Eastern Europe*—the most comprehensive guide to this renascent region, with more practical information and insider tips than any other. *Let's Go: Eastern Europe* brings our total number of titles, with their spirit of adventure and reputation for honesty, accuracy, and editorial integrity, to 21.

We've seen a lot in 35 years. *Let's Go: Europe* is now the world's #1 best selling international guide, translated into seven languages. And our guides are still researched, written, and produced entirely by students who know first-hand how to see the world on the cheap.

Every spring, we recruit over 100 researchers and 50 editors to write our books anew. Come summertime, after several months of training, researchers hit the road for seven weeks of exploration, from Bangkok to Budapest, Anchorage to Ankara. With pen and notebook in hand, a few changes of underwear stuffed in our backpacks, and a budget as tight as yours, we visit every *pensione*, *palapa*, pizzeria, café, club, campground, or castle we can find to make sure you'll get the most out of *your* trip.

We've put the best of our discoveries into the book you're now holding. A brand-new edition of each guide hits the shelves every year, only months after it is researched, so you know you're getting the most reliable, up-to-date, and comprehensive information available. The budget travel world is constantly changing, and where other guides quickly become obsolete, our annual research keeps you abreast of the very latest travel insights. And even as you read this, work on next year's editions is well underway.

At *Let's Go*, we think of budget travel not only as a means of cutting down on costs, but as a way of breaking down a few walls as well. Living cheap and simple on the road brings you closer to the real people and places you've been saving up to visit. This book will ease your anxieties and answer your questions about the basics—to help *you* get off the beaten track and explore. We encourage you to put *Let's Go* away now and then and strike out on your own. As any seasoned traveler will tell you, the best discoveries are often those you make yourself. If you find something worth sharing, drop us a line. We're at Let's Go, Inc., 1 Story Street, Cambridge, MA, 02138, USA (e-mail: letsgo@delphi.com).

Happy travels!

Table of Contents

Gain 500 pounds within minutes.

Sometimes there's no such thing as unwanted pounds. At those times, it's nice to know that with Western Union you can receive money from the States within minutes, in case the situation arises. Plus it's already converted into pounds.

So just call either the toll-free number in London, 0-800-833-833*, or the United States, 1-800-325-6000*, and then pick up your money at any Western Union location.

Traveling can be a lot easier if you're packing a few extra pounds.

WESTERN UNION | MONEY TRANSFER
The fastest way to send money worldwide.^{SM}

List of Maps

Acknowledgments

This book could not have been completed without Pete Keith's sharp editing, willing assistance, and respectful oversight. Liz Stein and Alexis Averbuck were always patient when I hounded them with production queries. I could not have navigated the byzantine arcana of Phone Day without Emily Hobson and Dan Glover. While I grew increasingly frazzled, Lisa retained a cheerful equanimity when helping me with last minute entries. Erica proofread assiduously, and did not poke me once. Unsolicited, Steve arrived with snacks when they were most needed. Miranda shared in my late-night delirium. Sean helped me solve many a dilemma.

Jen Cox and Jim Ebenhoh always stayed up to watch *120 Minutes*. Their warmth, companionship, and encyclopedic knowledge of punk rock and pop culture enriched my summer significantly. Stuart SM Sutcliffe (a.k.a. the third Toddler) was never more than a phone call away; he unhesitatingly provided confidence, levity, and rhythmic acumen. I am indebted to Alp Aker, who taught me to play the bass. Like Holmes, Alp's "lounging languid figure" belies an incisive mind; in our many conversations, he always sought to exercise linguistic care. Generic constraints prevent me from expressing my utter gratitude to and affection for my friends, too many of whom summered in far-flung locales. According me their unreserved respect, my parents and sister have given me constant love and support.

—J.E.C.

HOW TO USE THIS BOOK

London: An Introduction fills you in on London's history, politics, architecture, art, music, manners, and mores. **Essentials** offers practical advice for before you go and after you arrive. **Planning Your Trip,** with its information on necessary documents, useful maps, and currency, will help you think ahead. Here we offer special tips and resources for students, seniors, families, women, people with disabilities, and other travelers with specific needs. **Getting There** gives tips about budget travel to London. **Once There** provides information on useful organizations in London, emergency services, and the layout of the city. We cover the Underground, bus and other services that will help you get around.

In the **Accommodations** section, hostels, halls of residence, and B&Bs are listed in order of value, based on price, location, safety, and comfort. **Food and Drink** includes restaurant reviews organized by neighborhood and accompanied by a full list cross-referenced by type of food, price, hours, and atmosphere. We also provide a detailed list of pubs, tearooms, and groceries. Organized by neighborhood, the **Sights** section gives a sense of the hidden and not-so-hidden treasures in London's maze. **Museums,** from the National Portrait Gallery to Madame Tussaud's, have their own section. London's film, theatre, music, dance, and sports fill the **Entertainment** section. **Shopping,** entertainment for some, includes music stores, England's famous-name department stores, markets, and more. Our section on **Bisexual, Gay, and Lesbian London** offers information on social services and on entertainment. For those hwo want to explore more of England, our many **Daytrips** include university towns, mystic monuments, and sea side resorts as well as practical information on getting around by rail, bus, car, foot, or thumb. Check out our **Appendices** for a list of Bank Holidays and Blue Plaque Houses, musts for any traveler in the know.

Researcher-Writers

Vivian Lin   *London*

Vivian applied her boundless energy and relentless perfectionism to the task of learning London, and came up with some unanticipated results. An artist she encountered while checking pub listings almost painted her as a cherub. While her editor's band toiled away in certain obscurity in a damp Somerville basement, Vivian and Roz almost got signed to a record label, even though Roz has yet to learn to play her instrument. Making her way through Islington, Camden Town, Bloomsbury, and other hipster haunts, Vivian occasionally got carded, but this never prevented her from capturing the city in vivid, accurate, and conscientious detail. Vivian's urbanity will only be deepened by studying at SOAS this fall; we hope that she will send us postcards as perceptive as her copybatches were.

Mimi Schultz   *London*

Mimi evinced an unprecedented enthusiasm for the regions south of the Thames; the Docklands will never be the same again. City planners and enterprising capitalists could not hide their development schemes from Mimi; the success of her penetrating inquiries proves that behind every awesome power station there lurks a lesson to be learned about the contours of the city. In her peregrinations, Mimi consorted with Marxists, co-opers, *Time Out* bar reviewers, and Bad Grrls (or at least acquired their literature), yet still managed to send in detailed, evocative, and voluminous copy batches in which her affinity for both the city and the challenge of researching was palpable. Both as a roomate and as a researcher, Mimi has helped others view cities through illuminating new prisms.

Andy Liu   *Oxford*
Kelli Rae Patton   *Stratford-upon-Avon, Cambridge, Canterbury, Deal, Dover, Rye,*
                          Brighton, Arundel, Portsmouth, Salisbury, Stonehenge, Bath

STAFF

Editor	Julie E. Cooper
Publishing Director	Pete Keith
Production Manager	Alexis G. Averbuck
Production Assistant	Elizabeth J. Stein
Financial Manager	Matt Heid
Assistant General Manager	Anne E. Chisholm
Sales Group Manager	Sherice R. Guillory
Sales Department Coordinator	Andrea N. Taylor
Sales Group Representatives	Eli K. Aheto
	Timur Okay Harry Hiçyılmaz
	Arzhang Kamerei
	Hollister Jane Leopold
	David L. Yuan
President	Lucienne D. Lester
General Manager	Richard M. Olken

Don't forget to write.

Now that you've said, "Let's go," it's time to say
"Let's get American Express® Travelers Cheques." If they are lost or
stolen, you can get a fast and full refund virtually anywhere you
travel. So before you leave be sure and write.

London: An Introduction

At first, London is kind to the expectations of visitors stuffing their mental baggage with bobbies and Beefeaters, nursery rhymes and "Masterpiece Theatre," Sherlock Holmes and history books. The Thamescape is still bounded by the over-familiar Big Ben in the west and the archetypical Tower Bridge in the east; St. Paul's and the Tower of London pop up in between. The relatively small area embraced by the Underground's Circle Line seems filled to bursting with the "big sights." In some neighborhoods, rows of reassuringly English Victorian terraced houses seem to extend endlessly. And the whole world and all its double-decker red buses do seem to spin around the mad whirl of Piccadilly Circus.

But even the most timid of tourists will notice that for some reason, those tube lines spider out a long way from the Circle Line—central London is just a speck on the Greater London map. Beyond Tower Bridge looms the glossy, pyramid-tipped Canary Wharf skyscraper, centerpiece of the world's largest and most controversial redevelopment. Those clunky cabs are actually state-of-the-art traffic-dodging equipment, able to turn 360 degrees in a smaller space than any other car on the road. The Victorian doorway inscribed with an Anglican piety may belong to a Sikh or a Muslim in a city internalizing its imperial past. And glance between the bus fenders at peers and punks swirling around Piccadilly, or at a newsagent overflowing with music and style mags, to know that "culture" means more than the Royal Opera.

What makes London not just "quite interesting" but enthralling can be found partly in this a tension between the close quarters of central London and the expansive boroughs; between the cluttered, "familiar," and sometimes fictional past of the heritage industry and a riotously modern present.

■ HISTORY

In the aftermath of the Great Fire of 1666, as most of London lay an ashy wasteland, ambitious young architect Christopher Wren presented his blueprints for a new city to Charles II. Wren envisioned broad avenues and spacious plazas: London would no longer be a medieval hodgepodge of streets and buildings. But the pragmatic king was well aware that the plan, which took no account of existing property lines, would incense local landowners. So he vetoed Wren's design and the city was rebuilt in the same piecemeal way that it had arisen.

Personal enterprise and ownership have defined London from its founding as the Roman Empire's farthest outpost. Although Roman officials laid out merely the skeleton of a town in 43 AD—a bridge, roads, a mint—the city soon became a thriving purchase and shipping hub for wool, wheat, and metals. Within just a few years, Tacitus described the new Londinium as "a great trading center, full of merchants." With the Romans for protection, the locals were able to concentrate on commerce. But in 61 AD, the Romans failed to prevent Queen Boudicca's Iceni warriors from attacking, looting, and burning the town. To protect it from future raids, the Romans built a large stone fort on the edge of the town. In 200 AD, they added a wall and a wooden stockade, but in 410, with Rome in decline, they left altogether.

London slipped into a period of decay. Celts, Saxons, and Danes squabbled over it until 886 AD, when King Alfred the Great of Wessex recaptured the city. The Danes managed to seize the city from Alfred's successor, Ethelred the Unready. In response, Ethelred enlisted the help of his better-prepared friend Olaf (later a saint), who led a fleet up the Thames to the bridge in 1014. Inventive Olaf tied ropes to the bridge supports and rowed away, pulling the rickety bridge into the river. The

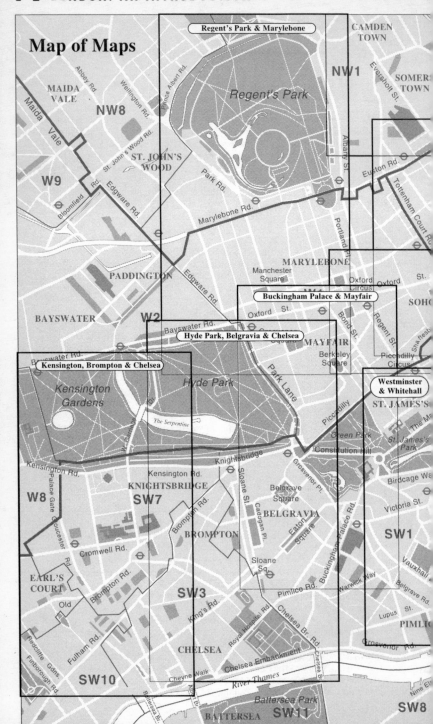

Map of Maps

Regent's Park & Marylebone

CAMDEN TOWN

NW1

SOMER TOWN

MAIDA VALE

NW8

Regent's Park

Abbey Rd.

Wellington Rd.

Prince Albert Rd.

Everisholt St.

St. John's Wood Rd.

ST. JOHN'S WOOD

W9

Maida Vale

Bloomfield Rd.

Edgware Rd.

Park Rd.

Albany St.

Euston Rd.

Tottenham Court Rd.

Marylebone Rd.

Portland Pl.

PADDINGTON

Edgware Rd.

MARYLEBONE

Manchester Square

Oxford Circus

Oxford

St.

SOHO

BAYSWATER

W2

Bayswater Rd.

Buckingham Palace & Mayfair

Oxford St.

Bond St.

Regent St.

Shaftesbury

Bayswater Rd.

Hyde Park, Belgravia & Chelsea

MAYFAIR

Berkeley Square

Piccadilly Circus

Kensington, Brompton & Chelsea

Kensington Gardens

Hyde Park

Park Lane

Piccadilly

Westminster & Whitehall

ST. JAMES'S

The Mall

The Serpentine

Green Park

St. James's Park

Constitution Hill

S. Carriage Dr.

Kensington Rd.

Palace Gate

W8

Kensington Rd.

KNIGHTSBRIDGE

SW7

Knightsbridge

Sloane St.

Grosvenor Pl.

Birdcage Wa

Victoria St.

SW1

Gloucester Rd.

Cromwell Rd.

Brompton Rd.

Belgrave Square

Cadogan Pl.

Buckingham Palace Rd.

EARL'S COURT

Old

Brompton Rd.

BROMPTON

Eaton Square

BELGRAVIA

Warwick Way

Belgrave Rd.

Redcliffe Gdns.

Finborough Rd.

Fulham Rd.

SW3

King's Rd.

Sloane Sq.

Pimlico Rd.

Lupus St.

PIMLIC

CHELSEA

Royal Hospital Rd.

Chelsea Br. Rd.

Grosvenor Rd.

SW10

Cheyne Walk

Chelsea Embankment

River Thames

Chelsea Br.

Nine

BATTERSEA

Battersea Park

SW11

SW8

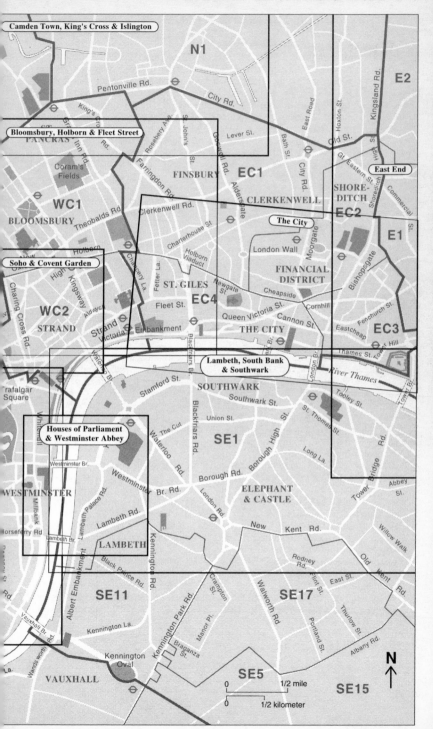

Camden Town, King's Cross & Islington

N1

E2

Pentonville Rd.

City Rd.

East Road

Hoxton St.

Kingsland Rd.

Bloomsbury, Holborn & Fleet Street

King's Cross Rd.

Lever St.

Bath St.

Old St.

Gt. Eastern St.

High St.

Commercial St.

East End

PANCRAS

Coram's Fields

Roseberry Ave.

St. John's

Goswell Rd.

City Rd.

FINSBURY

EC1

SHORE-DITCH

Shoreditch High St.

EC2

E1

WC1

Farringdon Rd.

CLERKENWELL

BLOOMSBURY

Theobalds Rd.

Clerkenwell Rd.

Aldersgate

The City

Holborn

Charterhouse St.

London Wall

Moorgate

Bishopsgate

Holborn

Chancery La.

Holborn Viaduct

FINANCIAL DISTRICT

Soho & Covent Garden

Fetter La.

ST. GILES

Newgate St.

Cheapside

Fenchurch St.

Charing Cross Rd.

High Kingsway

Fleet St.

EC4

Cornhill

EC3

WC2

Aldwych

Queen Victoria St.

Cannon St.

Eastcheap

STRAND

Strand

Victoria Embankment

THE CITY

Tower Hill

Trafalgar Square

Blackfriars Br.

London Br.

Thames St.

Tower Br.

Lambeth, South Bank & Southwark

River Thames

Whitehall

Stamford St.

SOUTHWARK

Tooley St.

Houses of Parliament & Westminster Abbey

The Cut

Union St.

Southwark St.

St. Thomas St.

Waterloo Rd.

Blackfriars Rd.

SE1

Tower Bridge Rd.

Westminster Br.

Borough High St.

Long La.

Abbey St.

WESTMINSTER

Westminster Br. Rd.

Lambeth Palace Rd.

Borough Rd.

London Rd.

ELEPHANT & CASTLE

Willow Walk

Millbank

Lambeth Rd.

New Kent Rd.

Horseferry Rd.

Lambeth Br.

LAMBETH

Rodney Rd.

Old Kent Rd.

Black Prince Rd.

Kennington Rd.

Flint St.

SE11

Albert Embankment

Kennington Park Rd.

Crampton St.

Manor Pl.

Walworth Rd.

SE17

Portland St.

Thurlow St.

Albany Rd.

Vauxhall Br. Rd.

Kennington La.

Braganza St.

N

VAUXHALL

Kennington Oval

SE5

SE15

0   1/2 mile

0   1/2 kilometer

POLITICS

Danes fell into the Thames—and the nursery rhyme "London Bridge is Falling Down" was born.

William the Conqueror arrived in London after his brief engagement at Hastings in 1066. He promptly proved his loyalty, building the White Tower both to protect and govern his citizens. Under more stable administration, the city began to rebuild itself economically and politically. It gained a municipal government under Richard I, and the right to elect a yearly mayor under John I. The merchant guilds, which arose after the Norman Conquest, took charge of elections and other municipal functions, regulating the quality of goods and taking care of sick or elderly workers.

Overseas trade and inland culture gained new momentum under the astute guidance of Elizabeth I. Joint stock ventures like the Virginia Company sent the British flag across the seas. Playwrights and poets amused commoners in the outdoor theatres of Southwark. Coffeehouses cropped up, brewing business deals alongside literary and political discussions. Natural disasters ravaged the city—the Plague in 1665 and the Great Fire in 1666—but Londoners energetically rebuilt.

In the 18th and 19th centuries, the city became increasingly crowded. Rampant growth worsened structural problems that the weak government was unable to address: most notably, horse-drawn traffic jams and street pollution. Private enterprise stepped into the gap; the first underground tube line was financed entirely by private backers. But the London County Council, created in 1889, provided a more substantial solution to expansion woes. It developed public motor-buses to reduce congestion and passed the Clean Air Act in 1935. The grimy, foggy streets that Holmes and Watson once rattled down would never be the same again.

As Britannia's rule expanded under Victoria, London enthusiastically took up its position as the center of the Empire. The 1851 Great Exhibition and the Crystal Palace in which it was housed were meant to demonstrate British supremacy in industry and science, as were the South Kensington museums created under Prince Albert's tutelage.

The world wars of the next century tested the endurance and common spirit of Londoners. After WWI, the "Homes for Heroes" program, which failed to deliver fully its promise of adequate housing, nevertheless expanded the map of London fourfold. And in World War II, Londoners rallied against the Germans and their bombs. "We would rather see London laid in ruins and ashes than that it should be tamely and abjectly enslaved," Winston Churchill declared in 1940. During the Battle of Britain, the city endured bombing every night except one for three straight months. When Hitler finally transferred the Luftwaffe to the Russian front, London emerged battered but still defiant.

After the war, there were once again those who had great plans for the city, and they were more successful than Christopher Wren. In 1944, the city gained the right to purchase all areas razed by the bombing; on this land they built hundreds of blocks of towering Council housing. In 1947 the Town and Country Planning Act provided for the creation of a "green belt" on the outskirts of the city. While the London Building Act of 1939 limited heights of buildings to 100 ft. "unless the Council otherwise consent," the office blocks of central London seem to suggest that the Council has otherwise consented quite a bit. These days Londoners have grown concerned about the excesses of high-rise development, regarding the "dream homes" in postwar blocks of flats as blighted . The council was overhauled in 1965, becoming the Greater London Council. Castigated by Conservatives as a den of the "loony left," the Council was controversially abolished in 1986 under Margaret Thatcher, leaving London with no elected governing body. The functions formerly discharged by the GLC have since devolved onto local councils.

■ POLITICS

Ever since a few barons bullied King John into agreeing to the *Magna Carta* in 1215—give or take a 17th-century regicide—political and social change has occurred (relatively) calmly in Britain. Artists, writers, and philosophers have traditionally served in politics. William Pitt, Benjamin Disraeli, and Winston Churchill chastised opponents and praised friends with eloquence and grace.

When a minor sex scandal does arise, the press tracks it for weeks. The steamy Profumo affair, on which the film *Scandal* was based, involved some high-profile House of Lords types and a few call girls. The British sex scandal took an interesting turn before the 1992 election, when the revelation of an affair by Liberal Democrat leader Paddy Ashdown shot his opinion poll ratings up by 15%. In 1993, the peculiarities of British political scandal met the (equally peculiar) intricacies of British libel law; when the *New Statesman* accused John Major of having an affair with a society caterer, Major promptly sued for libel, placing the magazine in a precarious financial position.

In the British system, the Prime Minister is not directly elected. Instead, general elections are held to choose a Parliament, and the leader of the majority party is formally invited by the Queen to form a government. In the Conservative Party, the party leader is chosen by Tory MPs; John Major is MP for Huntingdon, Cambridgeshire. Labour's more complicated process includes MPs, rank-and-file members, and trade union block votes. On July 21, 1994, Tony Blair became the head of the opposition Labour party. (Although MPs represent specific districts, they are not always native sons and daughters; selection and "de-selection" of candidates are controlled by the central parties.)

The main third party, the Liberal Democrats, was formed from the old Liberal Party and the Social Democratic Party, a moderate group that broke away from Labour in 1981; the LDs, led by Paddy Ashdown, champion proportional representation, a bill of rights, and open government, as well as libertarian economics. Other important small parties include the Greens, the Scottish Nationalist Party, and Plaid Cymru (the Welsh nationalist party). The main opposition party is constantly poised to move into office; it forms a "shadow cabinet" that mirrors the Cabinet in government. The Prime Minister has the power (technically the monarch's) to dissolve Parliament and call a general election at any time, but must do so within five years of the last one.

As political power moved from the House of Lords to the House of Commons during the 19th century, Parliament became a voice for the whole nation. It granted suffrage in grudging increments, but made social welfare a priority by the beginning of the 20th century. The dismal industrial conditions of the late 19th and early 20th century prompted not only moderate governmental regulation, but also clamors for change. Trade-union organization gained its modern form during the strike of the East London dockers in 1889, crystallizing a tradition which continues in the London of today. In 1906, the almost two million union members found political voice in the newly-formed Labour party. During the same period, British women, led by suffragette Emmeline Pankhurst, sought their own political rights; they gained limited suffrage in 1918 and full voting rights in 1928.

After World War II, the Labour Party introduced a national health system and nationalized industries, and initiated a period of vaguely social-democratic "consensus." Some thirty years later, politics took on a less humanistic tone, when Reaganite Margaret Thatcher brought the country's movement towards socialism to an abrupt halt. She claimed to have revitalized the nation's economy, increased competitiveness, and created a new style of affluence for the money-managers, but left growing social tensions, staggering dole lines (Britain's form of welfare), and a tattered educational system in her wake. One of her most controversial (and last) actions as Prime Minister was to abolish tax rates based on property value in favor of rates based on citizenship, levied on all adults over 18 regardless of their ability to pay—a poll tax. Euphemistically referred to by the government as "Community Charge," this tax is an undeniably regressive form of legislation which many fear will drive the poor to remove themselves from the electoral register to avoid payment. Thatcher's replacement, John Major, was confirmed in a close general election in 1992. Elected as a right winger, Major is now a self-described centrist. This confusion about his stance is fundamental to his political profile: critics complain that he tries to please everyone and fails, of course, to entirely please even one of the many and multiplying factions. One thing few disagree on is the fact that Major has replaced Thatcher's voluble resistance to the European Economic Community (EEC) with cautious negotiation.

London's own financial arrangements are undergoing significant changes. Privatization initiated by the Thatcher/Tory government in the 80s is still happening today. One by one many of the enterprises owned by the state—plane, rail, tube, buses, gas and electric, phone, mail, BBC, etc.—are being sold to private companies. Privately run companies are being allowed to enter the market in competition, thus pitting, for example, British Airways vs. Virgin Atlantic and BBC vs. ITV, and the everyday lives of Londoners (and tourists) are being radically affected.

■ ARCHITECTURE

"London is not ugly," artist Gustave Doré repeated fondly and frequently in 1870 as he toured the city. London may not be ugly, but it often seems a confused muddle of structures. Gracious buildings from all architectural periods co-exist, creating a madcap but endearing skyline. The Angles and the Saxons began the confusing story of English building with a style that combined severe Roman and simple Celtic. They built small monasteries and churches with several towers and wooden or stone roofs. The Normans brought the first distinctive national style in the 11th century: churches with endlessly long naves and rectangular east wings. These Romanesque elements survive in the 12th-century church of St. Bartholomew the Great.

In the Middle Ages, Gothic architecture became the design of choice for clerical buildings. Ribbed vaulting, pointed arches, and flying buttresses became immensely popular. The predecessor to today's St. Paul's Cathedral was one of Europe's largest Gothic churches. But after Henry VIII broke with Rome and confiscated the monasteries, Gothic architecture—strongly associated with Catholicism—fell out of favor. Court Architect Inigo Jones introduced Italian stylings: English manor houses began to be laid out symmetrically and surrounded by manicured gardens. Inspired by Andrea Palladio's buildings in Italy, Jones spread the Palladian style throughout 17th-century England. He coated James I's Banqueting House in Whitehall with gleaming Portland stone, constructed the airy Covent Garden Piazza, and built the first classical church in England for Charles I's Spanish fiancée.

The Great Fire of 1666 provided the next opportunity for large-scale construction. Christopher Wren built 51 new churches, flooding the skyline with a sea of spires leading up to St. Paul's, his masterwork. St. Paul's was Wren's final church—he used the earlier ones as experiments to work out anticipated design problems.

The lyrical styles begun by Jones and Wren continued to shape London's architecture for much of the next century. Other designers, like James Gibbs, Colin Campbell, and William Kent, refined their styles and integrated them with the new baroque trend sweeping the Continent. The tower and steeple plan of St. Martin's-in-the-Fields proved a popular model for Gibbs' colonial churches, particularly in the United States. Kent, a painter, designed the walls and pseudo-Pompeiian ceiling of Kensington Palace, and the interior of the Palladian Chiswick House. Campbell built early mansions such as Burlington House, now home of the Royal Academy.

By the late 1700s, builders yearned for something more exotic. Tired of London's stout brick face, John Nash covered the town with fanciful terraces and stucco façades. He wanted to create a massive garden city for the nobility. His plan was never realized in full, but the romantic pediments, triumphal arches, and sweeping pavilions of Regent's Park provide a glimpse of his rich vision. The discovery of Pompeii and Lord Elgin's pilfering of the Parthenon inspired the next trend—fake greek and Roman ruins. Architects Robert Adam, William Chambers, and John Soane went on columnic rampages, grafting Doric, Tuscan, Ionic, and Corinthian pillars onto a variety of unlikely structures.

ART

This enthusiasm for Neoclassicism faded under the reign of Victoria. Victoria's dark propriety and the Romantics' flair combined to usher in a spirited Gothic revival: pubs, villas, and banks were oddly festooned with Italian Gothic pillars. The design contest for the new House of Commons in 1894 required that the style be Gothic or Elizabethan. And an immense Gothic cathedral rose at St. Pancras Station. While many architects insisted on bringing back Gothic, others ushered in Italianate Renaissance, French and Dutch forms, still others latched onto Tudor, and some lonely pioneers discovered new building possibilities in iron and glass. Sir Joseph Paxton created the splendid Crystal Palace for the exposition of 1851. The inspirational (1600 ft. long) building burned down at the time of Edward's abdication.

After World War II, the face of building in London, perhaps exhausted by the demolition of the war, took a harsher turn. The 1951 Festival of Britain, a centennial celebration of the Great Exhibition and postwar "Tonic to the Nation," created such buildings as the Royal Festival Hall. The hopes of postwar utopian planning, and their varying degrees of fulfillment, are embodied in the vast and slightly interplanetary Barbican Centre. Then came the early sixties and a building boom in which the post-Blitz face of the City was established. Hulking monoliths now neighbor Victorian door pillars and spiraling chimneys. The medley of building continues: modern, neoclassical, and/or post-modern. Lloyd's of London's 1986 tower, decked on the *outside* with elevators and ducts. Contemporary London continues to be the city planner's nightmare—the frenetic development south of the Thames and in the Docklands will surely usher in new architectural styles.

■ ART

Religious art went out of vogue with the Reformation in the 16th century, distinguishing Britain from its still-Roman Catholic counterparts. An early republican revolution (Cromwell's in 1649) led to a more diverse set of patrons of British art; not only were the royals patrons, but also the gentry and the members of the rising middle classes.

Despite these distinguishing marks, many of its early stars were imported. In the 16th century, the German Hans Holbein worked in London as the official painter to the king. A century later, Sir Anthony Van Dyck played the same role, painting dramatic royal portraits of Charles I. Partly in reaction to these foreign artists who had helped shape the conventions of British painting, 18th-century painter and Londoner William Hogarth prided himself on his own Englishness. *A Harlot's Progress* and *A Rake's Progress,* two series of morally instructive engravings, established his reputation and broadened the audience for British art.

From the mid-18th to mid-19th century, portraiture continued to thrive under the influence of painters Thomas Gainsborough and Joshua Reynolds. The Royal Academy Reynolds founded now holds summer Academy exhibits in Piccadilly. The mid-18th century also saw the emergence of British landscape painting. London was home to J.M.W. Turner, who painted mythic, light-filled landscapes in both watercolor and oil paint. His visual records of his travels, including a set of engravings entitled *Picturesque Views of England and Wales,* secured his fame. In the same period, John Constable lovingly painted the smaller details of English landscape.

This period was followed by an eclectic visual feast ranging from William Blake's fantastical paintings and illustrations, to the jewel-like paintings of the Pre-Raphaelites John Everett Millais, Dante Gabriel Rossetti, and Edward Burne-Jones, to the Pop Art and later 'Op' Art of the 60s. Disturbing meat-filled portraits by Francis Bacon and the oddly unrealistic "realism" of Lucien Freud transformed Britain's tradition of portraiture in the last half of this century.

London is filled with art forms other than painting and engraving, including sculpture, photography, and constantly reinvented mixtures of media. Britain's sculptural tradition can be traced in London's architectural details, stone and brass tomb carvings, as well as in its abundant public monuments. Beginning in the 1930s, Henry Moore's rounded and abstracted human forms and Barbara Hepworth's carved elemental materials catapulted modern British sculpture into international fame. During the same period, Bill Brandt's photographs (collected in *The English at Home* and *Night in London*) described London and the English in visual essays. British photography since then has ranged from the intensely personal work of radical feminist Jo Spence to Nick Wapplington's photos of working-class interiors and the families that live in them.

■ MUSIC

Britain was long considered "a land without music," for while the continent blossomed into the fervid creativity of 19th-century Romanticism, Britain withdrew. The lion's share of British musical achievement was produced during the Renaissance, Restoration, and the 20th century.

The arts flourished during the reign of Elizabeth I. In the midst of a country torn by religious differences, Byrd composed magnificent pieces for both the Anglican and Roman Churches; Morley, Weelkes, and Wilbye took up (and enhanced) the madrigal just as it was about to be abandoned in its native Italy. John Dowland, perhaps the most famous composer of the Elizabethan Age, created melancholic lute music. Britain had only one well-known composer through the 18th and 19th centuries, Henry Purcell, whose opera *Dido and Aeneas* endures as a masterpiece. As was the case in the visual arts, Britain attracted some of the great artists: Handel considered Britain his home after 1713, and the British certainly consider him one of their own. Mozart composed his first symphony in Chelsea and Haydn's last was named "London."

In the late 19th century, the grand operettas of W.S. Gilbert and Arthur Sullivan satirized contemporary political blunders and social mores. The two collaborated successfully on such perennial favorites as *The Mikado, H.M.S. Pinafore,* and *The Pirates of Penzance.* Art music began a "second renaissance" under Edward Elgar, while Gustav Holst (*The Planets*) adapted the methods of neoclassicism to folk materials and to a Romantic temperament. William Walton and Ralph Vaughan Williams created a modernist tradition in English music in the early 20th century. More recently, Benjamin Britten's *Peter Grimes* made modern opera accessible to a wide range of audiences; Michael Tippett, composer of four powerful symphonies and *A Child of Our Time*, followed Britten's lead.

If the western world's pop music could ever be said to have a center, London is it: other cities have sounds and scenes, but in London each hip neighborhood has its own cast of musical characters and styles. National trends are made and unmade by the London-based music weeklies, *NME* (New Musical Express), *Melody Maker,* and *Sounds*; this makes the British music world more volatile, and more centralized, than its counterparts in other nations. An unknown band can release a single, make "single of the week," graduate to the papers' front covers, put out a million-selling CD, and vanish again within eight months.

London brought the "British Invasion" bands of the mid-60s to ears worldwide: the Beatles, of course, were Liverpudlians, but the Rolling Stones, the Kinks, and the Who all started in London's environs. (Mick Jagger, in fact, was briefly a student at the London School of Economics.) Mod and psychedelic booms from '66 to '68 produced a flurry of great tunes. White British adapters of American blues—most famously the Yardbirds—spawned guitar heroes like Eric Clapton (Cream) and Jimmy Page (Led Zeppelin), whose antics and technical skills dominated the mass markets as the 70s opened.

Working-class kids had meanwhile organized into all-encompassing subcultures based on music and dress: "rockers," who wore leather and liked American R&B, fought "mods" who wore long coats, rode scooters, took speed, and listened to the Who. "Skinheads" borrowed from Jamaican reggae and Anglo-Caribbean ska; later generations of skins would splinter into socialist and repellently right-wing factions, both propelled by stripped-down rock called "oi."

While David Bowie flitted through personas and prog-rock held the world hostage, mid-70s "pub rock" groups tried to return the form to the people, preparing the ground for punk. Malcolm McLaren, a King's Road entrepreneur, organized the Sex Pistols to get publicity for his outrageous boutique, "Sex,"; equipped with Vivienne Westwood's clothes and Johnny Rotten's snarl, the Pistols changed music and culture forever, first in Chelsea, then in London, then in the industrialized world. Bored school leavers, failed pub-rockers, and latter-day Situationists picked up both the Pistols' primitive musical attack and their spiked hair and safety-pinned ears.

When the Pistols cursed out presenter Bill Grundy on live national TV in December of '76, all hell broke loose: mainstream newspapers rushed to condemn "punk rock," which only gave it more steam. London was deluged with bands. Teenaged Marion Elliot ran away from school, renamed herself Poly Styrene, and started X-Ray Spex, whose only album was both a tuneful romp through consumer culture and an aching critique of it. Sax player Lora Logic, kicked out of X-Ray Spex, found her niche at Rough Trade: at first a reggae store, then a distributor, Rough Trade became a record label itself, specializing in unconventional, thought-out rock. As a record shop, Rough Trade is still the best around. Elvis Costello, Squeeze, and the Jam found that punk had cleared the ground for smart pop, which stayed persistently and bitingly English even as it took over world charts.

The winsome pop of Britain's mid-80s didn't all come from London, but Felt, Biff Bang Pow! and their shared label, Creation, were based in the same city as the weeklies that made them semi-famous. Unemployed kids and easy access to the drug Ecstasy made London the capital, if not the birthplace, of rave culture's all-night, all-day, sweaty, anaesthetic gatherings, and the electronic music that accompanied them.

Pure pop and talented dissonance continue to emanate from London. Dar Treacy's TV Personalities still break hearts from their base in the capital, the trendy, eclectic Too Pure record label operates from Camden Town, and Riot Grrrl bands like Huggy Bear and Pussycat Trash articulate a feminist message of women's empowerment. London's assembly of ethnic and expatriate cultures is finally affecting its pop—a rapper called Apache Indian merges South Asian *bhangra* music with his rhymes, and traditional South Asian drones meet ferocious electric guitars in an exciting, and excruciatingly self-conscious, new band called Cornershop.

■ LITERARY LONDON

Geoffrey Chaucer, the son of a well-to-do London wine merchant, initiated the tradition that British tales commence in London. The pilgrims in *Canterbury Tales* set off from Tabard Inn in Southwark on the south bank.

Ben Jonson held sway in the English court scene of the early 17th century. He planned balls for Queen Elizabeth and her friends, creating original music, choreography and special effects. Meanwhile, William Shakespeare (and his colleagues Marlowe, Jonson, and Webster) catered to the common folk in the circular theatres across the river in Southwark, the heart of the red light district.

Many writers found London a degenerate, morally disturbing place. John Donne, who became Dean of St. Paul's in 1621, wrote poetry while meting out advice to his parishioners. He set his first and fourth satires in London, drawing attention to urban evils. As a market for books developed in the 1700s, literary society began to resemble today's marketplace of trends: it welcomed Alexander Pope as a prodigy at the age of 17, but his disillusionment came quickly. In London, "nothing is sacred...but villainy," he wrote in the epilogue to his *Satires*. Pope drank away his gloom with professional genius Samuel Johnson in the Cheshire Cheese pub, while Boswell scurried about looking for crumbs. Daniel Defoe, Henry Fielding, and Samuel Richardson also explored themes of urban injustice, using journalism, satire and sermons as their tools.

Poets of the Age of Reason fantasized about a classic city different from the crime-ridden one that they inhabited, but none actually moved away. London remained a

M
E
D
I
A

haven for publishing and literary cliques still wrestling with ideas of social justice. In the early 18th century, Joseph Addison and Richard Steele attacked urban ills from a new perspective by creating a new literary genre: the *Tatler* and *Spectator* carried political and moral essays to subscribers.

As a grey haze settled over the city's houses and the beggars on the streets swelled into an army, the wretched state of the city became inescapably apparent. Charles Dickens followed his characters through 19th-century London's back streets and prisons. Even these fictional people began to notice that too much time in industrialized London did wretched things to one's nerves. The Romantic poets had the same idea; they abandoned the classical idealization of the urban and left the city. Keats and Wordsworth lived in Hampstead and Westminster, both distant suburbs at the time. Shelley wrote, "Hell is a city much like London," and Blake doubted the existence of a new Jerusalem "amongst these dark Satanic mills."

By the end of the 19th century, when reforms began to mitigate the effects of industrialization, some writers turned to purely aesthetic issues. In the 1890s, W.B. Yeats joined the London Rhymers' Club. Relentlessly quotable Oscar Wilde proclaimed that art could only be useless. But fellow dramatist and Fabian socialist George Bernard Shaw's politics influenced his vision of art; he wrote plays more didactic than decadent.

In 1921, T.S. Eliot turned London into his angst-ridden, modern *Waste Land,* an "Unreal City." The poem follows a crowd over London Bridge into the City, wondering how many of them the war has "undone." Both Eliot and Yeats did their time in the high modernist Bloomsbury group. This erudite crowd included Virginia Woolf, Vanessa and Clive Bell, economist John Maynard Keynes, and novelist E.M. Forster. Meanwhile, a penniless George Orwell was meeting street people and telling yarns of urban poverty in his ultimate tale of budget travel, *Down and Out in Paris and London.*

Orwell's warped future London in *1984*—derived largely from an all-too-contemporary bombed-out and rationing city—cast a shadow of gloom into the second half of this century. But aside from the disturbing visions of Anthony Burgess, much of London's modern literature is bright and often witty. Kingsley Amis and his son Martin Amis write deft satirical novels. London has become a publishing center for writers in English from the former colonies and other lands, such as Salman Rushdie, V.S. Naipaul, and Timothy Mo. Questions of London's future European and world status aside, a glance at recent titles says it all about writers' metropolitan fascinations: Amis' *London Fields,* V.S. Pritchett's *London Perceived,* Doris Lessing's *London Observed.* Writers keep coming to the irresistible town—as a publishing center and an inexhaustible topic, they seem unable to avoid it.

■ MEDIA

In your search for British culture, don't forget the radio and television stations of the BBC. As well as the more serious-minded *Masterpiece Theatre,* Britain exports *Monty Python's Flying Circus, Are You Being Served,* the time-traveling *Dr. Who,* and programs ranging from *Benny Hill* and his host of scantily clad women to the more subtle political satire of *Yes, Minister.*

British news programs cover political developments (and the debates in both Houses) in much greater detail than their American counterparts. In Britain, all of this is advertisement-free—TV owners in England pay a license fee that supports the BBC. The BBC's quasi-governmental associations have not hampered innovation, even as politicians of left and right are each certain that it's an agent of the other.

British radio offers the BBC World Service, constant and comprehensive national and international news. On a lighter note, *The Archers,* a radio drama that dates from 1951, still plays on. As do game shows on which the British intelligentsia show off their Oxford- and Cambridge-educated minds, their facility with words, and their very British humor. For those who like a more leisurely pace, ball by ball coverage of cricket matches can be found on the *Test Match Special.*

▩ Essentials

■■■ PLANNING YOUR TRIP

■ USEFUL ADDRESSES AND PUBLICATIONS

Although the amount of things to do in London can seem overwhelming, there are a number of offices and agencies that are more than willing to give out information. The free pamphlets and brochures available at tourist offices, hotels, and museums will help you develop a clearer idea of how you want to spend your trip.

TOURIST OFFICES

British Tourist Authority (BTA), 551 Fifth Ave, Suite 701, New York, NY 10176-0799 (tel. (212) 986-2200). Other U.S. branches in **Chicago, Atlanta,** and **Los Angeles.** In **Canada,** 111 Avenue Rd. #450, Toronto, Ont. M5R 3J8 (tel. (416) 925-6326). In **Australia,** The University Centre, 210 Clarence St., Sydney NSW 2000 (tel. (02) 267 4555). Publishes helpful accommodations guides, including *Stay on a Farm, Stay With a British Family,* and detailed hotel, guesthouse, and B&B guides. Other useful publications include *First Stop Britain,* a student kit which includes maps and their *London Guide,* and the ever-popular pub guide. The **British Travel Bookshop,** in their New York office, will send you their mail-order catalog upon request.

CONSULATES AND HIGH COMMISSIONS

British Consulates: In **U.S.,** British Embassy, 3100 Massachusetts Ave. NW, Washington, DC 20008 (tel. (202) 462-1340); consulates at 845 Third Ave., New York, NY 10022 (tel. (212) 745-0200); Marquis One Tower #2700, 245 Peachtree Center Ave., Atlanta, GA 30303 (tel. (404) 524-5856); 33 North Dearborn St., Chicago, IL 60602 (tel. (312) 346-1810); First Interstate Bank Plaza #1990, 1000 Louisiana, Houston, TX 77002 (tel. (713) 659-6270); and 11766 Wilshire Blvd. #400, Los Angeles, CA 90025-6536 (tel. (310) 477-3322). Call the Embassy for additional consulate addresses. In **Canada,** British High Commission, 80 Elgin St., Ottawa, Ont. K1P 5K7 (tel. (613) 237-1530). In **Australia,** British High Commission, Commonwealth Ave., Yarralumla, Canberra, ACT 2600 (tel. (616) 270 6666). In **New Zealand,** British High Commission, 44 Hill St., Wellington 1 (tel. (644) 472 6049).

USEFUL TRAVEL ORGANIZATIONS

The following budget travel organizations typically offer discounted flights for students and youths, railpasses, ISICs and other identification cards, hostel memberships, travel gear, travel guides, and general expertise in budget travel.

Campus Travel, 52 Grosvenor Gardens, London SW1W 0AG (tel. 730 8832; fax 730 5739). Tube: Victoria. Competitive fares. Open Mon.-Fri. 8:30am-6:30pm, Sat. 9am-8pm, Sun, 10am-5pm. Also at **UCL Union,** 25 Gordon St. Tube: Euston. Open Mon.-Tues. and Thurs.-Fri. 9:30am-5pm, Wed. 10am-5pm.

Council on International Educational Exchange (CIEE), 205 East 42nd St., New York, NY 10017 (tel. (212) 661 1414). A private, not-for-profit organization, CIEE administers work, volunteer, and academic programs around the world. **Council Charter,** 205 East 42nd St., New York, NY 10017 (tel. (212) 661 0311 or (800) 800-8222). A subsidiary of CIEE, Council Charter offers inexpensive charter and other airfares. **Council Travel,** a subsidiary of CIEE, is an agency specializing in student and budget travel. 41 U.S. offices, including ones in New York, Boston, Los Angeles, Chicago, and San Francisco. In **London:** 28A Poland St., WIV 3DB (tel. 437 7767). Tube: Oxford Circus. London office open Mon.-Wed. and Fri. 9am-6pm, Thurs. 9am-7pm, Sat. 10am-5pm.

TOP 5 Ways to Save Money While Traveling

5. Ship yourself in a crate marked "Livestock." Remember to poke holes in the crate.

4. Board a train dressed as Elvis and sneer and say "The King rides for free."

3. Ask if you can walk through the Channel Tunnel.

2. Board the plane dressed as an airline pilot, nod to the flight attendants, and hide in the rest room until the plane lands.

1. Bring a balloon to the airline ticket counter, kneel, breathe in the helium, and ask for the kiddie fare.

But if you're serious about saving money while you're traveling abroad, just get an ISIC--the International Student Identity Card. Discounts for students on international airfares, hotels and motels, car rentals, international phone calls, financial services, and more.

CTS Travel, 220 Kensington High St., W8 (tel. 637 5601 for travel in Europe, 323 5180 or 323 5130 for travel world-wide). Tube: High St. Kensington. Open Mon.-Sat. 9am-5pm, Sun. 10am-5pm. Also at 44 Goodge St., W1. Tube: Goodge St.

Educational Travel Centre (ETC), 438 North Frances St., Madison, WI 53703 (tel. (800) 747-5551, fax (608) 256-2042). Budget travel agency. Write for their free pamphlet *Taking Off.*

International Student Exchange Flights (ISE), 5010 East Shea Blvd., #A104, Scottsdale, AZ 85254 (tel. (602) 951-1177).

Let's Go Travel, Harvard Student Agencies, Inc., 53-A Church St., Cambridge, MA 02138 (tel. (800) 5-LETS GO or (617) 495-9649). Offers railpasses, HI/AYH memberships, ISICs, FIYTO cards, guidebooks, maps, bargain flights, and a complete line of budget travel gear. See catalog insert.

National Express: (tel. 730 0202 or 730 8235). Additional office at Piccadilly (13 Regent St., SW1; tel. 925 0189). National Express's Eurolines division specializes in coach and train travel all over Europe, including Russia and Eastern Europe. Open Mon.-Fri. 9am-6pm, Sat. 9am-4pm.

Rail Europe, Inc., 230 Westchester Ave., White Plains, NY 10604 (tel. (800) 438-7245, fax (914) 682-2821). Sells all Eurail products and passes, national railpasses, and rail tickets. Up-to-date info. on the Chunnel; call (800) 94-CHUNNEL.

STA Travel: 5900 Wilshire Blvd., Ste. 2110, Los Angeles, CA 90036 (tel. (800) 777-0112 in the U.S.) A student and youth travel agency with over 100 offices around the world. 11 offices in the U.S., including: 297 Newbury St., **Boston,** MA 02116 (tel. (617) 266-6014); 48 E. 11th St., **New York,** NY 10003 (tel. (212) 477-7166); 2401 Pennsylvania Ave., **Washington,** DC 20037 (tel. (202) 887-0912); and 51 Grant Ave., **San Francisco,** CA 94108 (tel. (415) 391-8407). In **London,** 86 Old Brompton Rd. SW7 3LQ (tube: South Kensington) and 117 Euston Rd. NW1 2SX (tel. 937 9921 for European travel). London offices open Mon.-Fri. 8am-8pm, Sat. 10am-4pm, Sun. 10am-2pm.

Trailfinders: 42-50 Earl's Ct. Rd., W8 (tel. 937 5400). Tube: High St. Kensington. Busier branch at 194 Kensington High St., W8 (tel. 938 3232; tube: High St. Kensington). Travel services. Information and vaccination section for those using London as a stopover for long haul flights. Both branches open Mon.-Wed. and Fri.-Sat. 9am-6pm, Thurs. 9am-7pm; Sun. (telephone only at Earl's Ct.) 10am-2pm.

Travel CUTS (Canadian University Travel Services Limited): 187 College St., **Toronto,** Ont. M5T 1P7 (tel. (416) 798-CUTS, fax (416) 979-8167). Canada's national student travel bureau and equivalent of CIEE, with 40 offices across Canada. In **London,** 295-A Regent St. W1R 7YA (tel. 637 3161). London office open Mon.-Fri. 9am-6pm, Sat. 10am-5pm.

Unitravel: 117 North Warson Rd., St. Louis, MO 63132 (tel. (800) 325-2222, fax (314) 569-2503). Budget travel agency.

YHA Travel Office: 14 Southampton St., WC2 (tel. 836 8541). Tube: Covent Garden. Branch at 174 Kensington High St., W8 (tel. 938 2948; tube: High St. Kensington). Complete travel services. Bookshop offers an extensive selection of travel guides, including *Let's Go,* to every country under the sun. Both branches open Mon.-Wed. 10am-6pm, Thurs.-Fri. 10am-7pm, Sat. 9am-6:30pm.

HOSTEL MEMBERSHIP

The 6,000 official youth hostels worldwide will normally display the **Hostelling International (HI)** logo (a blue triangle) alongside the national hostel association symbol. A one-year Hostelling International (HI) membership allows you to stay at youth hostels all over Britain for much less than you would spend in B&Bs or hotels. Despite the name, you need not be a youth. For the most part, membership must be acquired through the HI affiliate in one's own country. Some hostels sell them on the spot. The HI guides (*Vol. 1: Europe and the Mediterranean* and *Vol. 2: Africa, America, Asia, Australia, and New Zealand)* list HI hostels (US$11 each).

HI also offers an **International Booking Network,** which allows you to make confirmed reservations at any of the HI hostels (US$2 fee). Credit card (MC or Visa) guarantee is required (contact the offices listed below). Memberships are available from some travel agencies and from the following national HI affiliates:

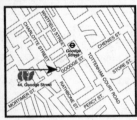

Hostelling International (HI): headquarters and information, 9 Guessens Rd., Welwyn Garden City, Hertfordshire AL8 6QW, England (tel. (01707) 332 487).

American Youth Hostels (AYH): 733 15th St. NW, Ste. 840, Washington, DC, 20005 (tel. (202) 783-6161, fax (202) 783-6171). 1-year membership US$25, under 18 $10, over 54 $15, family cards $35.

Australian Youth Hostels Association (AYHA), Level 3, 10 Mallett St., Camperdown, New South Wales, 2050 (tel. (02) 565 1699, fax (02) 565 1325). Fee AU$40, renewal $24, under 18 fee and renewal $12.

Hostelling International—Canada (HI-C): 400-205 Catherine St., Ottawa, Ont. K2P 1C3 (tel. (613) 237-7884, fax (613) 237-7868). One-year membership CDN$26.75, under 18 $12.84, two-year $37.45.

Youth Hostels Association of England and Wales (YHA): Trevelyan House, 8 St. Stephen's Hill, St. Albans, Hertfordshire AL12DY (tel. (01727) 855 215; or 14 Southhampton St., Covent Garden, London WC2E 7HY (tel. (0171) 836 1036. Enrollment fees are £9 adult, £3 under 18.

Youth Hostels Association of New Zealand (YHANZ), P.O. Box 436, 17 Gloucester St., Christchurch 1, New Zealand (tel. (03) 379 9970, fax (03) 365 4476). Annual memberships: senior (adult) NZ$34, youth (15-17) NZ$12, under 15 free. Rates are lower for 2- and 3-year memberships. Life membership NZ$240.

Youth Hostels Association of Northern Ireland (YHANI): 22-32 Donegall Rd., Belfast BT12 5JN, Northern Ireland (tel. (01232) 324 733, fax (01232) 439 699).

BOOKS, GUIDES, MAPS, ETC.

Bon Voyage!, 2069 W. Bullard Ave., Fresno, CA 93711-1200 (tel. (800) 995-9716, from abroad (209) 447-8441, CompuServe 70754, 3511). Annual mail order catalog offers a range of travel products: books, luggage, converters, maps, etc.

The College Connection, Inc., 1295 Prospect St., La Jolla, CA 92031 (tel. (619) 551-9770, fax (619) 551-9987). Publishes *The Passport,* a free booklet listing hints about every aspect of traveling and studying abroad. Sells railpasses with enhancements to college students.

Forsyth Travel Library, P.O. Box 2975, Shawnee Mission, KS 66201 (tel. (800) 367-7984, fax (913) 384-3553). Call or write for their catalog of maps, guidebooks, railpasses, timetables, and travel gear. MC, Visa, Discover.

Hippocrene Books, Inc., 171 Madison Ave., New York NY 10016 (tel. (212) 685-4371, orders (718) 454-2360, fax (718) 454-1391). Free catalog. Publishes travel reference books and guides, maps, foreign language dictionaries and texts.

John Muir Publications, P.O. Box 613, Santa Fe, NM 87504 (tel. (505) 982-4078 or (800) 888-7504). Publishes excellent books by veteran traveler Rick Steves, including *Europe Through the Back Door* (US$18) and *Mona Winks: Self-Guided Tours of Europe's Top Museums* (US$17).

Superintendent of Documents, U.S. Government Printing Office, P.O. Box 371954, Pittsburgh, PA 15250 (tel. (202) 783-3238, fax (202) 275-2529). Run through the State Department; publishes a series of region-specific pamphlets.

Travelling Books, P.O. Box 521491, Salt Lake City, UT 84152 (tel. (801) 461-3345). Mail-order service specializing in travel guides, books, and accessories that make the armchair traveler weep with wanderlust. Free catalog.

Wide World Books and Maps, 1911 N. 45th St., Seattle, WA 98103 (tel. (206) 634-3453, fax (206) 634-0558). Wide selection of travel guides and maps.

■ DOCUMENTS AND FORMALITIES

Remember to file all applications several weeks or even months before your planned departure date. Most offices suggest that you apply in the winter off-season (Aug.-Dec.) for speedier service. When you travel, always carry on your person two or more forms of ID, including at least one photo ID. Many establishments, especially banks, require several IDs before cashing traveler's checks. It is useful to carry extra passport-size photos to affix to the various IDs you will eventually acquire.

ENTRANCE REQUIREMENTS

You must have a valid **passport** to enter Britain and to re-enter your country. Canadians, Australians, New Zealanders, and other non-visa Commonwealth nationals also require an **Entry Certificate** to enter Britain, available at the point of entry. Citizens of the U.S., Canada, Australia, and New Zealand may enter the U.K. without a visa. The standard **period of admission** is six months in Britain. To stay longer, you must show evidence that you can support yourself for an extended period of time, and a medical examination is often required. Admission as a visitor from a non-EU nation does not include the right to work, which is authorized only by the possession of a work permit (see Alternatives to Tourism). Entering Britain to study does not require a special visa, but immigration will want to see proof of acceptance by a British school, proof that the course of study will take up most of your time in the country, and proof that you can support yourself.

PASSPORTS

Before you leave, *record your passport number,* and keep it apart from the passport. If you lose your passport while traveling, tell the local police and your nearest consulate *immediately.* Carry an expired passport or a copy of your birth certificate in a separate part of your baggage; most importantly, carry a photocopy of your passport, or leave it with someone at home.

U.S. citizens may apply for a passport valid for 10 years (5 if under 18) at any one of several thousand federal or state courthouses or post offices authorized to accept applications, or at a U.S. Passport Agency. Refer to the "U.S. Government, State Department" section of the telephone directory or call your local post office. Passports are processed according to the departure date indicated on the application form. In March through August, processing may take even longer. File early. Your passport will be mailed to you; you may pay for express mail return. Passport Agencies offer on-the-spot **rush service,** if you have proof that you are departing within five working days (e.g. an airplane ticket). Abroad, a **U.S. embassy or consulate** can usually issue new passports, given proof of citizenship. Call the U.S. Passport Information's 24-hr. recorded message (tel. (202) 647-0518), which offers general information, agency locations, and business hours.

Canadian passport application forms in English and French are available at all passport offices, post offices, and most travel agencies. You can apply by mail by sending a completed application form with appropriate documentation and the CDN$35 fee to Passport Office, Foreign Affairs, Ottawa, Ont., K1A 0G3. The processing time is approximately five business days in person and three weeks through the mail. Service is usually faster in winter. For additional information, call the 24-hour number at (800) 567-6868 (in Toronto call 973-3251, in Montreal call 283-2152). Refer to the booklet *Bon Voyage, But . . .* for a list of Canadian Embassies, High Commissions and Consulates abroad, available free of charge from any passport office or from: Info-Export (BPTE), Foreign Affairs, Ottawa, Ont., KIA 0G2.

Australian citizens must apply for a passport in person at a local post office, a passport office, or an Australian diplomatic mission overseas. An appointment may be necessary. Applicants for **New Zealand passports** must contact their local Link Centre, travel agent, or New Zealand Representative for an application form. The standard processing time is 10 working days from receipt; applications marked "urgent" receive priority. The application fee is NZ$80 or an application submitted in New Zealand and NZ$130 for one submitted overseas (if under age 16, NZ$40 and NZ$65 respectively). **South African citizens** can apply for a passport at any Department of Home Affairs Office.

YOUTH AND STUDENT IDENTIFICATION

In the world of budget travel, youth has its privileges. Many expenditures, particularly for transportation and sights, can be substantially reduced with a student ID. Two main forms of student and youth identification are accepted worldwide; they are extremely useful, especially for their insurance packages.

The **International Student Identity Card (ISIC)** is the most widely recognized form of student ID; more than one million students have it. The ISIC gets you discounts on sights, theater tickets, museums, accommodations, train, ferry, airplane travel, and other services throughout the world. Ask about discounts even when none are advertised. The ISIC provides accident insurance of up to US$3000 per accident, US$10,000 for emergency medical evacuation, and US$100 per day of in-hospital care for up to 60 days, among other benefits. Cardholders have access to a toll-free Traveler's Assistance hotline whose staff can help in medical, legal, and financial emergencies overseas. Many student travel offices issue ISICs. The accompanying *ISIC Handbook,* lists by country some of the available discounts. In many cases, establishments will also honor an ordinary student ID from your college or university for student discounts. Because of the proliferation of phony and improperly issued ISIC cards, many airlines and some other services now require double proof of student identity.

The US$16 **International Teacher Identity Card (ITIC)** offers identical discounts, in theory, but because of its recent introduction many establishments are reluctant to honor it. The application process is the same as for an ISIC.

The **Federation of International Youth Travel Organisations (FIYTO)** issues its own discount card to travelers under 26 (students or not). Also known as the **International Youth Discount Travel Card** or the **GO 25 Card,** this one-year card offers many of the same benefits as the ISIC. Most organizations that sell the ISIC also sell GO 25. You receive a brochure listing discounts at purchase. Proof of birthdate (copy of birth certificate or passport or a valid driver's license) and a passport-sized photo with your name printed on the back are required. The fee is US$10, CDN$12, or £4. For more information, contact FIYTO at Bredgage 25H, DK-1260, Copenhagen K, Denmark (tel. +45 33 33 96 00, fax +45 33 93 96 76).

INTERNATIONAL DRIVER'S PERMIT

Unless you have a valid driver's license from an EU country, a foreigner who drives in Britain is required to have an International Driving Permit (IDP). You will not need an IDP for short-term travel: an American or Canadian license is valid for up to three months in Britain. Most car rental agencies do not require the permit, but after three months you will be required to have it by the police, and it can also serve as additional identification. A valid driver's license from your home country must always accompany the IDP.

Your IDP must be issued in your own country before you depart. U.S. license holders 18 and older can obtain an IDP, valid for one year, at any **American Automobile Association (AAA)** office or by writing to its main office, AAA Florida, Travel Agency Services Department, 1000 AAA Drive (mail stop 28), Heathrow, FL 32746-5080 (tel. (800) 222-4357 or (407) 444-4245, fax (407) 444-7823). For further information, contact a local AAA office. Alternatively, procure an IDP from the **American Automobile Touring Alliance,** Bayside Plaza, 188 The Embarcadero, San Francisco, CA 94105 (tel. (415) 777-4000, fax (415) 882-2141). Show a valid license and provide a completed application, two passport-size photos, and US$10. Canadian license holders 18 and over can obtain an IDP (CDN$10) through any **Canadian Automobile Association (CAA)** office, or by writing to CAA Toronto, 60 Commerce Valley Dr. East, Thornhill, Ont. L3T 7P9 (tel. (905) 771-3000, fax (905) 771-3046).

Most credit cards cover standard insurance. If you drive your own car or rent or borrow one, you will need a **green card,** or **International Insurance Certificate,** to prove that you have liability insurance. The application forms are available at any AAA or CAA office. You can also get one through the car rental agency or leasing dealer; most of them include coverage in their prices. Verify whether your auto insurance applies abroad; even if it does, you will still need a green card as proof.

CUSTOMS

Don't be alarmed by customs procedures. The many regulations of customs and duties hardly pose a threat to the budget traveler. Persons entering Britain must declare alcohol, tobacco, and perfume at the point of entry. A duty is placed on excessive quantities of these substances. Britain has very strict restrictions on imports: among those goods prohibited are controlled drugs, horror comics, fireworks, meat and poultry, fruits and vegetables, plants and plant material, and wood with bark attached. All animals brought into the country are subject to a six-month quarantine at the owner's expense. To avoid problems when carrying prescription drugs, make sure bottles are clearly marked, and have a copy of the prescription ready to show the customs officer. Britain does not limit the amount of currency you may bring in. Goods obtained that have had duty and tax paid in another EU country, within certain limits set out for personal use, will not be subject to additional customs duty.

Upon returning home, you must declare all articles acquired abroad and pay a duty on those articles that exceed the allowance established by your country. Holding onto receipts for purchases made abroad will help you establish values when you return home. It is wise to make a list (including serial numbers) of any valuables that you take with you from home; if you register this list with customs at the airport before departing, you'll avoid being charged import duties upon your return. Keep in mind that goods and gifts purchased at duty-free shops abroad are not exempt from duty at your point of return; you must declare these items.

For information about **U.K. customs,** contact Her Majesty's Customs and Excise, Custom House, Heathrow Airport North, Houslow, Middlesex, TW6 2LA (tel. (0181) 910 3600; fax (0181) 750 1549). *HM Customs & Excise Notice 1* explains the allowances for people traveling to the U.K.

U.S. residents returning from abroad must declare all merchandise acquired abroad, including gifts, articles bought in duty-free shops, and purchases for others. The first $400 worth of merchandise for personal or household use may be entered duty free ($400 exemption good once every 30 days). You may include in your personal exemption one liter of alcoholic beverages (21 and up only). You must declare all purchases, so it's wise to keep sales slips handy in carry-on luggage, in case Customs inspectors wish to verify items on your customs declaration. For more information, call or write for a copy of *Know Before You Go* from the U.S. Customs Service, Box 7407, Washington, D.C. 20044l (tel. (202) 927-6724).

U.S. citizens may **mail home** bona-fide, unsolicited gifts free of duty if they are worth less than $100; mark on the outside of your gift package: the item(s) contained in package, the fact that the contents are unsolicited gifts, and the value of the gift. Alcohol, tobacco, or perfume may not be sent through the mail. If your gift package exceeds the duty-free limit, the U.S. Postal Service will collect customs duties and handling charges in the form of "postage due" stamps; the duty cannot be prepaid. If you are mailing home personal items of American origin, mark clearly on the outside of the wrapping, "American goods returned" in order to avoid paying duty. Somewhat different regulations apply to foreign nationals living in the U.S.; see a copy of *Customs Hints for Visitors (Nonresidents)*.

Canadian citizens who remain abroad for at least one week may bring back up to CDN $300 worth of goods duty-free once every year. You are permitted to ship goods home under this exemption as long as you declare them when you arrive. For more information, write to Canadian Customs, 2265 St. Laurent Blvd., Ottawa, Ont., K1G 4K3 (tel. (613) 993-0534; call (800) 461-9999 from within Canada).

Each **Australian** citizen over age 18 may import AUS$400 of goods duty-free. For further information contact the Australian Customs Service, 5 Constitution Ave., Canberra, ACT 2601 (tel. (6) 275 6255; fax (6) 275 6989). Each **New Zealand** citizen may bring home up to NZ$700 worth of unsolicited gifts or goods intended for personal use duty-free. For more information, consult *New Zealand Customs Guide for Travelers* or *If You're Not Sure About It, DECLARE IT,* both available from customs offices, or contact New Zealand Customs, 50 Anzac Avenue, Box 29, Aukland

MONEY

(tel. (09) 377 35 20; fax 309 29 78). Each **South African** citizen may import duty-free up to a value of R500. For information, write to The Commissioner for Customs and Excise, Private Bag X47, Pretoria, 0001. South Africans in the U.S. should contact the South African Mission to the IMF/World Bank, 3201 New Mexico Ave. #380, NW, Washington, DC 20016 (tel. (202) 364-8320/1; fax 364-6008).

■ MONEY

CURRENCY AND EXCHANGE

US$1 = 0.65 British pounds	1£ = US$1.55
CDN$1 = £0.47	1£ = CDN$2.13
IR£1 = £0.98	1£ = IR£1.02
AUS$1 = £0.48	1£ = AUS$2.08
NZ$1 = £ 0.39	1£ = NZ$2.59
SAR1 = £0.18	1£ = SAR5.54

> A Note on Prices and Currency
> The information in this book was researched in the summer of 1994. Since then, inflation will have raised most prices at least 10%. The exchange rates listed were compiled on August 15, 1994. Since rates fluctuate considerably, confirm them before you go by checking a national newspaper.

Nothing is certain in London but expense.
—William Sherstone, *Curiosities of Literature,* 1791-3

Even those lucky enough to have money may have trouble holding on to it as they make their way through the web of commissions and conversion rates. Remember that pounds will be less costly in Britain than at home. Even so, converting at least US$50 will allow you to breeze past expensive airport exchange counter lines.

Observe commission rates closely when abroad. Banks will ordinarily offer better rates than those of travel agencies, restaurants, hotels, and the dubious bureaux de change. Don't be lured by bureaux that scream "No Charge—No Commission." If it makes you wonder how they make their money, just look at the rates.

The British pound sterling (£) is divided into 100 pence (100p). Coins are issued in denominations of 1p, 2p, 5p, 10p, 20p, 50p, and £1; notes are issued in denominations of £5, £10, £20, and £50. The terminology used in the old monetary system still lingers in street markets—a "shilling" is 5p, a "quid" is £1, and a "guinea" is £1.05. Be aware that while Scotland's pound notes are legal tender throughout the U.K., they are often not accepted, especially in London.

Most banks are closed on Saturday, Sunday, and all public holidays. Britain enjoys "bank holidays" several times a year (see Appendix for dates). (Usual bank hours in Britain are Mon.-Fri. 9:30am-3:30pm, although many banks, especially those in the center of London, are remaining open until 5pm or on Saturday mornings.)

American Express, 6 Haymarket, SW1 (tel. 930 4411). Tube: Piccadilly Circus. Message and mail services open Mon.-Fri. 9am-5pm, Sat. 9am-noon. Currency exchange open Mon.-Fri. 9am-5:30pm, Sat. 9am-6pm, Sun. 10am-5:45pm. Bring ID to pick up mail (60p; free for AmEx Cheque or cardholders). Other offices at Victoria Station (147 Victoria St., SW1; tel. 828 7411); Cannon St. (54 Cannon St., EC4; tel. 248 2671); Knightsbridge (78 Brompton Rd., SW3; tel. 584 6182); and at the British Tourist Centre. Lost or stolen Traveler's Cheques should be reported immediately (tel. 0800 52 1313; 24-hr.).

Late Night Currency Exchange: You'll find *bureaux de change* at airports, major rail stations, and central London tube stations. Most are open 8am-9pm, but the following have later opening hours. **Thomas Cook,** 15 Shaftesbury Ave., WC2. Tube: Piccadilly Circus. Open until 11pm. **Exchange International,** Victoria Station. Tube: Victoria. Open until 10pm. **Chequepoint** offers 5 24-hr. locations: opposite Marble Arch tube station; Coventry Street, tube: Piccadilly Circus;

What to do when your *money* is done traveling before you are.

Don't worry. With MoneyGram,℠ your parents can send you money in usually 10 minutes or less to more than 15,500 locations in 75 countries. So if the money you need to see history becomes history, call us and we'll direct you to a MoneyGram agent closest to you.

MoneyGram℠
INTERNATIONAL MONEY TRANSFERS.

USA: 1-800-MONEYGRAM • Canada: 1-800-933-3278 • France: (331) 47-77-70-00
England: (44) Ø*-71-839-7541 • Germany: (0049) Ø*-69-21050 • Spain (91) 322 54 55
When in Europe, contact the nearest American Express Travel Service Office.

220 Earl's Ct. Rd., tube: Earl's Ct.; Victoria Station; 2 Queensway, tube: Queensway. Expect to pay a hefty fee.

TRAVELER'S CHECKS

Traveler's checks are the safest way to carry large sums of money, since their value can be reimbursed if they are lost or stolen. The major brands can be exchanged at virtually every bank in Britain, sometimes without a commission. Traveler's checks are also accepted at the great majority of B&Bs, shops, and restaurants. Along with replacement services, many issuing agencies offer services such as refund hotlines, message replaying, travel insurance, and emergency assistance.

Sign your checks immediately when you purchase them; copy the **serial numbers** down and keep them in a safe place (*not* in your wallet or with the checks); also leave a photocopy with someone at home. Countersign checks *only* when you are ready to use them and when the store cashier is watching; carry your passport when you plan to use checks. Refunds on lost or stolen checks, while occasionally quick, are usually time-consuming. To accelerate the process and avoid red tape, keep **check receipts** and a **record of which checks you've cashed** separate from the checks themselves. Buying checks in small denominations (US$20 checks rather than US$50 ones or higher) is safer and more convenient.

The major brands are sold at agencies and banks everywhere. Of these, **American Express** Traveler's Cheques are perhaps the most widely accepted. In Britain, though, **Barclays** and **Thomas Cook** checks are just as widely recognized; Barclays may be the best choice if you are traveling only in Britain. If you will be visiting other countries in addition to Britain, you should buy your checks in U.S. dollars. Few currencies are as easily exchanged worldwide, and you will save yourself the cost of repeatedly converting currency. If you are visiting only Britain, you may be better off buying in pounds; sterling traveler's checks are often easier to cash. (Barclays will cash any sterling check for free, regardless of the issuer.) Few establishments will take checks issued in foreign currency without taking a hefty bite for themselves. The following companies offer checks in U.S. dollars or British pounds—often in both:

American Express: Call (800) 221-7282 in the U.S. and Canada, (0800) 521 313 in the U.K., (1800) 626 000 in Ireland, (008) 251 902 in Australia, (0800) 441 068 in New Zealand, and (612) 886-0689 in Sydney with questions or to report lost or stolen Cheques. Elsewhere, call U.S. collect (801) 964-6665) or Sydney collect (612) 886 0689. AmEx Traveler's Cheques are the most widely recognized worldwide and easiest to replace if lost or stolen. Checks can be purchased at American Express Travel Services Offices, banks, and AAA offices. AmEx offices cash their own Cheques commission-free and sell Cheques which can be signed by either of 2 people traveling together. Cheque and cardholders can also call the Global Assist Hotline (tel. (202) 783-7474 collect from overseas, (800) 554-2639 in the U.S.) for emergency medical, legal, and financial services. Services and offices are described in *The American Express Traveler's Companion* (free for customers).

Barclays Bank/Visa: Sells Visa traveler's checks. Commission varies by bank (1-3%). Any brand of Visa Travelers Checks can be reported lost at the general Visa number: in the U.S. or Canada, (800) 227-6811; in the U.K., 937 8091; from elsewhere call New York collect, (212) 858-8500. For Barclays info, call (800) 221-2426 in the U.S. and Canada; (202) 671 212 in the U.K. Barclays will cash Visa checks for free.

Citicorp: Sells Visa traveler's checks. For Citicorp information and to report lost checks, call (800) 645-6556 in the U.S. and Canada, 982 4040 in Britain, or collect from elsewhere (813) 623-1709. Commission varies by bank (1-2%). Check holders automatically enrolled for 45 days in Citicorp's **Travel Assist Hotline** (tel. (800) 523-1199), which provides English-speaking doctor, lawyer, and interpreter referrals along with lost check assistance. Citicorp's World Courier Service guarantees hand-delivery of traveler's checks anywhere in the world.

Mastercard International: Sells Mastercard travelers checks in 11 currencies. In the U.S. or Canada call (800) 223-9920, or collect (609) 987-7300; from overseas call (44) 733 502 995. Commission varies by bank (1-2%).

Thomas Cook: Sells Mastercard Traveler's Checks. Commissions nonexistent to low (0-2%). In the U.S. call (800) 223-7373 for refunds, (800) 223-4030 for orders. From elsewhere call collect (212) 974-5696.

CREDIT CARDS

Credit cards are widely accepted in London, although not in all restaurants and hotels, especially in the budget range. Try to pay for large purchases abroad by credit card; the credit card company gets a better exchange rate than you do. Note that the British "Barclaycard" and "Access" are equivalent to Visa and Mastercard, respectively. You can often reduce conversion fees by charging instead of changing traveler's checks. Additionally, with credit cards such as American Express, Visa, and Mastercard, associated banks will give you an instant **cash advance** in local currency as large as your remaining credit line. The terms of this arrangement follow the policy of the bank that issued the card. Unfortunately, in most cases you will pay mortifying rates of interest. Many banks in Britain allow you to withdraw money from **ATM** machines with a credit card; look for **American Express, Mastercard,** or **Visa** logos on machines. You must work this out with your bank beforehand, as money will come from your checking account. To report a **lost credit card** overseas, call American Express at (0800) 892 333; Visa at (410) 581 7931; or Mastercard at (314) 275 6690.

ELECTRONIC BANKING

Automatic Teller Machines (ATMs), operated by bank or credit cards, are not quite as prevalent in Britain as in North America, but most banks in the larger cities are connected to an international money network, either **Plus** (tel. (800) THE PLUS/843-7587) or **Cirrus** (tel. (800) 4CIRRUS/424-7787). Depending on the system that your bank at home uses, you will probably be able to access your own personal bank account whenever you're in need of funds. In the U.K., Midland Bank and National Westminster Bank are hooked into Cirrus. Along with credit cards, ATMs offer by far the best exchange rate; Cirrus does charge $5 to withdraw non-domestically, but the favorable rate will often outweigh this charge on larger withdrawals. Before you go, memorize your **PIN** numerically (rather than alphabetically) as ATM keypads may not have letters.

American Express card holders can sign up for AmEx's free Express Cash service through which you can access cash from your account at any ATM with the AmEx trademark, but each transaction costs a minimum US$2.50 (max. US$10) plus conversion fees and interest. For a list of ATMs where you can use your card, call AmEx at (800) CASH NOW (227-4669). Set up your Express Cash account a few weeks before you travel. **Visa** cards access ATM networks in 40 countries (usually Cirrus, but it varies with the issuing bank). Contact your issuer before you travel in order to get a **PIN** (personal identification number), essential for ATM use. **MasterCard** functions in essentially the same way as Visa. Don't rely too heavily on automation. There is often a limit on the amount of money you can withdraw per day, and computer network failures are not uncommon.

SENDING MONEY ABROAD

Sending money overseas is a complicated, expensive, and often extremely frustrating adventure. Do your best to avoid it; carry a credit card or a separate stash of emergency traveler's checks. The easiest way to obtain money from home is to bring an **American Express Card.** AmEx allows green-card holders to draw cash from their checking accounts (checkbook not required) at any of its major offices and many of its representatives' offices, up to US$1000 every seven days (no service charge, no interest). If someone feeds money into your account back home, you'll be set. Or you can wire money through the money transfer services operated by

Western Union (tel. (800) 325-6000 in North America, (0800) 833 833 in Europe) or American Express (tel. (800) 543-4080 in the U.S., (800) 933-3278 in Canada). Fees are commensurate with the amount of money being sent and, for American Express, the time it is requested in (10 min., overnight, 3-5 days). Western Union is generally cheaper but may take longer: US$29 to send $250, $40 for $500, $50 for $1000. U.S. Citizens can also have money sent to them abroad in dire emergencies by the State Department's Citizens' Emergency Center (tel. (202) 647-5225, after hours (202) 647-4000). The State Department will cable a modest amount of money to consular offices, which will then disperse it according to instructions. To send money through the State Department a person can drop it off there or cable money to the department through Western Union.

OPENING A BANK ACCOUNT

For a long stay in London, an English **sterling bank account** may be a convenient way to manage funds. But opening an account can be difficult. Fewer people in Britain have bank accounts than in America; many have Post Office savings accounts or nothing at all. Those working in the U.K. should not have too much trouble, but full-time students may have to try harder. If the obstacles prove too great, try a **building society,** the British version of a savings and loan—building societies are less likely to require proof of employment.

Most major banks require a stay in Britain of at least a year. The four main English banks all have oodles of branches in London, with the following head offices: **Barclays Bank,** 54 Lombard St., EC3 (tel. 621 1888); **Lloyd's Bank,** 71 Lombard St., EC3 (tel. 626 1500); **Midland Bank,** 27 Poultry, EC2 (tel. 260 8000); **National Westminster Bank,** 41 Lothbury, EC2 (tel. 606 6060). (Bank tube for all.) **Abbey National,** head office at 201 Grafton Gate East, Milton Keynes (tel. (0908) 343 000), has branches throughout London. Procedures vary somewhat from bank to bank; in all cases you should contact your home bank a few months before coming to London. Obtain a letter of introduction from your bank, and find out if it can make arrangements in advance for an account to be opened at a bank in the U.K., so that it is available for use on arrival. Once in London, it may be harder to have your home bank help you open an account. When opening an account here you must show your passport and your bank's letter of introduction, a letter from an employer confirming the tenure of employment in Britain and a regular salary, or a letter from your school (in Britain) confirming your status as a full-time student.

While proof of employment almost guarantees an account, students are screened rigorously. Students of American colleges studying abroad should contact their home school's bursar's office, which may have a special arrangement with a bank in London. When opening an account for a student, the bank generally requires a large deposit to be placed in the account, which could ideally support the student for the full period of study. Alternatively, they may accept proof that regular payments would be made into the account (e.g., from parents).

Once you have made your way through all the red tape, the bank will generally issue you a checkbook, a check guarantee card (vouching for checks of up to £50 or £100), and a cash machine card. They may be rather reticent about handing out credit cards to temporary visitors—which should not matter as long as you can arrange to have your own credit card bills paid back home. Note that Barclaycard acts as both a Visa card and a check guarantee card for Barclay's checks.

VALUE-ADDED TAX

Britain charges value-added tax (VAT), a national sales tax, on most goods and some services. VAT is 17.5% on many services (such as hairdressers, hotels, restaurants, and car rental agencies) and on all goods (except books, medicine, food, and children's clothes). The prices stated in *Let's Go* include VAT unless otherwise specified. Non-EC visitors to the U.K. can get a VAT refund through the Retail Export Scheme. Ask the shopkeeper for the appropriate form, which immigration officials will sign and stamp when you leave the country. To obtain the refund in cash, bring

HEALTH AND INSURANCE

your stamped form to the Tax Free refund desk in the airport. To obtain the refund by check or credit card, send the form back in the envelope provided and the shopkeeper will then send your refund; note, however, that a service charge will be deducted from your refund. Many shops have a puchase minimum of £50-75 which you will have to meet before they fill out a VAT form for you; stores may out you off because of the inconvenience, but insist and the prices you pay for goods will become much more reasonable. You must leave the country within three months of your purchase in order to claim back VAT.

■ HEALTH AND INSURANCE

Common sense is the simplest prescription for good health while you travel: eat well, drink enough, get enough sleep, and don't overexert yourself. All food is normally safe in Britain. Although no special innoculations are necessary for travel to Britain, be sure that your inoculations are up-to-date.

Always go prepared with any **medication** you regularly take and may need while traveling, as well as a copy of the prescription from your doctor and a statement of any preexisting medical conditions you may have, especially if you will be bringing insulin, syringes, or any narcotics into a foreign country. If you wear **glasses or contact lenses,** be sure to take an extra pair and to know your prescription.

Travelers with medical conditions that cannot be easily recognized (diabetes, epilepsy, heart conditions, allergies to antibiotics, etc.) may want to join the **Medic Alert Foundation,** P.O. Box 1009, Turlock, CA, 95381-1009. Call the 24-hour hotline at (800) 432-5378. Membership to the foundation provides the Medic Alert Identification Tag, an annually-updated wallet card, and hotline access. The **American Diabetes Association,** 1660 Duke St., Alexandria, VA 22314 (tel. (800) 232-3472) provides copies of the article "Travel and Diabetes" and diabetic ID cards, which carry messages in 18 languages explaining the carrier's diabetic status. Or contact **Diabetic Travel Services, Inc.,** which provides worldwide information on diabetic treatment and physicians (39 East 52nd St., New York, NY 10022).

The United States **Centers for Disease Control** provides general information on health for travelers and maintains an international travelers hotline (tel. (404) 332-4559; fax service (404) 332-4565; or write to the Centers for Disease Control and Prevention, CDC, 1600 Clifton Rd. NE, Atlanta, GA 30333). The CDC publishes the booklet *Health Information for International Travelers* (publication #HHS-CDC 90-8280, US$6), a global rundown of disease, immunization, and general health advice. Request the booklet by writing the Superintendent of Documents, P.O. Box 371954, Pittsburgh, PA 15250; tel. (202) 783-3238, fax (202) 275-2529).

All travelers must be concerned about **sexually transmitted diseases (STDs)**, especially **HIV infection;** HIV is the virus that leads to **AIDS** (Acquired Immune Deficiency Syndrome). To **protect yourself** from HIV infection and other STDs while traveling, follow all the precautions that you should follow at home. Never have unprotected sex with people you do not know or with people, even those you know well, that you are not certain are not HIV positive (on the basis of test results from six months after the person's last risky contact). If you have any questions about HIV and AIDS, you can call the U.S. **Centers for Disease Control** (CDC)'s main **AIDS hotline** number (English tel. (800) 342-2437, 7 days, 24-hrs.; TTD (800) 243-7889, Mon.-Fri. 10 am-10 pm; or Spanish tel. (800) 344-7432; 7 days, 8 am-2am). The United Nations' **World Health Organization** provides information on AIDS as well: in the U.S., call the switchboard at (202) 861-3200; in Europe, call 41 22 791 46 73 (Switzerland).

Contraception is available in most pharmacies. Women on the Pill should bring enough to allow for possible loss or extended stays, and should bring a copy of the prescription, since forms of the Pill vary a good deal. If you use a diaphragm, be sure that you have enough contraceptive jelly on hand. **Condoms** are sold at all drugstores, supermarkets, and convenience stores.

Abortion is legal in England. The **U.K. Family Planning Association** can provide you with information on contraception and abortion in Britain; write to 27-35 Mortimer St., London W1N 7RJ (tel. 580 9360, fax 436 3288). For general information on contraception, condoms, and abortion worldwide, contact the **International Planned Parenthood Federation,** European Regional Office, Regent's College Inner Circle, Regent's Park, London NW1 4NS (tel. 486 0741, fax 487 7950).

Beware of unnecessary coverage–your current policies might well extend to many travel-related accidents. Medical insurance (especially university policies) often cover costs incurred abroad, although Medicare's coverage is not valid in London. Canadians are protected by their home province's health insurance plan up to 90 days after leaving the country: check with the provincial Ministry of Health or Health Plan Headquarters. Australians are covered by Medicare in Britain; consult Medicare's brochure "Health Care for Australians Travelling Overseas" or write to the Comonwealth Dept. of Health, Housing and Community Services, GPO Box 9848 in your capital city. In general, homeowners' insurance (or your family's coverage) often covers theft during travel. Homeowners are generally covered against loss of travel documents (passport, plane ticket, railpass, etc.) up to $500.

ISIC and ITICs provide US$3000 worth of accident and illness insurance, US$100 per day up to 60 days of hospitalization, and up to $10,000 coverage for emergency medical evaluation; they also give you access to a toll-free Traveler's Assistance hotline whose multilingual staff can provide help in medical, legal, and financial emergencies overseas. In the United States, call (800) 626-2427; from abroad call collect (713) 267-2525.

Insurance companies usually require a copy of the police report for thefts, or evidence of having paid medical expenses (doctor's statements, receipts) before they will honor a claim, and may have time limits on filing. Always carry your policy numbers and proof of insurance. Check with each insurance carrier for specific restrictions. If your coverage does not include on-the-spot payments or cash transferrals, leave space in your budget for emergencies.

SAFETY AND SECURITY

Travelers can feel more safe in London than in many large American cities. After all, even the bobbies are unarmed. Few streets or tube stations are deserted, even at night. Reasonable precautions and common sense will ward off most bad fortune.

Keep all valuables on your person, preferably stowed away in a money belt or necklace pouch, which hide your money from prying eyes. Don't put money in a wallet in your back pocket. Women should sling purses over the shoulder and under the opposite arm. Carry all your treasured items (including your passport, rail-pass, traveler's checks and airline ticket) either in a money belt or neck pouch stashed securely inside your clothing. Never count your money in public and carry as little as possible. Keep a sharp eye out for fast-fingered pick-pockets, dastardly con artists, and conniving packs of hustlers masquerading as angel-faced children. Be alert in public telephone booths. If you must say your calling-card number, do so very quietly. Wherever you stow your belongings, try to keep your valuables on your person. Making photocopies of important documents (passport, ID, driver's license, health insurance policy, traveler's checks, credit cards) will allow you to replace them in case they are lost or stolen. Carry one copy separate from the documents and leave another copy at home.

Unattended packages will be taken, either by thieves or by the police, who are paranoid—and rightly so—about IRA bombs. Obey the constant warnings regarding suspicious packages, and leave nothing unattended.

London is a tourist-friendly city. It's hard to wander unwittingly into unnerving neighborhoods; these areas, in parts of Hackney, Tottenham, and South London, lie well away from central London. The areas around King's Cross/St. Pancras and Notting Hill Gate tube stations are a bit seedy at night. Avoid parks, heaths, and the river-banks in all areas after dark. Late trains on the tube out of central London are usually crowded and noisy. Waiting late at night at less central stations, on the other hand, can be unsettling. On night buses, sit on the lower deck next to the driver, who has a radio.

When walking after dark, stride purposefully on busy, well-lit roads. Keep to the right, facing oncoming traffic. Avoid shortcuts down alleys or across wasteground. Women may want to carry a rape alarm or whistle. For more safety tips, get *Positive Steps*, a Metropolitan Police leaflet, from the Positive Steps Campaign, P.O. Box 273, High Wycombe, Bucks. HP12 3XE (tel. (01494) 450 541), or order Maggie and Gemma Moss's *Handbook for Women Travellers* (see Women and Travel).

Especially if you are traveling alone, be sure that someone at home knows your itinerary. Never say that you're traveling alone. Steer clear of empty train compartments, and avoid large Underground stations after dark. Ask managers of your hotel, hostel, or B&B for advice on specific areas, and consider staying in places with a curfew or night attendant. Some cheap accommodations may entail more risks than savings; when traveling alone, you may want to forego dives and city outskirts.

A lesser-known but very real source of danger to foreign pedestrians in London is crossing the street. Despite the prominent "Look Right" signs, at least one American dies every year after looking the wrong way before stepping into the road. Look both ways.

In an emergency, call 999, a free call from any pay or card phone. The operator will ask whether you require police, ambulance, or fire service. This is the emergency number across England.

There is no sure-fire set of precautions that will protect you from all situations you might encounter when you travel. A good self-defense course will give you concrete ways to react to different types of aggression, but it might cost you more money than your trip. **Model Mugging,** a national organization with offices in several major North American cities, teaches a very effective, comprehensive course on self-defense (courses US$400-500). Call Model Mugging in the U.S. at (617) 232-7900) on the East Coast, (312) 338-4545 in the Midwest, or (415) 592-7300) on the West Coast. Community colleges frequently offer self-defense courses at more affordable prices. **The U.S. Department of State's** pamphlet *A Safe Trip Abroad* (US$1) summarizes safety information for travelers. More complete information may be found in *Travel Safety: Security and Safeguards at Home and Abroad*, published by **Hippocrene Books, Inc.,** 171 Madison Ave., New York, NY 10016 (orders tel. (718) 454-2366; fax (718) 454-1391).

■ WHEN TO GO

Traveling during the off-season will save you money. Airfares drop and domestic travel becomes less congested. You won't have to compete with squadrons of fellow tourists crowding hotels, sights, and train stations and driving up prices. Hotel owners generally consider November to March the off-season, although business may be slow enough in October, April, and May for you to bargain for a discount. For sights, October to April is the off-season and opening hours are shortened.

CLIMATE

> *I'm leaving because the weather is too good. I hate London when it's not raining.*
>
> —Groucho Marx, June 28, 1954

London weather, while often damp, stays mild, with an average temperature in the mid-60s (°F) in summer and in the low 40s (°F) in winter. May and June are the sunniest months, July and August the warmest, and October and November the rainiest. December and January have the worst weather of the year—wet, cold, and cloudy. Expect unstable weather patterns throughout the year; a bright and cloudless morning sky often precedes intermittent afternoon showers.

■ PACKING

Pack light; the rest is commentary. Remember that you can buy almost anything you'll need in London. One tried-and-true method of packing is to set out everything you think you'll need, then pack half of it—and pack twice the money.

For a long stay in London you might prefer a suitcase to a conspicuous backpack. If you'll be on the move frequently, go with the pack. Bring along a small daypack for carrying lunch, a camera, and valuables. Keep your money, passport, and other valuables with you in a purse, neck pouch, or money belt. Label every article of baggage both inside and out with your name and address. For added security, bring a combination lock for your main bag and for London hostel lockers.

Nothing will serve you more loyally in London than comfortable walking shoes and a folding umbrella. Bring a light sweater (even in summer), an alarm clock, and a raincoat. Despite its rainy reputation, London gets gruelingly sunny in summer; pack sunglasses. A single-sheet sleeping sack is free in all London HI hostels.

Any electrical gadget will need an adapter and a converter. The voltage in England is 240 volts AC. (North American appliances are 110 volts AC.) Converters and adapters are available worldwide in department and hardware stores (US$10-15).

If you take expensive **cameras** or equipment abroad, it's best to register everything with customs at the airport before departure. If you're coming from the U.S., buy a supply of film before you leave; it's more expensive in Britain. Unless you're shooting with 1000 ASA or more, airport security x-rays should not harm your pictures. Pack film in your carry-on, since the x-rays employed on checked baggage are much stronger. If you're bringing a laptop or notebook **computer,** be sure to have both computer and floppy discs hand-inspected, lest stray x-rays wipe out your as-yet-unpublished *chef-d'oeuvre.* Officials may ask you to turn it on, so be sure the batteries are fully loaded. A warning: Lost baggage is common, and not always retrieved. Keep all valuables in your carry-on.

■ SPECIFIC CONCERNS

WOMEN AND TRAVEL

Women exploring any area on their own inevitably face additional safety concerns. In all situations it is best to trust your instincts: if you'd feel better somewhere else, don't hesitate to move on. You may want to consider staying in hostels which offer single rooms which lock from the inside, or religious organizations that offer rooms for women only. Stick to centrally located accommodations and avoid late-night treks or rides on the Underground. Remember that hitching is *never* safe for lone women, or even for two women traveling together.

To escape unwanted attention, foreign women in London should follow the example of local women; in many cases, the less you look like a tourist, the better off you'll be. Look as if you know where you're going, and ask women or couples for directions if you're lost or if you feel uncomfortable. Your best answer to verbal harassment may be no answer at all. Seek out a police officer or a female passerby before a crisis erupts, and don't hesitate to scream for help. *Always* carry change for the phone, and enough extra money for a bus or taxi. Carry a whistle on your key-chain, and don't hesitate to use it in an emergency. **London Rape Crisis Centre,** P.O. Box 69, WC1 (tel. 837 1600) offers a 24-hour rape crisis hotline. These warnings and suggestions should not discourage women from traveling alone—don't take unnecessary risks, but don't lose your spirit of adventure either.

Particularly good for travel to London is the *Women's Guide to London* (Virago), by Josie Barnard (£9.99). The **London Women's Centre** at Wesley House, 4 Wild Ct., WC2 (tel. 831 6946; tube: Holborn), is an umbrella organization that houses a variety of political, ethnic, leisure, and support groups for women. The female-staffed **Audre Lorde Clinic,** at the Ambrose King Centre, Royal London Hospital, E1 (tel. 377 7312; tube: Whitechapel) offers screenings for STDs, HIV tests, and breast exams (open Fri. 9:30am-12:30pm). **Lady Cabs** (tel. 272 1992) is a north London-

based women's taxi service. For more general information on women and travel, consult these publications:

Handbook For Women Travelers, by Maggie and Gemma Moss. Encyclopedic and well-written. £9. From Piaktus Books, 5 Windmill St., London W1P 1HF (tel. 631 0710).

A Journey of One's Own, by Thalia Zepatos. Eighth Mountain Press, US$15. The latest thing on the market, interesting and full of good advice, with a specific and manageable bibliography of books and resources.

Wander Women, 136 N. Grand Ave. #237, West Covina, CA 91791 (tel. (818) 966-8857. A travel and adventure networking organization for women over 40; publishes the quarterly newsletter *Journal 'n Footnotes*. Membership US$29.

Women Travel: Adventures, Advice & Experience, by Miranda Davies and Natania Jansz. Penguin, US$13. Information on specific foreign countries plus a decent bibliography and resource index.

OLDER TRAVELERS AND SENIOR CITIZENS

Proof of senior citizen status is required for many discounts listed. Seniors are eligible for a wide array of discounts on transportation, museums, movies, theater, concerts, restaurants, and accommodations. Look for the book *Unbelievably Good Deals and Great Adventures That You Absolutely Can't Get Unless You're Over 50,* by Joan Rattner Hellman (US$8).

Elderhostel, 75 Federal St., 3rd floor, Boston, MA 02110-1941 (tel. (617) 426-8056). You must be 60 or over and may bring a spouse. Programs at colleges and universities in over 47 countries on varied subjects which generally last a week.

Gateway Books, 2023 Clemens Road, Oakland, CA 94602 (tel. (510) 530-0299; fax (510) 530-0497; orders (800) 669-0773). Publishes *Get Up and Go: A Guide for the Mature Traveler* (US$11) and *Adventures Abroad* (US$13), which offer general hints for the budget-conscious senior who is considering a long stay abroad.

National Council of Senior Citizens, 1331 F St. NW, Washington, DC 20004 (tel. (202) 347-8800). Memberships are US$12 a year, $30 for three years, or $150 for a lifetime. Hotel and auto rental discounts, a senior citizen newspaper, use of a discount travel agency, and supplemental Medicare insurance (if you're over 65).

Pilot Books, 103 Cooper St., Babylon, NY 11702 (tel. (516) 422-2225). Publishes *The International Health Guide for Senior Citizens* (US$5, postage $1) and *The Senior Citizens' Guide to Budget Travel in Europe* (US$6).

TRAVELERS WITH DISABILITIES

Transportation companies in Britain are remarkably conscientious about providing facilities and services to meet the needs of travelers with disabilities. Notify a bus or coach company of your plans ahead of time, and they will have staff ready to assist you. **British Rail** offers a discounted railcard for British citizens only. If you don't have a railcard but are traveling in your own wheelchair or are blind and traveling with a companion, you are still eligible for certain discounts and services. With advance notification, BR will set aside a convenient spot for your wheelchair. Not all stations are accessible; write for the pamphlet *British Rail and Disabled Travellers.* **National Express** (bus travel) also offers some discounts. Several **car rental agencies** can have hand-controlled cars available provided you give them advance notice. Britain imposes a six-month quarantine on all animals entering the country—this includes seeing-eye dogs. The owner must also obtain a veterinary certificate (consult the nearest British Consulate for details). You can write to the British Tourist Authority for free handbooks and access guides.

Useful guides to London for people with disabilities are Nicholson's *Access in London,* a guide to accommodations, transport, and accessibility compiled by researchers with disabilities, available in any well-stocked travel shop (about £3.50). *London for All* is a booklet on transport, tours, and hotels published by the London Tourist Board and available at tourist Information Centres. *Door to Door,* published by Her Majesty's Stationery Office (49 High Holborn, WC1; tel. 211 5656; tube: Holborn), is also helpful. For **travel by Underground,** pick up the booklet *Access to the Underground* for 70p from Tourist Information Centres and London Transport Information Centres, or by post from from the Unit for Disabled Passengers (London Regional Transport, 55 Broadway, London SW1H 0BD; tel. 918 3312). London Transport's 24-hour travel information hotline is also useful (tel. 222 1234).

The **"Arts Access"** section at the beginning of the London telephone books details special services available at theatres, cinemas, and concert halls around London. Call 936 3436 with Arts Access questions, or **Artsline,** 5 Crowndale Rd., NW1 (tel. 388 2227), for entertainment accessibility information (Mon.-Fri. 9:30am-5:30pm). The **Society of West End Theatre** publishes the highly useful *Disabled Access Guide to London's West End Theatres.* To obtain a copy, write to the society at Bedford Chambers, The Piazza, Covent Garden, WC2E 8HQ. **Shape** (tel. 700 8138) offers very cheap tickets to accessible arts events, as well as providing transport and escorts to these events.

For general information, phone the **Disability Information and Advice Service** (tel. 275 8485), the **Disability Information Service** (tel. 630 5994; Mon.-Fri. 10am-4pm), or the **Greater London Association for the Disabled** (tel. 274 0107).

The following organizations provide general information and guides.

American Foundation for the Blind, 15 W. 16th St., New York, NW 10011 (tel. (212) 620-2147). Open Mon.-Fri. 9am-2pm. Provides ID cards (US$10); write for an application or call the Product Center at (800) 829-0500. Also call the Product Center to order AFB catalogs in braille, print, or on cassette or disk.

Directions Unlimited, 720 North Bedford Rd., Bedford Hills, NY 10507 (tel. (800) 533-5343 or (914) 241-1700; fax (914) 241-0243). Specializes in arranging individual and group vacations, tours, and cruises for those with physical disabilities.

Facts on File, 460 Park Ave. S., New York, NY 10016 (tel. (800) 829-0500 or (212) 683-2244 in AK and HI). Publishers of *Access to the World* (US$17), a guide to accessible accommodations and sights.

Flying Wheels Travel Service, PO Box 382, 143 W. Bridge St., Owatonne, MN 55060 (tel. (800) 535-6790; fax (507) 451-1685). Arranges international trips for groups or individuals in wheelchairs or with other sorts of limited mobility.

Graphic Language Press, PO Box 270, Cardiff by the Sea, CA 92007 (tel. (619) 944-9594). Publishers of *Wheelchair Through Europe* (US$13, postage included). Comprehensive advice for the wheelchair-bound travelers.

The Guided Tour, Elkins Park House #114B, 7900 Old York Road, Elkins Park, PA 19117-2339 (tel. (215) 635-2637 or (800) 738-5841). Organizes year-round travel programs for persons with developmental and physical challenges as well as those geared to the needs of persons requiring renal dialysis.

Mobility International, USA (MIUSA), PO Box 10767, Eugene, OR 97440 (tel. (503) 343-1284 voice and TDD; fax (503) 343-6812). International headquarters in Britain, 228 Borough High St., London SE1 1JX, (tel. 403 5688). Contacts in 30 countries. Information on travel for those with physical disabilities. Membership costs US$20 per year, newsletter $10. They also sell the periodically updated and expanded *A World of Options: A Guide to International Educational Exchange, Community Service, and Travel for Persons with Diabilities.*

Society for the Advancement of Travel for the Handicapped, 347 Fifth Ave. #610, New York, NY 10016 (tel. (212) 447-7284; fax (212) 725-8253). Publishes quarterly travel newsletter and pamphlets (free for members , US$3 for nonmembers), which contain advice on trip planning for people with disabilities. Annual membership is US$45, students and seniors US$25.

Twin Peaks Press, PO Box 129, Vancouver , WA 98666-0129 (tel. (206) 694-2462 or (800) 637-2256 MC and Visa orders; fax (206) 696-3210). Publishers of *Travel for the Disabled,* with tips and lists of accessible tourist attractions (US$20). Also publishes *Directory for Travel Agencies of the Disabled* (US$20), *Wheelchair Vagabond* (US$15), and *Directory of Accessible Van Rentals* (US$10).

BISEXUAL, GAY, AND LESBIAN TRAVELERS

The following organizations and publications provide general travel information. For more information specific to London, see Bisexual, Gay, and Lesbian London.

Are You Two...Together? A Gay and Lesbian Travel Guide to Europe, published by Random House and available at bookstores (US$18). A terrific guide filled with entertaining anecdotes and handy tips for gays and lesbians traveling in Europe. Includes a section on London.

Ferrari Publications, PO Box 37887, Phoenix, AZ 85069, tel. (602) 863-2408. Publishers of *Ferrari's Places of Interest* (US$16), *Ferrari's Places for Men* (US$15) , *Ferrari's Places for Women* (US$13), and *Inn Places: US and World-wide Gay Accommodations* (US$15). Available in bookstores, or by mail order (postage US$3.50 for the first item, $0.50 for each additonal item).

Giovanni's Room, 345 S. 12th St. Philadelphia, PA 19107, tel. (215) 923-2960, fax (215) 923-0813. A feminist, lesbian, and gay bookstore with mail-order service.

Renaissance House, PO Box 533, Village Station, New York, NY 10014, tel. (212) 674-0120, fax (212) 420-1126. A comprehensive gay bookstore with mail-order.

Spartacus International Gay Guides, published by Bruno Gmunder, Postfach 301345, D-1000 Berlin 30, Germany (tel. 49 (30) 25 49 82 00). Lists of bars, restaurants, hotels, and bookstores around the world catering to gay men.

Women Going Places (US$14). An international women's travel and resource guide emphasizing women-owned enterprises, geared toward lesbians.

The Pink Plaque Guide to London, by Michael Elliman and Frederick Roll. Walks covering some of London's more unconventional heroes and heroines. £7.

KOSHER AND VEGETARIAN TRAVELERS

See the Food introduction and listings under "Kosher" and "Vegetarian" in the restaurant section.

Jewish Chronicle Publications, 25 Furnival St., London EC4A 1JT England, tel. 405 9252, fax 831 5188. Publishers of *The Jewish Travel Guide,* which lists synagogues, kosher restaurants, and Jewish institutions in over 80 countries. Available in the United States from Sepher-Hermon Press, 1265 46th St., Brooklyn, NY 11219, tel. (718) 972-9010, US$12, postage US$1.75.

Jewish Vegetarian Society, 855 Finchley Rd., NW11 (tel. (0181) 455 0692).

Vegetarian Society of the UK, Parkdale, Dunham Rd., Altringham, Cheshire WA14 4QG, tel. (0161) 928 0793.

Vegetarian Times, Orders only (800) 435-9610. Publishes, in addition to the *Times*, the *European Vegetarian Guide to Restaurants and Hotels.*

TRAVELERS WITH CHILDREN

Children under two generally fly free on domestic flights and for 10 percent of the adult fare on international flights (this fare does not necessarily include a seat). 2 to 12 usually fly half price. Most sights and many accomodations in London have reduced fees for children, sometimes listed under the name "concessions." You may want to refer to the following publications, and remember to check *Time Out*'s listings for events of interest to children:

Lonely Planet Publications, Embarcadero West, 155 Philbert St., Suite 251, Oakland, CA 94607, (510)-893-8555 or (800)-275-8555, fax (510)-893-8563. Publishes *Travel with Children* by M. Wheeler (US$10.95, postage US$1.50 in the U.S.).

John Muir Publications, P.O. Box 613, Santa Fe, NM 87504 (800)-285-4078. The *Kidding Around* series of illustrated books for children includes a book on London that could be educational and distracting on long trips (US$10-13).

Mason-Grant Publications, P.O. Box 6547, Portsmouth, NH 03802 (tel. (603) 436 1608, fax (603) 427 0015). Publishes *Take Your Kids to Europe* by Cynthia W. Harriman (US$14), a budget guide geared towards family travel.

■ ALTERNATIVES TO TOURISM

If the often madcap, train-changing, site-switching pace of tourism loses its appeal, consider a longer stay in London. Study, work, or volunteering will help you get a better sense of parts of the city that are often hidden to the short-term visitor.

STUDY

It's not difficult to spend a summer, a term, or a year studying in London under the auspices of a well-established program. Enrolling as a full-time student, however, is somewhat more difficult; the requirements for admission can be hard to meet unless you attended a British secondary school, and often only a limited number of foreign students are accepted each year. For initial information on studying in Britain, contact the British Council office in your home country. You might also turn to CIEE's publications *Work, Study, Travel Abroad: The Whole World Handbook* or *Going Places: The High School Student's Guide to Study, Travel, And Adventure*. The following organizations and programs can also deluge you with information:

American Field Service Intercultural Programs (AFS), 220 East 42nd Street, 3rd Floor, New York, NY 10017. Call (800) 237-4636 or speak to Rory Vibar at the Program Information Office (tel. (212) 949-4242). Founded in 1947, AFS provides summer, semester, and year-long homestay exchange programs for high school students. Short-term adult programs are also offered. Financial aid.

The American Institute for Foreign Study, College Division, 102 Greenwich Avenue, Greenwich CT 06830 (tel. (800) 727 2437). For high school traveling programs, call (800) 888-ACIS. Organizes academic year, semester, summer, and academic quarter study abroad programs in London and many other cities worldwide. Programs are open to interested adults. Minority and merit scholarships.

Association of Commonwealth Universities (ACU), John Foster House, 36 Gordon Square, London WC1H 0PF (tel. 387 8572). Administers scholarship programs and publishes information about Commonwealth universities.

British Information Services, 845 3rd Ave., 9th Floor, New York, NY 10022 (tel. (212) 752-5747, fax (212) 752-5747). Gives information on study in Britain. Write for their free pamphlet, *Study in Britain*.

Cambridge Summer Program, University of New Hampshire, Hamilton Smith Hall, Durham, NH 03824 (tel. (603) 862-3962, fax (603) 862-3563). UNH sponsors a 6-week program in July and August at Gonville and Caius College, one of the 30 colleges comprising Cambridge University. Transfer credit for American students. Applicants must have completed 1 yr. of an undergraduate program.

Institute of International Education (IIE), 809 United Nations Plaza, New York, NY 10017-3580 (tel. (212) 984-5412); fax (212) 984-5358). Publishes several books on study abroad, including the free *Basic Facts on Foreign Study*. *Academic Year Abroad* (US$43, $4 postage) and *Vacation Study Abroad* (US$37, $4 postage) detail ober 3600 programs.

Inter-Study Programmes, 42 Milson St., Bath BA1 1DN (tel. (01225) 464 769, fax (01225) 444 104). In U.S., call their Boston office at (617) 391-0991. Offers semester- and year-long programs in Britain; handles all details between program institution and your home institution, including housing and credit transfer.

UKCOSA/United Kingdom Council for International Education, 9-17 St. Albans Place, London N1 0NX (tel. (0171) 226 3762, fax (0171) 226 3373). Advises prospective and current students on immigration, finance, and more .

Degree Programs

The first step in the multi-tiered process of applying to British universities is to send for the handbook, *How to Apply for Admission to a University* and an application form from **Universities Central Council on Admission** (UCCA), P.O. Box 28, Cheltenham, Glos. GL50 3SA (tel. 01242) 222 444). Generally, U.S. students must have completed two years' study at a U.S. university or college; British Information Services' pamphlet *Study in Britain* lists some schools that accept high school students. Applications for full-time undergraduate study in Britain must be made to

UCCA and should arrive by December 15 of the year preceding admission (by Oct. 15 for applicants who wish to be considered by Oxford or Cambridge). Regulations vary for students who already have a BA and wish to study in Britain; write directly to the school concerned to find out its preferences. (Graduate applications should be filed by mid-March of the year preceding admission.)

"Home students" (British students, or students from other EC countries who have lived in the EC for three years immediately preceding the year of their admission) pay reduced, subsidized rates, but "overseas students" are hit with the real thing. In the 1994-95 academic year, you would expect to pay around £5550 for a year of humanities courses and £6000-7000 for other expenses, not including plane fare. The ACU states that it is not possible for a student to work her way through college and warns that a student may have to produce evidence of financial security to gain admittance. For outside funding, your best bet is to apply for international scholarships and fellowships; contact your university's study-abroad office. The book *Higher Education in the United Kingdom 1993-94: A Handbook for Students and their Advisers* ($33), revised every three years, rigorously discusses financial and other aspects of the British university experience. (Stocked in many college libraries in the U.S.; published by Oryx Press for the ACU, 4041 N. Central Ave. #700, Phoenix, AZ 85012; tel. (800) 279-6799 or (602) 265-2651.)

WORK

Becoming a part of the economy may be the best way to immerse yourself in a foreign culture. You may not earn as much as you would at home, but you should manage to cover your living expenses and possibly your airfare. A range of short-term opportunities are available, although obtaining a work permit may be difficult.

Permits

Unless you're a citizen of a Common Market or a British Commonwealth nation, you'll have a tough time finding a legal paying job. Citizens of British Commonwealth nations (including Canada, Australia, and New Zealand) who are between the ages of 17 and 27 may work in Britain during a visit without permits if the employment they take is "incidental to their holiday." Commonwealth citizens with a parent born in the U.K. may apply for a certificate of entitlement to the right of abode, which allows them to live and work in Britain without any other formalities.

Officially, you can hold a job in European countries only with a work permit, applied for by your prospective employer (or by you, with supporting papers from the employer). The real catch-22 is that normally you must physically enter the country in order to have immigration officials validate your work permit papers and note your status in your passport. This means that if you can't set up a job from afar and have the work permit sent to you, you must enter the country to look for a job, find an employer and have them start the permit process, then *leave* the country until the permit is sent to you (up to six weeks), and finally return and start work.

If you are a full-time student at a U.S. or Canadian university, the cleanest, simplest way to get a job abroad is through work permit programs run by CIEE and its member organizations (see above). For a US$125 application fee, CIEE can procure three- to six-month work permits (and a handbook to help you find work and housing) for Britain, France, Germany, Ireland, Spain and some non-European countries.

Au pair jobs, temporary volunteer positions, and jobs at work camps and farm camps do not require a work permit, although you wil need an entrance card or letter of invitation from the organization or individual concerned.

Finding A Job

While casual jobs—bar, restaurant, and hotel reception work, for example—are readily available (look in shop windows and for the advertisements posted in the windows of local tobacconists), wages are unlikely to be more than £3-4 per hour. Most students here do not work during termtime, so part-time jobs that fit in with a daytime study schedule may be harder to find. Advice can be found at a local university's work-abroad resource center.

Other Work Programs

Summer positions as tour group leaders are available with **Hostelling International. World Learning, Inc.** (see Study) has positions for group leaders world-wide. Applicants must be at least 24 and have established leadership abilities, language fluency, and in-depth overseas experience for the countries to which they apply. Group leaders have all their expenses paid and receive a US$200 honorarium.

Au pair positions are officially reserved for unmarried female nationals of Western European countries whose primary aim is to improve their English. However, native English speakers can sometimes obtain these jobs. Check the help-wanted columns of the *International Herald Tribune*. Generally, *au pairs* help a host family by taking care of the children and light housework for about five hours per day in return for room, board, and a small monthly stipend. Make sure you know in advance what the family expects of you. Applicants should also determine the details of hours per week, salary, and living accommodations before settling in with their family. **Childcare International, Ltd.** arranges *au pair* and nanny placements throughout Europe in selected host families. The organization prefers a 6-12 month placement but does arrange summer work. Write to Childcare International, Ltd., Trafalgar House, Grenville Place, London NW7 3SA (tel. (0181) 959 3611 or (0181) 906 3116; fax (0181) 906 3461).

Useful Publications

There are a number of books listing work-abroad opportunities. Start with CIEE's free booklet *Work Abroad*, then graduate to the excellent publications put out by Vacation Work. Their books are also available in bookstores in North America, through Travel CUTS or from Peterson's Guides (address below).

Addison Wesley publishes *International Jobs: Where They Are, How to Get Them*, by Eric Kocher. Addison-Wesley, Order Department, Jacob Way, Reading, MA 01867 (tel. (800) 358-566). US$15.

Peterson's Guides, 202 Carnegie Center, Princeton, NJ 08543 (tel. (800) 338-3282 or (609) 243-9111). Peterson's publishes The *1993 Directory of Summer Jobs in Britain* (US$16), which lists 30,000 jobs in Scotland, Wales, and England, including openings for office help, farm laborers, chambermaids, and lorry drivers, and *Work Your Way Around the World* (US$18), a conglomeration of information.

World Trade Academy Press, 50 East 42nd St., New York, NY 10017 (tel. (212) 697-4999) publishes *Looking for Employment in Foreign Countries* (US$16.50), giving information on federal, commercial, and volunteer jobs abroad and advice on resumes and interviews.

VOLUNTEERING

Volunteer jobs are readily available almost everywhere, and provide great opportunities to go places and meet people. You may receive room and board in exchange for your labor, and the work can be fascinating. The following organizations and publications can help you to explore possibilities. Organizations that arrange placement often charge high application fees in addition to workcamps' charges for room and board. Check listings in the *International Directory of Voluntary Work* (£8.95); obtain a copy from Vacation Work Publications, 9 Park End St., Oxford, OX1 1HJ, England (tel. (01865) 241 978; fax (01865) 790 885).

Council on International Educational Exchange (CIEE): the International Voluntary Service Department publishes *Volunteer! The Comprehensive Guide to Voluntary Service in the U.S. and Abroad* (US$9, postage US$1.50). See Useful Travel Organizations for more information.

The Service Civil International-Voluntary Service (SCI-VS), Route 2, Box 560B, Crozet, VA 22932 (tel. (804) 823 1826), arranges placement in workcamps for people over 18 or 16, depending on the camp. US$40 registration in the U.S.

Volunteers for Peace Inc. (VFP), 43 Tiffany Rd., Belmont, VT 05730 (tel. (802) 259-2759, fax (802) 259-2922, contact Peter Coldwell). VFP publishes the International Workcamp Directory, which is updated every year and can be ordered directly from them for US$10 (deductible from future program fees). The directory covers 40 countries, and placement is quick; reservations are generally confirmed within 3 days. Most volunteers register between mid-April and mid-May. Most workcamp fees are $150, and some are open to 16-18-year-olds for $175.

■■■ GETTING THERE

■ FROM NORTH AMERICA

The first challenge in European budget travel is getting there. Call every toll-free number and don't be afraid to ask about discounts. Have a knowledgeable travel agent guide you through the options; better yet, have several knowledgeable travel agents guide you. Travel agents might not want to do the legwork to find the cheapest fares (for which they receive the lowest commissions). However, students and people under 26 should never need to pay full price for a ticket. Seniors can also get mint deals; many airlines offer senior traveler club deals or airline passes and discounts for seniors' companions as well. Travel sections in Sunday newspapers often list bargain fares from the local airport. Outfox airline reps with the phone-book-sized *Official Airline Guide* (at large libraries); this monthly guide lists every scheduled flight in the world (including prices).

Most airlines maintain a fare structure that peaks between mid-June and early September. Midweek (Mon.-Thurs.) flights run much cheaper each way than on weekends. Leaving from a travel hub such as New York, Atlanta, Dallas, Chicago, Los Angeles, San Francisco, Vancouver, Toronto, Melbourne, or Sydney will generally

win you a more competitive fare than from smaller cities; the gains are not as great when departing from travel hubs monopolized by one airline, so call around. Flying to London is usually the cheapest way across the Atlantic. In 1994, the high-season, roundtrip fares to London rarely topped US$650, and off-season rates were much lower, often hovering around US$250.

Return-date flexibility is usually not an option for the budget traveler; except on youth fares purchased through the airlines, traveling with an "open return" ticket can be pricier than fixing a return date and paying to change it. Avoid one-way tickets, too: the flight to Europe may be economical, but the return fares can be outrageous. Whenever flying internationally, pick up your ticket in advance of the departure date and arrive at the airport several hours before your flight.

COMMERCIAL AIRLINES

Even if you pay an airline's lowest published fare, you may be spending hundreds of dollars. The commercial airlines' lowest regular offer is the **APEX** (Advance Purchase Excursion Fare); specials advertised in newspapers may be cheaper, but have correspondingly more restrictions and fewer available seats. APEX fares provide you with confirmed reservations and allow "open-jaw" tickets (landing in and returning from different cities). Reservations must usually be made at least 21 days in advance, with 7- to 14-day minimum and 60- to 90-day maximum stay limitations, and hefty cancellation and change-of-reservation penalties. For summer travel, book APEX fares early; by May you will have difficulty getting the departure date you want.

Most airlines no longer offer standby fares, once a staple of the budget traveler. Standby has given way to the **three-day-advance-purchase youth fare,** a cousin of the one-day variety prevalent in Europe. It's available only to those under 25 (sometimes 24) and only within three days of departure—a gamble that often pays off, but could backfire if the airline's all booked up. Return dates are open, but you must come back within a year, and once again can book your return seat no more than three days ahead. Youth fares in summer aren't really cheaper than APEX, but off-season prices drop deliciously. **Icelandair** (tel. (800) 223-5500 from the U.S.) is one of the few airlines which offer this 3-day fare. Check with a travel agent for details.

Virgin Atlantic (tel. (800) 862-8621 from the U.S.) offers a "Visit Europe" plan in conjunction with British Midland Airways to various cities in Europe, including London. A one-way ticket is US$109.

STUDENT TRAVEL AGENCIES

Students and persons under 26 with proper ID qualify for deliciously reduced airfares. These are rarely available from airlines or travel agents, but instead from student travel agencies like **Council Travel, STA, Travel CUTS, University Travel Network,** and **Let's Go Travel.** In 1994, peak season round-trip rates from the East Coast to even the offbeat corners of Europe rarely topped US$700, and off-season fares were considerably lower. Return date change fees also tend to be low (around US$50). Student travel agencies can also help non-students and people over 26, but may not be able to get the same low fares.

CHARTER FLIGHTS AND TICKET CONSOLIDATORS

Ticket consolidators resell at heavy discounts unsold tickets on commercial and charter airlines that might otherwise have gone begging. Look for their tiny ads in weekend papers (in the U.S., the Sunday *New York Times* travel section is best), and start calling them all. Unlike tickets bought through an airline, you won't be able to use these tickets on another flight if you miss yours, and you will have to go back to the consolidator—not the airline—to get a refund. Phone around and pay with a credit card; you can't stop a cash payment if you never receive your tickets. Find out everything you can about the agency you're considering, and get a copy of their refund policy in writing. Insist on a **receipt** that gives full details about the tickets, refunds, and restrictions; if they don't want to give you a clear summary, use a different company.

It's best to buy from a major organization that has experience in placing individuals on charter flights. One of the most reputable is the CIEE-affiliated **Council Charter,** 205 E. 42nd St., New York, NY 10017 (tel. (800) 800-8222); their flights can also be booked through Council Travel offices. Another good organization is **Unitravel,** 1177 N. Warson Rd., St. Louis, MO 63132 (tel. (800) 325-2222); they offer discounted airfares on major scheduled airlines from the U.S. to over 50 cities in Europe and will hold all payments in a bank escrow until completion of your trip. Also try **Interworld Travel,** Douglas Entrance, 800 Douglas Rd. #140, Coral Gables, FL 33134-3138 (tel. (800) 331-4456, in Florida (305) 443-4929); **Rebel,** 25050 Avenue Kearney #215, Valencia, CA 91355 (tel. (800) 227-3235); **Travac** (tel. (800) 872-8800); **Bargain Air,** 655 Deep Valley Dr. #355, Rolling Hills, CA 90274 (tel. (800) 347-2345, (310) 377-6349 in California, fax (310) 877-1824). The **Air Travel Advisory Bureau,** Strauss House 41-45, Goswell Rd. London EC1V7DN (tel. 636 2908), puts travelers in touch with the cheapest carriers out of London. **Brendan Tours,** 15137 Califa St., Van Nuys, CA 91411-3021 (tel. (800) 421-8446, in California (818) 785-9696, fax (818) 902-9876), allows you to buy as little as one day in advance and requires that you stay no more than 90 days; savings are greatest if you stay for less than 7 or more than 30 days. **AirTech Unlimited,** 584 Broadway #1007, New York, NY 10012 (tel. (212) 219-7000, fax 219-0666), requires you to be flexible about specific cities and to leave a two to five day window in which to travel; they also offer a courier service for one-week visits.

Consolidators sell a mixture of tickets; some are on scheduled airlines, some on **charter flights.** The theory behind a charter is that a tour operator contracts with an airline (usually a fairly obscure one that specializes in charters) to use their planes to fly extra loads of passengers to peak-season destinations. Charter flights thus fly less frequently than major airlines and have correspondingly more restrictions. They are almost always fully booked, schedules and itineraries may change at the last moment, and flights may be cancelled. Shoot for a scheduled air ticket if you can, and consider travelers' insurance against trip interruption.

Airhitch, 2641 Broadway, New York, NY 10025 (tel. 212) 864-2000) and 1415 Third St., Santa Monica, CA 90410 (tel. (310) 394-0550) advertises a similar service: you choose a five-day date range in which to travel and a list of preferred European destinations, and they try to place you in a vacant spot in a flight in your date range to one of those destinations. Check all flight times and departure sites only with Airhitch, but read *all* the fine print they send you and compare it to what people tell you. The Better Business Bureau of New York received complaints about Airhitch a few years ago; they still don't recommend them, but they don't discourage you from using them, either.

Last minute **discount clubs** and **fare brokers** offer members savings on European travel, including charter flights and tour packages. Research your options carefully. **Last Minute Travel Club,** 1249 Boylston St., Boston, MA 02215 (tel. (800) 527-8646 or (617) 267-9800) is one of the few travel clubs that does not require a membership fee. Other clubs are **Discount Travel International** (call (800) 555-1212 to find out their new (800) number; it has changed), **Moment's Notice** (tel. (212) 486-0503; US$25 annual fee), **Traveler's Advantage** (tel. (800) 835-8747; US$49 annual fee), and **Worldwide Discount Travel Club** (tel. (305) 534-2082; US$50 annual fee). For US$25, **Travel Avenue** will search for the lowest international airfare available and then discount it 5-17% (tel. (800) 333-3335.) The often labyrinthine contracts for all these organizations bear close study—you may prefer not to stop over in Luxembourg for 11 hours.

COURIER FLIGHTS

Those who travel light should consider flying to Europe as a courier. The company hiring you will use your checked luggage space for freight; you're left with the carry-on allowance. Watch for restrictions: most flights are round-trip only with fixed-length stays (usually short), you may not be able to travel with a companion, and most flights are from New York or Boston. Round-trip fares to Western Europe from the U.S. range from US$199-349 (during the off-season) to US$399-549 (during the summer). **Now Voyager,** 74 Varick St. #307, New York, NY 10013 (tel. (212) 431-1616), acts as an agent for many courier flights worldwide from New York, although some flights are available from Houston. They also offer special last-minute deals to such cities as London, Paris, Rome and Frankfurt which go for as little as US$299 round-trip. **Halbart Express,** 147-05 176th St., Jamaica, NY 11434 (tel. (718) 656-8279), **Courier Travel Service,** 530 Central Avenue, Cedarhurst, NY 11516 (tel. (516) 374-2299), **Able Travel** (tel. (212) 779-8530), and **Discount Travel International** (call (800) 555-1212 to find out what their new (800) is; it will have changed) are other courier agents to try. **Travel Unlimited,** P.O. Box 1058, Allston, MA, publishes a monthly newsletter that details all courier travel options. A one-year subscription costs US$25 (abroad US$35). If you have travel time to spare, **Ford's Travel Guides,** 19448 Londelius St., Northridge, CA 91324 (tel. (818) 701-7414), lists **freighter companies** that will take passengers for trans-Atlantic crossings. Ask for their *Freighter Travel Guide and Waterways of the World* (US$15).

You can work directly with courier companies in New York, or check your bookstore or library for handbooks such as *The Insider's Guide to Air Courier Bargains* (US$15). The *Courier Air Travel Handbook* (US$10.70) explains the ins and outs of traveling as an air courier and contains names, telephone numbers, and contact points of courier companies; it can be ordered directly from Thunderbird Press, 5930-10 W. Greenway Rd. #112, Glendale, AZ 85306, or by calling (800) 345-0096. *The Air Courier's Handbook* is published by Big City Books, P.O. Box 19667, Sacramento, CA 95819; order it from the publisher or from a bookstore.

■ FROM CONTINENTAL EUROPE

BY PLANE

Unless you're under 25, flying across Europe on regularly scheduled flights will eat up your budget; nearly all airlines cater to business travelers and set prices accordingly. If you are 24 or under, special fares on most European airlines requiring ticket purchase either the day before or the day of departure are a happy exception to this rule.

BY TRAIN

Most European trains are fast, punctual, and convenient. The train system is scheduled to be expanded in October 1994: the **Channel Tunnel** will provide direct autoroute, TGV, and bus travel from France to the U.K. Twin rail tunnels (operational for shuttle train and passenger vehicles) will whisk travelers from Paris to Coquelles to Folkestone to Waterloo Station in under 5 hours. While France will soon have superfast TGV's speeding along the route, it will be several years before high-speed rail is operational on the British side. All reports suggest that Chunnel prices will be competitive with airline prices; however, fares and discounts have not been made public yet. For more information, contact **European Passenger Services** (tel. (0181) 784 1333) or the **British Rail Main Switchboard** (tel. 928 5151).

On major lines, reservations are always advisable and often required, even if you have a railpass; make them at least a few hours in advance at the train station (usually less than US$3). The ultimate reference is the *Thomas Cook European Timetable* (US$34), which covers all major and many minor train routes in Europe.

TRAIN DISCOUNTS AND RAILPASSES

For those under 26, **BIJ tickets (Billets Internationals de Jeunesse),** sold under the Wasteels, Eurotrain, and Route 26 names, are an excellent alternative to railpasses. Available for trips within Europe, they save an average of 30-45% off regular second-class fares. Tickets are sold from point to point, with free and unlimited stopovers along the direct route of the ticket, with a two-month limit to complete your trip. You can buy BIJ tickets from student travel agencies. In the U.S., contact Wasteels at (407) 351-2537; in London call 834 7066. Note that **Eurailpasses** are not valid in Britain. All train-related inquiries should be directed to British Rail at 928 5100 (for **BritRail** information, see Daytrips).

BY FERRY

Stena-Sealink Line (tel. (01233) 647 047) and **P&O European Ferries** (tel. (0181) 575 8555) offer extensive ferry service across the channel between France (Calais, Cherbourg, and Le Havre) and England (Dover and Portsmouth), as well as crossings to Ostend, Belgium and Bilboa, Spain. Sealink ferries are the most frequent and take one and a half to one and three-quarter hours (22 trips/day from Dover to Calais; about £24 one way). Traveling by **hovercraft** is quicker (50 min.), but it must be booked in advance. **Hoverspeed** services depart from Boulogne for Dover, with extra craft operating to Ramsgate from Dunkerque during the summer. The service is suspended in rough weather. Contact **Travelloyd,** 8 Berkeley Sq., London SW1 for information on Transalpino's reduced rates on hovercraft services, or the British Rail Travel Centre, 4-12 Regent St., London SW1Y 4PQ.

■ FROM AUSTRALIA AND NEW ZEALAND

Travelers from Australia or New Zealand are best advised to visit a local branch of one of the budget travel agencies listed above. **STA Travel** is probably the largest international agency you will find: they have offices in **Melbourne** (tel. (03) 349 2411), 222 Faraday St., VIC 3053 and **Auckland** (tel. (09) 398 9995), 10 High St. STA fares between Sydney and London were US$875 each way in 1994; STA in London may be able to find cheaper fares. **British Airways** (tel. (0181) 564 1449 or 564 1450) and **Qantas** both fly direct from Australia to Britain, but you'll pay for the convenience: in the summer of 1994, the Sydney-London return route was AUS$2699 on B.A. Any national airline between Australia and Britain can offer somewhat cheaper connecting flights on one part of the route; most travelers reportedly take Singapore Air or other Far East-based carriers during the initial leg of their trip. Check with STA or another company for more comprehensive information.

■ GETTING IN AND OUT OF LONDON

FROM THE AIRPORT

With planes landing every 47 seconds, **Heathrow Airport** (tel. (0181) 759 4321), in Hounslow, Middlesex, is the world's busiest international airport. The *bureaux de change* in each terminal are open daily: Thomas Cook, Terminal 1 (tel. (081) 897 3351; open 24 hr.); International Currency Exchange, Terminal 2 (open 6am-11pm); and Travellers' Exchange Corporation, Terminals 3 (tel. (081) 897 3501) and 4 (tel. (081) 759 4449; both open 24 hr.). The easiest way to reach central London from Heathrow is by **Underground** (Piccadilly line, about 45 min. to central London), with one stop for terminals 1, 2, and 3 and one for terminal 4. To reach **Victoria Station,** transfer at Gloucester Rd. or South Kensington to a District Line or Circle Line train heading east. At Victoria, you'll find a blue **Tourist Information Centre** with an accommodations service, more currency exchange, and information about transportation connections (see Getting Around London below).

London Regional Transport's **Airbus** (tel. 222 1234) makes the one-hour trip from Heathrow to central points in the city, including hotels. The Airbus A1 runs to Victoria, stopping at Hyde Park Corner, Harrods, and Earl's Ct. tube station. Airbus A2 runs to Russell Sq., with stops at Euston Station, Baker St. station, Marble Arch, Paddington station, Queensway station, Notting Hill Gate station, and Holland Park. (Both buses run daily 6:30am-3pm every 20min. and 3-8pm every 30min. £5, children £3.) The double-decker Airbuses have plenty of room for luggage, and most are wheelchair accessible. A **National Express** bus (tel. 730 0202) goes from Heathrow to Victoria coach station (5:30am-8:30pm every 30 min., 1 hr., £6.50).

Most charter flights land at **Gatwick Airport** in West Sussex (tel. (0293) 535 353). A number of 24-hr. restaurants and *bureaux de change* are located in both the North and South Terminals. From Gatwick, take the BR Gatwick Express train to Victoria Station (35 min.; daily 5:30am-8pm every 15 min., 8pm-1am every 30 min., 1-4am every hr. on the hr.; £8.50, under 15 £4.25). Council Travel in London sells tickets for the Gatwick Express for £7.50, cheaper than at BR's ticket window—you get the convenience and speed of train travel at the same price as the bus. **National Express coaches** run between Gatwick and Victoria (5:30am-11pm every hr., 60 min., £7.50).

Taxis are not advisable, especially during rush hour. Fares from central London to Heathrow run at least £30; from central London to Gatwick, expect to pay £50-60. Travelers who are too loaded down with bulky bags to negotiate the stairs and escalators entailed by public transport should consider using **London Airways,** a private chauffeur service (tel. 403 2228). For a flat rate, London Airways will take up to four people from either airport to any central London destination (£15 per car from Heathrow, £25 per car from Gatwick; call for airport pickup in 15 min.).

Flights from the U.S. go into both Gatwick and Heathrow. Double check which airport your flight serves before you leave. Starting with American Airlines' service from Chicago, major international flights are now arriving in upstart **Stansted Airport,** northeast of London in Stansted, Essex (tel. (01279) 680 500). Stansted is served by British Rail's **Stansted Express** to Liverpool St. Station (40 min.; Mon.-Fri. 5:30am-11pm every 30 min.; Sat. 6:30am-11pm every 30 min.; Sun. 7am-11pm every 30 min.; £10, under 15 £5).

FROM THE TRAIN STATIONS

If you are leaving London by train, find out from which of the eight major stations (Charing Cross, Euston, King's Cross, Liverpool St., Paddington, St. Pancras, Victoria, or Waterloo) you will depart. The Underground links these stations, and its stops bear the same names as the train stations. For information about particular destinations in the U.K. and Ireland, call the numbers listed below, or consult the display pages in the British Telecom business and services phone book (under the heading "British Rail") for such services as "Talking Timetables" (automated scheduling information to specific destinations).

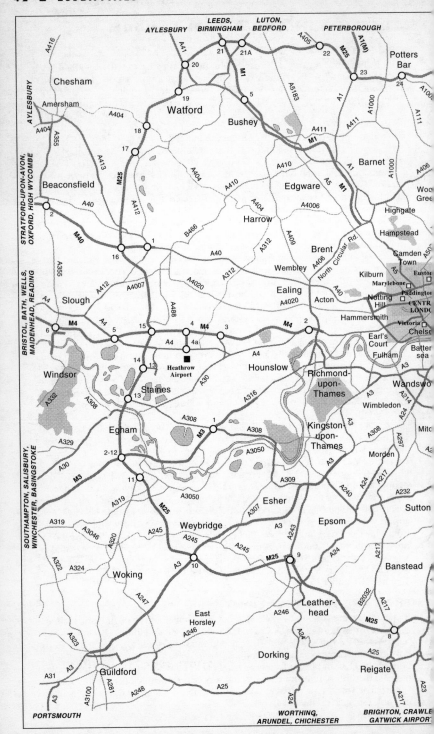

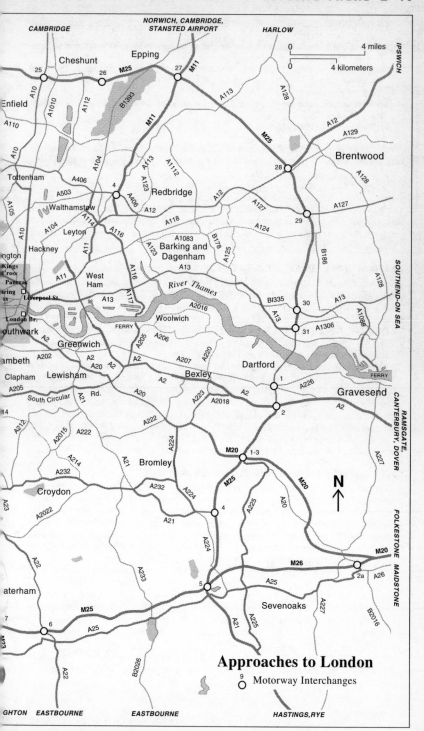

Approaches to London

○ Motorway Interchanges

To East Anglia, Essex, Southern England, Northeast, East, and **South London:** tel. 928 5100.

To the South Midlands, West of England, South Wales, West London, and **Republic of Ireland** via **Fishguard:** tel. 262 6767.

To the East and **West Midlands, North Wales, Northwest England, Scotland** via **West Coast, Northwest London, Northern Ireland,** and **Republic of Ireland** via **Holyhead:** tel. 387 7070.

To East and **Northeast England, Scotland** via **East Coast,** and **North London:** tel. 278 2477.

To Europe: tel. (0891) 888 731

British Rail runs **Travel Centres** at its mainline stations and at 12-16 Regent St. (tube: Piccadilly Circus); The Strand (tube: Charing Cross); Victoria St.; and King William St. (All open Mon.-Fri. 9am-5pm.)

To get a **Young Person's Railcard** (£16), you must be under 24 or a full-time student in the U.K. A **Senior Railcard** for persons over 60 also costs £16. Both will save you one-third on off-peak travel for one year. A **Network Card** gives the same discount for travel in the Network South East area. The **Network Rover** allows unlimited travel on Network Southeast for the daytripper (3 days on weekend £47; 7 days £69; children ½-price). Ask at any mainline station.

FROM THE BUS STATIONS

Victoria Coach Station (tube: Victoria), located on Buckingham Palace Rd., is the hub of Britain's denationalized coach network. **National Express coaches** (tel. 730 0202) service an expansive network which links cities big and small. Coaches are considerably less expensive than trains but also take longer. National Express offers a **Discount Coach Card** (£7) to students, youths 16-25, seniors, and disabled persons (30% discount). Other coach companies compete with National Express; their routes often overlap and prices are almost identical.

Much of the commuting area around London, including Hampton Court and Windsor, is served by **Green Line** coaches, which leave frequently from Eccleston Bridge behind Victoria Station. (For information, call (0181) 668 7261 Mon.-Fri. 8am-8:30pm, Sat.-Sun. 9am-5pm; or try the information kiosk on Eccleston Bridge.) Purchase tickets from the driver. Prices for day returns are higher before 9am Monday through Friday. Green Line discounts include the one-day **Rover** ticket (£6, valid on almost every Green Line coach and London Country bus Mon.-Fri. after 9am, Sat.-Sun. all day); and the **Three-Day Rover** (£16.50)

HITCHHIKING AND RIDE SHARING

Women, even in a group, should never hitchhike. Men should consider all of the risks involved before hitching. Anyone who values safety will take a train or bus out of London. Hitchers often check the University of London Union's ride board, on the ground floor of 1 Malet St., WC1 (tube: Russell Sq.), or ask at youth hostels for possibilities. Hitching can be quite difficult within central London and reasonably easy from places like Cambridge and Oxford to the city. Let's Go does not recommend hitchhiking as a safe means of transportation.

Freewheelers is a **"lift agency"** which can match you up to a driver going your way. Membership is required, and costs £10 per year. You must pay for five match-ups (each £1) in advance. The price for the trip itself is agreed between the passenger and driver based on fuel costs, approximately 3½p per mile. The agency requires that members abide by a safety procedure to confirm each other's identity, and keeps records of all members and matches made. Single-sex matching can be arranged. But Freewheelers does not take responsibility for members' safety—you are still getting in a car with a stranger. For more details, call (0191) 222 0090, or write to Freewheelers, Ltd., 25 Low Friar St., Newcastle upon Tyne, NE1 54E.

■■■ ONCE THERE

■ TOURIST OFFICES

London Tourist Board Information Centre: Victoria Station Forecourt, SW1 (tel. (0839) 123 432, recorded message only, 48p/min.). Tube: Victoria. Information on London and England, a well-stocked bookshop, theatre and tour bookings, and an accommodations service (a hefty £5 booking fee, plus 15% refundable deposit). Expect to take a number and wait at peak hours, around noon. Their cheapest rooms cost about £22, but most run around £25-30. Victoria Station center open daily 8am-7pm; Dec.-March Mon.-Sat. 8am-7pm, Sun. 8am-5pm. Additional tourist offices located at **Heathrow Airport** (open daily 9am-6pm; Dec.-March 9am-5pm), **Harrods,** and **Selfridges** department stores.

British Travel Centre: 12 Regent St., SW1. Tube: Piccadilly Circus. Down Regent St. from the Lower Regent St. tube exit. Run by the British Tourist Authority and ideal for travelers bound for destinations outside of London. Combines the services of the BTA, British Rail, and American Express (same rates for currency exchange as the main AmEx office, but shorter lines) with an accommodations service. For the latter, you pay a booking fee (£5) and a deposit (either 1 night's stay or 15% of the total stay depending on the place; does not book for hostels). Also sells maps, theatre tickets, books, and pamphlets translated into many languages. Pleasantly relaxed compared to LTB, but similarly long queues. Open Mon.-Fri. 9am-6:30pm, Sat. 9am-5pm, Sun. 10am-4pm; Nov.-April Mon.-Fri. 9am-6:30pm, Sat.-Sun. 10am-4pm.

City of London Information Centre: St. Paul's Churchyard, EC4 (tel. 606 3030). Tube: St. Paul's. Specializes in information about the City of London but answers questions on all of London. Helpful, knowledgeable staff. Open daily 9:30am-5pm; Nov.-March Mon.-Fri. 9:30am-5pm, Sat. 9:30am-12:30pm.

London Transport Information Offices: (24-hr. information line, tel. 222 1234). At the Heathrow, Victoria, Piccadilly Circus, Oxford Circus, Euston, Liverpool St., and King's Cross tube stops. Underground and bus travel, free maps.

■ EMBASSIES AND CONSULATES

All embassies and High Commissions close on English holidays.

United States Embassy: 24 Grosvenor Sq., W1 (tel. 499 9000). Tube: Bond St. Someone will always answer the phone. Embassy Travel Services at 22 Sackville St., W1 (tel. 439 7433). Tube: Piccadilly Circus. Travel Service office open Mon.-Fri. 10am-4pm.

Australian High Commission: Australia House, The Strand, WC2 (tel. 379 4334; in emergency, tel. 438 8181). Tube: Aldwych or Temple. Visa and passport inquiries tel. 438 8818. Open Mon.-Fri. 10am-4pm.

Canadian High Commission: MacDonald House, 1 Grosvenor Sq., W1 (tel. 629 9492). Tube: Bond St. or Oxford Circus. Visas Mon.-Fri. 8:45am-2pm.

Irish Embassy: 17 Grosvenor Pl., SW1 (tel. 235 2171). Tube: Hyde Park Corner. Open Mon.-Fri. 9:30am-5pm.

New Zealand High Commission: New Zealand House, 80 Haymarket, SW1 (tel. 930 8422). Tube: Charing Cross. Open Mon.-Fri. 10am-noon and 2-4pm.

South African Embassy, South Africa House, Trafalgar Sq. WC2 (tel. 930 4488). Tube: Charing Cross.

■ KEEPING IN TOUCH

It pleased him...to be able to go there from time to time when he was in London and to think, as he sat in solitude before his gas fire, that there was literally not a soul in the universe who knew where he was.
—Aldous Huxley, Antic Hay

MAIL

Air mail from London to anywhere in the world is speedy and dependable. A letter will reach the East Coast of the U.S. or urban Canada in about a week and may arrive in as few as three days. **Surface mail,** while much cheaper than airmail, takes up to three months to arrive. It is adequate for getting rid of books or clothing you no longer need in your travels. (See Customs.) In summer 1994, an airmail letter to destinations outside Europe cost 41p, a postcard 35p. The cheapest way to write overseas is by aerograms, which are sold in packs of six for £1.99, making them cheaper than postcards. Single aerograms are 36p. Postage for letters within the U.K. is 25p.

If you have no fixed address while in Britain, you can receive mail through the British post offices' **Poste Restante** (General Delivery) service. Mark the envelope "HOLD," and address it like this (for example): "Jane Doe, Poste Restante, Glastonbury, Somerset, England BA6 9HS." Include the county and the postal code if you know them. Try to have your Poste Restante sent to the largest post office in a region. When in London, send mail to Poste Restante, Trafalgar Square Post Office, 24-28 William IV St., London WC2N 4DL (tel. 930 9580; tube: Charing Cross; open Mon.-Sat. 8am-8pm). If you don't specify a post office, mail will be sent to either Trafalgar Square or London Chief Office, King Edward Bldg., EC1 (tel. 239 5047; tube: St. Paul's; open Mon.-Tues. and Thurs.-Fri. 8:30am-6:30pm, Wed. 9am-6:30pm).

Postcards and letters sent from the U.S. cost US40¢ and US50¢. The post office also sells aerograms for US45¢. Many U.S. city post offices offer Express Mail service, which sends packages under 8 oz. to major overseas cities in 40 to 72 hours (US$11.50-14). Private mail services provide the fastest, most reliable overseas delivery. **DHL, Federal Express,** and **Airborne Express** can get mail from North America to London in 2 days.

American Express also receives and holds mail for up to 30 days, after which they return it to the sender. If you want to have it held longer, just write "Hold for x days" on the envelope. The envelope should be addressed with your name in capital letters, and "Client Letter Service" should be written below your name. Most big-city American Express offices provide this service free of charge if you have their Traveler's Cheques, but some require that you be an AmEx cardholder. The free booklet *Traveler's Companion* contains the addresses of American Express offices worldwide, and can be obtained from any American Express office or by calling customer service at (800) 528-4800 (allow 6-8 weeks for delivery).

TELEPHONES

The country code for the U.K. when calling from abroad is **44.** Within London, if you are dialing from one 0171 or 0181 number to another, you don't need to dial the prefix. If you are dialing from 0171 to 0181 or vice versa (or from another phone code in Britain), you do. If you are dialing from outside Britain, you need only dial 171 or 181. **In Let's Go: London, numbers have 0171 codes unless otherwise noted.**

Major changes will be occurring to Britain's phone numbers on "Phone Day," April 16, 1995 at 1am. In England, all telephone codes starting 0 (virtually all codes) will start 01 (change from 071 to 0171). No service codes (such as 0800) will change. If you have general questions about Phoneday while in Britain, you can call the special BT Helpline at (0800) 010101. Since the new numbers could be used as of August 1, 1994, we have listed the new telephone codes everywhere in the guides. (If you come across a phone code that starts 0 rather than 01, we made a typo.) You should not encounter any problems using the codes we list before April 16; if you do, try dropping the initial "01" and replacing it with a "0."

The new, polite British payphone lights up with the words "Insert Money" as soon as you lift the receiver. Payphones do not accept the 1p coin, and often not the 2p or 5p. When the initial time period is exhausted, a series of beeps warns you to insert more money. For the rest of the call, the digital display ticks off your credit in penny increments so that you can plan ahead and insert more money. Unused coins are returned, but the phones do not give change, so use 10p and 20p coins.

More convenient than carrying tons of oversized English change is the **British Telecom (BT) Phonecard,** available in denominations of £2, £4, £10, and £20. (£20 cards have been known to contain only 100 10p units upon use). Phonecard phone booths (look for the green sign) are extremely common, except in rural areas; most phones accept change or phonecards, but not both. Cards are available everywhere; main post offices, almost any newsagent, or the W.H. Smith and John Menzies stationery chains stock them. BT calls are charged in 10p units. Newsagents also sell the **Mercury Phonecard,** available in the same denominations as the BT card, for use on the snazzy blue Mercury phones, usually located around tube stops. Mercury charges up to 20% less for its calls (including international and card calls) than BT. Mercury card calls are charged in 1p units. Mercury phones and some Telecom phones accept credit cards.

For international calls, dial the international code (00), the country code and (if necessary) the city code, and then the local number. The country code for the U.S. and Canada is **1,** Australia **61,** New Zealand **64,** Ireland **353,** and South Africa **27.** BT publishes a simple pamphlet telling visitors how to make international calls from any phone (available at tourist offices and most hotels, printed in several languages). Consider calling through U.S. long-distance companies, which offer significantly cheaper rates. To access a U.S. AT&T operator from Britain, dial their **USA Direct** number, (0800) 89 00 11. You can then call collect or with an AT&T calling card. Using an **MCI** (tel. (0800) 89 02 22) or **Sprint** (tel. (0800) 89 08 77) calling card will also reduce your costs. Calling collect costs much more. For Canadian Calling Card Holders, **Canada Direct** is (0800) 89 0016. Antipodeans should direct their inquiries to tel. 0102 in Australia or tel. 081 in New Zealand.

Get **reduced rates** for most international calls from Britain (Mon.-Fri. 8pm-8am; Sat.-Sun. all day; to Australia and N.Z., daily midnight-7am and 2:30-7:30pm). Within Britain, three rate periods exist: the lowest rates (Mon.-Fri. 6pm-8am, Sat.-Sun.); middle range (Mon.-Fri. 8-9am and 1-6pm); and most expensive (Mon.-Fri. 9am-1pm).

Important numbers in Britain include **999** for police, fire, or ambulance emergencies, **100** for the telephone operator, **192** for London and Britain directory inquiries, **155** for the international operator (this is a very expensive service), and **153** for international directory assistance. Directory assistance is free from public phones only. Translation assistance for international calls is available at 492 7222. Area codes for individual cities in Britain are listed in telephone directories. Telephone area codes range from three to six digits, and local telephone numbers range from three to seven. The code **(0800)** indicates a toll-free number. Before you call an advertised number beginning with **0898, 0836,** or **0077,** be aware that you will be charged at the highest, nay extortionate, rate.

■ EMERGENCY, HEALTH, AND HELP

Emergency medical care, psychological counseling, crash housing, and sympathetic support can often be found in London free of charge.

Britons receive largely free health care from the National Health Service (NHS). Foreign visitors do not, of course, get such favorable terms, but are nevertheless eligible for some free treatment, including: outpatient treatment in the Accident and Emergency (A&E) ward of an NHS hospital; treatment of communicable diseases (such as V.D., typhoid, or anthrax); and "compulsory" mental treatment.

Emergency (Medical, Police, and Fire): Dial 999; no coins required.

Police: Stations in every district of London, including: Headquarters, New Scotland Yard, Broadway, SW1 (tel. 230 1212; tube: St. James's Park); West End Central, 27 Savile Row, W1 (tel. 494 1212; tube: Piccadilly Circus); King's Cross, 76 King's Cross Rd., WC1 (tel. 704 1212; tube: King's Cross); Kensington, 72 Earl's Court Rd., W8 (tel. (081) 741 6212; tube: Earl's Ct.).

Hospitals: In an emergency, you can be treated at no charge in the A&E ward of a hospital. You have to pay for routine medical care unless you work legally in Britain, in which case NHS tax will be deducted from your wages and you will not be charged. Socialized medicine has lowered fees here, so don't ignore any health problem merely because you are low on cash. The following have 24-hr. walk-in A&E (also known as casualty) departments: **Westminster Hospital,** Dean Ryle St., Horseferry Rd., SW1 (tel. 746 8000; tube: Pimlico); **Eastman Dental Hospital,** 256 Gray's Inn Rd., WC1 (tel. 837 3646; tube: Chancery La. or King's Cross); **Royal London Hospital,** Whitechapel Rd., E1 (tel. 377 7000; tube: Whitechapel); **Royal Free Hospital,** Pond St., NW3 (tel. 794 0500; tube: Belsize Park or BR: Hampstead Heath); **Charing Cross Hospital,** Fulham Palace Rd. (entrance St. Dunstan's Rd.), W6 (tel. (0181) 846 1234; tube: Baron's Ct. or Hammersmith); **St. Thomas' Hospital,** Lambeth Palace Rd., SE1 (tel. 928 9292; tube: Westminster); **St. Bartholomew's Hospital,** West Smithfield (entrance on Giltspur St.), EC1 (tel. 601 8888; tube: Barbican or St. Paul's). For others look under "Hospitals" in the gray Businesses and Services phone book.

Pharmacies: Every police station keeps a list of emergency doctors and chemists in its area. Listings under "Chemists" in the Yellow Pages. **Bliss Chemists** at Marble Arch (5 Marble Arch, W1; tel. 723 6116) is open daily, including public holidays, 9am-midnight. **Boots Chemists** has branches throughout London: Oxford Circus (302 Regent St., tel. 734 9418) open Mon.-Fri. 8am-7pm, Sat. 9am-6pm; Victoria Station (inside train station, larger store in Victoria Place mall, tel. 931 9490) open Mon.-Fri. 8am-8pm, Sat. 9am-8pm; 254 Earl's Ct. Rd. (tel. 370 2232) open daily 8:30am-9pm; 127a Kensington High St. (tel. 937 9533) open Mon.-Fri. 8:30am-8pm, Sat. 9am-7pm; 961 Notting Hill Gate (tel. 727 4411) open Mon.-Fri. 9am-7pm, Sat. 9am-6pm. Boots also has branches in **Sainsbury** supermarkets.

Samaritans: 46 Marshall St., W1 (tel. 734 2800). Tube: Oxford Circus. Highly respected 24-hr. crisis hotline helps with all sorts of problems, including suicidal depression. A listening rather than advice service.

AIDS: National AIDS Helpline (tel. 0800 567 123; 24 hr.). Toll-free for information on testing, health care, or simply to answer questions and listen.

Women's Aid: 52-54 Featherstone St., EC1 (tel. 251 6537; 24 hr.). Will answer questions on issues of concern to women.

Rape Crisis Line: London Rape Crisis Centre, P.O. Box 69, WC1 (tel. 837 1600; 24 hr.). Call anytime, emergency or not, to talk to another woman, receive legal or medical information, or obtain referrals. Will send someone to accompany you to the police, doctors, clinics, and courts upon request.

Family Planning Association: 27-35 Mortimer St., W1 (tel. 631 0555). Tube: Oxford Circus. Informational services: contraception, pregnancy test and abortion referral. Open Mon.-Thurs. 9:30am-5pm, Fri. 9:30am-4:30pm. For abortion and family planning clinics, see "Medical Services" in *Time Out's* classifieds.

Alcoholics Anonymous: 11 Redcliffe Gdns., SW10 (tel. 352 3001). Tube: West Brompton. Information on meeting locations and times. Hotline answered daily 10am-10pm; answering machine from 10pm-10am.

Narcotics Anonymous tel. 498 9005. Hotline answered daily 10am-8pm.

Information for Travelers with Disabilities: Phone the **Disability Information and Advice Service** (tel.275 8485), **RADAR** (tel. 637 5400), the **Disability Information Service** (tel. 630 5994; Mon.-Fri. 10am-4pm), or the **Greater London Association for the Disabled** (tel. 274 0107) for general information.

Gay and Lesbian Information: see Gay and Lesbian London.

Salvation Army: 18 Thanet St., WC1 (tel. 383 4822). Tube: King's Cross/St. Pancras. Good reputation for advice and emergency short-term shelter.

Legal Advice: Release, 388 Old St., EC1 (tel. 729 9904; 24-hr. emergency number 603 8654). Tube: Liverpool St. or Old St. Specializes in criminal law and advising those who have been arrested on drug charges. Open Mon.-Fri. 10am-6pm. **Legal Aid Board,** 29-37 Red Lion St., WC1 (tel. 831 4209). Tube: Holborn. May provide legal advice and representation for minimal fees.

Citizen's Advice Bureaux: Holbron Library, Theobald's Rd., WC1 (tel. 404 1497). Tube: Holborn. Several branches dot London and offer advice on anything from housing advice to silencing your neighbor's doberman.

Discrimination: National Council for Civil Liberties, 21 Tabard St., SE1. Tube: Borough. Advising and campaigning organization for prevention of all types of discrimination and protection of civil rights. Advice through letters only.

Automobile Breakdown: AA Breakdown service, tel. 0800 887 766; 24-hr. RAC Breakdown Service, tel. 0800 828 282; National Breakdown, tel.499 0039.

Piccadilly Advice Centre, 100 Shaftesbury Ave., W1 (tel. 434 3773). Tube: Piccadilly Circus. Provides advice, information, and referrals to the "young, homeless, or new to London." Call to ask about soup-runs (free food) and night shelters. Open daily 2-6pm and 7-9pm.

National Association of Victims Support Schemes, Cranmer House, 39 Brixton Rd., SW9 (tel. 735 9166). Tube: Oval. The Association can send volunteers as soon as possible after you have been victimized by crime to provide emotional and practical support. Open Mon.-Fri. 9am-5:30pm.

St. Mary's Hospital Special Clinic, Praed St., W2 (tel. 725 1697). Tube: Paddington. Free and confidential drop-in clinic for STDs, including AIDS and HIV. Open Mon.-Tues., Thurs.-Fri. 9am-6pm and Wed. 10am-6pm.

Shelter Nightline: tel. (0800) 446 441. A volunteer-run helpline offering free advice on emergency accomodations. Open Mon.-Fri. 6pm-9am, Sat.-Sun. 24 hrs.

OTHER SERVICES

Baggage Storage: Students-Tourists Storage (tel. (0800) 622 244) has branches near all major tube, train, and coach stations. Dozens of cheap storage companies in the London area charge £3-5 per item per week (check the Yellow Pages under "Storage Service"). Lockers in train stations and airports are seldom available because of frequent bomb threats.

Library: Charing Cross Library, 4 Charing Cross Rd., WC2 (tel. 798 2051). Tube: Leicester Sq. Phone books, newspapers, photocopier, and used paperbacks (trashy best-sellers, mysteries, thrillers) for an unbeatable 10p. Open Mon.-Fri. 9:30am-7pm, Sat. 9:30am-1pm. See the Yellow Pages for a library near you.

Lost Property: If you lost it on the **Underground,** a **bus,** a **taxi,** or **British Rail,** see Getting Around. In all other cases, inquire at the nearest police station.

Phone Books: Not to be found in any phone booths. Try a library, post office, or directory assistance at tel. 192.

The Time: tel. 123.

The Weather: Weathercall (tel. (01891) 505 301) costs 39p per min. Mon.-Fri. 6pm-8am, Sat.-Sun. all day; 49p per min. at other times.

■ PUBLICATIONS ABOUT LONDON

London's daily newspapers, also the national dailies, divide themselves into "quality" and "tabloid" papers. Among the qualities, also known as broadsheets because of their dimensions, the **Times** is the oldest, with a reputation as the voice of the Establishment. The **Daily Telegraph** built its circulation, the largest among the qualities, with a slightly lower price and a petty conservatism. The **Guardian,** once the Manchester Guardian, tries to be all things to all soft-leftists, but its slightly off mod design (and its arts coverage) is more distinctive than its politics (but for American travelers, the Guardian has some of the best U.S. commentators). Both the Times and the Guardian face competition from the widely-acclaimed "non-partisan" **Independent,** founded in 1986, when it was a magnet for distinguished and disaffected quality journalists, many from the Times. The **Financial Times** supplements its City and industry news with praised international reporting; purportedly a favorite of "realistic" leftists.

At the low end of where the Telegraph leaves off, the **Daily Mail** picks up, as one of the aspiring "middle-market" tabloids: mixes of chatty columns and shopping and how-to tips—and fiercely conservative opinion. Its look-alike competitor is the pro-government **Daily Express.** The **Evening Standard,** the only purely local paper, is a middle-market tabloid that succeeds in breaking the posh-pop boundary; the same pinstripes squinting at the Times in the morning will be seen unfurling a Standard on the Tube ride home. Devoted to London, the Standard is also valuable for its nightly entertainment listings.

Dipping into the 20p per copy range, the **Sun** and the **Daily Mirror** conceal pin-up photos in a thin envelope of jingoistic frenzy—and in case you can't tell, the Sun

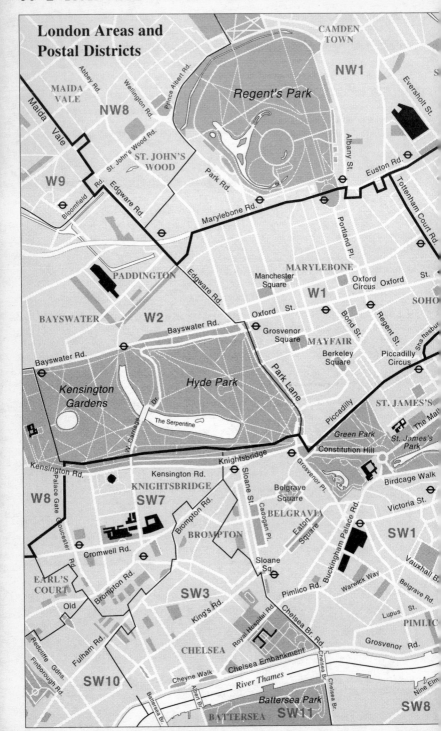

London Areas and Postal Districts

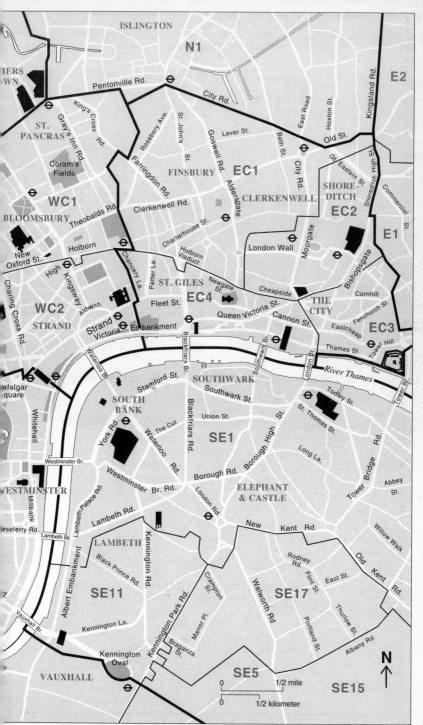

(owned by Rupert Murdoch) is the "conservative" paper and the Mirror the "Labour-party" paper.

You'll run into **The Big Issue** on most street corners. Partially written by the homeless, it is sold by homeless vendors who keep most of the cover price from copies they sell. While most of the news is old, the paper often has interesting features on local issues. Homesick Americans can buy the Sunday **New York Times** and the **International Herald Tribune** from many newsagents for £6.

The indispensible publication for the tourist who wants to get the most out of London is the weekly **Time Out,** with it's comprehensive entertainment listings. Londoners depend on it. You'll find everything here: theater information, concerts, club nights, sales, television schedules, book and music reviews, films, gay and lesbian happenings, and insightful features on London culture. Also worth a look are the British lifestyle magazines, **Arena,** and the resolutely hi, yet erudite **The Face.**

■ DETAILS

TIME, WEIGHTS AND MEASURES

1 meter (m) = 1.09 yards	1 yard = 0.92m
1 kilometer (km) = 0.621 mile	1 mile = 1.61km
1 gram (g) = 0.04 ounce	1 ounce = 25g
1 kilogram (kg) = 2.2 pounds	1 pound = 0.45 kg
1 "stone" (weight—of man or beast only) = 14 pounds	1 pound = .71 stone
1 liter = 1.057 U.S quarts	1 U.S quart = 0.94 liter
1 liter = 0.88 Imperial quarts	1 Imperial quart = 1.14 liter
1 Imperial gallon = 1.193 U.S. gallons	1 U.S. gallon = 0.84 Imperial gallon
1 British pint = 1.19 U.S. pint	1 U.S. pint = 0.84 British pint

Though Greenwich Mean Time (GMT) is the standard by which much of the rest of the world sets its clocks, the British have a system of their own, with Winter Time (=GMT) and British Summer Time (late March-late Oct.; 1 hr. later than GMT). This time change is a week out of sync with other daylight savings time changes, but British time is usually five hours ahead of Eastern North American time.

■■■ ORIENTATION

■ LAYOUT

Greater London is a colossal aggregate of distinct villages and anonymous suburbs, of ancient settlements and modern developments. As London grew, it swallowed adjacent cities and nearby villages, chewed up the counties of Kent, Surrey, Essex, Hertfordshire, and Middlesex. "The City" now refers to the ancient, and much smaller, "City of London," which covers but one of the 620 square miles of Greater London. London is divided into boroughs and into postal code areas. The borough name and postal code appear at the bottom of most street signs. Areas or neighborhoods are more vaguely delineated, but correspond roughly to the numbered postal areas; the district names are used frequently in non-postal discourse.

Most of the sightseer's London falls within the five central boroughs: the **City of London,** the **City of Westminster, Kensington and Chelsea, Camden,** and **Islington.** This region north of the river Thames is bounded roughly by the Underground's Circle line. The center of most visits to London is usually the **West End,** an area primarily within the borough of the City of Westminster. The West End incorporates the elegant Georgian façades of Mayfair, the crowded shopping streets around Oxford Street, the vibrant labyrinth of gay- and fashion-conscious Soho, and

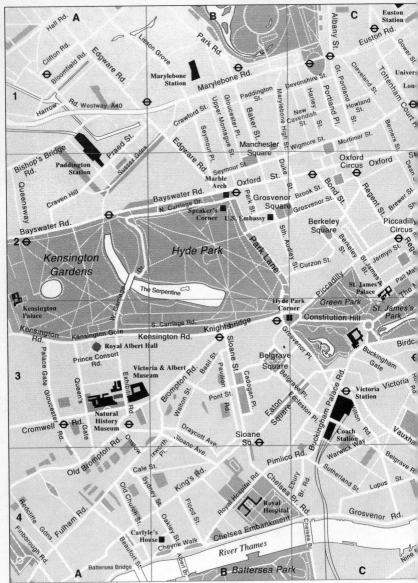

Central London: Major Street Finder

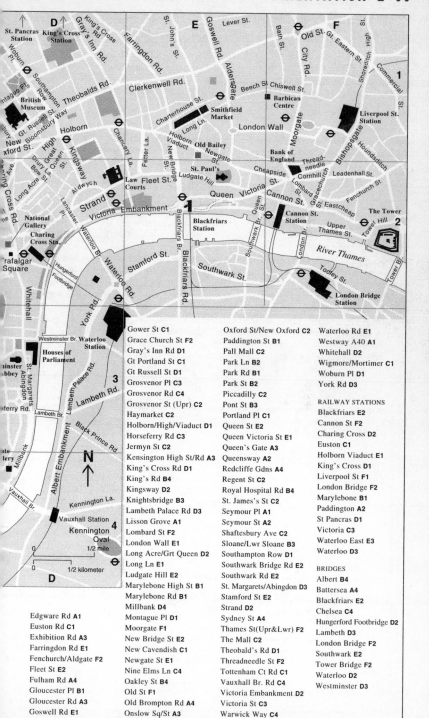

Gower St **C1**
Grace Church St **F2**
Gray's Inn Rd **D1**
Gt Portland St **C1**
Gt Russell St **D1**
Grosvenor Pl **C3**
Grosvenor Rd **C4**
Grosvenor St (Upr) **C2**
Haymarket **C2**
Holborn/High/Viaduct **D1**
Horseferry Rd **C3**
Jermyn St **C2**
Kensington High St/Rd **A3**
King's Cross Rd **D1**
King's Rd **B4**
Kingsway **D2**
Knightsbridge **B3**
Lambeth Palace Rd **D3**
Lisson Grove **A1**
Lombard St **F2**
London Wall **E1**
Long Acre/Grt Queen **D2**
Long Ln **E1**
Ludgate Hill **E2**
Marylebone High St **B1**
Marylebone Rd **B1**
Millbank **D4**
Montague Pl **D1**
Moorgate **F1**
New Bridge St **E2**
New Cavendish **C1**
Newgate St **E1**
Nine Elms Ln **C4**
Oakley St **B4**
Old St **F1**
Old Brompton Rd **A4**
Onslow Sq/St **A3**

Oxford St/New Oxford **C2**
Paddington St **B1**
Pall Mall **C2**
Park Ln **B2**
Park Rd **B1**
Park St **B2**
Piccadilly **C2**
Pont St **B3**
Portland Pl **C1**
Queen St **E2**
Queen Victoria St **E1**
Queen's Gate **A3**
Queensway **A2**
Redcliffe Gdns **A4**
Regent St **C2**
Royal Hospital Rd **B4**
St. James's St **C2**
Seymour Pl **A1**
Seymour St **A2**
Shaftesbury Ave **C2**
Sloane/Lwr Sloane **B3**
Southampton Row **D1**
Southwark Bridge Rd **E2**
Southwark Rd **E2**
St. Margarets/Abingdon **D3**
Stamford St **E2**
Strand **D2**
Sydney St **A4**
Thames St(Upr&Lwr) **F2**
The Mall **C2**
Theobald's Rd **D1**
Threadneedle St **F2**
Tottenham Ct Rd **C1**
Vauxhall Br. Rd **C4**
Victoria Embankment **D2**
Victoria St **C3**
Warwick Way **C4**

Waterloo Rd **E1**
Westway A40 **A1**
Whitehall **D2**
Wigmore/Mortimer **C1**
Woburn Pl **D1**
York Rd **D3**

RAILWAY STATIONS
Blackfriars **E2**
Cannon St **F2**
Charing Cross **D2**
Euston **C1**
Holborn Viaduct **E1**
King's Cross **D1**
Liverpool St **F1**
London Bridge **F2**
Marylebone **B1**
Paddington **A2**
St Pancras **D1**
Victoria **C3**
Waterloo East **E3**
Waterloo **D3**

BRIDGES
Albert **B4**
Battersea **A4**
Blackfriars **E2**
Chelsea **C4**
Hungerford Footbridge **D2**
Lambeth **D3**
London Bridge **F2**
Southwark **E2**
Tower Bridge **F2**
Waterloo **D2**
Westminster **D3**

Edgware Rd **A1**
Euston Rd **C1**
Exhibition Rd **A3**
Farringdon Rd **E1**
Fenchurch/Aldgate **F2**
Fleet St **E2**
Fulham Rd **A4**
Gloucester Pl **B1**
Gloucester Rd **A3**
Goswell Rd **E1**

the chic market in Covent Garden. All distances in London are measured from **Charing Cross,** the official center of London, on the south side of Trafalgar Square.

East of the West End, toward the City of London, lies **Holborn,** the center of legal activity, and **Fleet Street,** until recently the center of British journalism. Though the **City of London** is no longer the hub of central London, it continues to function as the financial heart of the metropolis. Here St. Paul's Cathedral is skirted by newer, taller buildings. The Tower of London, at the eastern boundary of the City, stands between central London and the vast **Docklands** building site stretching down the Thames—once port to the Empire, now attempting to show the face of a new commercial Britain.

Northeast of the West End, **Bloomsbury** harbors the British Museum, the core of London University, and scores of bookshops and art galleries. North and northwest of the West End, tidy terraces cling to the streets bordering Regent's Park in the districts of **Marylebone, Camden Town,** and **St. John's Wood. Islington** to the north east harbors an artsy intellectual image, and houses a growing gay community. One stage farther north, **Hampstead** and **Highgate** are separated from each other by the enormous Hampstead Heath. Two of London's most expensive residential areas, they command exceptional views of the city. Lying west of the West End, the faded squares of Paddington and Bayswater give way to Notting Hill, home each August bank holiday to the largest street carnival in Europe.

South and southwest of the West End, still in the City of Westminster, is the actual district of **Westminster.** This is England's royal, legislative, and ecclesiastical center, home of Buckingham Palace, the Houses of Parliament, and Westminster Abbey. Belgravia, packed with embassies, nestles between Westminster and the semi-gracious borough of **Kensington** and **Chelsea.** The shops of Knightsbridge and Kensington High Street, the excellent museums of South Kensington, the "posers" stalking the King's Road in Chelsea, and the Australians in and the large gay male population Earl's Court ensure this borough has no single image.

London's suburbs extend for miles in all directions. To the southwest, **Kew** luxuriates in its exquisite botanical gardens. In adjacent **Richmond** the expansive deer park brings wildlife to the capital. Towards the southeast, **Greenwich** takes pride in its rich navigational and astronomical history on the privileged path of the Prime Meridian. **Brixton,** just south of the river, is home to a large African and Caribbean community. Farther south lies the residential suburb of Wimbledon, site of the famed tennis tournament. Far out on the fringes of northeast greater London, ancient **Epping Forest** manages to preserve a degree of wildness and straddles the eastern and western hemispheres.

At times you'll need the ingenuity of Sherlock Holmes to find one of London's more obscure addresses. Some homeowners favor names rather than numbers, and the owner of a house on a corner is free to choose either street name as an address. Numbering starts at the end of the street nearest the center of London, but note that house numbers on opposite sides of large streets increase at different rates; house no. 211 may face no. 342. Numbers occasionally go up one side of the street and down the other. Some streets abruptly change names, disappear, and then materialize again after a hundred yards, while others twist through and around greens. You might find yourself in a tangle of Eaton Mews, Eaton Square, Eaton Gate, Eaton Place, and Eaton Terrace. There are 31 variations on Victoria Road, and 40 streets named Wellington. To navigate this mess, get a comprehensive street map or guide with a complete index, such as **London A to Z** ("A to Zed," as streetwise Londoners call it), *ABC Street Atlas,* or Nicholson's *London Streetfinder* (from £2). Even if you only intend to stay in London for a week or so, the outlay is well worth it.

Postal code prefixes, which often appear on London street signs and in street addresses, may help you find your way. The letters stand for compass directions, with reference to the central district (itself divided into WC and EC, for West Central and East Central). All districts that border this central district are numbered "1." There are no S or NE codes.

ECI: Farringdon, Clerkenwell. **EC2:** Barbican, the City. **EC3:** Tower of London. **EC4:** Blackfriars, Fleet St., Temple, St. Paul's.
WCI: Bloomsbury. **WC2:** Charing Cross, The Strand, Holborn.
EI: Whitechapel. **EI4:** Limehouse, including much of Docklands.
WI: Mayfair, Piccadilly, Oxford St., Soho, Marylebone. **W2:** Paddington. **W6:** Hammersmith. **W8:** Kensington. **W9:** Maida Vale. **WI0:** North Kensington. **WII:** Notting Hill. **WI4:** West Kensington.
SEI: South bank of the River, including Southwark and Waterloo. **SE3:** Blackheath. **SEI0:** Greenwich. **SEII:** Lambeth.
SWI: Victoria, Westminster, Belgravia, Pimlico, The Mall. **SW2:** Brixton. **SW3:** Chelsea, Brompton. **SW4:** Clapham. **SW5:** Earl's Court. **SW6:** Fulham. **SW7:** South Kensington. **SW8:** South Lambeth. **SW9:** Brixton. **SW10:** West Brompton. **SWII:** Battersea.
NI: Islington. **N6:** Highgate.
NWI: Camden Town. **NW3:** Hampstead. **NW5:** Kentish Town. **NW8:** St. John's Wood.

■ GETTING AROUND

PUBLIC TRANSPORTATION

London's public transit system, operated by **London Regional Transport (LRT),** is impressively comprehensive. The **Underground** (known as the tube) is supplemented by **buses** and by **British Rail (BR)**. Because government subsidies for public transport are very low, London's public transport system is one of the most expensive systems to ride when compared to other European capitals, and even New York. Nevertheless, London Transport is the busiest system in Western Europe, and taking public transport is always cheaper than taking a taxi.

In general, fares on all modes of public transportation in Britain are either "single" (one way) or "return" (round-trip). "Period returns" require you to return within a specific number of days; "day return" means you must return on the same day.

Information on both buses and the tube is available (tel. 222 1234; 24 hr.). Pick up free maps and guides at **London Transport's Information Centres** (look for the lowercase "i" logo at information windows and on signs). You can find these well-staffed booths with information on buses, Underground trains, the Docklands Light Railway (DLR), British Rail's London routes, and night buses at Heathrow Airport, Euston and Victoria rail stations, and the following major tube stops: King's Cross, Piccadilly Circus, Oxford Circus, St. James's Park, Liverpool St., Hammersmith, and Heathrow Terminals 1, 2, 3 station (most open weekdays 8am-6pm; central London stations also have weekend hours). For information on how the buses and Underground trains are currently running, phone 222 1200 (24-hr.). London Transport's **lost property office** (tel. 486 2496) lies just down the road from Holmes and Watson at 200 Baker St., W1 (tube: Baker St.; open Mon.-Fri. 9:30am-2pm). Allow two working days for articles lost on buses or the tube to reach the office.

London is divided into six concentric transport zones. Central London, including most of the major sights, is covered by zone 1; Heathrow Airport takes off in zone 6. Fares depend on the distance of the journey and the number of zones crossed. The **Travelcard,** because of its price and flexibility of both its duration and the zones it covers, has been a must for budget travelers. It can be bought for one day, one week, or one month's worth of travel. One-day Travelcards have certain restrictions: they cannot be used before 9:30am Mon.-Fri., and are not valid on night buses (adult one-day Travelcard, zones 1 and 2, £2.70). The one-week and one-month Travelcards can be used at any time, and are valid for Night Bus travel. Note that you will need a passport-sized photo in order to purchase a one-week or one-month Travelcard. Photo booths can be found in major tube stations, including Victoria, Leicester Sq., Earl's Ct., and Oxford Circus (about £2 for 4 pictures). Most tourists will find the zones 1&2 cards the most useful and economical. All Travelcards can be used on the Underground, regular buses, British Rail (Network SouthEast), and the Docklands Light Railway. Travelcards can be purchased at Underground ticket offices, London Transport Information Centres, and PASS agents throughout the city; credit cards are accepted. (Adult 1 wk. Travelcard, zones 1&2, £13; adult 1 mo. Travelcard, zones 1&2, £50.) Passes offered to tourists through travel agents outside Britain can be more expensive than a regular card. Depending on the rate of exchange, the London Visitor Travelcards have cost slightly more than the equivalent card in London—and have covered more zones than most visitors are likely to need.

UNDERGROUND

The color-coded **Underground** railway system, or the **tube,** is the easiest way to get around London, with 273 stations (give or take) on 11 lines (Bakerloo, Central, Circle, District, East London, Hammersmith and City, Jubilee, Metropolitan, Northern, Piccadilly, and Victoria). Small but invaluable "Journey Planner" maps are available at all stations. The stylization reduces above-ground geographic accuracy, but greatly increases lucidity. The famous map was designed in the 1930's by Henry Beck, an engineer who patterned his creation to resemble a circuit's schematic.

Fares depend on the number of zones passed through—a journey wholly within central zone 1 will cost much less than a trip to a distant suburb. On Sundays and Bank Holidays (see Appendix), trains run less frequently. All transfers are free. Bicycles are allowed on the above-ground sections of the Circle, District, Metropolitan, and Piccadilly lines for a child's fare except during morning and evening rush hours.

You can buy your ticket either from the ticket window or from a machine. The ticket allows you to go through the automatic gates; keep it until you reach your final destination, where it will be collected by another machine. Be aware that inspectors are becoming rather strict about enforcing the tube's new on-the-spot £10 fine for travel without a valid ticket.

Most tube lines' **last trains** leave Central London between midnight and 12:30am; service resumes around 6am. The gap in service is bridged by Night Buses (see Buses below). The tube, unremittingly packed during rush hour (Mon.-Fri. roughly 7-10am and 4:30-7:30pm), earns its share of flak due to delays, dirt, and diverted trains; the Northern line has been nicknamed "the misery line" because of its rush hour bedlam. Bear in mind that some distant suburban stations close on Sundays and other off-peak periods. Smoking is not allowed anywhere in or on the tube.

Some of London's deepest tube stations were used as air-raid shelters during the Blitz. At the worst of the bombing, as many as 175,000 people took shelter in them in one night; some were unable or unwilling to leave for days on end. While some stations may still bring bomb shelters to mind (indeed many remain virtually unchanged since then), others are quite jazzy with their intricate, colorful mosaics, often cryptically related to their name. London Transport continues its tradition of stylish poster art by commissioning paintings from contemporary artists for its "By Tube" posters, and has expanded to posting poems by writers from Middle English scrawlers to contemporary versifiers inside tube cars, a project which has drawn the attention of public transit authorities around the world.

Many stations feature labyrinthine tunnels and steep staircases, so if you're carrying a lot of luggage, you might fare better on a longer route that requires fewer transfers. Fitness zealots may wish to tackle the 331-step climb at Hampstead station, London's deepest. If you find yourself suffering from vertigo on the endless escalator, take heart from the example set by wooden-legged "Bumper" Harris. When London Transport installed the first escalators at Earl's Court in 1911, they hired Bumper to ascend and descend all day, thereby encouraging weak-kneed passengers. And remember to stand to the right, and walk on the left on escalators, or risk a rude tumbling from commuters in full stride.

BUSES

The way to see London is from the top of a bus—the top of a bus, gentlemen.

—William Gladstone

If you're in a hurry, don't take a bus. Take the tube; it's faster, easier, and generally more consistent. However, being shuttled about underground tunnels can hardly match the majesty of rolling along the street enthroned on the front seats of the top of a double-decker. Riding the buses is a great way to orient yourself to the city's layout, and to soak up its atmosphere and its sights. A number of buses in central London provide excellent sight-seeing opportunities at discount rates. The #11 bus, originating in at Liverpool Street station, takes in St. Paul's, Fleet Street, the Strand, Trafalgar Square, Westminster, Sloane Square, and all of King's Road. Route #14 originates in Riverside-Putney and coasts down Fulham Road, past the South Kensington museums, Knightsbridge, Hyde Park Corner, Piccadilly Circus and Leicester Square, and terminates on Tottenham Court Road in Soho.

Unfortunately, double-decker **Routemaster** buses, with their conductors and open rear platforms, are being replaced to save money. On modern double-deckers and on single-deck "hoppa" buses, you pay your fare to the driver as you board, and you must have exact change. On Routemasters, take a seat and wait for the conductor, who can tell you the fare and let you know when to get off. Smoking is not permitted on London's buses. **Bus stops** are marked with route information; at busy intersections or complicated one-way systems, maps tell where to board each bus. A warning: each stop is marked with route numbers and only those buses stop there. On stops marked "request," buses stop only if you flag them down (to get on) or pull the bell cord (to get off). While waiting, you must form a queue (line up); bus conductors may refuse some passengers at the stop with withering looks of scorn during crowded periods. Service is notoriously sporadic during the daytime; it is perfectly common to wait 20 minutes, only to be greeted by a procession of three buses in a row. Regular buses run from about 6am to midnight.

Night buses (the "N" routes) now run frequently throughout London from 11pm until 6am. When the tube goes to sleep (last trains run between midnight and 12:30am), night buses provide an inexpensive and convenient alternative to taxis. All night bus routes pass through Trafalgar Square, and many stop at Victoria as well. London Transport's information offices put out a free brochure about night buses, which includes times of the last British Rail and Underground trains. Call London Transport's 24-hr. information line (tel. 222 1234) for fares and schedules.

The bus network is divided into four zones. In and around central London, one-way **fares** range from 60p to £1.20, depending on the number of zones you pass through. Be sure to carry change to pay your fare; drivers will not accept big bills. Travelcards purchased for the Underground are valid on buses; armed with a Travelcard, you can hop on or off as often as you like. **Bus passes** are also available on a weekly or monthly basis, but are generally less practical than the Travelcard; only slightly more expensive than a bus pass, a Travelcard is also valid on the Underground and the DLR.

If you're planning on utlizing the bus network, London Transport issues a free bus map for London called the *All-London Bus Guide,* which is available at most tube stations and LRT information offices. The *Central Bus Guide* is a more manageable pamphlet, describing only bus routes in zone 1. If you require more detailed information about bus routes, there are 35 different *Local Bus Guides* which will help you navigate specific regions and/or neighborhoods. To find out whether buses are running on schedule, or whether routes have changed, call 222 1200. To acquire free local guides, call 371 0247.

Wheelchair accessible **Mobility Bus** routes, numbered in the 800s and 900s, service most of London. **Stationlink,** a wheelchair accessible bus, travels hourly between the major train stations. For information on either service, call 918 3312.

DOCKLANDS LIGHT RAILWAY

The Docklands Light Railway (DLR), London's newest transport system, connects the flashy developments of the old docks with the City of London. The semiautomatic trains run on elevated tracks, providing an unusual perspective on both the dilapidation and the frenetic construction in the area. The tube's zone system applies to the DLR, and DLR lines appear on all tube maps. Fares are the same as for the tube. There are three lines, the **red line** running north-south (connecting with the tube at Bow Church and Stratford), the **green line** running west-east to merge with the red line (connecting with the tube at Bank, Shadwell, and Tower Hill/Gateway), and the new Beckton line, which starts at Poplar Station (on the red line) and extends five miles to the east. In order to accommodate the construction, trains run on limited schedules (Mon.-Fri. 5:30am-11:30pm); buses travel the routes (same price as trains) Mon.-Fri. 11:15pm-12:50am, Sat. 5:30am-midnight, and Sun. 7:30am-11:30pm. Bus #D8 covers the red line and #D9 the green line. Call the 24-hour **Docklands Travel Hotline** (tel. 918 4000) for information.

BRITISH RAIL

Most of London is fully served by buses and the tube. Some districts, however, notably southeast London, are most easily reached by train. The BR is speedy and runs frequently to suburbs and daytrip areas around London, functioning as a commuter rail that is often cheaper than the tube. Its old-fashioned compartments are roomy and comfortable. The North London Link, stretching across north London from North Woolwich to Richmond, often deposits travelers closer to sights (such as Keats's house) than the tube: trains (every 20 min.) scoot from Hampstead Heath to Kew in 25 minutes. However, BR is used by most visitors for its service from Gatwick Airport to Victoria (see Getting In and Out of London). Information on Network South East services is available at all mainline stations. The massive Victoria train station, the terminus for most Network South East lines, offers timetables on large revolving spindles for your perusal. At the travel and information center at Waterloo (tel. 620 1032; open Mon.-Sat. 7:30am-9pm, Sun. 9am-9pm), you can buy your own copy of any timetable (30p for each section of London, £7.50 for the full timetable). *London Connections,* a map of all tube and Network South East lines, is free and available at any tube station or information office. For 24-hr. information on Network South East, call 928 5100.

TAXICABS

In order to earn a license, London taxicab drivers must pass a rigorous exam called "The Knowledge" to demonstrate that they know the city's streets by heart; the route taken by a cabbie is virtually certain to be the shortest and quickest. Although the London cab appears clumsy and vaguely old-fashioned, these specialized vehicles comfortably seat five and are able to dart in and out of traffic jams unperturbed. Most of the distinctively shaped cabs are black, although a few come in other colors, including *Financial Times* pink and *Evening Standard* newsprint pattern.

You are most likely to find cabs at large hotels, or at major intersections, but cabs abound throughout Central London and are easy to hail except during rain. A taxi is available if its yellow light is aglow. You can catch a cab yourself or call a radio dispatcher for one (tel. 272 0272 or 253 5000, or look in the Yellow Pages under "Taxi"); beware that you may be charged extra for ordering a cab by phone. Drivers are required to charge according to the meter for trips under 6 mi., but for longer distances you must negotiate the price. A 10% tip is expected, with a surplus charge for extra baggage or passengers. Taxis in London are notoriously expensive. If you believe that you have been overcharged, get the driver's number.

Apart from the licensed cabs, there are countless **"minicab"** companies, listed in the Yellow Pages. *Ladycabs* (tel. 272 3019) has only female cabbies (Mon.-Wed. 7:30am-midnight, Thurs. 7:30am-1am, Fri.-Sat. 8:30am-2am, Sun. 10am-midnight), as does *My Fare Lady* (tel. (0181) 458 9200). Be sure to ask the price when you order a minicab, and reconfirm it. Reclaim **lost property** (tel. 833 0996) you have left in a taxi at 15 Penton St., N1 (tube: Angel; open Mon.-Fri. 9am-4pm).

BICYCLES

London's roads are in excellent condition, but on weekdays both the volume and temper of its traffic may seem homicidal. However, bicycling has its advantages, and there are few better ways to spend a Sunday than pedaling through the parks of the city. Great deals on second-hand bikes can be found at the General Auction (see below). Also check outdoor markets, classified ads, and the University of London's bulletin board at 1 Malet St., WC1 (tube: Russell Sq.). Bikes are allowed on BR trains; you may take a bike onto the above-ground sections of the Circle, District, Metropolitan, and Piccadilly line Underground trains (Mon.-Fri. 10am-4:30pm and after 7:30pm, Sat.-Sun. all day) but you will be charged a child's fare for it. Many London cyclists wear breathing masks while riding to lessen the effects of the miasmal fumes polluting the London streets. The *Green Screen* (£6) is a cheaper and less-effective mask, while the *Respro* (£20-25) is the mask of choice for cyclists in the know; both are available at virtually all bike shops.

Brixton Cycles Co-op, 435-7 Coldharbour Ln., SW9 (tel. 733-6055). Tube: Brixton. A veritable mecca of mountain bikes for the hard-core crunchers of London. Besides loads of literature on the latest bike races, routes, and bike-a-thon fundraisers in and outside the city, they also have a great message board where Brixton locals advertise for roommates, funk drummers, and political rallies. Open Mon.-Sat. 9am-6pm, Thurs. 9am-7pm.

General Auctions, 63 Garrat La., Wandsworth, SW18 (tel. (081) 874 2955). Tube: Tooting Broadway, then bus #44 or 220. Police auction as many as 50-100 used bikes here every Mon. at 11am. Prices range from £5 to £400. Examine bikes Sat. 10am-3pm, Mon. 10-11am. Examine the £1 ones with particular care.

Mountain Bike and Ski, 18 Gillingham St., SW1 (tel. 834 8933). Tube: Victoria. From the station, go down Wilton Rd. and turn right on Gillingham St. Mountain bikes £7/day, £13/weekend, plus £1/day for insurance. £50 deposit required. Open Mon.-Thurs. 8:30am-5pm, Fri. 8:30am-7:30pm, Sat. 8:30am-4pm. MC, V.

On Your Bike, 22 Duke St. Hill, SE1 (tel. 357 6958). Tube: London Bridge. 10-speeds £12/day, £13/weekend, £25/week. If you don't have insurance credit card deposit £150, with insurance £50. Mountain bikes £15/day, £30/weekend, £25-30/week, steep £200 deposit. Open Mon. 8am-5:30, Tues.-Thurs. and Sat.

9:30am-5:30pm, Fri. 9:30am-7pm; in winter Fri.-Wed. 10am-6pm, Thurs. 10am-8:30pm. Access, MC, V.

Scootabout Ltd., 59 Albert Embankment, SE1 (tel. 582 0055 or 582 9836). Tube: Vauxhall. Mopeds (50cc) from £25/day, £99.50/week, including helmet, insurance, luggage rack, and unlimited miles. Credit card or £100 deposit required. Call ahead. Open Mon.-Fri. 9am-6pm, Sat. 9am-1pm.

CARS

London is not the place to go poncing about in your Mini—parking is next to impossible, traffic is deplorable, gas is very expensive, and the gear shift (not to mention your car) is on the left. When all's said and done, you can bike, bus, tube, or walk more quickly and cheaply. **Renting a car** will not save you time, money, or hassle compared to public transport in London. Big rental firms like Avis and Hertz may be convenient, but they are quite expensive. Small cheap companies can be dodgy. Drivers must usually be over 21 and under 70. Make sure you understand the insurance agreement before you rent; some agreements require you to pay for damages that you may not have caused. If you are paying by credit card, check to see what kind of insurance your company provides free of charge. You have been warned.

BOATS

The **River Thames** no longer commands as much traffic as in the Middle Ages, but if you venture out in a boat you can still sense the pulse of a major lifeline. **Catamaran Cruisers** (tel. 987 1185) offers cruises with commentary. Tours run from Charing Cross to Tower and Greenwich piers (every 30min. 10:30am-6:15pm; Tower £2.50 each way, Greenwich £3 each way, children ½ price). A Discoverer pass for a day's unlimited travel on the routes is £7, children £3. Call the London Tourist Board's **Riverboat Line** (tel. 730 4812) for more info.

The following destinations are served by **Westminster Pier** (tube: Westminster):

Tower of London: every 20 min., 10:40am-5pm (tel. 930 4097; £3.60, £4.60 return).

Greenwich: every ½ hr. 10:30am-5pm; 40-50min. (tel. 930 4097; £4.60, £5.60 return).

Thames Barrier: daily at 10am, 11:15am, 12:45, 1:45, and 3:15pm; 75min. (tel. 930 3373; £4, £5.70 return, children £2.30, £2.85 return).

Kew: daily 10:15am, 11am, 11:45am, 12:30am, 2, 2:45, and 3:30pm; 90min. (tel. 930 4721; £5, £7 return).

Richmond: daily 10:30am and noon; 3hrs. (tel. 930 4721; £6, £8 return).

Hampton Court: daily 10:30am and noon; 3-4½hrs. (tel. 930 4721; £7, £9 return).

Regent's Canal runs along the north rim of Regent's Park, and sets the stage for many a leisurely walk or boat trip.

Jason's Trip, opposite 60 Blomfield Rd., Little Venice, W9 (tel. 286 3428). Tube: Warwick Ave. Runs daily motor barges on the canal through the park to Camden Lock and back. June-Aug. and Easter at 10:30am, 12:30, 2:30, and 4:30pm; otherwise daily at 12:30 and 2:30pm. £4, return £5; under 14 £2.75, £3.50 return; family return £15.

Zoo Waterbus, Little Venice, W9 (tel. 482 2550). Tube: Warwick Ave. Shuttles passengers to the zoo in Regent's Park, and farther along to Camden Lock. In summer on the hr. 10am-5pm; in winter, every 1½ hr. 10:30am-3pm. £3, return £4, one way including admission to zoo £7.30.

Jenny Wren, 250 Camden High St., NW1 (tel. 485 4433). Tube: Camden Town. Drifts from Camden Lock to Little Venice and back. Weekdays at 11:30am and 2pm; Sat. at 2pm and 3:30pm; Sun. at 11:30am, 2pm, and 3:30pm; 1½-hr. £4 return, children £3 return.

Accommodations

To sleep in London, however, is an art which a foreigner must acquire by time and habit.

—Robert Southey, 1807

With a bit of perseverance, finding a safe, clean, convenient place to spend the night in London is not terribly difficult. B&Bs, hostels, and halls of residence all eagerly welcome tourists during the summer. You should plan ahead to nab one of the more desirable rooms, particularly in July and August, as they are likely to fill up rather quickly.

Almost all budget accommodations in London provide a bed and some form of breakfast. Apart from this fundamental similarity, the various accommodations differ widely in quality and texture. **Youth hostels** offer the option of, but are often not restricted to, dormitory-style accommodations. Guests pay low rates for clean and basic lodgings with little privacy—dorms sleep anywhere from 4 to 16 people. Both **HI**-affiliated (Hostelling International) hostels and private hostels make up in friend-liness what they lack in privacy, and can be marvelous places for swapping informa-tion and finding traveling companions. Non-HI, or **private hostels,** feature inexpensive dormitory accommodations—usually without the lockout and curfew restrictions that HI hostels tend to have. Private hostel dorms often feature fewer beds per room, and the beds are not always bunk beds. In both types of hostel, every room contains a sink, with bathrooms in the hall. Hostels are definitely the cheapest option for those traveling alone.

However, visitors traveling in groups can enjoy privacy and other amenities at similarly low rates by sharing a double, triple, or quad at a **B&B.** The term "B&B" encompasses budget hotels of varying quality and personality. Some are nothing more than budget hotels that serve breakfast; don't expect snug, quaint lodgings. Rooms in these lesser-quality B&Bs are small, soulless, and provide few amenities (although you can always count on a sink and tea/coffee-making facilities). How-ever, some B&Bs are quite cozy, sporting warm comforters, charming decorative details, friendly management, and the occasional pet. As the character of B&Bs can be so divergent, it is advisable to investigate all of your options before choosing a hotel.

In London B&Bs, a **basic room** means that you share the use of a shower and toi-let in the hall. An **en suite room,** which contains both a private shower and toilet (or "W.C."), costs several pounds more. Occasionally an "en suite" room will have either a shower or a toilet (not both), so be sure to check. Be warned, however, that in-room showers are often awkward prefab units jammed into a corner. **Family room** in B&B lingo generally means a quad or quint with at least one double bed and some single beds.

Most B&Bs (and some hostels) serve the full **English breakfast**—eggs, bacon, toast, baked beans, and tea or coffee. **Continental breakfast,** on the other hand, means only some form of bread and hot beverage.

B&Bs generally take reservations (by phone, fax, or letter) with one night's deposit unless we state otherwise. Before committing yourself to a hotel, see the room and bathroom, and test the bed—its quality may have a huge impact on your stay. In winter, be sure to check whether the room will be heated. If you don't like climbing stairs, keep in mind that "first floor" means second floor to Americans. Some proprietors grant **rate reductions** for stays of several days or over a week; it's always worth asking. Even in high season, it doesn't hurt to try bargaining—with the ongoing recession, the less desirable B&Bs are struggling for business. All require payment in advance, and many accept credit cards. Off-season is from October through March (although September, April, and May are slow enough that you may be able to haggle for a few pounds' discount).

Most B&Bs in London cluster around the railway stations. Although abundant and convenient, rooms in these areas tend to be well-worn. Less obvious but equally convenient areas offer more humane surroundings. Don't be put off by B&Bs located in areas which seem removed, residential, or peripheral; rooms in these outlying areas are often well-decorated and in good repair, neighboring special pubs and restaurants that don't cater to an exclusively tourist crowd.

Halls of residence of the London colleges and polytechnics offer privacy in the form of small, spare singles. If you have a student ID, you can often find stupendous bargains at these halls; in some cases, you can get a private single for the same price that you would pay for a bed in a hostel dorm. Rates are a bit higher for those without student ID, but are still an affordable option for those traveling alone. A few halls have fantastic locations and beautiful grounds, but rooms generally become brighter and more spacious the farther you move from the center of town. Again, all rooms come with sinks.

Making advance reservations and sending deposits seems inconvenient, but ensures that your arrival is as anxiety-free as possible. In the summer months, advance reservations are essential (especially for single rooms), rescuing you from the grungiest of packed railway station B&Bs. Write, fax, or phone the hotel to check availability on the date you wish to stay. The proprietor should specify the deposit amount (usually one night's stay). The hotel will advise the best way to make the deposit. More and more hotels and most HI hostels accept credit card reservations over the phone, so if you don't have the time to make written reservations, it's well worth calling ahead. The **Tourist Information Centre Accommodations Service** at Victoria Station bustles during high season (See Essentials).

In the listings below, all prices are given per room, while prices for a bed in a dorm are listed per person. The accommodations near the top of the listing for each region generally offer more pleasant lodgings at a better price than those at the bottom of the listing.

LONG-TERM ACCOMMODATIONS

Finding a flat in London is easy. Finding a decent one, however, requires some effort. Consider renting a **bed-sit,** anything from a studio apartment to a small room in a private house, with access to a kitchen and bathroom. Bed-sits run at the very least £40 per week, and most landlords won't lease for less than a month.

The wonderful **University of London Accommodation Office** puts out lists of accommodations for summer stays beginning in June, and at Christmas and Easter. Visit the office at the University of London Senate House, Room 5, Malet St., WC1 (tel. 636 2818; tube: Russell Sq.; open Mon.-Fri. 9:30am-5:30pm), with a student ID. They list a range of studios, flats, and flatshares (about £35-60 per week), and all University of London residence halls. Most summer lets don't begin until late June or July.

Accommodations agencies generally charge one or two weeks' rent as a fee; it's in their interest to find high-priced accommodations, and in your interest to avoid their services whenever possible. **Jenny Jones Accommodation Agency,** 40 S. Molton St., W1 (tel. 493 4801; tube: Bond St.) charges the fee to the landlord instead of the tenant, and has bed-sits starting from £50 for something suburban. You may have to check several times for a central location (£70-80). Check which zone the flat is in; this will determine transport costs for your stay. (Open Mon.-Fri. 9:30am-2pm and 2:30-5:30pm.) **Flatsearch,** 68 Queensway, W2 (tel. 221 6335 or 221 5918; tube: Bayswater), has bed-sits from £65, concentrated in the Queensway/Bayswater area. They also rent flats in Chelsea and Kensington starting at £120 per week. For bedsits they charge a full week's rent as commission (open Mon.-Fri. 9:30am-5:30pm). **Universal Aunts,** P.O. Box 304, SW4 0NN (tel. 738 8937; fax 622 1914) has central locations for about £75-150 plus a service charge. For information about their flat-rental service, call 386 5900.

Various **independent landlords** lease blocks of flats to tourists throughout London; a short list of such landlords appears in the London Tourist Board's *Where to Stay in London*. The BTA's free leaflet *Apartments in London* leans toward the more expensive holiday apartments, but has some budget listings. Bulletin boards in small grocery shops frequently list available rooms and flats, as do the classified sections of the major newspapers. Call as early as possible when responding to advertisements in one of the larger papers. Beware of ads placed by accommodations agencies; they often try to sell you something more expensive when you call.

HI/YHA HOSTELS

Each of the eight Hostelling International/YHA hostels in London requires a **Hostelling International** or **Youth Hostel Association of England and Wales (YHA) membership card.** Overseas visitors can buy one at YHA London Headquarters or at the hostels themselves for £9. An **International Guest Pass** (£1.50) permits residents of places other than England and Wales to stay at hostel rates without joining the hostel association. After you purchase six Guest Passes, you attain full membership. A membership card for residents of England and Wales costs £9 for age 18 and over, £3 otherwise.

The cheerful staff members, often international travelers themselves, keep London HI/YHA hostels clean and refreshingly well-managed. They can also often provide a range of helpful information on the environs of the hostel. Plan ahead, since London hostels are exceptionally crowded. During the summer, beds fill up months in advance. In recent years, hostels have not always been able to accommodate every written request for reservations, much less on-the-spot inquiries. But hostels frequently hold some beds free until a few days before—it's always worth checking. To secure a place, show up as early as possible and expect to stand in line. With a Visa or Mastercard, you can book in advance by phone. Or you can write to the warden of the individual hostel. There is a new **central reservations number** for all London hostels (tel. 248 6547; open Mon.-Sat. 9:30am-5:30pm).

For hostel information, visit or call the jumbo-market **YHA London Information Office and Adventure Shop,** 14 Southampton St., WC2 (tel. 836 1036; tube: Covent Garden; open Mon.-Wed. 10am-6pm, Thurs.-Fri. 10am-7pm, Sat. 9am-6:30pm). Cardholders receive a 10% discount on anything in the Adventure Shop.

All hostels are equipped with large **lockers** that require a padlock. Bring your own or purchase one from the hostel for £2.50. London hostels do not charge for a sheet sleeping bag. Most have laundry facilities and some kitchen equipment. Theatre tickets and discounted attraction tickets are available.

Oxford Street, 14-18 Noel St., W1 (tel. 734 1618; fax 734 1657). Tube: Oxford Circus. Walk east on Oxford St. and turn right on Poland St.; hostel stands next to a 1989 mural entitled "Ode to the West Wind." Bang in the heart of London and Soho, it fills up in a flash. Reception open 7am-11pm. 24 hr. security; no curfew. 89 beds in small rooms of 2-4, with pink walls and worn blue carpets. Rooms have large storage lockers, but you must bring your own padlock. Superb location makes up for the expense: £16.70, under 18 £13.70. Continental breakfast £2.70. Facilities include a spacious TV lounge with plenty of comfortable chairs, a fully equipped kitchen with microwave, currency exchange, and a monitored baggage room. Book at least 2-3 wks. in advance; full payment required to secure a reservation. MC, Visa. Not recommended for those who have trouble climbing stairs.

Hampstead Heath, 4 Wellgarth Rd., NW11 (tel. (0181) 458 9054; fax (0181) 209 0546). Tube: Golders Green, then bus #210 or 268, or on foot by turning left onto Wellgarth after a ½-mi. walk along North End Rd. Serenely positioned at the edge of the Hampstead Heath extension. Despite its peaceful surroundings, this hostel can fall victim to school parties. No curfew. 200 beds in surprisingly sumptuous dorms. £13.90, under 18 £11.80. Restaurant (breakfast £2.60). Kitchen and laundry facilities. The big bonus is the lovely backyard and outdoor walkway covered with clinging grape vines. Video games and pool table. Partially wheelchair accessible. MC, Visa, Switch.

City of London, 36 Carter La., EC4 (tel. 236 4965; fax 236 7681). Tube: St. Paul's. From the City Information Centre on the opposite side of St. Paul's Cathedral, go left down Godliman St. Take the first right onto Carter Lane. This centrally located and newly refurbished hostel offers antiseptic cleanliness and a full range of services, including secure luggage storage, currency exchange, laundry facilities, TV, ticket sales for theatres and buses, and 24-hr. security. Crisp beige walls adorned with posters, new carpeting, and custodians striding purposefully through the halls contribute to the orderliness of this modern hostel. Reception open daily 7am-11pm. Rooms contain between 2 and 15 beds; the average room has 5 beds. Larger rooms feature the less-than-ideal triple-decker bunk beds which are ubiquitous in London hostels. Single-sex rooms available. Single or double £22, under 18 £18.50. Triple or quad £19, under 18 £16.50. Standard dorm (5-8 beds) £18.90, under 18 £15.90. Economy dorm (10-15 beds) £14, under 18 £11. Special weekly rates available Sept.-Feb. Breakfast included. A canteen offers inexpensive set lunches and dinners. Best to call at least a week in advance, especially for the economy rate dorms.

Earl's Court, 38 Bolton Gdns., SW5 (tel. 373 7083; fax 835 2034). Tube: Earl's Ct. Exit from the tube station onto Earl's Court Rd. and turn right; Bolton Gdns. is the 5th street on your left. A converted townhouse in a leafy residential neighborhood. 155 beds in rooms of 4-16. Reception open 7:30am-10:30pm. No curfew. Triple-decker bunk beds uniform to London hostels work particularly well in these airy rooms. All rooms single-sex. £16.90, under 18 £14.90. Continental breakfast. Well-stocked lounge has TV/VCR, Sega videogames, and a soda machine. Currency exchange. 24-hr. security. Cafeteria meals available 5-8pm. Kitchen and laundry access.

Holland House (King George VI Memorial Youth Hostel), Holland Walk, W8 (tel. 937 0748; fax 376 0667). Tube: High St. Kensington. Though the walk from High Street Kensington is approximately ½ mi. long, don't be fooled into thinking that the Holland Park station is any closer. The walk from High St. Kensington is *much* safer than the walk from Holland Park. Turn left when you exit the Kensington High Street station; continue walking and turn right onto Holland Walk. Pass the vast playing field and enter the park through the entrance on your left; a quick right leads you to the hostel. One half of the hostel is a restored Jacobean mansion, but you're just as likely to be sleeping in the other half, a late 60s cement block. A no-nonsense staff welcomes you 24 hrs. a day. No curfew or lockout. Rooms have anywhere from 1 to 20 beds; most (12, 13, and 20 bed dorms) feature cramped bunk beds unsuitable for the claustrophobia-prone. If you can't get room #17 (the only single), try for room #18, a dorm with a pleasing vaulted ceiling. All rooms single-sex. Linens provided. Adults £16.90, under 18 £14.90. Breakfast included. Personal lockers. Telephones, vending machines, TV lounge, *bureau de change*, study rooms, laundry. Dinner (£2-3). Kitchen facilities.

Highgate, 84 Highgate West Hill, N6 (tel. (0181) 340 1831). Tube: Archway. From the Archway stop take bus #210 or 217 to Highgate Village, or, on foot, leave the Junction Rd. tube exit, turn left immediately onto Highgate Hill, which leads to Highgate Village (¾ mi.). At Highgate Village, turn left onto South Grove (where the triangular bus bay is), a street that becomes St. Michael's Terr. and merges with Highgate West Hill. About 40min. from central London. A Georgian house in the middle of historic Highgate village. Out-of-the-way location and idyllic neighborhood make for a homey hostel. Reception open 8:45am-10am, 1pm-7pm, and 8pm-11:30pm. Midnight curfew; no lockout. 69 beds, 4-16 beds per room. Clean bathrooms have flowered curtains and pink floors. £11.75, under 18 £7.85. Breakfast, served early, £2.60. TV lounge, kitchen facilities. MC, Visa.

Rotherhithe, Island Yard, Salter Rd., SE1 (tel. 232 2114). Tube: Rotherhithe on the East London line; transfer onto this line from District or Hammersmith lines at Whitechapel or transfer from the DLR at Shadwell. A 15min. walk down Brunel Rd. then onto Salter. Welcome to *2001, A Space Odyssey* (you're officially in the Docklands, just across the Thames from the Isle of Dogs). Chrome, glass, and white stucco make this brand new 320-bed hostel a trip into futuristic living. No curfew. Complete facilities and tightly packed but immaculate rooms, mostly 2- or 6-bed. £16.50, under 18 £13.50. Breakfast £2.60. Restaurant, a roomy lounge with video games, and a bar. Wheelchair accessible. AmEx, MC, Visa.

Epping Forest, Wellington Hall, High Beach, Loughton, Essex 1G10 (tel. (0181) 508 5161). Tube: Loughton (zone 6, 45 min. from central London), or BR: Chingford (zone 5), then a good 2mi. walk through the forest. A taxi from the tube station costs £3 for 1 or 2 people—about 60p extra for additional passengers. A retreat from London havoc and prices. Set in the heart of 6000 remote acres of ancient woodland. Reception open 7-10am and 5-11pm. £6.70, under 18 £4.80. Simple washing facilities and no laundry, but large kitchen. Open April-Oct.

PRIVATE HOSTELS

Private hostels, which do not require a HI card, generally have a youthful clientele. Some have kitchen facilities. There are almost never curfews. Dorm prices in the listings below are per person.

■■■ BLOOMSBURY

Central University of Iowa Hostel, 7 Bedford Pl., WC1 (tel. 580 1121; fax 580 5638). Tube: Holborn or Russell Sq. From Russell Sq., head left and turn left onto Southampton Row, then turn right onto Russell Sq.; Bedford Pl. is the first left. On a quiet B&B-lined street near the British Museum. No curfew. Reception open 8am-1pm and 3-8pm. Bright, spartan rooms with bunk beds, new wood furniture, and bookshelves. Dorms (2-4 beds) £15.50. Continental breakfast. Laundry facilities, kitchen facilities, and a recently refurbished TV lounge. 2-week max. stay. Open mid-May to mid-Aug. MC, Visa.

Astor's Museum Inn, 27 Montague St., WC1 (tel. 580 5360; fax 636 7948). Tube: Holborn, Tottenham Ct. Rd., or Russell Sq. Off Bloomsbury Sq. International "grunge"-clientele compensate for standard dorms with slightly saggy bunk beds. Bathrooms are clean, but the showers are a bit low-tech. Reception open 24 hrs. No curfew. Co-ed dorms (2-8 beds) £13-18, £57-67 per week. Discounts available Oct.-March. Continental breakfast. Kitchen facilities, cable TV lounge, and game room. If they're full, they will direct you to 1 of 2 other Astor's hostels and pay for your tube fare. MC, Visa.

Tonbridge School Clubs, Ltd., corner of Judd and Cromer St., WC1 (tel. 837 4406). Tube: King's Cross/St. Pancras. Follow Euston Rd. to the site of the new British Library and turn left onto Judd St.; the hostel is 3 blocks down. Students with non-British passports only. For the true budget traveler, a clean place for sleep and hot showers. No frills and no privacy, but dirt cheap. Lockout 9:30am-10pm; use caution when walking in the area at night. Midnight curfew. Men sleep in basement gym, women in karate-club hall. Blankets and foam pads provided. Storage space for backpacks during the day, but safety is not guaranteed. £3.

■■■ PADDINGTON, BAYSWATER, AND NOTTING HILL GATE

Palace Court Hotel, 64-65 Prince's Sq., W2 (tel. 229 4747 or 4412; fax 727 9228). Tube: Bayswater or Notting Hill Gate. From Bayswater head left out of the station. Take a left on Moscow Rd. and then turn right onto Hereford Rd. From Notting Hill Gate head north up Pembridge Gdns., turn right on Pembridge Sq., then take a left on Hereford Rd. The hostel is on the corner of Hereford Rd. and Prince's Sq. Alternately, call ahead and arrange for the *complimentary shuttle service* to pick you up at Victoria Station and ferry you directly to the hostel. 100 beds. With free keg parties every Wed. night, a late night TV lounge, and an outdoor patio area, this well-located new hostel will doubtless play host to much boisterous activity.

Salmon pink corridors lead into airy, comfortable rooms with 2-6 beds, all with closet and washbasin. Bed in a 6-bed room £9, in a 4-bed room £10, in a double £12; corresponding weekly rates are £50, £55, and £60. Sheets and cozy duvets, washed daily, are included. English breakfast. "Fats," the restaurant, serves dinner for under £3. Lounge with pool table, TV/VCR, pay phone, beverages. Phone or fax in a reservation and call one day before arriving to confirm; they will only hold your place until 4pm.

Centre d'Echanges Internationaux, 61-69 Chepstow Pl., W2 (tel. 221 8134; fax 221 0642). Tube: Notting Hill Gate or Bayswater. From Notting Hill Gate, head up Pembridge Gdns., turn right on Pembridge Sq., then turn left on Chepstow Place. From Bayswater, head west on Moscow Rd., then turn right onto Chepstow Place. The hostel is on your right. 180 beds. A delightful Gallic atmosphere pervades this immaculate hostel in a chic residential area convenient to Portobello Rd. and Hyde Park. Bilingual staff welcomes an international clientele, half of whom hail from France. Rooms are spacious, well-kept, and cleaned frequently. Lockout 10am-5pm. No curfew. Sheets and lockers included. Dorm (8-12 beds) £14. Singles £25. Doubles £20 per person. Triples £17.50 per person. Off-season discounts. Stay a week and you'll only be charged for 6 nights. Breakfast included. Pay an extra £5 per night for a strange in-room shower that looks, and feels, like a closet. Study rooms, coffee and soda machines, pay phone, TV room, laundry. The hostel's recently renovated pink restaurant, serves dinners from £1.30-4.50. Elevators, but narrow hallways prevent the hostel from being entirely wheelchair accessible. Reservations are strongly recommended; you can call ahead to inquire about vacancies but only a deposit will hold your reservation. AmEx, MC, Visa.

Palace Hotel, 31 Palace Ct., W2 (tel. 221 5628; fax 243 8157). Tube: Notting Hill Gate or Queensway. From Notting Hill Gate, walk east until Notting Hill Gate turns into Bayswater, then turn left onto Palace Ct. From Queensway, walk west on Bayswater and take a right onto Palace Ct. The hostel is on your left. 90 beds. Young community atmosphere and bright dorm rooms make this great deal an excellent social space for enthusiastic hostelers. Snapshots of former guests posted on the walls testify to the good vibes. No curfew. Airy rooms with tall windows all house 8 (bunk)beds. Single-sex rooms often available. Linens and comforters included. £10 per night, £55 per week. English breakfast. No credit cards.

Quest Hotel, 45 Queensborough Terr., W2 (tel. 229 7782). Tube: Queensway. From the tube, take a left onto Bayswater; walk for 2 blocks and turn left onto Queensborough Terr. The hostel, a terraced house, is on your left. 95 beds. Communal, clean, and sociable; staff throws one theme party a month. No curfew. All rooms have 4-8 beds; 2 have terraces facing the street. There are usually 1 or 2 women-only rooms available. £11.50-13.50, includes continental breakfast. English breakfast £2. Pool room and kitchen. Key deposit £3. MC, Visa.

■■■ KENSINGTON, CHELSEA, AND EARL'S COURT

Albert Hotel, 191 Queens Gate, SW7 (tel. 584 3019; fax 823 8520). Tube: Gloucester Rd, or bus #2 from South Kensington. From the tube, it's a substantial walk for those carrying luggage; take a right on Cromwell and a left on Queen's Gate. The hotel is approximately ¼ mi. up Queen's Gate on your right, in tantalizing proximity to Hyde Park. The bus, which stops by the Royal Albert Hall on Kensington Gore, is much quicker. A porch with a portico leads into an elegant wood-paneled corridor. Stately lounges contain plush couches, a pool table, and color TV. 24-hr. reception. No lockout or curfew. Rooms range from large dorms to intimate twins, some with terraces, most en suite. Dorm £9.50-12. Twins £32. Quads £12 per person. Single-sex and mixed dorms. Continental breakfast. Laundry. Reserve ahead with 1 night's deposit. No credit cards.

Curzon House Hotel, 58 Courtfield Gdns., SW5 (tel. 581 2116; fax 835 1319). Tube: Gloucester Rd. Turn right onto Gloucester Rd., right again on Courtfield Rd., and right on Courtfield Gdns. Your lodgings will cost a bit more, but you will be amply repaid in cleanliness and friendliness. Tidy and cool, this hostel recently installed new showers. TV lounge features langour-inducing couches. Most rooms have tall ceilings and mammoth windows that overlook a gracious park. Singles £26. Doubles £38. Triples £45. Dorm £13. Weekly and seasonal discounts. Single-sex dorms only. Continental breakfast. Kitchen. Luggage storage.

Court Hotel, 194-196 Earl's Court Rd., SW5 (tel. 373 0027; fax 244 9870). Tube: Earl's Ct. Sister hostel at 17 Kempsford Gardens (tel. 373 2174). Very clean Australian-managed hostel. All single, double, and twin rooms have TV and tea/coffee set. Linens provided. Singles £18, £119 per week. Doubles £14 per person, £154 per week. Triples or more £12 per person, £177 per week. Off-season and long-term discounts. Full kitchen facilities and spacious TV lounge. Safe available for valuables. Key deposit £5. Reservations not accepted; call for availability.

The Inchmont Hotel, 25 Collingham Place, SW5 (tel. 370 2414; fax 244 8301). Tube: Earl's Court or Gloucester Rd. Two TV lounges pamper listless, dazed backpackers. Refreshed, backpackers then hit the hostel party circuit, leaving soporific quiet in their wake. Most rooms have 2 or 3 bunkbeds, large windows, and wash basins. Dorm £10 per day, £50 per week, £47.50 if you stay 2 wks. or more. Doubles £15 per person. Kitchen well-used; guests shop at nearby Sainsbury's.

Chelsea Hotel, 33-41 Earl's Ct. Sq., SW5 (tel. 244 6892 or 7395; fax 244 6891). Tube: Earl's Ct. Turn right onto Earl's Court Rd., then right again at Earl's Court Sq. 300 dorm beds in a mammoth succession of connected houses. Vegetating backpackers zone out in the lounge, which sports a satellite TV and a pool table. 24-hr. reception. No lockout or curfew. Stark rooms generally feature bunk beds. Sheets provided. Dorm £9. Doubles £11.50, with shower £12.50. Triples £12. Quads £11. Winter rates £1 lower; weekly rates 7 nights for the price of 6. Continental breakfast. £1 per day luggage storage; store valuables in downstairs safe for 50p. Laundry. Fax available. Reserve ahead in writing.

O'Callaghan's Hotel, 205 Earl's Court Rd., SW5 (tel. 370 3000). Tube: Earl's Court. This hotel doesn't aim to impress; with prices this cheap, it doesn't have to. O'Callaghan's thrives by simply providing a solid mattress and unlimited coffee. 24-hr. reception. Garishly colored rooms have big windows and bunk beds. Single-sex rooms only. Doubles/twins £10 per person. Quads £8 per person, £49 per week. Key deposit £5.

■■■ NEAR VICTORIA STATION

Elizabeth House (YWCA Hostel), 118 Warwick Way, SW1 (tel. 630 0741). Tube: Victoria. Turn left onto Buckingham Palace Rd., then left onto the Elizabeth St. Bridge, which turns into St. George's Dr. Hostel is at intersection with Warwick Way. Not for women only; students, and families with children over 5 welcome. Friendly staff diminishes the institutional atmosphere. Reception 24 hrs. Large, spartanly furnished rooms. Singles £21, £135 per week. Doubles £40-42, £250-270 per week; with bath £45, £290 per week. Dorm (3-4 single beds) £15 per person, £100 per week. Continental breakfast. TV lounges. Try to reserve at least a month ahead (£10 deposit). YWCA membership required (10p per week).

Victoria Hotel, 71 Belgrave Rd. SW1 (tel. 834 3077; fax 932 0693). Tube: Victoria or Pimlico. Closer to Pimlico; from the station, take the Bessborough St. (south side) exit and go left along Lupus St. Take a right at St. George's Sq.; Belgrave Rd. starts on the other side. 70 beds. Wire sculptures dangle in the reception area, open 24 hrs. Whimsical splashes of color brighten the standard rooms with bunk beds. Shower stalls are a bit dark, but generally clean. Coed dorms for 5 £14 per person. 6-person dorm £13 per person. 8-person dorm £11 per person. One 6-bed women-only dorm available £14 per person. Continental breakfast. Cozy kitchen, TV lounge, pool table lounge.

■■■ NORTH LONDON

International Student House, 229 Great Portland St., W1 (tel. 631 3223; fax 636 5565). Tube: Great Portland St. At the foot of Regent's Park, across the street from the tube station's rotunda. Unattractive 60s exterior hides a thriving international metropolis with its own films, concerts, discos, study-groups, athletic contests, expeditions, and parties. No curfew. 400 beds in doubles and singles. Well-maintained rooms with institutional furnishings. Many in the second building at 10 York Terrace East enjoy views of Regent's Park. Singles £23.40. Doubles £19.75 per person. Triples £16.60 per person. Quads (some with bunk beds) £12.35 per person. Discounts for HI members. Special monthly and long-term rates also available (about 250 beds are occupied by long-term residents.) English breakfast. Lockable cupboards, laundry facilities, money changing services (£3 flat fee). Key deposit £10. Reserve through main office on Great Portland St. usually at least 1 month ahead, earlier during academic year. Letter of confirmation required for long-term stays. MC, V. Foreign currencies accepted.

HALLS OF RESIDENCE

London's university residences often accommodate visitors for limited periods during the summer break and during Easter vacations. Many of these halls are characterized by boxlike rooms and institutional furniture. Reliably maintained and well-located, they substitute convenience for character. Most charge around £20 and contain all singles, offering more privacy than a hostel. Call well in advance (by April for July reservations), as conference groups tend to snatch up rooms early.

■■■ BLOOMSBURY

Carr Saunders Hall, 18-24 Fitzroy St., W1 (tel. 580 6338). Tube: Warren St. Turn right off Tottenham Ct. Rd. onto Grafton Way, then left onto Fitzroy St. A newer London School of Economics building. 134 single study bedrooms, 12 doubles. Singles £20.50. Doubles £41. English breakfast. L Self-catering apartments for 2-5 people also available across the street; all are fully furnished, complete with cooking utensils, crockery, and bed linen. Min. stay 4 nights. Doubles £33. Triples £48. Quads £62. Quints £75. Under 12 half price.

Connaught Hall, 36-45 Tavistock Sq., WC1 (tel. 387 6181; fax 383 4109). Tube: Russell Sq. Head left from the station and turn right onto Woburn Pl.; the first left is Tavistock Sq. Graceful London University Hall often filled by academic groups. Quiet atmosphere. Reception open Mon.-Sat. 8am-11pm, Sun. 9am-11pm. 200 small, single study bedrooms with wardrobes, desks, and tea-making facilities. Singles £19.50. English breakfast. Laundromat, reading rooms, private garden, and an elegant green marble lobby. Reservations rec. Open July-Aug.

John Adams Hall, 15-23 Endsleigh St., WC1 (tel. 387 4086; fax 383 0164). Tube: Euston. Heading right on Euston Rd., take first right onto Gordon St., and first left onto Endsleigh Gdns.; Endsleigh St. is the second right. Elegant London University building. Some rooms have small balconies overlooking street. 124 singles, 22 doubles. Reception open daily 7:30am-10pm. Singles £21.40. Doubles £37. English breakfast. Laundry facilities, TV lounge, ping-pong table, and quiet reading room. Open July-Aug., Easter. MC, Visa.

Passfield Hall, 1 Endsleigh Pl., WC1 (tel. 387 3584 or 387 7743). Tube: Euston. Head left on Euston Rd., then take the first right onto Gordon St. Endsleigh Pl. is the second left. A L.S.E. hall between Gordon and Tavistock Sq. Lots of summer students. Reception open 8am-midnight. 100 singles, 34 doubles, 10 triples; rooms vary in size, but all have desks and a phone which can only receive incoming calls. £20.50 per person. Under 12 half price. Laundry. Kitchen. English breakfast. Call by March/April for July. Open July-Sept., Easter. MC, Visa.

Canterbury Hall, 12-28 Cartwright Gdns., WC1 (tel. 387 5526). Tube: Russell Sq. Head right from the station, turn left onto Marchmont St., and Cartwright Gardens will appear just past Tavistock Pl. A smaller, older hall. No curfew. Organized groups hog most of the 230 small singles. Better than its neighboring halls because there's 1 bathroom (with bathtub) for every 2 singles. Singles £21.15.

English breakfast. Squash courts, tennis courts, 2 TV lounges, laundry facilities. Open July-Aug. and Easter. Best to call by end of March for July reservations.

Commonwealth Hall, 1-11 Cartwright Gdns., WC1 (tel. 387 0311). Tube: Russell Sq. (See directions to Canterbury Hall above.) Déjà vu—it's just like Canterbury and Hughes Parry Halls. 24-hr. porter, no curfew. 420 small singles with institutional decor. Singles with breakfast £18.50, with breakfast and dinner £22.50. Reservations without deposit. Squash and tennis, laundry facilities, ping pong, TV lounges, library, music rooms, and a pleasant bar (pint £1.20). Open July-Aug.

Hughes Parry Hall, Cartwright Gdns., WC1 (tel. 387 1477). Tube: Russell Sq. (See directions to Canterbury Hall above.) Mammoth modern London University hall with 300 smallish institutional singles. Singles with breakfast £18.50, with breakfast and dinner £22. Squash and tennis, laundry facilities, libraries, TV lounge, bar, 24-hr. porter. Reservations without deposit. Open July-Aug.

Rosebery Avenue Hall, 90 Rosebery Ave., EC1 (tel. 278 3251; fax 278 2068). Tube: Buses #19 and 38 from Piccadilly Circus, or a 10-15 min. walk from the Angel tube station down St. John St., which forks to the right for Rosebery Ave. Farther out of the way than other halls (although close to Islington). Reception open daily 8:30am-1pm and 2pm-midnight. Compact, carpeted bedrooms with desk, wardrobe, and shelves. Singles £20.50. Doubles £30 or £40. Discounts for stays over 3 wks. English breakfast. Bar, game lounge, laundry facilities, TV room, and small garden. Small kitchen suitable for snack-making. Open late June-Sept.

■■■ KENSINGTON, CHELSEA, AND EARL'S COURT

The **King's Campus Vacation Bureau,** 552 King's Rd., London SW10 OUA (tel. 351 6011; fax 352 7376), controls bookings for a number of residence halls where students of **King's College** of the University of London live during the academic year. Rooms are available from early June to mid-September. Two of the halls (King's College and Wellington) are available during Easter. All have 24-hour security, and offer breakfast, linen, soap, towel, and laundry facilities. Any form of student ID will get guests a discount of approximately £5 per night; guests have the option of taking this discount or the 10% discount open to *all* individuals staying 7 nights or longer.

Ingram Court, 552 King's Rd., SW10 (tel. 351 6513). Tube: Sloane Sq. or Fulham Broadway. From Sloane Sq., take the #11 or 22 bus to Lot's Rd. (in front of campus); or walk 10 min. from Fulham Broadway. This site, once a part of Sir Thomas More's estate, approximates an accommodations utopia. Besides having a green lawn and ornamental fish pond in a beautiful courtyard, Ingram is also near the World's End Distillery, a supreme watering hole (see Pubs). Singles £19.50, twin £15.25 per person. Continental breakfast.

Wellington Hall, 71 Vincent Sq., Westminster, SW1 (tel. 834 4740; fax 233 7709). Tube: Victoria, walk 1 long block along Vauxhall Bridge Rd.; turn left on Rochester Row. Charming Edwardian hall on pleasant, quiet square. Convenient to Westminster, Big Ben, Buckingham Palace, and the Tate Gallery, this hall is the most central and expensive of the King's College halls. Memorable oak panels and stained-glass windows in dining room. Singles £21.50, twin £16.25 per person. English breakfast. 2 lounges, library, conference room, and bar. Open Easter.

Lightfoot Hall, Manresa Rd. at King's Rd., SW3 (tel. 333 4898 or 351 6011 for booking; fax 333 4901). Tube: Sloane Sq. or South Kensington. From South Kensington, take bus #49; from Sloane Sq., bus #11 or 22. Prime location. Rooms in a modern, institutional block. With student ID, singles and doubles are £13 per person. Singles £20. Twins £16 per person. Continental breakfast not included at student rate. Satellite TV. Bar. Rooms may be available during school year.

Queen Elizabeth Hall, Campden Hill Rd., W8 (tel. 333 4255 or 333 4245 24-hr.; fax 937 7783). Tube: High St. Kensington. Walk 1 block west and 2 north from the tube. Look for the wrought-iron gate. There's one catch: this particular hall *only takes groups of 10 or more.* Set in a picturesque and rather ritzy location midway between Holland Park and Kensington Gardens. All rooms are singles or doubles, with hall baths. Singles £19.50. Doubles £15.25 per person. Continental breakfast. Squash, tennis courts, and pool table.

Other halls of residence not affiliated with King's College which let rooms include:

Queen Alexandra's House, Kensington Gore, SW7 (tel. 589 3635 or 589 4053). Tube: South Kensington, or bus #52 to Royal Albert Hall; the hostel is just behind the Royal Albert Hall. Women only. Magnificent Victorian building with Doulton tiling. Cozy rooms, mostly singles. £22. Continental breakfast. Kitchen, laundry, sitting room, and 20 piano-laden music rooms. Although the hall is only officially open to guests from mid-July to mid-Aug., a few beds may be open during the off-season; call ahead. Write weeks in advance for a booking form.

Fieldcourt House, 31-32 Courtfield Gdns., SW5 (tel. 373 0153). Tube: Gloucester Rd. Turn left onto Cromwell Rd. Stay on Cromwell Rd. and turn left on Collingham Rd. (at Sainsbury's), then right onto Courtfield Gdns. Fresh and elegant reception with spiral staircase. Recent renovations include a new kitchen space. Reception open 24 hrs. Dorm rooms large and spare, with high ceilings. Singles £14. Doubles £13 per person. Triples £12 per person. Quads £11 per person. 5-bed dorm £10 per person. 6-bed dorm £9 per person. Weekly and winter discounts. Continental breakfast. Major credit cards.

More House, 53 Cromwell Rd., SW7 (tel. 584 2040). Tube: Gloucester Rd. Exit left onto Gloucester Rd. then turn right on Cromwell Rd. Unmarked Victorian building across from Natural History Museum. Although it doubles as the West London Catholic Chaplaincy Center, the atmosphere is not particularly religious or sectarian, unless you attend voluntary chapel. Occasional Monty Python screenings in a somewhat dated lounge. Singles £21. Doubles £36. Triples £41. Dorms £11. Continental breakfast included. Laundry and kitchen facilities available. A non-profit "bar" downstairs serves some of the cheapest pints in London. Reserve ahead with a £10 non-refundable deposit deductible from final bill. £5 supplement for 1-night stays, 10% discount after a week. Open July-Aug. No credit cards.

■■■ NORTH LONDON

Hampstead Campus, Kidderpore Ave., NW3 (tel. 435 3564; fax 431 4402). Tube: Finchley Rd. or West Hampstead, or bus #13, 28, 82, or 113 to the Platt's Lane stop on Finchley Rd. Turn onto Platt's Lane then take an immediate right on Kidderpore Ave. Reserve through King's Campus Vacation Bureau (see above—Kensington, Chelsea, and Earl's Ct.). Beautiful surroundings and unparalleled prices (obscene with a student discount), with buildings ancient and modern. Herb gardens. Singles £13.25, twins £11.25 per person. Game rooms, music room, and TV lounge.

Walter Sickert Hall, 29 Graham St., N1 (tel. 477 8822). Tube: Angel. Exit the station heading left. Turn left onto City Rd.; Graham St. will be on the left after an 8min. walk. Right in Islington. This converted office building opened as a new City University dorm in March 1994. Fresh blue carpeting and white-painted halls. All rooms come with private toilet and shower, hot pot, and phone, and the furnishings include desks and bookshelves. About 50 singles and 4 twins. Singles £25. Doubles £40. Prices subject to change, so call ahead. Continental breakfast. TV rooms, laundry facilities, 24-hr. security. Open July-Sept.

University of North London, Arcade Hall, Holloway Rd. (Tube: Holloway Rd.) The University of North London offers self-contained flats with kitchens for groups of 4-6 people on a weekly basis. All reservations must be made at the **Accommodations Advisory Office,** Stapleton House, 277-281 Holloway Rd., N7 (tel. 753 5041), and all payments must be made in advance. £40 per person per week, with a deposit of £40 for each week's stay. (A flat deposit of £120 is charged for stays of over two weeks.) Open July-Sept.

LONG-TERM STAYS

Anne Elizabeth House Hostel, 30 Collingham Pl., SW5 (tel. 370 4821). Tube: Earl's Ct. Cross Earl's Court Rd. and go straight down Earl's Court Gdns. Keep going straight; at the intersection with Knaresborough, the road turns into Collingham Pl. Caters to the needs of travelers on extended stays: kitchen, laundry, and ironing board. In summer '94, renovations were underway. No curfew. Rooms have floral curtains and white wood furniture. Single-sex only. Singles £17.50-23; £110-145 per week. Doubles £14.75-19.75 per person; £95-125 per week. Triples £12.50-16.50 per person; £79-105 per week. Quads £9.50-11.50 per person; £58-70 per week. Quints £8-10 per person; £48-61 per week.

Lee Abbey International Students' Club, 57-67 Lexham Gdns., W8 (tel. 373 7242). Tube: Earl's Ct. Left onto the Earl's Court Rd., then right on Lexham Gardens. The club is on your right. You must be at least 18 to stay here. Student status is required during the school year. Accommodations of varying degrees of modernity; much of the decor has passed its prime. Some rooms en suite. Linens provided. Singles £96-136 per week. Doubles £87.85-105.70 per week. Triples £73.50-89.60 per week. English breakfast included, with the option of purchasing inexpensive weekly meal tickets. Inquire about reservations in advance.

YWCA Park House, 227 Earl's Court Rd., SW5 (tel. 373 2851). This high-security block provides long-term stays for single women 16-25. Min. stay 6 mo., max. stay 3 yrs. 117 beds. Guests rent single bedrooms in 2- to 3-bedroom flats with living room, kitchen, and bathroom. £60.50 per week. Telephones, laundry, and TV.

Central Club Hotel, 16-22 Great Russell St., WC1 (tel. 636 7512). Tube: Tottenham Ct. Rd. Take Tottenham Ct. Rd., then take the first right onto Great Russell St. Down the street from the British Museum. International atmosphere. Clean spacious rooms with basic furnishings. Hardwood floors, cable TV, phones (incoming calls only), hot pots in singles and doubles. Singles £33, £210 per week. Doubles £60.25, £386.50 per week. Triples, quads, and quints £16 per person. Rooms with private bath add £7.50. Monthly rates. Coffee shop downstairs. Laundry facilities, gym, hairdresser, and masseuse (once a week). MC, Visa.

BED AND BREAKFAST HOTELS

■ BED AND BREAKFAST AGENCIES

Bed and Breakfast (GB), P.O. Box 66, Henley-on-Thames, Oxon, England RG9 1XS (tel. (01491) 578803; fax (01491) 410806). In the U.S. call (800) 367 4668, fax (212) 689 0679. The most comprehensive service, covering all of London for £14 and up per night. Free annual mini-guide *How to Book a B&B in Britain*.

The Independent Traveller, Dinneford Spring, Thorverton, Exeter, England EX5 5NU (tel. (01392) 860 807; fax (01392) 860 552). Offers cottages, houses, and apartments for rent. Various price ranges, short or long stays. Also books B&Bs.

London Home-to-Home, 19 Mt. Park Crescent, Ealing, London W5 2RN (tel. and fax (0181) 566 7976). B&B in London homes. £19-25 per person. Family rooms.

■■■ BLOOMSBURY

Despite its proximity to the West End, Bloomsbury maintains a fairly residential demeanor. Gracious, tree-filled squares and a prime location (within Zone 1 on the tube) cause hotel prices to be a pound or two higher here. All Bloomsbury B&Bs accept reservations with one night's deposit, and nearly all have fax machines.

GOWER STREET

Budget hotels line one side of Gower St. (tube: Goodge St.). From the tube station head left on Tottenham Ct. Rd., turn right onto Torrington Rd., and take the third right onto Gower St. These hotels tend be smaller and more intimate than some of their peers, exuding charm and personality. With the British Museum just down the street and loads of scrumptious eateries around the tube station, Gower St. B&Bs offer the best combination of comfort and convenience in Bloomsbury.

Regency House Hotel, 71 Gower St., WC1 (tel. 637 1804; fax 323 5077). Well-decorated, color-coordinated rooms with telephone, hot pot, TV, and architectural detailing. Spotless bathrooms. Enclosed patio with solid teak benches. Currently in the process of creating more en suite rooms. Singles £27, with shower £37. Doubles £37, with shower £52. Triples £52, with shower £65. Quads £60. Quint £68. Breakfast included. Winter discounts. Book in advance. MC, Visa.

Arran House, 77-79 Gower St., WC1 (tel. 636 2186 or 637 1140; fax 436 5328). The relatively large rooms come with TVs and hot pots and are embellished with various precious details, like elegant moulding, Japanese lanterns, and non-working fireplaces. Well-lit hallways and spotless bathrooms. Visitors have access to the tidy garden, laundry facilities, and a cable TV lounge which feels like a private living room. Singles £28, with shower £33, with bath £38. Doubles £42, with shower £47, with bath £55. Triples £55, with shower £60, with bath £70. Quads £64, with shower £69, with bath £80. Quints £70. English breakfast. MC, Visa.

Ridgemount Hotel, 65-67 Gower St., WC1 (tel. 636 1141 or 580 7060). Bright, rooms with cheery pink bedspreads on firm beds. Lovingly maintained by a gracious Gaelic-speaking couple. Owners have recently doubled their capacity by taking over the hotel next door; ongoing renovations have augmented the quality of the hospitality. Radiantly clean throughout. Rooms with TV. Laundry facilities, a garden in back, and free tea and coffee in the TV lounge. Singles £26, with bath £35. Doubles £38, with bath £47. Triples £51, with bath £60. Quads £60, with bath £70. Quints £68. English breakfast. Call well in advance. No credit cards.

Garth Hotel, 69 Gower St., WC1 (tel. 636 5761; fax 637 4854). Some rooms charmingly furnished, others (mostly smaller) more standard. All come with TV; hot pot available upon request. Hallways and dining room are decorated with old wooden signs from inns and pubs—read the fine print for amusement. TV lounge. Singles £28, with bath £38. Doubles £40, with shower £50. Triples £52, with shower £60. Quads £64, with shower £70. Weekly rates about £5 cheaper per night. Full English breakfast or traditional Japanese breakfast. MC, Visa.

The Langland Hotel, 29-31 Gower St., WC1 (tel. 636 5801). Frequented by Japanese tourists. Clean, spacious rooms, sparsely furnished. Some with TV, some with shower. Cable TV lounge. Singles £28. Doubles £38, with shower £45. Triples £48, with shower £60. Quads £64, with shower £80. Winter discounts. English breakfast included; save £3-5 by passing it up. MC, Visa.

RUSSELL SQUARE

The grass grows a little greener and the traffic jams a little less on the other side of the British Museum—but the rates run a little higher. (Tube: Holborn or Russell Sq.)

Thanet, 8 Bedford Pl., WC1 (tel. 636 2869 or 580 3377; fax 323 6676). A dependable hotel. The well-kept rooms are simply furnished and spacious, and all come with TV, radio, phone, and hot pot. Rooms in the back overlook a peaceable patio. Singles £37, with bath £47. Doubles £49.50, with bath £62. Triples with bath £75. Quads with bath £85. Extensive English breakfast. MC, Visa.

Ruskin Hotel, 23-24 Montague St., WC1 (tel. 636 7388; fax 323 1662). From the Holborn tube station take Southampton Row, then the second left onto Great Russell St.; Montague St. is the second right. Scrupulously clean and well-kept rooms sport vaguely institutional motel-type furnishings and hot pots. TV lounge with books and elegant glass lamps. Pricier thanks to its position across the street from one side of the British Museum. Singles £36. Doubles £52, with bath £64. Triples £64, with bath £74. English breakfast. AmEx, MC, Visa.

Cosmo House Hotel, 27 Bloomsbury Sq., WC1 (tel. 636 4661 or 636 0577). From the Holborn tube station take Southampton Row, then the second left onto Bloomsbury Pl.; the hotel is on your right. Clean, comfortable rooms with color TVs and fringed pink lampshades that look like Rococo Batman logos. Furnishings are a bit worn. Rooms in the back overlook a tree-filled garden, while some in the front have small balconies looking out onto the square. TV lounge with beverage machines. Singles £27. Doubles £40. Triples £50. English breakfast. AmEx.

Celtic Hotel, 62 Guilford St., WC1 (tel. 837 9258). Go left when exiting the station. Take a left onto Herbrand St., and then left again onto Guilford. Basic, sparsely furnished rooms and clean facilities. Pastel color scheme gives the place a fresh feel, balancing out the darkly lit walkways. Front rooms can be a bit noisy. TV lounge. Singles £30.50. Doubles £42.50. English breakfast.

CARTWRIGHT GARDENS

Accommodations encircle the crescent-shaped Cartwright Gardens (tube: Russell Sq.). From the tube station, follow Marchmont St. for two blocks until Cartwright Gardens appears on the left. Enjoy the pleasant neighborhood feel provided by the private garden in the center; only local B&B guests and University hall residents have access to the gated lawns and tennis courts.

Euro Hotel and George Hotel, 51-53 and 58-60 Cartwright Gdns., WC1 (tel. 387 8777; fax 383 5044). Large rooms with cable TV, radio, hot pot, and phone. White walls and furnishings give the rooms a bright, airy feel. Euro Hotel contains the main dining room and reception; because the George Hotel is in a separate building (about 30 seconds away from the Euro), rates are about £3 cheaper. Full English breakfast. Euro rates: singles £32.50; doubles £45.50; triples £57; quads £70; under 13 £9.50 Mon.-Fri. George rates: singles £29.50, with shower £34.50, with bath £39.50; doubles £42, with shower £46.50, with bath £49.50; triples £52.50, with shower £58.50, with bath £65.50. Quads £66, with shower £70; quints with shower £80; children under 13 £8.50 each Mon.-Fri.

Jenkins Hotel, 45 Cartwright Gdns., WC1 (tel. 387 2067; fax 383 3139). Petite, genteel, family-run B&B featured in the Agatha Christie's "Poirot." Tidy rooms with pastel wallpaper, floral prints, phones, teapots, TV, hairdryers, and fridges. Some rooms boast (non-working) coal fireplaces. Singles £33, with bath £46. Doubles £46, with bath £56. Triples with bath £76. English breakfast. MC, Visa.

Crescent Hotel, 49-50 Cartwright Gdns., WC1 (tel. 387 1515; fax 383 2054). Family-run with care. Attractive and homey. Tea/coffee makers in each room, hair dryers and alarm clocks on request. TV lounge. Singles £34.50, with shower £38.50. Doubles £50.50, with bath £60.50. Quad £72, with bath £80. Family rooms available. Discounts for stays over one week. English breakfast. MC, Visa.

Mentone Hotel, 54-55 Cartwright Gdns., WC1 (tel. 387 3927; fax 388 4671). Pleasingly decorated with prints galore and cheerful chenille bedspreads. Bright, neat hallways. All rooms with color TV and tea/coffee makers. April-Oct.: singles £34, with bath £45-48; doubles £45, with bath £54; triples with bath £63; quads with bath £68-72. Reductions Nov.-March. MC, Visa.

Devon Hotel, 56 Cartwright Gdns., WC1 (tel. 387 1719; fax 833 0335). While its decor may not be as coordinated as that of its neighbors, the cozy rooms offer plenty of unexpected touches. An orange bedspread here, colorful curtains there, and unique pieces of furniture sprinkled about. Rooms come with TV and hot pot. Singles £32. Doubles £45, with bath £50. English breakfast.

ARGYLE SQUARE

The cheapest B&Bs cluster around tiny Argyle Sq. (tube: King's Cross/St. Pancras)—a strip of grass encircled by an insalubrious "neighborhood" comprised almost entirely of hotels. The area is frequented by prostitutes and drug-dealers late at night. Many of the "hotels" in this area are actually guest houses catering to low-income families whose long-term stays are subsidized by Camden Council. All of the hotels listed below accept tourists.

Hotel Apollo, 43 Argyle St., WC1 (tel. 837 5489; fax 916 1862). From the tube station take Euston Rd. and turn left onto Argyle St. Bright white with blue trim, this hotel stands out from the others on the street. Rooms come with lace curtains, TV, and relatively new furnishings. Singles £24. Doubles £32. English breakfast.

Salters Hotel, 3-4 Crestfield St., WC1 (tel. 837 3817; fax 837 7779). Leave King's Cross tube station by the Pentonville Rd./Grays Inn Rd. exit. Crestfield St. is the first right. Simply furnished rooms come with TV and radio. Perfect if you love the color red; otherwise the bright red curtains, rugs, and velvety hallway wallpaper may be overwhelming. TV lounge and bar. Singles £22, with bath £25. Doubles £30, with bath £40. Full English breakfast. AmEx, MC, Visa.

European Hotel, 11-12 Argyle Sq., WC1 (tel. 837 7159 or 278 3408). Crestfield St. turns into Argyle Sq. A recently refurbished hotel whose small rooms are brightened with TVs and matching decor. Plywood doors are a bit thin. Some rooms en suite. Singles £18-24. Doubles £26-30. Full English breakfast.

■■■ NEAR VICTORIA STATION

In exchange for fairly expensive accommodations, travelers checking in to the B&Bs around Victoria Station receive a convenient location, within close proximity to several of London's major attractions. In the summer, prudent visitors make reservations at least two weeks in advance. Don't hesitate to call even if you haven't reserved; you never know when a vacancy will open up. The competition grows so fierce around here that many will negotiate a reduced rate for long stays, especially in low season. Show reluctance to take a room, and you may see prices plummet.

From the Victoria tube station (Victoria St. exit), head left past the bus bays and around the corner onto Buckingham Palace Rd. Turn left onto Eccleston Bridge, which becomes Belgrave Rd. Beware that addresses higher than 45 are quite a long walk down Belgrave Rd., which continues on the other side of Warwick Sq. A ride on bus #24 from Victoria Station or a tube hop over to Pimlico Station is advisable.

Melbourne House, 79 Belgrave Rd., SW1 (tel. 828 3516; fax 828 7120). Past Warwick Sq. Closer to Pimlico than Victoria; from Pimlico station take the Bessborough St. (south side) exit and go left along Lupus St. Turn right at St. George's Sq.; Belgrave Rd. starts on the other side of the sqaure. The proprietors, who live on the premises, are justifiably proud of the cleanliness of their rooms. The modern, private showers have smashing water pressure and glass doors. Air fresheners add the perfect olfactory complement to the sparkling bedrooms, all of which come with TV, phone, and hot pot. Singles £22-25. Doubles with bath £45-55. Triples with bath £65-70. 2-room quads with bath £75-80. Winter discount. Full English breakfast with cereal option. Book ahead. MC, Visa.

Luna and Simone Hotel, 47-49 Belgrave Rd., SW1 (tel. 834 5897 or 828 2474), past Warwick Sq. Bus #24 stops at the doorstep, or walk from Pimlico. Immaculate and well-maintained; the facade is currently undergoing its triannual repainting. The rooms, decorated in shades of blue, all come with TV, phones, and firm mattresses. Singles £20-22. Doubles £30-34, with bath £40-48. Triples £39-45, with bath £42-54. Winter discounts. English breakfast. Luggage storage. MC,Visa.

Marne Hotel, 34 Belgrave Rd., SW1 (tel. 834 5195; fax 976 6180). Close to Victoria. Management arranges home stays for students in association with Homestay U.K. Some of the high-ceilinged rooms are adorned with lush brocade wallpaper. All rooms with TV. Showers unsparklingly functional. Singles from £25. Doubles £35, with bath £42. Triples £45. Discounts for stays over 5 nights. English breakfast. Laundry facilities. AmEx, Diners, MC, Visa.

Alexander Hotel, 13 Belgrave Rd., SW1 (tel. 834 9738). Very close to Victoria. A small, 12-room B&B. Dark and cozy rooms with nicked wood furnishings. All come with TV, radio, and private bath. The showers are a bit old, and the mirrors have begun to tarnish, but the bathroom tiles provide charming detail. Singles with bath £32. Doubles with bath £42. Full English breakfast. MC, Visa.

Belgrave House Hotel, 30-32 Belgrave Rd., SW1 (tel. 834 8620). Red leather furniture and chandelier in lobby try to give the place the air of a hotel. Large, dark rooms, most with TV. Private shower cubicles have doors. One of the cheaper hotels along the street; however, the hotel offers fewer amenities and a smaller Continental breakfast. Singles £25, with shower £30. Doubles £35, with shower £40. Triples £45. Quads £60. Winter discounts. Reservations (£10-20 deposit).

Dover Hotel, 44 Belgrave Rd., SW1 (tel. 821 9085; fax 834 6425). Small rooms include the full suite of extras: TV, clock/radio, phone, hair dryer, tea/coffee maker, and bath. Prefab furniture more like a motel than a "homey B&B," though the pink walls add a cheerful touch. Private showers with sliding glass doors. Some build-up in the grout, but bathrooms are basically clean. Singles £35. Doubles from £50. Triples from £60. Quads from £70. Quints from £80. Continental breakfast. AmEx, Diners, MC, Visa.

Easton Hotel, 36-40 Belgrave Rd., SW1 (tel. 834 5938; fax 976 6560). Sunny rooms, some with TV. Lounge with bar. White-painted stairwells are a bit scuffed. The dining room has the ambience of a fast food restaurant—the seats are attached to the tables, which are bolted to the floor. Singles £28, with bath £38. Doubles £38, with bath £48. Triples £48, with bath £56. Quads with bath £66. 3-room quint with bath £75. English breakfast. AmEx, Diners, MC, Visa.

Sidney Hotel, 74-76 Belgrave Rd., SW1 (tel. 834 2738 or 834 2860; fax 630 0973). Past Warwick Sq.; closer to Pimlico. Large rooms decorated with banal floral patterns all come with TV, radio, phone, and hot pot. The rooms aren't quite as exciting as the reception desk, which is beautifully decorated with raised columns and classically robed female figurines. Singles £34, with shower £39, with bath £48. Doubles £50, with shower £54, with bath £62. Triples with bath £73.50. Quads with bath £86. Rooms for 5 or 6 also available. Weekly rates and winter discounts. English breakfast. AmEx, MC, Visa.

ST. GEORGE'S DRIVE

Running parallel to Belgrave Rd., St. George's Drive (tube: Victoria or Pimlico), parallel to Belgrave Rd., tends to be quieter. From Buckingham Palace Rd., continue one block further past Eccleston Bridge. Turn left at Elizabeth Bridge, which turns into St. George's Drive. From Belgrave Rd., walk one block farther down Buckingham Palace Rd. before turning left onto Elizabeth St., which becomes St. George's Dr. B&Bs also line **Warwick Way,** which crosses both Belgrave Rd. and St. George's Dr. near Victoria.

Georgian House Hotel, 35 St. George's Dr., SW1 (tel. 834 1438). Terrific student discounts for rooms on the 3rd and 4th floors. Fresh lilies greet you in the reception area. Spacious rooms decorated with personality—some with ceiling mouldings, some with striped curtains, some with blond wood furnishings, some with armchairs. Showers vary as well, ranging from metal stalls in the corner to newly refurbished bathing units. All rooms come with TV, phone, and hot pot. Huge English breakfast includes fruit and cereal. Singles £26, £16 students, with shower £28, with bath £30. Doubles £36, £29 students, with shower £38, with bath £45. Triples £48, £40 students, with shower £51, with bath £54. Quads £60, with bath £68. MC, Visa.

Colliers Hotel, 95-97 Warwick Way, SW1 (tel. 834 6931 or 828 0210; fax 834 8439). Well-lit hallways and plain but bright rooms, with peach walls and salmon bedspreads. Some new showers, some old. TV in each room, beverage machine in the entrance. Singles £24, with bath £26. Doubles £32. Triples £45. Weekly rates. 8% discount for seniors. English breakfast. Diners, MC, Visa.

Arden House Hotel, 10-12 St. George's Dr., SW1 (tel. 834 2988; fax 976 6560). Victoria Station is uncomfortably close; light sleepers should bring earplugs. Spare rooms with minimal white furnishings, phones, and hair dryers. Singles £25, with bath £35. Doubles £35, with bath £45. Triples £45, with bath £55. Quad with bath £65. Weekly rates. English breakfast. AmEx, Diners, MC, Visa.

For a hotel off the noisy main thoroughfares, but still within walking distance of Victoria Station, try one of these:

Oxford House, 92-94 Cambridge St., SW1 (tel. 834 6467; fax 834 0225), close to the church. From St. George's Dr. (see directions above), turn right onto Clarendon St., then take the 1st left onto Cambridge St. Convenient to Victoria Coach Station. Set in a quiet residential area, it's more home-like than most B&Bs in the vicinity; indeed, the proprietors live here. Bask next to the cat in the cushy, plant-filled TV lounge—the hotel's menagerie will soon be augmented by a new pet rabbit. Commodious rooms with flowered wallpaper. Firm beds, new pastel double-lined shower curtains. Singles £28-30. Doubles £38-40. Triples £48-51. Quad £64-68. Fabulously well-prepared English breakfast. Reserve 3-4 weeks ahead.

Melita House Hotel, 33-35 Charlwood St., SW1 (tel. 828 0471 or 834 1387; fax 932 0988). Second left off of Belgrave Rd. from Pimlico station, or the #24 bus from Victoria, which stops around the corner on Belgrave Rd. French spoken. Pale pink walls make the rooms fairly pleasant, although the private bathrooms are rather small. TV in each room. Eclectic lending library will satisfy any taste. Full English breakfast served in the wood-paneled dining room. Singles £24, with shower £28, with bath £32. Doubles £36, with shower £40, with bath £45. Triples with shower £50, with bath £55. Quads with bath £65. Quints with bath £75. Discounts for stays over 1 week. MC, Visa (for reservations only).

Windsor Guest House, 36 Alderney St., SW1 (tel. 828 7922). From the Victoria Station end of St. George's Dr., take the 1st right onto Hugh St., then the 2nd left onto Alderney St. Also convenient to Victoria Coach Station. Simple B&B at an almost unbeatable price. Spacious rooms with TV and relatively new industrial carpeting; note, however, that there are no closets. Brown tiled bathrooms. Singles £20. Doubles £26. Triples £36. Quad £45. Occasional discounts. English breakfast served in a room which doubles as a TV lounge.

EBURY STREET

Historic Ebury Street lies west of Victoria Station in the heart of Belgravia, between Victoria and Sloane Sq. tube stations. Those who can afford to stay here will enjoy a peaceful respite away from the bustle of the station while remaining close to many of London's major sights. From Victoria, take Buckingham Palace Rd. and turn right onto Eccleston St., then take the second left onto Ebury St.

Eaton House Hotel, 125 Ebury St., SW1 (tel. 730 8781; fax 730 3267). Kind hosts serve up Belgravian comfort without Belgravian prices. Spanish spoken eagerly. Large, pastel rooms have sleek dark wood chairs, TV, and tea/coffee maker. Singles £28. Doubles £42. Triples £52. 10% discount in winter. English breakfast. AmEx, MC, Visa.

Westminster House, 96 Ebury St., SW1 (tel. 730 4302). Large bathrooms are ultra-clean, with glass doors on the showers. Pale pink and green rooms have tufted velvet headboards, TV, and tea/coffee makers. Singles £34. Doubles £44, with bath £48. Quads with bath £56. Discounts for stays over 1 week. English breakfast included. MC, Visa.

Pyms Hotel, 118 Ebury St., SW1 (tel. 730 4986). Presided over by one of the kindest proprietors in Belgravia. Serene white rooms with bouncy mattresses, a full coffee/tea set, fresh towels, and gossamer curtains. Immaculate bathrooms have polished glass doors. All rooms with TV, tea/coffee maker. Singles £40, with bath £55. Doubles £55, with bath £70. Triples £63. English breakfast. MC, Visa.

Astors Hotel, 110-112 Ebury St., SW1 (tel. 730 3811; fax 823 6728). Young Euro-clientele relaxes in floral elegance. Upmarket rooms are clean and color-coordinated. All have TV, washbasin, soap, and fresh towels. Singles £25-37, with facilities £45. Doubles/twins £50, with facilities £57. English breakfast. MC, Visa.

■■■ PADDINGTON AND BAYSWATER

These neighborhoods are located near many of London's finest attractions. Whiteley's, London's first large, indoor shopping mall, is within walking distance. Slightly decrepit B&Bs cluster around Norfolk Sq. and Sussex Gdns. As you travel west, the hotels increase in character. (Tube: Paddington, unless otherwise noted.)

Compton House Hotel and Millard's Hotel, 148-152 Sussex Gardens, W2 (tel. 723 6225 or 723 2939). Turn left when you exit Paddington Station, then make a left onto Spring St. and another left on Sussex Gdns. Hotel(s) on your left. Actually several hotels bought and renovated over the past 14 years. One of the most respectable and clean budget hotels in this area. Carpeted stairwells lead to breathable rooms, all with full tea/coffee set, washbasin, closet, and TV. Selected rooms house especially large beds. Single £25, with shower £30. Doubles £35, with shower £40. Triples £45-48, with shower £50-55. Convivial proprietor Hermes will negotiate prices for longer-term stays. Breakfast served in a dining room featuring warm wood paneling. AmEx, MC, Visa.

Ravna Gora, 29 Holland Park Ave., W11 (tel. 727 7725). Tube: Holland Park. Just southwest of the intersection of Ladbroke Grove and Holland Park Ave. The hotel's facade is rather inconspicuous; look carefully for the name written on the portico in small black letters. Sedate and family-run, with room for 50 guests. Convenient to, yet removed from, the open-air performances in Holland Park and the crowds of Portobello. 24-hr. reception. Single £27. Doubles £44, with shower and toilet £54. Triples £51, with shower and toilet £63. Quasd £64, with shower and toilet £76. Breakfast included. MC, Visa.

Hyde Park House, 48 St. Petersburgh Pl., W2 (tel. 229 1687). Tube: Queensway or Bayswater. From Queensway, take a right onto Bayswater, the turn right again onto St. Petersburgh Pl. From Bayswater, take an immediate left when exiting the station (onto Moscow Rd.), and then turn left again onto St. Petersburgh Pl. Just north of the new West End Synagogue and just east of the hulking St. Matthew's church, this inconspicuous B&B blends right into its quiet residential surroundings. Cozy, sun-filled rooms with TV and washbasin. Singles £20. Doubles £30. Breakfast included. Kitchen. Reservation with deposit. No credit cards.

Hyde Park Rooms Hotel, 137 Sussex Gdns., W2 (tel. 723 0225 or 723 0965). Recently renovated rooms are bright and airy. Larger rooms have puffy double beds. All come with TV and washbasin. Singles £20. Doubles £30. Family £15 per person. Discount for small children. Breakfast included; orange juice in the morning compensates for the miniscule bathrooms. MC, Visa.

Garden Court Hotel, 30-31 Kensington Gdns. Sq., W2 (tel. 229 2553; fax 727 2749). Tube: Bayswater. Just south of Westbourne Grove, relatively convenient to Hyde Park and Portobello. Refreshingly tasteful decor. Budget travelers can only afford the rooms without private toilets and showers. TVs and hairdryers in every room. Firm yet bouncy mattresses add to the "real" hotel ambience. Single £26, with facilities £38. Doubles £38, with facilities £51. Triples £49, with facilities £57. Quad £57, with facilities £62. Breakfast included. A plush common area with unlimited coffee/tea and TV keeps guests comfortable. MC, Visa.

Gower and Hopkins Hotel, 129 Sussex Gdns., W2 (tel. 262 2262). A touch more style than some of its neighbors; the bedroom decor is actually color-coordinated. Spacious rooms have phones, TVs, and radios. Singles £28, with shower £34. Doubles £19 per person, with shower £25 per person. Triple with facilities £20 per person. Rooms of 4-5 beds, with shower, £18 per person. Diners, MC, Visa.

Lords Hotel, 20-22 Leinster Sq., W2 (tel. 229 8877). Tube: Bayswater. Halls have high ceilings but tired wallpaper. Basic rooms are clean—some have balconies. Frequented by German students. Singles £24, with shower £30, with shower and toilet £40. Doubles £35, with shower £42, with shower and toilet £52. Triples £46, with shower £52, with shower and toilet £62. Quads £56, with shower £60, with shower and toilet £70. Continental breakfast included.

Ruddimans Hotel, 160 Sussex Gdns., W2 (tel. 723-1026). Unfinished wood paneling renders somewhat dark rooms cozy and warm. 24-hr. reception. White-glove clean, with washbasin and TV in room. Not much space to move around, though; bathrooms are miniscule. Singles £25, with shower and toilet £32. Doubles £38, with shower and toilet £45. Triples £17 per person. Quad (2 twin beds and a double bed) £18 per person. No credit cards.

Barry House Hotel, 12 Sussex Pl., W2 (tel. 723 7340; fax 723 9775). Amenable manager receives diverse international clientele. Bright rooms with TVs and kettles, and some with desks. Singles £30. Doubles £48, with shower £58. Triples (none without facilities) £60. Family room £50. For longer stays, discounts can be negotiated. English breakfast included. Safe available for valuables. Offers taxi and sight-seeing services. AmEx, MC, Visa.

Linden House Hotel, 6 Sussex Pl., W2 (tel. 723 985; fax 724 1454). Though the rooms feel like oppressive pink closets, they are simple and clean. All have TV, washbasin, and tea-coffee set. Rooms facing the front have higher ceilings and more light. Singles £28. Doubles £40. Triples £55. Quads £70. Bathroom in suite £12-18 extra for singles and doubles. 10% discount for one week's stay. English breakfast. One night's deposit to reserve room. MC, Visa.

Westpoint Hotel, 170-172 Sussex Gdns., W2 (tel. 402 0281). Friendly staff, anonymous rooms. Double beds are more like single beds with too few extra inches added on each side. Musty bedspreads and very little elbow-room, but basically clean, with a phone and a TV in every room. Singles £26, with shower £35. Doubles £35, with shower £46. Triples £17 per person, with shower £19 per person. Family quad (with shower only) £16 per person. Continental breakfast included. MC, Visa. Payment with AmEx costs 5% extra.

■■■ EARL'S COURT

Emerging from the tube station onto Earl's Court Rd., travelers carrying bags will be harassed by hustlers hawking the area's budget accommodations. The area feeds on the budget tourist trade, spewing forth travel agencies, souvenir shops, and currency exchanges. The area also has a vibrant gay and lesbian population.

The Piccadilly tube line travels directly between Heathrow and Earl's Court. Underground exits are on Earl's Court Rd. and Warwick Rd., which run parallel to each other: turn right from the Warwick St. exit to reach Philbeach Gdns; turn right from the Earl's Court exit to Barkston Gdns., where the hotels are more pleasant but more expensive, or to Earl's Court Square. Trebovir and Penywern Rd. run parallel to each other and perpendicular to the roads onto which the Underground exits, so the exit you need will be determined by the hotel's street number.

White House Hotel, 12 Earl's Ct. Sq., SW5 (tel. 373 5903). A dramatic staircase sweeps guests up to the spacious breakfast area, a glassed-in porch filled with small, white tables. An unprecedentedly high ceiling and twin mirrors add to the dining area's elegance. Windows open onto a small terrace overlooking verdant Earl's Ct. Sq. Bedrooms are basic, with lace curtains and washbasins. Singles £17.50. Doubles £30, with bathroom £35. Triples £35. Laundry.

Mowbray Court Hotel, 28-32 Penywern Rd., SW5 (tel. 373 8285 or 370 3690; fax 370 5693). Distinctive striped reception area leads to a lounge decorated in 70s swinger style, complete with a full bar and a cigarette machine. Amicable manager Tony proffers services to everyone who walks through the door: wake-up calls, tour arrangements, taxicabs, theater bookings, and dry cleaning are all available. Rooms are equipped with firm mattresses, towels, shampoo, hair dryer, TV, radio, trouser press, telephone, the Bible, and *The Teaching of Buddha*. Singles £30, with shower and toilet £38. Doubles £40, with shower and toilet £48. Triples £50, with shower and toilet £58. Family rooms for 4 people £62, with shower and toilet £70 ; for 5 £72, with shower and toilet £84; for 6 £86, with shower and toilet £94. Negotiable discounts. Superb continental breakfast. Suites with kitchens are on the way. Reserve ahead if possible; no deposit required. A lift serves all floors. AmEx, MC, Visa.

Rasool Court Hotel, 19-21 Penywern Rd., SW5 (tel. 373 8900; fax 244 6835). Top-floor rooms have unique sloping ceilings. Curious red lounge has red curtains, red couches, and red chairs. All rooms include TV, phone, desk, closet, and colorful wall-hangings. Singles £20, with shower £22, with shower and toilet £25. Doubles £30, with shower £33, with shower and toilet £36. Triples with shower £40, with shower and toilet £45. Continental breakfast. Reserve 3-4 weeks in advance; 1 night's deposit required. Major credit cards.

Oxford Hotel, 24 Penywern Rd., SW5 (tel. 370 5162 or 370 5163; fax 373 8256). Musty orange bedspreads and peeling paint are mitigated by soaring ceilings with flamboyant mouldings. The windowless lounge features color TV, and the dining room is clean and stylish. Singles £20, with shower £24, with bathroom and TV £32. Doubles £28, with shower £35, with bathroom and TV £40. Triples £36, with shower £40, with bathroom and TV £45. Quads £44, with shower £50, with bathroom and TV £55. Quints with bath and TV £62. Winter and weekly rates may be 10-15% lower. Reserve ahead. No credit cards.

Half Moon Hotel, 10 Earl's Ct. Sq., SW5 (tel. 373 9956; fax 244 6610). Graceful mirrors on every landing and inexpensive "basic" rooms compensate for the lax mattresses and worn bedspreads. Singles £19-22, with shower £25-27. Doubles £28-32, with shower £36-40. Triples £42, with shower £50. Continental breakfast.

Lord Jim Hotel, 23-25 Penywern Rd., SW5 (tel. 370 6071; fax 373 8919). If you don't mind small bedrooms and closed spaces, this hotel is a great deal. Halls freshly painted. Large-windowed lounge with TV. All rooms include phone, TV, and hairdryer. Singles £15-20, with shower £25-30. Doubles £24-30, with shower £35-40. Triples £30-40. Winter discount. Continental breakfast. Credit cards.

Albion Court Hotel, 1-3 Trebovir Rd., SW5 (tel. 373 0833 or 373 8035; fax 373 9998). A competent hotel in a convenient location. Most rooms have en suite bathrooms. Each room can receive incoming phone calls. Singles £25. Doubles £35. Triples £40-50. Quads or Quints £12 per person. Continental breakfast. This otherwise mundane hotel is spiced up by the presence of "Dreams," a downstairs disco. Rockin' with DJs, a full bar, and the occasional theme party, the disco is open Mon.-Wed. 5-11pm, Thurs.-Sat. 5pm-1am.

Philbeach Hotel, 30-31 Philbeach Gdns., SW5 (tel. 373 1244 or 373 4544; fax 244 0149). The largest gay B&B in England, popular with both men and women. Elegant lounge done in deep reds and jewel-tone teals sports Asian porcelain and varnished wood mouldings. A gorgeous garden and an award-winning restuarant ("Wild About Oscar," see Bi-, Gay, and Lesbian London) make up for what the surprisingly straightforward bedrooms lack in ambience. Singles £38-43. Doubles £48, with shower and toilet £58. Continental breakfast included. Condom vending machine. Advance booking recommended. Credit cards.

Beaver Hotel, 57-59 Philbeach Gdns., SW5 (tel. 373 4553; fax 373 4555). Rooms with facilities are too expensive to mention, but if you don't mind hall showers and you've been aching for a touch of luxury, look here. Plush lounge with polished wood floors and remote-control TV—a second lounge has a pool table. All rooms have desks, phones, firm mattresses, and coordinated linens. Singles £27. Doubles £38. Breakfast. AmEx, MC, Visa.

Mayflower Hotel, 26-28 Trebovir Rd., SW5 (tel. 370 0991; fax 370 0994). Decorated in a cacaphonous color scheme; a bright yellow canopy escorts you into a rather grey lobby. Adding auditory to stylistic cacaphony, the tube passes directly behind the hotel. Hebrew, French spoken. All rooms contain supportive mattresses, TVs, phones, and sparkling retro-bathrooms. Singles £35. Doubles £45. Triples £55. Quads £60. Continental breakfast. Major credit cards.

York House Hotel, 27-29 Philbeach Gdns., SW5 (tel. 373 7519; fax 370 4641). French, Spanish, and Arabic are spoken in this dependable hotel. Special features include a modish 60s-style TV lounge and a back yard in which to frolic. Hallway facilities are clean and spacious. Singles £25. Doubles £40, with shower and toilet £55. Triples £49, with shower and toilet £65. Quads £56. Long-term stays. English breakfast. Major credit cards.

Hotel Halifax, 65 Philbeach Gdns., SW5 (tel. 373 4153). A small gay hotel attracting an older, quieter clientele than the Philbeach hotel. Mostly men. Color TVs, radios, and basins in large, well-appointed rooms with firm mattresses. Singles £27-30. Doubles £40. Continental breakfast plus cereal and a boiled egg. Full payment upon arrival. 2 wks. notice usually secures reservations.

Hotel Flora, 11-13 Penywern Rd., SW5 (tel. 373 6514). Limited choice of clean, well-maintained rooms with various amenities: private facilities, color TV, hair dryer, phone, radio, and tea/coffee bar. Bar downstairs. Singles £28. Doubles £36-42. Triples £55. Continental breakfast.

■■■ KENSINGTON AND CHELSEA

These hotels will prove convenient for those who wish to visit the stunning array of museums that line the southwest side of Hyde Park. Prices are higher, but hotels here tend to be significantly more sober and comfortable than many at Earl's Court. Vicarage Gate lies off of Kensington Church St.

Abbey House Hotel, 11 Vicarage Gate, W8 (tel. 727 2594). Tube: Notting Hill Gate. A gracious entrance hall and wrought-iron banisters lend the feel of an elegant Victorian conservatory to this hotel. After a series of renovations, the hotel has achieved a level of comfort that can't be rivaled at these prices. A new tea room provides free hot beverages 24hrs. a day. Palatial rooms with color TVs, washbasin, Holofil pillows, fresh towels and soap, and billowing curtains. Bathrooms (none en suite) decorated with Laura Ashley furnishings. Singles £32. Doubles £52. Triples £62. Quads £72. Quints £82. Winter discounts. Weekly rates. English breakfast. Reserve a month ahead if possible. No credit cards.

Vicarage Hotel, 10 Vicarage Gate, W8 (tel. 229 4030). Tube: Notting Hill Gate. The entrance hall here is spotless, with classy red velvet and gold framing a sweeping staircase. The stately breakfast room is only surpassed by the small, comfortable, and immaculate bedrooms, which contain fancy wooden wardrobes and antique mirrors. Singles £32. Doubles £54. Triples £66. Quads £72. Negotiable winter rates. Ample English breakfast. Reserve. No credit cards.

Swiss House, 171 Old Brompton Rd., SW5 (tel. 373 2769; fax 373 7983 ext. 218). A hospitable outpost with a manicured garden. Fluffy comforters, ruffled curtains, and matching carpets in every room. TV, telephone, towels, and soap included. Some hall toilets graced with plants and potpourri—a gentle touch. Singles £32, with shower and toilet £48. Doubles or twins £48, with shower and toilet £60. Extra bed £10. Continental breakfast included.

Reeves Hotel for Women, 48 Shepherd's Bush Green, W12 (tel. (0181) 740 1158). Tube: Shepherd's Bush or Goldhawk Rd. From Goldhawk Rd. station, head right down Goldhawk Rd., which turns into Shepherd's Bush Green as it runs along Shepherd's Bush Common. The hotel will be on the right. 5 doubles and 7 singles available in the first hotel in Britain owned, managed, and run by women for women travelers. Rooms are inviting and comfortably furnished; all come with TV and hot pot. The breakfast room, tastefully decorated with modern fixtures, sits next to a cozy, fully licensed women-only bar (open every night to guests, open to non-residents Fri. 7:30pm-midnight). Garden patio in back. Parking available. Singles £25, with bath £29. Doubles £45, with bath £49. Substantial Continental breakfast. MC, Visa (5% surcharge for credit card payments).

Still farther south you can stay in trendy **Chelsea,** but you'll have trouble finding moderately priced hotels south of King's Rd.

Oakley Hotel, 73 Oakley St., SW3 (tel. 352 5599 or 6610; fax 727 1190). Tube: Sloane Sq. or Victoria, then bus #11, 19, or 22; or, Kensington, then bus #49. Turn left onto Oakley St. from King's Rd. at the Chelsea Fire Station. Just steps away from Cadogan Pier, Albert Bridge, Battersea Park, and shopping on King's Rd., this hotel is one of the best bargains in London. Lovely bedrooms with large windows, matching bedspreads, and lots of fresh air. Comfortable lounge with TV and VCR doubles as a dining room. Incredibly amiable staff invites guests to use the kitchen facilities at any hour of the day or night. Singles £17-19. Twins £30-34. Triples £42. Quads £50. Dorms (for women only) £11, £60-65 per week. Winter and long-term discounts. English breakfast. Reserve ahead. No credit cards.

The area around **Gloucester Road** (GLOSS-ter) is less staid than the adjacent South Kensington and Chelsea neighborhoods, and remains relatively convenient to the Kensington museums and attractions (tube: Gloucester Rd.). Occasionally, the lower-priced private hostels in this area prove as comfortable as the hotels.

Hotel Europe, 131-137 Cromwell Rd., SW7 (tel. 370 2336/7/8; fax 244 6985). Classy lounge with color TV and upscale decor. This is the place to stay if you want the look and feel of a "real" hotel at an affordable price. Singles £30, with shower and toilet £35. Doubles £40, with shower and toilet £45. Triples £45, with shower and toilet £55. Continental breakfast. AmEx, MC, Visa.

Sorbonne Hotel, 39 Cromwell Rd., SW7 (tel. 589 6636 or 589 6637; fax 581 1313). Convenient access to the V&A and Harrods. Decor evokes the backdrop of an early Peter Sellers movie. Most rooms have TV, hair dryer, and phone; en suite rooms add a small fridge. Fake plants lend an atrium feel to some rooms. Singles £30, with shower and toilet £45. Double £42, with shower and toilet £52. Triples £45, with shower and toilet £65. Family £72. Continental breakfast. Laundry and ironing available. No children under 10 allowed. Reserve (deposit).

■■■ NORTH LONDON

Dillons Hotel, 21 Belsize Pk., NW3 (tel. 794 3360). Tube: Belsize Park, then bus #268. Or head right on Haverstock Hill and take the 2nd left onto Belsize Ave., which becomes Belsize Pk. Spacious B&B in an affluent, tree-lined suburb. Conveniently right around the corner from a lane of shops, little restaurants, a laundromat, and a post office. 15 large and well-furnished rooms. Cheery yellow breakfast room and homey TV lounge with floral wall paper. Singles £22, with shower £27. Doubles £31, with bath £36. Discounts Nov.-March. Continental breakfast. Book one month ahead.

Frank and Betty Merchant, 562 Caledonian Rd., N7 (tel. 607 0930). Tube: Caledonian Rd., then 8-min. walk left out of station through dreary bit of north London. Easy tube and bus access to center of London. Three bedrooms available in a private house with no sign but a garden out front. Friendly proprietors. Guests tend to be repeat custormers who have gotten to know each other well over the years. Room for 5-8 people only. £15 per person. English breakfast. Book ahead.

CAMPING

Camping in London is not the most convenient of options. For one thing, you probably won't be in London. Even with a Travelcard, the cost of shuttling in and out might better be spent on a cheap (and rain-proof) hostel. Nevertheless, n summer months, the few campsites near London fill up. You'll have to make reservations one to two weeks in advance.

Tent City, Old Oak Common Lane, East Acton, W3 (tel. (0181) 743 5708). Tube: East Acton. Bus #12 or 52A. 6 mi. from central London. You can pitch your own tent, or sleep in one of the dormitory-size tents already set up and waiting for you here. Extremely friendly campsite, full of backpackers. Showers, snack bar, baggage storage, laundry, and cooking facilities. Deservedly popular. £5 per person, children £3. Open June-Aug. 24 hrs.

Hackney Camping, Millfields Rd., Hackney Marshes, E5 (tel. (0181) 985 7656). Bus #38 from Victoria or Piccadilly Circus to Clapton Pond, and walk down Millfields Rd.; or bus #22a from Liverpool St. to Mandeville St., and cross bridge to Hackney Marshes. 4 mi. from London. An expanse of flat green lawn in the midst of London's East End. Free hot showers, baggage storage, shop, snack bar, laundry, and cooking facilites. No caravans. Open June-Aug. 24 hrs. £4 per person, children £2.

Crystal Palace Caravan Club Site, Crystal Palace Parade, SE19 (tel. (0181) 778 7155). Tube: Brixton, then bus #2A or 3. BR to Crystal Palace. 8 mi. from London. Wonderfully close to the healthful activities at the Crystal Palace National Sports Centre. Showers and laundry facilities. 21-day max. stay. Wheelchair accessible. Open year-round. £3.50 per person, children £1.20. Parking fees: caravan £7, tent with car £4.50, tent with motorcycle £2.50, tent with walkers no charge. Lower fees during off-peak season (Oct.-April).

Food and Drink

While British cooking still persists in all its boiled glory, cuisines from around the world have breathed new life into English kitchens. The introduction of Lebanese, Greek, Indian, Chinese, Thai, Italian, Cypriot, African, and West Indian flavors has spiced London up considerably.

Of these different cuisines, London is perhaps most famous for its **Indian restaurants** most of which are quiet and dimly lit (except for the ever-popular Khan's, listed below); dishes here are spicier than their milder American counterparts. In general, Indian restaurants are cheaper around Westbourne Grove (tube: Bayswater) and Euston Square, and cheaper still on Brick Lane in the East End.

London's wealth of international restaurants shouldn't deter you from sampling Britain's own infamous cuisine. **Pubs** are a solid choice for cheap, filling English classics like meat pastries ("Cornish pasties" and "pies"), potatoes, and shepherd's pie (a meat mixture topped with mashed potatoes and baked). **Fish-and-chip shops** and **kebab shops** can be found on nearly every corner. They vary little in price but can be streets apart in quality. Look for queues out the door and hop in line.

In **restaurants,** watch the fine print: a perfectly inexpensive entree may be only one item on a bill supplemented with side dishes, shamefully priced drinks, VAT, minimum per-person charges, and an occasional 50p–£2 cover charge. You don't have to tip in those restaurants that include service charge (10-12½%) on the bill. And if the service has disappointed you, you can complain to the manager and then legally subtract part or all of the service charge.

For a cheaper alternative to restaurant dining, try a meal in a **caff**—the traditional British equivalent of a U.S. diner. Caffs serve an odd mix of inexpensive English and Italian specialties (£4.50-6 for a full meal). Interiors range from serviceable to dingy, and tables may be shared, but the food is often very good.

Sandwich shops are handy for a quick bite and differ little from their kind in any country. Many serve filling, inexpensive breakfast foods all day. If you're not ordering take-away, order at the counter and sit down; someone will bring your food to you. You leave your plate on the table and pay on your way out. No tip is necessary.

Cappuccino and espresso are available in all eateries, even the humblest sandwich shop and caff. If you want regular **coffee**, ask for a **filter coffee** or you'll invariably be served a cappuccino. **White coffee** is coffee with a good deal of milk in it, what Americans think of as a café au lait. As for **tea,** Brits assume it is taken with milk, so if you drink plain tea (or black coffee), specify this clearly. Because most people add milk, coffee in England tends to be brewed strong and dark. Iced coffee is unheard of in London, even in summertime.(If you see it on a menu, it is referring to a shake-like coffee and ice cream drink.) In almost every eatery, smoking is permitted at any table (with the exception of vegetarian and whole food restaurants, where it is banned entirely).

Open-air markets pop up all over central London, vending fresh produce and raw fish at lower prices than stores. **Groceries** and **supermarkets** provide by far the cheapest option for a filling snack. The **Restaurant Switchboard** (tel. (0181) 888 8080; Mon.-Fri. 9am-8pm, Sat. 10am-4pm) will provide good advice in choosing a restaurant for the price of a phone call, although their idea of a budget restaurant may not be yours. Budget travelers should remember that it is always cheaper to eat take-away, rather than having a sit-down meal. Almost all restaurants have **take-away** service; by eating your meal elsewhere, you can sometimes save up to 40% on service and VAT charges.

The restaurants are arranged both by type and by location. Restaurants—By Type provides a list of restaurants cross-referenced by food and features (including price, hours, and ambience). The "Splurge" category consists of restaurants where a typical entree costs more than £6. Every restaurant listed in this section is followed by

B Y   T Y P E

an abbreviated neighborhood label; turn to Restaurants—By Location for the full write-up. In the listings by location, the restaurants towards the top of the list tend to offer a better combination of taste, ambience, and value than the ones towards the bottom of the list. Starred restaurants are **Let's Go Picks,** and represent the restaurants that we would not want to miss on a trip to London. The following is a code to the abbreviated neighborhood labels:

B	Brixton		H	Hampstead
B&E	Bloomsbury and Euston		*HSK*	High St. Kensington
B&Q	Bayswater and Queensway		*I*	Islington
C	Chelsea		*K&HP*	Knightsbridge and
CG	Covent Garden			Hyde Park Corner
CH	Chinatown		*NH&LG*	Notting Hill and
City	The City			Ladbroke Grove
CT	Camden Town		*S&PC*	Soho and Piccadilly Circus
EC	Earl's Court		*SK*	South Kensington
EE	East End		*ST*	South of the Thames
			V	Victoria

RESTAURANTS—BY TYPE

ALL YOU CAN EAT

★ Chutney's, *B&E*
Indian Veg Bhelpoori House, *I*
Kohinoor, *CT*
Parson's Old Spaghetti Factory and Coffee House, *SK*
Phoenicia, *HSK*
Rasa Sayang, *S&PC*

AMERICAN REGIONAL

Aroma, *CG*
Brahms and Lizst, *CG*
Cagney's Restaurant, *B&E*
Jackets, *B*

AFRICAN

★ The Belair Diner, *NH&LG*
Calabash Restaurant, *CG*
★ Le Petit Prince, *CT*

ASIAN/PACIFIC REGIONAL

Friendly Diner, *CT*
Golden Triangle Vietnamese Restaurant, *CG*
Great Nepalese Restaurant, *B&E*
Kamayan, *EC*
The New Culture Revolution, *I*
Rasa Sayang, *S&PC*
Satay Gallery/Restaurant, *B*
★ Wagamama, *B&E*

CARIBBEAN

★ The Belair Diner, *NH&LG*
The Village, *B*

CAFÉS

Beverly Hills Bakery, *K&HP*
British Museum Café, *B&E*
El Café, *B&Q*
Café Casbar, *CG*
Café Deco, *EC*
Café Grove, *NH&LG*
Café Olé, *I*
Café Pushkar, *B*
Chives, *B&E*
★ Cooltan Arts Café, *B*
Coffee Cup, *H*
Everyman Café, *H*
Frank's Café, *CG*
Gallery Café, *NH&LG*
The Gallery Café Bar, *City*
The Garden, *NH&LG*
Gambarti, *B&E*
Grafitti Café, *S&PC*
Kim's Café, *B*
Leigh St. Café, *B&E*
Marino's, *B&E*
Mary Ward Café, *B&E*
Neal's Yard Dining Room, *S&PC*
October Gallery Café, *B&E*
The Pantry, *K&HP*
Perry's Bakery, *EC*
Piazza, *CG*
Portobello Café, *NH&LG*
Presto, *S&PC*
Ruby in the Dust, *CT*
Soho, *S&PC*
Spreads of Covent Garden, *CG*
The Stock Pot, *C*
Troubador Coffee House, *EC*
Wot the Dickens, *B&E*

CHINESE
Camden's Friend Restaurant, *CT*
Champagne, *B&E*
Chuen Cheng Ku, *CH*
The Dragon Inn, *CH*
Dumpling Inn, *CH*
Golden Gate Cake Shop, *CH*
Gambarti, *B&E*
Hong Kong Chinese Restaurant, *EC*
Kowloon Restaurant, *CH*
Lee Ho Fook, *CH*
Lido Chinese Restaurant, *CH*
Stick and Bowl, *HSK*
Wong Kei, *CH*
Yung's Restaurant, *CH*

CLASSIC ENGLISH
Also see Pubs section, page 109.
★ Café Olé, *I*
The City, *City*
Crown and Anchor, *City*
Everyman Café, *H*
Porter's, *CG*
Presto, *S&PC*
★ The Stockpot, *S&PC*

COFFEE SHOP/ BREAKFAST
Anthony's Patisserie, *B&E*
Benjy's, *EC*
The Café, *B&Q*
★ Café Olé, *I*
Chelsea Kitchen, *C*
Conduit Coffee House, *B&E*
Farmer Brown Café, *CG*
Prost Restaurant, *NH&LG*
The Snack Box, *V*
Up-All-Night, *SK*

FISH AND CHIPS
Alpha One Fish Bar, *S&PC*
Costas Fish Restaurant, *NH&LG*
The Fryers Delight, *B&E*
Geale's, *NH&LG*
Season's, *EC*
Upper St. Fish Shop, *I*

FRENCH
Ambrosiana Creperie, *SK*
Café Casbar, *CG*
★ Crêpe Van, *H*
Entre Nous, *C*
Soho, *S&PC*

GREEK AND MIDDLE EASTERN
Cosma's Taverna, *B&E*
Gaby's, *S&PC*
Manzara, *NH&LG*

Nontas, *CT*
Olive Tree, *S&PC*
Phoenicia, *HSK*

INDIAN/SOUTH ASIAN
Bengal Cuisine, *EE*
★ Chutney's, *B&E*
Diwana Bhel Poori House, *B&E*
Eastern Eye, *EE*
Govinda's, *S&PC*
Gupta Sweet Center, *B&E*
Indian Veg Bhelpoori House, *I*
★ Khan's, *B&Q*
Khan's of Kensington, *SK*
Kohinoor, *CT*
★ Mandeer, *S&PC*
★ Nazrul, *EE*
★ Planet Poppadum, *C*
Rhavi Shankar Bhel Poori House, *B&E*
Shampan, *EE*
Sheraz, *EE*
Star of India, *SK*
West End Tandoori, *S&PC*

ITALIAN
Arco Bars, *K&HP*
Centrale, *S&PC*
Frank's Café, *CG*
Il Falconiere, *SK*
★ Lorelei, *S&PC*
Mama Conchetta, *CT*
Mille Pini Restaurant, *B&E*
Palms, *CG*
Parson's Old Spaghetti Factory and Coffee House, *SK*
Piazza, *CG*
Piazza Bar, *S&PC*
Pollo, *S&PC*
Trattoria Aquilino, *I*
Trattoria Mondello, *B&E*

KOSHER/DELI
★ Bloom's, *EE*
The Nosherie, *City*
Rabin's Nosh Bar, *S&PC*

LIVE ENTERTAINMENT
★ Cooltan Arts Café, *B*
Cosma's Taverna, *B&E*
Pizza Express, *S&PC*
★ Troubador Coffee House, *EC*

OPEN LATE
Alpha One Fish Bar, *S&PC*
Grafitti Café, *S&PC*
Lido Chinese Restaurant, *CH*
Piazza Bar, *S&PC*

Up-All-Night, *SK*
Yung's Restaurant, *CH*

OUTDOOR DINING

Bar Escoba, *SK*
★ The Cherry Orchard Café, EE
Chive's, *B&E*
Conduit Coffee House, *B&E*
Gourmet Pizza Company, *ST*
Il Falconiere, *SK*
Jules Rotisserie, *SK*
Leigh St. Café, *B&E*
Scott's, *CG*
South Bank Brasserie, *ST*
The Stockpot, *S&PC*
Wot The Dickens, *B&E*
The Wren at St. James's, *S&PC*

PIZZA

Gourmet Pizza Company, *ST*
Parkway Pizzeria, *CT*
Pizza Express, *S&PC*
Pizzeria Franco, *B*

RUSSIAN

Borshtch 'n' Tears, *K&HP*

SANDWICHES

Anthony's Patisserie, *B&E*
★ Bloom's, *EE*
Chelsea Bun Diner, *C*
City Harvest, *V*
Diana's Diner, *CG*
Farmer Brown Café, *CG*
Giulio's Snack Bar, *V*
Knightsbridge Express, *K&HP*
Leigh St. Café, *B&E*
Mange Too, *CT*
Mima's Sandwiches and Salads, *K&HP*
Neal's Yard Bakery and Tea Room, *CG*
Phoenix, *B*
★ The Stockpot, *S&PC*
Stop Gap, *B*
Woolley's Wholefood and Take Away, *B&E*

SPANISH/ PORTUGUESE/TAPAS

Also see Pubs and Bars section on page 109.
Bar Escoba, *SK*
★ Bar Gansa, *CT*
Blanco's Restaurant, *EC*
Leadenhall Wine Bar and Restaurant, *City*
Oporto Restaurant, *NH&LG*
Sol y Sombra, *B&Q*

SPLURGE

Calabash Restaurant, *CG*
★ The Fire Station, *ST*
★ Mandeer, *S&PC*
Phoenicia, *HSK*
Porter's, *CG*
Soho, *S&PC*
South Bank Brasserie, *ST*
Star of India, *SK*
Young Cheng, *CH*
Yung's Restaurant, *CH*

SWEETS

Holborn Baker, *B&E*
Marine Ices, *CT*
Mille Feuilles, *CG*
★ Oporto Patisserie, *NH&LG*
Rumbold's Bakery, *CT*

TAKE-AWAY

Bloom's, *EE*
City Harvest, *V*
Conduit Coffee House, *B&E*
Croissant Express, *City*
Food For Thought, *CG*
The Fryers Delight, *B&E*
Futures, *City*
Gallery Café, *NH&LG*
Giulio's Snack Bar, *V*
Gupta Sweet Center, *B&E*
Hong Kong Chinese Restaurant, *EC*
Manzara, *NH&LG*
★ Neal's Yard Soup and Salad Bar, *CG*
Perry's Bakery, *EC*
★ The Place Below, *City*
★ Planet Poppadum, *C*
Season's, *EC*
Take-away Counter, *H*
Upper St. Fish Shop, *I*
Woolley's Whole Food and Take Away, *B&E*

THAI

Jewel of Siam, *P&Q*
Penang, *B&Q*
Tuk Tuk, *I*

VEGETARIAN

Aquarius, *SK*
Chelsea Bun Diner, *C*
★ The Cherry Orchard Café, *EE*
★ Chutney's, *B&E*
★ Cooltan Arts Café, *B*
★ Crank's, *CG*
Crank's Health Food, *B&E*
Diwana Bhel Poori House, *B&E*
★ The East-West Restaurant, *City*
Food for Thought, *CG*
Futures, *City*

Gaby's, *S&PC*
Gallery Café, *NH&LG*
Gomarti, *B&E*
Govinda's, *S&PC*
Greenhouse Vegetarian Restaurant, *B&E*
Indian Veg Bhelpoori House, *I*
★ Jacaranda, *B*
★ Mandeer, *S&PC*

Neal's Yard Bakery & Tea Room, *CG*
Neals' Yard Dairy, *CG*
★ Neal's Yard Soup and Salad Bar, *CG*
★ The Place Below, *City*
Rhavi Shankar Bhel Poori House, *B&E*
Woolley's Wholefood and Take Away, *B&E*
★ The Wren at St. James's, *S&PC*

RESTAURANTS—BY NEIGHBORHOOD

■■■ THE WEST END

Soho, Piccadilly, and Covent Garden offer an inexhaustible world of dining options. Take-away is always less expensive, and sandwich bars and cafés will gladly send you off with a substantial meal for under £3. The entire West End is easily accessed by Piccadilly Circus, Leicester Square, Covent Garden, Tottenham Court Road, and Charing Cross tube stations. Pay special attention to closing times; some vegetarian eateries close quite early.

SOHO AND PICADILLY CIRCUS

Scads of unimpressive pizza and fast food joints cluster around Piccadilly Circus. A trip a few blocks down Shaftesbury Ave. and left onto Wardour or Dean St. rewards the hungry with the smart cafés and cheaper sandwich shops of Soho. **Old Compton St.,** Soho's main drag, lies off Wardour St. one block north of and parallel to Shaftesbury Ave. For fresh fruit, check out old **Berwick Market** on Berwick St.

★ **The Stockpot,** 18 Old Compton St., W1 (tel. 287 1066), by Cambridge Circus. Tube: Leicester Sq. or Piccadilly. Beloved by locals, who pack the sidewalk tables, it's the cheapest place in Soho to soak up some style. A simply marvelous value. Omelettes £2.10-2.25. Entrees £2.10-3.85. Divine apple crumble drowned in hot custard 85p. Open Mon.-Sat. 8am-11:30pm, Sun. noon-11pm. Also at 40 Panton St.

Pollo, 20 Old Compton St., W1 (tel. 734 5917). Tube: Leicester Sq. or Piccadilly Circus. This restaurant/madhouse serves some of the best Italian values in Soho. Delicious tortellini with a variety of sauces £3.20. *Risotto* £3.15. Pizzas £3.30. Cold gazpacho £1.40. Open Mon.-Sat. 11:30am-11:30pm.

Gaby's Continental Bar, 30 Charing Cross Rd., WC2 (tel. 836 4233). Tube: Leicester Sq. Low on atmosphere. Don't be put off by the steaming food photos out front; great Middle Eastern and vegetarian food lies within. Deservedly famous salt beef sandwich £2.80. Hefty falafel sandwich and a large selection of salads, around £1.80. Open Mon.-Sat. 8am-midnight, Sun. 11am-10pm.

★ **Lorelei,** 21 Bateman St. W1 (tel. 734 0954). Tube: Tottenham Ct. Rd., Leicester Sq., or Piccadilly Circus. Dim wall lamps reveal a tidy Italian restaurant with a wistful-mermaid mural. Lorelei is the perfect place for an inexpensive oven-baked pizza and a bottle of red wine. Mushroompizza £3.90. The *Poorman* (tomato, garlic, and oregano) caters to the budget diner (£2.95). Open daily noon-11pm.

Presto, 4-6 Old Compton St., W1 (tel. 437 4006). Tube: Leicester Sq. Highly trendy caff/café combo where Derek Jarman reputedly eats his bubble and squeak. Very crowded at dinner; harried waitstaff serves up pastas £3-4. Breakfast from £2.50. Open Mon.-Sat. 9am-1am, Sun. 11am-midnight.

Govinda's, 9 Soho St. W1 (tel. 437 3662). Tube: Tottenham Ct. Road. Run by Hare Krishnas. Wholesome Indian vegetarian food, mostly under £3. They always have a few Italian dishes in the oven, plus a nice selection of herbal teas. Open Mon.-Sat. noon-7pm.

Rabin's Nosh Bar, 39 Great Windmill St., W1 (tel. 434 9913). Tube: Piccadilly Circus. Off Shaftesbury Ave. right by the Circus. Teensy restaurant serving tasty New York-style deli food. Preferred halting spot for cabbies and comedians. Fried *gefilte* fish £2.40. Bagel sandwiches £2-2.65. Open Mon.-Sat. 11am-8pm.

★ **The Wren at St. James's,** 35 Jermyn St., SW1 (tel. 437 9419). Tube: Piccadilly Circus or Green Park. Wholefood/vegetarian delights served in a Christopher Wren church. Tranquil and gorgeous for lunch or tea and cake in the shady courtyard. Casserole of the day with brown rice £3.25. Carrot cake £1.40. Pot of tea 80p. Open Mon.-Sat. 8am-7pm, Sun. 10am-5pm.

Olive Tree, 11 Wardour St., W1 (tel. 734 0808). Tube: Leicester Sq. Inexpensive Middle Eastern specialties in a restaurant whose decor evokes "Casablanca." Sweet anarchy is not on the menu, but many delicious eggplant dishes are; sample the *Baba Ganoush* or the *Imam Beyildi* (eggplant stuffed with brown rice, mixed vegetables, and herbs). Reassuringly wholesome chicken dishes come with mounds of rice. Open daily 11am-11pm.

★ **Mandeer,** 21 Hanway Place W1 (tel. 323 0660 or 580 3470). Tube: Tottenham Ct. Road. Color me Ayurvedic! Hidden in the upper reaches of Soho, Mandeer pampers those willing to spend £7-8 all-natural Indian vegetarian cuisine, and the chance to learn about owner Ramesh Patel's Science of Life. The deep-fried dishes (*samosas, bhajia*) remain light and relatively grease-free (under £2). Try the beans of the day (£3.50) or the *panir matter* (cheese cubes, peas, and onions in a spiced sauce, £4.50) both delicately spiced and complemented well by *pilau* rice (a hefty £2.50). Management insists "all you need is love and an open mind." Open Mon.-Sat. for lunch (self-service) noon-3pm, dinner 5:30-10pm.

Alpha One Fish Bar, 43 Old Compton St., W1 (tel. 437 7344). Tube: Leicester Sq. or Piccadilly Circus. Good, greasy fun. Big fish (fresh—"not a deep freeze on the premises") and great chips. Large cod £2.50. Chips 80p. Open Sun.-Thurs. 11:30am-1am, Fri.-Sat. 11:30am-2am.

Jimmy's Greek Taverna, 23 Frith St. W1 (tel. 437 9521). Tube: Picadilly Circus or Tottenham Ct. Rd. This is a carnivore's carnival—even the moussaka contains meat (£4.40). Still, it's fun, hot, and sweaty, and portions are heaping. All come with chips and salad. Open Mon.-Wed. 12:30-3pm, 5:30-11pm, Thur.-Sat. 12:30-3pm, 5:30-11:30pm.

Pizza Express, 10 Dean St., W1 (tel. 437 9595). Tube: Tottenham Ct. Rd. Popular spot for good, varied pizza (£3.15-5.30). The original branch of the best pizza chain in London. In addition to the food, they keep a tight jazz line-up Sun.-Thurs. from 8:30-midnight, Fri.-Sat. from 8pm-12:30am. Admission £4-12.50. Fun, appreciative crowd. Open daily noon-12:30am. There's a non-jazz location at 30 Coptic St. (Tube: Tottenham Ct. Rd. or Holborn).

Grafitti Café, corner of Whitcomb and Coventry St., W1 (tel. 839 1259). Tube: Leicester Sq. Metallic chairs and tables. Sandwiches both classic and gourmet (tarragon chicken, mozzarella with sun-dried tomato) are the featured food (£1.75-2.30). Fresh fuit smoothies £1.25. Open daily 24hrs.

Piazza Bar, 146 Charing Cross Rd, WC2. Tube: Tottenham Ct. Road or Leicester Square. This relaxed dive reposes on the northwestern border of Soho and cooks up delightfully inexpensive meals. Pasta with salad and bread £2.50. Pizza £1.50 per slice. Coffee £1. Fresh-cut sandwiches-to-go. Open 24hrs.

West End Tandoori, 5 Old Compton St., W1 (tel. 734 1057). Tube: Leicester Sq. A steaming dumbwaiter, unusual lighting, and languid Indian music add to the serene atmosphere. Chicken curry £4.75. Vegetarian dishes £3.50-.75. Service charge 10%. Open Mon.-Thurs. noon-2:30pm and 5:30pm-midnight, Fri.-Sat. noon–1am. MC, Visa.

Soho, 11-13 Frith St., W1 (tel. 494 3491). Tube: Leicester Sq. Sprawling café/bar and rotisserie with sidewalk tables and lots of "beautiful people." Order a coffee and observe, or splurge in the pricey restaurant upstairs. Grilled chicken with dijon and sage vinaigrette £5.50. Cappuccino £1. Downstairs open Mon.-Fri. 8am-1am, Sat. 11am-1am.

Rasa Sayang, 10 Frith St., W1 (tel. 734 8720). Tube: Leicester Sq. Unusual Indonesian food in a slickly decorated restaurant. Popular *kado kado* (vegetables in spicy peanut sauce) £4.80. While the main dishes are a bit pricey, the lunch special (entree with beer or wine) is a good deal at £5.

CHINATOWN

Dozens of traditional, inexpensive restaurants are crammed into London's Chinatown (tube: Leicester Sq.), which occupies the few blocks between Shaftesbury Ave. and Leicester Sq. Gerrard St., the pedestrian-only backbone of Chinatown, is one block south of Shaftesbury Ave. Because of the Hong Kong connection, Cantonese cooking and language dominate. Most restaurants serve *dim sum* every afternoon. **Kowloon Restaurant,** 21-22 Gerrard St., W1 (tel. 437 0148; bakery open daily noon-11:45pm) and **Golden Gate Cake Shop,** 13 Macclesfield St., W1, off Gerrard St. (open daily 10:15am-7:15pm) sell pork buns and other scrumptious Chinese pastries.

Chuen Cheng Ku, 17 Wardour St., W1 (tel. 437 1398). Some consider it one of the planet's best restaurants. Certainly one of the longest menus. *Dim sum* dishes (served until 6pm) £1.65. Dried and fried *Ho-Fun* noodles with beef £4.20. Open daily 11am-midnight. AmEx, MC, Visa.

Wong Kei, 41-43 Wardour St., W1 (tel. 437 3071). Three stories of notoriously harried waiters and the best value Chinese food in Soho. A waterfall trickles on the first floor and dumbwaiters zoom food up to the other floors. Solo diners should expect to share tables. Roasted pork and egg rice £2.40. Set dinner for £6. Heaping noodle dishes only £2. Open daily noon-11:30pm.

Dumpling Inn, 15a Gerard St., W1 (tel. 734 5161). This new restaurant is gaining a reputation as one of the more elegant Chinatown eateries. Hearty soups £2. *Dim sum* dishes £2-2.50. Open daily noon-midnight. AmEx, Access, MC, Visa.

Lee Ho Fook, 15-16 Gerrard St., W1 (tel. 439 1829). A popular and inexpensive *dim sum* restaurant with a more polished decor than most places in Chinatown. *Dim sum,* served noon-5pm daily, £1.60-2. Fried rice with pork £3.20. £5 min. at dinner. Service charge 11%. Open Sun.-Fri. noon-11:30pm, Sat. noon-midnight.

The Dragon Inn, 12 Gerrard St., W1 (tel. 494 0870). Plain, diner-like setting, and traditional Cantonese home cooking. Delicious *dim sum* dishes are served only noon-4:45pm daily. Noodles £3.50-5.50. Open Sun.-Thurs. 11am-11:45pm, Fri.-Sat. 11am-midnight.

Yung's Restaurant, 23 Wardour St., W1 (tel. 437 4986). Late-night Chinatown cuisine for a price. Sweet and sour chicken £5.80. Service charge 10%. Open daily noon-4:30am.

Lido Chinese Restaurant, 41 Gerard St., W1. Denizens of the *demi-monde* will want to frequent this late night eatery. Chicken, beef, and vegetable dishes £4-5.80. Dim sum £1.50. Open daily 11:30am-4:30am.

COVENT GARDEN

Covent Garden offers an enticing—but often expensive—array of eateries to playgoers and tourists in the heart of London's theater district. Tucked away from the tourist labyrinth, **Neal's Yard** (off Neal St.) overflows with sumptuous vegetarian digs amongst herbal healers and colorful window boxes. Beware that these restaurants, and many others in the area, close relatively early; keep an eye out for the inconspicuous brasseries that dot the area when searching for late evening dining options (tube: Covent Garden.)

★ **Neal's Yard Soup and Salad Bar,** 3 Neal's Yard, WC2. Take-away only from this simple vegetarian's fantasy land. 3-4 hot entrees daily, from eggplant pasta to *dal* dishes, £2.25-4. Tempting mix 'n' match salads from £1.20. If summer means anything, it's the opening of the frozen yogurt annex which creates multi-layered fresh fruity parfaits. Open Mon.-Sat. noon-6pm, Sun. noon-5pm.

Food for Thought, 31 Neal St., WC2 (tel. 836 0239). Verdant foliage decorates this tiny basement restaurant offering large servings of excellent vegetarian food at moderate prices. Soups, salads, and stir-fries. Tasty daily specials from £3.25. Take-away. Open Mon.-Sat. 9:30am-8pm, Sun. 10:30am-4:30pm.

Neal's Yard Dining Room, 14-15 Neal's Yard, WC2 (tel. 379 0298). Above the blue Remedies shop. A touch more expensive than the neighbors, but it's got indoor seating. Wide, intercontinental selection. Mexican tortilla heaped with cheese £3.10. Open Mon.-Fri. noon-8pm, Sat. noon-6pm.

Neal's Yard Bakery and Tea Room, 6 Neal's Yard, WC2 (tel. 836 5199). Sourdough, cheese and herb, and two-seed breads all go for 90p for a small loaf. No smoking. Open Mon.-Fri. noon-8pm, Sat. noon-6pm.

★ **Crank's,** 1 Market Place, WC2. This branch of the extremely popular and affordable vegetarian chain has a terrace overlooking one of the most happening piazzas in London. Most entrees, like penne pasta with salad or roasted vegetables with tofu and ginger, are under £4. Fresh juices. Open Mon.-Sat. 9am-8pm, Sun. 10am-7pm. (Also at 17-19 Great Newport St., WC2.)

Spreads of Covent Garden, 15A New Row, WC2 (tel. 379 0849 or 836 5359). This cramped pre-theater establishment is packed on Sat. evenings—go early, because they close early. Generous "Main Event" dishes, like the Texas Super Cheeseburger or fried cod with fries and salad, don't exceed £3. Unbelievable deals for vegetarians: lasagna £2.45, veggie burgers and omelettes under £2.50. Open Mon.-Sat. 8am-8:30pm, Sun. 10am-6pm.

Piazza, 93 St. Martin's La., WC2 (tel. 379 5278). At the corner of Cecil Ct. and St. Martin's La. Bags of pasta suspended from the ceiling, Italian opera, outdoor seating, and a gourmet buffet satisfy the voracious. No skimping—they grate the parmesan before your eyes, and the pasta is homemade. Lasagna £5. Capuccino. Breakfast served. Open Mon.-Thurs. 8am-midnight, Fri. 8am-1pm, Sat. 8am-2pm.

Scott's, corner of Bedfordbury St. and New Row, WC2 (tel. 240 0340). Enjoy generous sandwiches at the small outside tables or in the tiled interior seating area. Extremely crowded at lunchtime. Scott's prices range from moderate for sandwiches (£1.80-3.50) to somewhat more expensive for other starters and entrees. Wide selection of breads and pasties. Open daily 8am-11:30pm.

Frank's Café, 52 Neal. St., WC2 (tel. 836 6345). Delicate and delicious homemade pasta at bargain prices (£2.40-4). An attractive hybrid of the yuppie bar and the down-to-earth caff. All-day breakfast special £2.35. Open Mon.-Sat. 8am-8pm.

Market Café, 21 The Market, WC2 (tel. 836 2137). Downstairs near the Punch and Judy mob scene. A pink crypt-like space, with low arched ceilings and muted pastel murals. Stone-baked pizzas and crêpes, both sweet and savoury, £4.50-6. Primarily a crêperie; the *Camarguaise* contains asparagus, cheese, and ham, the *Normandie* contains apples, raisins in calvados, cinnamon, and whipped cream. Open daily 10am-midnight. Wine-bar/terrace upstairs, open 12am-"late." AmEx, Visa.

Mille Feuilles, 39 St. Martin's La., WC2 (tel. 836 3035). Dainty, floral atmosphere and delicious confections. Homemade cheesecake £1.95 per slice. Dreamy Dutch apple tart £1.75 per slice. 3 scoops of ice cream £2.20. Take-away available. Open Mon.-Thurs. and Sat. 9am-11pm, Fri. and Sun. 9am-11:30pm.

Golden Triangle Vietnamese Restaurant, 16 Great Newport St., WC2 (tel. 379 6330). A bright new restaurant with affordable entrees. Try the mouthwatering *Thit Ga Kho*, chicken with ginger and wine sauce, or the *Tom Sot Ca Chua*, stir-fried prawns with spring onion and chili, both under £6. Beef with rice noodles soup serves 2 for £3.90. Friendly staff helps diners unfamiliar with Vietnamese cuisine negotiate the menu. Open Mon.-Thurs. noon-3pm and 5-11pm, Fri.-Sun. noon-11pm. AmEx, MC, Visa.

Café Casbar, 52 Earlham St.., WC2 (tel. 379 7768). This trendy venue serves hot French bread sandwiches (£2.75-4.25) and a variety of appetizers and entrees (£3.50-7). Smoky and crowded at peak meal times. Open Mon.-Sat. 10am-9pm, Sun. noon-6pm.

Farmer Brown Café, 4 New Row, WC2 (tel. 240 0230). Country kitchen-style restaurant dishing out tried and true barnyard favorites. Reputed to be London's finest sandwich shop. Roast turkey sandwich £2.50, tuna salad £4.30. Open daily 7:30am-7:30pm.

Calabash Restaurant, 38 King St., WC2 (tel. 836 1976). In the basement of the Africa Centre. Full meals aren't especially cheap, but the meats and sauces are delicious. Pan-continental menu. Spicy fried plantains in tomato sauce appetizer

£2.30. *Doro wat* (chicken in hot pepper sauce served with eggs and rice or *ingera* bread) £6.95. Open Mon.-Fri. 12:30-3pm and 6-11:30pm, Sat. 6-11:30pm.

Porter's, 17 Henrietta St., WC2 (tel. 836 6466). Like a British version of T.G.I. Friday's. Hot pies with a delicious, dense crust and vegetables £7.95. Minimum charge £4. Open Mon.-Sat. noon-3pm and 5-11:30pm, Sun. noon-10:30pm

Aroma, 36a St. Martin's La., WC2 (tel. 836 5110). Next door to the London Coliseum. A hyper, up-beat, vaguely Southwestern café serving many foods at lip-smackingly low prices. Various frozen desserts are in effect, like iced coffee with Häagen Dazs ice cream (£2.25), and Ben&Jerry's ice cream (£3.75 a pint). Fruit salads and refreshing juices also available. Take-away 20-30p cheaper. Open Mon.-Fri. 8am-11pm, Sat. 9am-11pm, Sun. noon-9pm.

Brahms & Liszt, 19 Russell St., WC2 (tel. 240 3661). Restaurant upstairs, music downstairs (see Pubs). Hosting a popular bi, gay, and lesbian night, this is one of the hipper spots in the Covent Garden area. Restaurant serves upscale cuisine like poached salmon with lime, coriander, and new potatoes (£5.50). The food is cheaper downstairs—sexy finger foods include nachos (small £2.95, large £5.45) and BBQ chicken wings (£4.50). Restaurant open daily noon-10:30pm.

■■■ BLOOMSBURY AND EUSTON

Superb Greek, Italian, and vegetarian restaurants line Goodge Street, conveniently close to the British Museum. Northwest of Bloomsbury, around Euston Sq., a vast number of what many Londoners consider the city's best and most traditional Indian restaurants ply their trade. Try to avoid the restaurants on Woburn Pl., Southampton Row, and Great Russell St., which cater to swarms of tourists. Instead, look for the cheap eateries on and around Theobald's Rd., between the Russell Sq. and Holborn tube stops.

NEAR GOODGE STREET

This food-filled neighborhood (tube: Goodge St.) offers a gamut of culinary temptations, ranging from upscale French cuisine to informal Mediterranean fare, to modest sandwich shops and cafés. Goodge St. (to the right of the tube station) and Tottenham St. (to the left of the station) are the main culinary drags, but those who meander down side streets will make delicious discoveries.

Cranks Health Food, 9-11 Tottenham St., W1 (tel. 631 3912). London's original health food restaurant, founded in 1961, now a 6-store chain. Crisp blond wood and white brick interior; frosted glass atrium ceiling in rear. Large portions of vegetarian and vegan dishes made with fresh ingredients, including free-range eggs and organic flour. Cool jazz soundtrack makes this the perfect place for a relaxing late afternoon break. Salad platter (quiche or vegetable tart with 2 salads) £3.45. Carrot cake £1.15. Take away available. No smoking. Open Mon.-Fri. 8am-7:30pm, Sat. 9am-7:30pm.

Greenhouse Vegetarian Restaurant, 16 Chenies St. basement, WC1 (tel. 637 0838). Luscious aromas redolent of fresh pastas, salads, bean stews, and quiches waft through this demure restaurant. Dark wooden tables, black chairs, and candles create a warm ambience. Alternative student types will sacrifice smoking to eat here. Main courses £3.85, thick pizza £2.10, desserts 75p-£1.50. BYOB. Open Mon. 10am-7pm, Tues.-Fri. 10am-9pm, Sat. 10am-8pm, Sun. noon-3pm.

Trattoria Mondello, 36 Goodge St., W1 (tel. 637 9037). An array of zesty, but pricier, pasta dishes served in a rustic dining room with open-beam ceilings and discreet seating alcoves. Diverse clientele. Pastas and pizzas about £4.20, but specialties cost more. Cappuccino 90p. Open Mon.-Fri. noon-3pm and 5:30-11:30pm, Sat. noon-midnight. MC, Visa.

Cosma's Taverna, 29 Goodge St., W1 (tel. 636 1877). Dark and smoky, with a simulated grape arbor. The basement *taverna* features a small dance floor where patrons can join a belly dancer and smash plates late into the night. Former U. S. presidential hopeful Michael Dukakis once entered the fray here. Tasty lamb kebab £5.80. *Ouzo* £1.60. *Moussaka* £5.50. Open Mon.-Sun. noon-3pm and 5:30pm-midnight. *Taverna* open Wed.-Sat. 6pm-2am.

Marino's, 31 Rathbone Pl., W1 (tel. 636 8965). From Goodge St. turn left onto Charlotte St., which turns into Rathbone Pl. Restaurant and sandwich bar bustling with a young, hip crowd. Huge seating area, yet maintains a café feel. Perfect for lunch, an afternoon snack, or a cappuccino to read the paper by. Pizzas, omelettes, and grilled meats (£3.20-4.65). Salads and sandwiches (£1.60 and up). Take-away available. Open Mon.-Fri. 7am-7pm, Sat. 7am-4pm.

Champagne, 16 Percy St., W1 (tel. 636 4409). Go right down Tottenham Ct. Rd. when exiting the tube; Percy St. is on the right. Popular Chinese restaurant with wax candles and wax roses at every table. Depictions of meditative sages and serene waterfalls grace the walls. Filling 3-course lunch special (soup, entree, fried rice, sherbet) £4.50, £4.10 take-away. All-you-can-eat buffet £2.99 (Mon.-Fri. noon-2:30pm). Open Mon.-Sat. noon-midnight. Major credit cards.

Anthony's Patisserie, 20 Tottenham St., W1 (tel. 636 4730). A plain sandwich shop with a shocking array of fillings, including both smoked ham and liver paté. Curries, Greek dishes, jacket potatoes, samosas, and baked goods. Greek salad in pita £1.70. Breakfast special (egg, bacon, toast coffee) £1.95. Limited seating. Open Mon.-Fri. 7am-5pm.

NEAR EUSTON

Restaurants specializing in Western and Southern Indian cuisine cluster along Drummond St. (tube: Warren St. or Euston Sq.). Many are *bhel poori,* or vegetarian. From the Warren St. tube station, head up Hampstead Rd. until it meets Drummond St. From the Euston Sq. station, take N. Gower St. until Drummond St. crosses it.

Chive's, 1 Woburn Walk, WC1 (tel. 388 3479). Tube: Euston. In a quiet, tree-filled alley. This snug little café serves fresh pastries, jacket potatoes, and unique sandwiches (cream cheese and pineapple £1.30). A favorite of area dance students. Counter seating inside, shaded sidewalk seating outside. Open daily 7am-6pm.

Wot The Dickens, 3 Woburn Walk, WC1 (tel. 383 4813). Tube: Euston. Head right down Eversholt St., cross Euston Rd., and Woburn Walk will be on the left off of Upper Woburn place. White tiled and modern, this slick café draws lively crowds at lunchtime. Strong espresso and large sandwiches. Shaded sidewalk seating. Smoked salmon plate £2.40. Croissant and coffee take-away £1. Open Mon.-Fri. 7am-6:30pm, Sat. 9am-4pm.

★ **Chutney's,** 124 Drummond St., NW1 (tel. 338 0604). Tube: Warren St. A cheerful café serving vegetarian dishes from Western and Southern India. Bright paintings and spiral brass lamps decorate the walls. Lunch buffet Mon.-Sat. noon-2:45pm and Sun. noon-10:30pm, £3.95. *Dosas* (filled pancakes) £2.45-3.50. Take-away available 6pm-11:30pm. Open daily noon-2:45pm and 6-11:30pm.

Diwana Bhel Poori House, 121 Drummond St., NW1 (tel. 387 5556). Tube: Warren St. Tasty Indian vegetarian food in a clean and airy restaurant. Blond wood paneling and small framed tapestries define the ambience. The specialty is *Thali* (an assortment of vegetables, rices, sauces, breads, and desserts) £3.70-5.80. Lunch buffet, noon-2:30pm, includes 4 vegetable dishes, rice, savouries, and dessert (£3.95). BYOB. Open daily noon-11:30pm. Also at 50 Westbourne Grove (tube: Bayswater).

Rhavi Shankar Bhel Poori House, 133-135 Drummond St., NW1 (tel. 338 6458). Tube: Euston Sq. Bright red and green patterns adorn the yellow wallpaper at this Indian vegetarian restaurant. Most entrees £2.50-3.50. *Paper dose* (paper-thin crispy rice pancake served with rich vegetable filling, tangy *sambhar* sauce, and coconut chutney) £3.70. Delectable *nans* and *parathas*. Open daily noon-10:45pm.

Great Nepalese Restaurant, 48 Eversholt St., NW1 (tel. 338 6737). Tube: Euston. From the station head left up Eversholt St. Portion sizes as great as the Himalayas. In addition to tandoori cooking you can try Nepalese specialties like *bhutura* chicken, prepared with green herbs and spices (£4.50). Huge set lunch of tandoori chicken, rice, vegetable curry, bread, and beverage £5.50. Min. charge £5.50. Open Mon.-Sun. noon-2:45 pm and 6-11:30pm. Major credit cards.

Gupta Sweet Centre, 100 Drummond St., NW1 (tel. 380 1590). Tube: Warren St. Excellent Indian sweets and savories to take away. Delicious *chum-chum (*sweet cottage cheese) 30p. Samosa 30p. Open daily 11am-7:30pm.

AROUND RUSSELL SQUARE

Immediately around Russell Square and the British Museum, eateries are predictably dull and overpriced. A few blocks to the east, on Theobald's Road and Lamb's Conduit, non-touristy cafés and bakeries line pedestrian walkways.

★ **Wagamama,** 4 Streatham St., WC1 (tel. 323 9223). Tube: Tottenham Ct. Rd. Go down New Oxford St., taking a left onto Bloomsbury St. Streatham St. is the first right. "Positive Eating+Positive Living." A smash hit when it first opened in 1992, this noodle bar still packs the customers in, so be prepared to queue. Fast food-with a high-tech twist: waitstaff take your orders on hand-held electronic radios which transmit directly to the kitchen. Strangers sit elbow-to-elbow at long tables slurping happily from their massive bowls of ramen, like extras from the set of *Tampopo*. Pan fried noodles, rice dishes, and vegetarian soup bases also available. Noodles in various combinations and permutations £3.80-5.70. No smoking. Open Mon.-Fri. noon-2:30pm and 6-11pm, Sat. 1-3pm and 6-11pm.

October Gallery Café, 24 Old Gloucester St., WC1 (tel. 242 7367). Tube: Holborn. Take Southampton Row and turn right at Theobald's Rd. Old Gloucester St. is the first left. A high ceilinged café with wood floors and wicker seats. Adjacent to a gallery which features the work of young international artists. Exciting menu changes daily to reflect the changing, multi-cultural artwork on display. Entrees around £3.50. Gallery open Tues.-Sat. 12:30-5:30pm, lunch served in the café 12:30-2pm.

British Museum Café, in the British Museum, Great Russell St., WC1 (tel. 636 1555). Tube: Holborn, Russell Sq., or Tottenham Ct. Rd. Not as pricey as the cafés right outside the Museum, and the light foods and coffee are quite good. Scrumptious homemade cakes £1.25-1.75 per slice. Sandwiches £1.50-2.65. Coffee 90p. Open Mon.-Sat. 10am-4:30pm, Sun. 2:30-5:30pm.

Leigh St. Café, 16 Leigh St., WC1 (tel. 387 3393). Tube: Russell Sq. A bright student and local-filled café serving creative sandwiches and pastries. Elegant decor and marble tables inside, enclosed garden seating in back. Watch the four-person team prepare your food behind the counter. Brie sandwich with walnuts, California sultana, and cucumbers, £1.95, £2.15 with salad. Vegetable curry with rice £2.75. Samosa 70p. Italian ice cream 60p. Groups of 5 or more students can call ahead and receive a discount. Take-away available. Open Mon.-Sun. 8am-9pm.

The Fryers Delight, 19 Theobald's Rd., WC1. Tube: Holborn. One of the best chippies around. Popular with British Library scholars and assorted locals. Funky diner decor—ensconce yourself in red and green vinyl booths while you munch. Large portions of fish and chips just £2.85. Open Mon.-Sat. noon-10pm, until 11pm for take-away.

Mille Pini Restaurant, 33 Boswell St., WC1 (tel. 242 2434). Tube: Holborn. Take Southampton Row and turn right onto Theobald's Row. Boswell St. is the second left. Wine racks on the walls and chandelier lights (each bulb with its own private lampshade) provide the decor; sepia-tone floor tiles add a rustic feel. Terrific brick-oven pizza (£3.80-4.50), pasta (£4.50-4.80), and homemade ice cream. Business-people and lawyers tend to dominate at lunch; dinners see a younger crowd comprised of students, nurses from the nearby hospital, and locals. Take-away available. Open Mon.-Fri. noon-3pm and 6-11pm, Sat. 6-11pm.

Woolley's Wholefood and Take-Away, 33 Theobald's Rd., WC1 (tel. 405 3028). Tube: Holborn. Healthy and delicious picnic fare, mostly vegetarian. Interesting sandwiches, all under £2. Creative jacket potatoes (with ratatouille £2.30). Dried fruit, nuts, herbal tea, and muesli also for sale. One pretty white table in the pedestrian alleyway, if no one else takes it. Open Mon.-Fri. 7am-3:30pm.

Gambarti, 38 Lamb's Conduit St., WC1 (tel. 405 7950). Tube: Russell Sq. Fresh, green café with hanging plants and a red tiled floor. Enjoy an English breakfast (£2.25), sandwiches, or spaghetti (£3.10) in the rustic interior or outside on the pedestrian walkway. Vegetarian options and Danish pastries. Friendly service, but take-away is cheaper. Mon.-Fri. 7am-3pm.

Mary Ward Café, 42 Queen St., WC1 (tel. 831 7711). Tube: Russell Sq. Located in the Mary Ward Centre for Adult Education, on the corner of Cosmo Pl. and Old Gloucester St. A term-time café with a laid-back atmosphere and a mature clientele. The café occupies a former sitting room, with a high detailed ceiling, a fireplace, and a statue of a woman eating a muffin. Art work for sale covers the walls. Perfect for a cheap, light lunch. Stuffed eggplant £1.75. Macaroni with mushroom and garlic (with salad) £2.95. Coffee 55p. Menu changes daily. Closed July-late Sept. Open Mon.-Fri. 9:30am-8:30pm.

Cagney's Restaurant, 13 Cosmo Pl., WC1 (tel. 278 8498). Tube: Russell Sq. A bistro and kitschy pink shrine to the late James Cagney. Movie stills of the latter grinning, glowering, and crooning cover the walls. Quick service and terrific burgers, although they all have embarrassing names. "At Dawn I Die" (burger with chili) £4.35. Pasta £3.95-4.95. Clientele mostly older tourists. Open Mon.-Fri. and Sun. 11am-11:30pm, Sat. 5-11:30pm. Major credit cards.

Conduit Coffee House, 61 Lamb's Conduit St., WC1 (tel. 242 8707). Tube: Russell Sq. The ideal sandwich and coffee shop (although SM will find no conduits for sale). Booths inside, with additional seating in the skylit back area, and many tables outside. Cheerful service. Delicious breakfasts £1.50-2.50. Take-away sandwiches £1-1.75. Lunch combinations £2.50-4.50. Danish pastries 50p take-away, 80p sit-down. Open Mon.-Fri. 7am-5:30pm.

Holborn Baker, across from 50 Lamb's Conduit st., WC1 (tel. 405 4542). Tube: Russell Sq. Very cheap local bakery. Danishes, turnovers, and other basic pastries. Cupcake 25p. Jam tarts 25p. Gingerbread people 45p and 60p. Roast chicken sandwich £1.25. Take-away only. Open Mon.-Thurs. 8am-6pm, Fri. 8am-4pm, Sat. 8:30am-1pm.

■■■ VICTORIA, KENSINGTON, AND CHELSEA

VICTORIA

Culinary prospects in Victoria (tube: Victoria) are bleak. The avenues radiating north and east from the station (Buckingham Palace Rd., Victoria Rd., and Vauxhall Bridge Rd.) are populated with mediocre sandwich shops and chain restaurants with tourists on the brain. Follow the suits and count on local office workers to find the cheapest lunch spots.

City Harvest, 38 Buckingham Palace Rd., SW1 (tel. 630 9781). A fresher sandwich bar than most in the area, with chalkboard specials and a busy lunch take-away scene. Conventional sandwiches £1-1.40, fancy sandwiches £2.30-3. Several set breakfasts available for less than £4. Open Mon.-Fri. 7am-5pm, Sat.-Sun. 9am-3pm.

The Snack Box, 326 Vauxhall Bridge Rd., SW1. Directly across from the Apollo Victoria. A certain source of sustenance. If you've just stumbled out of Victoria Station, this may be your rude awakening to the "English breakfast"—set breakfast of one fried egg, bacon, beans, sausage, and toast £2.50. Stuffed potatoes £1.40-2.30. Large coffee 50p. Open Mon.-Sat. 6:30am-6:30pm.

Giulio's Snack Bar, 4 Palace St., SW1. Across the road from the Royal Mews. The cheapest sandwich take-away in the area; perfect for a picnic in St. James's Park. Sandwiches from 60p. Open Mon.-Fri. 7am-5pm.

KNIGHTSBRIDGE AND HYDE PARK CORNER

Epicurian stomachs-on-a-budget enticed by the sumptuous outlay of the Harrods food court may growl with disappointment at the dearth of affordable eateries near Knightsbridge (tube: Knightsbridge). Knightsbridge Green, northwest of Harrods off Brompton Rd., offers several sandwich shops, in addition to fresh fruit and vegetable stands where you can procure provisions for a picnic.

Mima's Sandwiches and Salads, 9 Knightsbridge Green, SW1 (tel. 589 6820). Understandably packed during lunch hours. Practically every sandwich under the sun, each £2 or less. Open Mon.-Sat. 7am-5:30pm.

Knightsbridge Express, 17 Knightsbridge Green, SW1 (tel. 589 3039). Proprietor George looks after the crowds who pack this upbeat eatery. The upstairs seating area is more placid. Most sandwiches £1-2. Sandwich platters with cole slaw and potato salad under £4. Open Mon.-Sat. 6:30am-5:30pm.

Arco Bars, 46 Hans Crescent, SW1 (tel. 584 6454). Cheap and relatively plentiful Italian food. Lunch special of pasta, wine, and coffee £4.25. Generously filled sandwiches on excellent bread (£1.75-3). Open Mon.-Fri. 7am-6pm, Sat. 8am-6pm.

Borshtch 'n' Tears, 46 Beauchamp Pl., SW3 (tel. 589 5003). Dining here can prove an evening's entertainment; the management scoffs at English reserve. Blinis & smoked salmon £4.95. Entrees £7-10. Try a shot from one of the 16 different vodkas in Baron Benno von Borshtch's bewildering collection. Live music nightly. Last orders at 1am. Cover £1. Service charge 10%. Open daily 6pm-2am.

Beverly Hills Bakery, 3 Egerton Terrace, SW3 (tel. 584 4401). A cozy café and bakery near the London Oratory. Everything baked on the premises with natural ingredients. Slices of sinuous key lime pie, carrot cake, and cheese cake £2.10, £1.80 take away. Individual muffins 90p, 12 muffins £4.50. Espresso 70p. Open Mon.-Sat. 7:30am-6:30pm, Sun. 8am-6pm.

The Pantry, on the ground floor of Harrods, Brompton Rd. A remarkably good-humored juice and pasta bar in the bowels of the upscale beast that is Harrods. The food is priced out of your range, but you can't get fresh, pulpy juices like these anywhere else in the vicinity. A rather risqué selection of nectars on tap: "Sex and Aphrodisiacs" combines carrots, lettuce, apple, and ginger. Mango juice £1.50.

SOUTH KENSINGTON

For budget dining, Old Brompton Rd. and Fulham Rd. are the main thoroughfares in this graceful area of London; although beware that there are few budget restaurants on Fulham Rd. between the station and Drayton Gardens. South Kensington tube station lies closest, but some of the restaurants below require a substantial hike from there; others can be easily reached from the Earl's Ct. tube station. Old Brompton Rd. is served by buses #74 and C1; Fulham Road by buses #14, 45a, and 211.

Ambrosiana Crêperie, 194 Fulham Rd., SW10 (tel. 351 0070). Airy storefront with cane chairs and small tables. Gourmet but friendly. Savory crêpes £4.60-6 (try the combination of salami, asparagus, onions, and cheese). Sweet crêpes slightly cheaper (peaches, *crème de caçao*, and ice cream £3.65). Open Mon.-Fri. noon-3pm and 6pm-midnight, Sat.-Sun. noon-midnight.

Jules Rotisserie, 6-8 Bute St., SW7 (tel. 584 0600; fax 584 0614). This lively restaurant with indoor and outdoor seating serves roasted free-range poultry in various permutations. ¼ chicken with potatoes or green salad £4.95. Daily vegetarian salad specials (small £2, large £3.75). Fresh-squeezed orange juice £1.20. Open daily 11:30am-11:30pm.

Bar Escoba, 102 Old Brompton Rd., SW7 (tel. 244 8662). Lively Spanish restaurant and bar; just a 10min. walk from the South Kensington tube. A comfortable place with indoor and outdoor seating, pseudo-Mexican decor, and an Indiana Jones pinball machine. *Tapas* £1.50-4. Grilled chicken breast with lemon and chili sauce, chips, and salad £8. Gazpacho £1.95. Full bar. Open daily noon-11pm.

Aquarius, 163 Old Brompton Rd., SW7 (tel. 244 8970). A spare vegetarian and whole-food restaurant in a quiet locale. Most entrees, like vegetable paella or Mexican bean stew (£5.50 each) combine lentils, beans, rice, pasta, and/or soya. Veggie burger with salad £3.55. Open Mon.-Sat. 8:30am-11pm, Sun. noon-10pm.

Up-All-Night, 325 Fulham Rd., SW10 (tel. 352 1998). Ferns, Art Deco fans, and sauna-style wooden booths. Stop in after a late double bill at the Paris Pullman cinema. The cuisine is hardly gourmet, but the milkshakes are thick and the WC grafitti edifying. Greek salad £3.30. ½-lb. burger with chili £5.95. Service charge 10%. 15% discount on entrees noon-8pm. Open daily noon-6am. AmEx, Visa.

Star of India, 154 Old Brompton Rd., SW5 (tel. 373 2901). Unusual decor, with chairs draped in fabric. Slightly expensive but superior Indian cuisine, primarily mildly spiced. Wide vegetarian selection. *Chicken roghan* £6.50. Tasty *lamb tikka* £7.25. Spicy potatoes £3.65. Open daily noon-3:30pm and 6-11:30pm.

Il Falconiere, 84 Old Brompton Rd., SW7 (tel. 589 2401). A bit of Italy on Old Brompton Rd.—complete with sidewalk tables, pink tablecloths, and untranslated menus. Pasta £3.95-5.50. Mixed salad with prawns, ham, chicken, and anchovies £6.50. Veal with mushrooms, cream, and brandy £6.50. Open Mon.-Sat. noon-2:45am and 6-11:45pm. Major credit cards.

Khan's of Kensington, 3 Harrington Rd., SW 7 (tel. 581 2900 or 584 4114). Tube: South Kensington. This restaurant's decoration is along standard lines; at least it won't distract you from the stunning food. Tandoori lamb chops £6.25. Vegetarian tandoori mushroom masala £4.95. Open Mon.-Sat. noon-2:30pm and 5:30-11:30pm, Sun. 1-3:30pm and 6:30-11:30pm. Major credit cards.

Parsons Old Spaghetti Factory and Coffee House, 311 Fulham Rd. SW10 (tel. 352 0651). Faux butterflies, numerous plants, and chalkboard specials decorate this almost-Californian eatery. In the summer the ceiling opens like a sun roof and you can pretend that you're in a convertible. All-you-can-eat pasta specials and free refills on coffee. Pesto with sundried tomatoes £3.95. Beef and Mushroom pie baked with Guinness £6.95. Open daily noon-1am, last orders at 12:30am (midnight on Sun.).

HIGH ST. KENSINGTON

There are few appealing options for eating in the area. If you've got more time than you have money, walk uphill to Notting Hill Gate, where the range of food options is noticeably wider and less expensive.

Phoenicia, 11-13 Abingdon Rd., W8 (tel. 937 0120). Save this acclaimed Lebanese restaurant for a special night. Small and down-to-earth; food in huge helpings. All-you-can-eat luncheon buffet (£8) served 12:15-2:30pm. Cover charge £1.40. Service charge 15%. Open Mon.-Sat. noon-midnight.

Stick and Bowl, 31 Kensington High St., W8 (tel. 937 2778). Cheap, quick, and good Chinese cuisine. When you're done, your waiter may politely kick you off your barstool to accommodate the waiting crowd. Crispy beef £3.60. Try a special mixed dish for £4 (includes spring roll, sweet-and-sour pork, fried rice and vegetables, and 1 exploding prawn). Special dishes made upon request. Min. £2. Open daily 11:30am-11:30pm.

CHELSEA

When hunger pangs strike during a promenade down **King's Road,** you can either sate your desires on the spot or consider a jaunt down a neighboring thoroughfare, where affordable restaurants abound. Buses #11 and 22 run the length of King's Rd. from the Victoria or Sloane Sq. tube stations. Almost every destination along King's Rd. requires a bus ride or a considerable walk. Alternately, turn right onto Sydney St. or Edith Grove and head towards Fulham Rd., which runs parallel to King's Rd., to access a cornucopia of culinary delights.

Chelsea Kitchen, 98 King's Rd., SW3 (tel. 589 1330). 5-10min. walk from the tube. Locals rave about the eclectic menu of cheap, filling, tasty food: chicken mushroom fricassee, *spaghetti bolognese*, and a Spanish omelette are each £2.30 or less. Cozy booth seating. When the weather is amenable, grab one of the front tables and watch the Sloanies pass you by. Breakfast served 8-11:25am. Open Mon.-Sat. 8am-11:30pm, Sun. noon-11:30pm. No credit cards.

The Stock Pot, 273 King's Rd., SW3 (tel. 823 3175). The minimum per person is £2.20, but most meals won't cost you more than that anyway. All entrees, from lamb chops to fillet of trout, under £3.50. Itching for roughage? Large salads with exciting embellishments like avocado, cottage cheese, or pineapple under £3. Open Mon.-Sat. 8am-midnight, Sun. 10am-midnight.

★ **Planet Poppadum,** 366 King's Rd., SW2 (tel. 823 3368 or 3369). This Balti brasserie and bar manages to incorporate seemingly incommensurate elements of Euro-chic, Indian take-away, and futuristic modern styling into a spicy new-wave South Asian synthesis. Hipsters crowd in late at night. Tikka-take away served up unfailingly from behind the restaurant's sushi-sleek counter. Most vegetarian and chicken dishes under £5. All entrees include complimentary salad, yogurt, mango chutney, mixed pickle sauce, and, from a galaxy far, far away, poppadum. Renowned *nan* bread £1.50. Open Mon.-Wed. 4pm-midnight, Thurs.-Sun. noon-midnight. MC, Visa.

Chelsea Bun Diner, 9a Limerston St., SW10 (tel. 352 3635), just off King's Rd. A vast selection of sandwiches overflowing with gourmet fillings like smoked salmon and avocado (£1.30-4) and vegetarian dishes (vegetable pancake or veggie pie with chips and peas £4.25). In summer, the glass windows in front open out into the street for delightful *al fresco* dining. £3.90 special includes soup and entree (choice of pasta or meat) and tea or coffee. Huge breakfast special £3.05 (2 eggs, bacon, sausage, tomato, toast, and tea or coffee). BYOB. Open Mon.-Sat. 7am-11:30pm, Sun. 11am-11:30pm.

Entre Nous, 488 King's Rd., SW3 (tel. 352 4227). Cosmopolitan French atmosphere at budget prices. Huge sandwiches on crusty bread £1.50-3. Quiche £2.50. Salads £2.80-3.50. Excellent steak-and-kidney pie £2.60. Open Mon.-Fri. 8am-6pm, Sat.-Sun. 10am-6pm.

My Old Dutch Pancake House, 221 King's Rd., SW3 (tel. 376 5650). Saturated with Holland ephemera, the restaurant is kitschy and fun. Gargantuan pancakes, both sweet and savoury, served on discus-sized platters. Cheese, onion, and mushroom pancake £4.95. Vanilla, sugar, and lemon pancake £2.95. Set lunch menu, available from noon to 4pm on weekdays, includes a pancake with your choice of three toppings, a waffle with whipped cream and sauce, and tea or coffee (£4.95). Fruit beer. Open Sun.-Mon. noon-11pm, Tues.-Thurs. noon-11:30pm, Fri.-Sat. noon-midnight.

■■■ EARL'S COURT

Earl's Court and Gloucester Road eateries cater generously to their tourist traffic (tube: Earl's Ct. unless stated otherwise). Earl's Court, a take-away carnival, revolves around cheap and palatable food. Groceries in this area charge reasonable prices; shops stay open late at night and on Sunday. The closer you get to the high-rise hotels around Gloucester Rd. Station, the more expensive restaurants become. Look for the scores of coffee shops and Indian restaurants on Gloucester Rd. north of Cromwell Rd. (especially near Elvaston Pl.).

Perry's Bakery, 151 Earl's Court Rd., SW5 (tel. 370 4825). Amiable Bulgarian-Israeli management prides itself on a somewhat eclectic menu and phenomenal fresh baked goods. Great for eat-in (a few tables), but less expensive for take-away. Flaky *borekas* (pastry filled with cheese) make a filing snack (with spinach, £1.40). Straight from Israel come *Mitzli* juices (60p) and falafel (£2) with know-how. For breakfast enjoy their croissant plus all-you-can-drink tea or coffee for £2. Challah loaves £1.50. Open daily 6am-midnight.

★ **Troubador Coffee House,** 265 Old Brompton Rd., SW5 (tel. 370 1434). Near the junction of Earl's Ct. and Old Brompton Rd. Copper pots and mandolins are suspended from the ceiling, and whirring espresso machines steam up the windows in this community café. Formerly a bastion of countercultural activity—Bob Dylan played here early in his career. Assorted snacks, soups, and sandwiches, under £4. Vast selection of coffee drinks. Live music (see Entertainment—Folk Music). Open daily 9:30am-11pm.

Season's, 111 Gloucester Rd., SW7 (tel. 244 8454). Tube: Gloucester Rd., or a 10-15 min. walk from Earl's Court area. A member of the National Federation of Fish Fryers. Popular 50s-style fish and chips joint fries only in pure groundnut oil to produce "the finest fish and chips available." Bustling take-away counter serves up everything from fried cod, plaice, and haddock (£2.50-2.70) to more pricey options like lemon sole (£3). Pea fritters or cheese and onion fritters 60p. Traditional fish and chips with salt and vinegar £3.30. They also do burgers, salads, sandwiches, cappuccino, and espresso. Open daily 6am-11pm

Benjy's, 157 Earl's Court Rd., SW7. Crowded with hungry hostelers who weren't sated by their "included" breakfast. Simple decor and noteworthy all-day breakfast specials. Load up for the day (or night) with the "Builder Breakfast" (bacon, egg, chips, beans, toast, 2 sausages), £3.30. The "vegetarian" suits smaller appetites (toast, 2 eggs, baked beans, £2.90). All fixed breakfasts come with all-you-can-drink tea or coffee. Open daily 5am-9:30pm.

Blanco's Restaurant, 214 Earl's Court Rd., SW5 (tel. 370 3101). A worn *tapas* bar. Red and black tiles, upright chairs, and vaguely Spanish prints on the wall. Many drink here once the pubs close. *Tapas* £1.75-4.50. Grilled trout £5.50. Veal escalope £6.95. Pint of lager £2. Open Mon.-Sat. noon-1am, Sun. noon-midnight.

Hong Kong Chinese Restaurant, 14 Hogarth Place, SW5 (tel. 373 2407). Only a second away from Earl's Ct. Rd. on a street saturated with inexpensive and occasionally strange (e.g. Ashbee's Austro-Anglo wine cellar) ethnic restaurants. Clean, sleek, and friendly, Hong Kong keeps almost all dishes under the £5 mark. Noodle dishes are generous at £3.50. Smiling service. Take-out available. Open Mon.-Sat. noon-11:30pm, Sun. noon-11pm.

Café Deco, 62 Gloucester Rd., SW7 (tel. 225 3286). Tube: Gloucester Rd. Chrome and marble decor attracts chic French students from a nearby language school. The food must make them feel right at home; delicate fresh fruit tarts (apple, peach, and pear £1.25, raspberry or strawberry £2.35) and croissants are the *spécialités de la maison.* Cappuccino £1.18; take away 94p. Open daily 8am-8pm.

Kamayan, 10 Kenway Rd., SW5 (tel. 244 0007). Bi-level Filipino restaurant with a few ceiling fans isn't for the sqeamish: squid, chicken, and fish are found together in many dishes. A tantalizing vegetarian option: *Ginatang Gabi*, yam, green beans, and pumpkin in coconut milk, £2.50. *Pancit Palabok* (rice vermicelli with eggs, ground pork, shredded smoked fish, and garlic with lemon) £3. *Salabat* (ginger tea) only 50p. Open daily noon-10pm.

■■■ NOTTING HILL AND LADBROKE GROVE

The many restaurants dotting the streets which radiate out from the Notting Hill Gate and Ladbroke Grove stations exude a certain "goodness" that is not readily found elsewhere. Dishes from around the globe can be found in the area's hearty, reasonably priced restaurants. Stylish coffee-houses and pastry shops cluster near the Ladbroke Grove station.

The Garden, 1 Hillgate St., W8 (tel. 727 8922, fax 727 8944). Tube: Notting Hill Gate. A small, tasteful establishment that serves the cheapest lunches around, The Garden feels like an old neighborhood institution even though it just opened. Plants, a fireplace, and a bookshelf tucked away tidily behind the espresso machine create an inviting atmosphere in which hip local youth seem to feel right at home. Go crazy and try the most expensive thing on the menu; it's not likely to exceed a trifling £2.50. Steaming homemade pasta with chicken and mushrooms, delicately spiced, is noteworthy at £2.25. Sandwiches on your choice of breads range from £1-1.95; try one of the creative tuna salads. Open Mon.-Sat. 8am-4pm.

★**Oporto Patisserie,** 62a Golborne Rd., W10 (tel. (0181) 960 9669). Tube: Ladbroke Grove. A thriving enclave of Portuguese culture, this *pastelana* serves delectable pastries crafted from Iberian ingredients. Locals of Portuguese and North African descent mingle with city kids and Portobello strays around crowded tables. Order a steaming toasted cheese croissant (85p) and it will melt in your mouth. Miraculously, these inexpensive baked goods can make a full meal. Open 8am-8pm daily.

Oporto Restaurant, same address as **O'porto Patisserie,** but enter on Wornington Rd., around the corner. On summer weekends enjoy a barbeque on the outdoor terrace of this full restaurant, or lounge with the locals by the bar or in the adjoining pool table room. Affordable *tapas*-sized dishes like *moelas* (chicken giblets cooked in gravy with cloves, £2.50) make a tasty treat. Occasional guitarist and *fado* singers. Open Tues.-Sat. noon-11pm, Sun. noon-3pm and 7-11pm.

★ **The Belair Diner,** 23 All Saints Road, W11 (tel. 229 7961). Tube: Westbourne Park or Ladbroke Grove. Behind a rust-red exterior, sample dishes from a variety of international cuisines while listening to a mix of funk and jazz music. The menu of this candle-lit restaurant is a jumble of well-prepared West Indian, South American, and African dishes. Most succulent are the *roti* dishes, in which curried beef, chicken, or vegetables are lovingly enveloped by a large pancake (£5.75 with side salad). Fried plantains £1.95. Open Mon.-Sat. noon-midnight, Sun. 6pm-midnight.

Manzara, 24 Pembridge Rd., W11 (tel. 727 3062). Tube: Notting Hill Gate. Ostensibly a take-away shop, Manzara actually seats 40 people. Aided by an international waitstaff, owner Sergio serves up excellent kebabs and succulent Turkish pastries. If you visit frequently enough, you'll earn a soft, winning grin from him every time you pass the shop. A variety of cold hors d'oeuvres are available (£3.35). Cappuccino 65p. Take-away available at slightly lower prices. Open Mon.-Sat. 8am-midnight, Sun. 10am-midnight.

Costas Fish Restaurant, 18 Hillgate St., W8 (tel. 727 4310). Tube: Notting Hill Gate. It's disturbing to watch your meal dumped in a vat of boiling oil, but the final product is ample consolation. Fish and chips £3.75, take-away £2.85. Prices increase if you sit down. Open Tues.-Sat. noon-2:30pm and 5:30-10:30pm.

Geale's, 2 Farmer St., W8 (tel. 727 7969). Tube: Notting Hill Gate. Spirited locals crowd this reputable wood-paneled restaurant. Geale's has won various awards for their consistently crisp fish and chips (around £3.50). Fresh fish is also available, priced by weight and today's market price. Often a wait—sit it out in the bar upstairs. Take-away available. Open Tues.-Sat. noon-3pm and 6-11pm.

Café Grove, 253 Portobello Rd., W11 (tel. 243 1094). Tube: Ladbroke Grove. On the second floor of a building overlooking the hustle and bustle that is Portobello Rd. House music pulses through this airy art gallery/coffeehouse. High ceilings, wood floors, and original art work on the walls add an aesthetic dimension to the culinary pleasures offered by the delicate sandwiches (£1.75-2.75) and omelettes (£3-5). No alcohol served, but you may bring your own. Sitting on the terrace requires a min. of £3.50 per person. Open Mon.-Fri. 9:30am-11pm, Sat. 10am-11pm, Sun. 10:30-11pm.

Prost Restaurant, 35 Pembridge Rd., W11 (tel. 727 9620). Tube: Notting Hill Gate. Delicate food in an upmarket setting. Entrees here might exceed your price limit, but Sunday brunch is a classy and affordable option. Ask for a table upstairs by the window, where you can admire the heavy curtains and rich green decor. Hot continental breakfast includes 2 fried eggs, 2 potato pancakes, sausage, and a grilled tomato (£4.50). Scrambled eggs and smoked salmon with toast £5.25. Open Tues.-Fri. and Sun. 11am-11pm, Sat. 10am-11pm. Major credit cards.

Gallery Café, 74 Tavistock Rd. Tube: Ladbroke Grove. An unpretentious vegetarian café just off Portobello Road south of the Westway. Typical lunch specials include lasagna, moussaka, or lentils with curry sauce (all heaping portions, all £2.50 with salad). Many locals eat here everyday for lunch. Take away is a few pence cheaper; diners can sit outside on the cement plaza. Open Mon.-Fri. 9am-7pm, Sat.-Sun. 10am-5pm.

Portobello Cafe, on the west side of Portobello Rd. just north of the Westway bridge. Rotating ceiling fans and floral table cloths create an unusually sedate atmosphere for a hipster joint. Breakfast served all day (£1.85-4.95). A variety of burgers are available, £1.85-4. Open Mon. 9am-5pm, Tues.-Thurs. 9am-11pm, Fri.-Sat. 8am-11pm, Sun. 10am-5pm.

■■■ BAYSWATER AND QUEENSWAY

The culinary options in this area tend to be less scintillating than those in the neighboring Notting Hill/Ladbroke Grove area; if you crave nuanced flavors and sophisticated ambience, consider dining there. However, the famished traveler should have no trouble finding a solid, inexpensive meal in Bayswater or Queensway. Check out one of the countless kebab and fish-and-chip shops that dot the streets, or head to Westbourne Grove (tube: Bayswater or Royal Oak) for large concentrations of competent South Asian restaurants.

★ **Khan's,** 13-15 Westbourne Grove, W2 (tel. 727 5240). Tube: Bayswater. Cavernous, noisy, and crowded, Khan's persists as the best bargain around for delicious Indian cuisine. The menu explains to diners that the distinctive flavor of each dish "cannot come from the rancid ambiguity called curry powder," but only from "spices separately prepared each day." They're not kidding—the chicken *saag* (chicken cooked with spinach, £2.95) contains piquant spices that are well complemented by flat *nan* bread (95p) or rice (£1.40). If you dip into one of the chutneys sitting expectantly on your table when you arrive, you will be charged 30p. Chicken *tikka masala* £3.50. Open daily noon-3pm and 6pm-midnight.

The Café, 106 Westbourne Grove, W2 (tel. 229 0777). Tube: Bayswater or Notting Hill Gate. No-nonsense British-style breakfasts (served all day) and lunches. Soothing in its unaffectedness, with a friendly, maternal waitstaff. Standard breakfast (bacon, beans, a fried egg, a grilled tomato, buttered bread, and coffee or tea) £3. Open 8am-8pm daily.

Jewel of Siam, 39 Hereford Rd., W2 (tel. 229 4363). Tube: Bayswater. Well-prepared Thai food in a contrived yet endearing setting. Entrees are pricey, but sumptuous appetizers (£3.50-4.50) and noodle lunch specials (under £5) are quite satisfying. *Tom yum hed* (mushroom soup with lemon grass and lime leaves) is a tangy bargain at £3.50. Open Mon.-Fri. noon-2:30pm and 6pm-11pm, Sat. 6pm-11pm, Sun. 6pm-10:30pm. AmEx, MC, Visa.

Sol y Sombra, 43 Hereford Rd., W2 (tel. 792 3369). Tube: Bayswater or Notting Hill Gate. Pretend you're in Spain for just one evening in this refreshing *tapas* restaurant and wine bar. Nibble at small platters of savory delight, like mushrooms in garlic sauce, £2.80. Those hardy souls more intrepid than our researcher will doubtless sample the *pulpo gallega* (octopus in olive oil and paprika), £5. Open daily noon-midnight.

Penang, 41 Hereford Rd., W2 (tel. 229 2982). Tube: Bayswater. The standard interior belies magnificent Malaysian and Thai cuisine. Chicken, beef, pork, and curries all £2.70-5.70. Open Mon.-Sat. 6pm-11:30pm, Sun. 6pm-11pm.

El Café, 38 Westbourne Grove, W2 (tel. 727 0107). Tube: Bayswater. A gaudy yet generous joint offering huge mugs of coffee. Individualized menus handmade (by computer) by the owner. Seated at a glittery formica table, enjoy hummus/kebab dishes (pita sandwiches £1.75, with salad £2.50), or breakfast any time of day (croissants with jam and tea £1.80, up to £3 for salmon and eggs). Open Mon.-Sat. 8am-10pm, Sun. 10am-9pm.

■■■ THE CITY OF LONDON

This area is splendid for lunch (when food is fresh for the options traders) and disastrous for dinner (when the commuters go home and the food goes stale). Pick up some fresh fruit from a vendor in **Leadenhall Market,** off Leadenhall St. on Gracechurch St. In general, food prices may be higher in the City since many of the customers are on expense accounts.

★ **The Place Below,** in St. Mary-le-Bow Church crypt, Cheapside, EC2 (tel. 329 0789). Tube: St. Paul's. Attractive and generous vegetarian dishes served to the hippest of City executives in the unexpectedly light atmosphere of a stone church basement. Menu changes daily. Quiche and salad £5.25. Savory tomato, almond, and saffron soup £2.70. Meals about £1.50 cheaper take-away or 11:30am-noon. Dinner is more expensive (£15 for a two-course meal and coffee). Open Mon.-Fri. 7:30am-3pm, dinner Thurs.-Fri. 6:30-10:30pm. £3.50 minimum per person, noon-2pm.

Croissant Express, Unit 20-22, Leadenhall Market, EC3 (tel. 623 8804). Tube: Bank. (Also at the Moorgate tube station.) Business-people line the narrow eating counter and consume fresh baked goods. Shiny glass exterior, bright tiled interior. Plain croissant 40p, sandwiches £1.55-2.10. Take note of the bargain Croissant Express special: 2 mini plain croissants, 2 mini *pains au chocolat*, and 2 mini *pains au raisins*, £1. Open Mon.-Fri. 7am-5pm.

★ **The East-West Restaurant,** 188 Old St., EC1 (tel. 608 0300). Tube: Old St. Sublime macrobiotic cooking. Original artwork enlivens the white walls. Blond wood furnishings provide a setting commensurate to the vivacious crowd, comprised of hip diners of various ages and ethnicities, which congregates here. Menu changes daily. Main meals, such as deep-fried tofu with sweet carrots or stuffed peppers with tahini sauce, come with vegetables and salad, in small (£4.50) or large (£6) portions. Open Mon.-Thurs. 11am-9pm, Fri.-Sat. 11am-10pm, Sun. 11am-4pm. Major credit cards.

Crown and Anchor, Hill House, Shoe La., EC4 (tel. 583 4180). Tube: Blackfriars. Younger executives ingest inexpensive food in this low-ceilinged but spacious pub. *Faux* bookshelves and warm stained glass lamps create a homey atmosphere. A beer and sports bar is currently being added downstairs. Quiche with salad and french bread £1.95. Barbequed chicken with rice £2.50. Open Mon.-Fri. 11am-11pm.

The Gallery Café Bar, Unit 1, 9 Leather La., EC1 (tel. 404 5432). Tube: Chancery La. A sleek café with floor-to-ceiling glass windows and marble tables. The Leather La. market is visible from both the indoor and the outdoor seating. The proprietor often volunteers information about notable local sights. Casual clientele. Sandwiches from £1, homemade pizza slices from £1.50. Open Mon.-Fri. 7am-4pm.

The Nosherie, 12 Greville St., EC1 (tel. 242 1591). Tube: Chancery La. Inset among the jewellers of Hatton Garden, this unassuming deli sells good kosher food to an older clientele. As close as you'll get in London to a New York-style deli. Salt beef sandwiches about £2.80. Minimum charge £3 per person noon-3pm. Open Mon.-Fri. 8am-4pm.

Futures, 8 Botolph Alley, EC3 (tel. 623 4529). Tube: Monument. Off Botolph La. Fresh take-away vegetarian breakfast and lunch prepared in a petite kitchen open to view. Daily main dishes, like stir-fry with rice or chili vegetables, £3.10. Tomato and basil pizza, £1.75. Open Mon.-Fri. 7:30-10am and 11:30am-3pm.

Leadenhall Wine Bar and Restaurant, 27 Leadenhall Market, EC3 (tel. 623 1818). Tube: Bank. The maroon and cream colored interior matches the festive elegance of the restored Victorian marketplace outside. Matisse prints grace the walls. Young executive crowd. Spanish *tapas* buffet; dishes £2.95-5.50. A sizeable portion of steaming *paella* for 2 £12.50 (available Tues. and Wed. only). Open Mon.-Fri. 11:30am-8:30pm, lunch served from 11:30am-3pm.

■■■ THE EAST END

London's East End is a bustling jumble of neighborhoods filled with restaurants serving a wide variety of traditional foods. The large number of South Asian restaurants differ greatly in decor, quality, and price.

★ **The Cherry Orchard Café,** 247 Globe Rd., E2 (tel. (081) 980 6678). Tube: Bethnal Green. A lovely un-Chekhovian restaurant run by Buddhists. Photo portraits line the peach and turquoise walls. A tranquil garden awaits in back. Menu changes daily. Entrees (like broccoli and almond filo pie) average £3.50. Mixed salads, cakes, and desserts available all day. Hot meals served Mon. and Thurs.-Fri. noon-3pm, Tues.-Wed. noon-7pm. Open Mon. and Thurs.-Fri. 11am-4pm. Tues.-Wed. 11am-7pm.

★ **Bloom's,** 90 Whitechapel High St., E1 (tel. 247 6001). Tube: Aldgate East. (Also at Golders Green.) A London institution, this traditional kosher restaurant sells good salt (corned) beef sandwiches for £3.20. *Haimishe* family atmosphere. The take-away counter also sells canned food. Popular on Sun. Open Sun.-Thurs. 11am-9pm, Fri. 11am-2pm.

ISLINGTON

★ **Nazrul,** 130 Brick La., E1 (tel. 247 2505). Tube: Aldgate East. Although the plush red booths are inviting, the rapid service means that you don't have to linger long if you're pressed for time. The meat served here is bought from a local halal shop and cooked fresh daily. Considering the size of the portions, prices are terrifically cheap; chicken dishes £2.35-2.80. 10% discount Sun. noon-5pm. No bar, but you may bring your own alcohol. Open Mon.-Thurs. noon-3pm and 5:30pm-midnight, Fri.-Sat. noon-3pm and 5:30pm-1am, Sun. noon-midnight.

Bengal Cuisine, 12 Brick La., E1 (tel. 377 8405). Tube: Aldgate East. Tapestries from Bangladesh, detailed china patterns, and plants lining the windowsills lend a more elegant tone to the pink table-cloth setting. Chicken curries £2.95-3.35. 10% discount for students with ID. Open daily noon-midnight.

Shampan, 79 Brick La., E1 (tel. 375 0475). Tube: Aldgate East. A tad more expensive and a bit more plush than its neighbors, but still very reasonable. Diverse clientele. Wide ranging menu specializes in Bangladeshi cuisine. Balti dishes from £5.25. Seafood dishes £4.95. Open daily noon-3pm and 6pm-midnight. Major credit cards accepted.

Sheraz, 13 Brick La., E1 (tel. 247 5755). Tube: Aldgate East. A newcomer to Brick Lane, Sheraz participates in a recent trend towards more upscale South Asian restaurants. Decor is stark, tasteful, and elegant. The menu is a tad pricey, with entrees averaging £4-6. Fully stocked bar. Open daily noon-3pm and 6pm-midnight. Major credit cards accepted.

Eastern Eye, 63a Brick La., E1 (tel. 375 1696). Tube: Aldgate East. Pink on the outside and pretty on the inside, this Tandoori restaurant specializes in Balti dishes, which are prepared using a special stir-fry process that allows you to choose the ingredients (from £4.95). Other specialties include minced lamb for £3.55. Halal food available. Open daily noon-midnight, although the restaurant occasionally closes during the late afternoon until 5:30pm. Major credit cards accepted.

■■■ ISLINGTON

Dress smartly for a meal in one of the many bistros that line Upper St., which runs to the right as you exit the tube station (tube: Angel). Be careful when seeking specific addresses, though, since Upper St. numbers ascend on one side of the street and descend on the other. Unfortunately, few budget restaurants can be found in this cutting-edge area; cheaper fare lurks in the take-away sandwich shops, bakeries, and chip shops of the less upscale Chapel Market (the 1st left off Liverpool Rd.).

★ **Café Olé,** 119 Upper St., N1 (tel. 226 6991). A hip pasta bar/café adorned with colorful ceramic plates and painted floral borders on the salmon walls. Bustling with Islington trendies of all ages, the atmosphere remains comfortable. Endless breakfast: egg, bacon, sausage, tomato, mushroom, black pudding, bubble and squeak, and toast £3.80. Vegetarian breakfast also available. Lunch menu offers pasta (£3.50) and salads (£3.50), in addition to sandwiches (£1-2.50). The selection of pastas and salads expands at dinner; all are offered in small (£3.95) or large (£4.95) portions. Open Mon.-Sat. 8am-11pm.

Upper St. Fish Shop, 324 Upper St., N1 (tel. 359 1401). A well-known chippy offering specials varied according to the day's catch. Comfortable wood-paneled and red-check tableclothed interior, but there is a £5 min. for eating in. Take-away costs half as much. Open Mon. 5:30-10pm, Tues.-Fri. noon-2pm and 5:30-10pm, Sat. noon-3pm and 5:30-10pm.

The New Culture Revolution, 42 Duncan St., N1 (tel. 833 9083). Exit right from the station and take the first right onto Duncan St. A dumpling and noodle bar with slick black tables, plush chairs, and Matisse prints on the walls. Dumplings and noodles come either fried or in soup base, cooked with a variety of different meats, fish, or vegetables. Soups are lightly seasoned; the fried dishes are zestier. Dumplings £3.50-4. Noodles £3.50-5.50. Open Mon.-Fri. noon-2:30pm and 6-11pm, Sat. 1-11pm. 20% off if you pay before 7pm. AmEx, MC, Visa.

Indian Veg Bhelpoori House, 92-93 Chapel Market, N1 (tel. 837 4607 or 833 1167). An unmistakable bargain—all-you-can-eat lunch buffet of 18 vegetarian dishes and chutneys for a startling £3.25. Dinner buffet £3.50. If it's good enough for Miss Asia, who dined here with Miss Philippines in 1991, it's good enough for you. Open noon-3pm and 6-11pm. MC, Visa

Tuk Tuk, 330 Upper St., N1 (tel.266 0837). Bright blue exterior hides a sleek modern Thai restaurant with black metal chairs and speckled red tables. A moped taxi sticks its nose out of a ceiling corner. *Pad thai* £4.50. Noodle or rice dishes £4.50-5.95. Open daily 6-11pm. AmEx, Visa.

Trattoria Aquilino, 31 Camden Passage, N1 (tel. 226 5454). This intimate restaurant, with its extensive menu of homemade pasta, is a gem. The native Italian staff jumps to the diner's every request. Posh appearance belies good prices. Pastas £2.60-4.40. *Pollo parmigiani* £4.85. Generous portions. Best for lunch or early dinner—there is a £6 min. after 6pm. 10% service charge. Open Mon.-Sat. 12:30-2:30pm and 6-11:30pm.

■■■ CAMDEN TOWN

Camden Town can be a bit grotty, especially in the wake of the weekend markets; however, glamourous cafés and international restaurants are magnetically attracted to **Camden High Street,** which runs south from the Camden Town tube station to Mornington Crescent, and north to Chalk Farm, becoming **Chalk Farm Road.** . Note that many pubs in the area offer solid meals at rather reasonable prices. (Tube: Camden Town, unless otherwise noted.)

Parkway Pizzeria, 64 Parkway, NW1 (tel. 485 0678). Exit the station to the right, then head left along Camden High St.; Parkway is the immediate right. Juicy pizzas served in a welcoming pizzeria off of the main thoroughfare. Parquet floor and cool Art Deco mirrors; the partially marbled green walls match the marble table tops. Pizza with capers, pine nuts, tomato, and mozzarella, £3.65. Take away available. £3 min. when the restaurant is full. Open daily noon-midnight.

★ **Bar Gansa,** 2 Inverness St., NW1 (tel. 267 8909). Exit the station to the right and head right; Inverness is the first left. A small *tapas* bar with cream-colored walls, decorated with bright prints and festive Spanish ceramics. Hip clientele of all ages linger over their food, coffee, and wine. Ham, eggs, and chips £3.95. *Tapas* £1.95-3.50. Grilled goat cheese sandwich £4. Outdoor seating. A produce market buzzes inside. Open Mon.-Thurs. 10:30am-11:45pm, Fri. Sat. 10:30am-midnight, Sun. 10:30am-11pm.

★ **Le Petit Prince,** 5 Holmes Rd., NW5 (tel. 267 0752). Tube: Kentish Town. French/Algerian cuisine served in a whimsically decorated café/bar/restaurant. Illustrations from Saint-Exupéry's *Le Petit Prince* dot the walls, which are painted to simulate a cartoon-purple night sky. Lighting fixtures are draped with charming painted screens. Generous plantain sauté starter £2.95. Vegetarian couscous £4.95. Lamb, chicken, and fish dishes are slightly more expensive, but come with unlimited couscous and vegetable broth. Lunch menu includes crêpes (£4.25-4.40) and a coriander, guacamole, and melted goat cheese sandwich (£3.95). Open daily noon-3pm and 7-11:30pm.

Ruby in the Dust, 102 Camden High St., NW1 (tel. 485 2744). Young crowd drawn by the slick decor and jazzy milieu. Dark wood furnishings, a distressed wood floor, and bright wall accents. Burgers £5.75-6.25, veggie burger £5.55. Pasta £4.75-6.25. Mexican burrito £6.35. Selection of newspapers to read if you're feeling antisocial. Also at 70 Upper St., Islington. Open daily 10am-midnight. MC, Visa.

Mange Too, 244 Kentish Town Rd., NW5 (tel. 485 7186). Tube: Kentish Town. The office workers queuing patiently at lunchtime know what they're waiting for. Aromatic interior, with a seating area in back and 2 tables outside. Massive and tasty club sandwiches £2.70-3.50. Large and varied salad bar £4. Min. charge £1.50 Mon.-Fri. noon-2pm. Open Mon.-Fri. 8:30am-6pm, Sat. 9:30am-5:15pm.

Mama Conchetta, 10 Kentish Town Rd., NW1 (tel. 813 0056). Homey *ristorante* and pizzeria, with fresh flowers on the small wooden tables and painted china on the walls. One wall is a false house facade, complete with two shuttered windows and the overhanging end of a red-tiled roof. Pizza £4-5.50, pasta £4.80-5.50. Open Tues.-Fri. noon-3pm and 6-11pm, Sat.-Sun. noon-11pm. MC, Visa.

Nontas, 16 Camden High St., NW1 (tel. 387 4579). Tube: Mornington Crescent or Camden Town. This wonderfully intimate restaurant is one of the best Greek venues in the city. The incomparable *meze* (£8.75) offers a seemingly interminable selection of dips, meats, and cheeses. Other Hellenic fare includes kebabs, £4.90-5.20. *Ouzerie* in front, with plush chairs and petite tables, serves pastries and snacks, like *baclava* (95p), *spanachopitta* (£1.05), and Turkish coffee (75p). Open Mon.-Sat. noon-3pm and 6-11:30pm. *Ouzerie* open Mon.-Sat. 8:30-11:30pm. AmEx, MC, Visa.

Camden's Friend Restaurant, 51a Camden High St. (tel. 387 2835). Tube: Mornington Crescent or Camden Town. Wash down Pekinese seafood and vegetarian cuisine with lethal cocktails. Chicken dishes £3.10-4.20. Vegetarian dishes £3.50-5.20. Rice and noodle dishes £1.20-4.60. Open Mon.-Sat. noon-2:30pm and 6pm-midnight, Sun. 6pm-midnight. AmEx, MC, Visa.

Kohinoor, 23 Camden High St., NW1 (tel. 388 4553). All-you-can-eat Sunday buffet is a super value at £5.50. Of equally good value is the set dinner, which includes a starter, a chicken or lamb dish, vegetable curry, bread or rice, and coffee, all for £5.50. Open daily noon-3pm and 6pm-midnight. AmEx, MC, Visa.

Friendly Diner, 7 Kentish Town Rd., NW1 (tel. 482 0901). Showy black marble façade, but plain diner-like interior with black and white parquet floor. Cheap Chinese and Vietnamese cuisine. Roast crispy pork £3.80. Rice dishes £3.20-4. Open Sun.-Thurs. noon-11:30pm, Fri.-Sat. noon-midnight.

Marine Ices, 8 Haverstock Hill, NW3 (tel. 485 3132). Tube: Chalk Farm. Head left when exiting the station. Superb Italian ice cream (£1 per scoop) and sundaes. *Vesuvius* (£4.85) can defeat even the most Herculean appetite. Massively popular with the Camden town *artistes.* Take-away ice-cream counter open Mon.-Sat. 10:30am-11pm, Sun. 10:30am-9pm. Large Italian restaurant next door, open Mon.-Fri. noon-3pm and 6-11pm, Sat. noon-11pm, Sun. 11am-8pm.

■■■ HAMPSTEAD

This affluent district in northern London has a faintly artsy bent. Traditional teahouses for ladies who lunch still do well amidst a number of pricey brasseries and cafés. The station (tube: Hampstead) is on the corner of Heath St. (right exit) and Hampstead High St. (left exit).

★ **Crêpe Van,** 77 Hampstead High St., NW3. Outside the King William IV pub. A Hampstead institution. Paper-thin Brittany crêpes made in front of your eyes by a real French crêpe-maker in the tiniest van imaginable. Both sweet fillings (including banana and Grand Marnier) and savory (spinach and garlic cream, mushroom and cheese) £2-3. Open Mon.-Sat. 1-11pm, Sun. 1:30-11pm.

Coffee Cup, 74 Hampstead High St., NW3 (tel. 435 7565). The place to be seen if you're young, rich, and trendy. Marble tables on the sidewalk are packed by noon. Open Mon.-Sat. 8am-midnight, Sun. 9am-midnight.

Everyman Café, Holly Bush Vale, NW3 (tel. 431 2123). The hip café-cum-restaurant of the renowned repertory movie house, the Everyman Cinema. Have a croissant or muffin (£1) before catching Orson Welles's *Othello.* Or, try an omelette (£4), truffle-oil poached eggs with wild mushrooms (£5.50), or warm chicken and oyster mushroom salad (£6.50) after taking in an odious Wim Wenders flick. Open Mon.-Fri. noon-midnight, Sat. 11am-midnight, Sun. 11am-11pm.

Rumbold's Bakery, 45 South End Rd., NW3 (tel. 794 2344), across from the BR Hampstead Heath station. Handy for visitors to Keats House which is just around the corner, and worth every step of the way if you come to Hampstead at all. First-rate gourmet pastries, often still warm from the oven. Chocolate croissant (drizzled with chocolate and dusted with powdered sugar) 65p. Apricot danish (with fresh apricot slices in the middle and a honey glaze) 60p. Sandwiches of the brie-and-smoked-salmon variety too. Open Mon.-Sat. 8am-5pm.

Take-away Counter, down the alley of the Hampstead Market fruit stall next to 78 Hampstead High St., NW3. Signboard on High St.'s sidewalk alerts you to the presence of another nameless Hampstead institution. Definitely the cheapest lunch within a 3-mi. radius. Workers eat their lunches on the benches across from the counter. Sandwiches an impossible 60p. Pastries 35p. Jacket potatoes 90p. Soda, tea, or coffee 35p. Open Mon.-Fri. 11:30am-6pm.

■■■ SOUTH OF THE THAMES

Currently the locus of massive new economic and cultural development, the regions south of the Thames are poised to become some of the most vibrant in all of London. Unfortunately for the budget diner, the upscale nature of much of this development means that while exciting eateries abound, many are not affordable. In the South Bank, the **Gabriel's Wharf** complex is a good place to grab lunch or a relaxing snack.

★ **The Fire Station,** 150 Waterloo Rd., SE1 (tel. 620 2226). Tube: Waterloo or Embankment and cross the Hungerford footbridge. A cavernous converted Victorian fire station (a former rave venue) houses an exquisite restaurant with a cactus terrace and an open kitchen. Chef Dan Evans crafts delectable dishes from seasonal ingredients, without using microwaves or freezers; ingredients are insanely fresh. Chalkboard menu changes twice daily. Fresh fish up to £8, but many dishes (like leek and marinated anchovies with salsa verde) under £6. An oyster bar is in the works. Open daily noon-2:30pm and 6:30-11pm. AmEx, MC, Visa.

Gourmet Pizza Company, Gabriel's Wharf, Upper Ground, SE1 (tel. 928 3188). Tube: Waterloo or Embankment and cross the Hungerford footbridge. A chain restaurant located in the thriving arts community of Gabriel's Wharf. Outdoor seating on the waterfront. Generous main-course salads £4-6; try the avocado, pine nut, and parmesan salad. Various crazy pizza flavors, including English Breakfast, Chinese Duck, Mexican Lime, and Smoked Salmon (£5-7.95). Open daily noon-4:30pm and 5-10:30pm. AmEx, Visa.

South Bank Brasserie, Gabriel's Wharf, 56 Upper Ground, SE1 (tel. 620 0596). Tube: Waterloo or Embankment and cross the Hungerfood footbridge. Superb location in a waterfront Victorian building with a wide view of the Thames and St. Paul's. Be forewarned that you'll pay for the view—vegetarian dishes are the most affordable, with crêpes and pasta for £5.95. Enjoy a glass of wine on the patio before a South Bank Centre performance. Open Mon.-Sat. 11am-1am, Sun. 11am-10:30pm.

■■■ BRIXTON

The area within a three block radius of the Brixton tube station has a wealth of budget dining options. The market is a perfect place to purchase fruits and vegetables, but you don't have to stray far from the action in the marketplace to enjoy an affordable sit-down meal. **Brixton Wholefoods,** 56-58 Atlantic Road (tel. 737 2210), sells a potpourri of grains, coffees, spices, juices, candles, and nuts.

★ **Jacaranda,** 11-13 Brixton Station Road, SW9 (tel. 274 8383). A lot of homecooked food for very little money. Main dishes like *fusilli* dripping with cheese, fresh tomatoes, and broccoli, or vegetarian gumbo with rice and okra £2-4. 4 kinds of foccacia, £2.75 each. Fruit juice, iced tea, and iced coffee available. Open Mon.-Sat. 9:30am-9pm, Sun. 11am-6pm—closing hours vary.

Pizzeria Franco, 4 Market Row, Electric Lane, SW9 (tel. 738 3021). A tiny restaurant in the heart of the vast market. Tasty oven-baked foundations (including mussels, mushrooms, and eggplant) topped with spicy tomato sauce, herbs, and different cheeses £3.20-£3.50. Most pizzas under £5. Have a double espresso (£1) and feel the market's pulse. Open Mon.-Tues. and Thurs.-Sat. 8:30-11:30am (for "morning coffee") and 11:30am-5pm full menu. Closed Wed. and Sun.

★ **Cooltan Arts Café,** The Old Dolehouse, 372 Coldharbour Ln, SW9 (tel. 737 2745). Left out of the station, left on Coldharbour Lane, and under the bridge: Cooltan's on your left. Besides offering weekly meditation sessions (see Offbeat Entertainment) and a monthly arts and crafts market (see Markets), The Cooltan Artists' Co-op runs a vegan and vegetarian café. It's a co-op, so both the menu and the chef change daily; the food will be wholesome and fresh regardless of who is at the helm. Participatory "Acoustic Vegan Café," Thurs. 8pm-2am. Storytelling and poetry Wed. 8pm-1am. Open Tues.-Fri. noon-6pm

Café Pushkar, Brixton Market, 16c Market Row, SW9 (tel. 738 6161). A great vegetarian staple in the midst of crazy Brixton Market. Daily specials. Casserole of the day £3.25. Carrot and fresh coriander soup £1.60. Plain or chocolate croissants are a steal at 75p. Open Mon.-Tues. and Thurs.-Sat. 9am-5pm.

Jackets, 423-427 Brixton Rd, SW9. Tube: Brixton. American fast-food decor. Veggies from Covent Garden and meat from the local butcher add a touch of home-made flavor to what might otherwise taste like something you'd find in a University mess hall. Steaming potatoes packed with whatever your heart desires: spicy Chili con carne, cheese, chicken curry, sweetcorn—all are meal-sized and all are under £2. They also make their own lemon cordial. Open Mon.-Sat. 11am-11:30pm, Sun. noon-11pm.

Kim's Café, Brixton Market, 15 Market Row, SW9 (tel. 924 9105). Casual diner garishly decked in red and green. Affable management makes you feel right at home. Shepherd's Pie and 3 vegetables £2.90. English breakfast £2.90. Open daily 7:30am-4:30pm.

Phoenix, 441 Coldharbour Lane, SW9 (tel. 733 4430). Simple dishes and friendly management=good place to eat lunch. Straightforward diner ambience, but Coldharbour locale guarantees that your fellow diners will be hip. No sandwich above £2. Hot meals like chicken cutlet with veggies £2.40. Open Mon.-Sat. 6:30am-5pm.

Stop Gap, 500A Brighton Terrace, SW9. Right behind Red Records on Brixton Road. Extremely affordable sandwich bar carries all the basics (cheese, tuna, sweetcorn) for under £2. Plentiful flyers and brochures keep you informed of all the happenings around the neighborhood. Open daily 8am-5pm.

Satay Gallery/Restaurant, 5-7 Vining St., SW9 (tel. 737 2046). Will move to the new Ritzy complex, on the corner of Coldharbour Lane and Brixton Road, in January 1995; the phone number will remain the same. Exotic entrees, like *ikan panggang* (pomfret—an Indo-Pacific butterfish—cooked in savory coconut sauce) under £6. Paintings cover the walls, and a chic crowd fills the place on weekends. Many vegetarian options. Lunch 25% off Sun. and Wed. Open for lunch Wed.-Sat. noon-3pm; for dinner Tues.-Thurs. 7-11pm, Fri.-Sat. 7pm-midnight; and Sun. noon-11pm.

The Village, 410 Brixton Rd., SW9 (tel. 274 6545). Full bar and restaurant has ultra-sleek silver and black furnishings. Big Paul Klee-esque mural decorates the wall. They serve up tasty Carribbean and vegetarian dishes like jerk chicken (£5) and Rasta Pasta. Fried plantains, a standard starter in this area of London, are £1.50. Happy hour daily 3-7pm. Jazz and funk on weekends starts at 9pm. Open daily noon-midnight.

GROCERIES AND SUPERMARKETS

The most economical source of food is the **supermarket.** Besides groceries (like bread, cheese, fresh fruit, canned foods—the budget traveler's indispensable staples), some also sell excellent deli and bakery goods and satisfying prepared dishes-like ham and cheese pasty, meat pie or quiche, lamb samosa, and chicken *tikka*.

Europa, Ubiquitous small grocery store chain that stays open later (until 11pm) and charges a bit extra. Look for the yellow and black sign.

Harrod's, Brompton Rd. (tube: Knightsbridge). Enormous, regal food halls offer almost everything under the sun at out-of-this-budget-world prices; visit if only to gawk.

Marks & Spencer, Oxford St. (tube: Marble Arch); Poland St. (tube: Oxford Circus); Liverpool St. (tube: Camden Town); Kensington High St. (tube: High St.

Kensington). A tad pricier than Sainsbury, but particularly renowned for its vast array of prepared foods and salads.

Safeway, King's Rd. (tube: Sloane Sq., then #11 bus); Kensington High St. (tube: High St. Kensington); Edgware Rd. (tube: Paddington); Liverpool St. (tube: Camden Town); in the Barbican Centre; Brunswick Shopping Centre (tube: Russell Sq.). Your basic supermarket.

Sainsbury, Victoria Rd. (near Victoria Station); Cromwell Rd. (tube: Gloucester Rd.); Camden Rd. (tube: Camden Town); gargantuan "Hypermarket" in Merton (tube: Collier's Wood). The store's own brand of everything is unbeatably cheap and high quality—there are even organic and wholefood products.

Tesco, Bedford St. (tube: Covent Garden); Goodge St.; Portobello Rd. (tube: Notting Hill Gate); near Paddington and Victoria Stations. Generic supermarket.

PUBS AND BARS

> *"Did you ever taste beer?"*
> *"I had a sip of it once," said the small servant.*
> *"Here's a state of things!" cried Mr. Swiveller, "She never tasted it—it can't be tasted in a sip!"*
> —Charles Dickens, The Old Curiosity Shop

"As much of the history of England has been brought about in public houses as in the House of Commons," said Sir William Harcourt. Even if you don't happen to witness history in the making, you can certainly absorb the spirit of this major social institution. Many pubs are centuries old, and each has its distinctive history, ambience, and regulars. The mahogany paneling, the soft velvet stools, and the brass accents emphasize that they are more than mere boozing sites. While taverns and inns no longer play the role of staging post for coach and horses, pubs remain meeting-places, signposts, bastions of Britannia, and ideal conversation spots.

Note that most pubs do not offer a **full bar** selection, but only serve beverages in the beer family. If you thirst for cocktails, hi-balls, or mixed drinks, you will have to seek out a bar, not a pub. The listings below include both bars and pubs; a careful perusal of the individual descriptions will allow you to discern which establishments are traditional pubs and which offer a full bar selection.

London's 7000 pubs are as colorful and historic as their counterparts throughout England, with clientele varying considerably from one neighborhood to the next. Pubs in the City pack in tourists and pinstripes at lunch. The taverns up in Bloomsbury tend to draw a mix of tourists and students, while those in Kensington and Hampstead cater to the trendy element. Around the wholesale markets, tradespeople grab pints as early as six in the morning.

In general, avoid pubs within a half-mile radius of an inner-city train station (Paddington, Euston, King's Cross/St. Pancras, and Victoria). They prey upon tourists by charging 20-40p extra per pint. For the best pub prices, head to the East End. Stylish, lively pubs cluster around the fringes of the West End. Many historic alehouses lend an ancient air to areas recently swallowed up by the urban sprawl, such as Highgate and Hampstead. Some pubs have serious theater groups performing upstairs, while others are meeting places for community groups, literary workshops, and other cultural organizations.

Pubs close miserably early. Even though laws were relaxed in 1988 (allowing pubs and restaurants to serve alcohol all day), the law still requires that they stay open for no more than 12 hours a day. Most pubs serve from 11am to 11pm Mon.-Sat. in order to get lunchtime and afternoon business. Sundays are more restricted, with most pubs open noon-3pm and 7-10:30pm.

A bell 10 minutes before closing time signifies "last orders." If you are still intent on finding a late-night drinking spot, the recent change in licensing laws now permits many licensed restaurants to serve alcohol until they close, even if it's midnight or 1am. For those who don't want to order food, *tapas* bars may prove the most convenient place to continue drinking. These ubiquitous restaurants have reasonable prices, and most will let you order drinks without food.

Beer is the standard pub drink. Many pubs are "tied" to a particular brewery and only sell that brewery's ales; "Free Houses" sell a wider range of brands. In either case, beer is "pulled" from the tap in a dizzying variety of ways. All draughts, ales, and stouts are served "warm"–at room temperature–and by the pint or half-pint. **Bitter** is the staple of English beer, named for the sharp hoppy aftertaste. **"Real ale,"** naturally carbonated (unlike most beer) and drawn from a barrel, retains its full flavor. Brown, mild, pale, and India pale ales—less common varieties—all have a relatively heavy flavor with noticeable hop. **Stout** is rich, dark, and creamy. Try standing a match on the silky foam head of **Guinness.**

If you can't stand the heat, try a **lager,** the European equivalent of American beer. Budweiser and Michelob, where available, cost at least 30% more than German and British brews. Bottled beer is always more expensive than draft. **Cider,** the wine of the English, is a potent apple drink. Among the more complex liquids appearing at a pub near you are the **shandy,** a refreshing combination of beer and fizzy lemonade; **black and tan,** beer and stout layered like a parfait; **black velvet,** a mating of Guinness and Champagne, and **snakebite,** a murky mix of lager and cider.

Those who don't drink alcohol should savor the pub experience all the same; fruit juices, colas, and sometimes low-alcohol beers are served. Buy all drinks at the bar—bartenders are not usually tipped. Prices vary greatly with area and even clientele. Generally, a pint will set you back £1.60-2.10. Along with food and drink, pubs often host traditional games, including darts, pool, and bar billiards, an ingenious derivative of billiards played from only one end of the table. More recently, a brash and bewildering array of video games, fruit (slot) machines, and extortionate CD jukeboxes has invaded many pubs.

Look before you buy pub food. Pubs now serve anything from curry to burgers, but standard English favorites remain your best bet. Quality and prices vary greatly with virtually no relation between the two. **Steak and kidney pie** or **pudding** is a mixture of steak and kidney, mushrooms, and pastry or pudding crust. A **cornish pasty** is filled with potato, onion, and meat. **Shepherd's pie** consists of minced beef or lamb with onion, saddled with mashed potatoes, and baked. A **ploughman's lunch** encompasses bread, cheese, and pickled onions. The very lucky may even find the early childhood favorites, **bangers and mash** (sausages and mashed potatoes) or **bubble and squeak** (cabbage and mashed potatoes).

For a selection of gay pubs, see Bisexual, Gay, and Lesbian London.

■■■ THE WEST END

Lamb and Flag, 33 Rose St., WC2, off Garrick St. Tube: Covent Garden or Leicester Sq. Rose St. is off Long Acre, which runs between the 2 tube stops. A formerly obstreperous pub where a mob of angry readers seized Augustan poet John Dryden and nearly beat him to death—just one of the events that earned it the name "Bucket of Blood." Today a fun local crowd spills onto the small alley streets in the evenings.

The Porcupine, Great Newport St. at Charing Cross Rd., WC2. Tube: Leicester Sq. The West End's most schizophrenic pub: young folks on the first floor generate smoke and noise, while their parents peck at tasty pre-theater pub meals (£4.50-7) upstairs.

Riki Tik, 23-24 Bateman St., W1 (tel. 437 1977). Tube: Leicester Square, Tottenham Ct. Rd., or Piccadilly Circus. A hyped, hip, and tremendously swinging bar specializing in flavored vodkas (£2 per shot). Try white chocolate or, for the brave, aniseed. Open Mon.-Sat. 11am-11pm; closed Sun.

Freud's, 198 Shaftesbury Ave., WC2 (tel. 240 9933). Tube: Tottenham Ct. Rd. or Covent Garden. A downstairs bar with leftover late-80s decor: concrete walls, slate tables, and art for sale. Conversations here can get a little pretentious; nevertheless, in the early evenings it is a comfortable place, even for the single traveler.

Beer £1.95-2.75. Cocktails £3.10-4.55. Limited selection of snack foods. Live jazz Sun. eve. Open Mon.-Sat. 11am-11pm, Sun. noon-10:30pm.

The Dog and Duck, 8 Bateman St., W1 (tel. 437 4447). Tube: Tottenham Ct. Rd. The smallest pub in Soho, it fills up with a "punter" (British jargon for "alternative") crowd. Fireplace in back.

The Dog House, 187 Wardour St., W1 (tel. 434 2116). Tube: Tottenham Court Road. An affordable, megacrowded, and very hip bar in a boldly-colored basement space. Inventive cocktails (with non-alcoholic options) and cheap but gourmet snack food.

Globe, 37 Bow St., WC2. Tube: Covent Garden. Turn right from the tube onto Long Acre, then right again on Bow St. Near the Royal Opera House—join orchestra members and kill the ringing in your ears. Depicted in Hitchcock's *Frenzy.*

Maple Leaf, 41 Maiden Lane, WC2. Tube: Covent Garden. Maiden Lane is parallel to and 1 block away from the Strand. London's Canadian pub. A good place to satisfy that late-night urge for a pint of Molson (£1.60) after an evening at the theater.

Round House, New Row at Bedford St., WC2. Tube: Leicester Sq. or Covent Garden. This pub is pleasant in the afternoons and late evenings, but the flood of office workers arriving shortly after 5pm will prevent visitors from seating themselves or breathing any fresh air. Even hard to find a place to rest your glass.

The French House, 49 Dean St., W1. Tube: Piccadilly Circus or Tottenham Ct. Rd. Charles de Gaulle made this diminutive pub his unofficial H.Q. Skip the unimpressive beer for some wine; Dylan Thomas downed a few here, but then again, he wasn't particularly choosy.

The Albert, 52 Victoria St., SW1. Tube: Victoria. Award-winning pub with terrific service and mouth-watering, costly food. Come early or late to miss the tourist dinner deluge. Last orders for food at 9:30pm

The Salisbury, 90 St. Martin's La., WC2. Tube: Leicester Sq. A Victorian pub with a blindingly polished decor; the ornate glass and gilt become increasingly bewildering as the beers slip down.

Sherlock Holmes, 10 Northumberland St., WC2. Tube: Charing Cross. Upstairs room is a replica of Holmes' 221b Baker St. den. A host of relics to thrill the Holmes fiend—the tobacco in the slipper, correspondence affixed to the mantelpiece with a dagger, and the head of the Hound of the Baskervilles. Inexpensive and cozy to boot—if you can bear the kitsch.

Belushi's, 9 Russell St., WC2 (tel. 240 3411). Tube: Covent Garden. One of the few places where Budweiser is served. Crowded with precious young things too young to appreciate the Blues Brothers posters plastering the walls. Burgers and bar snacks served. Open daily 11am-11pm.

Nag's Head, 10 James St., WC2. Tube: Covent Garden. A favorite of London's theater elite. The round, light beige booths recall airport lounges

Brahms & Liszt, 19 Russell St., WC2 (tel. 240 3661). Tube: Covent Garden. Live music downstairs headlines rock, blues, and soul Mon.-Sat. 10pm-1am, Sun. 7-10:30pm. Happy hour Mon.-Sat. 6-8:30 serves a full range of wines, cocktails, and beer. Free before 9pm, occasional £5 cover after.

Tin Pan Alley Bar, 7 Denmark St. WC2 (tel. 836 0032). Tube: Tottenham Ct. Road or Leiceister Sq. Wholeheartedly unpretentious and basic, it's on "The Music Street" where those in the know shop for Fender Musicmasters. Draft beers £2, bottled beers £2.25. Open Mon.-Sat. 11am-11pm.

■■■ KENSINGTON AND CHELSEA

World's End Distillery, on King's Rd. near World's End Pass (before Edith Grove). Tube: Sloane Sq. This pub isn't wedged shamefacedly into a street corner like most others; it stands alone, grandiose and cathedralesque. If the universe collapsed and nothing but the World's End remained, we would not weep. Rather, we would lounge in a soft leather booth and play one of the many board games offered here, or sit on a green velvet stool and peruse one of the old books shelved near the candle-lit mirror. Live music on Thurs. and Sun. nights.

Admiral Codrington, 17 Mossop St., SW3. Tube: South Kensington. This old, handsomely appointed pub with a peaceful patio off the back is brimming with girls in platform shoes and boys in baggy suits. An impressive collection of single-malt whiskey.

The Chelsea Potter, 119 King's Rd., SW3. Tube: Victoria then bus #11, 19, or 22. This pub's name marks its history as a haven for ramshackle Chelsea artists throwing pots and living on their trust funds. Noisy outdoor tables. Enthusiastic patrons watch sports on TV. Pints of Carlsberg lager under £2.

The Goat in Boots, 333 Fulham Rd., SW10. Tube: South Kensington. Young tipplers come for the loud music and cocktail bar, not for pub decor or ambience.

The Australian, 29 Milner St., SW3. Tube: Sloane Sq. This cricket pub is especially appealing during the summer season, when enthusiasts can watch the Test Match while sipping a pint of bitter.

Cadogan Arms, King's Rd. near Old Church St., SW3. Tube: Sloane Sq. or Victoria, then bus #11, 19, or 22. Invigorating and jovial. Try to ignore the farm implements hanging from the rafters above your head. No telly in the hotel? Catch the football match on the big one here. Large burgers £3.25.

The King's Head and Eight Bells, 50 Cheyne Walk, SW3. Take bus #11 down King's Rd., get off at Oakley St., walk toward the river, and turn right on Cheyne Walk. Richly textured 16th-century pub where Thomas More would have a jar with his dangerous friend Henry VIII. Carlyle's modest house is just around the corner.

Royal Court Tavern, Sloane Sq., SW1. Tube: Sloane Sq. The ideal place to banter about the coy state of French cinema. Patronized, appropriately, by a proto-intellectual but nattily dressed crowd. Food served daily noon-2:30pm and 6-10:15pm.

The Windsor Castle, 144 Campden Hill Rd., W8. Tube: Notting Hill Gate. Legend has it that you could once see the Castle from here, before the advent of industrial haze. The beer garden at the back makes this pub particularly memorable, as do the amiable bar staff and clientele.

■■■ EARL'S COURT

The King's Head, Hogarth Pl., SW5. Tube: Earl's Ct. From Earl's Ct. Rd., head east on Childs Walk or Hogarth Pl. Large and popular pub, but quieter than most in Earl's Ct. Besides real ale, this pub has a passable wine list.

The Prince of Teck, 161 Earl's Ct. Rd., SW5. Tube: Earl's Ct. An atmosphere like Venus—hot and oppressive. Some love it, some loathe it; either way, you'll sweat. Aussie headquarters. Door sign says it all: "G'day and welcome to the land of Oz."

The Scarsdale, 23 Pembroke Sq., W8. Tube: Earl's Ct. Walk up Earl's Ct. Rd. 3 blocks past Cromwell Rd., and turn left at Pembroke Sq. When you see people sitting outside in a sea of flowers and ivy, contentedly throwing back a few pints as they talk without the interruption of beeping fruit machines and screeching jukeboxes, well, you've found it.

■■■ BLOOMSBURY

The Old Crown, 33 New Oxford St., WC1 (tel. 836 9121). Tube: Tottenham Ct. Rd. A thoroughly nontraditional pub. Mustard yellow walls, faded pine-green bar, green plants, and funky brass crowns suspending the light fixtures from the ceiling. The lively mixed crowd spills out onto the outdoor seating, creating a babble of voices above the upbeat rock music playing in the background; quieter seating upstairs. Also a restaurant/café serving salads, hummus, tea, and Mexican specialites. Open Mon.-Sat. noon-11pm. Major credit cards.

The Lamb, 94 Lamb's Conduit St., WC1 (tel. 405 0713). Tube: Russell Sq. E.M. Forster and other Bloomsbury luminaries used to do their tippling here. Discreet cut-glass "snob screens"—holdovers from Victorian times—render this pub ideal for dangerous liaisons and illicit assignations. Limited outdoor seating. Hot food served noon-2:30pm.

The Sun, 63 Lamb's Conduit St., WC1 (tel. 405 8278). Tube: Holborn. One of London's largest selections of real ales on tap at this busy pub on a street of cafés and sandwich shops. Stately cast-iron fireplaces and hardwood floors; the wood furniture has a comfortably worn feel. Standard, relatively cheap pub fare. Mixed crowd of business people, older locals, and students.

Grafton Arms, 72 Grafton Way, W1 (tel. 387 7923). Tube: Warren St. Off the tourist trail, near Regent's Park. One of the best central London pubs for a relaxed pint. Caters to a lively London University student crowd. 8 real ales. Standard pub fare sold all day. Wine bar on rooftop patio. MC, Visa.

Museum Tavern, 49 Great Russell St., WC1 (tel. 242 8987). Tube: Tottenham Ct. Rd. High coffered ceiling; spacious, plush atmosphere. Karl Marx sipped *Bier* here after banging out *Das Kapital* across the street in the British Museum reading room. The Star Tavern, which formerly occupied this site, was one of Casanova's rendezvous spots. 17 beers on tap.

Lord John Russell Pub, 91 Marchmont St., WC1 (tel. 388 0500). Tube: Russell Sq. Around the corner from the Cartwright Gdns. hotels and halls. A simple, unassuming local pub. Comfortable indoor and outdoor benches seat a mixed crowd of locals, students, and tourists. A good place to go for a well-drawn pint of Guinness.

The Water Rats, 328 Grays Inn Rd., WC1 (tel. 837 9861). Tube: King's Cross/St. Pancras. Ordinary appearance belies radical historical connections—this used to be one of Marx and Engels' favorite haunts. Average pint £2.10. Moonlights as the Splash Club Wed.-Sat. nights, a venue for indie rock, punk, and occasional acoustic gigs. 3 bands a night. £5, concessions £3.

Princess Louise, 208 High Holborn, WC1 (tel. 405 8816). Tube: Holborn. This big pub isn't big enough to contain the jovial crowd that assembles after office hours. Built in 1872 and refurbished in 1891, this pub maintains its ornate Victorian grandeur—beautiful tiles and etched mirrors line the walls. Fancy plasterwork columns support a decadent scarlet ceiling trimmed in gold.

■■■ THE CITY OF LONDON

Black Friar, 174 Queen Victoria St., EC4 (tel. 236 5650). Tube: Blackfriars. Directly across from the station. The entire edifice stands as an Art Nouveau monument to the medieval monks whose vestments are celebrated in the pub's name. Intriguing nooks and crannies. Witty advice can be read from the walls of the back room, called "The Side Chapel." Average pint £1.90.

Cartoonist, 76 Shoe La., EC4 (353 2828). Tube: Chancery La. Headquarters for the Cartoonist Club of Great Britain. Decorated with appropriate hilarity, but the current pin-striped clientele are themselves ripe for caricature. Limited outdoor seating.

Ye Olde Cheshire Cheese, Wine Office Ct., 145 Fleet St., EC4 (tel. 353 6170). Tube: Blackfriars or St. Paul's. Once on Fleet St., watch out for Wine Office Ct. on the right; a small sign indicates the alley. A 17th-century pub which has retained the small-rooms layout characteristic of that era. Famous as Dr. Johnson's and Charles Dickens' hangout—artifacts and pictures highlight events that shaped this pub/restaurant's 300-year history. 5 bars and 3 restaurants contained in "the Cheese."

Sir Christopher Wren, 7 Paternoster Sq., EC4 (tel. 248 1708). Tube: St. Paul's. Tremendous smoked glass windows bestow instant atmosphere upon this pub/restaurant. Comfortable, plush booths inside, picnic tables outside. Relatively high food prices primarily reflect the pub's proximity to Wren's masterpiece. Daily special £4.80. Average pint £1.85. Open Mon.-Fri. 11am-9pm, Sat.-Sun. 11:30am-3pm.

■■■ THE EAST END

The Blind Beggar, 337 Whitechapel Rd., E1 (tel. 247 8329). Tube: Whitechapel. You may be sitting where George Cornell sat when he was gunned down by rival Bethnal Green gangster Ronnie Kray in 1966. Spacious pub with a conservatory and a garden. Middle-aged locals tipple here.

Clutterbuck's, 89 Whitechapel High St., E1 (tel. 247 5393). Tube: Aldgate East. Newly redone, the decor remains traditional, with a dark wood bar and patterned carpeting. Opens out onto the street, where locals sit around small tables. Students welcome. A pint of Clutterbuck's ale £1.10. Bottomless homemade soup with fresh nob £1.95. Open Mon.-Sat. 11am-11pm, Sun. noon-3pm.

■■■ CAMDEN TOWN AND ISLINGTON

Lock Tavern, 35 Chalk farm Rd., NW1. Tube: Chalk Farm or Camden Town. A high-ceilinged pub decorated with theater bills. Roof patio offers a view of the action at Camden Market. Lively, mixed crowd. Cheap pub fare.

Slug and Lettuce, 1 Islington Green, N1. Tube: Angel. Upper St. changes its name to Islington Green as it passes by the Green. Patrons of the Screen on the Green across the street conduct earnest dissections of *Casablanca*. Good observation post for spotting Islington trendies (inside or outside). Try upstairs for a comfy, cozy setting.

Engine Room, 78-9 Chalk Farm Rd., NW1 (tel. 916 0595). Tube: Chalk Farm. A rock-oriented bar frequented by local band members. Painted black outside, with grafitti art on the windows; inside, the walls are plastered with old music posters, vinyl platters, and movie ads. Pool table. Cheap pub fare.

Truman's, 202 Camden High St., NW1. Tube: Camden Town. Simple wood floor and benches. Frequented by black-clad alternative youth tired from shopping for Puma Clydes and Doc Martens at the Market.

Edinburgh Castle, 57 Mornington Terrace, NW1. Tube: Camden Town. Exit to the right and head left down Camden High St. Turn right on Delancey St. and follow it until it intersects with Mornington Terrace. A pub that feels like a living room, complete with stuffed chairs, hanging plants, and a fireplace. Pool table. Outdoor patio often crowded with deflated or elated sports teams from nearby Regent's Park. Reputedly also popular with Soho media types. Barbecue in summer.

Camden Head, 2 Camden Walk. Tube: Angel. Just past the tip of the Islington green. A beautiful pub with cut-glass windows and plush seats, founded in 1749. Popular with Isy's younger set. Wed. and Sat. the outdoor patio bustles with thirsty visitors taking a break from bargain-hunting at the market.

Minogues, 80 Liverpool Rd., N1. Tube: Angel. Liverpool branches left off of Upper St. directly across from the station. If you can't make the journey across the Irish sea, throw back a Guinness and slog through the *Irish Times* at one of London's most traditional Irish pubs. Occasional live Irish music.

■■■ HAMPSTEAD AND HIGHGATE

The Holly Bush, 22 Holly Mount, NW3. Tube: Hampstead. The quintessential snug Hampstead pub in a quaint cul-de-sac, serving real ale. The maze of glass and wood makes this place ideal for an illicit assignation.

King William IV, 77 Hampstead High St., NW3. Tube: Hampstead. Outside: the famed Crêpe Van (see Restaurants). Inside: the famed gay pub, very trendy for people of all ages.

Spaniards Inn, Spaniards End, NW3.. Tube: Hampstead, then bus #210 along Spaniards Rd. Upscale pub on the north edge of Hampstead Heath. Pub has provided garden in summer and hearth in winter since 1585. Dickens, Shelley, Keats, and Byron were patrons. Intriguing aviary.

The Bull and Bush, North End Way, NW3. Tube: Golders Green, then bus #210, or Hampstead tube and bus #268. Immortalized in the classic music hall song "Down at the Old Bull and Bush," though the spiffy young gentlemen who crowd the bar today seem unlikely to break into chorus.

The Flask Tavern, 77 Highgate West Hill, N6. Tube: Archway. Near the youth hostel. Enormously popular on summer evenings and at Sun. noontime. Sitting on the vast terrace outside, drink a toast to Karl Marx, Yehudi Menuhin, or any other

LET'S GO® TRAVEL

CATALOG

1995

WE GIVE YOU THE WORLD... AT A DISCOUNT

Discounted Flights, Eurail Passes,
Travel Gear, Let's Go™ Series Guides,
Hostel Memberships... and more

Let's Go Travel
a division of
Harvard Student
Agencies, Inc.

**Bargains
to every
corner of
the world!**

Travel Gear

A **Let's Go T-Shirt**.............................$10

100% combed cotton. Let's Go logo on front left chest. Four color printing on back. L and XL. Way cool.

B **Let's Go Supreme**..........$175

Innovative hideaway suspension with parallel stay internal frame turns backpack into carry-on suitcase. Includes lumbar support pad, torso, and waist adjustment, leather trim, and detachable daypack. Waterproof Cordura nylon, lifetime gurantee, 4400 cu. in. Navy, Green, or Black.

C **Let's Go Backpack/Suitcase**....................$130

Hideaway suspension turns backpack into carry-on suitcase. Internal frame. Detachable daypack makes 3 bags in 1. Waterproof Cordura nylon, lifetime guarantee, 3750 cu. in. Navy, Green, or Black.

D **Let's Go Backcountry I**..$210

Full size, slim profile expedition pack designed for the serious trekker. New Airflex suspension. X-frame pack with advanced composite tube suspension. Velcro height adjustment, side compression straps. Detachable hood converts into a fanny pack. Waterproof Cordura nylon, lifetime guarantee, main compartment 3375 cu. in., extends to 4875 cu. in.

E **Let's Go Backcountry II**............................$240

Backcountry I's Big Brother. Magnum Helix Airflex Suspension. Deluxe bi-lam contoured shoulder harness. Adjustable sterm strap. Adjustable bi-lam Cordura waist belt. 5350 cubic inches. 7130 cubic inches extended. Not pictured.

800-5-LETSGO

Discounted Flights

Call Let's Go now for inexpensive airfare to points across the country and around the world.

EUROPE • SOUTH AMERICA • ASIA • THE CARRIBEAN • AUSTRALIA •
AFRICA

Eurail Passes

urailpass (First Class)

days.....................................$498	*Unlimited rail travel anywhere*
onth (30 days)....................$798	*on Europe's 100,000 mile rail network.*
onths (60 days).................$1098	*Accepted in 17 countries.*

Eurail Flexipass (First Class)

A number of individual travel days   Any 5 days in 2 months.............$348
to be used at your convenience   Any 10 days in 2 months...........$560
within a two-month period.   Any 15 days in 2 months...........$740

rail Youthpass (Second Class)

days.....................................$398	*All the benefits of the Eurail Pass*
onth (30 days)....................$578	*at a lower price. For those passengers*
onths (60 days)...................$768	*under 26 on their first day of travel.*

Eurail Youth Flexipass (Second Class)

Eurail Flexipass at a reduced rate   Any 5 days in 2 months.............$255
for passengers under 26   Any 10 days in 2 months...........$398
on their first day of travel.   Any 15 days in 2 months...........$540

ropass (First & Second Class)

Class starting at................$280	*Discounted fares for those passengers*
nd Class starting at............$198	*travelling in France, Germany, Italy,*
more details......................CALL	*Spain and Switzerland.*

Hostelling Essentials

Undercover Neckpouch............$9.95
Ripstop nylon with soft Cambrelle back. Three
pockets. 6 x 7". Lifetime guarantee. Black or Tan.

Undercover Waistpouch.........$9.95
Ripstop nylon with soft Cambrelle back. Two
pockets. 5 x 12" with adjustable waistband.
Lifetime guarantee. Black or Tan.

H **Sleepsack..................................$13.95**
Required at all hostels. 18" pillow pocket.
Washable poly/cotton. Durable. Compact.

I **Hostelling International Card**
Required by most international hostels. For U.S.
residents only. Adults, $25. Under 18, $10.

J **Int'l Youth Hostel Guide.......$10.95**
Indispensable guide to prices, locations, and
reservations for over 4000 hostels in Europe
and the Mediterranean.

K **ISIC, ITIC, IYTC..........$16, $16, $17**
ID cards for students, teachers and those people
under 26. Each offers many travel discounts.

800-5-LETSGO

Order Form

Please print or type — Incomplete applications will not be processed

Last Name	First Name	Date of Birth

Street (We cannot ship to P.O. boxes)

City	State	Zip

Country	Citizenship	Date of Travel

(   )   -

Phone	School (if applicable)

Item Code	Description, Size & Color	Quantity	Unit Price	Total Price
		SUBTOTAL:		

Domestic Shipping & Handling		Shipping and Handling (see box at left):	
Order Total:	Add:	Add $10 for RUSH, $20 for overnite:	
Up to $30.00	$4.00	MA Residents add 5% tax on books and gear:	
$30.01 to $100.00	$6.00		
Over $100.00	$7.00	**GRAND TOTAL:**	
Call for int'l or off-shore delivery			

MasterCard / VISA Order	*Enclose check or money order payable to:*
CARDHOLDER NAME _____	**Harvard Student Agencies, Inc.**
CARD NUMBER _____	53A Church Street
EXPIRATION DATE _____	Cambridge, MA 02138

Allow 2-3 weeks for delivery. Rush orders guaranteed within one week of our receipt. Overnight orders sent via FedEx the same afternoon.

Missing a Let's Go Book from your collection?
Add one to any $50 order at 50% off the cover price!

Let's Go Travel
1-800-5-LETSGO

(617) 495-9649   Fax: (617) 496-8015
53A Church Street
Cambridge MA 02138

Highgate luminary whose name flits through your giddy brain. Hostelers tipple here as early as 11:30am.

Jack Straw's Castle, North End Way, NW3. Tube: Hampstead, then climb up Heath St. or take bus #268 to the door. By Whitestone pond. Massive timber-clad block, frequented by Dickens and a few German bombs. Sweeping view.

■■■ HAMMERSMITH AND PUTNEY

There is, in fact, reason to travel to Hammersmith or Putney for a drink: the pubs listed here are all on the waterfront, and have outdoor seating with expansive views of the Thames. The Victorian bridges arching across the river are often lit beautifully at night, making this area a popular evening destination. To get to any of the pubs on Upper Mall, come out of the station and head west on Blacks Road. Walk for 5 minutes, take any left (Angel Walk, Bridge Avenue), and you'll hit the river. To reach Lower Richmond Road pubs, take the tube to Putney Bridge (District Line) and cross the Putney Bridge. As you come off the bridge, Lower Richmond is on your right.

The Dove, 19 Upper Mall, SW6. Tube: Hammersmith. As authentic a threesome of rooms as you'll find. Make the trip to the 300-year old tavern for a delicious lunch overlooking the Thames.

Rutland Arms, Upper Mall, SW6. Tube: Hammersmith. Its red neon sign reflects onto the Thames. Very crowded with college-aged locals, looking good and getting hyper about soccer matches. All the ales, plus Budweiser.

Half Moon, 93 Lower Richmond Rd., SW15. Tube: Putney Bridge. A no-nonsense pub known for daily live music in the room at the back. Check *Time Out* for gig details.

Star and Garter, 4 Lower Richmond Rd., SW15. Tube: Putney Bridge. A veritable monument of a riverside pub. Roomy lounge is nearly always full; some prefer to drink outside, where the music is less deafening.

■■■ SOUTH OF THE THAMES AND BRIXTON

Babushka, 173 Blackfriars Road, SE1 (tel. 928 6179). Tube: Waterloo. A promising new bar. Much attention paid to decor, perhaps in response to upscale pretensions of clientele. Art. High ceilings. Bottled beers £2, wine £1.60 per glass. Spirits served. Live music (mostly jazz) Mon.-Sat. 6-9:30pm. Open Mon.-Sat. noon-11pm, Sun. noon-6pm.

Bar Central, 131 Waterloo Rd., SE1 (tel. 928 5086). Tube: Waterloo. Near the Old Vic. An electric blue facade welcomes the thirsty to this cosmopolitan full bar and brasserie. Barkeep will mix you any drink that you know the name of. Open Mon.-Sat. noon-midnight, Sun. noon-11:30pm.

The Brixtonian, 11 Dorrell Pl., SW9 (tel. 978-8870). Tube: Brixton. A cozy, artsy bar removed from the moving and grooving of the market area. Green picnic tables on the pedestrian walk outside can be ideal for a quiet, slow drink with a loved one. International beer selection includes Sapporo (Japan) and August (Russia), both £2.50. Occasional live jazz. Open Mon. 5:30pm-midnight, Tues.-Wed. noon-midnight, Thurs.-Sat. noon-1am.

George Inn, 77 Borough High St., SE1 (tel. 407 2056). Tube: London Bridge. A fine 17th-century galleried inn; the older equivalent of Victoria coach station. Now it's the last stop of the day for the suits of the South Bank. Drafts £1.60-2.20. Open Mon.-Sat. 11am-11pm, Sun. noon-3pm and 7pm-10:30 pm.

Studio Six, Gabriel's Wharf, 56 Upper Ground, SE1 (tel. 928 6243). Tube: Waterloo. Lots of outdoor tables at this delightful locale right on the waterfront. Perfect for a pre- or post-South Bank Centre engagement. Bottled imports of the Mexican variety £2, draft beers £1.65. A few inexpensive bottled wines dot the list. Open Mon.-Sat. 11am-11pm, Sun. noon-3pm and 7:30-10:30pm.

■■■ DOCKLANDS

The Angel, 101 Bermondsey Wall, SE16 (tel. 237 3608). Tube: Rotherhithe. A 17th-century pub with an indescribable view of the river to the Tower Bridge and the City. Intriguing trap doors (for smugglers) and a balcony in the back. One of the few remaining galleried inns on the river. Restaurant on the second story is slightly plusher than its pilgrim neighbor's.

The Dickens Inn, St. Katherine's Way E1 (tel. 488-2208). Tube: London Bridge or DLR Tower Gateway. Gorgeous riverside pub on St. Katherine's Dock. Flowers sprayed all over the terraces. Nice place to stop if you're checking out the Crown Jewels nearby.

The House They Left Behind, 27 Ropemakers Fields, E14 (tel. 538-5102). Tube: DLR Limehouse or Westferry. There's a titillating story behind the name of this small pub; visit Mr. M. Naughton, proprietor, and get a history lesson. Located just off historic Narrow Street.

Mayflower, 117 Rotherhithe St., SE16 (tel. 237-4088). Tube: Rotherhithe. Named in honor of the Pilgrims who embarked for the New World from this tavern in 1620. Nautical interior with wood paneling and views of the Thames from the second story and from the jetty, a beer garden overlooking the river. Open Mon.-Sat. until 11pm, Sun. until 10:30 pm.

Prospect of Whitby, 57 Wapping Wall, E1, London Docks (tel. 481-1095). Tube: Wapping. 600-year-old pub, the hangout of the diarist Samuel Pepys. Open ceilings and a rustic flagstone bar. Serious Thamescape. Riverside terrace and prohibitive upstairs restaurant.

Town of Ramsgate, 62 Wapping High St., E1 (tel. 488-2685). Tube: Wapping. A mere 300 years old. Some convicts were imprisoned in the cellar on the way to the Antipodes; others were chained to the bank to succumb to the tide, just beneath the pleasant garden. This country inn has cheap sandwiches and a wide variety of hot entrees at reasonable prices. Beer garden overlooking river.

TEA

One should always eat muffins quite calmly. It is the only way to eat them.

—Oscar Wilde, The Importance of Being Earnest

English "tea" refers to both a drink and a social ritual. Tea the drink is the preferred remedy for exhaustion, ennui, a row with one's partner, a rainy morning, or a slow afternoon. English tea is served strong and milky; if you want it any other way, say so. (Aficionados always pour the milk before the tea so as not to scald it.)

Tea the social ritual centers around a meal. Afternoon **high tea** includes cooked meats, salad, sandwiches, and pastries. "Tea" in the north of England refers to the evening meal, often served with a huge pot of tea. **Cream tea,** a specialty of Cornwall and Devon, includes toast, shortbread, crumpets (a much tastier sort of English muffin), scones, and jam, accompanied by delicious clotted cream (a cross between whipped cream and butter). Most Brits take short tea breaks each day, mornings ("elevenses") and afternoons (around 4pm).

London hotels serve afternoon set teas, often hybrids of the cream and high varieties, which are expensive and sometimes disappointing. You might order single items from the menu instead of the full set to avoid a sugar overdose. Cafés often serve a simpler tea (pot of tea, scone, preserves, and butter) for a lower price.

Louis, 32 Heath St., NW3 (tel. (01) 435 9908). This intimate Hungarian confectionary and tea room thrills with finger-licking Florentine (a candy conglomerate of almonds, cherries, and chocolate) £1.80. A variety of cakes, tarts, and teas are also available. Open daily 9:30am-6pm.

Georgian Restaurant, Harrods, Knightsbridge, SW1 (tel. 730 1234). Tube: Knightsbridge. A carefully staged event. Revel in bourgeois satisfaction as you demurely enjoy your expensive set tea inside or out on the terrace (£10.50). Tea served daily indoors 3:30-5:15pm.

The Muffin Man, 12 Wrights La., W8 (tel 937 6652). Tube: High St. Kensington. Everything you dreamed a tearoom could be: ruffled white curtains, flowered tablecloths, ferns galore, and a side patio. Simply delightful. Set cream tea £3.80. High tea £4.70. Min. £1.50 from 12:30-2:30pm. Open Mon.-Sat. 8am-5:30pm.

The Orangery Tea Room, Kensington Palace, Kensington Gardens, W8 (tel. 376 0239). Tube: High St. Kensington. Light meals and tea served in the marvelously airy Orangery built for Queen Anne in 1705. Two fruit scones with clotted cream and jam £3.15. Pot of tea £1.35. Trundle through the gardens afterward, smacking your lips. Open daily 10am-6pm.

Savoy, Strand, WC2 (tel 836 4343). The elegance of this music-accompanied tea is well worth the splurge. (Don't eat anything the day you go—you'll get as much as you can eat, and more, at the Savoy.) Enjoy the leisurely luxury. Set tea £14.85. Tea served daily 3-5:30pm.

WINE BARS

John Mortimer's fictional barrister Horace Rumpole, who drinks every afternoon at Pommeroy's Wine Bar, habitually orders a bottle of "Château Thames Embankment." Unlike Rumpole's brand, much of the wine served in London's sleek wine bars lives up to neither its price nor its pedigree. Wine bars tend to be dominated by people still in their workclothes (pinstripes and pumps). Most wine bars serve interesting, if expensive, continental food (main dishes around £6). Consume wine by the glass or by the bottle, but watch out for places with skimpy glasses—unfortunately a common ailment.

Balls Brothers, 2 Old Change Ct., St. Paul's Churchyard, EC4 (tel. 236 9921). Tube: St. Paul's. London's oldest wine bar chain supplies convincing atmosphere and dependability to bankers and tourists. Glasses of wine from £1.85. Also at Cheapside (tube: St. Paul's), Threadneedle St. (tube: Bank), Liverpool St., St. Mary's at Hill (tube: Monument) and Hay's Galleria, Tooley St., Southwark (tube: London Bridge). Open Mon.-Fri. noon-10:30pm.

Basil's, 8 Basil St., SW1. Tube: Knightsbridge. Good food in a relaxed setting, featuring some fine Australian and New Zealand wines. Its placid atmosphere is a relief after the upmarket scene in most wine bars. Live jazz Wed. and Fri. 7-11pm. Open Mon.-Fri. noon-3pm and 5:30-11pm, Sat. noon-3pm.

Downs Wine Bar, Arch 166, Bohemia Pl., E8 (tel. (0181) 986 4325). Bus #22 or 38 to Hackney Central BR station. Just off Mare St. Way out in the East End, but worth the trip to a relaxed bar frequented by casual locals. Built underneath the railway arches (trains occasionally rumble overhead), but cozy and tasteful. Simple pasta dishes hover around £6. House wine £7.25 per bottle, £1.60 for a glass. Open daily noon-3pm and 5-11pm.

Le Café Des Amis, Hanover Pl., WC2. Tube: Covent Garden. Gourmet food and drink served in a cozy brick alleyway northeast of Covent Garden. Phenomenal cheeseboard selection; cheese by the plateful £4.95. Desserts £3-3.50. Entrees £7-10. House wine £8.45 per bottle, £1.75 per glass. Open Mon.-Sat. noon-11pm.

Simpson's, 38½ Cornhill, EC3 (tel. 626 9985). Tube: Bank. Glistens with shiny brass and shiny wooden benches polished by countless besuited bottoms. Steak-and-kidney pie £3.95, spotted dick (steamed sponge pudding with raisins) £1.50. Wine from £1.80 per glass. Open Mon.-Fri. 11:30am-3pm.

Solange's Brasserie, 11 St. Martin's Ct., WC2. Tube: Leicester Sq. Between St. Martin's La. and Charing Cross Rd. French music, wine, menu, and accents. Desserts £3-3.50. Carafe £3.95. Service charge 12.5%. Open Mon.-Fri. noon-3pm and 5:30pm-midnight, Sat. 5:30pm-midnight.

■ Sights

Try to resist the temptation to pack every famous edifice and museum into your itinerary, whatever the length. Be realistic. Take a moment between monument-hopping to sit down in a pub or on a bench to get a second wind and plot your next move. You don't need to drag yourself to a major sight just because you feel you should. You could spend a lifetime in London just doing what interests you.

Because London is both a horizontal and a vertical city—the center having spread outwards, while new skyscrapers were built over old Roman ruins over the years—some of the most meaningful "sight-seeing" you can do is just to walk down the city streets. Hidden in and around the main sights can be found a serene chapel or an immense carnival, a museum of clocks, a deer park, an Indian film festival, or an exhibition of Masai arms.

Many if not most sights charging admission offer discounts to students (with ID), seniors, and children, often labelled together as "concessions." To avoid the crowds, try to get started as early as possible. If you're under financial constraints, remember that many of the best sights in London—including parks, historic buildings, and museums—are absolutely free.

TOURING

The characteristic of London is that you never go where you wish nor do what you wish, and that you always wish to be somewhere else than where you are.

—Sydney Smith, 1818

A good city tour can introduce you to the highlights of London, enabling you to decide where to focus your energies.

The **London Transport Sight-seeing Tour** (tel. 222 1234) provides a convenient, albeit cursory, overview of London's attractions from a double-decker bus. Tours lasting 1½ hrs. depart from Baker St., Haymarket (near Piccadilly Circus),Marble Arch (Speaker's Corner), and Victoria St. (near the station), and include Buckingham Palace, the Houses of Parliament, Westminster Abbey, the Tower of London, St. Paul's, and Piccadilly Circus. (Tours daily every ½hr. 9:30am-5:30pm; £9, under 16 £5. Pay the bus conductor.) Longer day trips are also available. For a different perspective, London Transport also operates **London by Night,** which whizzes by London's floodlit landmarks. It departs 7pm or 9pm from Victoria Station (£6, under 14 £4). Several ordinary buses also give a stunning view of the city; get the free *Central London Bus Guide* and pick a scenic route; bus #15 is an especially good bet.

Walking tours can fill in the specifics of London that bus tours run right over; with a good guide, a tour can be as entertaining as it is informative. Among the best are **The Original London Walks** (tel. 624 3978; £4, £3 for students and HI members, accompanied children under 15 free); **Historical Tours of London** (tel. (081) 668 4019; £4.50, concessions £3.50); and **City Walks of London** (tel. 700 6931), whose tours include the Londons of Shakespeare, Dickens, or the Beatles, "Legal London," and "The Trail of Jack the Ripper" (£4, concessions £3, accompanied children under 12 free). Leaflets for these and others are all too available in hotels and tourist information centers. For meeting times and details, see the "Around Town" section of the weekly *Time Out* magazine.

If glancing at London from the top of a bus is unsatisfactory, and locomotion by your own two feet seems daunting, a tour led by **The London Bicycle Tour Company** (tel. 928 6838) may be the happy medium. They offer two Sun. tours: the morning Greenwich Market excursion and the afternoon East End tour. Both depart from 56 Upper Ground, SE1 (Sun. 10am and 2:30pm, approximately 3 hrs, £9.95; independent bike £6.95 per day.)

Whether you tour alone or with a group, pay attention to the user-friendly land-marks around you. Kind-hearted souls have conveniently labeled and catalogued the unwieldy city. Since 1867, the historically minded have been marking the houses of prominent personages with Blue Plaques (see Appendix for list of Blue Plaque Houses). Oval plaques divide the city into administrative wards. Insurance compa-nies used to put firemarks on houses to identify insured houses to firemen. The red metal mailboxes bear the initials (frilly to the point of indecipherability) of the sov-ereign at the time of their making. K London's public squares, shopfronts, drinking fountains, and even wooden benches capture a fascinating record of the city's history.

■■■ WESTMINSTER ABBEY

Think how many royal bones
Sleep within this heap of stones;
For here they lie, had realms and lands,
That now want strength to stir their hands.

—*Francis Beaumont*

Neither a cathedral nor a parish church, Westminster Abbey (tube: Westminster) is a "royal peculiar," controlled directly by the Crown and outside the jurisdiction of the Church of England. As both the site of every royal coronation since 1066 and the final resting place for an imposing assortment of sovereigns, politicians, poets, and artists, the Abbey functions as a cross between a national church and a national honor roll. Burial in the abbey is the greatest and rarest official honor in Britain; over the last 200 years, space has become so limited that many coffins stand upright under the pavement.

Although the Abbey was consecrated by King Edward the Confessor on 28 December 1065, only the Pyx Chamber and the Norman Undercroft (now the West-minster Abbey Treasure Museum) survive from the original structure. Most of the present abbey was erected by Henry III during the 13th century to honor Edward. However, most of the stone visible in in the Abbey today is actually refacing which dates from the 18th century, as do the two **West Front Towers,** designed and built by Sir Christopher Wren and his Baroque pupil, Hawksmoor. The North Entrance, completed after 1850, is the youngest part of the Abbey. The entrance's Victorian stonework includes carved figures of dragons and griffins.

In the Abbey's narrow **nave,** the highest in all of England, a slab of Belgian marble marks the **Grave of the Unknown Warrior,** the one part of the Abbey no one may tread upon. Here the body of a World War I soldier is buried in soil from the battle-fields of France. A piece of green marble engraved with the words "Remember Win-ston Churchill" sits nearby, rather than among fellow prime ministers in Statesmen's Aisle. Parliament placed it here 25 years after the Battle of Britain, perhaps prompted by pangs of regret that Churchill's body lay buried in Bladon and not in the Abbey's hall of fame.

At the foot of the **Organ Loft,** a memorial to Sir Isaac Newton sits next to the grave of Lord Kelvin. Franklin Roosevelt, David Lloyd George, Lord and Lady Baden-Powell of Boy Scout fame, and the presumptive David Livingstone number among the elect remembered in the nave. "Rare Ben Jonson" is buried upright; on his deathbed he proclaimed, "Six feet long by two feet wide is too much for me. Two feet by two feet will do for all I want." On the hour, the Dean of the Abbey climbs the stairs of the pulpit and offers a timely prayer to this distinguished captive audience.

To see the rest of the abbey, visitors must enter through a gate at the end of the north aisle of the nave and pay admission (see below). **Musicians' Aisle,** just beyond this gate, contains the graves of the Abbey's most accomplished organists, John Blow and Henry Purcell, as well as memorials to the composers Elgar, Britten, Vaughan Williams, and William Walton.

Statesmen's Aisle, in the early Gothic north transept, has the most eclectic collection of memorials. Prime Ministers Disraeli and Gladstone couldn't stand each other in life, but in death their figures stand in symmetry flanking a large memorial to Sir Peter Warren, alongside Peel, Castlereagh, Palmerston, and others. Sir Francis Vere's Elizabethan tomb in the southeast corner of the transept features the cracked shells of his armor held above his body. A strange paving stone in front of the memorial bears no exalted name, only the unsentimental inscription, "Stone coffin underneath."

The **High Altar,** directly south of the north transept, has been the scene of coronations and royal weddings since 1066. Anne of Cleves, Henry VIII's fourth wife, lies in a tomb on the south side of the sanctuary, just before the altar. A series of crowded choir chapels fills the space east of the north transept.

Beyond these chapels stands the **Chapel of Henry VII** (built 1503-12), perhaps England's most upstanding piece of late perpendicular architecture. Every one of its magnificently carved wooden stalls, reserved for the Knights of the Order of the Bath, features a colorful headpiece bearing the chosen personal statement of its occupant. The lower sides of the seats, which fold up to support those standing during long services, were the only part of the design left to the carpenters' discretion; they feature cartoon-like images of wives beating up their husbands and other more pagan stories. Lord Nelson's stall was no. 20, on the south side. Latter-day members of the order include bellicose Americans Ronald Reagan and Norman Schwarzkopf. The chapel walls sport 95 saints, including the once-lovely Bernadette, who after praying to be saved from a multitude of suitors, grew a beard overnight. The chapel's elaborate ceiling was hand-carved after it had been erected. Henry VII and his wife Elizabeth, the least legitimate couple ever to ascend to England's throne, lie at the very end of the chapel. Charles II exhumed Oliver Cromwell's body from this part of the Abbey in 1661 and had it hanged and beheaded. Today only a simple memorial to Cromwell remains. Protestant Queen Elizabeth I (in the north aisle) and the Catholic cousin she had beheaded, Mary Queen of Scots (in the south aisle) are buried on opposite sides of the Henry VII chapel. Both, the verger insists, "put Britain back on its feet again."

The **Royal Air Force (RAF) Chapel,** at the far east end, commemorates the Battle of Britain. A hole in the wall in the northeast corner of the Air Force memorial, damage from a German bomb, has been deliberately left unrepaired.

Behind the High Altar, in the **Chapel of St. Edward the Confessor,** rests the Coronation Chair, on which all but two (Edward V and Edward VIII) English monarchs since 1308 have been crowned. The chair rests on the ancient **Stone of Scone** ("skoon"), rumored to be inextricably linked to the government of Britain. The legendary stone (some say it was the biblical Jacob's pillow) was used in the coronation of ancient Scottish kings; James I took it to London to represent the Union, and in the 1950s it was briefly reclaimed by Scottish nationalists. During the Second World War, it was hidden from possible capture by Hitler, and rumor has it that only Churchill, Roosevelt, the Prime Minister of Canada, and the two workers who moved the stone knew of its whereabouts. For coronation convenience, the chair sits next to the seven-foot-long State Sword and the shield of Edward III.

Numerous monarchs are interred in the chapel, from Henry III (d. 1272) to George II (d. 1760). Edward I had himself placed in an unsealed crypt here, in case he was needed again to fight the Scots; his mummy was carried as a standard by the English army as it tried to conquer Scotland. An engraving by William Blake commemorates the moment in 1774 when the Royal Society of Antiquaries opened this coffin in order to assess the body's state of preservation. Sick persons hoping to be cured would spend nights at the base of the Shrine of St. Edward the Confessor, at the center of the chapel. The king purportedly wielded healing powers during his life, and dispensed free medical care to hundreds with the laying on of his hands.

Visitors befuddled by the graves of arcane English monarchs may find the names on the graves and plaques in the **Poets' Corner** more recognizable. This little shrine celebrates those dead, canonized, and anthologized in the annals of English

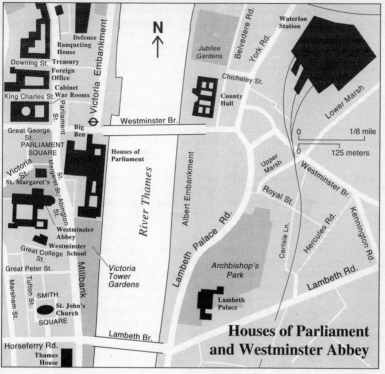

N

0   1/8 mile
0   125 meters

**Houses of Parliament
and Westminster Abbey**

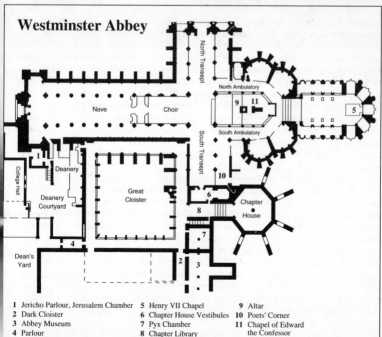

Westminster Abbey

North Transept

North Ambulatory

Nave   Choir

South Ambulatory

9   11

5

South Transept

College Hall

Deanery

Deanery
Courtyard

Great
Cloister

10

6

Chapter
House

8

7

Dean's
Yard

4

2   3

1 Jericho Parlour, Jerusalem Chamber   5 Henry VII Chapel   9 Altar
2 Dark Cloister   6 Chapter House Vestibules 10 Poets' Corner
3 Abbey Museum   7 Pyx Chamber   11 Chapel of Edward
4 Parlour   8 Chapter Library   the Confessor

WESTMINSTER ABBEY

literature. It begins with Geoffrey Chaucer, who was originally buried in the abbey in 1400—the short Gothic tomb you see today in the east wall of the transept was not erected until 1556. The lower classes of the dead poets' society, and those leading "unconventional" life-styles, often had to wait a while before getting a permanent spot in the Abbey; even the Bard remained on the waiting list until 125 years after his mortal coil was shuffled off. Oscar Wilde will be honored with a long overdue monument in Poet's Corner in 1995, the centenary of his conviction for homosexual activities. Floor panels commemorate Tennyson, T.S. Eliot, Dylan Thomas, Henry James, Robert Browning, Lewis Carroll, Lord Byron, and poets of World War I, all at the foot of Chaucer's tomb. Each one bears an appropriate description or image for puzzle solvers: D.H. Lawrence's publishing mark (a phoenix) or T.S. Eliot's symbol of death ("the fire and the rose are one").

The south wall bears tributes to Edmund Spenser, John Milton, and Ben "Johnson." A partition wall divides the south transept, its east side graced with the graves of Samuel Johnson and actor David Garrick, its west side with busts of William Wordsworth, Samuel Taylor Coleridge, and Robert Burns, in addition to a full-length William Shakespeare which overshadows the tiny plaques memorializing Jane Austen and the Brontë sisters. On the west wall of the transept, Handel's massive memorial looms over his grave next to the resting place of prolific Charles Dickens. On this side of the wall, you'll also find the grave of Rudyard Kipling and a memorial to that morbid Dorset farm boy, Thomas Hardy. Two non-poets are inexplicably included here: Old Parr, who reportedly lived to the age of 152, and "Spot" Ward, who once healed George II of a thumb injury.

The Abbey's tranquil **cloister** reposes in a special peace of its own. The entrance in the northeast corner dates from the 13th century, the rest of it from the 14th. The **Chapter House,** east down a passageway off the cloister, has one of the best-preserved medieval tile floors in Europe. The windows in the ceiling depict scenes from the Abbey's history. The King's Great Council used the room as its chamber in 1257, and the House of Commons used it as a meeting-place in the 16th century. Even today, it is the government and not the abbey that administers the Chapter House and the adjacent **Pyx Chamber,** once the Royal Treasury and now a plate museum.

Royal effigies (used instead of actual corpses for lying-in-state ceremonies) live in the **Westminster Abbey Treasure Museum.** The oldest, that of Edward III, has a lip permanently warped by the stroke that killed him. Those who knew Admiral Nelson found his effigy almost supernaturally accurate—perhaps because his mistress arranged his hair. The museum also includes an exhibit on the history of the Abbey as well as some historical oddities, including a Middle English lease to Chaucer and the much-abused sword of Henry V. (Chapter House open daily 10am-5pm; Pyx Chamber and museum open daily 10:30am-4pm. Combined admission £1, concessions 80p, children 50p.)

Enter through the cloisters on Great College St. to visit the 900-year-old **College Garden,** the oldest garden in England. (Open April-Sept. Tues. and Thurs. 10am-6pm; Oct.-March Tues. and Thurs. 10am-4pm; admission 20p; band concerts July-Aug. 12:30-2pm.) The **Brass Rubbing Centre** (tel. 222 2085) in the cloisters may also be worth a visit (open Mon.-Sat. 9am-5pm).

Those who enjoy amazingly informative discussions about architecture, fun gossip about the dead, and just a little sermonizing should take the excellent, all-inclusive Abbey Guided Super Tour (1½hr., £7) which takes visitors to otherwise inaccessible parts of the Abbey. (Tours depart from the Enquiry Desk in the nave Mon.-Fri. at 10am, 10:30am, 11am, 2pm, 2:30pm, and 3pm (except Fri.); Sat. at 10am, 11am, and 12:30pm.) To book one, inquire at the Abbey desk, call 222 7110, or write to Super Tours, 20 Dean's Yard, London SW1P 3PA. Portable tape-recorded commentaries in assorted tongues are available for £6. Photography is permitted only on Wednesday 6-7:45pm. (Westminster Abbey nave open Mon.-Sat. 7:30am-6pm, Wed. 6-7:45pm, Sun. in between services; free. Chapels and transepts open Mon.-Fri. 9am-4:45pm, also Wed. 6-7:45pm, Sat. 9am-2:45pm and 3:45-5:45pm;

admission £4, concessions £2, children £1; all parts of the abbey free Wed. 6-7:45pm.)

■■■ WESTMINSTER

The old city of Westminster, now a borough of London, once served as haven to a seething nest of criminals who sought sanctuary in the Abbey. A slum clearance program during Victoria's reign transformed the region into the array of brick and marble it is today. For the past 1000 years, Westminster has been the center of political and religious power in England. On weekdays, the streets still bear the traffic of civil service workers, who desert the area on weekends, leaving it to the crowds of tourists who flock here to see some of London's more monumental architecture.

In the environs of Westminster Abbey, **St. Margaret's** provides shelter from the storm. St. Margaret's has served as the parish church of the House of Commons since 1614, when Protestant MPs feared Westminster Abbey was about to become Catholic. John Milton, Samuel Pepys, and Winston Churchill were married here. The stained-glass window to the north of the entrance depicts a blind Milton dictating *Paradise Lost* to one of his dutiful daughters, while the stunning east window, made in Holland in 1501, honors the marriage of Catherine of Aragon to Prince Arthur. The post-WWII John Piper windows on the south side provide a marked contrast; entitled "Spring in London," they aptly consist of shades of gray. Beneath the high altar lies the headless body of Sir Walter Raleigh, who was executed across the street in 1618. The inscription on his memorial respectfully asks readers not to "reflect on his errors." William Caxton, Britain's first and most famous printer, is also buried here (open daily 9:30am-5pm when services are not being held).

On the south side of the abbey cluster the buildings of the **Westminster School,** founded as a part of the Abbey. References to the school date as far back as the 14th century, but Queen Elizabeth officially founded it in 1560. The arch in Dean's Yard is pitted with the carved initials of generations of England's most privileged schoolboys, among them Ben Jonson, John Dryden, John Locke, Christopher Wren, Edward Gibbon, and A.A. Milne.

The 14th-century **Jewel Tower,** a surviving tower of the medieval Westminster Palace, stands by the southeastern end of the Abbey, across from the Houses of Parliament. Formerly Richard III's loot warehouse and wardrobe, and later the Weights and Measures office, it now contains eclectic exhibits ranging from bits of the original Westminster Hall to a Norman sword dredged from the moat. (Tower open daily April-Sept. 10am-1pm and 2-6pm; Oct.-March 10am-1pm and 2-4pm. Admission £2.10, concessions £1.55, children under 16 £1.05.)

The **Victoria Tower Gardens,** immediately south of the Houses of Parliament, offer a secluded view of the Thames. Militant suffragettes Emmeline Pankhurst and her daughter are memorialized in the northwest corner of the gardens, and sticking out like a technicolor fang in the southern end is a Gothic-revival water fountain, opposite a bronze cast of Auguste Rodin's *The Burghers of Calais*. Just northeast of the Houses of Parliament, a dramatic statue of Boadicea commands attention at the corner of Victoria Embankment and Bridge Street. Queen Boadicea lead the local Iceni tribe in an English revolt against the Romans in 60 AD.

Four assertive corner towers distinguish former church **St. John the Evangelist,** now a chamber-music concert hall in nearby Smith Square, off Millbank at the south end of the Victoria Tower Gardens. Queen Anne, whose imagination was taxed by the task of directing the architects hired to build the 50 new churches she had founded by an Act of Parliament, supposedly upended a footstool and told Thomas Archer to build the church in its image. Dickens likened Archer's effort to a "petrified monster." Chamber music, choir, and orchestra concerts take place daily; tickets range from £4-15, with concessions starting as low as £3. (Box office tel. 222 1061; call ahead for details and concert times.) Any flurry of activity around the square is likely to be connected with no. 31, where the Central Office of the Conservative Party lurks, ready to swing into re-action down the road.

At Ashley Place, a few blocks down Victoria St. from Westminster proper is **Westminster Cathedral.** Not to be confused with the Anglican abbey, the Cathedral is the headquarters of the Roman Catholic church in Britain. The architecture is Christian Byzantine, in pointed contrast to the Gothic abbey. The structure was completed in 1903, but the interior has yet to be finished, and the blackened brick of the domes contrasts dramatically with the swirling marble of the lower walls. A lift carries visitors to the top of the rocket-like, striped brick bell tower for a decent view of the Houses of Parliament, the river, and Kensington. 1995 will witness the church's centenary celebration. (Lift open daily 9am-5pm; admission £2, concessions £1, families £5; cathedral open daily 7am-7pm).

■ ■ ■ THE HOUSES OF PARLIAMENT

The Houses of Parliament (tube: Westminster), oft-imagined in foggy silhouette against the Thames, have become London's visual trademark. For the classic view captured by Claude Monet, walk about halfway over Westminster Bridge, preferably at dusk and in purple fog. Like the government offices along Whitehall, the Houses of Parliament occupy the former site of a royal palace. Only Jewel Tower (see Westminster) and Westminster Hall (to the left of St. Stephen's entrance on St. Margaret St.) survive from the original palace, which was destroyed by a fire on October 16, 1834. Sir Charles Barry and A.W.N. Pugin won a competition for the design of the new houses. From 1840 to 1888, Barry built a hulking, symmetrical block that Pugin ornamented with tortured imitations of late medieval decoration—"Tudor details on a classic body," Pugin later sneered, before dying of insanity.

The immense complex blankets eight acres and includes more than 1000 rooms and 100 staircases. Space is nevertheless so inadequate that Members of Parliament (MPs) cannot have private offices or staff, and the archives—the original copies of every Act of Parliament passed since 1497—are stuffed into Victoria Tower, the large tower to the south. A flag flown from the tower (a signal light after dusk) indicates that Parliament is in session.

You can hear **Big Ben** in the slightly smaller northern tower but you can't see it; it's actually neither the tower nor the clock but the 14-ton bell that tolls the hours. Ben is most likely named after the robustly proportioned Sir Benjamin Hall, who served as Commissioner of Works when the bell was cast and hung in1858. Over the years Big Ben (the bell) has developed a crack. Each of the Roman numerals on the clock face measures two feet in length; the minute hands, 14 feet. The mechanism moving the hands is still wound manually. The familiar 16-note tune that precedes the top-of-the-hour toll is a selection from Handel's *Messiah*.

Unfortunately, access to Westminster Hall and the Houses of Parliament has been restricted since a bomb killed an MP in 1979. To get a **guided tour** (Mon.-Thurs.) or a seat at **Question Time** when the Prime Minister attends (Mon.-Thurs. 2:30-3:30pm), you need to obtain tickets—available on a limited basis from your embassy—or an introduction from an MP. Because demand for these tickets is extremely high, the most likely way of getting into the building is to queue to attend a debate when Parliament is in session. However, tours for overseas visitors can also be arranged by sending a written request to the Public Information Office, 1 Derby Gate, Westminster, SW1. The House of Commons Visitors' Gallery (for "Distinguished and Ordinary Strangers") is open during extraordinary hours (Mon.-Thurs. 2:30-10pm, Fri. 9:30am-3pm). The House of Lords Visitors' Gallery is often easier to access (open Mon.-Wed. 2:30pm-late, Thurs. 3pm-late, Fri. 11am-4pm). Visitors should arrive early, and be prepared to wait in the long queues by St. Stephen's Gate (on the left for the Commons, on the right for the Lords; free). Those willing to sacrifice the roar of the debate for smaller, more focused business can attend meetings of any of the various committees by jumping the queue and going straight up to the entrance. For times of committee meetings each week, call the House of Commons Information Office (tel. 219 4272). Both houses' business is announced daily in the major newspapers, and in a weekly schedule by St. Stephen's Gate. Many of the debates in both Houses are televised by the BBC—Americans will be astonished by the mayhem that ensues during Question Time. Note that the Visitors' Galleries are closed when the Houses are not in session: Easter week, summer recess (end of July-mid-Oct.), and a three-week winter recess during Christmas time.

After entering St. Stephen's Gate and submitting to an elaborate security check, you will be standing in St. Stephen's Hall. This chapel is where the House of Commons used to sit. In the floor are four brass markers where the Speaker's Chair stood. Charles I, in his ill-fated attempt to arrest five MPs, sat here in the place of the Speaker in 1641. No sovereign has entered the Commons since.

To the left from the Central Lobby and up the stairs is the **House of Commons' Strangers' Gallery.** Destroyed during the Blitz, the rebuilt chamber is modest, even anticlimactic. Most traditional features still remain, such as two red lines fixed two sword-lengths apart, which debating members may not cross. The Government party (the party with the most MP's in the House) sits to the Speaker's right, and the Opposition to his left. There are intentionally not enough benches in the chamber to seat all 650 members, to add a sense of huddled drama to the few occasions when all are present. Members vote by filing into **division lobbies** parallel to the chamber: ayes into the west, nays into the east. As they enter the chamber itself, they pass under **Churchill's Arch,** the half-destroyed stone doorway that the statesman insisted be left untouched as a reminder of Britain's war losses.

To enter the Lords' Gallery, go back through the Central Lobby, and pass through the Peers' corridor, whose walls are painted with scenes of Charles I's downfall. The ostentation of the **House of Lords,** dominated by the sovereign's Throne of State under a gilt canopy, contrasts with the sober, green-upholstered Commons' Chamber. Elaborate wall carvings divert attention from the speakers on the floor. The bewigged Lord Chancellor presides over the House from his seat on the Woolsack, stuffed with wool from all nations of the Kingdom and Commonwealth—harking back to a time when wool, like the Lords, was more vital to Britain. Yet the upper chamber is not entirely vestigial; it may amend bills and serves as the final court of appeal.

Outside the Houses is the Old Palace Yard, site of the untimely demises of Sir Walter Raleigh and the Gunpowder Plotter Guy Fawkes (the palace's cellars are still ceremonially searched before every opening of Parliament). To the north squats **Westminster Hall** (rebuilt around 1400), where high treason trials, including those of Thomas More, Fawkes, and Charles I, were held until 1825. The New Palace Yard is a good place to espy your favorite MPs as they enter the complex through the Members' entrance just north of Westminster Hall.

■■■ WHITEHALL

Whitehall was born in 1245 as York Place, residence for the Archbishops of York. Cardinal Wolsey enlarged York Place into a palace he thought fit for a king. Henry VIII agreed, and, after beheading Wolsey for treason, moved into his new London apartments of state, rechristened Whitehall in 1530. This gargantuan palace stretched all the way to Somerset House on the Strand, but William II resented an unnamed diplomat's description of Whitehall as "the biggest, most hideous place in all Europe," and relocated to a shiny new Kensington Palace. The rejected palace burned in 1698, and since then "Whitehall" (tube: Westminster or Charing Cross), stretching from Parliament St. to Trafalgar Sq., has become a synonym for the British civil service.

Conveniently enough, **Ten Downing Street** lies just steps up Parliament St. from the Houses. Sir George Downing, ex-Ambassador to The Hague (and the second person to graduate from Harvard College), built this house in 1681. Sir Robert Walpole, who is best remembered for his role in a series of vicious political satires, made it his official residence (as Prime Minister) in 1732. The exterior of "Number Ten" is decidedly unimpressive, especially from a distance, but behind the famous door spreads an extensive political network. The Chancellor of the Exchequer forecasts economic recovery from No. 11 Downing St., and the Chief Whip of the House of Commons plans Party campaigns at No. 12. Together, these three houses contain more than 200 rooms. Visitors have long been banned from entering Downing St., but Margaret Thatcher's decision to build threateningly protective gates for the Whitehall end did little to endear her to the British public.

The **Cabinet War Rooms** lurk at the end of King Charles St., near Horse Guards Rd. (see Museums). The rigorously formal **Cenotaph** honoring the war dead, usually decked with crested wreaths, stands where Parliament St. turns into Whitehall.

Just off Whitehall, at 6 Derby Gate, **New Scotland Yard** will probably fall short of crime-hounds' expectations. The second of three incarnations of the lair of those unimaginative detectives humbled by Sherlock Holmes and Hercule Poirot is nothing more than two buildings connected by an arch which currently contain government offices. The original Yard was at the top of Whitehall, on Great Scotland Yard, and the current New Scotland Yard is on Victoria St.

Henry VIII's **wine cellar** was one of the few parts of the palace spared in the fire of 1698. In 1953, the government erected the massive Ministry of Defense Building (nicknamed the Quadragon), just to the north, over Henry's cache. The cellar had to be relocated deeper into the ground to accommodate the new structure. Technically, visitors may view the cellar, but permission is dauntingly difficult to obtain (apply in writing to the Department of the Environment or the Ministry of Defense with a compelling story). Near the statue of General Gordon in the gardens behind the Ministry of Defense Building, you'll find the remnants of Queen Mary's terrace, built for Queen Mary II. The bottom of the steps leading from the terrace mark the 17th-century water level, reminding observers of the extent to which river transport determined the locations of 16th- and 17th-century buildings.

The 1622 **Banqueting House** (corner of Horse Guards Ave. and Whitehall), one of the few intact masterpieces of Inigo Jones, was the first true classical Renaissance building in England, and the only part of the original palace to survive the fire that consumed Whitehall. The Stuart kings held elaborate and narcissistic masques and feasts here, but the festivities ended on January 27, 1649 when King Charles I, draped in black velvet, was led out its doorway and beheaded. The allegorical paintings on the 60-foot-high ceiling (ironically the story of the happy reigns of James I and Charles I) are the handiwork of Rubens. A cautious James II supposedly placed the weather vane on top of the building to see if a favorable wind was blowing for William of Orange. From 1724 to 1890, the Banqueting House served as a Chapel Royal. These days the hall sees no executions, just some harmless state dinners (behind bulletproof glass) and the occasional concert. (Tel. 839 7569, open Mon.-Sat. 10am-5pm, but closed for government functions. Admission £2.90, concessions £2.25, children £1.90.)

On the west side of Whitehall north of Downing St. stand the **Horse Guards,** where two photogenic mounted members of the Household Cavalry keep watch daily from 10am to 4pm, although it is unclear what they are guarding—especially since the sentries themselves require the protection of constables, who usher tourists out of harm's way during the daily changing of the guard. (The head guard meticulously inspects the troops Mon.-Sat. at 11am and Sun. at 10am. The guard dismounts, with some fanfare, daily at 4pm. Crowds are usually thinner here than at Buckingham Palace. Closed Sat. in June.) Through the gates lies Horse Guards Parade, a large court (opening onto St. James's Park) from which the bureaucratic array of different architectural styles that make up Whitehall can be seen. **Beating the Retreat,** a must for lovers of pomp and circumstance, takes place here three or four evenings a week during the first two weeks of June (call 930 4466 for dates and ticket information). Beating the Retreat is merely a warm-up for **Trooping the Color,** in which the Queen gives the royal salute to the Root Guards. Trooping the Color takes place on the second Saturday in June and is, apparently, "the high point of London's ceremonial year."

■■■ THE MALL AND ST. JAMES'S

Just north of Buckingham Palace and the Mall, up Stable Yard or Marlborough Rd., stands **St. James's Palace,** the residence of the monarchy from 1660 to 1668 and again from 1715 to 1837 (tube: Green Park). The scene of many a three-volume novel and Regency romance, over the years this palace has hosted tens of thousands of the young girls whose families "presented" them at Court. Ambassadors and the elite set of barristers known as "Queen's Counsel" are still received "into the Court of St. James's." Only Henry VIII's gateway and clock tower and a pair of parading guards at the foot of St. James's St. still hark back to the Tudor palace; the guards' bayoneted rifles are a little too modern for comfort. You can visit Inigo Jones's fine **Queen's Chapel,** built in 1626, by attending Sunday services at 8:30 and 11:15am (Oct.-July). King Charles I slept for four hours in the palace's guardroom before crossing St. James's Park to be executed at the Banqueting House in 1649.

Henry VIII declared **St. James's Park** London's first royal park in 1532. Ever since, the park has been one of London's favorite places for a stroll. The fenced-off peninsula at the east end of the park's pond, Duck Island, is the mating ground for thousands of waterfowl. Near the bridge spanning the pond, plaques describe the flocks of rare ducks, geese, and other flying things. St. James's is also a good place to discover that lawn chairs in England are not free—chairs have been hired out here since the 18th century (rental 80p). For a good view of the guards who change at Buckingham Palace, wait between the Victoria Memorial and St. James's Palace from about 10:40 to 11:25am. You might miss the band (it usually travels down Bird-cage walk from Wellington Barracks), but you will also avoid the swarm of tourists.

The high-rent district around the palace has also come to be called St. James's. Bordered by St. James's Park and Green Park to the south and Piccadilly to the north, it begins at an equestrian statue of notorious madman George III on Cockspur St. off Trafalgar Sq. **St. James's Street,** next to St. James's Palace, runs into **Pall Mall**—the name derives from "pail-mail," a 17th-century predecessor of the noble game of croquet. Until Buckingham Palace was built, today's **Mall** (rhymes with "pal") was merely an endless field for the King to play the game on. Lined with double rows of plane trees, the Mall grandly traverses the space from Trafalgar Sq. to Buckingham Palace (tube: Charing Cross). Two monuments to Queen Victoria contribute to the Mall's grandeur: the golden horses of the **Queen Victoria Memorial,** near Buckingham Palace, and the massive **Admiralty Arch** opening onto Trafalgar Sq. (most striking when floodlit on summer nights).

Along the north side of the Mall lie the imposing façades of grand houses, starting with **Carlton House Terrace,** demolished, rebuilt, and remodeled since Nash erected it along the Mall as part of the 18th-century Regent's Park route; the statue on the terrace memorializes the "Grand Old Duke of York." The building became the office of the Free French Forces from 1940 to 1945 under the leadership of General Charles de Gaulle. It now contains the Royal Society of Distinguished Scientists and, perhaps the most exciting addition to the St. James area, the avant-garde **Institute of Contemporary Arts** (see Museums, Film, and Theatre). The ICA was established in 1947 to provide British artists with the kinds of resources and facilities then available only at the Museum of Modern Art in New York, and has been located in Carlton House since 1968.

Farther down on the Mall is **Marlborough House,** built by Sir Christopher Wren in 1710, but much altered since. The former residence of Queen Mary and Edward VII, it is now a centre for administration of the Commonwealth, and contains guest quarters for Commonwealth dignitaries visiting London. On the other side of St. James's Palace from Marlborough House at Stable Yard Rd. is **Clarence House,** the official residence of the Queen Mother. Behind Clarence House at Cleveland Row is **Lancaster House,** a splendid and extremely solid residence built for the Duke of York in 1841, which now hosts government and royal receptions.

Pall Mall and St. James's St., together with Jermyn St., parallel to Pall Mall to the north, flank what is perhaps the last bastion of the classic, dressed-to-oppress upper-class English man. At 70-72 Jermyn he will buy his shirts at Turnbull and Asser (one of Churchill's custom-made "siren suits" is on display). His bowler will be from Lock & Co. (ask politely to see their sinister-looking head measuring device), and his bespoke shoes will be the craft of John Lobb. Berry & Co. wine merchants supply the madeira, and Cuban cigars should really be bought at Robert Lewis, where Churchill had an account for sixty years. Escape the patrician solemnity of the area at Alfred Dunhill, 30 Duke Street (entrance on Jermyn); lurking upstairs above the staid merchandise is a riotously sublime **tobacco museum** (tel. 499 9566; open by appointment).

These Regency storefronts rub elbows with a number of famous London coffeehouses-turned-clubs. The coffeehouses of the early 18th century, whose political life was painted so vividly by Addison and Steele in their journal *The Spectator,* were transformed by the 19th century into exclusive clubs for political and literary men of a particular social station. The chief Tory club, the Carlton, at 69 St. James's St., was bombed by the IRA not long ago. The chief Liberal club, the Reform at 104 Pall Mall, served as a social center of Parliamentary power. In 1823, a Prime Minister and the presidents of the Royal Academy and the Royal Society founded the Athenaeum, on Waterloo Pl., for scientific, literary, and artistic men. Gibbon, Hume, Burke, and Garrick belonged to the Whig Brooks, founded in 1764 (60 St. James's St.).

Behind the statue of the Duke of York in Waterloo Pl. stand monuments to the Crimean War and its heroine, Florence Nightingale, who, in addition to nursing soldiers, pioneered the development of statistical and visual representations of information.

Around the corner from St. James's Palace stand royal medallists Spink's, and Christie, Manson, and Wodds Fine Art Auctioneers—better known as **Christie's,** 8 King St. (tel. 839 9060; tube: Green Park). The pamphlet describing the furniture, historical documents, and artworks being auctioned is scintillating but costs £10. Auctions, open to the public, are held most weekdays at 10:30am. **Sotheby's** also holds fine arts auctions, at 34 Bond St. (tel. 493 8080; tube: Bond St. or Oxford Circus). Amuse yourself on a rainy afternoon by watching the dealers do their bidding.

Between aristocratic Jermyn St. and Piccadilly, you can enter **St. James's Church** (tube: Green Park or Piccadilly Circus), a postwar reconstruction by Sir Albert Richardson of what Wren considered his best parish church. The exterior is unremarkable, but the interior is well worth a visit. Blake was baptized here, in the typical Wren single room interior, with galleries surrounding the main space. The work of Grinling Gibbons, Wren's master-carver, can be seen in the delightful flowers, garlands, and cherubs of the reredos, organ casing, and font (church open Mon.-Sat. 10am-8pm, Sun. noon-6pm).

■■■ BUCKINGHAM PALACE

I must say, notwithstanding the expense which has been incurred in building the palace, no sovereign in Europe, I may even add, perhaps no private gentleman, is so ill-lodged as the king of this country.
—Duke of Wellington, 1828

When a freshly crowned Victoria moved from St. James's Palace in 1837, Buckingham Palace, built in 1825 by John Nash, had faulty drains and a host of other leaky difficulties (tube: Victoria, and walk up Buckingham Palace Rd.; Green Park and St. James's Park are also convenient). Home improvements were made, and now, when the flag is flying, the Queen is at home, and you can visit her home.

After a recent debate about the proper way to subsidize the monarchy's senselessly posh existence—and because funds are needed to rebuild Windsor castle, which went up in flames in November 1992—Buckingham Palace finally opened to the public. Sort of. For only two months a year (most likely August and September) for the next four years, the palace will remain open to hordes of tourists. Not all of the Palace will be laid open; the tour is well roped-off from the working offices and private apartments. But visitors are able to stroll through the Blue Drawing Room, the Throne Room, the Picture Gallery (filled with Rubens, Rembrandts, and Van Dycks), and the Music Room (where Mendelssohn played for Queen Victoria), as well as other stately rooms.

In the opulent White Drawing Room, notice the large mirror to the left of the fireplace; it conceals a door through which the Royal Family makes a grand appearance before a formal dinner. Critics of the palace suggest it looks less like the home or even the office of the Queen and more like a museum, thus diminishing much of the excitement of seeing a monarch's living quarters. Indeed, the monarch scuttles off to Balmoral to avoid the plague of tourists descending upon her immaculate residence (palace open Aug.-Sept.; admission £8, seniors £5.50, children £4).

The 20th-century façade on the Mall is spectacularly uninteresting; the Palace's best side, the garden front, is seldom seen by ordinary visitors as it is protected by the 40-acre spread where the Queen holds her garden parties. Nasty-looking spikes and barbed wire atop the walls are designed to stop occasional forays by the Queen's admirers or potential assassins.

If you happen to visit the Palace on an off month, try to catch the chart-topping Kodak Moment for London tourists—the **Changing of the Guard,** which takes place daily from April to July, and only on alternate days from August to March. This cutback in the winter spectacle is attributed to budget constraints, but is generally interpreted as an attempt on the army's part to manipulate public opinion in favor of increased spending on the military. The "Old Guard" marches from St. James's Palace down the Mall to Buckingham Palace, leaving at approximately 11:10am. The "New Guard" begins marching as early as 10:20am. When they meet at the central gates of the palace, the officers of the regiments then touch hands, symbolically exchanging keys, et voilà—the guard is changed. The soldiers gradually split up to relieve the guards currently protecting the palace. The ceremony moves to the beat of royal band music and the menacing clicks of thousands of cameras. In wet weather or on pressing state holidays, the Changing of the Guard does not occur. To witness the spectacle, show up well before 11:30am and stand directly in front of the palace. You can also watch along the routes of the troops prior to their arrival at the palace (10:40-11:25am) between the Victoria Memorial and St. James's Palace or along Birdcage Walk. Throughout the day, a couple of guards pace back and forth methodically in front of the palace.

In the extravagant **Trooping the Colour** ceremony, held on the Queen's official birthday, a Saturday in early June, the colors of a chosen regiment are paraded ceremonially before her and her family. The parade in honor of the Queen brings out luminaries mounted on horses while somewhat less influential types putter about in limousines with little golden crowns on top. The actual ceremony takes place at Horse Guards Parade, followed by a procession down the Mall to the Palace, where she reviews her Household Cavalry and appears on the balcony for a Royal Air Force fly-by. The best view of all this is on TV, but you might catch a glimpse of the Queen in person as she rides down the Mall. Tickets for the event must be obtained through the mail. Write well in advance to the Household Division HQ, Horse Guards, SW1. If you don't get a ticket for the event, you may receive one for one of the rehearsals on the two preceding Saturdays. Since the Queen does not need to rehearse, these tend to be noticeably less crowded.

Down the left side of the Palace, off Buckingham Gate, an enclosed passageway leads to the **Queen's Gallery**. Selected treasures from the royal collection fill the rooms of this modern suite. The exhibition changes every few months, but you can usually catch a few of Charles I's Italian masters, George IV's Dutch still-lifes, Prince Albert's primitives, and occasionally some of the Leonardo da Vinci drawings from Windsor. In 1995 a special collection of Fabergé eggs and baubles will be on display (open until Dec. 22, 1994 Tues.-Sat. 10am-5pm, Sun. 2-5pm; opening times for 1995 have yet to be determined; admission £3, seniors £2, under 17 £1.50, family £7.50).

Also off Buckingham Gate stands the curious **Royal Mews Museum** (tel. 493 3175), which houses the royal coaches and other historic royal riding implements (open until Dec. 22 Wed. noon-4pm, last admission 3:30pm; opening times for 1995 have yet to be determined; admission £3, seniors £2, under 17 £1.50, family £7.50). A combined pass for the Gallery and the Mews may be purchased (£5, seniors £3.50, under 17 £2.20, family £12).

Nearby, you can drop in on the **Guards Museum** (tel. 930 4466, ext.#3271) at Wellington Barracks on Birdcage Walk, off Buckingham Gate (open Mon.-Thurs., Sat.-Sun. 10am-4pm; admission £2, students and children £1.20). The courtyard outside Wellington Barracks is probably the only place where you'll ever see the Guards at relative ease.

■■■ TRAFALGAR SQUARE AND CHARING CROSS

Unlike many squares in London, **Trafalgar Square** (tube: Charing Cross), sloping down from the National Gallery at the center of a vicious traffic round-about, has been public land ever since the razing of several hundred houses made way for its construction in the 1830s. **Nelson's Column,** a fluted granite pillar, commands the square, with four majestic, beloved lions guarding the base. The monument and square commemorate Admiral Nelson, killed during his triumph over Napoleon's navy off Trafalgar in Spain (the monument's reliefs were cast from French cannons).

Floodlights bathe the square after dark, when it fills up with eager tourists and club kids trying to catch the proper night bus home. Enthusiastic, even rambunctious New Year's celebrations take place here, including universal indiscriminate kissing.

At the head of the square squats the ordering façade of the **National Gallery,** Britain's collection of Old Masters (see Museums). A competition to design a new extension to the gallery ended in Prince Charles's denouncement of the winning entry as a "monstrous carbuncle" on the face of London, and the subsequent selection of a new architect. Philadelphian Robert Venturi's wing to the west of the main building is now open; the mock columns and pillars that echo the old building and even Nelson's Column are much discussed and generally liked.

The church of **St. Martin-in-the-Fields,** on the northeastern corner of the square opposite the National Gallery, dates from the 1720s. Designer James Gibbs topped its templar classicism with a Gothic steeple. The interior, despite the gilded and chubby cherubim, is simple, its walls relatively uncluttered with monuments. St. Martin, which has its own world-renowned chamber orchestra, sponsors lunchtime and evening concerts, as well as a summer festival in mid-July (lunchtime concerts begin 1:05pm; box office in the bookshop open Mon.-Sat. 11:30am-7:30pm, Sun. 11am-6pm; bookings tel. 702 1377 daily 12:30-2:30pm and 4:30-6:30pm; tickets £4-14; see Entertainment—Music for more information). The crypt has been cleared of all those dreary coffins to make room for a gallery, a book shop, a brass rubbing center, and a café that serves cappuccino with a baroque flair (open Mon.-Sat. 10am-9pm, Sun. noon-6pm; church open daily 7:30am-7:30pm). At 2:30pm on the first Saturday of every month a constitutional reform organization called **Charter 88** holds a rowdy "vigil" on St. Martin's steps, calling for a democratic written constitution for the U.K.

The original **Charing Cross,** last of 13 crosses set up to mark the stages of Queen Eleanor's royal funeral procession in 1291 ("charing" comes from "beloved queen" in French), was actually located at the top of Whitehall, immediately south of the present Trafalgar Square. Like many things, it was destroyed by Cromwell, and a replica now stands outside Charing Cross Station, which is just uphill from the Victoria Embankment. This spot used to be the pulsing heart of London life, as well as the geographical center of the city. "Why, Sir, Fleet Street has a very animated appearance," Samuel Johnson once remarked, "but I think the full tide of human existence is at Charing Cross." The full tide of traffic now engulfs the place, and the bronze statue of King Charles drowns in the ebb and flow of automobiles. The statue escaped the cross's fate with the aid of one wily John Rivett. He bought the statue "for scrap," and did a roaring trade in brass souvenirs supposedly made from the melted-down figure; it was in fact hidden and later sold, at a tidy profit, to Charles II.

■■■ PICCADILLY

All of the West End's major arteries—Piccadilly, Regent Street, Shaftesbury Avenue, The Haymarket—merge and swirl around Piccadilly Circus, the bright, gaudy hub of Nash's 19th-century London. Today the Circus earns its place on postcards with lurid neon signs, hordes of tourists, and a fountain topped by a statue everyone calls "Eros," though it was intended to be the Angel of Christian Charity in memory of the reformer, the Earl of Shaftesbury. Akin to New York's Times Square, silly Picadilly overflows with glam, glitz, and commerce.

The Circus was ground zero for Victorian popular entertainment, but only the façades of the great music halls remain, propped up against contemporary tourist traps. **London Pavillion,** 1 Piccadilly Circus, is a historic theatre recently converted into a mall (across the street from the Lillywhite's and Sogo stores). Inside the Pavillion lurks the nefarious **Rock Circus** (tel. 734 7203), a waxwork museum and revolving theatre dedicated to the history of rock-and-roll. Elvis, the Beatles, and Tina Turner stand among the 50 rock and pop artists eerily re-created as wax effigies. Infrared headsets pick up a CD soundtrack as you wander past each display (open Sun.-Mon. and Wed.-Thurs. 11am-9pm, Tues. noon-9pm, Fri.-Sat. 11am-10pm; admission £6.95, students and seniors £5.95, children £4.95, family of 4 £18.85).

The massive **Trocadero,** 13 Coventry Street (tel. 439 1791), also specializes in charging hapless tourists exorbitant rates for contrived entertainments. Once trapped in the Trocadero's vise-like grip, rapt hordes rush from the Guiness World of Records (tel. 439 7331), to Quasar—Serious Fun with a Laser Gun (tel. 434 0795), and Planet Hollywood (tel. 287 1000). After jogging through Alien War (see Offbeat Entertainment), a guided simulation of the movie *Aliens,* visitors fortify themselves with snacks purchased on the aptly named Food Street.

Aristocratic mansions once lined Piccadilly, a broad mile-long avenue stretching from Regent St. in the east to Hyde Park Corner in the west. The name derives from Piccadilly Hall, the 17th-century home of Robert Baker, an affluent tailor who did brisk business in the sale of "pickadills," frilly lace collars that were much in fashion in his day. The only remnant of Piccadilly's stately past is the showy **Burlington House** (across from 185 Piccadilly), built in 1665 for the Earls of Burlington and redesigned in the 18th century by Colin Campbell to accommodate the burgeoning **Royal Academy of Arts** (tel. 439 7438; tube: Piccadilly or Green Park). Founded in 1768, the Academy consists of 40 academicians and 30 associates who administer the exhibition galleries and a massive annual summer show, and maintain a free school of art (see Museums). The ambitious **Museum of Mankind** backs onto Burlington House behind the Royal Academy (see Museums).

An easily overlooked courtyard next to the Academy opens onto the **Albany,** an 18th-century apartment block renowned as one of London's most prestigious addresses. Built in 1771 and remodeled in 1812 to serve as "residential chambers for bachelor gentlemen," the Albany evolved into an exclusive enclave of literary repute. Lord Byron wrote his epic "Childe Harold" here. Other past residents include Macaulay, Gladstone, Canning, "Monk" Lewis, J.B. Priestley, and Graham Greene.

Piccadilly continues past imperious Bond Street, past the Ritz Hotel with its distinctive arcade and light-bulb sign, past the Green Park tube station, and past a string of privileged men's clubs on the rim of Green Park. At the gateway of the **Wellington Museum** in **Apsley House,** described by its first owner as "No. 1, London," the avenue merges into the impenetrable Hyde Park corner (see Museums). Apsley House was built by Robert Adam in the 1780s as the home of the Duke of Wellington. It will house an important collection of Spanish, Dutch, and Italian Old Masters (ransacked from Spain's Royal Collection when Wellington defeated the Bonapartes) when it opens in early 1995; until then, the most famous paintings are in the National Museum.

Running north from Piccadilly Circus are the grand façades of (upper) **Regent Street,** leading to Oxford Circus. The buildings and street were built by John Nash in the early 19th century as part of a processional route for the Prince Regent to follow from St. James's Park through Oxford Circus to his house in Regent's Park. The façades have changed since Nash's time, and today the street is known for the crisp cuts of Burberry raincoats and Aquascutum suits as well as Hamley's, the giant warehouse of Santa's goodies (see Shopping).

■■■ SOHO, LEICESTER SQUARE, AND CHINATOWN

For centuries, **Soho** was London's red-light district of prostitutes and sex shows. Though most of the prostitutes were forced off the streets by 1959 legislation, the peep shows and porn shops concentrated along Brewer St. and Greek St. ensure the continuation of a licentious tradition. Far from defining the flavor of Soho, however, the sex industry adds merely one small ingredient to the incredible cosmopolitan stew which is Soho today.

Loosely bounded by Oxford St. in the north, Shaftesbury Ave. in the south, Charing Cross Rd. in the east, and Regent St. in the west (tube: Leicester Sq., Piccadilly Circus, or Tottenham Ct. Rd.), Soho first emerged as a discrete area in the 1681 with the laying out of **Soho Square,** originally King Square (tube: Tottenham Ct. Rd., just off of Oxford St.). Grand mansions quickly sprang up as the area became popular with a fashionable set, famed for throwing extravagant parties. By the end of the 18th century, however, the leisure classes moved out, to be replaced by the leisure industries.Today, the square is a center of the film industry, and many of the area's storefronts contain film distributors, post-production and sound studios, editing rooms, and BBC offices.

Blurred by weather and cracked with age, a statue of Charles II (1681) presides over the **Soho Village Green.** His illegitimate son, the Duke of Monmouth, who rebelled against and was beheaded by Uncle James II, once commissioned a palatial house on this site; according to local legend, the district's current name comes from his rallying cry at the battle of Sedgemoor, *"Soe-hoe."*

Soho has a history of welcoming immigrants of various nationalities to its streets. The district was first settled by French Huguenots fleeing religious persecution after the revocation of the Edict of Nantes in 1685. In more recent years, an influx of settlers from the New Territories of Hong Kong have forged London's Chinatown south of Soho. A strong Mediterranean influence can also be detected in the aromas of espresso, garlic, and sizzling meats wafting through the area's maze of streets.

Perhaps contemporary Soho's most salient feature, especially on sunny days, is its vibrant **sidewalk café** culture. This culture is a recent development which marks an intentional departure from Soho's pornographic past. Five years ago Soho café and restaurant owners organized a well-funded renaissance, cleaning away some of the rubbish and sleaze to make room for London's hippest cafés and bars. An *alfresco* mecca, today's Soho overflows with media types (mostly in the film and TV industries), artists, writers, club kids, and posers. The area has a significant and visible gay presence; a concentration of gay-owned restaurants and bars has turned the region's central avenue, **Old Compton Street,** into the big gay heart of London.

Like the other SoHo in New York, Soho has become a stylish haunt for the (predominantly youthful, white, male, and fashionable) gay and the glamourous. Unfortunately, Soho's success may also cause its downfall. Attracted by the scent of money, large corporations and chain stores are moving in for the kill, threatening to destroy the area's distinct character. A branch of The Big Easy—a theme restaurant whose branches evoking the American South have been sprouting up elsewhere in London—has already invaded Old Compton St. Construction on what will be the biggest restaurant in Europe is currently underway. Slated to open in Sept. 1995, the 600-seater will take up two floors of what used to be the Marquee Club on Wardour St., a hotbed of rock celebrity in the 60s and 70s. To top it all off, the Manhattan Loft Corporation is building 37 luxury lofts above the imminent gastrodome. Only the fabulously rich will be able to afford the glamorous privilege of living in Soho, which is not currently a residential district.

Even the now well-entrenched and highly visible gay scene may be affected. Gordon Lewis, the owner of the Village and Yard gay bars (see Bisexual, Gay, and Lesbian London) and one of the most successful of the gay entrepreneurs who vitalized the Soho scene at the start of the 90s, is now ready to sell. Sadly, the people with the money to buy are the large breweries, who are eager to take back a chunk of the pink pound.

Though Soho may be facing yet another make-over (one which many fear will turn it into another Covent Garden), some traditions will remain, and its history cannot be changed. The eerie ruins of **St. Anne's Soho** on Wardour Street, which runs north through the offices of Britain's film industry from Shaftesbury Ave., remain from World War II. Leveled by German bombers in 1940, only Wren's anomalous tower of 1685 and the ungainly, bottle-shaped steeple added by Cockerell in 1803 emerged unscathed.

Since the 1840s, **Berwick St. Market** (parallel to the north end of Wardour St.) has rumbled with trade and far-flung Cockney accents. Famous for the widest and cheapest selection of fruits and vegetables in central London, the market has expanded to include cheap electrical appliances and a small selection of clothes (open Mon.-Sat. 9am-6pm). Nearby Meard Street yields an impression of Soho in its earlier, more residential days.

Running parallel to Regent St. is **Carnaby Street,** a notorious hotbed of 60s sex, fashion, and Mods. It witnessed the rise of youth culture and became the heart of what *Time* magazine called "Swinging London." Although Carnaby St. celebrates its 30th anniversary on Sept. 3, 1994, the chic boutiques and parading celebrities have long since left the area, which has lapsed into a lurid tourist trap crammed with stalls of junky souvenirs—though some of its more traditional denizens (like Iuderwicks, the oldest pipe-markers in London), have weathered the storms of fads and tourists alike.

Soho also has a rich literary past: Blake and Defoe lived on Broadwick St. (off Wardour St.), Thomas de Quincey (*Confessions of an English Opium Eater*) had bad trips in his houses on Greek and Tavistock St., and John Dryden lived at no. 43 Gerrard St. (in Chinatown). To the north, a blue plaque above the Quo Vadis restaurant at **28 Dean Street** locates the austere two-room flat where the impoverished Karl Marx lived with his wife, maid, and five children while writing *Das Kapital.*

Leicester Square, just south of Shaftesbury Ave., between Piccadilly Circus and Charing Cross Rd. (the pedestrian-only streets perpendicular to Charing Cross Rd. all lead to the square itself) is an entertainment nexus. Amusements range from very expensive, mammoth cinemas, to the free performances provided by the street entertainers, to the glockenspiel of the Swiss Centre (its 25 bells ring Mon.-Fri. at noon, 6, 7, and 8pm; Sat.-Sun. at noon and 2, 4, 5, 6, 7, and 8pm; ringing is accompanied by a moving model of herdsmen leading their cattle through the Alps), and the verbal banter between Hare Krishnas, Christian fundamentalists, and Ciaran, a beer-and-obscenities-spitting atheist. Not to mention the constant cacophony of tourist harangues produced by the throngs of visitors. (Though there's safety in crowds, watch out—within the first three months of 1994, 300 bag snatchers and 120 drug offenders were arrested in the square.)

On the north side of the square, at Leicester Place, the French presence in Soho manifests itself in **Notre-Dame de France** (tel. 437 9363). This church may not be architecturally distinctive, but those who venture inside will be rewarded with the exquisite Aubusson tapestry lining the inner walls. The tiny chapel built into the western wall features an arresting 1960 mural by Jean Cocteau (Masses in French Sat. 6pm, Sun. 10 and 11:30am). On the south side of the square, a small hovel and endless queue mark the **SWET half-price ticket booth,** where theatre tickets are sold for half price on the day of the show (see Theatre).

Cantonese immigrants first arrived in Britain as cooks on British ships, and London's first Chinese community formed around the docks near Limehouse. Now, however, London's **Chinatown** (known in Chinese as *Tong Yan Kai,* "Chinese Street") lies off the north side of Leicester Sq. Chinatown swelled with arrivals from Hong Kong in the 50s, and 50,000 more immigrants to Britain are expected as the colony's transfer to China approaches. Between the theatres of Shaftesbury Ave. and the cinemas of Leicester Sq., street signs in Chinese and pagoda-capped telephone booths spring up. **Gerrard Street,** the main thoroughfare, runs closest to Leicester Square tube station; the street where poet John Dryden once lived is now a pedestrian avenue framed by scrollworked dragon gates.

Chinatown is most vibrant during the year's two major festivals: the **Mid-Autumn Festival,** at the end of September, and the **Chinese New Year Festival,** around the beginning of February. For further information on festivals or Chinatown call the **Chinese Community Centre** at 44 Gerrard St., 2nd floor (tel. 439 3822). Those thirsty for eastern newspapers (in English or Chinese) should check out the bustling bookshop **Guanghua,** at 7 Newport Pl. (see Bookstores). The otherwise classical church of St. Martin-in-the-Fields in Trafalgar Sq. conducts a Chinese service every Sunday afternoon at 2:45pm.

■■■ COVENT GARDEN

The outdoor cafés, upscale shops, and slick crowds animating Covent Garden today bely the square's medieval beginnings as a literal "covent garden" where the monks of Westminster Abbey grew their vegetables. When Henry VIII abolished the monasteries in 1536, he bestowed this land upon John Russell, first Earl of Bedford. The Earl's descendants developed it into a fashionable *piazza* (designed by Inigo Jones) in the 1630s, giving London its first planned square.

Jones's **St. Paul's Church** now stands as the sole survivor of the original square, although the interior had to be rebuilt after bring gutted by a fire in 1795. Known as "the actor's church," St. Paul's is filled with plaques commemorating the achievements of Boris Karloff, Vivien Leigh, Noel Coward, and Tony Simpson ("inspired player of small parts"), among others. The church can only be entered through a little churchyard with entrances on Bedford, King, and Henrietta Streets. The misleading east portico facing the Covent Garden piazza never served as a door, but rather as a stage; an inscription marks it as the site of the first known performance of a Punch and Judy puppet show, recorded by Samuel Pepys in 1662 (open Mon. 8:30am-2:30pm, Tues.-Fri. 9:30am-4:30pm).

During the 1800s, a glass and iron roof was built to shelter the fruit, vegetable, and flower market which had rooted itself in the piazza. Though the wholesalers' carts left Covent Garden in 1974 for Nine Elms, south of the Thames, the Victorian architecture has remained to house the fashionable shops and expensive restaurants which sprouted during a tourist-oriented redevelopment. The Victorian Flower Market building in the south-east corner of the piazza now contains the **London Transport Museum** (see Museums). Markets selling crafts and antiques, the guaranteed crowds, and the omnipresent street performers enact a modern version of the jostling marketplace of yore.

The **Theatre Royal** and the **Royal Opera House** lend a feeling of civility to the area, adding pre-theatre and pre-concert-goers to the throng of visitors. These venues represent a long tradition of theatre in the Covent Garden area. The Theatre Royal (entrance on Catherine St.), was first built in 1663 as one of only two legal theatrical venues in London. Four previous incarnations were burnt down; the present building dates from 1812. The Royal Opera House (on Bow St.) began as a theater for concerts and plays in 1732. Also fire-prone, the present (and third) reincarnation now houses the Royal Opera and Royal Ballet companies.

Right across the street from the Royal Opera House stands **Bow Street Magistrates' Court** (which closed in 1992), the oldest of London's 12 magistrates' courts and home of the Bow Street Runners, predecessors of the city's present-day police. In the courthouse, novelist Henry Fielding and his brother Sir John presided over a bench famed for its compassion (in a time when compassion meant sentencing the perpetrator of petty theft to 14 years deportation to Australia rather than hanging).

The **Theatre Museum** sits to the south, on the corner of Russell and Wellington streets (see Museums). Nearby, a blue plaque at 8 Russell St. marks the site of Boswell's home, where he first met Dr. Johnson in 1763.

Even outside the renovated central market area, Covent Garden buzzes with activity. Curious stage-design shops cluster near the Opera House, and moss-covered artisans' studios stud the surrounding streets, interspersed with an odd assortment of theater-related businesses. Rose St. (between Garrick and Floral streets) leads to the notorious **Lamb and Flag** (see Pubs), supposedly the only timber building left in the West End. In this lively pub, Dryden was attacked and nearly murdered by an angry mob opposed to his writings.

On Great Newport St. to the west **The Photographers' Gallery** (see Museums) holds its reputation as one of London's major venues for contemporary photographic exhibitions. Long Acre and Neal St. bustle with diverse specialty shops, similar only in their high prices. The building at the corner of Earlham and Neal streets houses **Contemporary Applied Arts,** a showcase for contemporary British crafts, including furniture, ceramics, and jewelery (open Mon.-Wed. and Fri.-Sat. 10am-6pm, and Thurs. 10am-7pm).

Further up, Neal St. leads to **Neal's Yard,** a healthy hub of stores selling whole foods, cheeses and yogurts, herbs, fresh-baked breads, and homeopathic remedies. At the northern section of St. Martin's Lane, six streets converge at the **Seven Dials** monument (the seventh dial is the monument itself as a sundial). A replica of a 17th-century monument, the 1989 version is currently being restored.

■■■ MAYFAIR

The long-time center of London's blue-blooded *beau monde* was named for the 17th-century May Fair, held on the site of Shepherd's Market, a notorious haunt of prostitutes. Modern Mayfair has a distinctly patrician atmosphere; it is the most expensive property in the British version of *Monopoly*. In the 18th and 19th centuries, the aristocracy kept houses in Mayfair where they lived during "the season" (the season for opera and balls), retiring to their country estates in the summer. Mayfair is bordered by Oxford St. to the north, Piccadilly to the south, Park Lane to the west and Regent St. to the east (tube: Green Park, Bond St., or Piccadilly Circus).

Near what is now the Bond St. tube station, Blake saw mystical visions for 17 years on South Molton St. On busy Brook St., home to ritzy Claridge's Hotel, Handel wrote the *Messiah*. The reigning queen was born in a house (recently demolished) at no. 17 Bruton St. Laurence Sterne ended his life on haughty Bond St. (no. 39). Back in the 60s, on Davies Mews, Vidal Sassoon revolutionized hair styles at his first salon (now the Vidal Sassoon School—see Offbeat Entertainment).

Bond St. itself is the traditional address for the most prestigious shops, art dealers, auction houses, and hair salons in the city. Long-established shops, sporting crests indicating royal patronage, sell everything from handmade shotguns, to emerald tiaras, to antique furniture, to *objets d'art*. An array of art dealers and auctioneers with public galleries frequently offer special shows of exceptional quality. Starting at the New Bond St. end, **Sotheby's,** 34 New Bond St. (tel. 493 8080), displays everything from Dutch masters to the world's oldest condom before they're put on the auction block. Don't worry about sneezing away a million pounds when sitting in, as today's bidders use paddles (open Mon.-Fri. 9am-4:30pm). Modern art aficionados should also note the rugged Henry Moore frieze high up on the crest of the **Time/**

MARYLEBONE

Life Building, corner of Bruton St. At the **Marlborough Gallery** (entrance by Albemarle St.), the biggest contemporary names are sold; **Agnew's,** 43 Old Bond St., and **Colnaghi's,** 14 Old Bond St., deal in Old Masters.

Running west off Bond St., Grosvenor St. ends at **Grosvenor Square,** one of the largest of its breed in central London. Developed by Sir Richard Grosvenor in 1725, the central garden spreads across the site of Oliver's Mount, a makeshift barricade erected by the people of London in 1643 to repel Charles I's royalist army. The square, occasionally known as "little America," has gradually evolved into a U.S. military and political enclave since future President John Adams lived at no. 9 while serving as the first American ambassador to England in 1785. Almost two centuries later, General Eisenhower established his wartime headquarters at no. 20, and memory of his stay persists in the area's postwar nickname, "Eisenhowerplatz." From here you can see the humorless and top-heavy **U.S. Embassy** rising in the west, where protesters occasionally assemble to denounce the latest Yankee indiscretion.

West of Grosvenor Sq., a walk down **Park Lane,** the western border of Mayfair at Hyde Park, will take you by the legendary hotels that are sadly no longer up to *Let's Go* standards. The Hilton, Grosvenor House, and the Dorchester can be found here.

Tucked into the southwest corner where Park Lane meets Piccadilly is **Shepherd's Market,** once the site of the rowdy May Fair. During the 60s this tiny village-like area briefly revisited its rambunctious past, but has since been regentrified, teeming with swish pubs and shops. Dorothy Sayers's Lord Peter Wimsey shared his Piccadilly flat with trusty valet Bunter, while P.G. Wodehouse's "gentleman's gentleman" Jeeves babysat aristocrat Bertie Wooster in their fictional house on Half Moon St.

In the opposite (north-east) corner of Mayfair (tube: Oxford Circus), tiny **Hanover Square** provides a gracious residential setting for **St. George's Hanover Church,** where the *crème de la crème* of London society have married. Percy Bysshe Shelley, George Eliot, Benjamin Disraeli, and the soft-speaking Teddy Roosevelt came here to be married beneath the radiant barrel vault, with Handel's organ playing at their backs. The name **Savile Row** is synonymous with the elegant and excessively priced "bespoke" (custom-fitted and hand-sewn) tailoring that has prospered there for centuries. The Restoration playwright Sheridan, who lived at no. 14, was always impeccably turned out.

■■■ MARYLEBONE

Located between Regent's Park and Oxford St., the grid-like district of Marylebone (MAR-lee-bun) is dotted with decorous late-Georgian town houses. The name derives from "St. Mary-by-the-bourne," the "bourne" referring to the Tyburn or the Westbourne stream, both now underground. The eternally dammed Westbourne now forms the Serpentine in Hyde Park.

There's little to see in this well-kept, well-bred region of residences and office buildings, but Marylebone has had its share of notable denizens. Wimpole Street saw the reclusive poet Elizabeth Barrett write the fabulous *Sonnets from the Portuguese* before she eloped and moved in with Robert Browning. At different times, 19 York St. has been the home of John Milton, John Stuart Mill, and William Hazlitt. **Harley Street** is the address for Britain's most eminent doctors and specialists.

The area's most fondly remembered resident is Sherlock Holmes who, although fictitious, still receives about 50 letters per week addressed to his 221b Baker St. residence. The Abbey National Building Society currently occupies the site and employs a full-time secretary to answer requests for Holmes's assistance in solving mysteries around the world. The official line is that Holmes has retired from detective work and is keeping bees in the country. The **Sherlock Holmes Museum,** located at 239 Baker St. (marked "221b") will thrill Holmes enthusiasts with the meticulous re-creation of the detective's lodgings (see Museums).

Ever since the redoubtable **Madame Tussaud,** one of Louis XVI's tutors, trekked from Paris in 1802 carrying wax effigies of French nobles decapitated in the

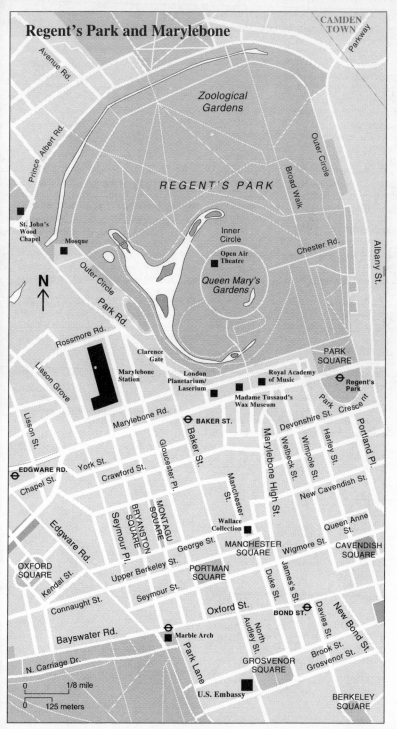

Regent's Park and Marylebone

CAMDEN TOWN

Parkway

Avenue Rd.

Prince Albert Rd.

Zoological Gardens

Outer Circle

REGENT'S PARK

Broad Walk

St. John's Wood Chapel

Mosque

Inner Circle

Open Air Theatre

Chester Rd.

Albany St.

N

Outer Circle

Park Rd.

Queen Mary's Gardens

Rossmore Rd.

Lisson Grove

Clarence Gate

Marylebone Station

London Planetarium/ Laserium

Royal Academy of Music

PARK SQUARE

Regent's Park

Park Crescent

Madame Tussaud's Wax Museum

Lisson St.

Marylebone Rd.

BAKER ST.

Devonshire St.

Portland Pl.

EDGWARE RD.

Chapel St.

York St.

Crawford St.

Gloucester Pl.

Baker St.

Marylebone High St.

Welbeck St.

Wimpole St.

Harley St.

New Cavendish St.

Edgware Rd.

MONTAGU SQUARE

BRYANSTON SQUARE

Seymour Pl.

George St.

Manchester St.

Wallace Collection

MANCHESTER SQUARE

Wigmore St.

Queen Anne St.

CAVENDISH SQUARE

OXFORD SQUARE

Kendal St.

Upper Berkeley St.

PORTMAN SQUARE

Connaught St.

Seymour St.

Oxford St.

Duke St.

James's St.

BOND ST.

Davies St.

New Bond St.

Bayswater Rd.

Marble Arch

Park Lane

North Audley St.

GROSVENOR SQUARE

Brook St.

Grosvenor St.

N. Carriage Dr.

U.S. Embassy

BERKELEY SQUARE

0   1/8 mile

0   125 meters

Revolution, her eerie museum on Marylebone Rd. (with an adjacent Planetarium) has been a London landmark (see Museums). Boris Becker, Cher, Archbishop Desmond Tutu, and Voltaire number among the luminaries re-created in life-size wax models.

Oxford Street, the southern border of Marylebone, passes through Oxford Circus, Bond St., and Marble Arch tube stations. Arguably London's major shopping boulevard, it's jam-packed with shops (ranging from cheap chainstores to the posh boutiques around Bond St.), crowds, and fast-food stands. Off Oxford St., pleasant **James's St.** (tube: Bond St.) lures passersby with one café after another—a good place for people-watching from a sidewalk table. Off James's St., Manchester Sq. holds the **Wallace Collection,** a must-see for fans of Dutch art (see Museums).

■■■ HYDE PARK AND KENSINGTON GARDENS

Totalling 630 acres, **Hyde Park** and the contiguous **Kensington Gardens** constitute the largest open area in the center of the city, earning their reputation as the "lungs of London." Henry VIII used to hunt deer here. At the far west of the Gardens, you can drop your calling card at **Kensington Palace** (tel. 937 9561; tube: Kensington High St. or Queensway), originally the residence of King William III and Queen Mary II and recently of Princess Margaret. Currently, the Princess of Wales, the little princes, and other stray members of the royal family live in the palace. A museum of uninhabited royal rooms (the State Apartments) and regal memorabilia includes a Court dress collection, with Di's wedding gown prominently displayed (palace open Mon.-Sat. 9am-5:30pm, Sun. 11am-5:30pm; admission £3.75, students and seniors £3, children £2.50). A walk west of the palace along Kensington Palace Gdns., one of London's most opulent thoroughfares, reveals embassies and the homes of a crew of millionaires.

The Round Pond east of the palace plays the ocean to a fleet of toy sailboats on weekends. The statue of Peter Pan, actually modelled from a girl, stands near the Italian fountains on the west bank of the Serpentine. The **Serpentine,** a lake carved in 1730, runs from these fountains in the north, near Bayswater Rd., south towards Knightsbridge. From the number of people who pay the £2.50 (children £1) to sunbathe at the fenced-off Serpentine beach (the Lido), one would think the sun shone more brightly there than anywhere else in London. Harriet Westbrook, P.B. Shelley's first wife, numbers among the famous people who have drowned in this human-made "pond." A bone-white arch derived from a Henry Moore sculpture stands on the northwest bank, but the best view is from across the water.

The **Serpentine Gallery** (tel. 402 6075), in Kensington Gardens, often hosts interesting exhibitions of contemporary works, as well as art workshops (gallery open daily 10am-6pm; parks open Mon.-Fri. 10am-6pm, Sat.-Sun. 10am-7pm; off-season Mon.-Fri. 10am-dusk, Sat.-Sun. 10am-4pm; free). Be careful not to get locked in after the park closes; those who do may be obliged to scale a rather large wall.

On the southern edge of Kensington Gardens, the Lord Mayor had the **Albert Memorial** built to honor Victoria's beloved husband, whose death Victoria mourned for nearly 40 years. Considered a great artistic achievement when first unveiled in 1869, the extravagant monument now seems an embarrassing piece of imperial excess. Unfortunately, you will be unable to judge for yourself since the Albert Memorial will be under designer scaffolding for another five years as it undergoes restoration. Across the street, the **Royal Albert Hall,** with its ornate oval dome, hosts the Promenade Concerts (Proms) in summer (see Entertainment). Also built to honor the Prince Consort, the hall is simpler than the memorial, and features a frieze of the "Triumph of the Arts and Sciences" around its circumference. Rotten Row (a corruption of *Route du Roi,* "king's road") was the first English thoroughfare to be lighted to prevent crime. However, this east-west path through southern Hyde Park,

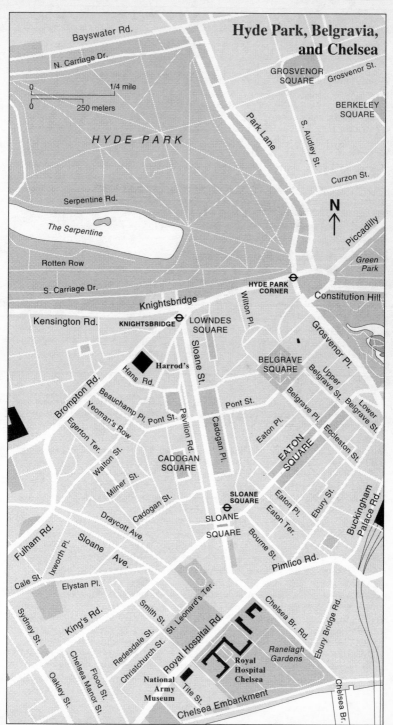

Hyde Park, Belgravia, and Chelsea

like the rest of the park, remains dangerous at night. There is a police station about 300 yards north of the Serpentine.

Speakers' Corner, in the northeast corner of Hyde Park (tube: Marble Arch, not Hyde Park Corner), is the finest example of free speech in action anywhere in the world. The **Marble Arch** is built on the exact site where the public gallows of Tyburn rested until 1783. Hangings here drew immense crowds who jeered and threw stones and rotting food at the unfortunate criminals (some of whom had done as little as steal a shilling's worth of goods) as they rolled in carts to the "Triple Tree," which stood at the present corner of Bayswater and Edgware Rd. Nowadays, on Sundays from late morning to dusk, and on summer evenings, soapbox revolutionaries, haranguers, madmen, and evangelists scream about anything from Kierkegaard to socialism to knitting. Test your patience and your vocal chords and go heckle with the best of them. At the southern end of Hyde Park cluster a group of statues: a Diana fountain, the "family of man," a likeness of Lord Byron, and a fig-leafed Achilles dedicated to Wellington and "inscribed by his countrywomen." Nick-named the "Ladies' Trophy," it was London's first nude statue. Royal park band performances take place in the bandstand 200 yards from Hyde Park Corner, in the direction of the Serpentine (June-Aug. Sun. 3 and 6pm).

■■■ KENSINGTON, KNIGHTSBRIDGE, AND BELGRAVIA

Kensington, a gracious and sheltered residential area, reposes between multi-ethnic Notting Hill to the north and chic Chelsea to the south. **Kensington High Street,** which pierces the area, has become a shopping and scoping epicenter. Obscure specialty and antique shops fill the area along Kensington Church Street to the north, Victorian-era museums and colleges dominate South Kensington, while the area around Earl's Court has mutated into something of a tourist colony while retaining a substantial gay population.

Take the tube to High St. Kensington, Notting Hill Gate, or Holland Park to reach **Holland Park,** a gracious peacock-peppered garden. Holland House (see Accomodations—Youth Hostels), a Jacobean mansion built in 1606 lies on the park's grounds. Destroyed in World War II, the house has since been restored and turned into a youth hostel. Holland Park also contains formal gardens, an open-air amphitheater, and a number of playgrounds. The park boasts cricket pitches, public tennis courts, and the Kyoto Gardens, a traditional Japanese garden.

Two petite exhibition galleries, the **Ice House** and the **Orangery,** blossom in the middle of the park. They mount free displays of contemporary painting and ceramics by local artists. The flag-ridden **Commonwealth Institute** stands by the park's southern entrance on the High St. (see Museums).

The curious **Leighton House,** 12 Holland Park Rd. (tel. 602 3316), lies a block west. Devised by the imaginative Lord Leighton in the 19th century, the house is a presumptuous yet amusing pastiche. The Arab Hall, with inlaid tiles, a pool, and a dome, is a hodgepodge of plundered Middle Eastern art. Now a center for the arts, Leighton House features concerts, receptions, and other events in the evenings, as well as frequent contemporary art exhibitions. An excellent taped commentary (£2.25) helps you find your way around (house open Mon.-Sat. 11am-5pm; free).

To reach the grandiose **South Kensington museums,** take the tube to the South Kensington station or the #49 bus from Kensington High St. The **Victoria and Albert Museum** and the **Natural History Museum** (both on Cromwell Road), and the **Science Museum** (on Exhibition Road) all testify on a grand scale to the Victorian mania for collecting, codifying, and cataloguing. The Great Exhibition of 1851 funded many of these monumental buildings, built between 1867 and 1935.

Brompton Oratory, just east of the V&A, is a showpiece of Italian art and architecture. H. Gribble built the aggressively Roman Baroque edifice in 1884 and

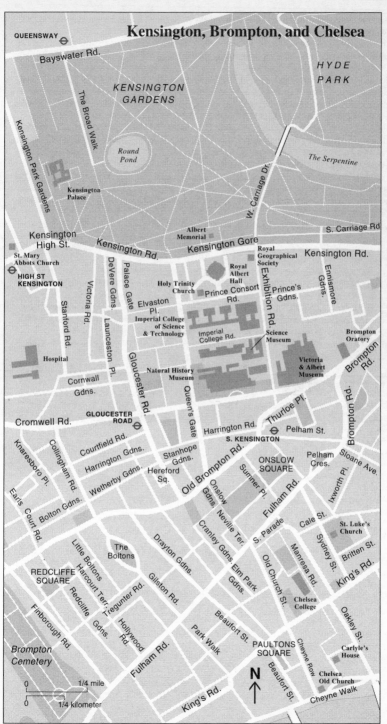

Kensington, Brompton, and Chelsea

QUEENSWAY ⊖

Bayswater Rd.

HYDE PARK

KENSINGTON GARDENS

The Broad Walk

Kensington Park Gardens

Round Pond

The Serpentine

W. Carriage Dr.

Kensington Palace

S. Carriage Rd

Albert Memorial

Kensington High St.

Kensington Rd.

Kensington Gore

Kensington Rd.

St. Mary Abbots Church

HIGH ST KENSINGTON ⊖

Royal Geographical Society

Royal Albert Hall

Ennismore Gdns.

DeVere Gdns.

Palace Gate

Holy Trinity Church

Prince Consort Rd.

Exhibition Rd.

Prince's Gdns.

Victoria Rd.

Stanford Rd.

Elvaston Pl.

Imperial College of Science & Technology

Imperial College Rd.

Science Museum

Brompton Oratory

Launceston Pl.

Gloucester Rd.

Hospital

Natural History Museum

Queen's Gate

Victoria & Albert Museum

Brompton Rd.

Cornwall Gdns.

Cromwell Rd.

GLOUCESTER ROAD ⊖

Harrington Rd.

Thurloe Pl.

Pelham St.

Knaresboro' Pl.

Collingham Rd.

Courtfield Rd.

Harrington Gdns.

Stanhope Gdns.

S. KENSINGTON ⊖

ONSLOW SQUARE

Pelham Cres.

Sloane Ave.

Earls Court Rd.

Bolton Gdns.

Wetherby Gdns.

Hereford Sq.

Old Brompton Rd.

Onslow Gdns.

Sumner Pl.

Fulham Rd.

Ixworth Pl.

Cranley Gdns.

Neville Ter.

Elm Park Gdns.

S. Parade

Cale St.

St. Luke's Church

Drayton Gdns.

Old Church St.

Manresa Rd.

Sydney St.

Britten St.

King's Rd.

The Boltons

Little Boltons

Harcourt Terr.

Redcliffe Gdns.

Tregunter Rd.

Gilston Rd.

Hollywood Rd.

REDCLIFFE SQUARE

Finborough Rd.

Fulham Rd.

Park Walk

Beaufort St.

Chelsea College

Cheyne Row

Oakley St.

Carlyle's House

Brompton Cemetery

PAULTONS SQUARE

Beaufort St.

King's Rd.

N ↑

Chelsea Old Church

Cheyne Walk

0 — 1/4 mile
0 — 1/4 kilometer

cluttered its interior with Italian statues; the enormous Renaissance altar in the Lady Chapel came from Brescia. The church affirms its reputation for fine music during its Sunday Latin Masses (oratory open 6:30am-8pm).

Various royal institutions of learning and culture are located north of Cromwell Rd. These august bodies include the Imperial College of Science, the Royal College of Music, the Royal College of Art, the uncharacteristically rotund **Royal Albert Hall** (see Entertainment), the Royal School of Needlepoint, and the **Royal Geographical Society.** The Society, just east of the Albert Hall, displays 800,000 maps and the explorer Stanley's boots (open Mon.-Fri. 10am-1pm and 2-5pm; free).

Patrician **Knightsbridge** manages to be wealthy and groomed without being forbidding. Knightsbridge is defined most of all by London's premier department store, **Harrods.** Founded in 1849 as a grocery store, by 1880 Harrods employed over 100 workers. In 1905 the store moved to its current location; today it requires 5000 employees to handle its vast array of products and services. Extravagance is their specialty. Besides an encyclopedic inventory, Harrods also contains a pub, an espresso bar, a salt beef bar, a champagne and oyster bar, a juice bar, and, naturally, a tourist information center (open Mon.-Tues. and Sat. 10am-6pm, Wed.-Fri. 10am-7pm; see Shopping).

Belgravia was first constructed as an area to billet servants after the building of Buckingham Palace in the 1820s, but soon became the haughty bastion of wealth and privilege it is today. Belgravia lies south of Hyde Park, ringed by stately Sloane St. to the west, Victoria Station to the south, and Buckingham Palace Gdns. to the east. The spacious avenues and crescents of the district center on **Belgrave Square,** 10 acres of park surrounded by late Georgian buildings that were the setting for *My Fair Lady.* Nearby **Eaton Square** was one of Henry James's London favorites. Residential Belgravia presents a quieter, more dignified façade than busier Knightsbridge or Mayfair. Money has refined and dehumanized the area, as embassies and big corporations take over imposing buildings, and apartments become the *pied-à-terres* of wealthy executives.

■■■ CHELSEA

Chelsea has always been one of London's flashiest districts—Thomas More, Oscar Wilde, and the Sex Pistols have all been resident at one time or another. It used to be that few streets in London screamed louder for a visit than the **King's Road.** Mohawked UB40s and pearl-necklaced Sloane Rangers (the awfully loose English equivalent of preppies) gazed at trendy window displays and at each other. While the hordes still flock here on Saturday afternoons to see and be seen, the ambience is drastically muted; most ertswhile scenesters look like they are desperately trying to recapture a past that they have only read about.

Symbolic of the street's recent metamorphosis from the center of a dynamic youth culture into a respectable shopping district is the chameleonic storefront at 430 King's Road, World's End. At this address in the 70s, impressario Malcolm McLaren and designer Vivienne Westwood masterminded a series of trendy boutiques which capitalized on the subcultural fashions then in vogue, like the Teddy Boy look. Let it Rock, Too Young To Live Too Fast To Die, and Seditionaries were some of the shop's various incarnations; the shop's most important incarnation was **Sex,** the punk clothing store in which the Sex Pistols (and, some would argue, punk rock) were born. Ripped clothing, safety pins, and bondage gear as fashion originated here. While Westwood still displays her designs in a boutique at this address, she now sells fabulously expensive couture garments. Ironically, the boutique's current neighbor is the Chelsea Conservative Club.

While no longer the epicenter of the punk rock youthquake, Chelsea remains a brilliant area for strolling. If you're pressed for time, be aware that the tube is practically nonexistent around here, so you'll have to rely on **buses** (#11 or 22).

Any proper exploration of Chelsea begins at **Sloane Square.** The square takes its name from Sir Hans Sloane (1660-1753), one of three collectors whose artifacts made up the original collections of the British Museum. The nearby **Royal Court Theatre** debuted many of George Bernard Shaw's plays. Until 1829, King's Rd., stretching southwest from Sloane Sq., served as a private royal thoroughfare from Hampton Court to Whitehall. Today the street is a commercial thoroughfare where overpriced restaurants, historic pubs, and the **Chelsea Antique Market** (253 King's Road) lurk amid many boutiques.

Off King's Rd., Chelsea becomes cozier, the closest thing to a village that central London now possesses. By the river stands Wren's **Royal Hospital** (1691), founded by Charles II for retired soldiers and still inhabited by 400 army pensioners. Former soldiers, in uniforms changed only slightly from 18th-century versions, welcome visitors to the spacious grounds and splendid buildings (open Mon.-Sat. 10am-noon and 2-4pm, Sun. 2-4pm; free).

East of the Hospital lie the **Ranelagh Gardens** (usually open until dusk). Here 18th-century pleasure-seekers spent their evenings watching pageants and fireworks and imbibing to excess. The **Chelsea Flower Show** blooms here the third week in May (Tues.-Fri.), but even Royal Horticultural Society members have trouble procuring tickets for the first two days. The **National Army Museum** stands directly west of the hospital, along Royal Hospital Rd. (see Museums).

Cheyne (pronounced "chainy") **Walk, Cheyne Row,** and **Tite Street** formed the heart of Chelsea's artist colony at the turn of the century. Watch for the blue plaques on the houses; J.M.W. Turner moved into a house in Cheyne Walk, and Edgar Allan Poe lived nearby. Mary Ann Evans (a.k.a. George Eliot) moved into no. 4 just before her death. Dante Gabriel Rossetti kept his highly disreputable *ménage* (which included peacocks and a kangaroo) in no. 16, where he doused himself with chloral hydrate and hammered the image of the artist as nonconformist into the public mind. Nos. 19 to 26 cover the ground that used to be Chelsea Manor, where Queen Elizabeth I once lived. Both Mick Jagger and Keith Richards got satisfaction on the Walk in the 60s. The area's arbiter of the aesthetic, Oscar Wilde, reposed stylishly at 34 Tite St. from 1884-1895 and was arrested for homosexual activity at Chelsea's best-known hotel, the Cadogan (75 Sloane St.). John Singer Sargent, James MacNeill Whistler, Radclyffe Hall, and Bertrand Russell also lived on Tite St. Today, fashionable artists' and designers' homes line the street, though the area is too expensive for it to remain a true bastion of bohemian culture.

At the west end of Cheyne Walk lies the **Chelsea Old Church,** partially designed by Sir Thomas More. Henry VIII is reported to have married his third wife here before the official wedding took place. The friendly verger will point out **Crosby Hall** down the street, a 15th-century hall that was More's residence in Bishopsgate before it was moved, stone by stone, to its present position in 1910 (church open daily 10am-1pm, 2pm-5pm; phone first).

Chelsea's famed resident Thomas Carlyle crafted his magnificent prose on Cheyne Row. On this miraculously quiet street colored by flowers and tidy houses, **Carlyle's House,** 24 Cheyne Row (tel. 352 7087), has remained virtually unchanged since the Sage of Chelsea expired in his armchair. Inside this small Queen Anne home, glass cases shield his books and manuscripts; family portraits and sketches ornament the walls—which he had doubled in thickness, vainly hoping to keep out noise. In his attic study Carlyle wrote and rewrote *The French Revolution* after John Stuart Mill's chambermaid accidently burned his first draft (open April-Oct. Wed.-Sun. 11am-5pm; admission £2.75, children £1.50; last admission 4:30pm).

■■■ NOTTING HILL

Notting Hill is one of London's most diverse neighborhoods; a variety of racial and ethnic groups currently call the area home, as do many hip young people. On the area's lively streets, trendy places to eat and shop ply their trade among dilapidated stores, wafts of incense, and Bob Marley posters. The region explodes with exuberant festivity every summer during the Notting Hill Carnival.

The scenery that surrounded the village of Notting Hill in the mid-19th-century (a few cornfields, a meadow, an occasional lane) has changed drastically since the Great Western Railway opened up North Kensington to development in 1838. The Ladbroke family commissioned high society architects to develop the area, whereupon upper middle class families quickly took up residence in spacious neoclassical mansion houses. Residential Ladbroke Grove was recently rendered infamous as the haunt of repulsive dart-playing Keith Talent in Martin Amis's novel *London Fields*.

Commercial **Portobello Road,** the area's lively main thoroughfare, runs parallel to Ladbroke Grove. Now the site of one of London's most popular weekly markets, Portobello has hosted side-shows, fortune-tellers, conjurers, and charlatans selling miracle elixirs since the early Victorian age.

Irish and Jewish immigrants were the first to occupy the poor areas of "Notting Dale" in the late 19th century, but the 1930s saw the arrival of Fascist demonstrations against Jews and local immigrant groups. Inter-ethnic tension culminated in the 1950s when Teddy-Boy gangs engaged in open warfare against Afro-Caribbean immigrants; the devastating riots that ensued are depicted in Colin MacInnes's novel *Absolute Beginners* (later made into a movie musical starring David Bowie).

Amy Garvey (Marcus's widow) helped the Black community on Notting Hill survive the various onslaughts against it. Today the multi-ethnic area sees little racial animosity. **Golborne Road** is home to vibrant North African and Portuguese communities, and the area is dotted with many traditional bakeries and family restaurants.

Presently, it's the **Portobello Market** (tube: Ladbroke Grove) every Saturday that brings additional energy to the area. Starting on the southern end near Notting Hill Gate, various antique stores and thriving galleries line Portobello Road. As the idler wanders further north, antiquarians give way to fresh fruit, vegetable, and baked goods stalls. Finally, near Lancaster Road and the Westway (the overhead highway), stalls sell second-hand clothing (including second-hand Doc Martens in really good condition for as little as £5-10), collector's vinyl, and various desirable trinkets.

In between Ladbroke Grove and Portobello Road, running parallel to both, is **Kensington Park Road,** home to eccentric specialty shops and (occasionally contrived) trendy restaurants. Here the encouragingly eclectic character of the neighborhood is quite visible; the self-congratulatory Body Shop is right across the street from a tattoo parlor and the Anglo-Yugoslavian Butcher.

Notting Hill celebrates its vital existence more than usual on the August Bank Holiday Monday and the preceding Sunday, during the **Notting Hill Carnival,** Europe's biggest outdoor festival. A parade of steel drummers, fantastic costumes, skanking followers, and dancing policemen is the highlight. African-Caribbean music reverberates through the streets. The more highbrow **Portobello Festival** in early June celebrates film, theatre, art, and music in the area (tel. 229 7981 for information)

■■■ CAMDEN TOWN AND REGENT'S PARK

In the 18th century, Camden Town was still only farmland and cattle fields owned by the Lord Chancellor Charles Pratt, Earl of Camden. Though he began some minor building projects in the area around Camden High St., the town really started to develop with the opening of the Regent's Canal in 1820, bringing with it timber and coal wharves, family-run breweries, saddlers, picture-framers, and the like. By the 19th century, Camden Town was a solid working-class district, spliced with railways and covered in soot. Charles Dickens spent his childhood here, crowded in a four-room tenement with his extended family at 16 (now 141) Bayham St. The experience served as the model for the Cratchit family in *A Christmas Carol*. Waves of Irish, Cypriot, Greek, Italian, and Portuguese immigrants brought a diversity to the area that persists to this day.

Contemporary Camden Town is a stomping ground for trendy youth of all subcultural affiliations. Trends are instigated and abandoned at the **Camden Markets,** now London's fourth-largest tourist attraction, which draws 200,000 funky visitors each weekend (tube: Camden Town; see Shopping). Opened in 1974 with only four stall holders, the markets now cram in hundreds of bohemian vendors catering to an international youth culture. Though the area is renowned for its shoes and boots, anything and everything can be found here, and the clientele reflects the diversity of the goods. Straggly-haired neo-hippies, black-clad goths, pierced punks, clean-cut preppies, and even thirty-something couples (complete with little kids) all add to the madness of the markets on weekends.

To avoid the scene, go on a weekday, when panhandlers and scurrying students are the worst you'll have to contend with. Though the markets will be closed, the area's restaurants and cafés, second-hand and young designer fashion stores, and specialty shops (including one of London's best left-wing bookstores, a gay sex and fetish-wear shop, London's only stored dedicated to folk music, and a 3-story emporium of the-artist-formerly-known-as-Prince paraphernalia, owned by the purple monarch himself) still offer plenty of fodder for more relaxed browsing.

Although parts of Camden Town have turned into genteel residential enclaves, the area has for the most part resisted gentrification, as the scruffy storefronts on High St. and dilapidated warehouses along Regent's Canal will attest. The market crowds leave behind a recurrent wake of litter that lines the curbs, and Arlington House, the largest dole house in Europe, stands around the corner from the tube station.

Just south of Camden Town lies the 500-acre **Regent's Park** (tube: Regent's Park, Great Portland St., Baker St., or Camden Town; open 5am-dusk). Larger than either Hyde Park or Kensington Gardens, and full of lakes, promenades, and Dakotan open spaces, the park has become a popular spot for family cricket and football matches. On Sundays from June through August, you can hear tubas and trumpets entertain at the bandstand, or see performances in the **Open Air Theatre** near Queen Mary's Gardens (see Entertainment). Take a boat ride on the park's lake (£1.25), or, if you're feeling romantic, navigate your own (rowboat for max. 4 people £5.50, available daily 10am-dusk).

Laid out in 1812 by John Nash for the Prince Regent (the future George IV), the park is edged on three sides by majestic Nash terraces. The recently restored Regency terraces present a magnificent façade. The cream-colored porticoed and pillared buildings have been home to the likes of H.G. Wells (17 Hanover Terrace) and Wallis Simpson (7 Hanover Terrace). **Regent's Park Canal,** part of the Grand Union Canal, dips around the unprotected north side of the park and into neighboring Paddington. From "Little Venice" (Tube: Warwick Avenue), you can take a leisurely trip down the canal (see Essentials—Getting Around).

The park's most popular attraction historically has been the privately owned **London Zoo** (tel. 722 3333; tube: Camden Town, or Baker St.; bus #274 from either station takes you almost to the door), located in the northeast quadrant. Despite a long period of near financial collapse, the zoo—Britain's largest—survived, and today you can see two giant pandas, rare Asian lions, a poisonous black mamba named Fang, and an aquarium with sharks and piranhas. The zoo has the added attraction of some terrific modern architecture; don't miss the elegant double-helix ramps at the center of the Penguin Pool, designed by Lubetkin in 1934. In August 1994, the zoo will reopen its enlarged and updated Children's Zoo. (Open daily 10am-5:30pm; Oct.-March daily 10am-4pm. Admission £6.50, concessions £5, under 15 £4, families £17.50.)

Within the park's Inner Circle, the delightful **Queen Mary's Gardens** erupt in color in early summer. The rose garden, which stays open until dusk, dazzles with 20,000 blooms. North of Regent's Park stands **Primrose Hill,** long a favorite spot for picnics and kite-flying. (It is also the site of a pagan rite conducted by druids on the Autumn Equinox.) On a clear day you can see as far as the Surrey Downs.

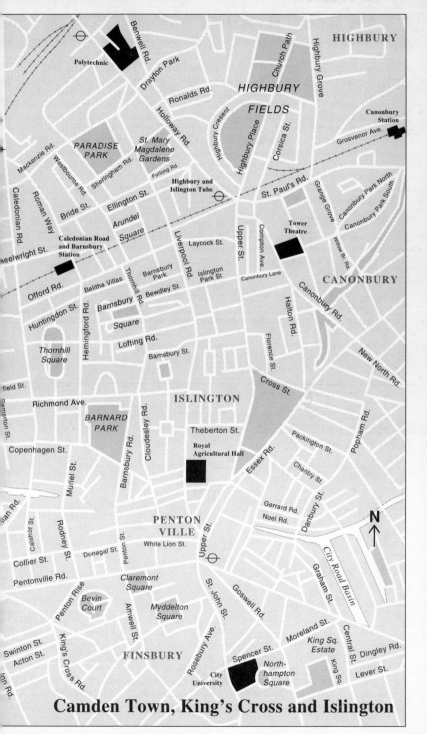

Camden Town, King's Cross and Islington

■■■ BLOOMSBURY

During the first half of the 20th century, Bloomsbury gained its reputation as an intellectual and artistic center, due largely to the vitalizing presence of the famed Bloomsbury Group, which included biographer Lytton Strachey, novelist E.M. Forster, economist John Maynard Keynes, art critic Roger Fry, painter Vanessa Bell (sister of Virginia Woolf), and, hovering on the fringe, T.S. Eliot, the eminent British poet from St. Louis. Although very little of the famed intellectual gossip and high modernist argot still emanates from 51 Gordon Square, where Virginia Woolf lived with her husband Leonard, the area has maintained an earnestly intellectual atmosphere. Even after the Bloomsbury Group's disintegration, young artists and radicals still populated the area, giving rise to the term "Bloomsbury bluestockings" to describe modern young women who smoked, drank, and defied the restrictive rules of behavior then current for women.

Today, the British Museum and the University of London guarantee a continued concentration of cerebral activity in the area. The **British Museum** makes an appropriate Bloomsbury centerpiece; forbidding on the outside but quirky and amazing within, it contains the remains of 2 million years' worth of world history and civilization, in addition to sheltering the enthralling British Library until construction is completed on its new home (see Museums).

Buildings of the **University of London** pepper the streets to the north of the Museum. Excluded from the Anglican-dominated universities at Oxford and Cambridge, Jeremy Bentham and a group of dissenters founded **University College** on Gower St. in 1828. They modeled the curriculum after those of German research universities, banned the teaching of theology, and admitted Catholics and Jews. Rumor has it that an embalmed Bentham (or at least his clothed skeleton) resides in a closet there and is rolled out for meetings of the trustees. University College was chartered (along with King's College in The Strand) as the University of London in 1836, making London the last major European capital to acquire a university. In 1878, the University became the first to admit women to its degree courses. The university's administrative headquarters and library reside in **Senate House**, the white concrete tower (1933) dominating Malet St.

To the north, close to the former houses of Strachey and Keynes, stands the **Percival David Foundation of Chinese Art,** 53 Gordon Sq. (tel. 387 3909; tube: Russell Sq. or Goodge St.), a connoisseur's hoard of fabulously rare ceramics. Sir David presented his collection to the University of London in 1950, and it is currently administered by SOAS (the School of Oriental and African Studies). Waft by the intricate fan bequeathed in 1930 by the last emperor of China to his English tutor, Sir Reginald Johnston, and be sure to save time for the illuminating Ming Gallery on the top floor (open Mon.-Fri. 10:30am-5pm; free).

To the northeast along Euston Rd., **St. Pancras Station** (tube: King's Cross/St. Pancras) rises as a monument to Victorian prosperity over a neighborhood of present-day decay. This red-brick neo-gothic fantasy, completed in 1867, opened in 1874 as the Midland Grand Hotel. In 1890 the hotel opened the first smoking room for women in London. After serving as an office building from 1935 until the early 1980s, the now abandoned building faces an uncertain future.

Next door, the sprawling new (and controversially ugly) **British Library** is still under construction, although it is due to open in 1996-7. Plans and models of the modern, tiered, red-brick library can be viewed in the intriguing Library galleries in the British Museum.

Up St. Pancras Rd., past the station's red brick effluvia, **St. Pancras Old Church** sits serenely in its large and leafy garden. Mary Godwin first met Shelley here in 1813 by the grave of her mother, Mary Wollstonecraft. Rumor has it that believing her mum died during her birth, Godwin insisted that Shelley make love with her on the grave. Parts of the church date from the 11th century.

Directly northeast of the British museum, **Russell Square** squares off as central London's second-largest, after Lincoln's Inn Fields. T.S. Eliot, the "Pope of Russell

Square," hid from his emotionally ailing first wife at no. 24 while he worked as an editor and later director of Faber and Faber, the famed publishing house.

Bernard Street leads east to Brunswick Square, sight of the **Thomas Coram Foundation for Children** (40 Brunswick Square, tel. 278 2424; tube: Russell Square). Thomas Coram, a retired sea captain, established the Foundling Hospital for abandoned children here in 1747. In order to raise funds, he sought the help of prominent artists, including William Hogarth, who, in addition to serving as a governor of the hospial, donated paintings and persuaded his friends to do the same. The composer Handel also lent a hand, giving the hospital an organ and performing in a number of benefit concerts. Although the hospital was torn down in 1926, its art treasures remain, displayed in a suite of splendidly restored 18th-century rooms. Several canvases by Hogarth mingle with works by Gainsborough, Benjamin West, and Roubiliac, a cartoon by Raphael, and a signed manuscript copy of the *Messiah*. The adjacent Governor's Court Room, with its ornate ceilings and rococo plaster work, houses a poignant collection of tokens and trinkets left with the foundlings admitted to the hospital before 1760 (open Mon. and Fri. 1:30-4:30pm; admission £1, art students and seniors 50p).

Across from the Foundation lies **Coram's Fields** (93 Guilford St., tel. 837 6138), 7 acres of old Foundling Hospital grounds which have been preserved as a children's park, complete with a menagerie of petting animals, an aviary, and a paddling pool for kids under five. No dogs allowed—no adults, either, unless accompanied by a child (open Easter-Oct. daily 9am-8pm, Nov.-March daily 9am-5pm; free).

Charles Dickens lived at 48 Doughty St. (east of Russell Sq., parallel to Gray's Inn Rd.) from 1837 to 1839, scribbling parts of *The Pickwick Papers, Nicholas Nickleby, Barnaby Rudge,* and *Oliver Twist.* Now a four-floor museum and library of Dickens paraphernalia, the **Dickens House** (tel. 405 2127; tube: Russell Sq. or Chancery La.) holds an array of prints, photographs, manuscripts, letters, and personal effects. The rusty iron grill mounted on a basement wall was salvaged by the author from the Marshalsea Jail, a notorious debtor's prison where Dickens's father did time for three months in 1824 while his young son labored in a shoe-black factory (open Mon.-Sat. 10am-5pm, last entry 4:30pm; £3, students £2, children £1, family £6).

To the south of the British museum, the shrapnel-scarred Corinthian portico of Hawksmoor's 18th-century church, **St. George's, Bloomsbury** looms in Bloomsbury Way. Completed in 1730 according to Hawksmoor's design, a statue of George I crowns the heavy steeple which was modelled on the tomb of King Mansolos in Turkey. Inside, novelist Anthony Trollope was baptized before the magnificent gilded mahogany altar, where Dickens set his "Bloomsbury Christening" in *Sketches by Boz* (open sporadically: "We try to keep the church open all day, but we can't leave it unattended").

At the corner of Little Russell St. and Coptic St., a modern day **Pizza Express** (reputed to be the best pizza chain in London) has very tastefully adapted itself to fit its shell, a well-preserved Victorian dairy. Even if you do pass on the pizza, poke your head in for a peek at the tiled interior and the brilliant blue glass windows on the inside wall (open daily 11:30am-midnight).

Directly west of the museum, Bedford Square remains one of London's best-preserved 18th-century squares. All of the doorways of what are now offices are framed with original pieces of Coade Stone, an artificial stone manufactured outside of London. Further west, the residential calm is interrupted by Tottenham Ct. Rd., lined with furniture and electronics shops. To the north, the 580ft **Telecom Tower** rears up over Fitzrovia, emitting TV and radio waves.

Despite the historical aura which suffuses the area today, Bloomsbury is still a locus of innovation. Several community centers provide venues and resources for alternative cultural activity. Particularly noteworthy are the **Drill Hall Arts Center** (see Entertainment—Fringe theatres), **The Place** (see Entertainment—Opera and Ballet), and the **October Gallery** (24 Old Gloucester St., off of Queen St.) a small venue which mounts the works of young, international artists (tel. 242 7367; open

Tues.-Sat. 12:30-5:30pm). Similarly, **Gay's The Word Bookshop** (see Bi, Gay, and Lesbian London) adds its own slant to the collection of traditional, second-hand, and rare bookstores that recall Bloomsbury's historical role as a center of book trade.

St. Giles-in-the-Fields, a modest rectangular church surmounted by a beautiful Flitcroft tower (1731), rises above a 1687 Resurrection relief and a lush churchyard on St. Giles High St. John Wesley and his brother Charles preached from the pulpit here between 1743 and 1791. George Chapman, the celebrated translator of Homer and inspirer of Keats, lies buried beneath a heroic tomb attributed to Inigo Jones in the north aisle. The children of numerous London literati came here to be baptized, including Milton's daughter (and patient reader) Mary and Byron's daughter Allegra (open Mon.-Fri. 9am-4:30pm).

■■■ ISLINGTON

Lying in the low hills just north of the City of London, Islington (tube: Angel or Highbury and Islington) began as a royal hunting ground. Islington was first absorbed into London by fugitives from the Plague, and later by industrialization and trade along the Regent's Canal.

Islington first became "trendy" during the late 17th century when its ale houses and cream teas made it a popular hang-out for the wealthy. A century later, however, the rich began to move out, leaving the area to deteriorate. In more recent times, Islington was one of London's first areas to undergo regentrification; it established itself as an academic and artistic haven by the 1930s, serving as home to writers such as George Orwell, Evelyn Waugh, Douglas Adams, and Salman Rushdie.

Today, Islington is one of the hottest neighborhoods in London. Often likened to New York City's Greenwich Village and SoHo, the area is favored by trendy, style-conscious, and well-to-do Londoners, sometimes criticized for their artsy self-indulgence. Many of the more stylish University of London students and professors live here, alongside several ethnic communities including Turkish, Irish, Italian, and Bengali residents. As the number of gay pubs in the area attests, Islington is also home to a large gay community. (Chris Smith, the only voluntarily out Member of Parliament, was elected from this area.)

A refurbished 19th-century chapel at 44a Pentonville Road now houses the **Crafts Council,** the national organization for the promotion of contemporary crafts. In addition to the Crafts Council Gallery, the building also contains a picture library with slides of British works, a reference library, a gallery shop, and a café. The council sponsors fantastic temporary exhibitions. 1994 shows included *True to Type* (an introduction to letterpress printing, featuring the works of 15 small presses), and *What is Jewelry?* (a cross-cultural and historical look at the function and style of jewelry in society; from the end of Nov.-Jan. 22 1995). Take advantage of the free admission; not only are the main exhibition galleries wonderfully air-conditioned, but the building's lighting fixtures, furniture, clocks, floors, door handles and lettering have been designed by contemporary artisans, creating an aesthetically appealing exhibition space. (Tel. 278 7700. Tube: Angel; exit the station to the left and take the first right onto Pentonville Rd. Open Tues.-Sat. 11am-6pm, Sun. 2-6pm. Wheelchair accessible.)

To the north, well-attended street markets **Chapel Markets** and **Camden Passage**, to the left and right of Upper St., offer fresh produce and cheap clothing, and expensive antiques, respectively (see Shopping).

The **Business Design Centre** at 52 Upper St. is hard to miss. The modern-looking glass façade belies its origin as the Royal Agricultural Hall, completed in 1861. Known as "the Aggie," the Hall's large, enclosed space served as the site for a wide range of crafts exhibitions, animal shows, meetings, Christmas fêtes, military tournaments, circuses and the World's Fair. All was happy and glorious until the start of World War II, when the government took over the Hall to use it as an office building. In the 1970s, the Hall was sold to a property developer who hadn't realized that the historic building could not legally be demolished; he in turn sold the site to the

Islington Council in 1976. The future of the building seemed uncertain. In 1985, however, the Hall was purchased by a commercial developer, and after a year and a half of restoration, it re-opened in 1986 as the Business Design Centre, part office building, part trade market, and, marking a return to its golden past, part exhibition complex. Annual exhibits include Fresh Art (July 21-31, 1994), a showcase for recent fine arts graduates, and New Designers (July 7-17, 1994), a springboard for commercial and consumer design students. (Call 359 3535 for information and details; many exhibitions charge admission.)

At the south end of Islington Green, a statue of Sir High Myddleton commemorates the man who built the 40-mile New River Canal in 1613. Running between Canonburg Rd., and St. Paul's Rd., the canal originally brought water down to London from Herfordshire.

Those interested in the history of Islington should visit the **Museum Gallery** at 268 Upper St. (tel. 354 9442), which sponsors local history (and local artists') exhibitions. (Open Wed.-Fri. 11am-3pm, Sat. 11am-5pm, Sun. 2-4pm. Tube: Highbury and Islington.) Also indispensible is the **Islington Tourist Information Centre** at 44 Duncan St. (tel 278 8787), with its friendly staff, free pamphlets, reference books, and information on local guided walks. (Open Mon.-Sat. 10am-5pm. Tube: Angel; exit right and take the first right.)

Islington's increasingly youthful inhabitants, known as the N1 *cognoscenti*, tout Islington as "the West End without the tourists, Covent Garden without the crap." Boasting dozens of cafés and bistros, several active and critically-acclaimed "fringe" theaters, starring the **King's Head** and the **Old Red Lion** theaters among others (see Theatre), a concentration of popular gay pubs, and a reputable repertory cinema, it's not hard to see why the area has drawn such a loyal following.

■■■ HOLBORN AND THE INNS OF COURT

The historical center of English law lies in an area straddling the precincts of Westminster and the City and surrounding long and litigious High Holborn, Chancery Lane, and Fleet Street. The Strand and Fleet St. meet at the **Royal Courts of Justice** (tel. 936 6000; tube: Temple or Aldwych—rush hours only), a wonderfully elaborate Gothic structure designed in 1874 by architect G.E. Street for the Supreme Court of Judicature. While historical legal costumes are on display, most visitors come to view the courts in action (courts and galleries open to the public Mon.-Fri. 9am-4:30pm; court cases start at 10:30am).

Barristers in the City are affiliated with one of the famous **Inns of Court** (Middle Temple, Inner Temple, Lincoln's Inn, and Gray's Inn), four ancient legal institutions which provide lectures and apprenticeships for law students and regulate admission to the bar. The tiny gates and narrow alleyways that lead to the Inns are invisible to most passersby. Inside, the Inns are organized like colleges at Oxford, each with its own gardens, chapel, library, dining hall, common rooms, and chambers. Most were founded in the 13th century when a royal decree barred the clergy from the courts of justice, giving rise to a new class of professional legal advocates. Today, students may seek their legal training outside of the Inns, but to be considered for membership they must "keep term" by dining regularly in one of the halls.

South of Fleet St., the labyrinth of the **Temple** (tube: Temple) encloses the prestigious and stately Middle and Inner Temple Inns. They derive their name from the clandestine, elusive, crusading Order of the Knights Templar, who embraced this site as their English seat in the 12th century. The secretive, bellicose order dissolved in 1312, and this property was eventually passed on to the Knights Hospitallers of St. John, who leased it to a community of common law scholars in 1338. Virtually leveled by the Germans in the early 1940s, only the church, crypt, and buttery of the Inner Temple survive intact from the Middle Ages.

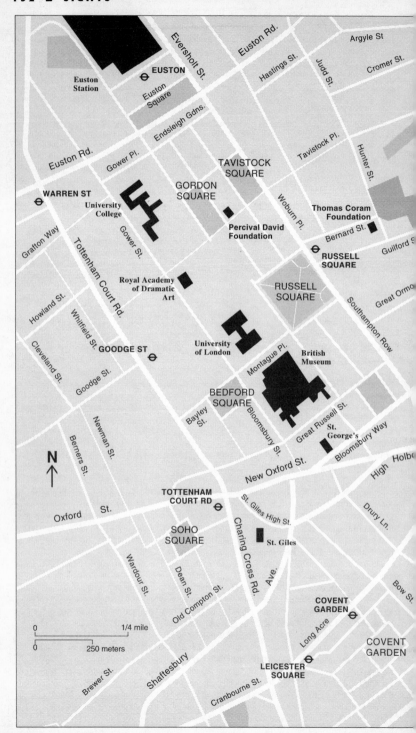

EVERSHOLT St.
Euston Rd.
Argyle St
Hastings St.
Cromer St.
Judd St.

Euston Station
EUSTON
Euston Square

Endsleigh Gdns.

Euston Rd.
Gower Pl.

Tavistock Pl.
Hunter St.

TAVISTOCK SQUARE

WARREN ST
GORDON SQUARE

Grafton Way

University College

Woburn Pl.

Thomas Coram Foundation

Percival David Foundation

Bernard St.

RUSSELL SQUARE

Guilford S

Gower St.

Tottenham Court Rd.

Royal Academy of Dramatic Art

RUSSELL SQUARE

Great Orm

Southampton Row

Howland St.

Whitfield St.

Cleveland St.

University of London

GOODGE ST

Goodge St.

Montague Pl.

British Museum

BEDFORD SQUARE

Bayley St.

Bloomsbury St.

Great Russell St.

St. George's

Bloomsbury Way

High Holb

N

Berners St.

Newman St.

New Oxford St.

Drury Ln.

Oxford St.

TOTTENHAM COURT RD

St. Giles High St.

SOHO SQUARE

Charing Cross Rd.

St. Giles

Wardour St.

Dean St.

Old Compton St.

Ave.

Bow St

COVENT GARDEN

0   1/4 mile
0   250 meters

Long Acre

COVENT GARDEN

LEICESTER SQUARE

Brewer St.

Shaftesbury

Cranbourne St.

Bloomsbury, Holborn, and Fleet Street

Acton St.

King's Cross Rd.

Lloyd Baker St.

Rosebery Ave.

Goswell Rd.

City University

Gray's Inn Rd.

Farringdon Rd.

Exmouth Market

Cyrus St.

Mecklenburg

Calthorpe St.

Wren St.

Mount Pleasant

Compton St.

St. John St.

Lamb's Conduit St.

Doughty St.

Great James St.

Dickens' House

John St.

Clerkenwell Rd.

FARRINGDON

Cowcross St.

Theobald's Rd.

Gray's Inn

Leather Lane

Hatton Garden

Farringdon Rd.

Charterhouse St.

Red Lion St.

Greville St.

CHANCERY LANE

Smithfield Market

Long Lane

High Holborn

HOLBORN

Sir John Soane's Museum

Chancery Lane

Fetter Ln.

New Fetter Ln.

Holborn Viaduct

Lincoln's Inn

London Silver Vault

Dr. Johnson's House

Old Bailey

Lincoln's Inn Fields

Kingsway

Bream's Bldgs.

Shoe Lane

Portugal St.

Carey St.

Public Records Office

LUDGATE CIRCUS

Ludgate Hill

Royal Courts of Justice

St. Dunstan's

Fleet St.

St. Brides

New Bridge St.

St. Clement Dane's

The Temple

1

Bouverie St.

Tudor St.

Blackfriars Station

Aldwych

Arundel St.

Essex St.

Middle Temple Ln.

King's Bench Wk.

2

4

City of London College

BLACK-FRIARS

St. Mary-le-Strand

ALDWYCH

3

Temple Ave.

Somerset House

Embankment

Blackfriars Br.

Lancaster Pl.

Victoria

TEMPLE

1 Temple Church of St. Mary
2 Inner Temple Gardens
3 Middle Temple Gardens
4 Middle Temple Hall

Held in common by both the Middle and Inner Temples, the **Temple Church** is the finest of the few round churches left in England. It contains gorgeous stained-glass windows, a handsome 12th-century Norman doorway, an altar screen by Wren (1682), and ten arresting, armor-clad stone effigies of sinister Knights Templar dating from the 12th and 14th centuries. Be sure to note the menacing and grotesque heads lining the circular wall surrounding the effigies. Author Oliver Goldsmith, whose late-night revelry at the Temple often irritated his staid neighbor, Blackstone, lies buried in the yard behind the choir (open erratically Wed.-Sat. 10am-4pm, Sun. 1-4pm).

According to Shakespeare (*Henry VI*), the red and white roses that served as emblems throughout the War of the Roses were plucked from the Middle Temple Garden. On Groundhog Day in 1601, Shakespeare himself supposedly appeared in a performance of *Twelfth Night* in **Middle Temple Hall,** a grand Elizabethan dining room in a building on Middle Temple Lane, just past Brick Ct. (not open to the public). **Fountain Court** contains its 1681 namesake, restored in 1919. Nearby, a handful of London's last functioning gas lamps illuminate Middle Temple Lane.

Back across Fleet St., on the other side of the Royal Courts, **Lincoln's Inn** (tube: Holborn) was the only Inn to emerge unscathed from the Blitz. The lawyers of Lincoln's Inn were mocked by John Donne's rhyming couplets in his *Satire: On Lawyers.* New Square and its cloistered churchyard (to the right as you enter from Lincoln's Inn Fields) appear today much as they did in the 1680s. The **Old Hall,** east of New Sq., dates from 1492; here the Lord High Chancellor presided over the High Court of Chancery from 1733 to 1873. The best-known chancery case is that of Jarndyce and Jarndyce, whose life-sapping machinations are played out in the many pages of *Bleak House.* Dickens knew well what he described, having worked as a lawyer's clerk in New Court just across the yard. To the west, Tudor-style **New Hall** houses a 19th-century mural by G.F. Watts and a lugubrious collection of legal portraits. Built in 1497, the adjacent library is London's oldest. John Donne, William Pitt, Horace Walpole, and Benjamin Disraeli number among the many luminaries associated with Lincoln's Inn. (See the porter at 11a Lincoln's Inn Fields for admission to the halls; irregular opening policies.) **Sir John Soane's Museum** sits smugly on the north side of Lincoln's Inn Fields, London's largest square; it's the house bedecked with sculpture amidst a row of plain buildings (see Museums).

Gray's Inn (tube: Chancery La.), dubbed "that stronghold of melancholy" by Dickens, stands at the northern end of Fulwood Pl., off High Holborn. Reduced to ashes by German bombers in 1941, Gray's Inn was restored to much of its former splendor during the 1950s. The Hall, to your right as you pass through the archway, retains its original stained glass (1580) and most of its ornate screen. The first performance of Shakespeare's *Comedy of Errors* took place here in 1594. Francis Bacon maintained chambers here from 1577 until his death in 1626, and is the purported designer of the magnificent gardens.

Of the nine Inns of Chancery, only **Staple Inn's** building survives (located where Gray's Inn Rd. meets High Holborn; tube: Chancery La.). The half-timbered Elizabethan front, with its easily recognized vertical striping, dates from 1586. Devoted son Samuel Johnson wrote "Rasselas" here in one week to pay for his mother's funeral. For those who can't get enough of the fascinating Inns of Court, "Legal London" **walking tours** are held every Monday and Wednesday at 2pm and 11am respectively (tel. 624 3978; £4, students £3).

South of Gray's Inn and east of Lincoln's Inn stands the **Public Records Office** and its museum (tel. (081) 876 3444) on Chancery La., where William the Conqueror's *Domesday Book,* a statistical survey of England written on animal skins, outclasses the rest of the exhibits. The museum's lone room offers other scraps of British parchment salvaged from the confetti mills of time, like contracts for buildings and statistics on child labor. The exhibits are drawn from the office's vast collection and are rotated regularly (museum open Mon.-Fri. 9:30am-4:45pm; free).

■■■ FLEET STREET

Named for the one-time river (now a sewer) that flows from Hampstead to the Thames, Fleet Street (tube: Blackfriars or St. Paul's) was until recently the hub of British journalism. Once a hive of journalistic activity, Fleet Street is now just a famous name and a few (vacated) famous buildings. In 1986 the *Times,* which moved to cheaper land at Wapping, Docklands, initiated a mass exodus from the street. The *Daily Telegraph* abandoned its startling Greek and Egyptian revival building, moving to Marsh Wall in 1987. The *Daily Express,* once the occupant of an Art Deco manse of chrome and black glass on Fleet St., now headlines in Blackfriars. Rupert Murdoch's *The Sun* also moved to Wapping at this time, using the move as an excuse to shift to non-union labor. (In looking for addresses of the following sights, beware that, like many English streets, Fleet St. is numbered up one side and down the other.)

The tiered spire of Wren's **St. Bride's** (1675), near 89 Fleet St., became the inspiration for countless wedding cakes thanks to an ingenious local baker. Dubbed "the printers' church" because the first printing press with moveable type was housed here in 1500, it boasts a ceiling adorned with shiny gold rosettes and scrollery. Post-Blitz excavations of its ancient crypt have revealed traces of a late Saxon cemetery, the foundation of a 6th-century Roman structure, and the ruins of several earlier churches. Also underground, a musty collection of relics and rocks calls itself a museum, alongside an exhibit detailing the evolution of printing in Fleet St. (open Mon.-Fri. 8:30am-5pm, Sat. 9am-5pm, Sun. 9am-7:30pm).

A few blocks down the street, opposite 54 Fleet St., a large white sign labels the alleyway entrance to Johnson's Court. Inside the alley, more discreet signs point the way to **Samuel Johnson's House,** 17 Gough Square (tel. 353 3745). Follow the signs carefully; Carlyle got lost on his way here in 1832. This dark brick house was Dr. Johnson's abode from 1749 to 1758. Here he completed his *Dictionary,* the first definitive English lexicon, even though rumor falsely insists that he omitted "sausage." Johnson buffs will not find many original documents here, but they can carry home bookmarks bearing his image. Tours are self-guided, but the knowledgeable curator is eager to supplement your visit with anecdotes about the Great Cham and his hyperbolic biographer, James Boswell (open Mon.-Sat. 11am-5:30pm; Oct.-April Mon.-Sat. 11am-5pm; admission £3, students, children, and senior citizens £2).

A few more blocks down Fleet St., the neo-Gothic **St. Dunstan-in-the-West** holds its magnificent lantern tower high above the banks surrounding it. The chimes of its curious 17th-century clock are sounded on the quarter hour by a pair of hammer-wielding, mechanical giants. A statue of Elizabeth I (one of the few contemporary likenesses of the Queen) rises above the vestry door. The three 16th-century effigies leaning against the porch may represent King Lud, the mythical founder of London, and his sons. In the central archway, you can see a rough carving of poet-priest John Donne. Both Donne and his biographer Izaak Walton maintained close ties with the church of St. Dunstan.

About a block down the street, at no. 17 Fleet St. (tube: Temple), a half-timbered house dating from 1610 perches above the gateway to the Temple Church (see Holborn and Inns of Court). The stairs leading up to **Prince Henry's Room** (tel. (081) 294 1158) are just to the left of the gate. The one room consists of an ornate but monochromatic 17th-century ceiling (arguably London's finest example of Jacobean plaster-work), richly carved mahogany paneling, and Samuel Pepys memorabilia (open Mon.-Sat. 11am-2pm; free).

■■■ THE STRAND

Hugging the embankment of the River Thames, **The Strand** (tube: Charing Cross, Temple, or Aldwych—rush hours only) has fared ill through London's growth. Once lined with fine Tudor houses, today this major thoroughfare curves from Trafalgar Square through a jumbled assortment of dull commercial buildings. All the sights are at the Aldwych and Temple end of the street.

Somerset House, a magnificent Palladian structure built by Sir William Chambers in 1776, stands on the site of the 16th-century palace where Elizabeth I resided during the brief reign of her sister Mary. Formerly the administrative center of the Royal Navy, the building now houses the exquisite **Courtauld Collection** (see Museums) and the less exquisite offices of the Inland Revenue.

Just east of the Courtauld, **St. Mary-le-Strand's** slender steeple and elegant portico rise above an island of decaying steps in the middle of the modern roadway. Designed by James Gibbs and consecrated in 1724, the church overlooks the site of the original Maypole, where London's first hackney cabs assembled in 1634. Parishioner Isaac Newton laid claim to the pole for a telescope stand. Inside, the baroque barrel vault and altar walls reflect Gibbs' architectural training in Rome. The intricate floral moldings were crafted by brothers John and Chrysostom Wilkins, who received a mere 45p for each elaborate bloom (open Mon.-Fri. 11am-3:30pm). Across the street, newsreaders pompously intone "This is London" every hour from Bush House, the nerve center of the **BBC**'s worldwide radio services.

To the east stands handsome **St. Clement Danes** (tel. 242 8282), whose melodious bells get their 15 seconds of fame in the nursery rhyme "Oranges and lemons, say the bells of St. Clement's." Children get their 15 minutes of fruit when oranges and lemons are distributed in a ceremony near the end of March. Designed by Wren in 1682, the church was built over the ruins of an older Norman structure reputed to be the tomb of Harold Harefoot, leader of a colony of Danes who settled the area in the 9th century. In 1720, Gibbs replaced Wren's original truncated tower with a slimmer spire. Although German firebombs gutted the church in 1941, the ornately molded white stucco and gilt interior has been restored, contrasting beautifully with the rich darkness of the wooden pews. This official church of the Royal Air Force has marble floors inlaid with brass squadron medallions, but the altarpiece painting and twisted hanging brass lamps are more aesthetically pleasing. A crypt-*cum*-prayer-chapel houses an eerie collection of 17th-century funerary monuments. Samuel Johnson worshipped here, and a statue of the Doctor strikes a bizarre pose outside the church (open daily 8am-5pm). Outside the front entrance, the recently erected "Bomber" Harris memorial has attracted controversy; Col. Arthur Harris masterminded the devastating firebombing of civilian Dresden in World War II.

The nearby Gothic giant houses the Royal Courts of Justice (see Holborn and Inns of Court). **Twining's Teas** (tel. 353 3511) brews at 216 The Strand, near the Fleet St. end of the road. It is both the oldest business in Britain still operating on original premises and the narrowest shop in London (open Mon.-Fri. 9:30am-4:30pm). Just east stands the only Strand building to survive the Great Fire, the **Wig and Pen Club,** 229-230 The Strand, which was constructed over Roman ruins in 1625. Frequented by the best-known barristers and journalists in London, the Wig and Pen is, in the sage words of the *Baltimore Sun,* "a window through which you can see Fleet Street in all its aspects." The club is open to members only, though a passport-toting overseas traveler can apply for free temporary, if not actively encouraged, membership. If you have the nerve, walk up the ancient, crooked staircase—the only remnant of the original 17th-century house. Backpackers beware: the doorman will haughtily reject denim-bedecked budget travelers.

The **Temple Bar Monument** stands in the middle of the street where The Strand meets Fleet St., marking the boundary between Westminster and the City. The Sovereign must still obtain ceremonial permission from the Lord Mayor to pass the bar and enter the City here.

To the south, the **Embankment** (tube: Charing Cross or Embankment) runs along the Thames, parallel to The Strand. Between the Hungerford and Waterloo Bridges stands London's oldest (though non-indigenous) landmark, **Cleopatra's Needle,** an Egyptian obelisk from 1450 BC, stolen by the Viceroy of Egypt in 1878. A sister stone stands in Central Park in New York. Fairly near Trafalgar Sq., the **Savoy Chapel** (1505) on Savoy Hill—an appendage of Savoy Palace, inhabited after

1268 by John of Gaunt—provides a respite from the traffic and sensationalistic journalism of Fleet St. (tel. 836 7221; open Tues.-Fri. 11:30am-3:30pm).

■■■ THE CITY OF LONDON

Until the 18th century, the City of London was London; all other boroughs and neighborhoods now swallowed up by "London" were neighboring towns or outlying villages. Enclosed by Roman and medieval walls, the City had six gates, whose names survive: Aldersgate, Aldgate, Bishopsgate, Cripplegate, Newgate, and Ludgate.

Today, the one-square-mile City of London is the financial center of Europe. Each weekday 350,000 people surge in at 9am and rush out again unfailingly at 5pm, leaving behind a resident population of only 6000. Today's City hums with activity during the work week, is dead on Saturdays, and seems downright ghostly on Sundays. At the center of the City, the massive Bank of England controls the nation's finances, and the Stock Exchange makes the nation's fortune. Proliferating cranes, office building sites, and rising share indices bore witness to the British "economic resurgence" of the late 80s, while the panic in such City stalwarts as Lloyd's of London is testimony to the non-recovery of the early 90s. Terrorist attacks in the recent past have prompted the government to regulate traffic into the City; all vehicles must enter from one of eight streets where they are then checked for bombs. These security measures have exacerbated the City's traffic congestion.

The City owes much of its graceful appearance to Sir Christopher Wren, who was the chief architect working after the fire of 1666 almost completely razed the area. In his diary, Samuel Pepys gives a moving firsthand account of the fire that started in a baker's shop in Pudding Lane and leapt between the overhanging houses to bring destruction upon the City. Afterwards, Charles II issued a proclamation that City buildings should be rebuilt in brick and stone, rather than highly flammable wood and thatch. Wren's studio designed 52 churches to replace the 89 destroyed in the fire, and the surviving 24 churches are some of the only buildings in the City from the period immediately following the Great Fire. A host of variations on a theme, they gave Wren a valuable chance to work out problems of design that would come up as he rebuilt St. Paul's Cathedral. The original effect of a forest of steeples surrounding the great dome of St. Paul's must be his greatest contribution to London's cityscape; unfortunately, the modern skyscrapers so energetically condemned by amateur city planner Prince Charles now obscure that effect. Most of the City's churches have *irregular or random opening times*.

Perhaps the most important secular structures of the City are the buildings of the **Livery Companies.** The companies began as medieval guilds representing specific trades and occupations, such as the Drapers and the Fishmongers. These guilds played a role in fixing trade standards; today many also contribute to charity and sponsor educational programs. New guilds, like the information technologists, have formed to keep up with changing times. The 84 **livery halls** are scattered around the square mile. Most halls do not open to the public; those that do require tickets. The City of London Information Centre (see below) receives a batch of tickets in February, but they disappear rapidly. Inquire there for the current opening situation. Some halls sponsor spring celebrations, and a few hold fascinating exhibits—for example, a showing of the finest products of London's goldsmiths.

The **City of London Information Centre,** St. Paul's Churchyard (tel. 332 1456; tube: St. Paul's) can give you up-to-date details on all of the City's attractions. (Open daily 9:30am-5pm; Nov.-March Mon.-Fri. 9:30am-5pm, Sat. 9:30am-12:30pm.) A 24-hour on-line "Leisure Data Base" is located just outside of the Information Centre. Simply touch the computer screen to access information that falls into one of the following categories: kids, sports, attractions, the countryside, days out in London, and the Barbican. Information can be accessed by subject, event, or venue; detailed descriptions, listings, and directions make this a useful resource.

The oldest part of London, the City is home to many municipal traditions. One of the largest is the **Lord Mayor's Show,** on the second Saturday of November, a glittering parade of pomp and red velvet to the Royal Courts of Justice in celebration of London citizens' right to elect their Lord Mayor. Information and street plans are available from the City of London Information Centre starting in mid-October. One of the newer traditions is July's **City of London Festival,** which jam-packs the churches, halls, squares, and sidewalks of the area with music and theater (see Entertainment).

Although currently devoted to the business of making money, the City offers an unusual number of free attractions. Most of the specialized museums in the area are free, and many of the churches sponsor free weekly lunchtime music recitals (usually starting at 1:10pm). Keep an eye out for the many vestpocket parks which dot the City—perfect places to munch on a take-away lunch. On weekends the activity dies down, leaving the City practically deserted; many of the pubs and restaurants close down. However, the museums and some of the Wren churches remain open on Sundays, giving visitors a chance to contemplate the City architecture without being crushed by umbrellas and briefcases.

■ BANK TO LUDGATE: WESTERN SECTION

The few remaining stones of the Roman **Temple of Mithras,** Queen Victoria St. (tube: Bank or Mansion House), dwell incongruously in the shadow of the Temple Court building. Discovered during construction work and shifted a few yards from its original location, the temple still retains a recognizable outline. Down Queen Victoria St., **St. Mary Aldermary** (so called because it is older than any other St. Mary's church in the City) towers over its surroundings. A rare Gothic Wren, it is especially notable for its delicate fan vaulting. The bells that recalled London's old Mayor Dick Whittington to London rang out from the church of St. Marie de Arcubus, replaced by Wren's **St. Mary-le-Bow,** Cheapside, in 1683. The range of the Bow bells' toll is supposed to define the extent of true-blue Cockney London.

St. James Garlickhythe, on Upper Thames St., gets its name from the garlic once sold nearby. Its modest Hawksmoor steeple is dwarfed by the huge Vintners Place development across the street. To the west on Queen Victoria St. stands a rare red-brick Wren church with an elegant cupola, **St. Benet's.** Just across the street, the **College of Arms** rests on its heraldic authority behind ornate gates. The College regulates the granting and recognition of coats of arms, and is directed by the Earl Marshal, the Duke of Norfolk. The officer-in-waiting at the Earl Marshal's stately paneled Court Room can assess your claim to a British family coat of arms. (Open Mon.-Fri. 10am-4pm.) Farther west, at 146 Queen Victoria, **St. Andrew-by-the-Wardrobe** (tube: Blackfriars) was originally built next to Edward III's impressive Royal Stores. Now the church cowers beneath the Faraday building, the first building allowed to exceed the City's previously strict height limit.

Queen Victoria St. meets New Bridge St. in the area known as Blackfriars, in reference to the darkly clad Dominican brothers who built a monastery there in the middle ages. Shakespeare acted in James Burbage's theater here in the late 1500s. Ludgate Circus, to the north, is now the noisy site of major redevelopment. A peaceful haven is offered by **St. Martin-within-Ludgate,** a Wren church on Ludgate Hill untouched by the Blitz. The square interior boasts some fine Grinling Gibbons woodwork, and the slim spire still pierces the dome of St. Paul's when seen from Ludgate Circus, just as Wren intended.

Around the corner, the **Old Bailey** (tel. 248 3277; tube: St. Paul's), technically the Central Criminal Courts, crouches under a copper dome and a wide-eyed figure of justice on the corner of Old Bailey and Newgate St.—infamous as the site of Britain's grimmest prison. Trial-watching persists as a favorite occupation, and the Old Bailey fills up whenever a gruesome or scandalous case is in progress. You can enter the public Visitors' Gallery and watch bewigged barristers at work (Mon.-Fri. 10am-1pm and 2-4pm; entrance in Warwick Passage off of Old Bailey). When court is not in session (July-Sept.), the building is closed. Cameras, large bags, and backpacks may not be taken inside. The Chief Post Office building, off Newgate to the north, envelops the enthralling **National Postal Museum** (see Museums). The reticent yet rewarding **Postman's Park** is nestled behind obscuring gates across the street from the Post Office. Those who venture into this serene nook will find a noteworthy sculpture of a minotaur by Michael Ayrton.

Further east on Angel St. and Gresham St., going left up Aldermanbury, huddles the **Guildhall** (tel. 606 3030), a cavernous space where dignitaries were once tried for treason. An improbable mix of high Gothic and modish 60s concrete, the building currently serves as the City's administrative center and houses the town clerk, a library, offices, and the **Guildhall Clock Museum** (see Museums). Monuments to national figures like Nelson, Wellington, and Pitt stand in the Great Hall, while busts of other famous personages peer down sternly from the walls above. (Open daily 10am-5pm; Oct.-April Mon.-Sat. 10am-5pm.) The **Public Library** specializes in subjects pertaining to the history of London, including City church manuscripts, family geneaologies, and early maps. Recent acquisitions include books on Victorian women and a grammar of English dialects. Visitors are free to browse through the collection of books, but are not permitted to take them out of the library. (Open Mon.-Sat. 9:30am-5pm.)

■ THE BARBICAN AND NORTHERN SECTION

The **Barbican Centre,** which opened in 1972 and covers 60 acres, stands as one of the most impressive and controversial post-Blitz rebuilding projects (tube: Barbican or Moorgate). Widely considered an architectural symbol of the brutalism of the postwar landscape, the Barbican is also acknowledged as a vital cultural center. A city unto itself, the labyrinthine complex of residential apartments and offices shelters the **Royal Shakespeare Company,** the **London Symphony Orchestra,** the **Museum of London,** the **Guildhall School of Music and Drama,** and the **Barbican Art Gallery** (see Entertainment and Museums). **St. Giles Church** and the **City of London School for Girls** stand in the complex's unexpectedly verdant central courtyard, whose artificial lakes and planned gardens temper the Barbican's relentless urbanity.

The Silk Street pedestrian entrance to the complex is currently under reconstruction, although the entrance's canopy and statues of the nine muses should be in place by fall 1994. In response to the mass confusion heretofore caused by the Centre's maze of high level walkways, new index signs and color-coded carpets are currently being installed. In addition, the floors are being renumbered, so that the ground level floor will be called level 0, not level 5. These changes will hopefully make the centre easier to navigate.

In order to reach **St. Bartholomew the Great,** one must enter through an exceedingly narrow Tudor house located on Little Britain. Parts of the church date from 1123, although 800 years of alteration have much embellished it. Note the almost jarring contrast between the colorfully tiled floor and the somber gray of the medieval walls inside. (Open Mon.-Thurs. 8am-4:30pm, Fri. 10:45am-4:30pm, Sun. 8am-8pm.) For an early pint, try one of the pubs around **Smithfield,** a meat and poultry wholesale market since the 12th century. (Market open daily 5am-noon; some surrounding pubs open at 7am.) Smithfield's associations with butchery antedate the meat market. Scotsman William Wallace and rebel Wat Tyler rank among those executed here in the Middle Ages. It was also among Queen Mary's favorite Protestant-burning sites.

Charterhouse (tel. 253 9503), a peculiar institution first established as a priory and converted in 1611 to a school and hospital for poor gentlemen, stands on the edge of Charterhouse Sq. The school has moved to Surrey, but the fine group of 15th- to 17th-century buildings still houses around 40 residents, who must be bachelors or widowers over 60. (Tours April-July Wed. at 2:15pm. Nominal charge for charity.)

Just north of the square, up St. John's St. and off Clerkenwell Rd., stands **St. John's Gate.** On the ground floor, a museum commemorates the volunteer St. John Ambulance Brigade. (Open Mon.-Fri. 10am-5pm, Sat. 10am-4pm.) Another museum presents the history of the medieval knights of St. John and the role they played in the Crusades. Their 1140 priory was one of the first hospitals in Europe. One-hour tours of the 1504 gate, the church, and the 12th-century crypt are given (Tues. and Fri.-Sat. 11am and 2:30pm; £2.50 donation requested).

■ BANK TO THE TOWER: EASTERN SECTION

The massive windowless walls and foreboding doors of the **Bank of England** enclose four full acres (tube: Bank). The present building dates from 1925, but the eight-foot-thick outer wall is the same one built by eccentric architect Sir John Soane in 1788. The only part open to the public is the plush **Bank of England Museum** (see Museums). Its neighbors, the **Stock Exchange** and the **Royal Exchange** are not open to visitors. **St. Margaret Lothbury** (down Throgmorton St.), Wren's penulti-mate church, contains a sumptuous carved wood screen (1689). Most of the church's furnishings have been conglomerated from demolished City churches. A couple of blocks north, the **National Westminster Tower** hovers at over 600 feet; until recently, it was Britain's tallest skyscraper.

The 1986 **Lloyd's** building and **Leadenhall Market,** off Leadenhall St., supply the most startling architectural clash in the City. The ducts, lifts, and chutes of Lloyd's are straight out of the 21st century. This futuristic setting houses the **Lutine Bell,** which is still occasionally rung—once for bad insurance news, twice for good. In contrast, across a narrow alley the ornate cream and maroon fittings of Victorian Leadenhall Market emerge. A food market has stood here since the Middle Ages.

Behind the imposing, tautological **Mansion House,** home of the Lord Mayor, stands **St. Stephen Walbrook** (on Walbrook). Arguably Wren's finest, and alleg-edly his personal favorite, the church combines four major styles: the old-fashioned English church characterized by nave and chancel; the Puritan hall church, which lacks any separation between priest and congregation; the Greek-cross-plan church; and the domed church, a study for St. Paul's. The Samaritans, a social service group that advises the suicidal and severely depressed, was founded here in 1953. The mysterious cheese-like object in the center is actually the altar. Sculpted by Henry Moore, it is as controversial as you think it is.

The church of **St. Mary Woolnoth,** at King William and Lombard St., may look odd without a spire, but the interior proportions and the black and gilt reredos con-firm the talents of Wren's pupil Nicholas Hawksmoor. The only City church untouched by the Blitz, it "kept the hours" in Eliot's *Waste Land*. **St. Mary Abchurch,** off Abchurch Lane, provides a neat domed comparison to St. Stephen's—its mellow, dark wood and baroque paintings contrast with St. Stephen's bright airy interior.

Before even the most basic rebuilding of the city, Wren designed a tall Doric pil-lar. Completed in 1671, the simply-named **Monument** lies at the bottom of King William St. (tube: Monument). Supposedly, the 202-foot pillar stands exactly that many feet from where the Great Fire broke out in Pudding Lane on September 2, 1666, and "rushed devastating through every quarter with astonishing swiftness and worse." High on Fish Street Hill, the column offers an expansive view of London. Bring stern resolution and £1 to climb its 311 steps. (Open Mon.-Fri. 9am-6pm, Sat.-Sun. 2-6pm; Oct.-March Mon.-Sat. 9am-4pm.)

Over the river near the Monument the current **London Bridge** succeeds a slew of ancestors. The famed version crowded with houses stood from 1176 until it burned in 1758. The most recent predecessor didn't fall down; in 1973 it was sold to an American millionaire for £1.03 million and shipped, block by block, to Lake Havasu City, Arizona. **St. Magnus Martyr,** on Lower Thames St., stands next to the path to the 12th-century London Bridge, and proudly displays a chunk of wood from a Roman jetty. According to T.S. Eliot, the walls of the church "hold inexplicable splendor of Ionian white and gold," a soothing contrast to the forlorn (and former) Billingsgate fish market next door. The deserted trading floors there pine for the bustle and carp transported to the new Billingsgate in Docklands.

St. Mary at Hill, Lovat Lane, is a typical Wren church with a surprisingly convincing reworking of the old interior by early Victorian craftsmen, and an even more convincing contemporary reconstruction project. **St. Dunstan-in-the-East,** St. Dunstan's Hill, suffered severe damage in the Blitz; only Wren's amazing spire remains. The ruins have been converted into a gorgeous little garden that makes a fine picnic spot. Covered in green, the remaining walls demarcate a secluded oasis in the middle of the City.

Pepys witnessed the spread of the Great Fire from atop **All Hallows by the Tower,** at the end of Great Tower St. Just inside the south entrance is an arch from the 7th-century Saxon church, discovered in 1960. To the left, the baptistery contains a striking wood font cover by Grinling Gibbons. At the tiny **St. Olave's** in Hart St., an annual memorial service is held for Pepys, who is buried here with his wife. According to a 1586 entry in the church's Burial Register, Mother Goose is also interred here. Across the street, Seething Lane Gardens is perfect for a take-away lunch.

■■■ ST. PAUL'S CATHEDRAL

Sir Christopher Wren's domed masterpiece dominates its surroundings even as modern usurpers sneak up around it. St. Paul's has become a physical and spiritual symbol of London. Prince Charles and Lady Diana broke a 200-year tradition of holding royal weddings in Westminster Abbey so they could celebrate their ill-fated nuptials here. The current edifice is the third cathedral to stand on the site; the first cathedral was founded in 604 and destroyed by fire in 1089. The second and most massive cathedral was a medieval structure, one of the largest in Europe, topped by a spire ascending 489 feet. Falling into almost complete neglect in the 16th century, the cathedral became more of a marketplace than a church, and plans for its reconstruction were in the works well before the Great Fire. Wren had already started drawing up his grand scheme in 1666 when the conflagration demolished the cathedral, along with most of London, and gave him the opportunity to build from scratch.

Both the design and the building of the cathedral were dogged by controversy. Like his Renaissance predecessors, Wren preferred an equal-armed Greek cross plan, while ecclesiastical authorities insisted upon a traditional medieval design with a long nave and choir for services. Wren's final design compromised by translating a Gothic cathedral into baroque and classical terms: a Latin Cross floor plan with baroque detailing. Wren's second model received the King's warrant of approval (and is thus known as the "Warrant Model"), but still differed from today's St. Paul's. The shrewd architect won permission to make necessary alterations as building proceeded and, behind the scaffolding, Wren had his way. The cathedral was topped off in 1710; at 365 feet above the ground, the huge classical dome is the second-largest free-standing dome in Europe.

In December 1940, London burned once again. On the night of the 29th, at the height of the Blitz, St. Paul's was engulfed by a sea of fire. This time it survived. Fifty-one firebombs landed on the cathedral, all swiftly put out by the heroic volunteer St. Paul's Fire Watch; a small monument in the floor at the end of the nave honors them. Two of the four high-explosive bombs that landed did explode, wrecking the north transept; the clear glass there bears silent testimony.

Dotted with sculptures, bronzes, and mosaics, St. Paul's makes a rewarding place for a wander. Above the choir, three neo-Byzantine glass mosaics by William Richmond, done in 1904, tell the story of creation. The stalls in the **Choir,** carved by Grinling Gibbons, narrowly escaped a bomb, but the old altar did not. It was replaced with the current marble High Altar, covered by a St. Peter's-like *baldacchino* of oak, splendidly gilded. Above looms the crowning glory, the ceiling mosaic of *Christ Seated in Majesty.* A trial mosaic adorns the east wall of **St. Dun-stan's Chapel,** on the left by the entrance. On the other side of the nave in the **Chapel of St. Michael and St. George** sits a richly carved throne by Grinling Gibbons, made for the coronation of William and Mary in 1710. Along the south aisle hangs Holman Hunt's third version of *The Light of the World,* allegedly the most well-traveled picture in the world. Monuments to the mighty abound—Wellington, Nelson, Kitchener, and Samuel Johnson are all remembered here.

The **ambulatory** contains a statue of poet John Donne (Dean of the cathedral 1621-1631) in shrouds, one of the few monuments to survive from old St. Paul's. Also in the ambulatory is a modern sculpture of the Virgin Mary and Baby Jesus by Henry Moore. One month after the arrival of Moore's sculpture, entitled *Mother and Child,* guides insisted a name plaque be affixed to the base, as no one knew what it was meant to represent. Britain restored the former **Jesus Chapel** after the Blitz and dedicated it to U.S. soldiers who died during World War II. The graceful and intricate choir gates were executed by Jean Tijou early in the 18th century.

The **crypt,** saturated with tombs and monuments, forms a catalogue of Britain's officially "great" figures of the last two centuries, including Florence Nightingale and sculptor Henry Moore. (A few remnants made it through the Great Fire, including a memorial to Francis Bacon's father Nicolas.) The massive tombs of the Duke of Wellington and Nelson command attention; Nelson's coffin, placed directly beneath the dome, was originally intended for Cardinal Wolsey. A bust of George Washington stands opposite a memorial to Lawrence of Arabia. Around the corner lounges Rodin's fine bust of poet W.F. Henley (1849-1903). **Painter's Corner** holds the tombs of Sir Joshua Reynolds, Sir Lawrence Alma-Tadema, and J.M.W. Turner, along with memorials to John Constable and the revolutionary William Blake. Nearby, a black slab in the floor marks Wren's grave, with his son's famous epitaph close by: *Lector, si monumentum requiris circumspice* (roughly, "If you seek his monument, just look around you").

The display of **models** of St. Paul's details the history of the cathedral in all of its incarnations. Creating the great model of 1674, the star exhibit, cost as much as constructing a small house. In these models you can see how the upper parts of the exterior walls are mere façades, concealing the flying buttresses which support the nave roof (audiovisual presentations every ½ hr. 10:30am-3pm; crypt open Mon.-Sat. 8:45am-4:45pm).

Going up St. Paul's proves more challenging than going down: 259 steps lead to the vertiginous **Whispering Gallery,** on the inside base of the dome. During your ascent, look for the 18th-century grafitti carved into the stairwell. Words whispered against the wall whizz round the sides. A further 118 steps up, the first external view glitters from the **Stone Gallery,** only to be eclipsed by the uninterrupted and incomparable panorama from the **Golden Gallery,** 153 steps higher at the top of the dome. The monolithic Bankside power station dominates the South Bank, overshadowing its neighbor to the left, a small white building that housed Wren during his massive construction projects; the Victorian-Gothic extravaganza of St. Pancras station struts to the north, laced with the greenery of Hampstead Heath. Before descending, take a peek down into the cathedral through the glass peephole in the floor; Nelson lies buried more than 400 feet directly below. (Tube: St. Paul's. Cathedral open for sightseeing Mon.-Sat. 8:30am-4pm; crypt and ambulatory open Mon.-Sat. 8:45am-4:15pm; galleries open Mon.-Sat. 10am-4:15pm. Admission to cathedral, ambulatory, and crypt £3, students £2.50, children £2. Admission to cathedral, ambulatory, crypt, and galleries £5, students £4, children £3.)

St. Paul's Churchyard, a fine picnic spot popular since Shakespeare's day, is surrounded by railings of mostly unappreciated interest; they were one of the first applications of cast iron. The modern St. Paul's Cross marks the spot where the papal pronouncement condemning Martin Luther was read to the public.

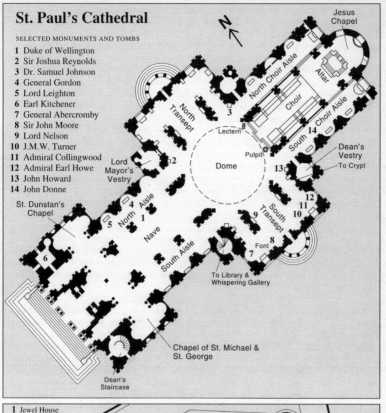

St. Paul's Cathedral

SELECTED MONUMENTS AND TOMBS

1 Duke of Wellington
2 Sir Joshua Reynolds
3 Dr. Samuel Johnson
4 General Gordon
5 Lord Leighton
6 Earl Kitchener
7 General Abercromby
8 Sir John Moore
9 Lord Nelson
10 J.M.W. Turner
11 Admiral Collingwood
12 Admiral Earl Howe
13 John Howard
14 John Donne

Jesus Chapel
North Choir Aisle
Altar
Choir
South Choir Aisle
North Transept
Lectern
Pulpit
Dome
Dean's Vestry
To Crypt
Lord Mayor's Vestry
St. Dunstan's Chapel
North Aisle
Nave
South Aisle
South Transept
Font
To Library & Whispering Gallery
Chapel of St. Michael & St. George
Dean's Staircase

ST. PAUL'S CATHEDRAL

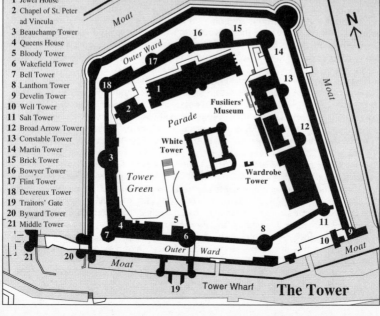

1 Jewel House
2 Chapel of St. Peter ad Vincula
3 Beauchamp Tower
4 Queens House
5 Bloody Tower
6 Wakefield Tower
7 Bell Tower
8 Lanthorn Tower
9 Develin Tower
10 Well Tower
11 Salt Tower
12 Broad Arrow Tower
13 Constable Tower
14 Martin Tower
15 Brick Tower
16 Bowyer Tower
17 Flint Tower
18 Devereux Tower
19 Traitors' Gate
20 Byward Tower
21 Middle Tower

Moat
Outer Ward
Fusiliers' Museum
Parade
White Tower
Wardrobe Tower
Tower Green
Moat
Outer Ward
Moat
Tower Wharf
The Tower

■■■ THE TOWER OF LONDON

The Tower of London, the largest fortress in medieval Europe and the palace and prison of English monarchs for over 500 years, is soaked in blood and history. Its intriguing past and striking buildings attract over two million visitors per year. The oldest continuously occupied fortified building in Europe, "The Tower" was founded by William the Conqueror in 1066 in order to protect—and command—his subjects. Not one but 20 towers stand behind its walls, though many associate the image of the **White Tower,** the oldest one, with the Tower of London. Completed in 1097, it overpowers all the fortifications that were built around it in the following centuries. Originally a royal residence-*cum*-fortress, it last housed James I, and has subsequently served as a wardrobe, storehouse, public records office, armory, and prison.

The various towers connect by massive walls and gateways, forming fortifications disheartening to visitors even today. Richard I, the Lionheart, began the construction of defenses around the White Tower in 1189. Subsequent work by Henry III (1216-72) and Edward I (1272-1307) brought the Tower close to its present condition.

Two rings of defenses surround the White Tower. On the first floor of the White Tower nests the **Chapel of St. John,** dating from 1080, the finest Norman chapel in London. Stark and pristine, it is the only chapel in the world with an "aisled nave and encircling ambulatory," a balcony where women were allowed to join the otherwise men-only chapel services. Failed arsonist Guy Fawkes of the Gunpowder Plot was tortured beneath this chapel.

On the **Inner Ward,** the **Bell Tower** squats on the southwest corner. Since the 1190s, this tower has sounded the curfew bell each night. Sir Thomas More spent some time here, courtesy of his former friend Henry VIII, before he was executed in the Tower Green.

Along the curtain wall hovers the **Bloody Tower,** arguably the most famous, and certainly the most infamous, part of the fortress. Once pleasantly named the Garden Tower, due to the officers' garden nearby, the Bloody Tower supposedly saw the murder of the Little Princes, the uncrowned King Edward V and his brother (aged 13 and 10), by agents of Richard III in 1483. The murder remains one of history's great mysteries; some believe that Richard was innocent and that the future Henry VII arranged the murders to ease his own ascent. Two children's remains found in the grounds in 1674 (and buried in Westminster Abbey) have never been conclusively identified as those of the Princes. Sir Walter Raleigh did some time in the prison here off and on for 13 years and occupied himself by writing a voluminous *History of the World Part I.* Before he got round to writing Part II, James I had him beheaded.

Henry III lived in the adjacent **Wakefield Tower,** largest after the White Tower. The crown kept its public records and its jewels here until 1856 and 1967 respectively, although Wakefield also has its own gruesome past. Lancastrian Henry VI was imprisoned by Yorkist Edward IV during the Wars of the Roses and was murdered on May 21, 1471 while praying here. Students from Cambridge's King's College, founded by Henry, annually place lilies on the spot of the murder.

Counterclockwise around the inner **Wall Walk** come the **Lanthorn, Salt, Broad Arrow, Constable,** and **Martin** towers, the last scene of the self-styled "Colonel" Thomas Blood's bold attempt in 1671 at stealing the Crown Jewels. Martin's lower level now houses a small exhibit of **Instruments of Torture.** The inner ring comes full circle, completed by the **Brick, Bowyer** (where, according to Shakespeare's constantly accurate *Richard III,* the Duke of Clarence died after being drowned in Malmsey wine), **Flint, Devereux,** and **Beauchamp** towers.

Within the inner ring adjoining the Bell Tower lurks the Tudor **Queen's House** (which will become the King's House when Prince Charles ascends to the throne). The house has served time as a prison for some of the Tower's most illustrious guests: both Anne Boleyn and Catherine Howard were incarcerated here by charming hubby Henry VIII; Guy Fawkes was interrogated in the Council Chamber on the upper floor; and in 1941, Hitler's Deputy Führer Rudolf Hess was brought here after parachuting into Scotland. The only prisoners remaining today are the clipped ravens hopping around on the grass outside the White Tower; legend has it that without the ravens the Tower would crumble and a great disaster would befall the monarchy. The ravens even have a tomb and gravestone of their own in the grassy moat near the ticket office.

Although more famous for the prisoners who languished and died here, the Tower has seen a handful of spectacular escapes. The Bishop of Durham escaped from Henry I out a window and down a rope. The unfortunate Welsh Prince Gruffyd ap Llewelyn, prisoner of Henry III in 1244, apparently had not learned his knots properly—his rope of knotted sheets broke and he fell to his death.

Prisoners of the highest rank sometimes received the honor of a private execution rather than one before the spectators' benches of Tower Hill, just east of the present tube station. A block on the Tower Green, inside the Inner Ward, marks the spot where the axe fell on Queen Catherine Howard, Lady Jane Grey, Anne Boleyn, and the Earl of Essex, Queen Elizabeth's rejected suitor. Sir Thomas More, "the king's good servant but God's first," was beheaded in public. The nearby **Chapel of St. Peter ad Vincula** (St. Peter in Chains) was once called "the saddest place on earth" by Lord Macaulay; the remains of prisoners were transported here after their executions. The decapitated bodies of Henry VIII's two executed queens lie beneath the altar and in the crypt. (Entrance to the chapel by Yeoman tour only. See below.)

The prisoners may be gone, but the weapons and armor remain. An expansive display from the **Royal Armouries,** testifying to Henry VIII's fondness for well-molded metal suits, takes up three floors. To find a glut of arms and weaponry, visit the **New Armouries** to the east. (The **Oriental Armoury,** which houses weapons from Asia, has been moved to Fort Nelson to make room for the expanded Crown Jewels display.)

The prize possessions of the Tower and of England, the **Crown Jewels** pull in the crowds. Oliver Cromwell melted down much of the original royal treasure; most of the collection dates from after Charles II's Restoration in 1660. You may have seen thousands of pictures of the crowns and scepters before, but no camera can capture the dazzle. The **Imperial State Crown** and the **Sceptre with the Cross** feature the Stars of Africa, cut from the Cullinan Diamond. Scotland Yard mailed the precious stone third class from the Transvaal to London in an unmarked brown paper package, a scheme they believed was the safest way of getting it to England. **St. Edward's Crown,** made for Charles II in 1661, is only worn by the monarch during coronation.

The Tower is still guarded and inhabited by the Yeoman of the Guard extraordinary, popularly known as the "Beefeaters." (The name does actually derive from "eaters of beef"—well-nourished domestic servants.) To be eligible for Beefeaterhood, a candidate must have at least 22 years honorable service in the armed forces.

Visitors enter the Tower through the **Byward Tower** on the southwest of the **Outer Ward,** which sports a precariously hung portcullis. The password, required for entry here after hours, has been changed every day since 1327. German spies were executed in the Outer Ward during World War II. Along the outer wall, **St. Thomas's Tower** (after Thomas à Becket) tops the evocative **Traitors' Gate,** through which boats once brought new captives.

The whole castle used to be surrounded by a broad **moat** dug by Edward I. Cholera epidemics forced the Duke of Wellington to drain it in 1843. The filled land became a vegetable garden during World War II but has since sprouted a tennis court and bowling green for inhabitants of the Tower.

Free, entertaining tours of about one hour, given every half hour by Yeomen, start outside Byward Tower (tube: Tower Hill; open Mon.-Sat. 9:30am-5pm, Sun. 2-5pm; Nov.-Feb. Mon.-Sat. 9:30am-4pm; admission £6.70, students and seniors £5.10, children £4.40, families £19). Try to avoid the phenomenal Sunday crowd—queues start around noon. The best times to visit are Mondays and Tuesdays. Once inside, expect to queue for 20 to 30 minutes for entry to the Crown Jewels. For tickets to the **Ceremony of the Keys,** the nightly ritual locking of the gates, write in advance to Resident Governor, Tower of London, EC3 (inquiries, tel. 709 0765).

Tower Bridge, a granite and steel structure reminiscent of a castle with a drawbridge, is a familiar sight. A new exhibition inside the bridge explains its history. The one hour and 15 minute-long tours include a walk across the upper level of the bridge. (Open daily April-Oct. 10am-6:30pm, Nov.-March 10am-5:15pm. Admission £5, children £3.50.)

■■■ THE EAST END

Today London's East End continues a trajectory that began 300 years ago, when the areas directly east and northeast of the City of London first served as a refuge to those who either weren't welcome in the City, or who didn't want to be subject to the City's jurisdictions. During the 17th century, this included political dissenters, religious orders, the French Huguenots, and Protestants fleeing religious persecution in France. By 1687, 13,000 Huguenots had settled in Spitalfields, the area northeast of the City of London (which takes its name from a long-gone medieval priory, St. Mary Spital). The silk-weaving Huguenots soon built a reputation for the quality of their cloth—but as they attracted rich customers, they also began to attract resentment from surrounding communities.

The East End has maintained its status as a relatively poor section of London with a history of racial conflict. A large working-class population moved into the district during the Industrial Revolution, soon followed by a wave of Jewish immigrants fleeing persecution in Eastern Europe who settled around **Whitechapel.** The success some attained as clothing manufacturers drew the attention of the British Union of Fascists, who instigated anti-Semitic violence which culminated in the "Battle of Cable Street" in 1936. A mural on St George's Town Hall (236 Cable St.; tube: Shadwell) commemorates the victory against bigotry won in the streets that day.

Other major communities which have since moved in and out of the area include the Irish, the Chinese, and the Somalis. In 1978, the latest immigration wave brought a large Muslim Bangladeshi community to the East End. At the heart of this community is **Brick Lane** (tube: Aldgate East), a street lined with Indian and Bangladeshi restaurants (see Food and Drink), colorful textile shops, and grocers stocking ethnic foods. (To reach Brick Lane, head left up Whitechapel as you exit the tube station; turn left onto Osbourne St., which turns into Brick La.) Most street signs in the area are written in Arabic as well as English. On Sundays, vibrant market stalls selling books, bric-a-brac, leather jackets, and salt beef sandwiches flank this street and Middlesex St., better known as **Petticoat Lane**—its original name, drawn from the street's historical role as a center of the clothing trade; a prudish Queen Victoria gave the street the more respectable, official name it bears today (see Shopping: Street Markets). At Fournier St., a former church now holds a mosque; on Friday afternoons after prayer the street fills with chatter. The **East London Mosque,** 84-86 Whitechapel Rd. (tel. 247 1357; tube: Aldgate East), was London's first to have its own building. To visit the mosque, set up an appointment.

Even the communities that have since moved out of the East End have not vanished without leaving some trace behind. **Christ Church,** Commercial St., E1 (tel. 377 0287; tube: Aldgate East; exit the station left, and turn left onto Commercial St.), was begun by Hawksmoor in 1714 as part of Parliament's Fifty New Churches Act of 1711. The Act had been created to combat nonconformism against the Church of England; thus, the construction of Christ Church in Spitalfields was a reaction against the Huguenot Protestantism. Today, the church sponsors the **Spitalfields Music Festival** of classical music during the last three weeks of June (box office tel. 377 0287); its crypt serves as a rehabilitation center for alcoholics. At the **Dennis Severs House,** 18 Folgate St. (tel. 247 4013; left off Commercial St., past Christ Church), you can visit the historically recreated home of a family of Huguenot silk-

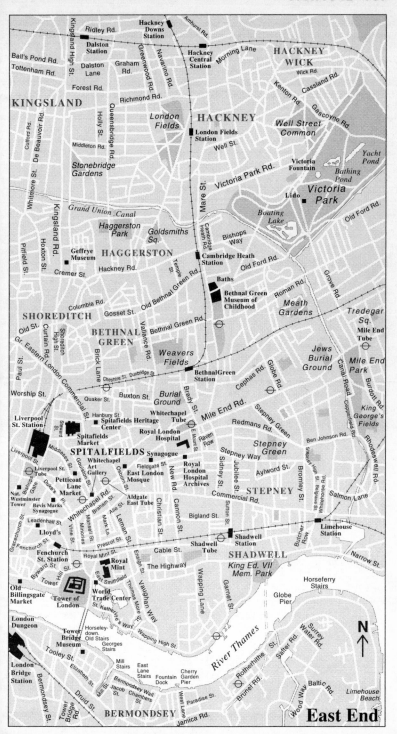

East End

weavers who lived there from 1724 to 1919 (open first Sun. of each month 2-5pm; admission £5).

Most of the Jewish community has moved on to suburbs to the north and west of central London, like Stamford Hill and Golders Green (see Greater London), but notable remnants of the former East End community include the renowned kosher restaurant **Bloom's** (see Food) and the city's oldest standing synagogue, **Bevis Marks Synagogue,** (tel. 626 1274, Bevis Marks and Heneage La., EC3; tube: Aldgate: from Aldgate High St. turn right onto Houndsditch; Creechurch La. on the left leads to Bevis Marks). Although Bevis Marks is geographically situated in the heart of the City of London, its spirit lies in the East End. Founded in 1701 by Joseph Avis, the synagogue was first opened to serve the Spanish and Portuguese Jewish Congregation and has since served as a place of worship for many eminent figures from Anglo-Jewish history. Set back in a secluded courtyard, the huge wooden portal of the well-preserved synagogue beckons visitors to "take a step back in time" (organized tours Sun. and Tues. 11:30am, Mon., Wed., and Fri. noon).

In today's East End, scattered deserted warehouse spaces and airy studios house the brushes and oils of the area's 6000 artists. Some of their work, much of which focuses on the experience of the East End's nonwhite population, occasionally hangs on the high white walls of the **Whitechapel Art Gallery,** on Whitechapel High St., which holds temporary exhibitions of such artists as Frida Kahlo and Piotr Nathan (see Museums).

Part of the East End's great attraction is that the numerous small but interesting sights it offers are free. **Spitalfields Heritage Centre,** 17-19 Princelet St., E1 (tel. 377 6901; tube: Aldgate East, Shoreditch, or Liverpool St.; Princelet St. bisects Brick Lane), is dedicated to research on local immigrant communities. Housed in an 1870 synagogue, it still displays a wooden ark, pulpit, and seats (free; call for opening hours).

Spitalfields Farm, Weaver/Pedley St., E1 (tel. 247 8762; tube: Shoreditch), is a genuine working farm in the middle of the city where you can buy produce and plants. During the summer and on Sundays, enjoy the farm and crafts activities, go for a pony ride or feast at a barbecue (open Tues.-Sun. 10am-1pm and 2-6pm; free). The **Spitalfields Market** at Commercial and Brushfield St. (tel. 247 6590; tube: Liverpool) offers craft and antique stalls, special retail shops, an international food hall (including London's first organic food market), indoor sports including roller hockey, and changing art exhibitions under three acres of glass-covered space (open Mon.-Fri. 11am-3pm, Sun. 9am-3pm; Sun. is the best time to go). The Sunday morning flower and plant market on **Columbia Road** (tube: Old St. or Shoreditch; take Old St. to Hackney Rd., Columbia Road is on the right) is also worth a visit (open Sun. 8:30am-1pm). **Englefields Limited,** Cheshire St., E2 (tel. 739 3616; tube: Shoreditch; turn right onto Brick Lane, then right onto Cheshire St.) is the oldest pewter cast manufacturer in London—some molds have been in use almost 300 years—you can still watch the pewter being hand made (call to ask about availability of free tours).

An overdramatized aspect of the East End's history is its association with London's most notorious criminals. Jack the Ripper's six murders took place in Whitechapel; you can tour his trail with a number of different guided walk companies, all of which offer a Jack the Ripper tour every evening (see Sights: Touring). More recently, cockney Capone twins Ron and Reggie Kray ruled the 60s underworld from their mum's terraced house in Bethnal Green. Ron wiped out an ale-sipping rival in broad daylight in 1966 at the **Blind Beggar** pub at Whitechapel Rd. and Cambridge Heath Rd.

Along Cambridge Heath Rd. lies the **Bethnal Green Museum of Childhood** (see Museums). North past Bethnal Green, and beyond the wafts of curry on Brick Lane, stretch the expanses of **Hackney** which mesh into **Clapton** and farther north, **Stoke Newington.** Traditionally known as a community of "Londoners' stock," Hackney now ever-adapts to its growing Caribbean, African, and Turkish populations—Brixton without the hype and the tube line. West Indian beef patty shops and thumping night clubs, as well as discount clothing, food, and shoe stores line the main drags of Mare St. and Lower Clapton Rd. The community center at the **Harriet Tubman House,** 136 Lower Clapton Rd., E5 (tel. (0181) 985 6649), acts as a gathering place, an information center, and as the Sam Uriah Morris Society's small black history museum (BR: Clapton; from Liverpool St. take Upper Clapton Rd. down to Lower Clapton Rd.; open sporadically).

■■■ THE SOUTH BANK

A hulk of worn concrete and futuristic slate, the South Bank gestures defiantly at the center of London from across the Thames. Housing the British terminus of the imminent **Channel Tunnel,** this region is currently poised to become one of London's most dynamic. Major commercial development, which anticipates the Chunnel's eventual flourishing, is currently underway. To the untutored eye, this area initially appears confusing and dismal, especially on the average cloudy London day. The massive **South Bank Centre** is the predominant architectural eyesore; yet behind this hulking facade lurks London's most concentrated campus of artistic and cultural activity (tube: Waterloo, then follow signs for York Rd.; or Embankment and cross the Hungerford footbridge).

The region south of the Thames has long been home to entertainment, much of it bawdy; until the English Civil Wars, most of this area fell under the legal jurisdiction of the Bishop of Winchester, and was thus protected from London censors. The region stayed almost entirely rural until the 18th-century Westminster and Blackfriars bridges were built. Until the post-WWII development began, the area was a den of working-class neighborhoods, dark breweries, smoky industry, and murky wharves through which suburbanites passed on their way into the city.

Contemporary development began in 1951 during the Festival of Britain, the centenary of the Great Exhibition of 1851, when the **Royal Festival Hall** was built. A veritable eruption of construction ensued, producing the many concrete blocks that comprise the Centre: the **National Film Theatre,** the **Hayward Gallery** and **Queen Elizabeth Hall** complex, and the **Royal National Theatre.** Recent calls for a demolition and replacement of the Queen Elizabeth Hall and the Hayward Gallery have prompted many to declare their fondness for the complex. More recent additions to the South Bank landscape include the **Jubilee Gardens,** planted for the Queen's Silver Jubilee in 1977, which stretch along the Embankment.

The 3000-seat Royal Festival Hall and its three auditoriums (Olivier, Lyttleton, and Cottlesoe) are home to the Philharmonia and London Philharmonic Orchestras, the English National Ballet, and host to countless others; its chamber-musical sibling is the Queen Elizabeth Hall (see Entertainment—Music and Dance). The National Theatre (see Entertainment—Theatre), opened by Lord Olivier in 1978, promotes "art for the people" through convivial platform performances, foyer concerts, lectures, tours, and workshops. The Hayward Gallery (see Museums) on Belvedere Rd. houses imaginative contemporary art exhibitions. Multicolored posters displaying Russian titles and Asian warriors distinguish the entrance to the National Film Theatre (see Entertainment—Film), directly on the South Bank. The Film Theatre also operates the innovative **Museum of the Moving Image** (see Museums).

Today the South Bank teeters on the brink of a second development explosion precipitated by community planners, the expansion of city boundaries, and, most importantly, the opening of the **Channel Tunnel.** Waterloo station has been designated the London terminus of the "Chunnel," and Nicholas Grimshaw's spectacular new blue and silver international terminal will be many visitors' introduction to Britain. Having suddenly become the neighborhood that links Britain to the continent, the South Bank is in a period of flux.

Tycoon Richard Branson (of Virgin records/airlines fame) has already teamed up with a Japanese firm to buy the former **County Hall,** a formidable Renaissance edifice with a massive riverfront façade. The Hall was headquarters of the London County Council from 1913 until 1965, and of the Greater London Council, until it was controversially abolished in 1986. Branson and friends plan to build a ritzy hotel in the Hall. The London Underground Ltd. has already started tearing up earth in order to expand the Jubilee Line, so commuters will have an easier time getting in and out of the city; this project won't be completed for another three years. Economic development has not supplanted cultural development; the British Film Institute plans to build a new IMAX Cinema where the Waterloo Bull Ring currently confuses motorists.

The most colorful recent changes in the South Bank landscape result from the unflagging efforts of a non-profit development company, **Coin Street Community Builders (CSCB).** In 1984 CSCB bought 13 previously derelict acres, upon which they have since erected a park and riverside walkway, seven housing cooperatives, and a designer crafts market at **Gabriel's Wharf** (tel. 620 0544). Gabriel's Wharf is a great place to watch original crafts being fashioned while grabbing a snack after a visit to the National Theatre.

CSCB's next renovation project, the OXO Tower, is adjacent to Gabriel's Wharf. Formerly the headquarters of a company that produced meat extract, the Art Deco tower is notable for its clever subversion of rules that prohibited permanent advertising on buildings; architects built the tower's distinct geometric windows in the shape of the company's logo. By Spring 1995, CSCB's renovated **OXO Tower Wharf** will be a frenetic hub of South Bank activity. A meticulously planned potpourri of rooftop cafés, retail outlets, designer workshops, performance spaces, and residential flats make this the most innovative community-minded structure in recent London history.

Numerous pedestrian pathways are being planned for the region which will make it easier to get to the jumbled stalls of the **Cut Street Market** near Waterloo station. The market's old character has waned as ambitious development projects consume more of the area's residential neighborhoods, but prices have stayed low, and used-book sellers and curiosity stands have maintained the district's flavor.

Farther along Waterloo Rd., the magnificently restored **Old Vic** (tel. 928 7616), former home of Olivier's National Repertory Theatre, now hosts popular seasons of lesser-known classics and worthy revivals. The smaller **Young Vic** (see Entertainment—Theatre) is just a bit further down the road.

The **Christ Church Tower** of 1876 rises above a mundane block of office buildings at the corner of Kennington Rd., directly across from Lambeth North tube station. **Lambeth Palace** (tube: Lambeth North), on the Embankment opposite the Lambeth Bridge, has been the Archbishop of Canterbury's London residence for seven centuries. Although Archbishop Langton founded it in the early 13th century, most of the palace dates from the 1800s. The palace's notable exterior includes the entrance at the 15th-century brick Morton's Tower, and Lollard's Tower, where John Wyclif's followers were thought to be imprisoned (open by prior arrangement only; contact Lambeth Palace, Lambeth Palace Road, SE1). East on Lambeth Road is the **Imperial War Museum** (see Museums).

■■■ SOUTHWARK AND BANKSIDE

Across London Bridge from the City lies Southwark (SUTH-uk), a distinctive area with a lively history (tube: London Bridge). The area around the **Borough High St.,** also called "the Borough," has existed—with the exception of minor changes—for nearly two thousand years. Until 1750, London Bridge was the only bridge over the Thames in London, and the highway leading to it had many travelers who liked to stop at the inns lining the road. The neighborhood has historically been associated with entertainment from the days of bear-baiting to the even more vicious pleasures of Defoe's *Moll Flanders*. **Bear Gardens,** located along the bank of the Thames, received its name from the bear-baiting arena which stood there in Elizabethan times.

But Southwark's greatest "vice" has always been theatre. Shakespeare's and Marlowe's plays were performed at the **Rose Theatre,** built in 1587 and rediscovered

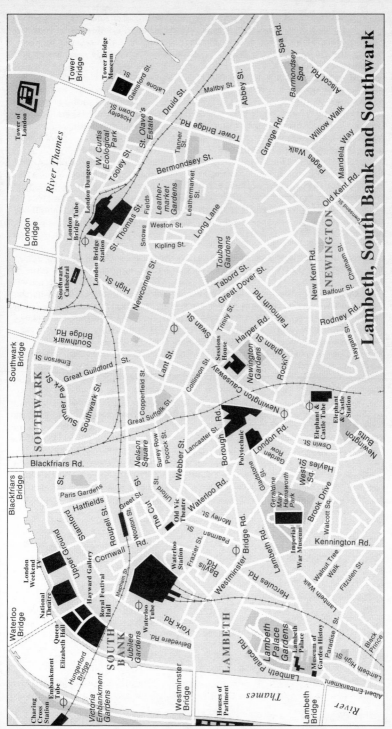

SOUTHWARK AND BANKSIDE

Lambeth, South Bank and Southwark

during construction in 1989. The remnants are to be preserved and displayed underneath a new *Financial Times* office block at Park St. and Rose Alley. The remains of Shakespeare's **Globe Theatre** were discovered just months after those of the Rose. While privately owned, the remains of the Globe can be viewed under an elevated building on Park street.

A project spearheaded by filmmaker Sam Wanamaker is underway to build a "new" Globe on the riverbank. This Globe replica was scheduled to open on Shakespeare's birthday, April 23, 1995, but a dearth of funds has pushed the opening date back to August 1995. The replica will be part of the **International Shakespeare Globe Centre,** a vast complex which will ultimately contain a second theatre, an exhibition gallery, an archival library, an auditorium, and various shops, and will be located directly across the Thames from St. Paul's Cathedral.

The **Shakespeare Globe Museum,** 1 Bear Gardens Alley (tel. 928 6342), a gallery devoted to Southwark history, concentrates on the history of the Globe. Models and text trace the development of the Elizabethan stage from the first purpose-built playhouse in 1756 to the closing of the Globe in 1642. The museum is scheduled to become obsolete on August 1, 1995, when its exhibits will be subsumed into those of the new Globe Centre (open Mon.-Sat. 10am-5pm, Sun. 2-5:30pm; admission £3, students £2). Follow the signs from the London Bridge tube to Bear Gardens; it's quite a long walk.

On the road to the Globe Museum squats the **Liberty of the Clink** (tel. 403 6515). The Bishop of Winchester's Court had jurisdiction over these 70 acres of Bankside land, which for several hundred years made up London's red-light district. "The Clink" was the Bishop's private prison for London's criminals. Henry Barrowe and John Greenwood, the early Separatists, were imprisoned here before being hanged (exhibition open Oct.-April daily 11am-5pm; May-Sept. 10am-6pm, closes later Sat.-Sun; admission £2, students £1, families £5).

An awesome architectural monolith looms menacingly over the Clink and the new Globe construction site. The huge, terrible **CEGB Power Station**'s windowless tower rises to the height of 325 feet. Designed by Giles Gilbert Scott in the late forties, the building was under construction for 13 years. Finally opened in 1960, the station abruptly ceased operation in 1980, its method of generating power having been rendered obsolete by brash, technological upstarts. After more than a decade of inactivity, the tower is now the object of much-deserved attention; by the year 2000, the tower will become the new home of the Tate Gallery's **Modern Art Museum.** The Tate plans to pour £80 million into the project, which will doubtless bolster the south-of-the-Thames' ascendant cultural domination over London.

At Montague Close near the bridge rises the less intimidating tower of **Southwark Cathedral** (tel. 407 2939), after Westminster Abbey probably the most striking Gothic church in the city; it is certainly the oldest. Mostly rebuilt in the 1890s, only the church's original 1207 choir and retro-choir survive. The glorious altar screen is Tudor, with 20th-century statues. The church is dotted with interesting stone and wood effigies which have explanatory notes. Shakespeare is believed to have rested here between 1599 and 1611. His brother Edmund was buried in the church in 1607. Medieval poet John Gower is buried here in a colorful tomb. This was the parish church of the Harvard family, and a chapel was dedicated in 1907 to the memory of John Harvard, who had been baptized in the church exactly three hundred years before. For the hungry worshipper, the cathedral also has a restaurant, Chapter House Restaurant, managed by Pizza Express Ltd. (open Mon.-Fri. 10am-4:30pm).

Just a couple of blocks southeast, your hair will rise and your spine will chill at **St. Thomas's Old Operating Theatre,** 9a St. Thomas St. (tel. 955 4791), a carefully preserved 19th-century surgical hospital. Rediscovered in 1956, it is the only known example of a pre-Victorian operating theatre. See the wooden table where unanesthetized patients endured excruciatingly painful surgery, or travel through the herb garret and museum (open Mon., Wed., Fri. 12:30-4pm, or by appointment; admission £1, concessions 60p).

If your appetite for the macabre is not sated by the minutia of early medicine, the **London Dungeon** awaits buried beneath the London Bridge Station at 28 Tooley St. (see Museums). Not for the squeamish, this dark, dank maze of more than 40 exhibits recreates horrifying historical scenarios of European execution, torture, and plague.

Moored on the south bank of the Thames just upstream from Tower Bridge, the World War II warship **HMS Belfast** (tel. 407 6434) led the bombardment of the French coast during D-Day landings. The labyrinth of the engine house and the whopping great guns make it a fun place to play sailor. Mind your head. You can take the ferry that runs from Tower Pier on the north bank to the Belfast whenever the ship is open, or take the tube to London Bridge. Follow Tooley St. from the London Bridge, past the London Dungeon, and look for the signs (open daily 10am-5:20pm, Nov.-March 19 10am-4pm; admission £4, students £3, children £2, family £10; ferry one way 50p, return £1, students one way 30p, return 60p). East of Tower Bridge, the bleached Bauhaus box of the **Design Museum** perches on the Thames (see Museums).

Hundreds of stalls selling antiques have been located in the **Bermondsey Market** on Bermondsey Abbey St. since 1949. Go early (the serious traders arrive at 5am) on Friday morning to catch the best bargains. **Hays Galleria** (tel. 626 3411), Bankside between Hay's Lane, Battlebridge Lane and Tooley St. (tube: London Bridge), occupies the reconstructed Hay's Wharf. Underneath the glass and steel barrel-vaulted roof, the galleria houses restaurants, shops, and sculpture, including a spectacular giant kinetic sculpture by David Kemp called *The Navigators* which combines water jets and all the accoutrements of Britain's nautical past.

■■■ BRIXTON

The genteel Victorian shopping and residential district of SW9 (tube: Brixton) became the locus of a Caribbean and African community following large-scale Commonwealth immigration in the 1950s and 1960s. Brixton gained unexpected notoriety in mid-April 1981, when fierce riots broke out pitting locals against police. Newspaper headlines screamed about "The Battle of Brixton," and alarmist copy spoke of "Bloody Saturday," simmering fires, charred buildings, molotov cocktails, and widespread looting. Hanif Kureishi's film *Sammie and Rosie Get Laid* investigates the private lives of educated leftists who live at the margins of riots similar to the Brixton riots.

There has been much speculation since as to the cause of the riots. Some locals argue that as the black population in Brixton grew, so did police harassment, and boiling resentment finally turned to aggression. Many compare the Brixton riots to the race-related riots which rocked major American cities in the 1960s. Reagan-clone Margaret Thatcher attributed the riots to "copycat hooliganism" and said that "nothing but nothing" justified them.

One optimistic theory asserted that a vibrant commerce would emerge from the post-riot shambles. Brixton has certainly revived since 26 of its buildings were destroyed by fire that April. The firms "Backing Brixton" on the railway bridge testify to this revitalization.

Yet radicalism still thrives in Brixton. Outside the tube station revolutionaries let a thousand different militant newspapers bloom. Meetings of dub poets, Black Muslims, neo-Marxists, and Rastafarians continuously transpire here. Posters advertising these events confront you as you exit the station; as compelling as these posters are the aromas of baked meat patties, incense, and cocoa bread that emanate from the market.

Most of the activity in Brixton centers around the **Brixton Market** at Electric Ave., Popes Rd., and Brixton Station Rd. (see Shopping—street markets). Step out of the station and you're practically at the market's heart. One of the market's main arteries inspired Eddie Grant to "take it higher" in the early-Eighties techno-reggae hit, "Electric Avenue." Shoppers from all over London mix with local crowds among vendors of food, clothing, and junk. Street preachers preach, performers busk, and waves of music pour out of the record shops. Choose from among the stalls of fresh fish, vegetables, and West Indian cuisine, or browse through the stalls of African crafts and discount clothing.

Nearby, on the corner of Coldharbour and Atlantic, is the **Black Cultural Archives,** 378 Coldharbour Lane, SW9 (tel.738 4591; fax 738 7168). The result of post-riot initiatives begun in Brixton in the early 1980s, the archives mounts small but informative exhibits on black history and local issues in a downstairs gallery. Upstairs, books, documents, clippings, and photographs relating to the black presence in Britain are catalogued and stored.

Brixton is currently slated for commercial development that promises to alter the neighborhood's character. In early 1995 the **Ritzy Project** development, at the corner of Coldharbour and Brixton Roads, will be completed; the multi-purpose complex will house a 5-screen art-cinema (Europe's largest), 20 new flats, and several restaurants. The complex will provide a much needed outlet for artistic creativity in the area, although some have warranted fears that the development will encourage gentrification.

Brixton is a fascinating neighborhood for aimless wandering. Browse through the area's numerous record stores, starting at **Red Records** at 500 Brixton Rd., and you will find the latest in hip hop, ragga, and socca (see Shopping—records). Spend a moment reading the radical graffiti ("Smash the Nazis by any means necessary," "Defend the life of Dr. Guzman in Peru") and enjoying the sound of water trickling down the small colored fountain in the area's **central plaza,** on Effra Street near Coldharbour.

For information on upcoming concerts, festivals, and other goings-on in the Brixton area, stop by the **Lambeth Town Hall,** located at Brixton Hill and Coldharbour Lane. They also hold information on meetings of community groups.

Greater London

Lo, where huge London, huger day by day,
O'er six fair counties spreads its hideous sway.
                                                    —Jane Austen, *The Golden Age*

London has tended to expand horizontally rather than vertically. Far-flung villages, swallowed up by this sprawl, resolutely maintain their own identities amidst sheets of mundane commuter housing. London is the world's largest capital in area, and Londoners take pride in calling it home, be it in the West End or Enfield. London Transport and British Rail cover Greater London thoroughly; most areas are accessible without a car.

■■■ HAMPSTEAD AND HIGHGATE

The urban villages of Hampstead and Highgate, poised on hills north of Regent's Park, seem entirely detached from central London. To get to Hampstead, take the tube to Hampstead or BR to Hampstead Heath. To reach Highgate, take the tube to Archway, then bus #210 or 217 to Highgate Village. Either trip takes at least half an hour from the center of London.

Hampstead, 1005 years old, has traditionally been a refuge for artists. But nary an artist can be found today on its tidy streets lined with Jaguars, designer boutiques, and Georgian townhouses. The sheer affluence of the place overwhelms; half of the restaurants are French, and even the McDonald's has slick Italian black-lacquered chairs. The town exudes old money and refinement, and is still populated by London's elite. Those wealthy enough to live here include former Labour Party leader Michael Foot, authors John Le Carré, G. G. Franey, and Margaret Drabble, earnest thespians Emma Thompson and Kenneth Branaugh, Sting, and George Michael.

While some might find Hampstead's conspicuous opulence oppressive, the area is undoubtedly beautiful with its well-pruned trees, serene flowers, and charming narrow streets. Escape from the city and come here for a cream tea at **Louis,** 32 Heath Street (see Food and Drink), or a leisurely stroll in summer.

The major sight of interest, nestled in the midst of Hampstead, is **Keats House,** Keats Grove, one of London's finest literary shrines. To get there from the Hampstead tube station, head left down High St. for several blocks, turn left down Downshire Hill, and then take the first right onto Keats Grove. (The BR Hampstead Heath station is much closer.) Before dashing off to Italy to breathe his last consumptive breath and die in true Romantic-poet style, John Keats pined here for his next-door fianceé, Fanny Brawne. He allegedly composed "Ode to a Nightingale" under a plum tree here—the distant ancestor of the one growing in the garden today. The house is furnished as it was during Keats's life, complete with his manuscripts and letters (open Mon.-Fri. 2-6pm, Sat. 10am-1pm and 2-5pm, Sun. 2-5pm; Nov.-March Mon.-Fri. 1-5pm, Sat. 10am-1pm and 2-5pm, Sun. 2-5pm; free). The **Keats Memorial Library** (tel. 435 2062) next door contains a unique collection of books on the poet's life, family, and friends (open by appointment only).

Now a National Trust property open to the public, **Fenton House,** Windmill Hill (tel. 435 3471), exhibits a collection of 18th-century porcelain and early keyboard instruments still used for occasional concerts. (For permission to play them, apply in writing to the Warden, Windmill Hill, London NW3 6RT.) You can see the walled garden and orchard free of charge. To get there, cross the street onto Holly Bush Hill, then bear right at the fork onto Hampstead Grove (house open Mon.-Wed. 1-6:30pm, Sat.-Sun. 11am-5:30pm; admission £2.50). Farther up Hampstead Grove and a left turn onto Admiral's Walk takes visitors to the **Admiral's House,** Admiral's Walk, which tries to simulate a ship, but fails quite miserably to do so.

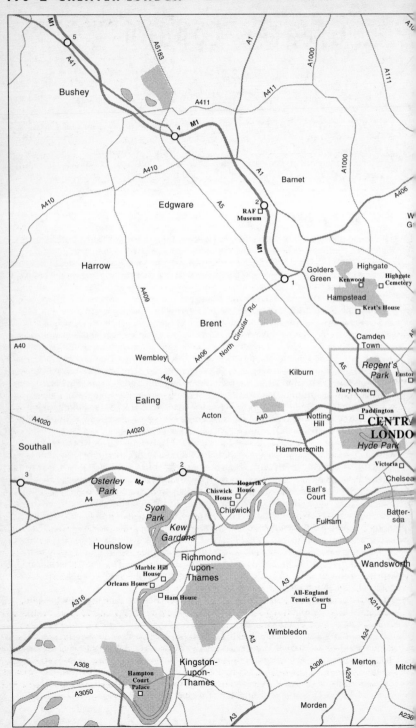

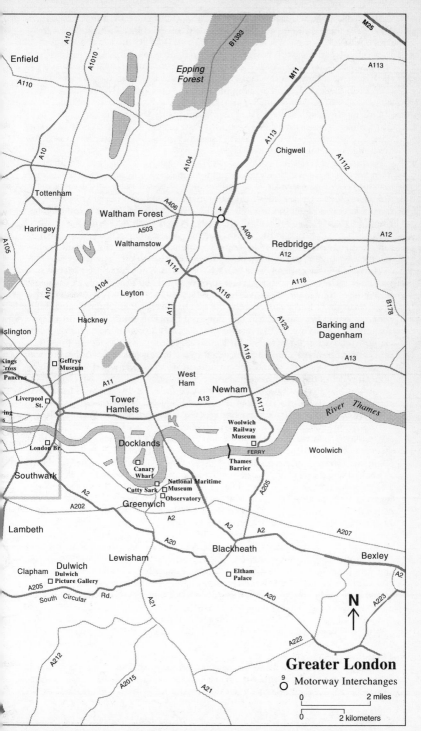

Greater London

○ Motorway Interchanges

0 — 2 miles
0 — 2 kilometers

N ↑

The idyllic walk to **Burgh House,** Flask Walk (tel. 431 0144), is much more satis-fying than the exhibitions of the Hampstead Museum inside. Just a few narrow streets and cobblestone sidewalks away from the High St., the town is transformed into a country village, with flowers everywhere and birds chirping in the boughs of commandingly large trees. Stop for lunch or a peaceful cup of tea at **The Buttery** in the basement of Burgh House. Head left on Hampstead High St. and take the first left onto Flask Walk (a pedestrian shopping arcade; house open Wed.-Sun. noon-5pm; Buttery open Wed.-Sun. 11am-5:30pm).

Church Row, off Heath St., vehemently retains its 18th-century style and digni-fied terraces. The narrow alleyways off the Row hark back to the days of Mary Pop-pins, complete with small, overflowing secret gardens. The painter John Constable lies buried in St. John's churchyard down the row.

Hampstead Heath (tube: Belsize Park) separates the Hampstead and Highgate from the rest of London. Once a hangout for outlaws, it now attracts docile picnick-ers and kite flyers; however, it is unadvisable to wander the heath alone at night. The heath remains the wildest patch of turf in London; you can get lost here, but dog-walkers will know the way out. On a hot day, take a dip in **Kenwood Ladies' Pond, Highgate Men's Pond,** or the *outré* **Mixed Bathing Pond.** Women may expose their top halves at the Ladies' Pond as long as they remain lying down. In July, 1994, gay protestors held a "strip-off" demonstration at the men's pond to pro-test the Corporation of London's introduction of a "trunks-on" policy.

Kenwood House, Hampstead La. (tel. (081) 348 1286), a picture-perfect exam-ple of an 18th-century country estate, presides over the heath. This airy mansion now houses the **Iveagh Bequest** (see Museums). Chief justice Lord Mansfield, the original owner of Kenwood, decreed the end to slavery on English soil. Mansfield's progressive policies did not win him universal popularity and, after destroying his abandoned townhouse in Bloomsbury, the Gordon Rioters pursued him north to Hampstead. Luckily for him (and for Kenwood House), his pursuers stopped for a drink at the **Spaniard's Inn** on Spaniards Rd. (see Pubs), and a responsible publican made sure they got too drunk to continue. In summer, Kenwood hosts a hugely popular series of **outdoor concerts** (see Entertainment—Music) in which top-flight orchestras play from a bandshell across the lake (tube: Archway or Golders Green, then bus #210 to Kenwood). From Hampstead High St., bus #268 goes to Golders Green (Kenwood open daily 10am-6pm; Oct. to mid-April daily 10am-4pm.; free).

Parliament Hill, on the southeastern tip of the heath, marks the southern bound-ary between Hampstead and Highgate and commands a gorgeous view of London, sweeping from the Docklands to the Houses of Parliament. The height of the hill, some say, owes much to the piles of corpses left here during the Plague. The bones of ancient Queen Boudicca also reputedly lie here. It was toward this hill that Guy Fawkes's accomplices fled after depositing explosives under the House of Com-mons in 1605, hoping for a good view of the explosion. To get there from the end of Keats Grove, turn right onto South End Rd., take the first left onto South Hill Pk., bear right at the fork, and bear left at the next fork.

To get from Hampstead to Highgate, walk across the heath or up Hampstead La. **Highgate Cemetery,** Swains La., is a remarkable monument to the Victorian fasci-nation with death. Its most famous resident, rather inaptly, is Karl Marx, buried in the eastern section in 1883. An unmistakably Stalinist bust, four times life size, was placed above his grave in 1956 and attracts pilgrims from everywhere. Death makes for strange bedfellows; novelist George Eliot lies buried nearby. The magically spooky western section contains some of the finest tombs. (Eastern Cemetery open Mon.-Fri. 10am-4:45pm, Sat.-Sun. 11am-4:45pm. Admission £1.50. Western Ceme-tery access by guided tour only Mon.-Fri. at noon, 2pm, and 4pm, Sat.-Sun. hourly from 11am to 4pm. Admission £2. Camera permit £1, valid in both sections. No tri-pods or video cameras allowed.)

Waterlow Park, immediately north of the cemetery, affords a gorgeous setting in which you can shed the urban grime of London and the Victorian gloom of the graveyard next door. The sociable ducks never turn down a good feed. By the eastern entrance, **Lauderdale House,** supposedly once home to Nell Gwyn, mistress of Charles II, now serves light snacks and lunches, but no oranges.

Highgate Village stands 424 ft. above the River Thames. You can climb Highgate Hill for a breathtaking panoramic view of London. On the way up, you will pass **Dick Whittington's Stone,** where 600 years ago the young, poor Dick heard the Bow Bells calling him back to London—"Turn again, Whittington, thrice Lord Mayor of London." He turned, went back to London, and was thrice Lord Mayor. His petrified cat stands guard. From Archway tube station, take the Junction Rd. exit and head left around the corner onto Highgate Hill, which goes up for ¾ mi. to the village—or wait there for bus #210 (which stops near Dick Whittington's Stone en route).

Once in Highgate Village, turn left onto South Grove at the triangular bus depot. Here hides **The Grove,** an avenue of late 17th-century houses secluded behind magnificent elms. Poet and critic Samuel Taylor Coleridge lived at no. 3 for the last 18 years of his life, entertaining Carlyle, Emerson, and sundry other visitors.

Descend from the heights into the depths of the subconscious in South Hampstead. Leaf through the pages of Sigmund's diary at the **Freud Museum,** 20 Maresfield Gdns., (see Museums).

■■■ GOLDERS GREEN

North of Hampstead, Golders Green is a small and quiet residential area that is the center of London's Jewish community. While Stamford Hill, to the east of Golders Green, is the heartland of the Orthodox community, it is in Golders Green that Jewish culture is visible in the streets. However, places of interest are spread out over a large area poorly served by public transport. The tube to Golders Green, bus #268 from Hampstead High St., and bus #210 from Archway tube all deposit visitors at the intersection of North End Way and **Golders Green Road,** a wide shopping strip of mundane stores and a surprising number of Chinese restaurants; Jewish eateries and Hebrew/English signs only begin to appear several blocks away from the tube/bus station.

At no. 111a, **Yossi's Nosh** (tel. (0181) 455 6777) sells blintzes (£2.45), hummus and pita (£2.15), and Middle Eastern food (open Sun.-Thurs. noon-11pm, Fri. noon-3pm). At no. 130, busy **Bloom's** restaurant and take-away, a branch of the famous Whitechapel restaurant, is one of several shops on the block selling foodstuffs supervised kosher by the London *Beth Din.* "Think Tradition! Remember— Kosher!" admonishes the Bloom's motto; Neil Diamond, Bob Dylan, Golda Meir, and various royals have sampled *kneidlach* soup, *latkes,* and *gefilte* fish at this *fleischig* haven (tel. (0181) 455 3003/1338; open Sun.-Thurs. 9:30am-2am, Fri. 9:30am-3pm, Sat. sundown-4am). Israeli-owned **Carmelli's Bagels,** 126-128 Golder's Green Rd., is a popular spot for a Saturday night dairy meal; upscale *glatt* kosher Israeli cuisine can be had at **Dizengoff,** 118 Golder's Green Rd. (tel. (0181) 458 7003). Also on Golder's Green Rd. are stores selling "Elite" and "Osem" brand foodstuffs imported from Israel—this is the place to find Bazooka gum with Hebrew cartoons, a treat prized above all others by Hebrew school students the world over.

Down at 146a, **Jerusalem the Golden** sells a hodgepodge of Jewish children's books and arts and crafts (tel. (0181) 455 4960; open Mon.-Thurs. 9:30am-6pm, Sun. and Fri. 9:30am-5pm). The strongest Jewish presence is in the shops lining Finchley Rd. between Alberon Gdns. and Portsdown Ave. **The Jewish Chronicle,** the world's oldest Jewish newspaper, provides information on Jewish events around London (tel. 405 9252).

The ashes of Freud, in his favorite Greek vase, are kept at the **Golders Green Crematorium,** Hoop Lane Rd., NW11 (tel. (0181) 455 2374; open daily 8am-7pm). Other celeb ashes and memorials include Marks and Spencer founder and Zionist Lord Sieff, rocker Marc Bolan, and *Dracula* creator Bram Stoker. To pay your respects, walk under the tube's bridge, then turn right at the first traffic light (at the church) onto Hoop Lane Rd.

DOCKLANDS

■■■ DOCKLANDS

London Docklands, the largest commercial development in Europe, has utterly changed the face of East London within the space of 10 years. Developers have poured tons of steel, reflective glass, and money onto the banks of the Thames east of London Bridge. A new Fleet Street and an inchoate heavyweight financial center have risen from the ruins of the once deserted dockyards of Wapping, Surrey Docks, and the Isle of Dogs. However, the region's frenetic progress has a dismally regressive underside; recently, racist agitators have attempted to threaten the area's immigrant communities, and many Londoners wonder whether the nearly unrestricted authority of the private company responsible for the region's development might facilitate decisions which adversely effect the region's low-income communities.

Londinium, already a prominent port in Roman times, sprouted wharves and quays that spread east from the City during the Middle Ages; Royal Dockyards were established at Deptford and Woolwich in 1515. As London grew in importance, the docks grew with it, stretching miles down the Thames, until they had become the powerful trading center of the British Empire. During World War II, the Blitz obliterated much of the dockland area, whilst the war seriously diminished Britain's world influence. As the sun set on the empire, the docks continued to do good business until the early 60s. Then the advent of container transport and modern shipping methods rapidly rendered the docks obsolete—by 1982 all had closed, leaving sweeping tracts of desperate dereliction.

As part of the Thatcher government's privatization program, redevelopment of the area was handed over to the private sector—in the form of the **London Docklands Development Corporation (LDDC)**—along with a generous helping of public funds. Since then, the LDDC has been at the helm of what it calls "the most significant urban regeration program in the world." The all-powerful company is answerable only to Parliament and the Department of the Environment; however, local councils retain responsibility for housing, highway, and education decisions.

Building has taken place on a phenomenal scale, but the task of populating new office space with businesses initially lagged behind. Hesitantly at first but now more steadily, big businesses have begun to take up residence in the area, filling in the previously empty floors of shiny new skyscrapers. The area is not only populated by wealthy entrepreneurs ferried to work every day on executive launch motorboats that zoom across the Thames. After a disastrous recession slump, the Docklands are now poised for a new housing boom. Low-cost housing communities are springing up all over the southern bank of the Thames, especially on the Isle of Dogs. Hopefully this housing will benefit the local residents, many of whom feel that they have been displaced by the new development, and view the LDDC as a callous agent of gentrification.

Docklands covers a huge expanse, from the Tower to Greenwich. The best way to see the region is via the **Docklands Light Railway (DLR)** (tel. 918 4000), a futuristic driverless, totally automatic elevated rail system. The DLR is slow but smooth, and affords a panoramic view which helps you put the huge expanse of the Docklands into perspective. All tickets, Travelcards, and passes issued by London Transport, London Underground, and BritishRail are vaild on the DLR provided they cover the correct zones. The wheelchair-accessible DLR is replaced by bus on weekends and after 9:30pm on weekdays (see Essentials—Getting Around).

The first stop for any tour of the Docklands should be the **Docklands Visitors Centre** (tel. 512 1111; DLR: Crossharbour, then left up the road). Loads of brochures hide behind the information desk, the most useful being the *DLR Tourist Guide,* which includes a map of the area, points of interest, and DLR info. A huge room is devoted to informing visitors about the history of the Docklands and its future, using photos, charts, maps, architects' plans, and a tearfully inspiring propaganda video (open Mon.-Fri. 8:30am-6pm, Sat.-Sun. 10am-4:30pm). Other Docklands information desks are at the Tower Hill/Gateway and Island Gardens stops. A separate **Museum of Docklands** is in the works; until then, a section in the Museum of London counts as the Docklands museum (call the Museum of Docklands Project, tel. 515 1162, for an update).

Also at the Crossharbour stop are the **London Arena,** a 12,000-seat concert and sports venue recently purchased by the US company that runs the Los Angeles Coliseum and the Louisiana Superdome, and the **Island History Trust** (tel. 987 6041), a museum and photo archives recounting the history of the Isle of Dogs and the immigrant communities that have lived here (off the road just past the Visitors' Centre; open Tues.-Wed. 1:30-4:30pm; free).

Recently these immigrant populations have been beleaguered by poor public housing policy, and victimized by a spate of racist activity. The **Millwall** neighborhood, just southwest of the Crossharbour DLR stop, is where the fraught relationship between Chinese and Bangladeshi immigrants and right wing agitators is most visible. In 1994, locals feared that members of the right-wing National Party would try to intimidate Bangladeshi residents so that they would be afraid to vote. While this did not happen, the racial tension testifies to the lingering presence of social problems which the massive new development has not ameliorated.

In the 19th century, the docks and factories of the **Isle of Dogs** (not an island, but a peninsula on the Thames named after the hounds of Edward II that once resided here) churned with activity. After its heyday during the Industrial Revolution, it declined along with the rest of the Docklands. Now, however, the most furious building is taking place here, notably the 800-ft. **Canary Wharf** skyscraper, Britain's tallest. The pyramid-topped building, which contains shops, restaurants, a concert hall, and a visitor center, is virtually the emblem of the Docklands (visitor center open Mon.-Sat. 10am-6pm). Also at the shiny new marble-bedecked Canary Wharf stop is a slick food court where office workers lunch and Canary Wharf Pier (where the Riverbus stops; see Essentials—Getting Around). In 1993, when Canary Wharf remained largely unoccupied due to the recession, Spiral Tribe, an underground rave-coordinating organization, attempted to use the building as a rave venue but were thwarted by the police.

On the southern end of the Isle of Dogs, the pastoral expanses of **Mudchute Park** come as a relief after the human-made modernity of the new Docklands (DLR: Mudchute). Here are 32 acres of grassy knolls, plus horses to ride and farm animals to pet at **Mudchute Farm,** Pier St., E14 (tel. 515 5901; open daily 9am-5pm). At the southern end of the line, **Island Gardens** offers a sweeping view of Greenwich across the river. You can walk through the chilly foot tunnel (the steps at either end are quicker than waiting for the lift) and take in some of the sights (see Greenwich and Blackheath).

Getting off at **Shadwell** station, you'll see the old dock community: drab brick housing, dusty streets, traditional pubs, caffs, and pie-and-mash shops. Note the stark contrast between these economically depressed areas and the sleek, newly developed regions; many Londoners believe that this contrast testifies to the largely unregulated LDDC's greed and lack of social responsibility. Hopefully, brightening economic forecasts for the Docklands as a whole will bring relief to areas like Shadwell. Southwest of the station, down Cannon St. Rd. and a right onto The Highway, is the turreted **St. George in the East** (1714-26), whose plain façade and tower can be seen from several stops away on the DLR (open daily 9am-5pm). The work of Wren disciple Nicholas Hawksmoor, it was bombed in the war but restored and given a modern interior in 1964.

Across The Highway, the new face of Docklands appears in the form of **Tobacco Dock,** a generic shopping mall (tel. 702 9681) that strives to attract tourists with two replica pirate ships. *The Three Sisters* explains the history of piracy (admission £2.50, students, seniors, and children £1.50), while *The Sea Lark* has a *Treasure Island* theme (admission £1; mall open daily 10am-5pm). On Wapping Wall, a 16th-century pub, **Prospect of Whitby,** looks over the river.

From the Westferry stop, turn left onto West India Dock Rd., then left onto Three Colt St. for another Hawksmoor church, **St. Anne's** (built 1712-24), which presides over a leafy churchyard. This is the sister church of St. George-in-the-East; its clock face comes from the workshop which provided Big Ben's face. The church's Victorian organ was the winner of the organ prize at the Great Exhibition of 1851 (tel. 987 1502; open Sun. 3-4:30pm and by appointment).

The Limehouse and Westferry stops cover the historic **Limehouse** neighborhood, where dock and factory workers once lived. The legacy of Limehouse's 19th-century Chinese community can be seen in the Chinese restaurants along West India Dock Rd. The famous Narrow Street along the Thames is an official conservation area, where many Georgian houses can be seen. At 76 Narrow Street, **The Grapes,** the pub Dickens described in "Le Jolly Fellowship Porters," maintains its original ambience. Just east of narrow street on Ropemaker's fields lies **The House They Left Behind,** a pub famed as a Joseph Conrad haunt.

■■■ GREENWICH AND BLACKHEATH

In a nation whose livelihood is dependent upon the waves, the village of Greenwich stands on hallowed ground, at a point where the Thames runs wide and deep. Although the village functioned historically as the eastern water approach to London, Greenwich (GREN-idge) is synonymous with time in modern-day minds. After Charles II authorized the establishment of a small observatory here in 1675 "for perfecting navigation and astronomy," successive royal astronomers perfected their craft to such a degree that they were blessed with the Prime Meridian in 1884.

In addition to the maritime and astronomical traditions, Greenwich also lays claim to a bit of royal history: in Tudor times, it was the site of one of Henry VIII's palaces, and he, as well as his daughters Mary and Elizabeth (each of whom became queens) were born here.

When industrialization hit Britain in the 19th century, Greenwich somehow manages to stay out of the developmental fray. As a result, the streets around the pier feel very quaint (if somewhat touristy), with their tiny storefronts, pubs, and cafés. Greenwhich also offers numerous corner markets, with vendors peddling everything from Jimmy Hendrix CDs to African carvings and leather bomber jackets. On summer Sundays, the village streets are taken over by the young, old, bold, and beautiful seeking the ultimate bargain at the **Greenwich Market,** at Greenwich Church St. and College Approach (open in summer Sat.-Sun. 9am-6pm; in winter Sat. 9am-5pm). In addition to this covered crafts market, Greenwich boasts an **Antique Market** on Burney St., which sells antiques, books, and various bric-a-brac (open Sat.-Sun. 8am-4pm).

Genteel terraces now encircle **Greenwich Park,** used as a burial ground during the 1353 plague. The shriveled trunk of an oak tree on the east side of the park (now fenced off and covered in ivy) marks the spot where Henry VIII frolicked with an 11-fingered Anne Boleyn. The garden in the southeast corner of the park combines English garden and fairy tale, with a wild deer park thrown in for good measure.

Ranger's House sits in the southwest. Originally built for an admiral in 1688, it was given to the Park Ranger in 1815. Today it contains the Suffolk Collection of Jacobean portraits and the Dolmetsch Collection of antique musical instruments. The newer Architectural Study Centre holds a substantial collection of architectural details from 18th- and 19th-century London dwellings. (Open April-Oct. daily 10am-6pm; Nov.-March Wed.-Sun. 10am-4pm. Admission £2, concessions £1.50, children £1; price includes a taped tour. Wheelchair accessible.) In summer, bands perform at Greenwich Park as a part of the **Royal Park Band** performance series. Free shows begin at 3 and 6pm (every Sun. June-Aug.) and take place in the bandstand north of the gardens. From the last week of July to the middle of August, the young and the young at heart can see puppet shows in the playground at the northeast corner of the park (Mon.-Sat. at 11:30am and 2:30pm). The Children's Boating Pool next to the playground (open daily 10am-dusk) gives kids a chance to unleash pent-up sea-faring energy accumulated in the nearby museums.

At the top of the hill in the middle of the park stands the **Old Royal Observatory** (tel. (0181) 858 1167), disguised by Sir Christopher Wren. Only select parts are open to the public. Flamsteed House, with its unique, octagonal top room contains Britain's largest refracting telescope and an excellent collection of early astronomi-cal instruments—astrolabes, celestial globes, and orreries—displayed with almost comprehensible explanations. The **Prime Meridian** is marked by a brass strip in the observatory courtyard. Jump from west to east in an instant. Greenwich Mean Time, still the standard for international communications and navigation, is displayed on an over-120-years-old clock. The red time ball, used since 1833 to indicate time to ships on the Thames, drops daily at 1pm. In 1894, an anarchist blew himself up while trying to destroy the observatory, and Polish sailor Joseph Conrad used the bizarre event as the seed for his novel *The Secret Agent.* (Open Mon.-Sat. 10am-6pm, Sun. noon-6pm; in winter Mon.-Sat. 10am-5pm, Sun. 2-5pm. Admission £3.95, con-cessions £2.95, children £2.75. Planetarium shows Mon.-Sat. at 11:30am,. noon, 12:30, 2, 2:30, 3pm, 3:30, and 4pm. Shows last about ½hr. Planetarium tickets £1.50, children £1. 45-min. sound guide to the observatory £2.)

Just outside the observatory, you can share a splendid view of the Thames with a statue of General Wolfe (conqueror of French Canada) kindly donated by the Cana-dian government. At the foot of the hill is the **National Maritime Museum** (see Museums).

The museum forms the west addition to **Queen's House** (tel. (0181) 858 4422), the 17th-century home which was started for James I's wife, Anne of Denmark, who unfortunately died before construction was completed. The house was finished for Henrietta Maria, the wife of Charles I. Designed by the age's master architect, Inigo Jones, it is England's first Palladian villa, known to the Queen as her "house of delights." The house has been renovated and now exhibits sumptuous 17th-century furnishings, rich silk hangings, and an art collection. (Open May-Sept. Mon.-Sat. 10am-6pm, Sun. noon-6pm; Oct.-April Mon.-Sat. 10:30am-3:30pm, Sun. 2:15-4pm. Tours are given every 15min. Admission £3.95, under 16 £2.95. Closed Jan. 1995 for maintenance.)

Charles II commisssioned Wren to tear down the Royal Palace of Placentia and to construct the **Royal Naval College** (tel. (0181) 858 2154) in its place. Because it was situated directly between the Queen's House and the river, the College was constructed in two halves, so as to leave the Queen with an unobstructed view. Stop in to see James Thornhill's frescoed optical illusions in the Painted Hall. In the chapel hangs Benjamin West's painting of a shipwrecked St. Paul. (Open Fri.-Wed. 2:30-5pm; free; services Sun. at 11am.)

By the River Thames in Greenwich, the **Cutty Sark,** one of the last great tea clip-pers, anchors in dry dock. The ship (whose name, meaning "short shift," comes from Burns's poem "Tam O'Shanter") conveyed 1.3 million pounds of tea on each 120-day return trip from China. In the prime of its sea-going days, between 1869 and 1938, it set new records for speed. The decks and crews' quarters have been restored, and exhibits describing the history of the Pacific trade have been added. The vessel is also filled with the largest collection of ships' figureheads in the world (Tel. (0181) 858 2698; open Mon.-Sat. 10am-6pm, Sun. noon-6pm; in winter Mon.-Sat. 10am-5pm, Sun. noon-5pm. Admission £3.25, concessions £2.25, families £8.)

The **Gypsy Moth IV** rests nearby. In this tiny 54-ft- long craft, the 66-year-old Sir Fran-cis Chichester spent 226 days sailing solo around the globe in 1966-67 (tel. (0181) 853 3589; open April-Oct. Mon.-Sat. 10am-6pm, Sun. noon-6pm; last entry ½hr. before closing; admission 50p, concessions 30p).

A show at the **Greenwich Theatre** (Croom's Hill, SE18) can be a relaxing conclu-sion to a day spent traipsing about galleries. The season runs from April to August; August 1994 featured the London debut of Wendy Wasserstein's *The Sisters Rosensweig.* (Box office tel. (0181) 858-7755, performances Mon.-Fri. at

7:45pm, Sat. at 2:30 and 7:45pm; tickets £7-14.50, students and seniors £5.50-6.50.)

At 10-12 Crooms Hill, across from the theatre, you'll find the **Fan Museum** (tel. (0181) 305 1441), which opened in 1991 as the first and only museum in the world dedicated to the history, art, craft, and coquetry of the fan. The museum occupies two restored Georgian houses that share a Japanese-style garden at the back. (Open Tues.-Sat. 11am-4:30pm, Sun. noon-4:30pm; admission £2.50, seniors and children £1.50; Tues. 2-4:30pm free for the disabled; wheelchair accessible.).

The most picturesque (and appropriate) passage to Greenwich is by boat. Cruises to Greenwich pier depart from the Westminster (tel. 930 4097), Charing Cross (tel. 987 1185), and Tower (tel. (0181) 305 0300) piers (see Essentials—Getting Around for times and prices). Because of changing tides, always call to confirm times. The crew provides valuable commentary on the major sights along the voyage. Trains leave from Charing Cross, Cannon St., and London Bridge for Greenwich (less than 20min., day return £2.80). The DLR whizzes from Tower Gateway to Island Gardens (16min., Mon.-Fri. only). From there Greenwich is just a 10-minute walk through the foot tunnel. When the DLR is not in service, bus D9 runs from the Island Gardens station to Bank Station. Bus #188 runs between Euston and Greenwich stopping at Kinsway, Aldwych, and Waterloo. If you plan on seeing all of the major sites, it's a good idea to buy a "passport ticket" for admission to the Observatory, National Maritime Museum, Queen's House, and the *Cutty Sark*. The ticket is good for up to one year (passport £7.95, children £5.45, families £14.95). The friendly **Greenwich Tourist Information Centre,** 46 Greenwich Church St., SE10 (tel. (0181) 858 6376; open daily 10am-5pm, with reduced winter hours) will go out of their way to arrange a variety of afternoon tours (£2.50-3, 1-1½ hr.).

Just on the south side of Greenwich Park lies **Blackheath,** a large sloping field where Wat Tyler and his fellow peasants revolting over a poll tax congregated in 1381. The **Royal Blackheath Golf Club,** constituted in 1766 and founded on the common much earlier, is the world's oldest; James I was known to take an occasional bash here with his three wood. Standard highwayman problems once plagued Blackheath, but the fine houses near the common have since made it one of the more fashionable addresses in South London. Daniel Day Lewis was a recent resident, living on the near-by Croom Hill, a well-preserved 17th-century street. A traditional site for royal celebrations, Blackheath still holds fairs on Bank Holidays, and is the starting point every spring for the **London Marathon,** the largest 26-miler in the world.

Eltham Palace graces the slopes southeast of Blackheath, and remains one of the finest examples of pre-Elizabethan architecture in England. 14th-century kings spent their Christmases here, and the palace's sturdy composition and game-filled woods made it a favorite 15th-century royal haunt. However, after the Civil War (1642-60), the palace was left to deteriorate, and when it was restored in 1934, only the hall and the bridge over the moat survived. Open hours are sporadic (normally open April-Sept. Thurs. and Sun. 10am-6pm, Oct.-March Thurs. and Sun. 10am-4pm, but call ahead.)

A bit farther down the river, the steel and concrete **Thames Barrier** (tel. (0181) 854 1373, 1 Unity Way, Woolwich SE18), the world's largest movable flood barrier, is the reason that London no longer enjoys the exciting high tides of yesteryear. Constructed during the 1970s, the barrier spans 520m and consists of 10 separate movable steel gates; when raised, the main gates stand as high as a five-story building. A visitors' center has a working model of the barrier, in addition to exhibits explaining its history (open Mon.-Fri. 10:30am-5pm, Sat.-Sun. 10:30am-5:30pm; admission £2.50, seniors and children £1.55). From Charing Cross take BR to Charlton Station; from there it's a 15-minute walk. Alternatively take the boat from Greenwich pier (25min.; 75min. from Westminster pier). Call 930 3373 for details of Westminster service; (0181) 305 0300 for Greenwich. Farther yet along the curving river, on the north bank, is the **North Woolwich Old Station Museum** (BR: North Woolwich; see Museums).

■■■ KEW GARDENS

After days of sight-seeing in central London, the **Royal Botanic Gardens** (tel. (0181) 940 1171) at Kew provide a restorative breath of fresh air. Yet another example of the Empire's encyclopedic collecting frenzy, the Royal Botanic Gardens at Kew display thousands of flowers, plants, bushes, fruits, trees, and vegetables from the world over, spread over 300 perfectly maintained acres. Founded in 1759 by Princess Augusta, Kew gradually grew in size until it became a royal park in 1841.

Traveling west towards Kew on the District line, you will begin to see green fields instead of old brick railway bridges. The walk from the Kew tube station to the gardens takes you through Kew village, a sedate, gentrified neighborhood sporting tiny shops, traditional architecture, and luxury automobiles.

The gardens comprise several buildings and sections, each containing different exhibits. The moist and tropical **Palm House,** a unique masterpiece of Victorian engineering built in 1848, will stun you with the revelation that bananas are in fact giant herbs. Climb the white spiral stairs to the upper gallery for the toucan's-eye view. In 1991 a **Marine Display,** opened by HRM Princess Margaret, was added to the basement of the glassy Palm House. The beautifully-lit aquariums let you watch batfish and porcupine puffer fish interact with colorful sea kelp.

Although replete with voluptuous fronds, the Palm House is dwarfed by its younger Victorian sibling, the **Temperate House.** The climate here nurtures 3000 species, arranged according to geographical origins in its 50,000 square feet. The lush South American Rainforest species section surpasses all others.

As an English garden, Kew would not be complete without its **pagoda** (in the southeast corner of the park), designed by William Chambers in 1762 as testimony to Britain's fascination with the Orient.

On the opposite side of the park from the pagoda, the **Princess of Wales Conservatory** allows you to browse through ten different tropical climates; it's just a few steps from a rainforest to an arid desert. The award-winning pyramidal design not only allows the building to rise from the hedges without disruption, but it also conserves energy remarkably well. Don't miss the spectacular giant waterlilies or the amiable pineapple family.

In the northeastern section of the gardens stands **Kew Palace.** Built in 1631 but leased as a royal residence since 1730, this inconspicuous summer home of King George III and Queen Charlotte has evolved into a small museum depicting the vagaries of late 18th-century monarchical life. You can spend hours with the royal toy collection inside or the well-documented herb garden out back; wander by the lilacs made famous by Noyes's poem "Go down to Kew in lilactime." (Palace open daily 11am-5:30pm. Admission £1, students and seniors 75p.)

West of the Palace, the park rambles on in a controlled state of wilderness. Solitary benches sit secluded among groves of trees, and small grassy clearings provide perfect picnic spots. Comical signs posted along the way warn that some paths are not suitable for high heels.

Other points of interest at the gardens include the **Marianne North Gallery,** a small but interesting collection of 19th-century paintings, the **Rhododendron Dell** (built by Capability Brown), and the **Waterlily House.**

The calming way to reach Kew is by boat from Westminster pier (every 30min. 10:30am-3:30pm, 1½hr., £7, return £9) and the cheapest way is by tube or BR North London line (Kew Gardens station, zone 3). Should you opt to drive, plenty of parking is available outside the gardens. (Gardens open Mon.-Fri. 9:30am-6:30pm, last admission 6pm, Sat.-Sun. and bank holidays 9:30am-7:30pm, last admission 7pm. Glasshouses and galleries open Mon.-Fri. 9:30am-7:30pm, Sat., Sun., and bank holidays 9:30am-6pm. Call to confirm closing times as they may vary by season. Admission £4, student and seniors £2, children 5-16 £1.50, under 5 free, admission during last open hour £1.50. No bikes, dogs, radios, or ballgames. Tours leave Victoria Gate daily except Thurs. at 11am and 2:30pm, £1, concessions 50p.) Kew hosts jazz and classical music concerts sporadically in the summer; ticket prices run £9-15. Call the gardens for more information.

■■■ SYON PARK

Syon Park (tube: Gunnersbury, zone 3), just across the Thames from Kew in Brent-ford (walk across Kew Bridge and left along London Rd., or BR: Syon Lane), harbors stately **Syon House** (tel. (081) 560 0881). This is the last hulking mansion left in London still under its original hereditary ownership. The castellated exterior of the house is Tudor, built to incorporate the buildings of a monastery where Queen Catherine Howard was imprisoned before her execution in 1542. In 1553 owner-ship of the house passed to the Duke of Northumberland, who offered the crown to his daughter-in-law Lady Jane Grey here. Not a week later, Mary Tudor took back the house, and the Duke's head. The house reverted to the Northumberlands in 1594, and they still own it today.

The mansion's perfect interior was created by Robert Adam in 1766. The Ante-room, a green marble and gilt extravaganza, is dazzling; the Long Gallery has a more balanced elegance (house open April-Sept. Wed.-Sun. 11am-5pm, Oct. Sun. noon-5pm; admission £3.25, children, students, and seniors £2.50). The stately gardens around Syon House can be enjoyed daily 10am to dusk (admission £2.25, conces-sions £1.75). On the park grounds you'll find a six-acre rose garden, landscaped by Capability Brown, and the world's largest collection of historic British cars (open 10am-5pm, Nov.-Feb. 10am-4pm; admission £3). Joint tickets for both Syon House and Syon Park are £4.74, concessions £3.50.

Also in the vicinity, the **London Butterfly House** has over 1000 butterflies flying "free," as well as some less pleasant insects (open 10am-5pm; Nov.-March 10am-3pm; admission £2.50).

■■■ RICHMOND

Ever since Henry I came up the Thames in the 12th century, Richmond has preened its royal pedigree. Although Henry VII's Richmond Palace, built in 1500, was demol-ished during Cromwell's Commonwealth, the town has not lost its dignified sheen; the 18th-century houses around **Richmond Green** make it possibly the most serene park in or around London.

The **Richmond Tourist Information Centre,** in the old Town Hall on Whittaker Ave., has complete information on Richmond and surrounding areas (tel. (0181) 940 9125; BR or tube: Richmond; open Mon.-Sat. 10am-6pm, Sun. 10:15am-4:15pm, reduced winter hours). The **Museum of Richmond** (tel. (0181) 332 1141) in the same building is an excellent local museum with exhibits on famous inhabitants, from actor Edmund Kean to writers George Eliot and Virginia Woolf (open Tues.-Sat. 11am-5pm, Sun. 2-5pm, closed Sun. Oct.-April, admission £1, children 50p). The **Richmond Festival** (tel. (0181) 332 0534) in the first week of July explodes with music, dance, and children's activities, much of it free.

Most of Richmond's sights are scattered around the actual village. **Richmond Park,** atop Richmond Hill, is Europe's largest city park. Its 2500 acres were once a royal hunting ground, and are still home to several hundred nervous deer who share the grounds with thousands of tourists and the Royal Ballet School, housed in the Palladian White Lodge. The Isabella Plantation woodland garden, deep inside the park, bursts with color in the spring, when its azaleas and rhododendrons come into bloom. Patient anglers fish in nearby Pen Pond, while model boats sail across Adam's Pond.

Quinlan Terry designed the controversially Neoclassical development on the river near Richmond Bridge. Across Richmond Bridge, on Richmond Rd., the gleaming cube of **Marble Hill House** (tel. (081) 892 5115; Richmond BR or tube, then bus #33, 90B, or 290) perches on the Thames, amid vast trimmed lawns. Like its contemporary Chiswick House, it is a villa inspired by both Palladio and Inigo Jones. Marble Hill House was built in 1729 for Henrietta Howard, George II's mistress. The Great Room, on the first floor, is lavishly decorated with gilt and carvings by James Richards and the original Panini paintings of ancient Rome. During the summer, a series of outdoor concerts are held on the grounds. (See Entertainment; house open daily April-Oct. 10am-6pm; Nov.-March Wed.-Sun. 10am-4pm; free.)

On nearby Orleans Road, the remains of the 18th-century **Orleans House** (tel. (081) 892 0221; Richmond BR or tube, then bus #33, 90B, or 290) hold a gallery of art and artifacts of local history. Only the Octagon Room survives from the original house, which put up with the Duc D'Orleans (the future King Louis Philippe) for three years in the 19th century (open Tues.-Sat. 1-5:30pm, Sun. 2-5:30pm; Oct.-March Tues.-Sat. 1-4:30pm, Sun. 2-4:30pm; free).

On some summer days, a small passenger ferry (30p) runs between Marble Hill Park (next to Orleans House) and **Ham House,** on Ham Street (tel. (081) 940-1950; Richmond BR or tube, then bus #65 or 371). Built in 1610, this house was lavishly "modernized" during the late 1960s by the Duke of Lauderdale and his wife, who had inherited the house from her father, Charles I's "whipping boy." (As part of his "reward" for taking all the future king's punishments whenever he misbehaved, he received the lease to the Ham estate when he became an adult.) The house and gardens have been newly restored; go to take tea in the Orangery and enjoy the surrounding water meadows. (Open April-Oct. Mon.-Wed. 1-5pm, Sat. 1-5:30pm, Sun. 11:30am-5:30pm; Nov.-Dec. Sat.-Sun. 1-4pm. Admission £4, children £2.)

During the summer, Richmond can also be reached by a boat from Westminster (see Getting Around—Boats) which stops at Richmond on its way to Hampton Court. Boats leave Westminster Pier at 10:30am, 11:15am, and noon. The trip takes 2-3 hours (adult one-way £6; adult roundtrip £8). The upriver boat service only runs from the Monday before Easter until the end of September.

■■■ HAMPTON COURT

Compared to Buckingham Palace's drab facade, Hampton Court (tel. (0181) 781 9500 or (0181) 781 9666 for recorded information and special events) seems better fit for royalty. Cardinal Wolsey built it in 1514, showing Henry VIII by his example how to act the part of a splendid and all-powerful ruler. Henry learned the lesson well and confiscated the Court in 1525, when Wolsey fell out of favor. Today, the palace stands in three parts. The first and most endearing, designed by Wolsey, adapted the Renaissance style with a free hand. The windows wander over the wine-dark brick, disdaining formal symmetry.

By 1535, Henry had converted to Anglicanism and English chauvinism, and Wolsey's Renaissance designs seemed tainted with Catholicism. Henry's **Great Hall,** monumental but empty, harkens back to the Middle Ages. Look for the stained-glass window depicting Henry VIII surrounded by the coats of arms of his six unfortunate wives. When working correctly, the **Astronomical Clock** in Anne Boleyn's Gateway indicates the hour, day, month, phase of the moon, and approximate time for high tide at London Bridge; its sun revolves around the earth.

When William and Mary ascended to the throne in 1689, they commissioned Wren to demolish the entire building and build a highly symmetrical, more spacious palace that would rival Versailles. Luckily, Wren ran out of money. The palace's east facade and classical **State Apartments,** whose windows peer out over the cloisters of **Fountain Court,** remain as some of the best records of his work. Thus, the imprints left by Hampton Court's earliest inhabitants account for its uniqueness: a quirkily harmonious blend of 16th-century motifs and 18th-century classicism.

Hampton Court looks best from the outside. Inside, you can see two curiosities of Renaissance art: the **tapestries** woven from the Raphael cartoons in the Victoria and Albert Museum, and a roomful of grisaille work originally by Mantegna but poorly repainted in the 18th century. You'll also find a selection of paintings from the royal collection. Note the intriguing ceilings, woodwork, and ornaments, especially in the downstairs kitchen and cellars. The **King's Apartments** are newly restored after a 1986 fire; cool down with a snack in Elizabeth I's Privy Kitchen (open 10am-5pm in the summer).

Sixty marvelous acres of Palace gardens are open and free, and contain some highly celebrated amusements, including the famous **maze** (open March-Oct.), a hedgerow labyrinth first planted in 1714 that served as the prototype for such later structures as Stanley Kubrick's Overlook Hotel; the great vine planted in 1769 that still produces grapes and now encloses a whole room with its foliage; and the indoor tennis court (built in 1529), still used by "real tennis" purists. Henry's is one of only four courts left in England designed for this early squash-like brand of the game (open March-Oct.). Also note the exhibit of Tijou's ironwork gates, left freestanding for the most part, and admirable from all sides. (Hampton Court open Mon. 10:15am-6pm, Tues.-Sun. 9:30am-6pm; Oct.-March Mon. 10:15am-4:30pm, Tues.-Sun. 9:30am-4:30pm; last admission 45min. before closing. Admission to palace, courtyard, cloister, and maze £7, concessions £5.30, under 16 £4.70, under 5 free, families £19.30. Admission to maze only £1.75, under 16 £1.10.)

BR runs trains from Waterloo to Hampton Court every half-hour (35 min., day return £3.60). From the first Mon. before Easter until the end of Sept., a boat runs from Westminster Pier (See Getting Around—Boats) to Hampton Court, leaving in the morning at 10:30am, 11:15am, and noon, and returning from Hampton Court at 3, 4, and 5pm. The trip takes 3-4 hours one way (adult one way £7, roundtrip £9).

■■■ CHISWICK

Six miles west of central London, the riverside village of Chiswick was long ago engulfed by London's suburban sprawl. Today, two houses of great historical and artistic interest stand out among the gentle homes of the bourgeoisie.

Lord Burlington hired architect William Kent to execute his designs, heavily influenced by Andrea Palladio's studies of ancient buildings and his Villa Rotunda in Vincenza. The Palladium style of **Chiswick House** (tel. (0181) 995 0508; BR: Chiswick or tube: Turnham Green, Gunnersbury, or Chiswick Park) took English society by storm when it was built in 1729. Lord Harvey, a contemporary freelance critic, sneered, "You call it a house? Why? It is too small to live in, and too large to hang from one's watch." But the day's notables were more than happy to see and be seen when Burlington entertained at Chiswick.

The striking exterior with its magnificent staircases is best viewed from the Burlington Rd. entrance. Inside, the most notable rooms are on the first floor, including the Dome Saloon, still crowded with works of art collected by Burlington. Elaborate ceilings top the Red, Green, and especially the Blue Velvet rooms. Watch out for the perfectly cubical rooms–a standard Palladian device. The gardens, laid out by Kent, mix traditional ordered and manicured horticulture with serendipitous spontaneity (open April-Sept. daily 10am-1pm, 2-6pm; Oct.-March Wed.-Sun. 10am-1pm, 2-4pm; admission £2.30, concessions £1.70, under 16 £1.15).

Just northeast of the Chiswick House grounds, on Hogarth La., artist and social critic William Hogarth lived in a more modest abode. **Hogarth's House** (tel. (0181) 994 6757; follow Burlington La. north to Chiswick Sq. and go left at the Hogarth Roundabout; the house is about 200 yards down Hogarth La.), which Hogarth called his "country box by the Thames," has been refurbished after decades of neglect, and now makes a proper home to some of his best paintings and engravings. Follow the descending path of ruin in *A Harlot's Progress* or *Marriage à la Mode*, and turn from the degradation of *Gin Lane* to the prosperity of *Beer Street*. The original of *The Rake's Progress* is at Sir John Soane's Museum, Lincoln's Inn Fields (see Museums; house open Mon. and Wed.-Sat. 11am-6pm, Sun. 2-6pm; Oct.-March Mon. and Wed.-Sat. 11am-4pm, Sun. 2-4pm; closed last 2 weeks of Sept. and last 3 weeks of Dec.; free).

■■■ WINDSOR AND ETON

Royalty is an unfortunate national obsession, and **Windsor Castle** (tel. (01753) 868 286 or (01753) 831 118 for 24-hr. information line) contains the majestic ingredients—chivalry and pageantry, ramparts, and busbied guardsmen—from which the regal mythology has been constructed. The castle dominates this river town of cobbled lanes and tea shops surrounded by the 4800-acre Great Park, far away from London in the farming country of Surrey. Built by William the Conqueror as a fortress rather than as a residence, it has grown over nine centuries into the world's largest inhabited castle. You can saunter blithely in and out of its labyrinthine terraces, and enjoy beautiful views of the Thames Valley.

Windsor is notorious to contemporary visitors as the site of a fire which helped make 1992 an *annus horribilis* for the royal family, and reduced the extent to which the public involuntarily subsidizes the royals' senselessly posh existence. The influential conflagration blazed for nine hours on November 20, 1992, and was only extinguished through the efforts of 225 firefighters and 39 fire engines. Six rooms and three towers were destroyed or badly damaged by smoke and flames, although 80% of the state rooms escaped harm. Consequently, admission to the castle grounds has been jacked up in an attempt to raise the funds needed to repair the fire damage; visitors pay once upon entering the grounds, and will pay again if they chose to visit certain wings of the castle.

Visitors touring the intact sections of Windsor will see **St. George's Chapel** (tel. (01753) 865 538) rising across the courtyard as they first enter the castle grounds. The chapel is a sumptuous 15th-century building with delicate fan vaulting and an amazing wall of stained glass dedicated to the Order of the Garter (open Mon.-Sat. 10am-4pm, Sun. 2-4pm; admission £3; students, seniors, and children £1.80; family of 5 £6). Here Henry VIII rests in a surprisingly modest tomb near George V, Edward IV, Charles I, and Henry VI. A ceremonial procession of the Knights of the Garter, led by the Queen, takes place here in June. As you walk up by the Round Tower, whose foundations have recently been shifting, keep an eye out for the stone hippo in the moat garden.

Past the gargoyles of Norman Gate, built by Edward III, at the castle's top end, you can visit the elegantly furnished **state apartments** (admission £4, seniors £2.50, children £1.50). These formal rooms are richly decorated with artwork from the massive Royal Collection, including works by Holbein, Rubens, Rembrandt, and an entire room of Van Dycks. (The state apartments are closed Dec. 22-Jan. 2.) In the same wing is **Queen Mary's dolls' house**, an exact replica of a palace on a tiny scale, and the **Gallery** (tel. (01753) 831 118), where temporary exhibitions are shown. Windsor's impressive changing of the guard takes place at 11am. (Grounds open daily 10am-5pm; Nov.-March daily 10am-4pm; state apartments, dolls' house, and gallery open daily 10am-5pm; Nov.-March daily 10am-4pm. Admission to the grounds Mon.-Sat. £8, Sun. £5; over 60 Mon.-Sat. £5.50, Sun. £3.50; under 17 Mon.-Sat. £4, Sun. £2.50; family of 4 Mon.-Sat. £18, Sun. £11.50. Last admission 1 hr. before closing.)

Follow the road that bears left around royal grounds to come to the entrance to **Windsor Great Park,** a huge expanse of parkland where deer graze and the royals ride. The Long Walk leads through the park towards the Copper Horse statue. At the other end of the park lie the Savill Gardens and the Smith's Lawn polo fields, where accident-prone Prince Charles used to play. Windsor's old town is directly across the road from the castle gate.

About 15 minutes down Thames St. and across the river is **Eton College,** the preeminent public (that is, private) school founded by Henry VI in 1440. Eton boys still wear tailcoats to every class, and solemnly raise one finger in greeting to any teacher on the street. Wellington claimed that the Battle of Waterloo was "won on the playing fields of Eton": catch a glimpse of the uniquely brutal "Wall Game" and see why. Eton has molded some notable dissidents and revolutionaries—Percy Bysshe Shelley, Aldous Huxley, George Orwell, and even former Liberal Party leader Jeremy

Thorpe. John Le Carré taught here, and Denys Finch-Hatton, portrayed in *Out of Africa* by Robert Redford, is memorialized in the bridge by the cricket pitches. The Queen is the sole (honorary) female Old Etonian—although each of Eton's houses has a resident "dame," an elderly matron who possesses domestic skills that Eton boys aren't expected to cultivate.

Wander around the schoolyard, a central quadrangle where teenaged boys have frolicked for centuries. A statue of Henry VI, and the school's chapel, an unfinished cathedral, occupy this space. The central area is surrounded by the 25 houses which shelter approximately 1250 students; those who get the best exam results get the best rooms.

Beyond the courtyard lie the picturesque **cloisters** and a comical museum explaining some of the antiquated traditions that obscure the school's modern educational mission. Don't let the 15-minute propaganda film convince you that all Eton students speak seven languages and play three instruments, however. (Yard, cloisters, and museum open July-Aug. daily 10:30am-4:30pm; May-June and Oct.-March daily 2-4:30pm; admission £2.20, children £1.50.)

It costs one or two more pounds on a tour to see more of the school. **Lower school,** one of the oldest classrooms currently in use in the world, dates from 1443. Students still hold Latin prayers here every Sunday night. Above, naughty students still face the Head Master in a room whose walls are carved with the names of former scholars.

In 1996, the venerable edifices of Windsor castle and Eton will be joined by a decidedly more whimsical construction, **Lego World at Windsor.** This magical wonderland, "a different sort of pleasure park for children and their families," promises to include Lego playscapes, Lego cities, and a lake (made of water, not Lego) for boating. The Lego World Information Center (tel. (0753) 621 621) anxiously awaits your queries.

For those interested in a longer stay in the Windsor/Eton vicinity, there is an **HI hostel** at Edgeworth House on Mill La. (tel. (0753) 861 710; fax (0753) 832 100). The hostel is a 20-minute walk from the Windsor/Eton central station; walk along the river heading west from the station. Meals, kitchen facilities, and laundry are available. £8.70, under 18 £5.80.

British Rail (tel. 262 6767) serves Windsor and Eton Central station and Windsor and Eton Riverside station, both of which are near Windsor Castle (street signs point the way unmistakably). Trains leave from Victoria or Paddington via Slough or directly from Waterloo to Riverside (every 30min., 45min., cheap day return £5). Green Line **coaches** (tel. (0181) 668 7261) #700, 701, and 702 also make the trip from their station on Eccleston Bridge, behind Victoria Station (70-90min., day return £4.35-5.50). The **tourist office** (tel. (01753) 852 010) is in the Central station (open Easter-Sept. daily 10am-4pm).

■■■ SOUTHALL

London's largest South Asian community congregates in Southall, about 10 mi. west of central London (BR: Southall). Don't expect a garish Little India theme-park; the streets here are lined with the same charmingly gabled and gardened Victorian homes found in many other suburbs. But South Road and Broadway are also filled with Asian restaurants, grocers, and sweet shops. Video stores burst with the latest classics from the prolific Indian film industry, and every other window displays mannequins modeling dazzling saris. Get your *nan* bread mix, fresh cumin, and mango chutney at the morning **market** on Fridays and Saturdays.

While the East End is home to many Muslims, Sikhs concentrate in Southall. Many worship at the **Guru Granth Gurdwara** temple on Villiers Rd., in a former church (non-Sikhs may not enter). Colored light bulbs festoon the façade of the Hindu **Vishwa Temple,** 2 Lady Margaret Rd.

Museums

Rainy days, although quite numerous here, will not suffice for London's museums—you may find yourself drawn indoors even in the best of weather.

Museums tend to be the most peaceful weekday mornings. Admission to major collections is usually free, but many museums, no longer heavily subsidized by the government, now charge or request a £1-2 donation. Most charge for special exhibits and offer student and senior citizen discounts ("concessions"). The last few years have witnessed the birth of a number of expensive theme museums, with elaborate sound systems and computers supplementing more traditional exhibits.

The **London White Card** is a discount card which allows you unlimited access to participating museums for a period of three or seven days. The card can be purchased at any of the participating museums, including the V&A, the Science Museum, the Natural History Museum, and the Courtauld Institute. The card will only afford you substantial discounts if you plan to visit *many* museums, or if you plan to visit a particularly expensive museum more than once (3-day card £10, £25 for families. 7-day card £20, £50 for families.)

■ BRITISH MUSEUM

The sheer volume of the British Museum's collections stands as a comprehensive document of the political, military, and economic power of the British Empire. Founded in 1753, the museum began with the personal collection of the physician Sir Hans Sloane. In the following decades, the museum became so swollen with gifts, purchases, and Imperialist spoils that a new building had to be commissioned. Robert Smirke drew up the design in 1824. Constructed over the next 30 years, the neo-classical building is still home to the museum today.

The British Museum's national archaeological collections recapitulate the glory days of Egypt, Asia, Greece, Rome, and prehistoric and medieval Europe. The museum also houses superb temporary exhibitions of its coin and medal, and print and drawing collections. The **British Library's** galleries share the building now, but its most famous manuscripts (the *Magna Carta*, the Gutenberg Bible, etc.) and most current stacks are due to move with the rest of the library to a new building in St. Pancras in 1996-7.

Wandering through 2½ mi. of galleries may frustrate even the most die-hard museum-goer. To catch the main attractions, buy the £2.50 short guide; for a more in-depth look, introductory books on specific parts of the collection are available for about £5. **Guided tours** (£6; 1½hrs.) cover the highlights, and can be booked for groups no larger than 10 at the information desk or by phone at 323 8599.

From the main entrance on Great Russell St., the British Library galleries are to the right. In the **Manuscript Room,** the **English Literature** displays include manuscripts from *Beowulf* (c. 1000) and the *Canterbury Tales* (1410), as well as the scrawlings of Jonson, Jane Austen, Elizabeth Barrett Browning, James Joyce, Virginia Woolf, and Philip Larkin, to name just a few. **Biblical displays** include ravishing illuminated texts and some of the oldest surviving fragments (the *Codex Sinaiticus* and the *Codex Alexandrinus)*, 3rd-century Greek gospels, and the Celtic *Lindesfarne Gospels*. The **Historical Documents** section proffers epistles by, among others, Henry VIII, Elizabeth I, Churchill, Napoleon, and Jeremy Bentham. Two copies of the *Magna Carta* get their very own cases. Lenin's application for a reader's ticket is signed under the pseudonym "Jacob Richter." **Music displays** show off works by Handel, Beethoven, and Stravinsky. Other cases offer curious **maps** from ancient times to the 18th century. The "Manuscript of the Month" case offers a rare chance to view a manuscript of current interest or pertinence not normally on display.

The **King's Library,** built between 1823 and 1826 to house George III's library, now contains (in addition to George III's books) an exhibit on early printing history and displays of printed books, most notably the Gutenberg Bible and Shakespeare's First Folio. Manuscripts from around the world fill the display cases in the south end of the gallery. Samples of Chinese calligraphy, early Japanese printed books, manuscripts in Hebrew and Arabic, and Sanskrit scriptures provide glimpses into the role of books in various cultures. Although you'll need a reader's pass in order to study in the circular **Reading Room** where Marx wrote *Das Kapital*, visitors are allowed to see the room briefly Mon.-Fri. at 2:15pm and 4:15pm.

The outstanding **ancient Egypt** collection occupies rooms on the ground and upper floors. Entering the ground floor gallery, one is greeted by two of the many imposing statues of Amenophis III. To the left rests the **Rosetta Stone,** discovered in 1799 by French soldiers. Its Greek text enabled Champollion to finally crack the hieroglyphic code. The head of Ramses II, famed for his arrogance towards Joseph and higher beings in Exodus, dominates the northern section of Room 25. Among the sculptures, the sublime royal head in green schist (1490 BC) stands out. The asexual representation of the latter has left scholars to debate whether it represents dominatrix Queen Hatshepsut or her successor, King Tuthmosis. In the side gallery 25a, don't miss three of the finest and best known Theban tomb paintings. While famed as one of the most "human" of the daunting sculptures in the collection, the black granite Sesostris III remains more noteworthy for its ears than its warmth. To the right of the virile Ramses (reputed father of 150), in a side gallery, glistens the gold of the inner coffin of priestess Henutmehit. The central gallery is filled with tributes to the animal world, including the tiny blue hippo. The upstairs Egyptian gallery contains brilliant sarcophagi and grisly mummies, and an ancient body "desiccated by the dry, hot sand." Delicate papyri include the *Book of the Dead of Ani.*

The **Assyrian galleries,** wedged between Egypt and Greece, are renowned for the reliefs from Nineveh (704-668 BC), illustrating a campaign in southern Iraq. Room 16's entrance is guarded by the five-legged, human-headed bulls, made to look stationary from the front, mobile from the side.

The **Greek antiquities** exhibits are dominated by the **Elgin Marbles,** 5th-century BC reliefs from the Parthenon, now residing in the spacious Duveen Gallery. In 1810, Lord Elgin procured the statues and pieces of the Parthenon frieze while serving as ambassador to Constantinople. The museum claims that Elgin's "agents removed many sculptures from the Parthenon with the approval" of unnamed "authorities" for the price of £75,000. Later, for reasons of financial necessity, he sold them to Britain for £35,000. Every so often, the Greeks renew their efforts to convince the British government to return the marbles. Carved under the direction of ancient Greece's greatest sculptor, Phidias, the marbles comprise three main groups: the frieze, which portrays the most important Athenian civic festivals; the metopes, which depict incidents from the battle of the Lapiths and Centaurs (symbolizing the triumph of "civilization" over "barbarism"); and the remains of large statues that stood in the east and west pediments of the building.

Other Greek highlights include the complete Ionic façade of the Nereid Monument, one of the female caryatid columns from the Acropolis, and two of the Seven Wonders of the Ancient World. Once crowded by a four-horse chariot, the **Mausoleum at Halicarnassus** gained such fame in antiquity that it coined the word "mausoleum" in many European languages. The second wonder is the **Temple of Artemis,** built to replace the one buried by Herostratus in 356 BC to perpetuate his name in history.

Among the many sculptures of the **Roman antiquities,** the dark blue glass of the **Portland Vase** stands out. The inspiration for ceramic designer Josiah Wedgwood, the vase has tenaciously survived a series of mishaps and reconstructive operations which took place even before the vase was dug up in 1582. When it was discovered, the base had already been broken and replaced. In 1845, it was shattered by a drunken museum-goer; when it was put back together, 37 small chips were left over. Since then, the vase has been beautifully reconstructed twice, with more left-over chips being reincorporated each time. The scene depicted is an enigma; controversy still rages among experts over a Ph.D. student's recent interpretation of it as the depiction of an ancient poem.

The **Roman-Britain** section includes the **Mindenhall Treasure,** a magnificent collection of 4th-century silver tableware. With a diameter of almost two feet and weighing over 18 pounds, the aptly named Great Dish impresses with its size and elaborate decorations. Nearby crouches **Lindow Man,** an Iron Age Celt supposedly sacrificed in a gruesome ritual and preserved by peat-bog. The **Sutton Hoo Ship Burial,** an Anglo-Saxon ship buried (and subsequently dug up) in Suffolk complete with an unknown king, is the centerpiece of the **Middle Ages** galleries.

The majority of the museum's **Oriental Collections** reside in the recently refurbished Gallery 33. The gallery's eastern half is dedicated to the Chinese collection, renowned for its ancient Shang bronzes and fine porcelains, and the western half is filled by Indian and Southeast Asian exhibits, which include the largest collection of Indian religious sculpture outside of India. Upstairs, the collection continues with a series of three galleries displaying Japanese artifacts, paintings, and calligraphy.

In addition to their prodigious permanent collections, the British Museum and British Library both also put on a number of temporary exhibits (1994's exhibits included *Beauty and Banknotes: Images of Women on Paper Money* and *Russian Avant-Garde Books 1912-1934*), special gallery talks, and slide lectures, many of which are free. 1994 also witnessed the opening of two new museum galleries: **Renaissance to the 20th Century** and the **Mexican Gallery.**

The museum is located at Great Russell St., WC1 (tel. 636 1555 or 580 1788 for recorded information; tube: Tottenham Ct. Rd., Goodge St., Russell Sq., or Holborn). The rear entrance, with access to certain galleries, is on Montague St. For recorded information on wheelchair accessibility, call 637 7384. Persons who are blind or visually-impaired should enquire about the tactile exhibits; a **touch tour** of Roman sculptures is given in room 84 in the basement—ask about it at the main information desk. (Open Mon.-Sat. 10am-5pm, Sun. 2:30-6pm. Admission is free, but the larger, special exhibits cost £3, concessions £2. See Food and Drink for information on the tasty British Museum Café.)

■ NATIONAL GALLERY

The National Gallery maintains one of the world's finest collections of Western painting, especially strong in works by Rembrandt, Rubens, and Renaissance Italian painters. The Berggruen Collection of works from the turn of this century, including many Impressionist works and a large selection of Picassos, has been temporarily loaned to the National. The Tate Gallery has joint custody of the British Collection.

You can spend days in this maze of galleries, renovated and rehung in 1992. A helpful guide is the **Micro Gallery,** a computerized, illustrated catalogue which cross-references works any way you want, can print out a free personal tour mapping out the locations of the paintings you want to see (open Mon.-Sat. 10am-5:30pm, Sun. 2-5:30pm).

The National's collection is divided into four color-coded sections; paintings within these sections are arranged by school. The collection starts in the new Sainsbury Wing, to the west of the main building, designed by postmodern Philadelphian Robert Venturi. Amid fake ceiling supports and false perspectives hang works painted from 1260 to 1510. Early Italian paintings such as Botticelli's *Venus and Mars,* Raphael's *Crucifixion,* and Leonardo da Vinci's famous *Virgin of the Rocks* are framed by the arches and columns of the new building. In Van Eyck's *Arnolfini Marriage,* Van Eyck himself is in the mirror; is the bride pregnant?

Paintings from 1510 to 1600 are found in the **West Wing,** to the left of the Trafalgar Sq. entrance. Titian's *Bacchus and Ariadne* displays his mastery of contrast. Stormy El Grecos are featured here as well. *The Ambassadors* contains a cunning blob that resolves itself into a skull when viewed at the proper back-breaking angle. Strong collections of Rembrandt and Rubens adorn the **North Wing**—Rembrandt's young and old self-portraits make a fascinating contrast. Placid Claude and Poussin landscapes are routed by the unabashed romanticism of Caravaggio and Velázquez. Van Dyck's *Equestrian Portrait of Charles I* headlines the State Portrait room.

The **East Wing,** to the right of the main entrance, is devoted to painting from 1700 to 1920, including a strong English collection. The natural light provides the perfect setting for viewing the paintings; many, such as Turner's *Rain, Steam, and Speed* (note the tiny jackrabbit running alongside the train), seem to acquire a special luminosity. Gainsborough's tight *Mr. and Mrs. Andrews* and Constable's rustic *The Hay Wain* whet the appetite before the Impressionists clamor for attention. Impressionist works include a number of Monet's near-abstract waterlilies, Cézanne's *Old Woman with Roses,* and Rousseau's rainswept *Tropical Storm with a Tiger.* Picasso's *Fruit Dish, Bottle, and Violin* (1914), the National Gallery's initial foray into the abstract, has since been joined by another room of Picasso's work.

The National Gallery holds frequent special exhibitions in the basement galleries of the Sainsbury Wing, which usually cost £2-4. Free hour-long guided tours which introduce visitors to the collection's major works depart from the Sainsbury wing at 11:30am and 2:30pm Monday through Friday, and 2pm and 3:30pm on Saturday. The National shows free films about art every Monday at 1pm in the lower-floor theatre, and lectures take place in the afternoons (Tues.-Fri. at 1pm, Sat. at noon). On Wednesdays in the summer the Gallery stays open until 8pm; musical performances in the Sainsbury foyer begin at 6pm. For more information on lectures and films contact the Education department at 389 1744.

The gallery is located in Trafalgar Sq., WC2 (tel. 389 1785 or 839 3526 for recorded information; tube: Charing Cross or Leicester Sq.). Disabled access is on the north side at the Orange St. entrance. (Open Mon.-Sat. 10am-6pm, Sun. 2-6pm. Free.)

■ NATIONAL PORTRAIT GALLERY

This unofficial *Who's Who in Britain* began in 1856 as "the fulfillment of a patriotic and moral ideal"—namely to showcase Britain's most officially noteworthy citizens. The museum's declared principle of looking "to the celebrity of the person represented, rather than to the merit of the artist" does not seem to have affected the quality of the works displayed—many are by such top portraitists as Reynolds, Lawrence, Holbein, Sargent, and Gainsborough.

The 9000 paintings have been arranged more or less chronologically. The earliest portraits hang in the top story—solemn Thomas More, maligned Richard III, venerated Elizabeth I, and canny Henry VII. Charles II is here, surrounded by his wife and mistresses. Follow the flow of British history through the galleries: from the War of the Roses (Yorks and Lancasters), to the Civil War (Cromwell and his buddies), to the American Revolution (George Washington), to imperial days (Florence Nightingale), and on to modern times (Margaret Thatcher).

Level four, dedicated to Henry VIII and predecessors, cherishes the Holbein cartoon of the king. Famous geologists, politicians, reformers, and fops populate the Victorian section, along with literary figures, among them Tennyson, Thackeray, and Dickens. Charming "informal" portraits of the royal family are displayed on the mezzanine; check out the incredibly unflattering portrait of Prince Charles.

The first floor is jammed with displays of the 20th century, from Churchill to Peter Gabriel; the modern works take more amusing liberties with their likenesses. The museum sucessfully melds together different media of portraiture, like sculpture, sketches, caricatures, and photographs. Some of the early black and white photographs are especially arresting; the deceptiveness of scale in Robert Howlett's 1857 portrait of Isambard Brunel taunts viewers.

The gallery often mounts temporary displays. The annual British Petroleum Portrait Award brings out a selection of works from England's most promising artists (on display June-Sept.).

Informative lectures begin at 1:10pm Tuesday through Friday, 3pm on Saturday. Check the monthly schedule for locations.

These people are only a third of the 150 students who bring you the *Let's Go* guides. With pen and notebook in hand, a few changes of underwear stuffed in our backpacks, and a budget as tight as yours, we visited every *penstone*, *palapa*, pizzeria, café, club, campground, or castle we could find to make sure you'll get the most out of *your* trip.

We've put the best of our discoveries into the book you're now holding. A brand-new edition of each guide hits the shelves every year, only months after it is researched, so you know you're getting the most reliable, up-to-date, and comprehensive information available.

But, as any seasoned traveler will tell you, the best discoveries are often those you make yourself. If you find something worth sharing, drop us a line. We're at Let's Go, Inc., 1 Story Street, Cambridge, MA 02138, USA (e-mail: letsgo@delphi.com).

H A P P Y   T R A V E L S !

The gallery portrays at St. Martin's Pl., WC2, just opposite St. Martin's in the Fields (tel. 306 0055; tube: Charing Cross or Leicester Sq.; open Mon.-Fri. 10am-5pm, Sat. 10am-6pm, Sun. 12-6pm; free, except for some temporary exhibits £1-3.) The new Orange St. entrance has a wheelchair ramp, and there is a lift to all floors. Sign-interpreted talks are now a regular feature: for more information, call extension #216.

■ TATE GALLERY

The Tate Gallery opened in 1897 expressly to display contemporary British art. Since then, the gallery has widened its scope, obtaining a superb collection of British works from the 16th century to the present and a distinguished ensemble of international modern art. Novices need not fret: the new captions and introductory notes in each gallery are extremely thorough.

The Tate's **British collection** starts with a room at the far end of the gallery devoted to 16th- and 17th-century painting. The parade of Constables includes the famous views of Salisbury Cathedral, and a number of Hampstead scenes dotted with the requisite red saddle splashes. George Stubbs's enlivening landscapes and sporting scenes lead to Gainsborough's landscapes and Sir Joshua Reynolds's portraits. Don't miss the visionary works of poet, philosopher, and painter William Blake, or the haunting images of Sir John Everett Millais, one of the three founding members of the Pre-Raphaelite Brotherhood.

The paintings in each of the 30 rooms of the main gallery are organized chronologically and grouped by theme, offering a clear perspective on the development of British art, from early landscapes and portraits through Victorian, pre-Raphaelite, and Impressionist paintings. At this point, the rooms begin to emphasize the relationship between British and foreign art movements, thus providing the perfect segue into the Tate's outstanding **modern collection** of international 20th-century art. Sculptures by Henry Moore, Epstein, Eric Gill, and Barbara Hepworth, in addition to Rodin's **The Kiss,** are found in the Cuveen Sculpture Galleries, the central hall of which leads to the start of the British collection. Modern paintings and sculptures are displayed in subsequent rooms: the works of Monet, Degas, Van Gogh, Beardsley, Matisse, and the Camden Town Group (Sickert, Bevan) hang to the left of the entrance. Paintings by members of the Bloomsbury Group, Picasso, Dalí, and Francis Bacon, sculptures by Modigliani and Giacometti, and samples of the styles that have dominated since the 1950s—Constructivism, Minimalism, Pop, Super-realism, and Process Art—lie to the right of the central hall.

The Tate's 300-work J.M.W. Turner collection resides in the **Clore Gallery.** Architect James Stirling designed the annex to allow natural light to illuminate both the serenity of *Peace—Burial at Sea* and the raging brushstrokes of gale-swept ocean scenes. The collection covers all of Turner's career, from early, dreamy landscapes such as *Chevening Park* to the later visionary works, in which the subject is lost in a sublime array of light and color.

Although the layout of the galleries does not change, the displays are changed annually, so that different facets of the Tate's exhaustive collection can be emphasized. The Tate also hosts a series of temporary exhibits in the downstairs galleries.

Free tours run Mon.-Fri. at 11am for British Art before 1900, noon for Highlights of the Collection, 2pm for Early Modern Art, and 3pm for Later Modern Art; the Highlights of the Collection tour is also given Sat. at 3pm and Sun at 3:45pm. Free lectures are given Monday through Saturday at 1pm, Sunday at 2:30pm. The Tate puts on some of the most important special exhibitions in the world, both in the main building and in the Clore Gallery, for which an admission fee is charged. The Tate is located at Millbank, SW1 (tel. 821 1313; tube: Pimlico; open Mon.-Sat. 10am-5:50pm, Sun. 2-5:50pm; free).

■ VICTORIA AND ALBERT MUSEUM

Housing the best collection of Italian Renaissance sculpture outside Italy, the greatest collection of Indian art outside India, and the world center for John Constable studies, the mind-bogglingly inclusive V&A has practically perfected the display of fine and applied arts. Founded in 1899 by Queen Victoria, the museum took on its eclectic contours when the original curators were deluged with objects donated for exhibition from every epoch and region of the world. Easily the most enchanting museum in London, the V&A lets you saunter through the histories of art, design, and style in its 12 acres of galleries.

The vast scope of the museum's permanent collection is astonishing, but this fact does not stop the V&A from putting up consistently ground-breaking **temporary exhibitions;** watch for the enthusiastically hyped "Street Style: From Sidewalk to Catwalk, 1940 to Tommorow" (Nov. 94-Feb. 95).

While there are a million possible trajectories through the V&A's corridors, you might consider beginning your visit with the ground floor galleries. Reopening in late 1995 after extensive renovation, the stars of the **Renaissance collection** are the famed *Raphael Cartoons*—seven of the 10 large, full-color sketches (scenes from the Acts of the Apostles) done by Raphael and his apprentices as tapestry patterns for the Sistine Chapel. The endless galleries of Italian sculpture include Donatello's *Ascension* and *Madonna and Child*. The **Medieval Treasury,** in the center of the ground floor, features well-displayed vestments, plate, stained glass, and illuminations. The most spectacular treasure is the domed Eltenburg Reliquary.

Plaster cast reproductions of European sculpture and architecture (the 80-ft.-tall Column of Trajan from Rome; the façade of the Santiago Cathedral in Spain; Michelangelo's *Moses, Dying Slave, Rebellious Slave,* and *David*) occupy rooms 46A-B on the ground floor. Next door, test the knowledge you've gained here to distinguish impostors from the real things in the **Fakes and Forgeries gallery.**

The **dress collection,** also on the ground floor, traces popular and elite clothing fashions from 17th-century shoes to the latest John Galliano confection. Focused primarily on Western women's garb, this exhibit documents the vagaries of sartorial design and textile technology—and implicitly documents changing gender roles. Expansive and edifying, this collection displays both the mantua, a mid-18th century dress so restrictive that women who wore it had trouble walking through doorways, and the metallic nylon "longest minidress" that underfed Kate Moss wore to the British Design Awards. Women can count their fully intact ribs in thankful glee that they are no longer subject to the corsets and stays of 200 years ago; however, lest they think that fashion has become emancipatory, the precipitous purple mock-crocodile platform shoes that tripped Naomi Campbell up during a recent Westwood runway show are also displayed.

The V&A's formidable **Asian collections** have recently been supplemented by the Nehru Gallery of Indian Art and the T.T. Tsui Gallery of Chinese Art. The **Nehru gallery** contains splendid examples of textiles, painting, Mughal jewelry and decor, and revealing displays on European imperial conduct. You can see Tippoo's Tiger, a life-sized wooden musical automaton that simulates groans and roars while consuming a European gentleman, alluded to by John Keats in his poem *The Cap and Bells.* The simply elegant **Tsui gallery** divides its 5000-year span of Chinese art into six areas of life—Eating and Drinking, Living, Worship, Ruling, Collecting, and Burial. Objects are displayed in the context in which they were originally used. Treasures include the Sakyamuni Buddha and an Imperial Throne. The **Toshiba Gallery of Japanese Art** has a prime collection of lacquer art, as well as traditional armor and intriguing contemporary sculpture.

The V&A's displays of **Islamic Art** are punctuated by the intricacies of Persian carpets and Moroccan rugs. The collection's most breathtaking carpet, completed in Azerbaijan in 1540, is perhaps the largest carpet that you will ever see.

The first floor holds the sizeable collection of **British art and design.** Shakespeare immortalized the immense Great Bed of Ware (room 54) in *Twelfth Night.* Cool, dim room 74, "1900-1960," exhibits the best in modern British design, including works by Wyndham Lewis, Charles Rennie Mackintosh, and Eric Gill. International design classics—mostly chairs—grace "Twentieth Century Design."

The **jewelry collection** (rooms 91-93—actually a pilfer-proof vault!), so unwieldy that it has been annotated in bound catalogues instead of posted descriptions, includes pieces dating from 2000 BC. The **National Art Library,** located on the first floor, houses numerous Beatrix Potter originals as well as first editions of Winnie the Pooh adventures.

The new **Frank Lloyd Wright gallery** on the second floor of the Henry Cole Wing illustrates Wright's philosophy of Organic Architecture. The Wright-designed interior of the Kauffmann Office, originally commissioned for a Pittsburgh department store, is the V&A's first 20th-century period room.

The exquisitely redesigned **Glass Gallery** recently reopened in room C-131. Vases, bowls, pipes, and brandy bottles provide a colorful and effulgent assault on visitors' eyes. A sophisticated electronic labeling system allows visitors to retrieve extensive details about any piece in the gallery by entering a code into a computer.

Photography aficionados will want to visit the **Print Room** (#503 in the Henry Cole Wing), a provisional home for photography until the V&A opens a full-fledged photography gallery in 1998. The print collection encompasses both the incipient stages of the medium and the most contemporary products. Sander, Arbus, and Freidlander are all represented here.

John Constable's prodigious collection of weather studies resides on the sixth floor of the Henry Cole Wing. For those whose tastes run smaller, room 406 showcases English and Continental **portrait miniatures** (including Holbein's *Anne of Cleves* and *Elizabeth I*).

The V&A offers scores of special events. Introductory museum tours are offered Monday through Saturday at 11am, noon, 2pm, and 3pm; Sunday at 3pm. Theme tours are offered Monday through Saturday at 11:30am, 1:30pm, and 2:30pm. Both tours last approximately one hour. Individual lectures of V&A summer courses can be attended for partial tuition: contact the Education Services Department (tel. 938 8638). Numerous free lectures throughout the summer cover anything from Impressionism to Japanese quilt technique. Fantastic 45-minute tours for children ages 6-11 depart from the museum's main entrance; call for details. In keeping with Henry Cole's original vision of the museum as functional, the V&A often provides special "gallery trail" guides for children; inquire at the information desk.

The **New Restaurant,** on the ground floor of the Henry Cole Wing, serves a wide range of meals. On Sunday mornings the restaurant hosts a jazz brunch, which features live music and full English breakfast or lunch (11am-3pm; £7.50).

The V&A is located on Cromwell Rd., SW7 (tel. 938 8500, 938 8441 for 24-hr. recorded information, or 938 8349 for current exhibitions; tube: South Kensington or buses #C1, 14, and 74; open Mon. noon-5:50pm, Tues.-Sun. 10am-5:50pm; free; suggested donation £4.50, concessions £1). Most of the museum is wheelchair accessible; wheelchair users are advised to use the side entrance on Exhibition Rd. Gallery tours and taped tours are available for the visually impaired.

■ OTHER MAJOR COLLECTIONS

Accademia Italiana delle Arti, 24 Rutland Gate, SW7 (tel. 225 3474, fax 589 5187). Tube: Knightsbridge or South Kensington. From Knightsbridge, head west along Knightsbridge Rd. and take a left onto Rutland Gate. A small museum housing changing exhibits of art and artifacts. Everything from the memorable 1993 exhibit "Hurrah for the Bra" to an exploration of Michelangelo's Casa Buonarroti. Open Tues. and Thurs.-Sat. 10am-5:30pm, Wed. 10am-8pm, Sun. noon-5:30pm. £5, students and seniors £2.50, children 5-12 £1, under 5 free.

Bank of England Museum, Threadneedle St., EC2 (tel. 601 5792 or 601 5545). Tube: Bank. Entrance on Bartholomew Lane, left off of Threadneedle St. Housed in the Bank of England. Enter the museum through a grandly domed entrance foyer with a mosaic floor where an attendant in red tails waits to receive you. A cultural history of banknotes and check-writing. Absorbing forgery exhibits, in addition to a display of arms once used to defend the bank and a collection of ancient Roman pottery. Open Mon.-Fri. 10am-5pm, Sun. 11am-5pm; Oct.-Easter Mon.-Fri. 10am-5pm. Free.

Barbican, Barbican Centre, EC2 (tel. 638 8891). Tube: Barbican. A community arts center, the Barbican hosts free concerts, art exhibitions, and library displays in its labyrinthine network of foyers. Summer 1994 exhibits included "Strictly Textiles," a group show of works in fabric. The Centre also houses the Barbican Art Gallery, which charges an admission fee. "Who's Looking at the Family," a display of pictures by over 30 European and American photographers, was shown in 1994. Open Mon. and Wed.-Fri. 10am-6:45pm, Tues. 10am-5:45pm, Sun. and holidays noon-6:45pm. £4.50, students and senior citizens £2.50, Mon.-Fri. after 5pm, £2.50.

Bethnal Green Museum of Childhood, Cambridge Heath Rd., E2 (tel. (0181) 980 2415). Tube: Bethnal Green. The V&A's annex for its collection (weighted towards the Victorian era) of toys, dolls, board games, and puppets. Displays also include children's books, costumes, and nursery furniture. The doll houses provide an interesting architectural and social history. Open Mon.-Thurs. and Sat. 10am-5:50pm, Sun. 2:30-5:50pm. Free.

Bramah Tea and Coffee Museum, The Clove Building, Maguire St., Butlers Wharf, SE1 (tel. 378 0222, fax 378 0219). Tube: Tower Hill or London Bridge, or DLR: Tower Gateway. Follow directions to the Design Museum and turn right onto Maguire St. Appropriately located in the spot on Butlers Wharf that used to see 6000 chests of tea unloaded each day. Find out why Britain became a nation practically defined by its tea-drinking habits and how Nestlé and General Foods tried to seduce Brits with the lure of an instant caffeinated beverage. Great assortment of teapots. Cafeteria serves up eye-opening cups of coffee and tea (60p), a pot of tea (£1), or tea w/scones (£3). £3, concessions and under 14 £1.50, family £6. Group discounts. Shop vends anything related to the hot brown beverage.

Cabinet War Rooms, Clive Steps, King Charles St., SW1 (tel. 930 6961 or 735 8922). Tube: Westminster. Follow the signs from Whitehall. Churchill and his cabinet ran a nation at war from this secret warren of underground rooms. See the room where Churchill made his famous wartime broadcasts and listen to cuts of some of his speeches. Spot the transatlantic hotline disguised as a loo. Free but rather slow cassette guides available. Open daily 10am-6pm. Last entrance 5:15pm. £3.90, seniors £3, students £2.80, under 16 £1.90, families £10.

Commonwealth Institute, Kensington High St., W8 (tel. 603 4535). Tube: High St. Kensington. Celebrates the far-flung outposts of the British Commonwealth under a roof of suitably Zambian copper. Malaysian paper crafts, Indian musical instruments, and Asian film are all featured. Excellent frequent art exhibits in the main hall, and dance and music performances in the evenings (often free). Crawls with schoolchildren. Exhibits open Mon.-Sat. 10am-5pm, Sun. 2-5pm. £1, concessions 50p, children under 5 free.

The Courtauld Institute, Somerset House, the Strand, WC2 (tel. 873 2549), across from the corner of Aldwych and the Strand. Tube: Temple or Aldwych (rush hour only). An intimate 11-room gallery displays mostly Impressionist and post-Impressionist masterpieces. The collection features some of the most famous works by Cézanne, Degas, Gauguin, Seurat, and Renoir, plus Van Gogh's *Portrait of the Artist with a Bandaged Ear,* and Manet's *Bar aux Folies Bergère.* The Institute's other collections include early Italian religious works—key works by Botticelli, Rubens (*Descent from the Cross*), Bruegel, Cranach (*Adam and Eve*), and Modigliani; as well as Oskar Kokoschka's stunning *Prometheus Triptych.* Open Mon.-Sat. 10am-6pm, Sun. 2-6pm. £3, concessions £1.50.

The Design Museum, Butlers Wharf, Shad Thames, SE1 (tel. 403 6933 or 407 6261). Tube: London Bridge, then follow signs on Tooley St, or Tower Hill and cross the Tower Bridge. Housed in an appropriately Bauhausy box on the river, this museum is dedicated to mass-produced classics of culture and industry, such as the automotive bombshell dropped by the Citroën DS in the 1950s. Happily, you *can* sit in some of the century's most influential chairs. Sub-aquatic cameras and minimalist cutlery are also displayed. Library open by appointment. Open Mon.-Fri. 11:30am-6pm, Sat.-Sun. noon-6pm. £4.50, concessions £3.50.

Dulwich Picture Gallery, College Rd., SE21 (tel. (0181) 693 5254). From Victoria, take the BR to West Dulwich (10min., day return £1.60). Head right on Park Row/ Dulwich Common, then left (after passing Dulwich College) on College Rd. England's first public art gallery with a decent, rather unfocused collection. Sir John Soane, who designed the museum's quarters in 1811, included a mausoleum for the gallery's founders, whom you can visit in the center of room 6. The collection is strongest on portraits (Lely, Gainsborough, Reynolds), Dutch landscapes (Cuyp), and religious Italian works (Tiepolo), although it also houses three Rembrandts, a couple of minor Rubens, a few Poussins, and a very fine studio-of-Velázquez *Philip IV.* Thieves fancied Rembrandt's *Jacob III de Gheyn* so much that it was stolen on four separate occasions (it has since been recovered). Open Tues.-Fri. 10am-5pm, Sat. 11am-5pm, Sun. 2-5pm. £2, students £1, children free.

Freud Museum, 20 Maresfield Gdns., NW3 (tel. 435 2002). Tube: Finchley Rd. Head right from the tube station down Finchley Rd. and take the fifth left onto Trinity Walk; Maresfield Gdns. is at the end of the street. A re-creation of the home where Freud spent a year after escaping Nazi Vienna. The museum includes the library and study where he completed some of his most influential works. Open Wed.-Sun. noon-5pm. £2.50, students £1.50.

Geffrye Museum, Kingsland Road, E2 (tel 739 9893). Tube: Liverpool St., then bus #22A or 22B north. This humble but absorbing little museum meticulously chronicles the English home interior, from Elizabethan times to the height of the Linoleum Age in the fifties. Excellent temporary exhibits. Open Tues.-Sat. 10am-5pm, Sun. 2-5pm. Free.

Guildhall Clock Museum, in the Guildhall Library, Aldermanbury, EC2 (tel. 260 1868). Tube: Bank, St. Paul's, or Moorgate. "The Worshipful Company of Clockmakers" presents a well-labeled collection of pocket watches, jeweled watch keys, and a few curiosities. Mary Queen of Scots' macabre silver skull-shaped watch is notable—she checked the time by opening the jaw and looking inside its mouth. The one-room museum also includes an exhibit from "The Worshipful Company of Makers of Playing Cards," featuring a deck designed by Erté. Open Mon.-Fri. 9:30am-4:45pm. Free.

House of Detention, Clerkenwell Close, EC1 (tel. 253 9494). Tube: Farringdon. Located in the basement of what was once the busiest prison in London. Visitors travel down dark ventilation tunnels to view the prison wash-house, kitchen, and cells. Life-sized mannequins and educational displays illustrate 300 years of criminal history in London. The haunting music and the low-ceilinged darkness can leave you feeling edgy. 15min. taped tours available. Open daily 10am-6pm. £3, students £2, families (2 adults, 2 children) £8.

Imperial War Museum, Lambeth Rd., SE1 (tel. 416 5000). Tube: Lambeth North or Elephant & Castle. Do not be misled by the jingoistic resonance of the name; this museum is a moving reminder of the brutal human cost of war. The atrium is filled with tanks and planes; the eloquent testimony to war's horror is downstairs. Gripping exhibits illuminate every aspect of two world wars, in every medium possible. The Blitz and Trench Experiences recreate every sad detail (even smells); veterans and victims speak through telephone handsets. The powerful Belsen exhibit documents the genocide of the concentration camps and the story of the rescue and rehabilitation of survivors. Documents worth seeing include the "peace in our time" agreement that Neville Chamberlain triumphantly brought back from Munich in 1938, and Adolf Hitler's "political testament," dictated in the chancellery bunker. Upstairs, the art galleries keep fine examples of war painting, such as Sargent's *Gassed, 1918.* Open daily 10am-6pm. £3.90, students £2.90, children £1.95, families £10.50. Free daily 4:30-6pm.

Institute of Contemporary Arts, the Mall, SW1 (tel. 930 3647 or 930 3647 for recorded information). Tube: Piccadilly Circus or Charing Cross. Entrance is located on the Mall at the foot of the Duke of York steps. Vigorous outpost of the avant garde in visual and performance art. 3 galleries, a cinema featuring first-run independent films, experimental space for film and video, theatre, seminars and lectures (£2-5.50), video library, and readings (call for schedule). Recent "ICA Talks" have featured Mario Vargas Llosa and Eve Kosofsky Sedgewick. Galleries open Sat.-Thurs. noon-7:30pm, Fri. noon-9pm. £1.50.

The Iveagh Bequest, Kenwood House, Hampstead Heath, Hampstead La., NW3 (tel. (0181) 348 1286). Tube: Archway or Golders Green, then bus #210 to Kenwood. An outstanding collection of 18th-century British portraiture and furniture, with a few fine works by Dutch masters, including Vermeer's *Guitar Player* and the last of Sir Joshua Reynolds for his fans. Open daily 10am-6pm; Oct. to mid-April 10am-4pm. Free. Admission charged for special visiting exhibitions.

Jewish Museum, 129 Albert St., NW1 (tel. 388 4525). Tube: Camden Town. Exit the station to the right and head left. Take the first right onto Parkway; Albert St. will be on the left. A collection of antiques, manuscripts, and paintings documenting Jewish history, with a special focus on the history of Jews in London from 1066 to the present. As the museum recently relocated, it is advisable to call ahead to confirm opening times and admission costs. Open Sun.-Thurs. 10am-4pm. £2.50.

London Dungeon, 28-34 Tooley St., SE1 (tel. 403 0606). Tube: London Bridge. An inexplicably popular spectacle. Gory waxwork displays of medieval disease and decomposition; bogus historical commentary attempts to justify the stomach-churning reconstructions. Take a walk through the "Jack the Ripper Experience" to see the ghastly trail of blood this killer left on the streets of Victorian East London. The management declines responsibility for ensuing nightmares. Open daily 10am-6:30pm, Oct.-March 10am-5:30pm. £6.50, under 14 £6.50, students £5.50.

London Transport Museum, Covent Garden, WC2 (tel. 379 6344). Tube: Covent Garden. On the east side of the Covent Garden piazza. Reopened in Dec. 1993 after 9 months and £4 million worth of renovations, the museum now boasts two new mezzanine floors, two new air-conditioned galleries, and a variety of interactive video displays. Although much of the ground floor traffic flows through a maze of historic trains, trams, and buses, the museum offers much more than a history of London's public transport vehicles. In addition to high-tech displays like the subway simulator, low-tech exhibits provide a thought-provoking cultural history: see how the expansion of the transportation system fed the growth of suburbs (one of the keys to why Hampstead is wealthier than Islington). London Transport design also features prominently throughout: learn about the history of the Johnston typeface you see everywhere on the tube. Don't miss the excellent temporary exhibits, drawn largely from the museum's photo, map, and poster archives. First-class museum shop sells London Transport posters and postcards. Opens daily 10am-6pm, last admission 5:15pm. £3.95, concessions £2.50, families £10, special group rates available. Wheelchair accessible. MC, Visa.

Madame Tussaud's, Marylebone Rd., NW1 (tel. 935 6861). Tube: Baker St. The classic waxwork museum, founded by an *emigré* aristocrat who manufactured life-size models of French nobility who met their demise at the guillotine. Models are disconcertingly lifelike; best-looking awards go to Nelson Mandela and Harrison Ford, with an honorable mention to Cher in all of her synthetic glory. Visitors may also be disconcerted by the museum's layout, which is occasionally illogical. The more macabre exhibits, like the display of famous psycopaths and wife-murderers from English history, are essentially gratuitous titillation designed to keep the crowds rolling in. And roll in they do; one of the U.K.'s top tourist attractions, Madame Tussaud's is best visited in the morning to get a good view of the most popular collections. To avoid the horrific queues, form a group with at least nine fellow sufferers and use the group entrance. Open Mon.-Fri. 10am-5:30pm, Sat.-Sun. 9:30am-5:30pm. £7.40, children £4.75, seniors £5.50, families (2 adults, 2 children) £19.95. A distinctive green dome shelters the adjacent **Planetarium.** Ride the Space Trail through a model universe and watch a Star Show. £4.20, children £2.60, seniors £3.25, families £11. Combined admission £9.95, children £6.25, seniors £7.55, families £25.95.

Museum of London, 150 London Wall, EC2 (tel. 600 3699 or 600 0807 for 24-hr. info.). Tube: St. Paul's or Barbican. Located amongst old Roman walls and chaotic building sites, exhibits in themselves. This fabulously engrossing museum tells the story of the metropolis from its origins as Londinium to the present. Comprehensive exhibits outline London's domestic, political, religious, cultural, industrial, sartorial, and medical histories. An oasis flourishes at the museum's center:

the Nursery Garden, a living history of the nursery trade in London (the garden closes at 5:20 pm). Free historical lectures given Wed.-Fri. 1:10pm. Open Tues.-Sat. 10am-6pm, Sun. noon-6pm, last entry 5:30pm. Open Bank Holidays Mon. 10am-6pm. £3, students £1.50, families £7.50, free after 4:30pm. Wheelchair accessible.

Museum of Mankind, 6 Burlington Gdns., W1 (tel. 328 8043). Tube: Green Park or Piccadilly Circus. The Burlington Arcade next to the Royal Academy leads right to the museum. The ethnographic collection of the British Museum, it includes a mass of engrossing artifacts, primarily from non-Western cultures. Annual exhibits re-create the lifestyles of ancients and moderns, featuring everything from everyday tools to ritual objects. Useful introductory gallery gives a cross-section of the permanent collection, which includes Mexican turquoise mosaics, African pipes, British Columbian stone carvings, and Sioux war bonnets. Check out the amazing feathered image, found by Captain Cook, representing a Hawaiian god with a mohawk. Films Tues.-Fri. at 1:30 and 3pm. Open Mon.-Sat. 10am-5pm, Sun. 2:30-6pm. Free.

Museum of the Moving Image (MOMI), South Bank Centre, SE1 (tel. 928 3232 or 401 2636 for 24-hr. information). Tube: Waterloo, or Embankment and cross the Hungerford footbridge. MOMI and the National Film Theatre, both appendages of the British Film Institute, are housed in a phenomenal building on the South Bank. The entertaining museum charts the development of image-making with light, from Chinese shadow puppets to film and telly. Costumed actor-guides lead you through interactive exhibits—act out your favorite western, read the TV news, or watch your own superimposed image fly over the River Thames. The camera-shy will enjoy countless clips and famous props, from the slapstick of the silents to the gaudy days of "Dr. Who." Open daily 10am-6pm; last entry 5pm. £5.50, children 5-16 £4, disabled £4, students with ID £4.70, family £16. Prices are subject to review in Jan. 1995.

National Maritime Museum, Romney Rd., Greenwich, SE10 (tel. (0181) 858 4422). BR: Greenwich. Set picturesquely in Greenwich, the museum documents the history of British sea power—in effect, the history of British power up to World War I. The lower floors display underwater discoveries, such as hand-painted charts and 17th-century models of wooden warships, as well as the coat in which Horatio Nelson was struck down by a French sniper at Trafalgar. Open Mon.-Sat. 10am-6pm, Sun. noon-6pm; in winter Mon.-Sat. 10am-5pm, Sun. 2-6pm. £3.75, concessions £2.75.

National Postal Museum, London Chief Post Office, King Edward Building, King Edward St., EC1 (tel. 239 5420). Tube: St. Paul's. Drawer after vertical drawer of delicate stamps are not the only attractions that this compact museum offers. Displays include samples of unadopted stamp designs, life-sized mannequins sporting dapper postal uniforms, and toy models of delivery trucks and pillar boxes. The astute visitor will learn about the legendary Rowland Hill, and the untutored will be initiated into the mysteries of pneumatic postage. The historical review of mail-sorting machines and postal codes includes early-20th-century posters from the Post Office's many campaigns for correct addressing. Open Mon.-Fri. 9:30am-4:30pm. (The museum will be closed April 25-May 6, 1995.) Free.

Natural History Museum, Cromwell Rd., SW7 (tel. 938 9123 or 938 9242 for group bookings). Tube: South Kensington. A tremendous cathedral of a museum, combining monumental medieval styling with a modern iron and steel framework. The museum's personality is split between a glorious but ultimately dull Victorian past (the encyclopedic frenzy is only slightly diluted—see the world's largest collection of metalliferous ores) and a high-tech present (buttons, levers, and microscopes galore). Permanent exhibits include "Discovering Mammals," "Creepy Crawlies," "Ecology: A Greenhouse Effect," "Primates" (the lifestyle and behavior of everything from the lemur to the human being), and the superb dinosaur exhibits, with tantalizing computer displays and relatively realistic life-size models. The interactive Discovery Centre for children and other hands-on enthusiasts is matchless. Open Mon.-Sat. 10am-6pm, Sun. 11am-6pm. £5, concessions £2.50, families (up to 2 adults and 4 children) £13.50. Free Mon.-Fri. 4:30-6pm, Sat.-Sun. 5-6pm. Wheelchair accessible.

Old Operating Theatre Museum, 9a St. Thomas St., SE1 (tel. 955 4791 or (0181) 806 4325). Tube: London Bridge. A truly bizarre little museum off the beaten tourist track. Built in 1821 for the treatment of poor women, this wooden operating amphitheatre was abandoned for many years before being renovated as a museum. Amputated body parts preserved in jars rest next to surgical tools. Open Tues.-Sun. 10am-4pm. £2.

Pollock's Toy Museum, 41 Whitfield St., W1 (tel. 636 3452). Tube: Goodge St. Housed above a modern toy shop in a maze of tiny, 18th-century rooms congested with antique playthings of every size and description, including Eric, the oldest known teddy bear (b. 1905) and "Blow Football," a toy based on scientific principles. Elaborate toy theatres take center stage in one room. The exhibits appeal largely to the nostalgia of adults, but precocious children are also bound to enjoy. Open Mon.-Sat. 10am-5pm, last admission 4:30pm. £2, under 18 75p, under 18 free on Sat. AmEx.

Royal Academy, Piccadilly, W1 (tel. 439 7438), across from no. 185. Tube: Green Park or Piccadilly Circus. The academy frequently hosts traveling exhibits of the highest order. Space for these shows has recently been enlarged by high-tech architect Norman Foster. The whopping annual summer exhibition is a British institution where the works of established and unknown contemporary artists are reviewed at the deliberate rate of 10 per min. Reynolds, Gainsborough, Constable, and Turner were members of the Academy in its heyday. Open daily 10am-6pm. Admission usually £5, students and seniors about £3, under 18 about £2. Summer exhibitions £4.50, students and seniors £3, under 18 £2.25. Advance tickets occasionally necessary for popular exhibitions.

Royal Festival Hall Galleries, Royal Festival Hall, South Bank Centre, SE1 (tel. 928 3002). Tube: Waterloo, or Embankment and cross the Hungerford footbridge. (See Entertainment—classical music.) Photography and architecture are this gallery's primary art forms. Hosts the South Bank Photo Show during the summer months. Occasional jazz concerts in the foyer. Open daily 10am-10:30pm. Free.

Science Museum, Exhibition Rd., SW7 (tel. 938 8008 or 938 8080). Tube: South Kensington. The Science Museum can enlighten you on subjects ranging from the exploration of space to papermaking to basic topology. The museum's introductory exhibit romps through a "synopsis" of science since 6000 BC, lingering over the steam-powered Industrial Revolution that vaulted Britain to imperialist world domination. Launch Pad, a special hall of child-run experiments on the first floor, is irresistible to kids of all ages. Other permanent exhibits include "Food for Thought," which demonstrates the impact of technology on food, and the excellent Flight Gallery of aeronautics. Don't miss the striking Bertone B.A.T. car display of of Franco Scaglione's revolutionary aerodynamic mobiles built with Alfa Romeo parts; they look like they're aquadynamic, too. The "Glimpses of Medical History" exhibit is not for the squeamish. Open Mon.-Sat. 10am-6pm, Sun. 11am-6pm. £4.50, concessions (students, children, and seniors) £2.40, under 5 and people with disabilities free. Free daily 4:30-6pm.

Shakespeare's Globe Museum, Bear Gardens, SE1 (tel. 928 6342). Tube: London Bridge. Theatre memorabilia, balsa-wood replicas of Elizabethan theatres, and a full-size stage upstairs. The museum is also in the midst of an ongoing project to build an exact copy of the Globe Theatre on an adjacent parking lot. Open Mon.-Sat. 10am-5pm, Sun. 2-5:30pm. £3, concessions £2.

The Sherlock Holmes Museum, 239 Baker St. (marked "221b"), W1 (tel. 935 8866). Tube: Baker St. Sir Arthur Conan Doyle actually occupied this house for an unspecified period of time in the late 1800s. Students of Holmes' deductive method will be intrigued by the museum's meticulous re-creation of his storied lodgings. Upstairs is a display of "artifacts" from the stories. Leaf through a hilarious selection of letters Holmes has received in the last few years; one hard-to-fool American student writes, "My teacher's making me write to you even though everyone knows you're 6 feet under. I feel so stupid." You are encouraged to try on the deerstalker cap and cloak. Open daily 9:30am-5:30pm. £5, under 17 £3.

Sir John Soane's Museum, 13 Lincoln's Inn Fields, WC2 (tel. 405 2107). Tube: Holborn. Soane was an architect's architect, but the idiosyncratic home he designed for himself will intrigue even lay-persons. Window-sized, inset, and convex mirrors placed strategically throughout the house for lighting effects also create skewed angles and weird distortions. The columns in the Colonnade room support a room-within-a-room above. Famous artifacts on display include Hogarth paintings, the massive sarcophagus of Seti I, and casts of famous buildings and scupltures from around the world. Look for the little numbers on the objects and art works; Soane catalogued everything himself. Open Tues.-Sat. 10am-5pm; lecture tour Sat. at 2:30pm (arrive by 2pm). Free.

The Story of Telecommunications, 145 Queen Victoria St., EC4 (tel. 248 7444). Tube: Blackfriars. Dedicated to the preservation and presentation of 200 years' worth of telecommunications history, this 2-story museum buzzes with activity. Interspersed with displays of Victorian phones, publicity ads from the 1920s and 30s, and optical fibre technology are a number of cacaphonous hands-on exhibits popular with children. You can print out a telegram, fax yourself, or call someone at the other end of the museum. Open Mon.-Fri. 10am-5pm. Wheelchair accessible with prior arrangement. Free.

Theatre Museum, 1e Tavistock St., WC2 (tel. 836 7891). Tube: Covent Garden. Public entrance on Russell St., off the east end of the Covent Garden piazza. This branch of the V&A contains Britain's richest holding of theatrical memorabilia; see numerous 19th-century Shakespearean daggers before you. Exhibits also include models of historical and present-day theaters, as well as other stage-related arts, such as ballet, opera, puppetry, the circus, and rock music. Evocative photograph collection and eccentric temporary exhibits. Box office just inside the door sells tickets to West End plays, musicals, and concerts with negligible mark-up in most cases. Box office open Tues.-Sat. 11am-8pm, Sun. 11am-7pm. Museum open Tues.-Sun. 11am-7pm. £3; students, seniors, and under 14 £1.50; family £7.

The Wallace Collection, Hertford House, Manchester Sq., W1 (tel. 935 0687). Tube: Bond St. Founded by various Marquises of Hertford and the illegitimate son of the fourth Marquis, Sir Richard Wallace, the museum overflows with an embarassment of riches, particularly in Dutch and Rococo art. Outstanding are Hals's *The Laughing Cavalier,* Delacroix's *Execution of Marino Faliero,* Fragonard's *The Swing,* and Rubens' *Christ on the Cross*. Landscapes, interiors, portraits, and genre scenes from the major Dutch Golden Age artists hang near a passel of Rubens oil sketches (drafts of some of his most famous works). Several wall-sized Bouchers, multitudes of Greuze, and many Watteaus show the Rococo at its most flamboyant. Numerous encounters with the Other are depicted in the collection of French Orientalist painting. Also home to the largest armor and weaponry collection outside of the Tower of London. Open Mon.-Sat. 10am-5pm, Sun. 2-5pm. Guided tours Mon.-Tues. 1pm, Wed. 11:30am and 1pm, Thurs.-Fri. 1pm, Sat. 11:30am, Sun. 3pm. Free.

Wellington Museum, Apsley House, on the north side of Hyde Park Corner, W1 (tel. 499 5676). Tube: Hyde Park Corner. Due to reopen in 1995. This building was enlarged and altered in 1828 to provide a suitable home for the Duke of Wellington, hero of the Battle of Waterloo and Prime Minister-to-be. The building now displays relevant memorabilia.

Whitechapel Art Gallery, Whitechapel High St., E1 (tel. 377 0107). Tube: Aldgate East. The high-ceilinged and sunny galleries of the Whitechapel contain no permanent collection, but host some of Britain's (and Europe's) most daring exhibitions of contemporary art. Recent exhibits have included the work of Lucian Freud and Franz Kline. A show of Cuban art is planned for 1995. Exhibitions often focus on the multi-ethnic East End community; the Whitechapel Open Exhibit showcases artists from the area. After touring the galleries, unwind with a beverage and a baked good in the Whitechapel Art Gallery Cafe. Open Tues. and Thurs.-Sun. 11am-5pm, Wed. 11am-8pm. Free, but donations are appreciated.

Winston Churchill's Britain at War, 64-66 Tooley St., SE1 (tel. 403 3171; fax 403 5104). Tube: London Bridge. A macabre reconstruction of the London WWII experience, including a surprisingly realistic Blitz blackout scene. Crouch in a shelter, wear a gas mask, pick your way through rubble. Fun. Open daily 10am-5pm. £5, concessions £3.75, family £13.

Entertainment

When a man is tired of London, he is tired of life; for there is in London all that life can afford.

—Samuel Johnson, 1777

On any given day or night, Londoners and visitors can choose from the widest range of entertainment a city can offer. Suffering competition only from Broadway, the West End is the world's theatre capital, supplemented by an adventurous "fringe." Music scenes range from the black ties of the Royal Opera House to Wembley mobs and nightclub raves. The work of British filmmakers like Derek Jarman, Sally Potter, and Mike Leigh—often available in the States only on video—is shown in cinemas all over the city. Dance, comedy, sports, and countless unclassifiable happenings can leave you poring in bewilderment over the listings in *Time Out* (£1.50) and *What's On* (£1). **Kidsline** (tel. 222 8070) answers queries on children's events (Mon.-Fri. 4-6pm). **Artsline** (tel. 388 2227) provides information about disabled access at entertainment venues across London (Mon.-Fri. 9:30am-5:30pm).

■■■ THEATRE

The stage for a national dramatic tradition dating from Shakespeare's day, London maintains unrivalled standards in theatre. The renowned Royal Academy for the Dramatic Arts draws students from around the globe. Playwrights such as Tom Stoppard and Alan Ayckbourn premier their works in the West End; class-conscious political dramas, younger writers, and performance artists uphold a vibrant "fringe" scene; and Shakespearean and Jacobean revenge tragedies are revived everywhere. Tickets are relatively inexpensive; the cheapest seats in most theatres cost about £8, progressing upward to £22 for orchestra seats. Previews and matinees cost a few pounds less, and many theatres offer dirt-cheap **student/senior standbys** (indicated by "concs," "concessions," or "S" in newspaper and *Time Out* listings)—around £7 shortly before curtain with ID (come two hours beforehand to be sure of a seat). **Day seats** are sold to the public from 9 or 10am on the day of the performance at a reduced price, but you must queue up even earlier to snag one. If a show is sold out, returned tickets may be sold (at full price) just before curtain. Most theatres also offer senior citizen discounts on advance ticket purchases for weekday matinees. For the latest on standbys for West End shows, call the **Student Theatreline** (tel. 379 8900; updated from 2pm daily).

"Stalls" are orchestra seats. "Upper Circle" and "Dress Circle" refer to balcony seats above the stalls. "Slips" are seats along the top edges of the theater; usually the cheapest, they often have restricted views of the stage. The "interval" is the intermission. Programs are never free; these large, glossy booklets cost £1.50-2. Matinees are on weekdays and Saturday at 2, 2:15, 2:30, or even 3pm. Evening performances start between 7:15 and 8pm.

The **Leicester Square Ticket Booth** sells tickets at half-price (plus £1.50 booking fee) on the day of the performance, but carries only tickets for the West End, Barbican, and National Theatre. Tickets are sold from the top of the pile, which means you can't choose a seat and the most expensive seats are sold first. Lines are the worst on Saturday (open for matinees Mon.-Sat. noon-2pm, for evening shows 2:30-6:30pm; cash only; max. 4 per person). If you schlep to a box office in person, you can select your seats from the theatre seating plan (box offices usually open 10am-8pm). Reserve seats by calling the box office and then paying by post or in person within three days, or by calling the **First Call booking office** (tel. 497 9977; booking fee for some shows) for West End shows. Credit card holders can charge the tickets over the phone but must produce the card when picking up tickets.

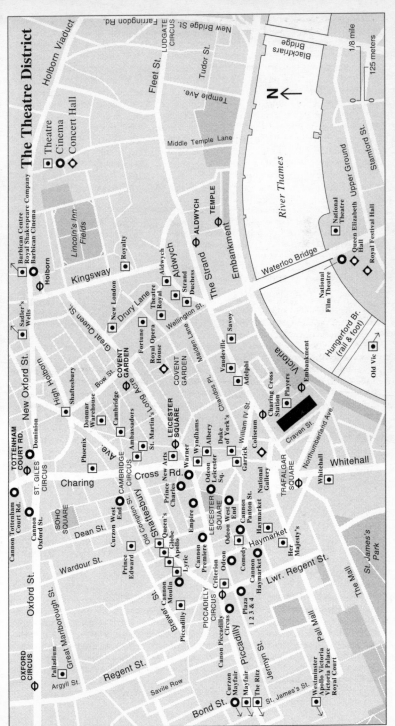

The Theatre District

■● Theatre
◎ Cinema
◇ Concert Hall

Patronize ticket agencies only if you're desperate—they can, and will, charge whatever they like. Avoid package-deal specials cooked up for tourists, and be aware that many shows around Piccadilly are tawdry farces and sex shows. For big-name shows, try to get tickets months in advance. Write or call first to the theatre box office; failing this, try **Keith Prowse** (tel. 631 4604), London's largest ticket agency (which also has an office at 234 W. 44th St., New York, NY 10036; tel. (800) 669-7469) or **Ticketmaster** (tel. 344 4444). These agencies charge a standard fee.

Aside from what's going on inside them, many West End theatres themselves form part of the city's fabric. The **Theatre Trust** has protected many historic theatres from demolition; landmarks include the Theatre Royal, Haymarket, the Albery, the Palace, the Criterion, the Duke of York, Her Majesty's, the Shaftesbury, the Savoy, and the Palladium. The most historic theatre of them all, Shakespeare's **Globe Theatre,** exists only as a carefully preserved excavation site and foundation. The Shakespeare Society of America is negotiating to buy the site and build a replica of the original theatre; at the same time, a replica down the street is nearly finished.

Barbican Theatre, Barbican Centre, EC2 (tel. 628 2295 for 24-hr. information or tel. 638 8891 for reservations). Tube: Barbican or Moorgate. London home of the Royal Shakespeare Company. Tickets for the main theatre, the **Barbican,** £7.50-22; weekday matinees £6-12; Sat. matinees and previews £8-16. Student and senior citizen standbys bookable in person or by telephone from 9am on the day of the performance, £6.50-8 (1 per person). Fascinating futuristic auditorium; each row of seats in the Barbican has its own side door through which patrons enter the theatre (there are no aisles). The forward-leaning balconies guarantee that no one sits farther than 65ft. from center stage, and every seat in the house gives a clear view. Stick around at the interval to watch the shiny metal safety curtain seal off the stage. Jacobean, Restoration, and experimental contemporary works in the tiny black-box second theatre, **The Pitt,** evenings and Sat. matinees £15, previews £13, midweek matinees £12. Student and senior citizen standbys available from 9am the day of the performance, £6.50. There are always several signed and audio-described performances during the run of each show. Box office (on Level 5 of the Centre) open daily 9am-8pm. Major credit cards.

Royal National Theatre, South Bank Centre, SE1 (tel. 928 2252). Tube: Waterloo, or Embankment and cross the Hungerford footbridge. The brilliant repertory companies in the **Olivier** and **Lyttleton** theatres (£6-22) put up classics from Shakespeare to Ibsen as well as mainstream contemporary drama. The smaller **Cottesloe** (£6-14) plays with more experimental works like Kushner's *Angels in America*. All 3 theatres are well-raked and have widely spaced rows, so even the rear balcony seats offer an unobstructed view of the stage. 40 day seats in each of the 3 theatres (Olivier, Lyttleton, and Cottesloe) reduced to £7-13 at 10am on day of performance. General standby seats sold from 2hr. before performance at £8-10; student and senior standby 45min. before show £6. Senior citizen matinees £9. Platform performances by major theatre figures and writers (lectures or dramatic selections) presented as pre-play appetizers (£3.50, students and seniors £2.50). The complex features live music, exhibitions, and other free activities. The National's outstanding **bookshop** has the widest selection in London for plays and books about theatre (open Mon.-Sat. 10am-11pm). **Backstage tours** Mon.-Sat. £3.50, concessions £2.50; call 633 0880 for times. **Box office** open Mon.-Sat. 10am-8pm.

WEST END THEATRES

Descriptions of what was playing in 1994 are included to give each theatre's flavor. Except for the huge musicals, don't expect to find these shows playing in 1995.

Adelphi Theatre, The Strand, WC2 (tel. 344 0055 for Ticketmaster). Tube: Charing Cross. Lloyd Webber's latest extravaganza—*Sunset Boulevard.* £17.50-36.

Albery Theatre, St. Martin's La., WC2 (tel. 867 1115). Tube: Leicester Sq. Oscar Wilde's *Lady Windemere's Fan.* £10-22.50.

Aldwych Theatre, Aldwych, WC2 (tel. 836 6404). Tube: Covent Garden or Aldwych—rush hours only. High-quality. *An Inspector Calls* by J.B. Priestley. £7.50-22.

Apollo Victoria Theatre, Wilton Rd., SW1 (tel. 828 8665). Tube: Victoria. *Starlight Express.* £10-30.

Criterion Theatre, Piccadilly Circus, W1 (tel. 839 4488). Tube: Piccadilly Circus. Alternative line-ups. The Flying Karamazovs in *Juggle and Hyde.* £6.50-12.50.

Dominion Theatre, Tottenham Ct. Rd., W1 (tel. 580 8845). Tube: Tottenham Ct. Rd. Revival of *Grease* originally starring Debbie Gibson. Such a big hit that it's running until Sept. 1995 (even though Debbie is gone). £7.50-25.

Donmar Warehouse, Earlham St., WC2 (tel. 867 1150). Tube: Covent Garden. David Mamet's *Glengarry Glen Ross,* £8-18.

Drury Lane Theatre Royal, Catherine St., WC2 (tel. 494 5062). Tube: Covent Garden. *Miss Saigon,* £5.75-30. Until April 1995.

Duke of York's Theatre, St. Martin's La., WC2 (tel. 836 5122). Tube: Leicester Sq. *The Rocky Horror Show,* £8.50-22.50.

Globe Theatre, Shaftesbury Ave., W1 (tel. 494 5065). Tube: Piccadilly Circus. An adaptation of Feydeau's *An Absolute Turkey (Le Dindon),* £9.50-25.

Her Majesty's Theatre, Haymarket, SW1 (tel. 494 5050). Tube: Piccadilly Circus. *Phantom of the Opera,* £9-30.

London Palladium Theatre, Argyll St., W1 (tel. 494 5020). Tube: Oxford Circus. *Fiddler on the Roof,* £7.50-27.50.

Lyric Hammersmith, King St., W6 (tel. (0181) 741 2311.) Tube: Hammersmith. High-quality repertory in the Main House. Ibsens's *The Lady from the Sea,* £7.50-15. More far-out doings in the Studio (tel. (0181) 741 8701). A modern adaptation of *Macbeth,* £7, concesssions £5.

Lyric Shaftesbury Theatre, Shaftesbury Ave., W1 (tel. 494 5045). Tube: Piccadilly Circus. *Five Guys Named Moe,* a jazz musical, £5-27.50.

New London Theatre, Drury Lane, WC2 (tel. 405 0072). Tube: Covent Garden. *Cats.* Until Jan. 1995. Tickets £10.50-30.

Old Vic, Waterloo Rd., SE1 (tel. 928 7616). Tube: Waterloo. Historic, famed repertory company in one of the most beautiful performance spaces in London. Mostly contemporary plays fetch phenomenal reviews. *900 Oneonta* written and directed by David Beaird. Tickets £7.50-14.50.

Open Air Theatre, Inner Circle, Regent's Park, NW1 (tel. 486 2431 or 486 1933 for credit card bookings). Tube: Baker St. or Regent's Park. Mostly Shakespeare; you have to sit in the front to catch every word. Bring a blanket and a bottle of wine. Performances in summer Mon.-Tues. and Fri. at 8pm; Wed.-Thurs. and Sat. at 2:30 and 8pm. Plays other than the regular feature presentation are performed on Sun. at 8pm. Previews in late May at reduced prices.

Palace Theatre, Shaftesbury Ave., W1 (tel. 434 0909). Tube: Leicester Sq. *Les Miserables.* Tickets £7-30.

Prince Edward Theatre, Old Compton St., W1 (tel. 734 8951). Tube: Leicester Sq. *Crazy for You.* Tickets £11.50-30.

Prince of Wales Theatre, Coventry St., W1 (tel. 839 5987). Tube: Piccadilly Circus. *Copacabana,* £20-30.

Royal Court Theatre, Sloane Sq., SW1 (tel. 730 1745). Tube: Sloane Sq. Challenging, inventive productions. The petite **Theatre Upstairs** (tel. 730 2554) puts on consistently fine, original fringe shows.

St. Martin's Theatre, West St., WC2 (tel. 836 1443). Tube: Leicester Sq. Agatha Christie's *The Mousetrap* in its 5th decade, £8-20.

Savoy Theatre, The Strand, WC2 (tel. 836 8888). Tube: Charing Cross. Usually hosts the English National Ballet in summer.

Victoria Palace Theatre, Victoria St., SW1 (tel. 834 1317). Tube: Victoria. *Buddy,* the musical biography of Buddy Holly, £6-25.

Wyndham's Theatre, Charing Cross Rd., WC2 (tel. 867 1116). Tube: Leicester Sq. David Storey's *Howe,* £9-22.

FRINGE

"The fringe" is what Londoners dub the dozens of smaller, less commercial theatres that don't belong to the Society of West End Theatres. Born in the avant-garde late

THEATRE

1960s, the fringe today runs the gamut from amateur community productions to top-notch experimental dramas. Although the fringe is scattered all over London and its suburbs, several of the best theatres can be found in Islington. Ticket prices are much lower than in the West End (£4.50-10). All offer student and senior citizen's discounts in advance or at the door—no standby necessary.

Almeida Theatre, 1a-1b Almeida St., N1 (tel. 359 4404). Tube: Angel or Highbury & Islington. A highly notable theatre. The summer new opera series with the English National Opera generates rave reviews from critics. Ian MacDairmaid is a director here. Doubles as an avant-garde music showcase. The same managers run the excellent wine bar next door. Box office open Mon.-Sat. 10am-6pm.

Arts Threshold, 17 Gloucester Terr., W2 (tel. 262 1629). Tube: Paddington, then #27 bus. The resident company is an Edinburgh theatre festival winner. Pay what you can on Tues.

Battersea Arts Centre (BAC), Old Town Hall, 176 Lavender Hill, SW11 (tel. 223 2223). BR: Clapham Junction. One of the top fringe venues, with innovative productions and talented new playwrights. Main and 2 studio stages with "mainstream" (radical corruptions of Shakespeare and other canonical texts) and experimental works, plus improv in the Arts Café. In autumn holds British Festival of Visual Theatre. Pay what you can on Tues. Tickets £6-7.50.

The Bush, Bush Hotel, Shepherd's Bush Green, W12 (tel. (0181) 743 3388). Tube: Goldhawk Rd. or Shepherd's Bush. Above a busy Irish pub. Critically acclaimed. Box office open Mon.-Sat. 10am-7pm. Tickets around £6-10.

Café Theatre, Ecology Centre, 45 Shelton St., WC2 (tel. 240 9582). Tube: Covent Garden. Home of the Artaud Theatre Company, which presents Artaudian shows on one stage; on the other stage, Sartre's comedy *Intimacy* is the longest-running show on the fringe. Tickets £3.50-5.

Drill Hall Arts Centre, 16 Chenies St., WC1 (tel. 637 8270). Tube: Goodge St. Politically active productions, often with a gay slant. Includes many adaptations from other media. Delicious vegetarian restaurant downstairs.

Etcetera Theatre, Oxford Arms, 265 Camden High St., NW1 (tel. 482 4857). Tube: Camden Town. Experimental, inventive scripts by new playwrights. Tickets £5-7.

The Gate, The Prince Albert, 11 Pembridge Road, W11 (tel. 229 0706). Tube: Notting Hill Gate. In 1994 this pub-theatre with a big reputation hosted the London New Plays Festival. A Greek Trilogy marathon will run into late 94 (*Electra, Orestes,* and *Iphigenia in Aulis*). Box office open Mon.-Fri. 10am-6pm.

Greenwich Theatre, Crooms Hill, SE10 (tel. (0181) 858 7755). BR: Greenwich. Multicultural, experimental works, in addition to classics like *Alice in Wonderland*. Tickets £6.50-9.50.

Hampstead Theatre, Avenue Rd., Swiss Cottage Centre, NW3 (tel. 722 9301). Tube: Swiss Cottage. One of London's oldest small theaters: notable alumni/ae include John Malkovich.

Holland Park Open Air Theatre, Holland Park, W14 (tel. 602 7856). Tube: Holland Park or High St. Kensington. Mainstream shows share the open-air stage with opera and ballet in the summer.

Institute of Contemporary Arts (ICA) Theatre, Nash House, The Mall, W1 (tel. 930 3647). Tube: Piccadilly Circus or Charing Cross. One of the least conventional: some plays without dialogue, some based on political themes or dreams. Tickets prices (£1.50-7) include entrance to galleries, café, and bar.

King's Head, 115 Upper St., N1 (tel. 226 1916). Tube: Highbury & Islington or Angel. A Very Big Deal. The slightly ramshackle atmosphere of this pub theatre is well-known among dedicated London theatre-goers. Kenneth Branagh and Ben Kingsley are alumni. Occasional lunchtime performances. Some plays run £2-4, others £5-9.

New End Theatre, 27 New End, NW3 (tel. 794 0022). Tube: Hampstead. Reputable new works presented by various local companies. Plays range from Isaac Bashevis Singer to modern mysteries about Jesus.

Old Red Lion, St. John's St., N1 (tel. 837 7816). Tube: Angel. Yet another of Islington's gems, the Lion is one of the top fringe theatres and usually presents intriguing plays by new writers.

Oval House, 52-54 Kennington Oval, SE11 (tel. 582 7680). Tube: Oval. Flamboyant, provocative productions include Steven Dykes's *Visitation*. £3-7.

Shakespeare Globe Site, Bankside, SE1 (tel. 620 0202). Tube: London Bridge. Entrance on Emerson St. Shakespeare plays, often with members of Britain's most prestigious companies, are sometimes presented with proceeds towards the reconstruction of Shakespeare's Globe Theater.

Soho Poly, 16 Riding House St., W1 (tel. 636 9050). Tube: Oxford Circus. Reputation for bizarre yet realistic drama. Fosters many young and aspiring writers.

Theatre Royal Stratford East, Gerry Raffles Sq., E15 (tel. (0181) 534 0310). Tube: Stratford. Acclaimed and popular new drama.

Theatre Upstairs, Royal Court, SW1 (tel. 730 2554). Tube: Sloane Sq. This highly experimental theatre barely survived the late 80s, but persists as a home for consistently good plays and performances.

Tricycle Theatre, 269 Kilburn High Rd., NW6 (tel. 328 1000). Tube: Kilburn. A favorite among locals—some good avant-garde performances. Best-known for new Black and Irish playwrights. Occasionally dance or music on Sun.

Young Vic, 66 The Cut, SE1 (tel. 928 6363). Tube: Waterloo. Inland from the actual river bank. Theatre in the round. Besides giving new talent a crack at the classics, they sponsor a community-oriented summer festival—everything from masked Balinese dancers to schoolkids doing Chekhov. Box office open Mon.-Fri. 9am-5pm. Now adapting Bruno Shultz's *Street of Crocodiles*.

Lunchtime theatre productions are generally less serious than evening performances, but at £2-4 they're a great way to start the afternoon. (Most productions start around 1:15pm.) Check the lunchtime listings at the end of *Time Out's* theatre section. The **King's Head** (see above) is probably the most successful at daytime shows. **St. Paul's Church,** at the central marketplace in Covent Garden, often has lunchtime theatre on its steps. In summer, call **Alternative Arts** (tel. 287 0907 or 437 9828) for information on their street theatre around the city; they've performed *War and Peace* entirely inside a motorcycle sidecar. If you can scrape together a group of 12-17 on a weekday evening, you can follow a **Tube Theatre** (tel. 586 6828) comic posing as a bumbling commuter onto the trains and watch the real-life reactions; "performances" Mon.-Fri. 7pm; tickets £12 per person.

Every two years (next in 1995) the **London International Festival of Theatre (LIFT)** moves in. For four weeks in June and July, theatres all over the city host the best mainstream and avant-garde productions from all over the world, such as the Beijing Youth Opera, Hanoi water-puppetry, New York's Wooster Group, and an installation in a truck that roams through London's streets (tel. 413 1459).

■■■ FILM

London's film scene offers everything from Arnold Schwarzenegger to French existentialism, from Hollywood dramas to Asian documentaries. The degenerate heart of the celluloid monster is Leicester Square, where the most recent hits premiere a day before hitting the chains around the city. West End first-run screens include the **Empire** (tel. 437 1234), **Odeon Leicester Sq.** (tel. 930 3232), the **Warner West End** (tel. 437 3484), all at Leicester Sq. tube; the **Odeon Haymarket** (tel. 839 7697; tube: Piccadilly Circus), and the **MGM Oxford St.** (tel. 636 0310; tube: Tottenham Ct. Rd.). All have recorded messages detailing times and exorbitant ticket prices.

Thousands of films pass through the capital every year, old and new. Newspapers have listings, while *Time Out* covers both commercial films and the vast range of cheaper alternatives—late-night films, free films, "serious" films, and repertory cinema clubs. Also worth perusing are the ICA and NFT monthly schedules, available on-site (see below). Cinema clubs charge a small membership fee. This fee (usually 30p-£1.50) entitles cardholders and one guest to reduced admission; some cards

FILM

work at more than one cinema. Fees and cards make cinemas "clubs," and "clubs" can legally serve liquor—most cinemas have bars and many have restaurants. For evening performances buy your ticket early, or book in advance, especially on weekends. Many cinemas have assigned seating; ushers will help you find your place. Big theatres often charge different prices for different seats. Most London moviehouses charge £5-9, but many charge £3 all day Monday and for matinees Tuesday through Friday. For a mainstream first-run, go to the following inexpensive cinema:

The Prince Charles, Leicester Pl., WC2 (tel. 437 8181 or 437 7003). Tube: Leicester Sq. Shows scads (4 per day) of relatively recent Hollywood features sprinkled with classics for only £1.50, evenings and weekends £2.

Repertory theatres include:

Electric Cinema, 191 Portobello Rd., W11 (tel. 792 2020). Tube: Ladbroke Grove or Notting Hill Gate. The first Black cinema in Britain. Past screenings include ground-breakers like *Menace II Society*, *The Posse* by Mario van Peebles, and *Sankofa*, winner of the 1993 African Cinema Festival. Tickets £5. Discounted tickets (£4) available Mon.-Thurs. for students, seniors, and children; bring ID.

Everyman Cinema, Hollybush Vale, Hampstead, NW3 (tel. 435 1525). Tube: Hampstead. Double and triple bills based on either a theme or an obscure celluloid figure. Special seasonal runs; membership 60p per year. Tickets £4.50 Mon.-Fri., £5 Sat.-Sun.; students Mon.-Fri. £3.50.

French Institute, 17 Queensberry Pl., SW7 (tel. 589 6211). Tube: South Kensington. Excellent French masterpieces, usually subtitled. Tickets £4, students £3.

Gate Cinema, Notting Hill Gate, W11 (tel. 727 4043). Tube: Notting Hill Gate. Recent art films. Featured directors include Wim Wenders, Jane Campion, Derek Jarman, and Stephen Soderbergh. Tickets £5.50, students before 6pm Mon.-Fri. £3. Rotating Sunday matinees, £4.

Goethe Institute, 50 Prince's Gate, Exhibition Rd., SW7 (tel. 411 3400). Tube: South Kensington. Old German classics (generally without subtitles) and a sprinkling of U.S. favorites. Tickets £5.

Institute of Contemporary Arts (ICA) Cinema, Nash House, The Mall, W1 (tel. 930 3647). Tube: Piccadilly Circus or Charing Cross. Cutting-edge contemporary cinema, plus an extensive list of classics. Frequent special programs celebrating the work of a single director; recent tributes have lauded Rainer Fassbinder and Peter Greenaway. Tickets £6.50; concessions, Mon. screenings, and first screenings Tues.-Fri. £5. Experimental films and classics in the *cinémathèque; £4.*

London Film-maker's Co-op Cinema, 42 Gloucester Ave., NW1 (tel. 586 8516). Tube: Camden Town or Chalk Farm. Devoted to avant-garde and British films. Some double bills. Membership £3.50 per year, 50p per day. Tickets £3.50, students £2.50.

MGM Swiss Centre, Leicester Sq., WC2 (tel. 439 4470). Tube: Leicester Sq. or Piccadilly Circus. New French films with subtitles. Hidden around the left side of the centre. £6, children £3.50, concessions £3.50 before 6pm Fri., Mon. £3.

Minema, 45 Knightsbridge, W1 (tel. 235 4225). Tube: Knightsbridge or Hyde Park Corner. Small screen behind a tiny door, showing reborn art classics and popular foreign films as well as "commercial art." Tickets £6.50, students £3.50.

National Film Theatre (NFT), South Bank Centre, SE1 (tel. 928 3232 for box office). Tube: Waterloo, or Embankment and cross the Hungerford footbridge. The NFT is one of the world's leading cinemas, screening a mind-boggling array of film, television, and video in its three auditoria. Program changes daily but is arranged in seasonal series which highlight the work of a single director, country, or genre. Home of the London Film Festival, held in Nov. For daily ticket availability, call 633 0274. Tickets £4.35; under 16 admitted to select performances for £3.15; students, seniors, the unemployed, and registered disabled can buy tickets the day of the performance for £3.15. Members receive discounted tickets, mailings, and priority bookings. Box office open daily 11:30am-8:30pm.

Phoenix, 52 High Rd., N2 (tel. (0181) 883 2233 or 444 6789). Tube: East Finchley. Double bills mix and match European, American, and Asian mainstream hits and classics. Comfortable auditorium. Children's cinema club on Sat. mornings. £4.50, afternoons £3, students (Sat. night) £3, children £2, seniors £2.50.

Renoir, Brunswick Centre, Brunswick Sq., WC1 (tel. 837 8402). Tube: Russell Sq. British bohemian and popular foreign-language films (subtitled). £5.50; first showing £4, first showing for students £2.50.

Riverside Studios, Crisp Rd., W6 (tel. (0181) 748 3354). Tube: Hammersmith. A random mix of British prestige work, documentaries, and Fellini. Housed in a remodeled film studio. £3.75, students £2.60.

Screen on Baker St., 96 Baker St., NW1 (tel. 935 2772). Tube: Baker St. Slightly off-beat European and American films. All day Mon. and first screening Tues.-Fri. £3.50. Other screenings £5. MC, Visa.

Screen on the Green, Islington Green, N1 (tel. 226 3520). Tube: Angel. Revived and topical foreign classics as well as mainstream Hollywood. Trendy north London clientele. First show Mon.-Fri. £3.50, Fri.-Sat. £4.50, late night £5.

Screen on the Hill, 203 Haverstock Hill, NW3 (tel. 435 3366). Tube: Belsize Park. Just like its cousins above: a mix of art-house and wide-release. Good coffee. Ticket £5, first show Mon.-Fri. £3.50. £5, first show Mon.-Fri. £3.50.

Smoking cinemas include:

Cinema Fumée, in the Brixton Academy, 211 Stockwell Rd., SW9 (tel. 924 9999). Tube: Brixton. A cinematic celebration of the cancer stick, where 800 people watch cult flicks fortnightly, have a fag, and feel no guilt. If you forget to bring a pack, no worries: there will be cigarette girls vending Death brand cigarettes. Launched Aug. 5 1994, the success may be overwhelming, call to check dates and movies. £6.50.

Notting Hill Coronet, On Notting Hill Gate Rd., (tel. 727 6705). Tube: Notting Hill Gate. Opposite McDonald's. A 396-seater dive with a quirk: it's London's last smoking cinema. Perhaps it won't last long. Second-run mainstream films. £5.75, children £2.75.

■■■ MUSIC

Everyone from punk-rockers to opera fiends can exploit the richness of the London music scene. Unparalleled classical resources include five world-class orchestras, two opera houses, two huge arts centers, and countless concert halls. The rock scene, home of the London Underground of the late 60s, birthplace of the Sex Pistols and punk in the 70s, blessed with the Television Personalities and Soul II Soul in the 80s, and lately with 90s ragga remixes and Stereolab.

Summer is the best time for festivals and outdoor concerts, but the entire calendar offers enough music to satisfy and deafen you. Check the listings in *Time Out*. Keep your eyes open for special festivals or gigs posted on most of the city's surfaces, and for discounts posted on student union bulletin boards.

CLASSICAL

London's world-class orchestras provide only a fraction of the notes that fill its major music centers. London has been the professional home of some of the greatest conductors of the century—Sir Thomas Beecham, Otto Klemperer, and Andre Previn—as well as fertile ground for Britain's greatest composers.

Barbican Hall, Barbican Centre (tel. 638 4141 or tel. 638 8891 for box office). Tube: Barbican or Moorgate. Houses the venerable **London Symphony Orchestra.** The Barbican also welcomes a number of guest artists; in July 1994, the Kronos Quartet played a series of concerts. Tickets £5-29. Student and senior citizen standby tickets sold shortly before the performance.

Blackheath Concert Halls, 23 Lee Rd., Blackheath, SE3 (tel. (0181) 463 0100). Tube: Blackheath. Attracts top performers southeast year-round. In June, one of the Greenwich Festival sites (see below). Tickets £3.50-20; reductions for students and seniors.

Royal Albert Hall, Kensington Gore, SW7 (tel. 589 8212). Tube: South Kensington. Exuberant and skilled, the **Proms** (BBC Henry Wood Promenade Concerts) never fail to enliven London summers. Every day for 8 weeks July-Sept. an impressive roster of musicians performs routinely outstanding programs including annually commissioned new works. Camaraderie and craziness develop in the long lines for standing room outside. The last night of the Proms traditionally steals the show, with the massed singing of "Land of Hope and Glory" and "Jerusalem." Don't expect to show up at the last minute and get in; a lottery of thousands determines who will be allowed to paint their faces as Union Jacks and "air-conduct" in person. Gallery £2, arena £3—join the queue around 6pm; tickets £4-16, sometimes £4-21 for special performances. Box office open daily 9am-9pm; or try Ticketmaster at 379 4444.

Royal Festival Hall, South Bank Centre (tel. 928 8800 for box office). Tube: Waterloo, or Embankment and cross the Hungerford footbridge. The **London Philharmonic** and the **Philharmonia Orchestra** play in this vast hall in the hive of cultural activity that is the South Bank Centre. Conductors for the 94-95 season include Franz Welser-Most, Bernard Haitink, Klaus Tennstedt, Mariss Jansons, and Zubin Mehta. Booking for the summer season begins in early May. Tickets £4-28. Standbys for students, children, seniors, and the unemployed, when available, are sold on the day of the performance at the lowest ticket price; call 633 0932 after 10:30am. Box office open daily 10am-9pm. AmEx, Diners Club, MC, Visa.

St. John's, Smith Square, converted church just off Millbank (box office tel. 222 1061). Tube: Westminster. A schedule weighted toward chamber groups and soloists. Tickets £4-16, usually reduced for students and seniors.

Wigmore Hall, 36 Wigmore St., W1 (tel. 935 2141). Tube: Bond St. or Oxford Circus. Small, elegant, and Victorian. Many young artists make their debut here. Sponsors a summer festival in addition to its master concerts and chamber music series. Tickets £4-20; 1hr. standbys at lowest price. In summer, Sun. morning coffee concerts greet enthusiasts at 11:30am; tickets £5.50, coffee free.

The two main locations of the Barbican and the Royal Festival Hall, as well as the South Bank's smaller halls, the **Queen Elizabeth Hall** and the **Purcell Room,** play host to a superb lineup of groups, including the **Academy of St. Martin-in-the-Fields,** the **London Festival Orchestra,** the **London Chamber Orchestra,** the **London Soloists Chamber Orchestra,** the **London Classical Players,** and the **London Mozart Players,** in addition to diverse national and international orchestras. Vladimir Ashkenazy's **Royal Philharmonic Orchestra** performs at both the Barbican and the South Bank, and the **BBC Symphony Orchestra** pops up around town as well. Although the regular season ends in mid-July, a series of festivals on the South Bank in July and August take up the slack admirably, offering traditional orchestral music along with more exotic tidbits (tickets £3-20). Festivals include:

City of London Festival, box office at St. Paul's Churchyard, London EC4 (tel. 248 4260). Tube: St. Paul's. Explosion of activity around the city's grandest monuments: music in the livery halls, singing in churches, plays at various venues, grand opera, art exhibitions, and a trail of dance winding among the monuments. First 3 weeks of July. Box office open Mon.-Fri. 9:30am-5:30pm. Many events free, others £3.50-35. Information from early May at box office.

Greenwich Festival, (tel. (0181) 317 8687). Stages performances all over the Greenwich area in June. Free-£10.

Kenwood Lakeside Concerts, at Kenwood, on Hampstead Heath (tel. (0181) 348 1286 or 973 3427 for booking or 379 4444 for Ticketmaster booking—no booking fee). Tube: Golders Green or Archway, then bus #210; or East Finchley, then take a free shuttle bus to Kenwood (5-7pm, and after concerts until 10:45pm). The concerts are on the North side of Hampstead Heath. 45 years of top-class outdoor performances, often graced by firework displays and laser shows. Every summer Sat. (Mid-June-early Sept.) at 7:30pm, music floats to the audience from a performance shell across the lake. Reserved deck chairs £10-15, students and seniors £8-12. Grass admission £8.50-11, students and seniors £5.50-9. If the "outdoor" part is more important to you than the "concert," you can listen from afar for free. Limited free parking available.

Lufthansa Baroque Festival, main site at St. James's Church, Piccadilly (tel. 734 4511). Tube: Piccadilly Circus. In June, the early moderns swoop down on the city. Tickets £5-15.

Marble Hill House, (tel. 973 3427 or 413 1443 for booking). Tube/BR: Richmond, then bus #33, 90, 290, H22, or R70. Hosts outdoor concerts in summer Sun. at 7:30pm. Bring a blanket, and picnic on the grounds of this stately house. Members of the audience eat anything from cheese sandwiches in Tupperware to salmon on alabaster. (July-Aug.)

Medieval and Renaissance music still commands a following in England; many London churches offer performances of both liturgical and concert music, often at lunchtime. Premier among them are **St. Martin-in-the-Fields,** Trafalgar Sq. (tel. 976 1926 or 839 1930; tube: Charing Cross); **St. James's Piccadilly** (see above); **St. Bartholomew the Great** (tel. 601 5171; tube: Barbican); **St. Bride's,** Fleet St. (tel. 353 1301; tube: Blackfriars). **St. Paul's boys' choir** sings at the cathedral's Sunday 5pm service. Concerts are usually free. Also watch for the **Academy of Ancient Music,** the **Early Music Consort of London,** and the **Praetorius Ensemble.**

Artists from the **Royal College of Music,** Prince Consort Rd., SW7 (tel. 589 3643) and the **Royal Academy of Music,** Marylebone Rd., NW1 (tel. 935 5461) play at their home institutions and at the main city halls. Concerts at these schools are often free—call for details. Check with the **University of London Union,** 1 Malet St., WC1 (tel. 580 9551; tube: Goodge St.) for on-campus music there.

OPERA AND BALLET

Dance Days festival, Battersea Arts Centre (tel. 223 2223). A diverse and energetic show of contemporary and folk dance for 2 weeks in July. Call for details.

Embankment Gardens Opera Season. Tube: Embankment. Popular open-air opera. Visit the Embankment Gardens for completely free *al fresco* opera, usually performed in the afternoon and early evening. Check *Time Out* for details.

Holland Park Theatre, box office in the Visitor Centre (tel. 602 7856). Tube: Holland Park. Open-air opera from a number of companies June-July, in both English and the original languages. In summer, also outdoor opera. £10-15.

London Coliseum, St. Martin's La., WC2 (tel. 836 3161). Tube: Charing Cross or Leicester Sq. The **English National Opera's** repertoire leans towards the contemporary, and all works are sung in English. Seats in the Coliseum £6-43; standby tickets £10-15 available from 10am on day of performance—technically only 1 ticket per person waiting in line. In summer, when the ENO is off, the **English National Ballet** and visiting ballet companies perform here. Tickets £8-43; student and senior citizen discounts by advance booking only. Coliseum box office open Mon.-Sat. 10am-8pm.

The Place, 17 Duke's Rd., WC1 (tel. 387 0031). Tube: Euston. Fringe and experimental dance is the focus. £4-12.50.

Royal Festival Hall, South Bank Centre, SE1 (tel. 928 8800 for booking). Tube: Waterloo, or Embankment and cross the Hungerford footbridge. Visiting ballet companies grace the stage year-round. In addition to their regular productions at the London Coliseum, the English National Ballet occasionally performs here; tickets for these performances £7-32.

Royal Opera House, at Covent Garden, Box St., box office at 48 Floral St., WC2 (tel. 240 1911 or 240 1066). Tube: Covent Garden. The **Royal Opera** performs in this grand old venue. Standbys—"amphitheatre" seats in back with decent view—£8.25-13 from 10am on performance day; when available, student standbys about £10 1hr. before performance (tel. 836 6903 for recorded info); upper slips—on uncomfortable benches with view of about half the stage—from £2. The **Royal Ballet** also performs at the Royal Opera House. Tickets £2.25-54. At 10am on day of show, 65 amphitheatre seats go on sale (strictly 1 per person; lines often long;

£6-8.50). When available, standbys for students and senior citizens sold 1hr before curtain; call 836 6903. Box office open Mon.-Sat. 10am-8pm.

Sadler's Wells Theatre, Rosebery Ave., EC1 (tel. 278 8916). Tube: Angel. The principal stage for **visiting dance troupes** ranging from Twyla Tharp to national folk companies. Tickets £4-35; student discounts available. 50 stall tickets reserved for sale on performance day.

ROCK, POP, JAZZ, AND FOLK

London generates and attracts almost every type of performer under the sun: the clubs and pubs of the capital offer a wide, strange, and satisfying variety of musical entertainment. Often, thrash metallists play the same venue as Gaelic folk singers: check weekly listings carefully. *Time Out* and *What's On* have extensive listings and information about bookings and festivals. You can make credit card reservations for major events by calling **Ticketmaster** (tel. 379 4444); if you do not buy your tickets directly from the venue's box office, you may be charged a booking fee.

Rock and Pop

Major venues for rock concerts include the indoor **Wembley Arena** and the huge outdoor **Wembley Stadium** (tel. (0181) 900 1234; tube: Wembley Park or Wembley Central), the **Royal Albert Hall** (see Classical); the **Marquee,** and the **Forum** (see below). In the summer, many outdoor arenas such as **Finsbury Park** become venues for major concerts and festivals (see also Dance Clubs).

Astoria, 157 Charing Cross Rd., WC2 (tel. 434 0403). Tube: Tottenham Ct. Rd. Hot and sweaty hard rock, but the patrons don't seem to mind. £7-14.

Borderline, Orange Yard, off Manette St., WC2 (tel. 734 2095). Tube: Leicester Sq. or Tottenham Ct. Rd. British record companies use this basement club to test new rock and pop talent. £3-10. Live music 8:30-11pm, dancing 11pm-3am.

Brixton Academy, 211 Stockwell Rd., SW9 (tel. 326 1022). Tube: Brixton. Time-honored and rowdy venue for a wide variety of music including rock, reggae, rap, and "alternative." 4000 capacity. Recent gigs include Violent Femmes, Ice Cube, and foxy bachelors Stone Temple Pilots. £9-15. Box office takes cash only—book ahead with a credit card. Box office open Mon.-Fri. 10am-7pm, Sat. 11am-6pm.

Fairfield Halls, Park La., Croydon, Surrey (tel. (0181) 688 9291). BR: East Croydon. Large venue for festivals and concerts. £5-11.

Forum, 9-17 Highgate Rd., NW5 (tel. 284 2200). Tube: Kentish Town. Night bus N2. Top notch audio system in a popular venue which was formerly the Town-and-Country Club. Open daily 7-11pm. £7.50-17.50.

Garage, 20-24 Highbury Corner, N5 (tel. 607 1818). Tube: Highbury and Islington. Night bus N92. Club-slash-performance space with decent views. Rock, pop, and indie bands most nights. £4-11. Music starts 9pm.

Hackney Empire, 291 Mare St., E8 (tel. (0181) 985 2424). Tube: Bethnal Green then bus #253 north or BR: Hackney Downs or Hackney Central. Not much to look at, but its East End location attracts ragga and roots lovers for live tunes and wicked DJs. Also host to popular comic routines like the Caribbean duo Bello and Blacka. £3-12. Hours vary by show.

Half Moon Putney, 93 Lower Richmond Rd., SW15 (tel. (0181) 780 9383). Tube: Putney Bridge. Rocking pub with a mix of rock, jazz, and folk. Near the Thames. £3-5. Open daily from 8:30pm.

Hammersmith Apollo, Queen Caroline St., W6 (tel. (0181) 741 4868). Tube: Hammersmith. Big 50s building hosts mainstream rock. £11-25.

London Palladium, 8 Argyll St., W1 (tel. 494 5020). Tube: Oxford Circus. They've hosted Lou Reed. Open 6:45-10:30pm. Music usually starts 7:30. £8.50-29.

The Marquee, 105 Charing Cross Rd., WC2 (tel. 437 6601). Tube: Leicester Sq. or Tottenham Ct. Rd. A loud, busy showcase for the latest bands: hundreds churn through each month. £5-7. Open daily 7pm-midnight.

Mean Fiddler, 24-28 Harlesden High St., NW10 (tel. (0181) 961 5490). Tube: Willesden Junction. Night bus N18. Cavernous club with high balconies and good bars, strangely mixing country & western, folk, and indie rock. £5-10. Open Mon.-Sat. 8pm-2am, Sun. 7:30pm-1am. Music begins 9-9:30pm.

Powerhaus N1, 1 Liverpool Rd., N1 (tel. 837 3218). Tube: Angel. Also accessible by Night buses N92 and N96. Quirky mix of live indie rock and folk music in a converted pub. The recently revitalized Raincoats have played here. £4-6. Open Mon.-Thurs. 8pm-2am, Fri.-Sat. 8pm-3am, Sun. 7-11pm.

Rock Garden, The Piazza, Covent Garden, WC2 (tel. 836 4052). Tube: Covent Garden. Great new bands play nightly. £5, before 11pm. £4, Sun. lunchtime £2. Open Mon.-Sat. 7:30pm-3am, Sun. noon-3pm and 7:30pm-midnight.

Royal Albert Hall, Kensington Gore, SW7 (tel. 589 8212). Tube: Gloucester Rd., Knightsbridge, or South Kensington. #52 bus goes directly to RAH (both a day and night bus.) Elton John, Elvis Costello, Eric Clapton, and others. Box office open daily 9am-9pm.

Shepherd's Bush Empire, Shepherds Bush Green, W12 (tel. (0181) 740 7474). Tube: Shepherds Bush. Hosts dorky cool musicians like David Byrne and the Proclaimers. 2000 capacity, with 6 bars. £6-20.

Wembley Stadium and **Wembley Arena,** Empire Way, Wembley (tel. (0181) 902 8833. Tube: Wembley Park or Wembley Central. A football (soccer) stadium. Take a pair of binoculars. Possibility of inclement weather. Could really suck. Open 7:30pm-11pm selected nights. Admission £14-25. The **Arena** is the largest indoor venue in London, serving high-priced refreshments. Open 6:30-11pm selected nights. £15-25.

The Venue, 2A Clifton Rise, New Cross, SE14 (tel. (0181) 692 4077). Tube: New Cross, Night Bus N77. Getting to be a big indie scene. Dancing goes late into the night. Open Fri.-Sat. 7:30pm-2am; music starts 9:30pm. £5-6.

Jazz

In the summer, hundreds of jazz festivals appear in the city and its outskirts, including the **Capital Radio Jazz Parade** (July; tel. 379 1066), the **North London Festival** (June-July; tel. (0181) 449 0048), and the **City of London Festival** (July; tel. 248 4260). Ronnie Scott's, Bass Clef, and Jazz Café are the most popular clubs. Jazz clubs often stay open much later than pubs, and so are ideal spots for tippling into the wee hours.

100 Club, 100 Oxford St., W1 (tel. 636 0933). Tube: Tottenham Ct. Rd. Strange mix of traditional modern jazz, swing, and blues. Staged one of the Sex Pistols' first London gigs. Discount for groups of 5 or more. £5-8. Open Mon.-Thurs. 7:30pm-midnight, Fri. 7:30pm-3am, Sat. 7:30pm-1am, Sun. 7:45-11:30pm.

606 Club, 90 Lots Rd., SW10 (tel. 352 5953). Tube: Fulham Broadway, or buses #11 and 22 or Night bus N11. Blossoming talent bops along with household names in diverse styles. Open Mon.-Sat. 8:30pm-2:30am, Sun. 8:30-11:30pm. Music Mon.-Wed. 9:30pm, Thurs. 10 pm, Fri.-Sat. 10:30pm, Sun. 10pm. £4, Fri.-Sat. £4.50.

Bass Clef, 35 Coronet St., N1 (tel. 729 2476 or 729 2440), off Hoxton Sq. Tube: Old St, Night bus N96. Hosts African and Latin performers. Call for a reservation or arrive early. £3-7. Open daily 7:30pm-2am.

Bull's Head, Barnes Bridge, SW13 (tel. (0181) 876 5241). Tube: Hammersmith, then bus #9. A waterside pub renowned for good food and modern jazz and funk. £3.50-7. Open Mon.-Sat. 11am-11pm, Sun. noon-3pm and 7-10:30pm. Music starts at 8pm, and at lunchtime on Sun.

Jazz Café, 5 Parkway, Camden Town, NW1 (tel. 284 4358 or 916 6000 for box office). Tube: Camden Town, Night bus N93. Top new venue in a converted bank. Classic and experimental jazz. £7-12. Open Sun.-Thurs. 7pm-midnight, Fri. 7pm-3am, Sat. 7pm-1am.

Jazz at Pizza Express, 10 Dean St., W1 (tel. 437 9595). Tube: Tottenham Ct. Rd. Packed, dark club hiding behind a pizzeria. Fantastic groups, and occasional greats; get there early. £3.50-12.50. Music 9:30pm-1am. (See Food and Drink.)

Palookaville, 13a St. James St., WC2 (tel. 240 5857). Tube: Covent Garden. Relaxed restaurant and wine bar with cool live jazz ensembles and an intimate dance floor. Free to diners, £3 after 9:30pm Thurs.-Sat. Music nightly 8:45pm-1:30am.

Pizza on the Park, 11 Knightsbridge, Hyde Park Corner, SW1 (tel. 235 5550). Tube: Hyde Pk. Corner. Another Pizza Express branch that hosts mainstream jazz musicians. Open daily 8am-midnight. Music starts 9:15pm. £8-15.

Ronnie Scott's, Frith St., W1 (tel. 439 0747). Tube: Leicester Sq. or Piccadilly Circus. The most famous jazz club in London. Expensive food and great music. Candles on every small table, and great faded photographs of jazz legends who've played Ronnie Scott's. Ronnie himself, a legend in his own time, still hosts. Waiters masterfully keep noisy clientele from ruining the music by politely telling them to shut up. Open fabulously late—the music just keeps going. Rock/soul/world music on Sun. £12. Book ahead or arrive by 9:30pm. Music starts 9:30-10pm. Open Mon.-Sat. 8:30am-3am.

Folk and Roots

To a large extent, folk music in London means Irish music. But aside from the Celtic variety, the term "folk" covers a whole host of musical hybrids including acoustic folk rock, political tunes, folky blues, and even English country-western. Some of the best are free, but welcome donations or consumption.

Acoustic Room, at The Mean Fiddler, 24-28 Harlesden Hight St., NW10 (tel. (0181) 961 5490). Tube: Willesden Junction. Superb acoustic rock/folk performers, with a decidedly younger, "alternative" slant. £4-5. Open Mon.-Sat. 8pm-2am, Sun. 7:30pm-1am.

Africa Centre, 38 King St., WC2 (tel. 836 1973). Tube: Covent Garden. Music and dance from Africa. More like a cultural center than a club. £7. Open Fri.-Sat. 10pm-3am.

Archway Tavern, Archway Roundabout, N19 (tel. 272 2840). Tube: Archway. Sponsors a mix of groups with Irish accents. Free-£1.50. Open Mon.-Sat. from 9:30pm, Sun. from 9pm.

Bunjie's, 27 Litchfield St., WC2 (tel. 240 1796). Tube: Covent Garden. Packed vegetarian restaurant with folk and hard-to-classify folk genre-crossing groups; lively, dancing audience. Wed. is best. £3, students £2.50. Open Mon.-Sat. 8-11pm.

Cecil Sharpe House, 2 Regent's Park Rd., NW1 (tel. 485 2206). Tube: Camden Town, Night buses N2, N29, N93. Regents canal-side view. Happening folk scene, with singing and dancing. £3-5. Open Thurs.-Sat. 7:30pm-11pm.

Forge Folk & Blues Club, at Andy's Workshop, 27 Denmark St., WC2 (tel. 836 0899). Tube: Tottenham Ct. Rd. Sometimes snags premier folk acts. Wed. is Acoustic Blues night. £3.50-5. Open Tues.-Sat. from 8:30pm.

Halfway House, 142 The Broadway, West Ealing, W13 (tel. (0181) 567 0236). Tube: Ealing Broadway, Night bus N50, N89. Irish, Cajun, and blues. Open Mon.-Thurs. 11am-11pm, Fri. 11am-midnight, Sat. noon-3pm, 7-10:30pm. Free.

Troubadour Coffee House, 265 Old Brompton Rd., SW5 (tel. 370 1434). Tube: Earl's Ct. Acoustic entertainment is served up in a warm café. Bob Dylan played here early in his career. On Wed. the café becomes the "Institute for Acoustic Research." Folk and jazz Fri.-Sat. £4.50, concession £3.50. Open 8pm-11pm.

Weavers, 98 Newington Green Rd., N1 (tel. 226 6911). Tube: Highbury and Islington. Well-respected folk and country acts. £2-6. Open Mon.-Sat. 8:30pm-midnight, Sun. 7:30pm-midnight.

■■■ DANCE CLUBS

London pounds to 100% Groovy Liverpool tunes, ecstatic Manchester rave, home-town soul and house, imported U.S. hip-hop, and Jamaican ragga. Check out the 12" bins at record stores for the obscure dub mixes that dominate the playlists. Fashion evolves and revolves: flares and platforms have been supplanted by little-girl t-shirts, silver mini-skirts, and Puma Clydes. The most expensive dance halls freak out their patrons with virtual-reality video shows and cyberpunk games.

Many clubs host a variety of provocative one-nighters (like "Get up and Use Me") throughout the week. In fact, it's the night's event and not the physical location that counts in deciding where to rave. If you're looking for a truly underground dance experience, keep your ear to the ground. While news of serious raves travels exclusively by word of mouth, they can attract thousands of revelers in the know, who congregate in abandoned warehouses or in open fields outside the city.

Remember that the tube shuts down two or three hours before most clubs and that taxis can be hard to find in the wee hours of the morning. Some late-night frolickers catch "minicabs," little unmarked cars that sometimes wait outside clubs (see Essentials—Getting Around). Arrange transportation in advance or acquaint yourself with the extensive network of night buses (tel. 222 1234 for information). Listings include some of the night bus routes that connect to venues outside of central London, but routes change and a quick double-check is recommended.

As always, check listings in *Time Out* and *What's On*. In addition, many record stores in Brixton and in Soho (on Berwick St.) post flyers and handbills advertising dance-club events. For more gay and lesbian entertainment, see Bisexual, Gay, and Lesbian London below.

Africa Centre, 38 King St., WC2 (tel. 836 1973). Tube: Covent Garden. On weekends, "Club Limpopo" features DJ Wala's African grooves and a live set. Used to be a Soul II Soul hangout, as mentioned on their hit from *Vol. I*. The Africa Centre is an arts center rather than a full-time club. £6-7. Open 9pm-3am.

Bar Rumba, 36 Shaftesbury Ave., W1 (tel. 287 2715). Tube: Piccadilly Circus. New Latin dance club and bar is making spicy salsa waves. Call to find out about their Latin dance sessions. £3-6. Open 10pm-3am.

The Camden Palace, 1a Camden High St. NW1 (tel. 387 0428). Tube: Camden Town. Night buses N2, N29, or N90. Enormously popular with tourists and Brits alike, especially on Wed., when "Twist and Shout," and 50s-60s music predominates. Admission £2-10. Open Tues.-Thurs. and Sat. 9pm-2:30am, Fri. 9pm-6am.

Club 414, 414 Coldharbour Ln., SW2. Tube: Brixton. Groove to melodic deep house, underground, and garage at this lesser-known dance venue. Downstairs offers laser lights; upstairs is "melo melo" chill-out floor. Usually open 10 or 11pm-6 or 7 am.

The Electric Ballroom, 184 Camden High St., NW1 (tel. 485 9006). Tube: Camden Town. Night bus N2, N29, N90, or N93. Cheap and fun. *Time Out* described Saturdays as "probably London's best rock, Gothic, and Glamour punk night." Most of the clientele here refuse to wear natural fibers. £5, members £4.

The Fridge, Town Hall Parade, Brixton Hill, SW2 (tel. 326 5100). Tube: Brixton. Night bus N2. A serious dance dive with a multi-ethnic crowd. Jazzie B from Soul II Soul got his start here and now he's back every Fri. night. Stylish 21+ crowd. Features Telly psychedelia and twisting dance cages. Immensely popular weekly "Love Muscle" every Sat. night crowds with busy mixed-gay clientele. The Fridge cools down during the summer months. Open 10pm-4 or 6 am.

The Garage, 22 Highbury Corner, N5 (tel. 607 1818). Tube: Highbury and Islington. Night bus N19, N73, N96. Local club specializing in indie rock. Saturday nights women only. £3-6. Open daily 7:30pm-2am.

Gossips, 69 Dean St., W1 (tel. 434 4480). Tube: Piccadilly Circus or Tottenham Ct. Rd. A dark basement club renowned for a wide range of great one-nighters. Anything goes, from heavy metal to ska to psychedelia to reggae. Call ahead for details; music and crowd changes on a nightly basis. Hard Club 92 (Wed.) still claims to be the place for "Euros and trendy weirdos," while the notorious Gaz's Rockin' Blues (now in its 12th year) on Thurs. is highly recommended for its ska, blues, and soul. £3-8. Open Mon.-Sat. 10pm-3:30am.

Hippodrome, Charing Cross Rd., WC2 (tel. 437 4311). Tube: Leicester Sq. Infamously enormous, expensive, loud, and tourist-ridden. Witching-hour laser shows. £6-12; leave your blue jeans and trainers behind. Open Mon.-Sat. 9pm-3:30am.

Iceni, 11 White Horse St., W1 (tel. 495 5333). Tube: Green Park. Off Curzon Street. 3 beautiful floors of deep funk entertainment. They also have board games for those who can't keep the beat. £5-8. Open Wed.-Sat. 10pm-3am.

Legends, 29 Old Burlington St., W1 (tel. 437 9933). Tube: Green Park, Piccadilly Circus, or Oxford Circus. Smart, beautiful people. Excellent one-nighters in this dark chrome-lined dance club. Wed. is swingbeat night, Thurs. is "A Brand New Kiss Night" with soul, swing, and boogie classics. £3-15. Open Wed.-Sat. 10pm-3:30am.

Maximus, 14 Leicester Sq., WC2 (tel. 734 4111). Tube: Leicester Square. On Thursdays this venue goes back to its roots as a mirrored disco for "Soul Kitchen." £5-10. Open Wed.-Thurs. 10:30pm-3am, Fri.-Sat. 10:30pm-6am, Sun. 9:30pm-3am.

Milk Bar, 12 Sutton Row, W1 (tel. 439 4655). Tube: Tottenham Ct. Rd. Opposite Astoria. Small club with weird white and silver decor. Especially popular on Wed. Crazy drag revue Fri. £4-10. Open Mon.-Sat. 10pm-3am, Sun. 7:30pm-midnight.

Ministry of Sound, 103 Gaunt St., SE1 (tel. 378 6528). Tube: Elephant & Castle. Night buses N12, N62, N65, N72, N77, N78. Oh-so-hip, oh-so-out-of-everyone's-price-range. Tight door policy keeps Hyper-Hyper in business. London's attempt to outdo New York. Hit its zenith in 1992 but still packs in the crowds. Fri. £12, Sat. £15. Open Fri. Midnight-8am, Sat. midnight-9am.

Raw, 112a Great Russell Street, WC1. Tube: Tottenham Ct. Rd. Thursday "Indie and Alternative Sounds" (they call it Cabbage Patch) play 2 dance floors. First room plays the Breeders and Lemonheads; room 2 plays old school rap. £3-5. Open 10:30pm-3am.

Subterania, 12 Acklam Rd., W10 (tel. (0181) 960 4590). Tube: Ladbroke Grove. This is where it's at—directly beneath the Westway flyover. Relaxed, multi-ethnic crowd comes to dance to wicked house and garage music. Club classics and "90s disco." Crucial on Fri. and Sat. midnight onwards. £5-8. Open daily 10pm-3am.

United Kingdom, Buckhold Rd., SW18 (tel. (0181) 877 0110. BR: Wandsworeth Town or N88 Night bus. Brand-new club far removed from the kitsch of the West End–go if you feel the need for a long trip. Euro-style techno and trance. Open Fri.-Sat. 10pm-6am. £10.

The Vox, 9 Brighton Terrace, SW9 (tel 737 2095). Tube: Brixton. Behind Red Records on Brixton Road. "Institute of Dubology" rages every Thursday night 10pm-3am with dub chemists like Rootsman and Trans-spiritual Express Iyahbingi Drummers. Most nights headline dub, techno, and psycho-trance. £3-6. Open until 3am, Fri.-Sat. until 6am.

The Wag Club, 35 Wardour St., W1 (tel. 437 5534). Tube: Piccadilly Circus. Funky multi-level complex with bars and an eatery amongst throngs of dancers in platforms. Once clubland's crowning glory, it still hosts popular one-nighters. Soul on Wed., "Progressive," garage, and house music on Thurs., hip hop/funk on Sat. Mon.-Thurs. £4-6, Fri. £8, Sat. £10. Open Mon.-Thurs. 10:30pm-3:30am, Fri.-Sat. 10:30pm-6am.

■■■ LITERARY LIFE

Bookstores, especially **Waterstone's** and **Compendium** (see Shopping—Bookstores), hold frequent readings by major authors. The Institute of Contemporary Arts (see Museums—Other Major Collections) also hosts readings. As always, check the "Books and Poetry" listings in *Time Out*.

Brixton Poets, The Prince Albert, Coldharbour Lane, SW2 (tel. 701 9608). Tube: Brixton. Chaotically poetic performance group, new members always welcome. Tues. 9pm. Free.

Circle of Consciousness, Assembly House, 292 Kentish Town Rd., NW5 (tel. 372 0418). Tube: Kentish Town. Performance poetry, with music, theater, and comedy thrown in on the side. Thurs. 8:30pm, £2.

Islington Poetry Workshop, Community Room, Gillespie Neighbourhood Office, 102 Blackstock Rd., N4 (tel. 281 2369). Tube: Finsbury Park. Warm and supportive group of writers who encourage newcomers to bring along their poetry for reading and discussion. Meetings Wed. 7:30 pm. £8, shared by all attending.

Poetry Round, Periquite Hotel, 33-44 Barkston Sq., SW5 (tel. 373 7851). Tube: Earl's Ct. Poetry workshop–bring poems and copies for readings and criticism. Mon. 8pm. £2.50, concessions £1.50.

The Poetry Society, 22 Betterton St., WC2 (tel. 240 0810). Tube: Covent Garden. Along with The Voice Box, the other main venue for readings. £4, students £3.

Terrible Beauty Workshop, Troubadour Coffee House, 265 Old Brompton Rd., SW5 (tel. 835 2282). Tube: Earl's Ct. For all kinds of poetry, including prose poems and experimental work. Established writers often present their work. £3, concessions £2.50. Meetings Mon. 8-10pm.

Vertical Images, Victoria, Mornington Place, NW1 (tel. (0181) 340 5807). Tube: Mornington Crescent. Poetry readings alternating with poetry workshops (bring copies of your poems for readings and critiques.) Sun. 8pm, Free.

The Voice Box, Level 5, Red Side, Royal Festival Hall, SE1 (tel. 921 0906). Tube: Waterloo. Frequent readings of international prose and poetry by renowned writers, plus special events and festivals. *Literature Quarterly,* their free listings brochure, has a complete schedule and useful descriptions of the readers. £2.50-£5, students £1.50-3. The **Poetry Library** (tel. 921 0943) has the largest collection of 20th-century poetry in Britain, as well as poetry magazines, audio and video recordings, and an information board where contests and workshops are posted. Open daily 1am-8pm. Membership is free (bring ID and current address).

■■■ OFFBEAT ENTERTAINMENT

London, that great cesspool into which all the loungers and idlers of the Empire are irresistibly drained.
—Sir Arthur Conan Doyle, "A Study in Scarlet"

If you've got the cash, you can indulge in luxuries like rowing boats in the pond at Regent's Park or dodging aliens in Piccadilly Circus. If you haven't, there are other options for entertainment that won't break the budget traveler's bank.

Alien War, The Trocadero, 13 Coventry St., W1 (tel. 439 1791). Tube: Piccadilly. For 20 min. of non-stop laughs interspersed with an occasional blood-curdling scream, venture through Sigourney Weaver's dreamscape space pod. For £6.95 (more fun for your money than a Leicester Square movie) you'll be led through a maze of corridors pumped thick with dry-ice by a good-looking actress or actor in futurist-army fatigues. Luckily they carry laser guns, because you will inevitably be attacked by funny people wearing replicas of the original "Alien" costume. Open daily until midnight.

City Farms: Goats, ducks, rabbits, sheep, poultry, and sometimes cattle, horses, and donkeys bleat, quack, baa, moo, and cluck for you at **Kentish Town,** Grafton Rd., NW5 (tel. 482 2681; tube: Kentish Town; open daily 9:30am-5:30pm); **Freight Liners,** Sheringham Rd., N7 (tel. 609 0467; tube: Highbury & Islington; open Tues.-Sun. 11am-5pm); **Hackney,** 1a Goldsmith's Row, E2 (tel. 729 6381; tube: Shoreditch, then bus #6, 48, or 55; open Tues.-Sun. 10am-4:30pm); **Stepping Stones,** Stepney Way, E1 (tel. 790 8204; tube: Whitechapel; open Tues.-Sun. 9:30am-6pm); and **Surrey Docks,** Rotherhithe St., SE16 (tel. 231 1010; tube: Surrey Quays; open Tues.-Sun. 10am-5pm). Call to confirm opening times. All are free.

College of London Fashion, 20 John Povices St., W1 (tel 629 9401). Tube: Oxford Circus. If you want some pampering and have a few quid and a few hours to spare, offer yourself to the students at the LCF's beauty-therapy department, where they learn how to give everything from cathiodermie to pedicures. Prices (to cover the cost of products used) start from £2.50. Open Mon.-Fri. 9am-8pm.

The College of Psychic Studies, 16 Queensberry Pl., SW7 (tel. 589 3292). Tube: South Kensington. Eager for you to become their newest subject. Unlock your true self through graphoanalysis, harness universal wisdom and release life blocks (karmic or otherwise) with regression therapy, or achieve that eternally sought-after harmony between body and spirit through aromatherapy. Open Mon.-Thurs. 10am-7:30pm, Fri. 10am-4:30pm; closed most of Aug.

Conway Hall, Red Lion Sq., WC1 (tel. 242 8032). Tube: Holborn. Spend the day of rest engaged in radical activities. Atheist lectures Sun. morning, chamber music Sun. evening. The evidence suggests that Socialists, New Agers, and other suspicious characters convene here. Free Sun. lectures at 11am, sometimes also at 6:30pm, Oct.-mid-July. Chamber music at 3pm, £3.50

The Cooltan, in the Old Dolehouse, 372 Coldharbour Lane, SW9 (tel. 737 2745). Tube: Brixton. Offers meditation classes, usually on Friday nights 7-9pm; donations accepted For information call the co-op, or contact Friends of the Western Buddhist Order (tel. 673 5570). A variety of other classes, like life-drawing, T'ai Chi Ch'uan, yoga, and drum workshops, are offered; call for details.

Daily Mail and **Evening Standard,** Northcliffe House, 2 Derry St., W8 (tel. 938 6000). Tube: High St. Kensington. See an issue of one of these tabloids in production. For information write to the Personnel Administrator, Hammondsworth Quays Ltd., Surrey Quays Rd., SE16 1PJ.

Islington Arts Factory, 2 Parkhurst Rd., N7 (tel. 607 0561). Tube: Holloway Rd. Exit left onto Holloway Rd. Turn left onto Camden Rd., which leads to the corner of Camden and Parkhurst. Music, art, and dance studios available for hire. (The Factory itself offers classes and sponsors small exhibitions; they also have a darkroom.) For £5.50 per hour (in the daytime) you can rent a music room fully equipped with a drum set, P.A., and mikes. (£3 annual membership fee required.) Open Mon.-Fri. 10am-10pm, Sat. 10am-6pm.

Porchester Baths, Queensway, W2 (tel. 792 3980 or 792 2919). Tube: Bayswater or Royal Oak. In the Porchester Centre. A Turkish bath with steam and dry heat rooms and a swimming pool. Built in 1929, the baths are an Art Deco masterpiece of gold and marble. Rates are high (3hr. £15.40), but devoted fans keep taking the plunge. Men bathe Mon., Wed., and Sat.; women bathe Tues., Thurs., and Fri. Open Mon.-Sat. 10am-10pm. Open Sun. 10am-4pm (women only), 4-10pm (mixed couples). Swimwear must be worn at all times.

Radio and TV Shows. Become part of a live studio audience. Get free tickets for the endless variations on "Master Mind." Write to the **BBC Ticket Unit,** Broadcasting House, Portland Pl., W1; **Thames TV Ticket Unit,** 306 Euston Rd., NW1; or **London Weekend Television,** Kent House, Upper Ground, SE1.

Speakers' Corner, in the northeast corner of Hyde Park. Tube: Marble Arch. Crackpots, evangelists, political activists, and more crackpots speak their minds and compete for the largest audience every Sun. 11am-dusk. (See Sights—Hyde Park.)

Vidal Sassoon School of Hairdressing, 56 Davies Mews, W1 (tel. 629 4635). Tube: Bond St. Become your own offbeat entertainment. Cuts, perms, and color at the hand of a Sassoony. Cut and blow dry £8.50, with student ID £4.50. All-over tint £10.50. Make sure you have about 3hrs. to spare. Open Mon.-Fri. 10am-3pm.

■■■ SPORTS

SPECTATOR SPORTS

Association Football

Many evils may arise which God forbid.
—King Edward II, banning football in London, 1314

Football (soccer) draws huge crowds—over half a million people attend professional matches in Britain every Saturday. Each club's fans dress with fierce loyalty in team colors, and make themselves heard with uncanny synchronized cheering. Mass violence and vandalism at stadiums has dogged the game for years. Ninety-five people were crushed to death in Sheffield in 1989 after a surge of fans tried to push their way into the grounds. Matters have improved; still, visitors may feel more comfortable buying a seat rather than standing on "the terraces."

The season runs from mid-August to May. Most games take place on Saturday, kicking off at 3pm. Allow time to wander through the crowds milling around the stadium. London has been blessed with 13 of the 92 professional teams in England. The big two are **Arsenal,** Highbury, Avenell Rd., N5 (tel. 359 0131; tube: Arsenal) and **Tottenham Hotspur,** 78 High Rd., W17 (tel. (0181) 808 3030; BR: White Hart

Lane). But the football scene is very partisan and favorites vary from neighborhood to neighborhood. Tickets are available in advance from each club's box office; many now have a credit card telephone booking system. Seats cost £10-23. England plays occasional international matches at Wembley Stadium, usually on Wednesday evenings (tel. (0181) 900 1234; tube: Wembley Park).

Rugby

The game was spontaneously created when a Rugby College student picked up a soccer ball and ran it into the goal. Rugby has since evolved into a complex and subtle game. **Rugby League,** a professional sport played by teams of 13, has traditionally been a northern game. The only London side is **Fulham,** Crystal Palace National Sports Centre, SE19 (tel. (0181) 778 0131; BR: Crystal Palace). Wembley Stadium (tel. (0181) 902 8833) stages some of the championship matches in May. A random *mêlée* of blood, mud, and drinking songs, "rugger" can be incomprehensible to the outsider, yet aesthetically exciting nonetheless. The season runs from September to April. The most significant contests, including the Oxford vs. Cambridge varsity match in December and the springtime five nations championship (featuring England, Scotland, Wales, Ireland, and France) are played at **Twickenham** (tel. (0181) 892 8161; BR: Twickenham). First-rate games can be seen in relaxed surroundings at one of London's premiere clubs such as **Saracens,** Dale Green Rd., N14 (tel. (0181) 449 3770; tube: Oakwood), and **Rosslyn Park,** Priory La., Upper Richmond Rd., SW15 (tel. (0181) 876 1879; BR: Barnes).

Cricket

Cricket remains a confusing spectacle to most North Americans. The impossibility of explaining its rules to an American has virtually become a national in-joke in England. Once a synonym for civility, cricket's image has been dulled. The much-used phrase, "It's just not cricket," has recently taken on an ironic edge. While purists disdain one-day matches, novices find these the most exciting. "First class" matches amble on rather ambiguously for days, often ending in "draws." .

London's two grounds stage both county and international matches. **Lord's,** St. John's Wood Rd., NW8 (tel. 289 1615; tube: St. John's Wood), is *the* cricket ground, home turf of the Marylebone Cricket Club, the established governing body of cricket. Archaic stuffiness pervades the MCC; women have yet to see the inside of its pavilion. **Middlesex** plays its games here (tickets £6-7). Tickets to international matches cost £15-40 (booking essential). The **Oval,** Kennington, SE11 (tel. 582 6660; tube: Oval), home to **Surrey** cricket club (tickets £7), also fields Test Matches (tickets for internationals £15-40; book ahead).

Rowing

The **Henley Royal Regatta,** the most famous annual crew race in the world, conducts itself both as a proper hobnob social affair (like Ascot) and as a popular corporate social event (like Wimbledon). The rowing is graceful, though laypeople are often unable to figure out what on earth is going on. The event transpires on the last weekend in June and the first in July. Saturday is the most popular and busiest day, but some of the best races are the finals on Sunday. Public enclosure tickets (£4 for the first two days, £5 for the last three) are available by the river (the side opposite the station) or write to the Secretary's Office, Regatta Headquarters, Henley-on-Thames, Oxfordshire, England RG9 2LY (tel. (01491) 572 153). Take BR from Paddington to Henley, or Green Line coach #390 from Victoria (1½hr., day return £7).

The **Boat Race,** between eights from Oxford and Cambridge Universities, enacts the traditional rivalry between the schools. The course runs from Putney to Mortlake on a Saturday in late March or early April. Old-money alums, fortified by strawberries and champagne, sport their crested blazers and college ties to cheer the teams on. Bumptious crowds line the Thames and fill the pubs (tube: Putney Bridge or Hammersmith; BR: Barnes Bridge or Mortlake). Call (0181) 748 3632 for more information.

Tennis

For two weeks starting in late June, tennis buffs all over the world focus their attention on **Wimbledon.** If you want to get in, arrive early—9am the first week, 6am the second; the gate opens at 10:30am (get off the tube at Southfields or take one of the buses from central London which run frequently during the season). Entrance to the grounds (including lesser matches) costs £5-7, less after 5pm. If you arrive in the queue early enough, you can buy one of the few show court tickets that were not sold months before. Depending on the day, center court tickets cost £10-30, court 1 tickets £9-24. Other show courts (courts #2, 3, 13, 14), where top players play their early rounds, cost £6-16. Other courts have first-come, first-served seats or standing room only. Get a copy of the order of play on each court, printed in most newspapers. If you fail to get center or court 1 tickets in the morning, try to find the resale booth (usually in Aorangi Park), which sells tickets handed in by those who leave early (open from 2:30pm; tickets only £2). Also, on the first Saturday of the 1992 championships, several hundred extra center court tickets were put up for sale; a new "tradition" that has since continued. Call (0181) 944 1066 for recorded information during the tournament.

For details of the 1995 championships call the All England Club (tel. (0181) 946 2244) or send a self-addressed stamped envelope between August 1 and December 31, 1994 to **The All England Lawn Tennis and Croquet Club,** P.O. Box 98, Church Rd., Wimbledon SW19 5AE. Topspin lob fans mustn't miss the **Wimbledon Lawn Tennis Museum** (tel. (0181) 946 6131), located right on the grounds (open Tues.-Sat. 11am-5pm, Sun. 2-5pm; call ahead to check near tournament time).

Horses

The **Royal Gold Cup Meeting** at **Ascot** takes place each summer in mid-June. An "important" society event, it is essentially an excuse for Brits of all strata to indulge in the twin pastimes of drinking and gambling while wearing silly hats. The Queen takes up residence at Windsor Castle in order to lavish her full attentions on this socio-political vaudeville act. (The enclosure is open only by invitation; grandstand tickets £8.50-20, Silver Ring £3; tel. (01344) 222 11). In July, the popular George VI and Queen Elizabeth Diamond Stakes are run here, and during the winter Ascot hosts excellent steeplechase meetings (BR from Waterloo to Ascot). Top hats, gypsies, and Pimms also distinguish the **Derby** ("darby"), run in early June at **Epsom** Racecourse, Epsom, Surrey (tel. (01372) 726 311; grandstand tickets £9-20). More accessible, less expensive summer evening races are run at **Windsor,** the racecourse, Berkshire (tel. (01753) 865 234; BR: Windsor Riverside; admission to tattersalls and paddock £10), and **Kempton Park Racecourse,** Sunbury-on-Thames (tel. (01932) 782 292; BR: Kempton Park; admission to grandstand £13, Silver Ring £4).

In late June, **polo** aficionados flock to the **Royal Windsor Cup,** The Guards Polo Club, Smiths Lawn, Windsor Great Park (tel. (01784) 437 797; BR: Windsor & Eton Central; admission £15 per car). You can stand on the "wrong" side of the field for free, or hobnob in the clubhouse for a £10 day membership.

Greyhound Racing

Greyhound racing—a.k.a. "the dogs"—is the second most popular spectator sport in Britain, after football. It's a quick and easy way to lose money—races last all of 20 seconds. Almost all races start at 7:30pm. Races are held year-round at **Hackney** and **Wimbledon Stadiums, Walthamstow** (tel. (0181) 531 4255), and **Wembley** (tel. (0181) 902 8833). In late June, Wimbledon hosts the **Greyhound Derby,** nephew to its horseracing uncle (tel. (0181) 946 5361). Admission for most races starts at £2.50.

PARTICIPATORY SPORTS

Time Out's Guide to Sport, Health, & Fitness (£5.50) can give you more complete information on the sports listed below and many others. For general fitness during your visit, **London Central YMCA,** 112 Great Russell St., WC1 (tel. 637 8131; tube:

Tottenham Ct. Rd.), has a pool, gym, weights, and offers weekly membership for £27, off-peak weekly membership (use after 4pm prohibited) £20 (open Mon.-Fri. 8am-10pm, Sat.-Sun. 10am-10pm). **The Sportsline** answers queries on a vast range of clubs and locations (tel. 222 8000; Mon.-Fri. 10am-6pm).

Swimming

Dive into the **Britannia Leisure Centre,** 40 Hyde Rd., N1 (tel. 729 4485; tube: Old Street), an unashamedly sensational aquatic playground replete with a towering flume, fountains, and monstrous inflatables (open Mon.-Fri. 9am-10pm, Sat.-Sun. 9am-6pm; admission £2.25). Outdoor bathers may prefer the popular **Serpentine Lido** (tel. 724 3104; tube: Knightsbridge), a chlorinated lake in Hyde Park with surprisingly luxurious changing rooms and a kiddie pool and sandpit for children (open May-Sept. daily 9am-5pm; admission £3, deck chairs 50p). Indoorsy types might take shelter in the beautiful Edwardian **Chelsea Sports Centre,** Chelsea Manor St., SW3 (tel. 352 6985; tube: Sloane Sq.) or lounge in their adjacent solarium (open Mon.-Fri. 7:30am-10pm, Sat. 8am-5pm and 6-10pm, Sun. 8am-6:30pm; last entry 5:45pm; admission £1.80, children 66p). The pool at the **University of London Union,** 1 Malet St., WC1, is closer to the center of town; you don't usually need a UL ID (open during term-time Mon.-Fri. 9:30am-7pm, Sat. 9:30am-4pm, Sun. [women only] 1-5pm; admission 80p). The centrally located **Oasis Baths,** 32 Endell St., WC2 (tel. 831 1804; tube: Covent Garden or Holborn), possess an outdoor pool as well as an indoor pool that churns to the beat of nightly aqua aerobics classes (open Mon.-Fri. 7:30am-8pm, Sat.-Sun. 9:30am-5pm; admission £2.30, children 75p).

Tennis

If you weren't wild-carded for Wimbledon, London does have alternatives. Private tennis clubs offer the plushest facilities, but are expensive and often require you to be the guest of a member. **Public courts** vary in quality; all cost about £3-5 per hour. You'll have to call ahead and book three days in advance. Hard courts include **Battersea Park** (tel. (0181) 871 7542; BR: Battersea Park); **Holland Park** (tel. 262 5484; tube: South Kensington); **Lincoln's Inn Fields** (tel. 405 5194; tube: Holborn); **Parliament Hill,** Hampstead Heath (tel. 485 4491; BR: Gospel Oak); and **Regent's Park** (tel. 935 5729; tube: Regent's Park).

Squash

While London is honeycombed with squash courts, the vast majority reside within private health and racquet clubs that charge £200-400 for an annual membership plus steep hourly court fees. Visitors and casual players can, however, use the courts maintained by the city's numerous sports centers on a "pay as you play" basis; most charge around £6 per hr. plus around 70p for equipment rental. The **Chelsea Sports Centre,** Chelsea Manor St., SW3 (tel. 352 6985); the **Queen Mother's Sports Centre,** 223 Vauxhall St., SW1 (tel. 798 2125); the **Sobell Sports Centre,** Homsey Rd., N7 (tel. 609 2166); and the **Saddlers Sports Centre,** Goswell Rd., EC1 (tel. 253 9285) are all reasonably priced, centrally located, and open to the public. (For details see Health and Fitness Centres below.)

Basketball

Basketball in England remains very much an American game. Competition takes place only at a club level. Playoffs take place at the **Crystal Palace National Sport Centre** (tel. (0181) 778 0131; BR: Crystal Palace). The **English Basketball Association** (Calomax House, Lupton Ave., Leeds, W. Yorks.; tel. (01532) 496 044) can direct you to the club in your area or tell you where to find a court. National League games are played every Saturday and Sunday. The **London Jets** play at the Sedwick Centre (tel. 481 5123) near Aldgate East tube station, while the **Brixton Topcats** play at the Brixton Recreation Centre, Station Rd., SW9 (tel. 274 7774). Tube: Brixton. Call to see if you can join in a pick-up game.

Cycling

Traffic and pollution interfere with the art of cycling during the day. Setting out for a late-night ride is probably your best bet for a jaunt within the city. The Mall makes a great late-night criterion track. Cycling on Sundays can be more tolerable (especially in the weekend wasteland of the City), but still requires a good deal of care and skill.

On Your Bike, 52 Tooley St. (tel. 378 6669; tube : London Bridge), rents bikes by the day, weekend, or week. **Brixton Cycles Co-op,** 435-37 Coldharbour Ln. (tel. 733-6055; tube: Brixton), is a friendly mountain bike mecca. If you just want to get a cheap bike fixed, go to **Bike Peddlers,** 50 Calthorpe St., WC1 (tel. 278 0551; tube: Russell Sq.), for friendly service and an inexpensive repair . Most bike rental shops also rent locks, "green screens" (anti-pollution face masks), water bottles, and reflector lights. **Bike Events** (tel. (01225) 310 859) has information on bikeathons and charity races that cycling enthusiasts can participate in.

Health and Fitness Centers

London is blessed with over 200 public sports and fitness centers. The few listed below are some of the most central and comprehensive; consult the yellow pages under "Leisure Centers" for more exhaustive listings, or call the local borough council for a list of centers near you.

Chelsea Sports Centre, Chelsea Manor St., SW3 (tel. 352 6985). Tube: Sloane Sq. or South Kensington. Activities: aerobics, badminton, basketball, bowls, canoeing, dance, football, lacrosse, martial arts, racquetball, roller skating, squash, swimming, tennis, volleyball, weight training, and yoga. Special facilities: sauna, solarium, and spa baths. No membership or admission charge. Gym card £6 annually for use of weights, or pay each time. Activities £1.80-3.60. Open Mon.-Fri. 7:30am-10pm, Sat. 8am-10pm, Sun. 8am-6:30pm.

Jubilee Hall Recreation Centre, Tavistock St., WC2 (tel. 836 4835), on the south side of Covent Garden. Tube: Covent Garden. Regular classes and activities include weight lifting, yoga, martial arts, gymnastics, dance, badminton, and aerobics. Special facilities include a sauna, solarium, and an alternative sports medicine clinic. Crowded with West End office workers at lunchtime. Annual membership £50. Admission free to members; £1.50 for nonmembers plus £2.50-3.50 for activities. Open Mon.-Fri. 7:30am-10pm, Sat.-Sun. 10am-5pm.

Queen Mother Sports Centre, 223 Vauxhall Bridge Rd., SW1 (tel. 798 2125). Tube: Victoria. Activities: aerobics, badminton, basketball, bowls, canoeing, diving, gymnastics, judo, other martial arts, racquetball, squash, swimming, trampolining, volleyball, and weight lifting. Special facilities: solarium, café, and bar. Equipment rental. Activities £2-5.50 per hour, but membership (£20.30 per year) required for anything but the pool. Open Mon.-Fri. 7:30am-10pm, Sat. 8am-6pm, Sun. 9am-6pm.

Saddlers Sports Centre, Goswell Rd., EC1 (tel. 253 9285). Tube: Barbican. Activities: aerobics, badminton, basketball, body conditioning, canoeing, cricket, fencing, racquetball, squash, swimming, tennis, volleyball, weight training, and yoga. Special facilities: sauna and solarium. 50m pool with 5 lanes. Young, casual clientele. No membership or admission charge. Activities £1.25-4. Open Mon., Wed., and Fri. 7:30am-9pm, Tues. and Thurs. 9am-9pm.

▪ Shopping

London does sell more than royal commemorative mugs and plastic police helmets.

For department stores and fashion outlets, try Oxford St., Knightsbridge, and Kensington; for expensive designer goods, Sloane St., Bond St., and Regent St.; for hip young clothes, Oxford Circus, Covent Garden, Kensington, and Camden; and for specialty stores, Bloomsbury and Covent Garden. London Transport's handy *Shoppers' Bus Wheel* instructs Routemaster shoppers on the routes between shopping areas (available free from any London Transport Information Centre). *Nicholson's Shopping Guide and Streetfinder* (£2.95) should suit bargain hunters seeking further guidance. Serious shoppers should read *Time Out's* massive *Directory to London's Shops and Services* (£6) cover to cover.

Prices descend during sale seasons in July and January. *Time Out*'s "Sell Out" section has listings of stores having sales. Tourists who have purchased anything over £50 should ask about getting a refund on the 17.5% VAT, although most shops have a VAT minimum. Another option is to save receipts and obtain a refund at the airport—be warned, the commission charged is not small. Many shops stay open late on Thursday. Many stores may be closed on Sunday.

■■■ DEPARTMENT STORES

Debenham's, 334 Oxford St. (tel. 580 3000). Tube: Oxford Circus. A bit more staid than Selfridges, but cheap. Open Mon.-Tues. 9am-6pm, Wed.-Fri. 9am-8pm, Sat. 9am-7pm.

Fenwick's, 63 New Bond St., W1 (tel. 629 9161). Tube: Bond St. Slightly more upmarket than John Lewis. Open Mon.-Sat. 9:30am-6pm, Thurs. 9:30am-7:30pm.

Fortnum & Mason, 181 Piccadilly, W1 (tel. 734 8040). Tube: Green Park or Piccadilly Circus. Liveried clerks serve expensive foods in red-carpeted and chandeliered halls at this renowned establishment. Queen Victoria naturally turned to Fortnum & Mason when she wanted to send Florence Nightingale 250 lbs. of beef tea for the Crimean field hospitals. Visit the costly but satisfying tea shop, or splurge on an ice cream sundae. Open Mon.-Sat. 9:30am-6pm.

Harrods, on Brompton Rd., near tube (tel. 730 1234). Tube: Knightsbridge. Their humble motto *Omnia Omnibus Ubique* ("All things for all people, everywhere") says it all. They can do everything from finding you a live rhinoceros to arranging your funeral. They stock more than 450 kinds of cheese, and pour an elegant afternoon tea. Open Mon., Tues., and Sat. 10am-6pm, Wed.-Fri. 10am-7pm.

John Lewis, off Oxford Circus (tel. 629 7711). A giant emporium worth visiting. Its sister shop, **Peter Jones** on Sloane Sq. (tel. 730 3434; tube: Sloane Sq.) is equally wide-ranging. Lewis has a price guarantee similar to Selfridges's. Both open Mon.-Wed. and Fri.-Sat. 9am-5:30pm, Thurs. 9:30am-8pm.

Liberty of London, south of Oxford Circus on Regent St. (tel. 734 1234). Tube: Oxford Circus. A prime exponent of the 19th-century arts and crafts movement, this is the home of the famous Liberty prints, found in every form from entire bolts of fabric to silk ties. The faux-Tudor building also houses a large variety of Eastern imports. Open Mon.-Tues. and Fri.-Sat. 9:30am-6pm, Wed. 10am-6pm, Thurs. 9:30am-7:30pm.

Marks & Spencer, near Bond St., Marble Arch, and High St. Kensington tube stations, as well as others across London (tel. 935 7954). Also known as Marks and Sparks. Sells British staples in a classy but value-conscious manner. The clothes err on the side of frumpy. Everyone British, including Margaret Thatcher, buys her underwear here. Open Mon.-Wed. and Sat. 9am-7pm, Thurs.-Fri. 9am-8pm. Hours vary slightly in more far-flung regions.

Selfridges, near the Bond St. tube station on Oxford St. (tel. 629 1234). An enormous pseudo-Renaissance building with a vast array of fashions, homewares, and foods. They'll refund the difference on any item found for less elsewhere. Open Mon.-Wed. and Fri.-Sat. 9:30am-7pm, Thurs. 9:30am-8pm.

■■■ CLOTHING

Clothing stores are clustered about several main shopping areas in London, making it easy to wander and browse. Kensington High St. has mid-range, popular chains, as does the length of Oxford St. Around the Bond St. tube station, Oxford St. becomes posher; here, Bond St. and South Molton St. are the main avenues. The streets around Covent Garden (Long Acre, Neal St.) are a mixture of mid-range and designer boutiques, with hip fashions and lots of shoestores. In Knightsbridge, on Brompton Rd. and Sloane St. (which extends all the way to Sloane Sq.), you'll find ritzy couture and designer stores. King's Rd. in Chelsea, once a haven for stylish, trendy clothes, is fading fast.

The cheapest and best array of second-hand and vintage clothes is at the stalls of Camden Market and Portobello Rd. (see Street Markets). Used-clothing stores include:

Accupuncture, 3 Tisbury Ct., W1 (tel. 437 4974), off of Wardour St., next to Village Soho. Tube: Piccadilly Circus. A tiny, hard-to-find, anarchically packed shop known for its vintage racks, 70s and 80s fashion gems, the occasional contemporary Westwood outfit and, crucial to the contemporary fashion scene, Adidas. Open Mon.-Sat. 11am-8pm.

American Classics, 20 Endell St., WC2 (tel. 831 1210). Tube: Covent Garden. Also at 400-404 King's Rd., SW10 (tel. 351 5229). Tube: Sloane Sq., then bus #11. Mostly denim and men's shirts and jackets. Open Mon.-Sat. 10am-6:30pm, Sun. noon-5pm.

Bluebird Garage, 350 King's Rd., SW3 (tel. 352 7215). Tube: Sloane Sq., then bus #11. More new than second-hand stalls; all sell hip and clubby garb. Stüssy and Jr. Gaultier are here. Open Mon.-Fri. 10am-6pm, Sat. 10am-6:30pm.

Cornucopia, 12 Upper Tachbrook St., SW1 (tel. 828 5752). Tube: Victoria. Also at 51 Chelsea Manor St., SW3 (tel. 352 7403), off King's Rd. Tube: Sloane Sq., then bus #11. The grande dame of period clothing shops, selling women's attire from 1910-1960. 1920s ball gowns start at £20. Open Mon.-Sat. 11am-6pm.

Flip, 125 Long Acre, WC2 (tel. 836 7044). Tube: Covent Garden. Dozens of 50s and 60s blouses and sweaters, plus the usual jeans and menswear. Open Mon.-Wed. and Fri.-Sat. 10am-7pm, Thurs. 10am-8pm, Sun. noon-6pm.

The Frock Exchange, 450 Fulham Rd., SW6 (tel. 381 2937). Tube: Fulham Broadway. Second-hand designer-wear in excellent condition. Open Mon.-Sat. 10am-5:30pm, in summer 10:30am-5pm.

Kensington Market, 49-53 Kensington High St., W8 (tel. 938 4343). Tube: High St. Kensington. Reasonable prices for used clothes and shoes, with a good selection of whatever's trendy at the moment, plus cheap denim and leather. Also new clubwear and accessories. Zandra Rhodes had a stall here in the 60s. Open Mon.-Sat. 10am-6pm.

Radio Days, 87 Lower Marsh, SE1 (tel. 928 0800). Tube: Waterloo. Fantastic selection of collectibles and memorabilia from the 1920s-1960s. Dresses, books, valises, and classic traveling trunks. Open Mon.-Fri. 10:30am-5pm, Sat. 11am-4pm, or by appointment.

"High street" fashion is what the British call trendy mainstream young clothes at reasonable prices sold in a number of chainstores and department stores.

Knickerbox, 93Oxford St., W1 (tel.287 0819). Tube: Bond St. Also at 9 Kensington Arc, W8; 28 Sloane St., SW1; and in most malls and tube station arcades. Reasonably priced lingerie, bodysuits, and even swimwear in natural fibers. Open daily 9am-7pm, Thurs. 9am-8pm.

Kookai, 360 Oxford St., W1 (tel. 499 4564). Tube: Bond St. Also at 123d Kensington High St., W8; 27a Sloane Sq., King's Rd., SW1; 5 Brompton Rd., SW3 (tube:

Knightsbridge). Not "high street" exactly—similar to Warehouse, but with a more designer feel and higher prices. Hip yet elegant. Open Mon.-Wed. and Fri.-Sat. 10am-7pm, Thurs. 10am-8pm.

Next, 189 and 327 Oxford St., W1 (tel. 494 3646). Tube: Oxford Circus and Bond St. Also at 54 Kensington High St., W8; 20 Long Acre, WC2; 13 King's Rd., SW3; 33 Brompton Rd., SW3 (tube: Knightsbridge); and in the Victoria Place mall. A sort of cross between The Limited and J. Crew—casual clothes for a wide range of ages. Open Mon.-Wed. and Fri.-Sat. 10am-6pm, Thurs. 10am-7:30pm.

Top Shop/Top Man, 214 Oxford St., W1 (tel. 636 7700). Tube: Oxford Circus. Also at 60-64 The Strand, WC2 (tube: Charing Cross), off Trafalgar Sq. Multi-story megastore with the trendiest of inexpensive fashions for men and women (in the basement), with something to suit every taste. The basement also carries other interesting labels and shoes. Open Mon.-Wed. and Fri.-Sat. 10am-6:30pm, Thurs. 10am-8pm.

Warehouse, 116 and 333 Oxford St., W1 (tel. 436 4179). Tube: Oxford Circus and Bond St. Also at 24 Long Acre, WC2 (tube: Covent Garden); Kensington High St., W8; 96 King's Rd., SW3. Slightly more alternative and more upmarket than Top Shop. Open Mon.-Wed. and Fri.-Sat. 10am-6pm, Thurs. 10am-7pm.

Devout shoppers come to London for shoes, where they find the coolest soles at decent prices. Especially important: Doc Martens are significantly cheaper in the U.K., where they're manufactured.

Dolci's, 82-4 and 181 and 333 Oxford St., W1 (tel. 580 1346). Tube: Tottenham Ct. Rd., Oxford Circus, and Bond St. Also at 40 Kensington High St., W8. Just as hip as Shelly's, but also stocks more conventional styles, foul-weather footwear, and dressy pumps. Cheaper too. Open Mon.-Wed. and Fri.-Sat. 10am-6:30pm, Thurs. 10am-7:30pm.

Office, 43 Kensington High St., W8 (tel. 937 7022). Tube: High St. Kensington. Also at 60 Neal St., WC2; 59 So. Molton St., W1 (tube: Bond St.); 221 Camden High St., NW1. Ultra-trendy mid-range chain patronized by chic black-clad types. Open Mon.-Sat. 9:30am-6:30pm.

Red or Dead, 36 Kensington High St., W8 (tel. 937 3137). Tube: High St. Kensington. Also at 33 Neal St., WC2; 186 Camden High St., NW1. They were hawking platforms long before the 70s revival. Not for budgeteers. Open Mon.-Fri. 10:30am-7:30pm, Sat. 10am-7pm, Sun 12:30-7pm

Shelly's, 159 Oxford St., W1 (tel. 437 5842). Tube: Oxford Circus. Also at 14 Neal St., WC2; 40 Kensington High St., W8; 124b King's Rd., SW3. The latest in shoes, and every style of Doc Martens in existence. Open Mon.-Wed. and Fri.-Sat. 9:30am-6:30pm, Thurs. 9:30am-8pm.

Some of the better-known British fashion designers and their ateliers:

Hyper-Hyper, 26-40 Kensington High St., W8 (tel. 938 4343). Tube: High St. Kensington. A mall of small boutiques exhibiting the work of more than 70 young British designers. Garments sold here have appeared in the pages of *Vogue* and *Elle*. The staff is so icy that the store needs no air-conditioning. Open Mon.-Wed. and Fri.-Sat. 10am-6pm, Thurs. 10am-7pm.

Maribov, 55 Pembridge Rd., W11 (tel. 727 1166). Tube: Notting Hill Gate. Owner Ginny makes each intricate piece of clothing by hand. Consequently, these one-of-a-kind clothes are a bit pricey. Exotica like velvet capes, tops made from vintage scarves, and chiffon tail-coats are par for the course at this unique boutique. Open Mon.-Sat. 10am-6pm. AmEx, MC, Visa.

Rifat Ozbek, 18 Haunch of Venison Yard, rear of 105 New Bond St., W1 (tel. 408 0625). Tube: Bond St. Former media darling who borrows from various ethnic costumes. Open Mon.-Sat. 10am-6pm.

Paul Smith, 23 Avery Row, W1 (tel. 493 1287), off of Brook St. Tube: Bond St. The seconds and out-of-season outlet for the witty yet elegant menswear store. Emphasis here tends towards stylish casual wear, with savings of up to 50% off regular retail prices. Open Mon.-Wed. and Fri.-Sat. 10:30am-6:30pm, Thurs. 10:30am-7pm.

Vivienne Westwood, 6 Davies St., W1 (tel. 629 3757). Tube: Bond St. Brilliantly radical, although more staid of late. Open Mon.-Wed. and Fri.-Sat. 10:30am-6pm, Thurs. 10:30am-7pm. Also an **outlet** at 40-41 Conduit St., W1 (tel 439 1109; tube: Oxford Circus). Save 30%on "used" ("used" meaing that they've been worn for shoots or down a catwalk) samples. Save as much as 75% on items from last year's collection. Open Mon.-Sat. 10:30am-6pm.

■■■ BOOKSTORES

In London, even the chain bookstores are wonders. An exhaustive selection of bookshops lines Charing Cross Rd. between Tottenham Ct. Rd. and Leicester Sq. and many vend secondhand paperbacks. Cecil Ct., near Leicester Sq., is a treasure trove of tiny shops. Establishments along Great Russell St. stock esoteric and specialized books on any subject from Adorno to the Zohar. The best places to look for maps and travel books are **Stanford's,** 12 Long Acre (tel. 836 1321; tube: Covent Garden; open Mon. and Sat. 10am-6pm, Tues.-Wed. and Fri. 9am-6pm, Thurs. 9am-7pm) and the **Travellers' Bookshop,** 25 Cecil Ct., WC2 (tel. 836 9132; tube: Leicester Sq.; open Mon.-Fri. 11am-7pm, Sat. 11am-6:30pm); also try Harrods and the YHA shop (see Specialty Shops below).

Bell, Book and Radmall, 4 Cecil Ct., WC2 (tel. 240 2161). Tube: Leicester Sq. A small antiquarian bookstore with a zippy staff, an exceptional selection of American and British first editions, and an impressive supply of sci-fi and detective novels. Fascinating original illustrations line the staircase (for sale, but forget it). Open Mon.-Fri. 10am-5:30pm, Sat. 11am-4pm.

Bookmongers, 439 Coldharbour La., SW9 (tel. 738 4225). Tube: Brixton. A second-hand bookstore with a healthy selection of works by African and Caribbean authors. Significant gay and lesbian novels section, and a section of modern classics by women authors. Open Mon.-Sat. 10:30am-6:30pm. No credit cards.

Compendium, 234 Camden High St., NW1 (tel. 485 8944). Tube: Camden Town. A good general selection, but specializes in postmodern literature, the left, occult, and all-around avant garde. Open Mon.-Sat. 10am-6pm, Sun. noon-6pm.

Dillons, 82 Gower St., WC1 (tel. 636 1577), near University of London. Tube: Goodge St. Also on The Strand near Trafalgar Square. The most graceful bookstore in London. Easier to navigate and about as complete as Foyles. Strong on academics, particularly history and politics. Fair selection of reduced-price and secondhand books, plus classical CDs and tapes. Open Mon.-Fri. 9:30am-7pm, Sat. 9:30am-6pm.Trafalgar Square branch open Mon.-Sat. 9:30am-9pm.

Foyles, 119 Charing Cross Rd., WC1 (tel. 437 5660). Tube: Tottenham Ct. Rd. or Leicester Sq. A giant warehouse of books—you'll get lost without a staffer's help. Open Mon.-Sat. 9am-6pm, Thurs. 9am-7pm.

Hatchards, 187 Piccadilly, W1 (tel. 437 3924). Tube: Green Park. Oldest and most comprehensive of London's bookstores, recently expanded. Come in for 10min., stay for 2hrs. Also at 150 King's Rd. (tel. 351 7649); 390 The Strand (tel. 379 6264); 63 Kensington High St., (tel. 937 0858); and Harvey Nichols in Knightsbridge (tel. 235 5000). Open Mon.-Fri. 9am-6pm, Sat. 9am-5pm.

Maggs Brothers Ltd., 50 Berkeley Sq., W1 (tel. 493 7160). Tube: Green Park. A bibliophile's paradise housed in a haunted (so the story goes) 18th-century mansion. Tremendous selection of 19th-century travel narratives, illuminated manuscripts, militaria, orientalia, maps, and autographs. Open Mon.-Fri. 9:30am-5:30pm.

National Theatre Bookshop, South Bank Centre, SE1. Tube: Waterloo, or Embankment and cross Hungerford footbridge. The widest selection in London for plays and books about theatre.

Pleasures of Past Times, 11 Cecil Ct., WC2 (tel. 836 1142). Tube: Leicester Sq. A friendly, fascinating shop crammed with the stuff of youthful enchantment: early children's books with exquisite color plates and engravings, adventure stories, fairy tales, antique postcards, Victorian valentines, and other vintage juvenalia. Open Mon.-Fri. 11am-2:30pm and 3:30-5:45pm.

Puffin Bookshop, The Market, Covent Garden (tel. 379 6465). A child and parents' delight. Open Mon.-Sat. 10am-8pm, Sun. noon-6pm.

Samuel French's, 52 Fitzroy St., W1 (tel. 387 9373). Theatre and opera books. Open Mon.-Fri. 9:30am-5:30pm.

Skoob Books, 15-17 Sicilian Ave., Southampton Row and Vernon Pl., WC1 (tel. 405 0030). Tube: Holborn. The best used bookstore in Bloomsbury; academic and general interest. Students receive a 10% discount. Open Mon.-Sat. 10:30am-6:30pm. AmEx, MC, Visa.

Southeran's of Sackville Street, 2-5 Sackville St., W1 (tel. 439 6151). Tube: Piccadilly Circus. Founded in 1815, Southeran's has established itself as an institution of literary London. Dickens frequented these unnervingly silent stacks, and the firm handled the sale of his library after his death in 1870. Strong departments include architecture and literary first editions. If you want to know how people traveled before the *Let's Go* era, check out their antiquarian travel narratives. Open Mon.-Fri. 9:30am-6pm, Sat. 10am-4pm.

Thomas Heneage & Co., 42 Duke St., SW1 (tel. 930 9223). Tube: Green Park. A truly outstanding collection of art books. Close to Christie's. Open Mon.-Fri. 10am-6pm.

Vintage Magazine Market, on the corner of Brewer and Great Windmill St. near Piccadilly Circus (tel. 439 8525). 50s magazines and film posters clutter this store. Open Mon.-Sat. 10am-7pm, Sun. 1-8pm.

Waterstone's, 121-125 Charing Cross Rd., WC1 (tel. 434 4291), next door to Foyles. Tube: Leicester Sq. A great many reliable branches, including 193 Kensington High St., W8 (tel. 937 8432); 99 Old Brompton Rd., SW7 (tel. 581 8523); 266 Earls Ct. Rd., SW5 (tel. 370 1616); 128 Camden High St., NW1 (tel. 284 4948). An extensive selection of paperbacks; calmer and friendlier than its neighbor, though also a little cramped. They mail books to the U.S. (open Mon. and Wed.-Fri. 9:30am-8pm, Tues. 10am-8pm, Sat. 9:30am-6pm, Sun. 11am-6pm; Kensington High St. open until 10pm Mon.-Fri.)

Zwemmers, 80 Charing Cross Rd., WC2 (tel. 379 7886). A three-store artbook empire. The Charing Cross branch specialized in photography and media. The 24 Litchfield St., WC2 branch focuses on fine and decorative arts and architecture. At 28 Denmark St., WC2, the emphasis is on Eastern European art (a small photography gallery hides away upstairs.) Open Mon.-Fri. 9:30am-6pm, Sat. 10am-6pm.

Alternative bookshops infiltrate the city:

Books for a Change, 52 Charing Cross Rd., WC2 (tel. 836 2315). Tube: Charing Cross. A bookstore and information centre jointly sponsored by the Campaign for Nuclear Disarmament, Friends of the Earth, the UN Association, and War on Want. The small fiction section is overshadowed by the surrounding sections focusing on green issues, third world development, and New Age health. Also stocks shirts and postcards. Open Mon-Fri. 10am-6:30pm, Sat. 10am-6pm.

Gay's the Word, 66 Marchmont St., WC1 (tel. 278 7654). Tube: Russell Sq. At Gay's the Word, well, gay's the word. Open Mon.-Fri. 11am-7pm, Sat. 10am-6pm, Sun. 2-6pm.

Kilburn Book Shop, 8 Kilburn Bridge, Kilburn High Rd., NW6 (tel. 328 7071). Tube: Kilburn. Features politically correct reading material. Open Mon.-Sat. 9:30am-5:30pm.

Silver Moon, 68 Charing Cross Rd., WC2 (tel. 836 7906). Tube: Leicester Sq. A radical feminist bookstore. An exhaustive selection of books by and about women, the largest lesbian department in Britain, and a complete stock of all Virago books in print. Open Mon.-Wed. and Fri. 10:30am-6:30pm, Thurs. 10:30am-8pm, Sat. 10am-6:30pm.

Timbuktu Bookshop, in the Black Cultural Archives, 378 Coldharbour Ln, SW9 (tel. 737 2770). Tube: Brixton. Features a small collection of both academic and spiritual books relating to people of African origin in the diaspora. Also carries local crafts and African clothing. Open (usually) Mon.-Fri. 10am-1pm and 2-4pm.

■■■ RECORD STORES

If a record can't be found in London, it's probably not worth your listening time. London, for years the hub of the English music scene, has a record collection to match. Corporate megaliths **HMV, Virgin,** and **Tower Records** fall over each other claiming to be the world's largest record store. Don't expect any bargains or rarities, and remember that when it comes to records, "import" means "rip-off." For rarities, secondhand, and specialist records, try the wealth of diverse shops scattered throughout the West End and the suburbs. At **Camden Town, Brixton, Ladbroke Grove,** or Soho's **Hanway Street,** you can have a good afternoon's browse in search of an obscure Dusty Springfield 45, or you just might stumble upon a £4 Duran Duran *Rio* only to discover after purchasing it that Simon LeBon signed the cover in silver metallic pen.

Black Market, 25 D'Arblay St., W1 (tel. 437 0478). Tube: Oxford Circus. One of many Soho dives frequented by aspiring DJs and serious spinners. Soul, swing, and hip hop in the basement, house/garage upstairs. Open Mon.-Sat. 10am-6:30pm.

Cheapo Cheapo Records, 53 Rupert St., W12 (tel. 437 8272). Tube: Piccadilly Circus. A warren of 70s and early 80s records at rock bottom prices. Open Mon.-Sat. 11am-10pm.

Dress Circle, 57 Monmouth St., WC2 (tel. 240 2227). Tube: Tottenham Ct. Rd. Specialists in theatre recordings of past greats and present performers. Memories in the Moonlight, Zero Mostel, Julie Andrews, Oh! I love a parade! Sheet music, books and videos too. Open Mon.-Sat. 10am-7pm.

Hand Spun Records, 45 Pembridge Rd., W11 (tel. 727 6306). Tube: Notting Hill Gate. This hip-hop hole-in-the-wall at the back of the "Have a Nice Day" clothing shop peddles a solid collection of R&B records, with a sideline in jazz. Open Mon.-Sat. 11am-6:30pm.

Honest Jon's, 278 Portobello Rd., W10 (tel. 969 9822). Tube: Ladbroke Grove. At Honest Jon's, heavily-postered walls declaim slogans like "Hail Caesar, Godfather of Harlem." This jumping joint has extensive Parliament-Funkadelic offerings and a jazz basement in which Blakey, Parker, and Mingus are only the tip of the iceberg. Open Mon.-Sat. 10am-6pm, Sun. 11am-5pm.

On the Beat, 22 Hanway St., W1 (tel. 637 8934). Tube: Tottenham Ct. Rd. Lots of alternative, used 45's, posters, magazines (tattered *Rolling Stones* from ages gone by) in a long narrow space. Open Mon.-Sat. 10am-5pm.

Plastic Passion, 2 Blenheim Crescent, W11 (tel. 229 5424). Tube: Notting Hill Gate. New Wave and punkish. Small, but extremely dedicated collectors. Open Fri.-Sat. 10am-6:30pm.

Record and Tape Exchange, 229 Camden High St., NW1 (tel. 267 1898). Tube: Camden Town. Branches at 38 Notting Hill Gate, W11, and 90 Goldhawk Rd., W12. Dirt-cheap 70s stuff in the basement. Fewer modern bargains. Open daily 10am-8pm.

Red Records, 500 Brixton Rd., SW2. Tube: Brixton. Specializes in rhythms and mixes of the African diaspora. From Remmy Ongala of Tanzania to the Mighty Sparrows of Trinidad, this place holds your ragga, hip-hop, lovers, soul, motown, or funk fave. Open Mon.-Sat. 9:30am-7pm.

Rhythm Records, 281 Camden High St., NW1 (tel. 267 0123). Tube: Camden Town. Secondhand reggae, ska, and dub. Limited but well-selected contemporary section. Open daily 9:30am-7pm.

Rough Trade, 130 Talbot Rd., W11 (tel. 229 8541). Tube: Ladbroke Grove. Birthplace of the legendary independent record label. Original snapshots of Johnny Rotten are casually tacked up on the wall next to old posters advertising concerts for Rough Trade bands like The Smiths, The Raincoats, and the X-Ray Spex. Punk rock encyclopedists post lists of their top-ten favorite bands/songs of all time; add your two cents' worth. Open Mon.-Sat. 10am-7pm.

Sarah's Jazz and Soul, 12 Berwick St., W1 (tel. 494 1081; fax 287 0022). Tube: Piccadilly Circus or Tottenham Ct. Rd. Huge selection from Europe, the U.S., and the whole world. They're "vinyl friendly" and swear they'll pay the best prices for your used goods. Open Mon.-Sat. 10am-6pm.

Sister Ray, 94 Berwick St., Soho W1 (tel. 287 8385, fax 287 1087). Tube: Piccadilly Circus or Tottenham Ct. Road. A high-class record store with a crazy selection of the latest in funk and rap, and up-and-comings in the Euro and U.S. indie rock scene. Unlike many record stores in the area, this place has embraced CDs with open arms. Open daily 10:30-7pm.

Soho Records, 3 Hanway St., W1 (tel. 580 4805). Tube: Tottenham Ct. Road. Autographed posters, Indie, significant collection of used 70s and 80s LP's. Cheapo section: 3 albums for £5—this section has losers like Elton John. Open Mon.-Sat. 10am-8pm, Sun. 1pm-7pm.

Vibe!, 36 Hanway St., W1P (tel. 580 8898). Tube: Tottenham Ct. Rd. Claustrophobic and cramped, but full of used vinyl and collector's 45s. Big 80s collection. Open Mon.-Sat. 11:30am-7pm.

Vinyl Solution, 231 Portobello Rd., W11 (tel. 229 8010). Tube: Ladbroke Grove. Hard-core and indie. Open Mon.-Sat. 10:30am-6:30pm.

■■■ SPECIALTY SHOPS

Hamley's, 188-196 Regent St., W1 (tel. 734 3161). Tube: Oxford Circus. London's largest toy shop offers 6 floors of every conceivable toy and game. Bring a leash for the kids. Open Mon.-Sat. 10am-6pm, Thurs. 10am-8pm.

Honour, 86 Lower Marsh, SE1 (tel. 401 8220). Tube: Waterloo. Fetish gear for the 90s: rubber, leather, and harnesses galore. A good resource for information on upcoming gothic, pagan, and fetish happenings.

Into You, 144 St. John St., EC1 (tel. 253 5085). Body adornment specialists. Nipple and belly-button piercing by Teena Marie.

The Museum Store, 37 The Market, WC2 (tel. 240 5760). Tube: Covent Garden. Collects and sells items found in museum stores around the world—everything from teddy bears to freeze-dried astronaut ice cream. Open Mon.-Sat. 10:30am-6:30pm, Sun. 11am-5pm.

The New Power Generation, 21 Chalk Farm Rd., NW1 (tel. 267 7751). Tube: Chalk Farm. A three-floor store dedicated to (and owned by) the artist formerly known as Prince. The first floor sells Prince merchandise, like symbol-adorned purple goblets; the basement sells Prince CDs; and at the top you'll find a funky snack bar. Open Mon.-Thurs 10am-5:30pm, Fri-Sun. 10am-6pm.

Sheeba, Brixton Market, at 396 Coldharbour La. (tel. 737 3558). Tube: Brixton. Satisfies the fancies of those interested in the culture of East Africa. Specializes in carvings and jewelry from Kenya, natural teas and spices from Ethiopia, and many more treasures from the continent. Open Mon.-Sat. 9:30am-6 or 7pm.

Smith and Sons Snuff Shop, 74 Charing Cross Rd., WC2. Tube: Leicester Sq. Tobacco enthusiasts will revel in the scent of this shop's 122 years of tobacco history. Open Mon.-Fri. 9am-6pm.

Stanley Gibbons, 399 Strand, WC2 (tel. 836 8444). Tube: Charing Cross. A funhouse of postal history books, collector phone cards, and stamps of every persuasion. Open Mon. 9:30am-5:30pm, Tues.-Fri. 8:30am-5:30pm, Sat. 10am-4pm.

■■■ MARKETS

STREET MARKETS

Brick Lane, E1. Tube: Aldgate East. Market with a South Asian flair: food, rugs, spices, bolts of fabric, and strains of sitar. Open Sun. 5am-2pm.

Brixton Market, Electric Ave., Brixton Station Rd. and Popes Rd., SW2. Tube: Brixton. Covered market halls and outdoor stalls sprawl out from the station. The wide selection of African and West Indian fruit, vegetables, fabrics, and records make Brixton one of the most vibrant, and hippest, markets. Also a remarkable number of stalls vending various colors and styles of hair extension pieces. The two indoor arcades are the Electric Arcade and the Granville Arcade, both with entrances off Atlantic Road. Open Mon., Tues., Thurs., and Sat. 8am-6pm, Wed. 8am-1pm, Fri. 8am-7pm.

Camden Markets, by Regent's Canal and along Camden High St., NW1. Tube: Camden Town. One of the funkiest, trendiest places to tap those Doc Marten soles and buy clothes, shoes, and Manic Panic hair dye. Highlights are the Camden Lock Market (corner of Chalk Farm Rd. and Camden Lock Pl.; open Tues.-Sun.), the Stables Market (past the Lock on Chalk Farm Rd.), and the Electric Ballroom (on the High St.; open Sun. 9am-5:30pm)—all with stalls of cool second-hand garb. Camden Town Bootleggers do a roaring trade, but check the quality of the tapes before buying. Open Sat.-Sun. 8am-6pm.

Camden Passage, Islington High St., N1. Tube: Angel. Turn right as you come out of the Underground, then bear right on narrow, pedestrian-only Islington High St. One of the biggest antique markets, plus prints and drawings. Open Wed. and Sat. 8:30am-3pm.

Chapel Market, N1. Tube: Angel. Turn left off Liverpool Rd., the street diagonally across from the tube towards the right. Emphasis on produce and flowers, but also household goods, those dubious electronics, and clothes, spiced with nuts and African music. A refreshing change from the trendy new face of Islington. Open Tues.-Wed. and Fri.-Sat. 8am-6:30pm, Thurs. and Sun. 8am-12:30pm.

The Cooltan, 372 Coldharbour Lane, SW9 (tel. (0181) 674 5309). Locals show off their creations in an Arts and Crafts market. You can too—call Orla to rent a stall, £6 in advance, £8 on the spot. First Sat. of every month, 10am-6pm.

Greenwich Market, Covered Market Sq., SE10, near the Cutty Sark. BR: Greenwich. A popular crafts market in a pastoral setting frequented by London lawyers on daytrips down the river. On Greenwich High Rd., the Open-Air Second-hand Market proffers vintage print dresses. Open Sat.-Sun. 9:30am-5pm.

Merton Abbey Mills, Merantun Way, SW19. Tube: Colliers Wood, and walk on Christchurch Rd. to Merantun Way past the SavaCentre, or South Wimbledon, and follow Morden Rd. to Merantun. An excellent, earthy crafts and clothes market on the river Wandle: brown rice yogurt, and Chinese food galore. Morden Hall Park (National Trust) just along the river. Open Sat.-Sun. 10am-5pm.

Petticoat Lane, E1. Tube: Liverpool St., Aldgate, or Aldgate East. A London institution—street after street of stalls, mostly cheap clothing and household appliances. The real action begins at about 9:30am. Open Sun. 9am-2pm; starts shutting down around noon.

Portobello Road, W11. Tube: Notting Hill Gate or Ladbroke Grove. High-quality antiques at high prices at the Notting Hill end of the street. Some call this "a place to visit your stolen silver"; others consider it nothing more than a tourist trap. Immortalized by Paddington Bear. Watch out for pickpockets. To the north, tourists thin out as antiques give way to produce and second-hand clothes stalls under the Westway flyover. A number of pricey vintagewear shops operate here. Antique market Sat. 7am-5pm. Clothes market Fri.-Sat. 8am-3pm.

TRADE MARKETS

London's fresh produce comes in through massive wholesale markets. These markets don't exactly roll out the red carpet for visitors, but they have wall-to-wall atmosphere. You won't find a more fascinating place to have a pint at 6:30am than near the trading. The new **Billingsgate** market (DLR: Canary Wharf or Poplar; open Tues.-Sat. 5:30-9am) removed its fishy smells from the old site by St. Magnus Martyr in the City. **Smithfield,** Charterhouse St., EC1 (tube: Farringdon or Barbican; open Mon.-Fri. 5am-9am), allegedly the largest meat market in the world, sells wholesale only. The market's name is derived from the "smooth field" upon which cattle were sold here in the mid-1800s. Pubs in the area wake up as early as the meat mongers and serve correspondingly flesh-filled breakfasts. The **New Covent Garden Market,** Nine Elms Lane, SW8 (tube: Vauxhall), handles London's fruit, vegetables, and flowers; traders only. **Borough Market,** Stoney St., SE1 (tube: London Bridge; open Mon.-Sat. midnight-10am), also barters in fruit and vegetables and allows casual visitors to look around. Once a medieval market held on London Bridge, it keeps moving due to flux in the Bankside area.

Bisexual, Gay, and Lesbian London

Travelers coming to London will be delighted by the range of London's very visible gay scene, which covers everything from the flamboyant to the cruisy to the mainstream. London presents a paradoxical mix of tolerance and homophobia. On the one hand, gay culture is so visible that an entire section of the general entertainment weekly *Time Out* is dedicated to Gay Listings; on the other, queer bashings and police arrests of cruisers are not uncommon occurences.

Britain suffers from a number of regressive laws, most notably Section 28, which prohibits local governments from "promoting" homosexuality. Additionally, the age of consent law for male homosexuals is 18 (recently lowered from 21), in contrast to the age of consent for heterosexuals, which is 16. Another developing issue involves the National Health Secretary's recent move to ban lesbian mothers and single women from the NHS's artificial insemination treatment.

Despite this negative political climate, gay communities thrive in London. Heavily gay-populated areas like Earl's Court, Islington, and Soho attest to the liveliness of the social scene; London also boasts an active network of political groups. Section 28 sparked an immediate call to action within the gay community, and the spirit of political activisim has not died out; July 1994 witnessed the launch of London's first Lesbian Avengers branch. The Labour Party has committed itself to repealing Section 28 as soon as it returns to power.

The gay community's center is the **London Lesbian and Gay Centre,** 67-69 Cowcross St., EC1 (tel. 608 1471; tube: Farringdon), a venue for a wide variety of meetings, as well as a disco, bar, restaurant, and gym (open Mon.-Tues. noon-11pm, Wed., Thurs., and Sun. noon-midnight, Fri.-Sat. noon-3am). **OutRage** (tel. 439 2381), the London version of Queer Nation, plans direct action and protests (meetings Thurs. 7:30pm at The Swiss Room, Central Club, 16 Great Russell St., WC1; tube: Tottenham Ct. Rd.). The London branch of **ACT-UP** (tel. 262 3121) meets weekly to organize direct action against businesses and institutions discriminating against people with AIDS.

With so many bisexual-, gay-, and lesbian-specific **periodicals** in London, it's easy to educate yourself to the current concerns of London's many gay communities. *Capital Gay* (free) mostly caters to men. *MX* is the best source of up-to-date information on the bar and club scene, and will help you pin down those protean one-nighters. *The Pink Paper,* Britain's national gay and lesbian newspaper, contains news, reviews, and features. *Pink Paper*'s bimonthly sister publication, *Shebang,* covers all aspects of lesbian life. *Gay Times* (£2) is the British counterpart to the *Advocate; Diva* (£2) is a monthly lesbian lifestyle magazine with an excellent mix of political and entertainment features, and good listings.

■ INFORMATION AND ADVICE LINES

Bisexual Helpline: tel. (0181) 569 7500. Tues.-Wed. 7:30-9:30pm.

Black Lesbian and Gay Helpline: tel. 837 5364. Thurs. 7-10pm.

Body Positive Helpline: tel. 373 9124. Daily 7-10pm. Support for HIV-positive people.

GALOP (Gay London Policing Group): tel. 233 0854. Mon.-Fri. 10am-6pm, 24-hr. answerphone. Advice, counsling, and support for gay men who have been harassed by the police.

Gay and Lesbian Legal Advice: tel. 253 2043. Advice on all topics, from basic discrimination to police harassment. Mon.-Fri. 7-10pm.

Irish Gay Helpline: tel. (0181) 983 4111. Mon. 7:30-10pm.

Jewish Lesbian and Gay Line: tel. 706 3123. Mon. and Thurs. 7-10pm.

Lesbian and Gay Switchboard: tel. 837 7324. A 24-hr. advice, support, and information service. Minicom facility for the deaf.

Lesbian Line: tel. 251 6911. Advice, information, and counselling referrals. Mon. and Fri. 2-10pm, Tues.-Thurs. 7-10pm.

National AIDS Helpline: tel. (0800) 567 123 (free). 24-hr. information and advice

Shakti: tel. 993 9001. The South Asian lesbian and gay network.

■ BARS, CAFÉS, PUBS, AND RESTAURANTS

The Angel, 65 Graham St., N1 (tel. 608 2656). Tube: Angel. Exit the station and head right, taking the first right onto Duncan St. At the end of Duncan, follow Vincent Terr. (which runs next to the Grand Union) straight to Graham St. A buzzing café/bar painted aquamarine and yellow for a vaguely Southwestern feel. One of few gay places with a consistently balanced male-female ratio. Eclectic menu of light meals, like Japanese noodles with stir-fry and tofu, all under £3. Salads and cakes under £2. Transparent juicer lets you watch as fresh juices are squeezed. Free live music Sun. Open Mon.-Sat. noon-midnight, Sun. noon-11:30pm.

Balans, 60 Old Compton St., W1 (tel. 437 5212). Tube: Leicester Square. Fiery flower arrangements and feral zebra-print lampshades create a relentlessly glamorous ambience in this brasserie/bar. Lunch, snacks, and *citron pressé* served. Full bar. Live blues, acoustic, and vocal performers Mon.-Sat. 11pm-1am. Open Mon.-Thurs. 9am-2am, Fri.-Sat 9am-2:30am, Sun 9am-1am.

The Bell, 257-9 Pentonville Rd., N1 (tel. 837 5617). Tube: King's Cross/St. Pancras. A disco bar with nightly themes. Well-dressed, friendly young crowd of both sexes. Mon. and Fri. are the **Cactus Club,** a country and western dance night. Dancing lessons 8-9pm (8pm-1am, £3). Wed. is **Pop Tarts**, with indie/alternative rock (9pm-2am; free before 10pm, then £1). Fri. is **Tribe**, a louder indie night (9pm-3am; £2-3). Sun. is the terrifically campy **Jo's Original Tea Dance** (5pm-midnight, £3).Open Mon. 9pm-1am, Tues.-Wed. and Sat. 9pm-2am, Thurs. 9pm-1:30am, Sun. 5pm-midnight.

The Black Cap, 171 Camden High St., NW1 (tel. 485 1743). Tube: Camden Town. North London's best-known drag bar. Live shows every night attract a mixed male and female crowd. When the shows aren't on, a DJ plays top-40 in the large.-Sat. noon-2am, Sun. pub hours). Especially crowded Sun. afternoon. Open Mon-Thurs. 9pm-2am; Fri.-Sat. 9pm-3am; Sun. noon-3pm, 7-midnight. Cover Tues.-Sat. £2-3.

The Box, Seven Dials, Monmouth St., WC2 (tel. 240 5828). Tube: Covent Garden. Small, intimate and stylish gay bar and brasserie in a removed section of Covent Garden. Trendy women-only "Girl Bar" every Sunday 7pm-late attracts nice girls, entice girls, shock girls, frock girls, cute girls, boot girls; £1 per pint till 9:30pm, £1.50 after. Serves delicate snacks and lunch foods like avocado mousse with toast and sweetbutter (£2.70). *Ciabatta* sandwich of cold roast beef, horseradish, watercress and cream cheese £4.80. Open Mon.-Sat. 11am-11pm, Sun 12:30-10:30pm.

Comptons of Soho, 53 Old Compton St., W1 (tel. 437 4445). Tube: Leicester Sq. or Piccadilly Circus. Soho's "official" gay pub, always busy with a large crowd of all ages. Horseshoe-shaped bar encourages the exchange of meaningful glances. Open Mon.-Sat. 11:30am-11:30pm, Sun. 7-10:30pm.

Crews, 14 Upper St. Martin's La., WC2. Tube: Leicester Sq. The largest and hottest bar for men in the West End. Expect to queue at the door. Open Mon.-Sat. noon-11pm, Sun. 7-10:30pm.

Drill Hall Women-Only Bar, 16 Chenies St., WC1 (tel. 631 1353). Tube: Goodge St. A much anticipated one-nighter located in the lobby of one of London's biggest alternative theatres. Dim lighting and red walls. Crowded, smoky, and laid back. Open Mon. 6–11pm.

Duke of Clarence, 140 Rotherfield St., N1 (tel. 226 6526). Tube: Angel, then bus #38, 56, or 73 up the Essex Rd. Rotherfield St. is the first right after the Essex Rd. and Canonbury/New North Rd. intersection. An unfortunate rarity, this is one of the few daily bars owned and run by women. A popular hang-out for local lesbians, both young and old. Open Mon.-Fri. 5:30-11pm, Sat. 6:30-11pm.

The Edge, 11 Soho Sq., W1 (tel. 439 1313). Tube: Tottenham Ct. Rd. Possibly the prime café/bar in which to pose and socialize in Soho; sleek gay male and straight customers spill out onto the sidewalk tables. Purple walls, plenty of metal trim, and a brassy bar decorate the 2 floors inside. Pricey food served until 5pm. Open Mon.-Sat. 8am-1am, Sun. 11am-10:30pm.

Fanny's, 305A North End Rd., W14 (tel. 385 9359). Tube: West Kensington. A basement bar with kitchy, 1950s decor for a predominantly female drinking club. Frequent money-saving happy hours (7-8pm), and nightly themes, including bisexual and TV/TS nights. Open Mon.-Sat. 7pm-late. £2 for nonmembers.

First Out Café/Bar, 52 St. Giles High St., WC2 (tel. 240 8042). Tube: Tottenham Ct. Rd. Off of New Oxford St. Despite the gaudy paint job and loud music, the crowd here is definitely casual. Order cheap, wholesome meals from the counter on the first floor and take a seat at the squiggly-shaped tables. Spicy peanut curry with rice, or fusilli in aubergine and tomato sauce, £2.95. Bar downstairs. Open Mon.-Sat. 10am-11pm, Sun. noon-10:30pm. Fri. night is Tattoo at First Out—women only in the bar 8-11pm.

Freedom, 60-66 Wardour St., W1 (tel. 734 0071). Tube: Piccadilly or Leicester Sq. A hyper-trendy Soho haunt frequented by a predominatly gay crowd. Stark white walls are decorated with jolting artistic graffiti. Fun £8.95 jugs of sangria are swimming with fresh fruit; "bar nibbles" (£3.20) are served with complimentary Miller Lite. Open Mon.-Sat. 9am-11pm, Sun. 9am-10:30pm.

Old Compton Café, 34 Old Compton St., W1 (tel. 439 3309). Tube: Leicester Sq. Open 24 hrs. in the geographic epicenter of Soho, this is *the* gay café. Tables and people (mostly male) overflow onto the street.

Silver Screen Café, 233 Earl's Ct. Rd. SW5 (tel. 370 5700). Tube: Earl's Ct. An unassuming restaurant by day, a happening bar by night. Former 5-star hotel chef serves no entree over £5. American-style Sun. brunch (pancakes, waffles, eggs benedict, etc.) served 1-7pm. Full bar. Occasional entertainment includes fire jugglers, python trainers, and acrobats. Bartender Sasha reports that Thurs. is women's night upstairs. Open Mon.-Sat. noon-11pm, Sun. 1-10:30pm.

Wilde About Oscar, 30-31 Philbeach Gdns., SW5 (tel. 835 1858 or 373 1244). Tube: Earl's Ct. In the garden of a gay B&B. A definite splurge, but its worth it; dine in a manicured garden. Candles, flowers, and few tables make for an intimate dining encounter. Starters, like breaded goat cheese with onion jam (£4.50), are generous, served on a bed of greens. Main courses are mostly Thai and French dishes. Open daily 7pm-midnight.

Wow Bar, at the Brixtonian Backyard, Neal's Yard, WC2 (tel. 240 2769). Tube: Covent Garden. Bar and Caribbean restaurant in trendy Covent Garden with weekly lesbian night on Sat. Reputedly a "lipstick" lesbian hang-out. Locals played it extremely cool when Martina Navratilova stopped by for a "quiet" drink in '94. Admission £1.50. Wow Bar open 8pm-late; restaurant open daily noon-midnight.

■ DANCE CLUBS

Bump, at Subterania, 12 Acklam Rd., W10 (tel. (0181) 960 45 90). Tube: Ladbroke Grove. Exit left and walk up Ladbroke Grove to Cambridge Gardens. Turn right on Cambridge Gardens, which turns into the pedestrian-only Acklam Rd. The club is under the Westway on your right. A sleek, but still eclectic crowd; good mix of gay men, lesbians, and straight couples. Large dance floor under a circular balcony bar. Open Sat. 10pm-3:30am; £6, free with flyer before 11pm, then £4.

The Fridge, Town Hall Parade, Brixton Hill, SW2 (tel. 326 5100). Tube: Brixton. "Love Muscle" on Sat. (10pm-6am) is the gay night at this hip club. Totally packed. The former theater's cavernous dance floor (that's for lesbians, not thespians!) still gets sweaty with the crowd of happy men and women dancing to house music. Open 10pm-6am. £9, £6 after 3am, £7 before midnight with flyer.

The Gardening Club, 4, The Piazza, Covent Garden, WC1 (tel. 497 3153). Tube: Covent Garden. Some mighty queer goings-on in the heart of Covent Garden. The cosmopolitan clientele groove to NY-style house, garage, and funk, and take breaks at the restaurant or cappuccino bar. Wed. is "She's Gotta Have It," a new women-only club night. (Open 10pm-3am, £4, £2 w/flyer, free before 11pm.) Sun. is the very popular "Queer Nation," for gay men, lesbians, and friends. (Open 9pm-2am. £6£5 w/ flyer, £4 concessions.)

G.A.Y., at London Astoria 2, 157 Charing Cross Rd., WC2 (tel. 734 6963). Tube: Tottenham Ct. Rd. A 3-nights-a-week pop extravaganza amidst chrome and mirrored disco balls. Emphatically unpretentious clientele (very mixed, in both gender and orientation). Hosts some big acts, including Bananarama. Open Mon., Thurs., Sat. 10:30pm-4am. Mon. £3, £1 w/ad or flyer; Thurs. £3, free before midnight w/student ID; Sat. £6.

Heaven, Villiers St., WC2 (tel. 839 3852), underneath The Arches. Tube: Embankment or Charing Cross (Villiers is off of the Strand). Still the oldest and biggest gay disco in Europe. Three dance floors, high-tech lighting, pool tables, bars, and a capacity of nearly 4000 means you'll never get bored. Wed. is the "Fruit Machine," a popular mixed gay night that feels a little less frenetic than the Sat. night crowd, plus The Powder Room for drag queens. (Open 10pm-3:30am; £6, £4 with flyer or before 11:30pm. Fri. is "Garage," for a mixed gay/straight crowd, plus the Dyke Shed upstairs. (Open 10:30pm-3:30am; £7.50, £6 before 11:30pm, £4 with flyer.) Open 10pm-4am, £8, £7 before 11:30pm.

Turnmills, 63B Clerkenwell Rd., EC1 (tel. 250 3409). Tube: Farringdon. Walk up Turnmill St. and turn right onto Clerkenwell Rd. The Turnmills building plays host to three hugely popular clubs. Sat. night is "Pumpin' Curls," a women's night where trendy clubbers enjoy sweaty dancing to hard house. Gay men allowed in as guests. (Open 10pm-3am, £5 or £10 joint ticket with "Trade"). At 3am, "Pumpin' Curls" turns into "Trade," a high-energy party for an attractive but no-attitude crowd that grinds to fierce house. Because of its late hours, "Trade" draws a diverse mix of late-night clubbers from places like Heaven, the Fridge, and Pumpin' Curls after they've all shut down. Get there early or late to avoid long queues, or get your ticket beforehand. (Open 3am-noon. £10. Tickets available at Rox on Old Compton St., Trax on Greek St., and the Dispensary on Newburgh St. Joint tickets at Pumpin' Curls and Heaven.) Sun. night at *ff*, music tends to be more techno, the crowd younger, male, and cruisy. (Open 9:30pm-5am. £7, £5 concessions before midnight.)

Up to the Elbow, fortnightly at the Laurel Tree, 113 Bayham St., NW1 (tel. 485 1383). Tube: Camden Town. Exit the station left, then cross to the right; Bayham is parallel to Camden High St. Housed in a small, black-painted, windowless (and hot!) room above the Laurel Tree pub, this club offers a blend of British and L.A. queercore, both DJ's and live, featuring bands like Mouthfull, Sapphic Sluts, and the "dragcore" group Desire. Indie indeed. Mixed crowd. Every other Fri. 9pm-late. £3, £2 concessions.

■ SHOPPING AND SERVICES

Clone Zone, 64 Old Compton St., W1 (tel. 287 3530). Tube: Piccadilly or Leicester Sq. Well-stocked shop for cards, books, clothes, sex toys, and gay-themed objects. Open Mon.-Sat. 11am-11:30pm, Sun. 1-7pm. Also at 1 Hogarth Rd., SW5 (tel. 373 0598; tube: Earl's Ct.). Open Mon.-Sat. 11am-11pm. AmEx, MC, Visa.

Don't Panic, 52 Dean St., W1 (tel 734 5363). Tube: Piccadilly or Leicester Sq. Dean St. is off of Shaftesbury. The company that came out with the famous "I can't even think straight" t-shirt. Printed hats, mugs, watches, pins, towels, etc. Open Mon.-Sat. 11am-10pm, Sun. noon-10pm. MC, Visa.

Gay's the Word, 66 Marchmont St., London WC1N 1AB (tel. 278 7654). Widest stock of gay and lesbian literature in England; mail order service available. Noticeboard, coffee area, discussion groups, and readings. Free map of "Gay London." Open Mon.-Fri. 11am-7pm, Sat. 10am-6pm, Sun. 2-6pm.

SH!, 22 Coronet St., N1 (tel. 613 5458). Tube: Old St. Head east on Old St. and turn left onto Pitfield St, Coronet will be off the right. A sex shop run by women, for women. Open Mon. and Wed.-Sat 11:30am-6:30pm.

Daytrips from London

London is a splendid place to live for those who can get out of it.
— Lord Balfour, Observer Sayings of the Week, 1 Oct. 1944

■ PRACTICAL INFORMATION FOR DAYTRIPPERS

GETTING AROUND

Trains

Britain's nationalized **British Rail** service is extensive but somewhat expensive. If you plan to travel a great deal within Britain, the **BritRail Pass** is a good buy. (Eurail-passes are *not* valid in Britain.) BritRail Passes are only available in the U.S. and Canada; *you must buy them before traveling to Britain.* They allow unlimited travel in England, Wales, and Scotland. In 1994, BritRail standard class Passes cost US$219 for eight days, $339 for 15 days, $425 for 22 days, and $495 for one month. Senior citizens pay US$199, $305, $379, and $445 respectively. Those between 16 and 25 pay US$179, $269, $339, or $395; children ages 5-15 pay one-half the corresponding adult fare. BritRail Travel also offers **Flexipasses,** which allow travel on a limited number of days within a specific time period.

Passes and additional information on discounts are available from most travel agents or BritRail Travel International's Reservation Centre, 1500 Broadway, 10th Floor, New York, NY 10036-4015 (tel. (212) 575 2667, fax (212) 575 2542). In Canada, write to 2161 Young St., Suite 812, Toronto, ON M4F386 (tel. (416) 484 0571).

British Rail in the U.K. does offer discounts for students/youth, seniors, and children. The **Young Person's Railcard** (£16, valid for one year) offers 1/3 off most fares, as well as some ferry discounts. You can buy this pass at major British Rail Travel Centres in the U.K. You must prove you're either between 16 and 23 (with a birth certificate or passport) or a full-time student over 23 at a British school, and submit two passport-sized photos. Those 60 and over can buy a **Senior Railcard** (£16) taking up to 1/3 off most fares; these are also available at major British Rail Travel Centres. Families have their own Railcard, as do wheelchair-bound travelers.

Coaches and Buses

The British distinguish between **buses,** which cover short local, rural, and city routes, and **coaches,** which cover long distances with few stops. *Let's Go* usually uses the term "buses" to refer to both of these services. Long-distance coach travel in Britain is definitely the least expensive option for travel within the U.K. **National Express** is the principal operator of long-distance coach services (for information contact Eurolines (tel. 730 0202), Grosvenor Gdns., London). Each county or region also has its own companies for rural service. Some coaches require advance reservation. Budget travelers should be on the look-out for regional coach passes, which offer unlimited travel in a certain area for a certain number of days. Those over 60 or between 16 and 25 are eligible for **Seniors'** and **Young Persons' Discount Coach Cards** (£7 per yr.), valid on National Express, reducing standard fares by about 30%. Local intra-city services (mostly fast and frequent minibus services) are provided by local companies in conjunction with county councils.

Cars and Caravans

The advantages of car travel speak for themselves. Disadvantages include high gasoline prices, the unfamiliar laws and habits associated with foreign driving, and the heinous exhaust that results from lax British emissions standards. The major difficulty that most North American drivers have in Britain is driving on the "wrong" side of the road—i.e. sitting on the right-hand side of the car and driving on the left side of the road. Be particularly cautious at roundabouts (rotary interchanges): give way to traffic from the right. British law requires drivers and front-seat passengers to wear seat belts; rear-seat passengers also should buckle up when belts are provided.

Speed limits are always marked at the beginning of town areas; upon leaving, you'll see a circular sign with a slash through it, signaling the end of the speed restriction. Speed limits aren't always strictly enforced, but note that many British roads are sinuous and single-track; drivers should use common sense.

Hiring (renting) an automobile is the least expensive option if you plan to drive for a month or less. For more extended travel, you might consider **leasing.** Prices range from £150 to £300 per week with unlimited mileage plus VAT; for insurance reasons, renters are required to be over 21 and under 70. **Europe by Car** will rent to younger people if the paperwork is done in advance in the U.S. All plans require sizable deposits unless you're paying by credit card. Make sure you understand the insurance agreement before you rent; some agreements require you to pay for damages that you may not have caused.

Several U.S. firms offer rental and leasing plans for Britain; try **Kemwel Group,** 106 Calvert St., Harrison, NY 10528-3199 (tel. (800) 678 0678); **Auto Europe,** #10 Sharp's Wharf, P.O. Box 1097, Camden, ME 04843 (tel. (800) 223 5555, fax (207) 236 4724); or **Europe by Car,** Rockefeller Plaza, New York, NY 10020 (tel. (800) 223 1516 or (212) 581 3040; student and faculty discounts available on rentals).

Bicycles

For information about touring routes, cyclists can consult tourist offices or any of the numerous books on cycling in Britain. The Cyclists' Touring Club, Cotterell House, 69 Meadrow, Godalming, Surrey GU7 3HS, England (tel. (01483) 417 217, fax (01483) 426 994) provides information, maps, and a list of bike rental firms in Britain. Annual membership is £24, under 18 £12, and family £40. The club's bi-monthly magazine, *Cycletouring and Campaigning,* is a valuable resource; they also publish an annual *Tours Brochure for Great Britain*.

British Rail lets you put your bike in the luggage compartment of most trains free of charge and store your bike at most stations for a nominal fee. See *The Rail Traveler's Guide to Biking by Train*, available from British Rail and at most stations.

Thumb

Adventurous daytrippers often hitchhike in parts of Britain outside of London. *Let's Go* does not recommend hitching. *A woman alone should not hitch.* Never accept a ride in the back of a two-door car. In an emergency, experienced hitchers will open the door; this usually surprises the driver enough to make him or her slow down. If a hitcher feels uneasy about the ride for any reason, he or she gets out at the first opportunity.

Vacation Work Publications publishes the *Hitch-Hikers' Manual: Britain,* which contains practical information on hitching laws, techniques, and the best places to hitch in 200 British towns (£3.95). For a copy of the book, contact Vacation Work, 9 Park End St., Oxford, England OX1 1HJ.

ACCOMMODATIONS OUTSIDE LONDON

A swift jaunt from the capital can easily turn into an extended tour. It may be more convenient not to return to London after each foray. Tourist information centers outside London provide aid in the search for rooms. These offices often have free lists of vacancies, which they will post on their doors after hours. For about £1, most offices will book you a place to stay. Most offer a "book-a-bed-ahead" service; for a fee of about £2, they will reserve you a room in the next town on your itinerary.

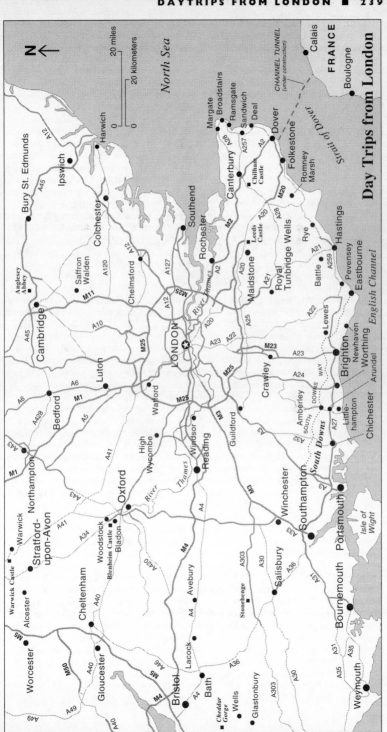

Day Trips from London

N←

20 miles
20 kilometers
0

North Sea

FRANCE
Calais
Boulogne

CHANNEL TUNNEL
(under construction)

Strait of Dover

Harwich

Bury St. Edmunds
Ipswich
A12
A45

Anglesey Abbey
Cambridge
A45

Saffron Walden
A120
Colchester
Chelmsford
A2

Southend
Rochester
A127
A12
M11
M25

Margate
Broadstairs
Ramsgate
Sandwich
Deal
Canterbury
A28
A257
A2
Dover
Folkestone

Chilham Castle
Romney Marsh
M20

A10
LONDON
River Thames
A20

Maidstone
Leeds Castle
A20
A21
A26
Royal Tunbridge Wells
Rye
Hastings
A21
A259
Battle
Pevensey
Eastbourne

Hastings

English Channel

Luton
A6
Bedford
M1
A5
Watford
M25

Windsor
High Wycombe
Reading
A41
A40

A25
A22
A23
Lewes
M23
A23
Crawley
A24
SOUTH DOWNS WAY
Amberley
Brighton
Newhaven
Worthing
Little-
hampton
Arundel
A27

Northampton
A43
M1
Stratford-
upon-Avon
Warwick
Warwick Castle
Alcester
A428
A6
A43
A41

Oxford
A34
Woodstock
Blenheim Castle
Bladon
A420
A40

River Thames
M4
A4
Guildford
A3
A32

Winchester
A3
South Downs
Southampton
A33
Chichester
Portsmouth
Isle of Wight

Cheltenham
A40
Gloucester
M50
A40
M5

Lacock
A4
Avebury
A36
Stonehenge
A303
A4
A30
Salisbury
A36
A303
A30

Bristol
Bath
A4
A46
A36

Cheddar Gorge
Wells
Glastonbury
A303

Bournemouth
A31
A35

Weymouth
A35
A31

Worcester
A49
A40
A49

■■■ OXFORD

Oxford University, England's first, was founded in 1167 by Henry II. Until then, the English had traveled to Paris to study. After his tiff with Thomas à Becket, Archbishop of Canterbury, Henry ordered the return of English students studying in Paris, so that "there may never be wanting a succession of persons duly qualified for the service of God in church and state." Oxford boasts among its graduates Sir Christopher Wren, Oscar Wilde, Indira Gandhi, and Hugh Grant; Christ Church alone has produced 13 prime ministers.

Oxford has no official "campus." The University's 40 independent colleges, where students live and learn, are scattered throughout the city; central libraries, laboratories, and faculties are established and maintained by the University. At the end of their last academic year, students from all the colleges come together for their "degree examinations," a grueling three-week process that takes place in the Examination Schools on High St. in late June and early July. The tourist office guide *Welcome to Oxford* (£1) and the tourist office map (20p) list colleges' public visiting hours (usually for a few hours in the afternoon; often curtailed neither with prior notice nor explanation). Christ Church, Magdalen, and New College charge admission; others may impose mercenary fees during peak tourist times.

Start your walking tour at Carfax, the center of activity, with a hike up the 99 spiral stairs of **Carfax Tower** (tel. 792 653) for an overview of the city. A free map of the rooftops ia available from the attendant at the bottom (open late March-Oct. daily10am-6pm; £1.20, children 60p).

Just down St. Aldates St. stands **Christ Church** (tel. 26492), an intimidating edifice that dwarfs the other colleges. "The House" has Oxford's grandest quad and its most patrician students. (Open Mon.-Sat. 9:30am-5:30pm, Sun. noon-5:30pm. Services Sun. 8am, 10am, 11:15am, 6pm; weekdays 7:15am, 7:35am, 6pm. £2.50; seniors, students, and children £1.) Christ Church's chapel is also Oxford's **cathedral,** the smallest in England. In the year 730, St. Frideswide, Oxford's patron saint, built a nunnery on this site in thanks for two miracles she had prayed for: the blinding of an annoying suitor, and his recovery. The cathedral's right transept contains a stained glass window (c. 1320) depicting Thomas à Becket kneeling in supplication, just before being hacked apart in Canterbury Cathedral. The 20-minute film shown continuously in the vestry (free) gives a concise history of the college and cathedral.

The Reverend Charles Dodgson (who wrote under the name Lewis Carroll) was friendly with Dean Liddell of Christ Church—and friendlier with his daughter Alice—and used to visit them in the gardens of the Dean's house next to the cathedral. The White Rabbit can be spotted fretting in the stained glass of the hall.

Curiouser and curiouser, the adjoining **Tom Quad** sometimes becomes the site of undergraduate lily pond dunking. The quad takes its name from **Great Tom,** the seven-ton bell in Tom Tower, which has faithfully rung 101 strokes (the original number of students) at 9:05pm (the original undergraduate curfew) every evening since 1682. Nearby, the fan-vaulted college **hall** bears imposing portraits of some of Christ Church's most famous alums—Charles Dodgson, Sir Philip Sidney, John Ruskin, John Locke, and W.H. Auden—in the corner by the kitchen.

Through an archway (to your left as you face the cathedral) lies **Peckwater Quad,** encircled by the most elegant Palladian building in Oxford. Look here for faded rowing standings chalked on the walls and for Christ Church's library, closed to visitors. The adjoining **Canterbury Quad** houses the **Christ Church Picture Gallery** (enter on Oriel Square and at Canterbury Gate), a fine collection of Italian primitives and Dutch and Flemish paintings. (Open Mon.-Sat. 10:30am-1pm and 2-5:30pm, Sun. 2-5:30pm; Oct.-March closes at 4:30pm. £1, students 50p. Visitors to gallery only should enter through Canterbury Gate off Oriel St.) Across St. Aldates at 30 Pembroke St., the **Museum of Modern Art** (tel. 722 733) exhibits works ranging from 10-foot-high floral hemp structures to photos of AIDS patients. (Open Tues.-Sat. 10am-6pm, Thurs. 10am-9pm, Sun. 2-6pm. £2.50, seniors, students, and children £1.50, free Wed. 10am-1pm and Thurs. 6-9pm. Wheelchair accessible.)

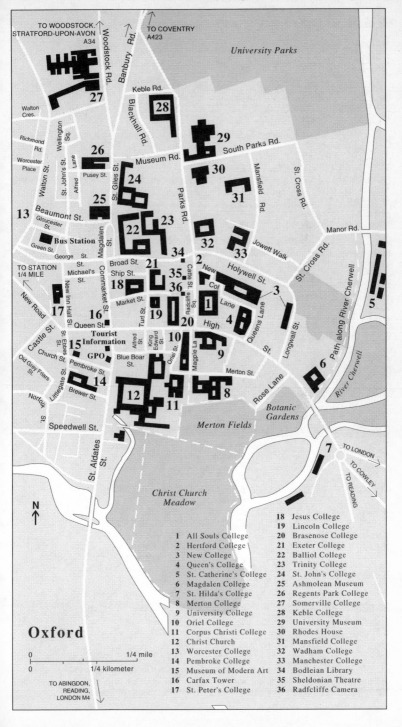

TO WOODSTOCK,
STRATFORD-UPON-AVON
A34

TO COVENTRY
A423

University Parks

Woodstock Rd.

Banbury Rd.

Keble Rd.

Walton
Cres.

Richmond
Rd.

Worcester
Place

Blackhall Rd.

Museum Rd.

South Parks Rd.

Mansfield Rd.

St. Cross Rd.

Wellington
Sq.

St. John's St.

Alfred Lane

Pusey St.

St. Giles St.

Parks Rd.

Jowett Walk

Manor Rd.

Beaumont St.

Gloucester
St.

Green St.

Bus Station

Magdalen St.

George St.

St.

TO STATION
1/4 MILE

St.
Michael's
St.

New Inn Hall St.

Broad St.

Ship St.

Cornmarket St.

Market St.

Turl St.

Catte St.

Holywell St.

New
Col
Lane

Radcliffe Sq.

High

St. Cross Rd.

Path along River Cherwell

Queens Lane

Longwall St.

New Road

Castle St.

St. Ebbes St.

Church St.

Pembroke St.

Old Grey Friars St.

Littlegate St.

Brewer St.

Norfolk
St.

Queen St.

Tourist
Information

GPO

Blue Boar
St.

Alfred St.

King
Edward St.

Oriel St.

Magpie La.

Merton St.

Rose Lane

River Cherwell

Speedwell St.

St. Aldates
St.

Merton Fields

Botanic
Gardens

TO LONDON

TO COWLEY

TO READING

Christ Church
Meadow

N

Oxford

0   1/4 mile
0   1/4 kilometer

TO ABINGDON,
READING,
LONDON M4

1 All Souls College
2 Hertford College
3 New College
4 Queen's College
5 St. Catherine's College
6 Magdalen College
7 St. Hilda's College
8 Merton College
9 University College
10 Oriel College
11 Corpus Christi College
12 Christ Church
13 Worcester College
14 Pembroke College
15 Museum of Modern Art
16 Carfax Tower
17 St. Peter's College
18 Jesus College
19 Lincoln College
20 Brasenose College
21 Exeter College
22 Balliol College
23 Trinity College
24 St. John's College
25 Ashmolean Museum
26 Regents Park College
27 Somerville College
28 Keble College
29 University Museum
30 Rhodes House
31 Mansfield College
32 Wadham College
33 Manchester College
34 Bodleian Library
35 Sheldonian Theatre
36 Radcliffe Camera

Oriel College is wedged between High and Merton St. (tel. 276 555). Oriel became a hotbed of the "Tractarian Movement" in the 1830s, when college clergy such as Keble and Newman tried to push the Anglican church back toward Rome (open daily 2-5pm). Behind Oriel, **Corpus Christi College** (tel. 276 700) surrounds a quad with an elaborate sundial in the center, crowned by a golden pelican (open daily 1:30-4:30pm).

Next door, **Merton College,** off Merton St. (tel. 276 310), features a fine garden; the college's 14th-century library holds the first printed Welsh Bible. The college is also home to the **Mob Quad,** Oxford's oldest, dating from the 14th century (college open Mon.-Fri. 2-5pm, Sat.-Sun. 10am-5pm).

The soot-blackened **University College** on High St. (tel. 276 602), up the crooked Logic Lane from Merton St., dates from 1249 and vies with Merton for the title of oldest college, claiming Alfred the Great as its founder (open July-Aug. daily 10am-6pm). Percy Bysshe Shelley was expelled from University for writing the pamphlet *The Necessity of Atheism,* but has since been immortalized in a prominent monument inside the college (to right as you enter from High St.). Farther down High St. on the right lies the **Botanic Garden,** a sumptuous array of plants that has flourished for three centuries (open daily 9am-5pm; glasshouses open daily 2-4pm; free).

With flowers lining the quads, a deer park on its grounds, the river watering its flank, and Addison's Walk (a verdant circular path) framing a meadow at one edge, **Magdalen College** (tel. 276 000) has traditionally been considered Oxford's handsomest. Its spiritual patron is alumnus Oscar Wilde—the place has always walked on the flamboyant side. Edward Gibbon declared the 14 months he spent here "the most idle and unprofitable of my whole career" (open July-Sept. daily 11am-6pm; other times Mon.-Fri. 2-6pm, Sat.-Sun noon-6pm. £1.50, children and seniors £1).

Just up High St. toward Carfax, a statue of Queen Caroline (wife of George II) crowns the front gate of **Queen's College** (tel. 279 120). Wren and Hawksmoor went to the trouble of rebuilding Queen's in the 17th and 18th centuries, with a distinctive Queen Anne style in glorious orange, white, and gold. A boar's head annually graces the Christmas table—supposedly to commemorate an early student of the college who, attacked by a boar on the outskirts of Oxford, choked his assailant to death with a volume of Aristotle.

Next to Queen's stands **All Souls** (tel. 279 379), a graduate college with a prodigious endowment. Candidates who survive the pre-admission exams get invited out to dinner, where it is ensured that they are "well-born, well-bred, and only moderately learned" (open Mon.-Fri. 2-4:30pm).

Turn up Catte St. to the **Bodleian Library** (tel. 277 000), Oxford University's principal reading and research library with over six million books and 50,000 manuscripts. Sir Thomas Bodley endowed the library's first wing in 1602 on a site that had housed university libraries since 1488; the institution has since grown to fill the immense **Old Library** complex, the round **Radcliffe Camera** next door, and two newer buildings on Broad St. As a copyright library, the Bodleian receives a copy of every book printed in Great Britain. There are four guided tours a day (£3). Admission to the reading rooms is by ticket only. If you can prove you're a scholar (a student ID may be sufficient, but a letter of introduction from your college is encouraged) and present two passport photos (which can be taken on the spot), the Admissions Office will issue a two-day pass for £2. You still won't be allowed access to the manuscripts division unless you are "formally enrolled in a graduate degree program" and/or have a letter from your institution explicitly specifying the necessity of the Oxford archives. (Library open Mon.-Fri. 9am-6pm, Sat. 9am-12:30pm.) Across Broad St. from the Bodleian you can browse at **Blackwell's,** the famously encyclopedic bookstore.

The **Sheldonian Theatre** (tel. 277 299), set beside the Bodleian, is a Roman-style jewel of an auditorium built by Wren as a university theatre and home of the **University Press.** Graduation ceremonies, conducted in Latin, take place in the Sheldonian. The cupola of the theatre affords an inspiring view of Oxford's dreaming spires (open Mon.-Sat. 10am-12:45pm and 2-4:45pm; Nov.-Feb. until 3:45pm; admission 50p, children 25p).

The gates of **Balliol College** (tel. 277 777), across Broad St. (open daily 2-5pm), still bear scorch marks from the immolations of 16th-century Protestant martyrs (the pyres were built a few yards from the college, where a small cross set into Broad St. rattles cyclists today). Housed in flamboyant pink and yellow neo-gothic buildings, Balliol is a mellow place that recently had a Marxist master.

Balliol students preserve a semblance of tradition by hurling bricks over the wall at their arch-rival, conservative **Trinity College** (tel. 279 900), on Broad St. (open daily 2-5pm). Trinity, founded in 1555, has a baroque chapel with a limewood altarpiece, cedar lattices, and angel-capped pediments.

Across Catte St. from the Bodleian, New College Lane leads to **New College** (tel. 279 555). So named because of its relative anonymity at the time of its founding by William of Wykeham in 1379, New College has become one of Oxford's most prestigious colleges. The accreted layers of the front quad reveal the architectural history of the college. Look for the exquisitely detailed misericords, carved by sympathetic carpenters into the pews to support monks' bottoms. A peaceful croquet garden is encircled by part of the **old city wall,** and every few years the mayor of the City of Oxford visits the college for a ceremonial inspection to ascertain the wall's good repair (open daily 11:30am-5pm; school term 2-5pm).

Turn left at the end of Holywell St. and then bear right on Manor Rd. to see **St. Catherine's** (tel. 271 700), one of the most striking of the colleges. Built between 1960 and 1964 by the Danish architect Arne Jacobsen, "Catz" has no chapel, and its dining hall was funded by Esso Petroleum (open daily 9am-5pm). At the corner of St. Cross and South Parks Rd., the **Zoology and Psychology Building** looms like a great concrete ocean liner. Many colleges hold athletic contests nearby on the **University Parks,** a refreshing expanse of green.

Walk through the **University Museum** (tel. 272 950), Parks Rd. (open Mon.-Sat. noon-5pm; free) to the **Pitt Rivers Museum** (tel. 270 927) and behold a wonderfully eclectic ethnographic and natural history collection that includes shrunken heads and rare butterflies (open Mon.-Sat. 1-4:30pm; free). Just up Banbury Rd. on the right, the **Balfour Buildings** house 1400 musical instruments from all over the world, including a working black leather violin (open Mon.-Sat. 1-4:30pm; free).

Keble College (tel. 272 727), across from the University Museum, was designed by architect William Butterfield to stand out from the sandstone background; the intricate and multi-patterned red brick is known as "The Fair Isle Sweater" (open daily 2-5pm). Through a passageway to the left, the **Hayward** and **deBreyne Buildings** squat on the tarmac like black plexiglass spaceships.

The imposing **Ashmolean Museum,** Beaumont St. (tel. 278 000), was Britain's first public museum when it opened in 1683. Its outstanding collection includes drawings and prints by Leonardo da Vinci, Raphael, and Michelangelo; copious French impressionist and Italian works; and Rembrandts, Constables, and assorted Pre-Raphaelites (open Tues.-Sat. 10am-4pm, Sun. 2-4pm; free). Ashmolean's **Cast Gallery,** behind the museum, stores over 250 casts of Greek sculptures (open Tues.-Fri. 10am-4pm, Sat. 10am-1pm; free).

A few blocks up St. Giles, as it becomes Woodstock Rd., stands **Somerville College** (tel. 270 600), Oxford's most famous women's college. (The oldest is Lady Margaret Hall.) Somerville's alumnae include Dorothy Sayers, Indira Gandhi, and Margaret Thatcher. Women were not granted degrees until 1920 and they still comprise only 38% of today's student body (open daily 2:30-5:30pm).

At the remote end of Beaumont St., you'll reach **Worcester College** (tel. 278 300). Derisively called Botany Bay, the college has attracted some of Oxford's more swashbuckling students, including confessed opium addict Thomas De Quincey and handsome poet Richard Lovelace. Worcester enjoys a large and dreamy garden and a lake shore where plays are staged in summer (open daily 2-6pm).

By far the most eccentric of Oxford's neighborhoods is the five blocks of **Cowley Road** nearest the Magdalen Bridge roundabout. The area is a living version of the

OXFORD

Whole Earth Handbook, a fascinating clutter of alternative lifestyles, small book-stores, and wholefood restaurants. North of Worcester College along Walton St., past the palatial **Oxford University Press** complex, lies the neighborhood of **Jericho.** A working-class suburb in the 19th century, the area has been redeveloped and today houses a people of various ethnicities.

The Oxford Story, 6 Broad St. (tel. 790 055 or 728 822), hauls visitors around on medieval-style "desks" through noisy dioramas recreating Oxford's past. Share the simple pleasures of a 13th-century student making merry with a wench; hear the cries of the bishops who were burned a few feet away on Broad St. (Open July-Aug. 9am-6:30pm, April-June and Sept.-Oct. 9:30am-5pm, Nov.-March 10am-4pm; £4.50, seniors and students £3.95, children £3.25.)

ORIENTATION AND PRACTICAL INFORMATION

Queen, High, St. Aldates, and Cornmarket Streets meet at right angles in **Carfax,** the town center. The colleges surround Carfax to the east along High St. and Broad St.; the bus and train stations lie to the west. Past the east end of High St. over Magdalen Bridge, the neighborhoods of **East Oxford** stretch along **Cowley Road** (marked "To Cowley" on some maps) and **Iffley Road** (marked "To Reading"). To the north along **Woodstock** and **Banbury Roads,** leafier residential areas roll on for miles past some of the more remote colleges.

Getting There: Local trains run hourly from London. **Intercity** trains leave from Paddington (1hr.; single £12.30, day return £12.40, period return £16.40). The **Oxford Tube** (tel. 772 250) sends buses from Grosvenor Gardens in London (1-6 per hr.; 1½ hr.; day return £6, students, children, and seniors £5.50).

Getting About: The **Oxford Bus Company** (tel. 711 312) operates the red double-deckers and lime-green "City Nipper" minibuses, as well as the CityLink service to London; **Oxford Minibus** (tel. 771 876) owns the checkered-flag minibuses and the Oxford Tube London service. Most local services board on the streets adjacent to Carfax; some longer-distance buses depart from the bus station. Abingdon Rd. buses are often marked "Red Bridge," and some Iffley Rd. buses are marked "Rose Hill." Fares are low (most about 80p single). Some companies issue **Compass** tickets, good for one day's travel (about £4), but companies disdain each other's tickets. You can also purchase weekly bus passes at Carfax travel or at the bus station.

Tourist Office: St. Aldates Chambers, St. Aldates St. (tel. 726 871 or 252 664 after hours). *Welcome to Oxford* (£1) is the official guide; *Vade Mecum* (£1), put out by Oxford undergrads, includes a helpful list of restaurants. Accommodations list 40p, comprehensive map 70p. Books rooms for £2.50 and a 10% deposit. Open Mon.-Sat. 9am-5pm, Sun. 10am-3:30pm.

Tours: 2hr. walking tours leave 7 times daily from the tourist office between 10:30am and 4pm (£3.20, children £2). **Spires and Shires** (tel. 513 998) runs 1½hr. tours every hour 11am to 4pm, leaving from the Trinity College gate on Broad St. (£3, children £2). Ubiquitous **tour buses** can be boarded anywhere between the train station and Magdalen College; **The Oxford Tour** charges £6.50, students £4.50, children £2 (tel. 790 522). Or take a tour from one of the many **student groups** (£2.50, students free). Some students will regale you with stories you won't hear on the official tours and will give you your money back if you're dissatisfied. Others won't. One tour every hour between 9am-5pm.

Accommodations Hotlines: After the tourist office closes, tel. 241 497 (East Oxford), 862 138 (West Oxford), 510 327 (North Oxford), 725 870 (South Oxford).

Postal Code: OX1 1ZZ. **Telephone Code:** 01865.

Train Station: Botley Rd. (tel. 722 333 for British Rail timetable), west of Carfax. Travel Centre open Mon.-Fri. 8am-7:30pm, Sat. 8am-6pm, Sun. 11am-6pm. Station open Mon.-Fri. 5:50am-8pm, Sat. 6:50am-8pm, Sun. 8am-8pm.

Bus Station: Gloucester Green (follow arrows from Carfax). **Oxford Tube** (tel. 772 250); **Oxford CityLink** (tel. 711 312, 772 250 for timetable); **National Express** (tel. 791 579), office open daily 8am-6:30pm. **Carfax Travel,** 138 High

St. at Carfax (tel. 726 172), books for National Express, as well as for British Rail and ferries. Open Mon.-Fri. 9am-5pm, Sat. 9am-1pm.

Taxi: Radio Taxi, tel. 242 424. **ABC,** tel. 770 681.

Bike Rental: Pennyfarthing, 5 George St. (tel. 249 368). Closest to town center. Rental £5/day; 3-speeds £10/week; deposit £25. Open Mon.-Sat. 8am-5:30pm.

Boat Rental: Oxford Punting Co., Folly Bridge (tel. (01223) 327 280), across from Head of the River pub. **Riverside Boating Co.,** Folly Bridge (tel. 721 600), behind Head of the River pub. **Magdalen Bridge Boat Co.,** Magdalen Bridge (tel. 202 643), east of Carfax along High St. **Salter Brothers,** Folly Bridge (tel. 243 421), offers cruises to Iffley and Abingdon, May-Oct.

Hospital: John Radcliffe Hospital, Woodstock Rd. (tel. 741 166). Take bus #10.

Emergency: Dial 999; no coins required. **Police:** St. AldatesSt. (tel. 266 000).

ACCOMMODATIONS

Book at least a week ahead, especially for singles, and expect to mail in a deposit. B&Bs line the main roads out of town, all of them a vigorous walk (15-20min.) from Carfax. The No. 300s on **Banbury Road,** fern-laced and domestic, stand miles north of the center (catch a Banbury bus on St. Giles St.). You'll find cheaper B&Bs in the 200s and 300s on Iffley Rd. and from No. 250-350 on **Cowley Rd.,** both served by frequent buses from Carfax. **Abingdon Road,** in South Oxford, is about the same price and distance, though less colorful.

HI Youth Hostel, Jack Straw's Lane, Headington (tel. 62997). Catch any minibus from the post office just south of Carfax (every 15min., last bus 11:10pm; 55p). 116 beds. Lockout 10am-1pm, curfew 11:30pm (though nightguard is on duty to let stragglers in). Well-equipped, with kitchen, lockers, and food shop. Close quarters and large lounges promote chatter. £8.70, under 18 £5.80.

Tara, 10 Holywell St. (tel. 244 786 or 248 270). The best B&B in town, situated among the colleges on the oldest medieval street in Oxford. Kind hearing-impaired proprietors, Mr. and Mrs. Godwin, lip-read and speak clearly, so there'll be no communication problems. Desks, basins, TVs, and refrigerators in every room; kitchenette on 2nd floor. Breakfast room a virtual museum of academic regalia and college coats-of-arms. Singles £25, doubles £38. Open July-Sept.; the rest of the year it fills up with students, but check anyway. Reserve at least 2 weeks in advance.

Bravalla, 242 Iffley Rd. (tel. 241 326). Sunny rooms hung with nonintrusive floral patterns and pastels. Singles £18-20, doubles with bath £36-42.

Whitehouse View, 9 Whitehouse Rd. (tel. 721 626), off Abingdon Rd. Only 10min. from Carfax. The size and decor of the rooms vary; ask to see a selection if you can. Excellent breakfasts. Doubles with TV £17-18.

Newton House, 82-84 Abingdon Rd. (tel. 240 561), a half mile from town center; take any Abingdon bus across Folly Bridge. TVs and dark, hulking wardrobes in every room. Doubles £35, with bath £45.

Old Mitre Rooms, 48 Turl St. (tel. 279 821). Lincoln College dorm rooms. 1 bathroom for every six people. Singles £18, doubles £35.20, with bath £38. Continental breakfast. Open July-early Sept. Inquire at the Mitre Pub and Restaurant at the corner of Turf and High St.

St. Hugh's College, St. Margaret's Rd. off Banbury Rd. (tel. 54642). Bedrooms, some of them enormous, in Victorian houses on Canterbury Rd. Singles £15-19, doubles £30-36. Continental breakfast probably won't sustain you for the vigorous walk into town. Open late June-Sept.

FOOD

Oxford's eateries seduce students fed up with college food. For fresh produce, deli goods, and breads, visit the **Covered Market** between Market St. and Carfax (open Mon.-Sat. 8am-5:30pm). Eat and run at one of the better take-aways: **Bret's Burgers,** in a shack on Park End St. (tel 245 229), near the train station, with delectable burgers and chips from £1.50 (open Sun.-Thurs. noon-11pm, Fri.-Sat. noon-11:30pm); or **Parmenters,** 58 High St. near Magdalen College, recognizable by the line out the door (apricot flapjacks 75p, carrot cake £1.15, sandwiches £1.30-2.75; open Mon.-Fri. 8:30am-5:30pm, Sat.-Sun. 9am-5:30pm).

The Nosebag, 6-8 Michael's St. (tel. 721 033). Heaping plates of salad and meat dishes served cafeteria-style for under £5, £6.50 at dinner. Open Mon. 9:30am-5:30pm, Tues.-Thurs. 9:30am-10pm, Fri.-Sat. 9:30am-10:30pm, Sun. 9:30am-9pm.

Chiang Mai, in an alley at 130A High St. (tel. 202 233). Spicy Thai food in half-timbered surroundings. Extensive vegetarian menu; entrees £4.30-6.50. Reserve ahead, especially on weekends. Open Mon.-Sat. noon-2:30pm and 6-11pm.

Cherwell Boathouse, Bardwell Rd. (tel. 527 46), off Banbury Rd., 1 mi. north of town. Romantically perched on the leafy bank of the Cherwell. 3-course meals. Well-loved wine list. Expect to spend the entire evening; book well in advance. Dinner usually under £20, and worth every penny. When you're finished, rent a punt next door and drift off into the watery night. Open Tues.-Sat. 6:30-10pm, Wed.-Sun. noon-2pm.

Munchy Munchy, 6 Park End St., (tel. 245 710), on the way into town from rail station. Stark wooden decor and silly name redeemed by spirited cooking and energetic proprietress. Different dishes daily, all Indonesian or Malaysian (£5-8). Open Tues.-Sat. noon-2pm and 5:30-10pm.

Polash Tandoori Restaurant, 25 Park End St. Delicious Indian cuisine served in a quiet setting near the train station. Vegetable dishes under £2.50. Sunday lunch buffet £6.95 per person. Open Mon.-Thurs. noon-2:30pm and 6-11:30pm, Fri.-Sat. noon-2:30pm and 6pm-midnight, Sun. noon-11:30pm.

Heroes, Ship St. (tel. 723 459). Packs in student clientele and serves up yummy sandwiches with a super selection of stuffings, £1.60-2.65. Open Mon.-Fri. 8am-7pm, Sat. 8:30am-5pm, Sun. 10am-5pm. Breakfast 8-11am.

For those staying at B&Bs across Magdalen Bridge, there are a number of cheap and tasty restaurants along the first four blocks of Cowley Rd. **Hi-Lo Jamaican Eating House,** 70 Cowley Rd. (tel. 725 984), **Kashmir Halal,** 64 Cowley Rd. (tel. 250 165), and **The Pak Fook,** 100 Cowley Rd. (tel. 247 958), are all good bets. Or keep an eye out for the legendary **kebab vans** that roll into town after hours—usually at Broad St., High St., Queen St., and St. Aldate's.

PUBS

Turf Tavern, 4 Bath Pl., off Holywell St. A 13th-century building, intimate and relaxed until the student crowd turns it into a mosh pit. Beers, punches, ciders, and country fruit wines. Open Mon.-Sat. 11am-11pm; Sun. noon-3pm, 7-10:30pm.

The Eagle and Child, 49 Giles St. Known to all as the Bird and Baby, this archipelago of pleasant panelled alcoves moistened the tongues of C.S. Lewis and J.R.R. Tolkein. *The Hobbit* and *The Chronicles of Narnia* were first read aloud here. Open Mon.-Fri. 11am-2:30pm, 5:30-11pm; Sat. 11am-2:30pm and 6-11pm; Sun. noon-2:30pm and 7-10:30pm.

The Bear, Alfred St. Since 1242. 5000 ties from England's brightest and most boastful cover every flat surface but the floor. Food served noon-3pm and 6-8pm; no dinner Sun. and Mon. Open Mon.-Sat. noon-11pm, Sun. noon-2:30pm and 7-10:30pm.

The Blue Boar, 11 Wheatsheaf Yard, off Blue Boar St. The hammering music will drive you out onto the terrace for a fine view of a blackened stone wall. Right behind Christ Church; packed with students. Open Mon.-Thurs. noon-3pm and 5:30-11pm; Fri.-Sat. noon-11pm; Sun. 10:30am-3pm and 7-10:30pm.

The Kings Arms, Holywell St. Oxford's unofficial student union, with a few refugee scholars from the New Bodleian across the street. Open Mon.-Sat. 10:30am-11pm; Sun. 10:30am-3pm and 7-10:30pm.

ENTERTAINMENT

Oxford shuts down fairly early, and public transit vanishes by 11pm. Look for posters, check the bulletin boards at the tourist office, or pick up a free copy of *This Month in Oxford.* The tourist office also prints a daily event sheet in summertime.

Throughout the summer, college theatre groups stage productions in gardens or in cloisters. Try to attend a concert or an evensong service at one of the colleges, or a performance at the **Holywell Music Rooms. City of Oxford Orchestra,** the city's professional symphony orchestra (tel. 252 365), plays a subscription series in the Sheldonian Theatre and college chapels throughout the summer (shows at 8pm; tickets £7-17, students 25% discount). They also have Sunday coffee concerts. The year-long **Music at Oxford** series plays in halls throughout the city; for information, call 864 056 or write to 6A Cumnor Hill, Oxford OX2 9HA.

The **Apollo Theatre,** George St. (tel. 244 544), presents a wide range of performances, including comedy, drama, rock, jazz, and the Royal Ballet (tickets from £7, students and seniors £2 discount). The **Oxford Playhouse,** Beaumont St. (tel. 798 600) puts on bands, dance troupes, and the Oxford Stage Company (tickets from £5, children and seniors £2 discount, students gets best available seat from 2 hrs. before the show for £5, Wed.-Thurs. £3). The **Oxford Union,** St. Michael's St., and **The Old Fire Station** on George St. (tel. 794 494) feature more avant-garde work.

The **Jericho Tavern,** at the corner of Walton and Jericho St. (tel. 54502), features local rock bands (open Mon.-Sat. 11am-3pm and 6-11pm; cover charge £3.50-5). **The Jolly Farmers,** Paradise St. (tel. 793 759), is Oxfordshire's only gay and lesbian pub, featuring occasional comedy, female impersonators, and male strippers. Take Queen St. from Carfax, turn left on Castle St., then right on Paradise St. Open Mon.-Sat. noon-11:30pm; Sun. noon-3pm and 7-10:30pm.

A favorite pastime in Oxford is **punting** on the River Thames (known in Oxford as the Isis) or on the River Cherwell (CHAR-wul). Don't be surprised if you suddenly come upon **Parson's Pleasure,** a small riverside area where men sometimes sunbathe nude. Female passersby are expected to open their parasols and tip them at a discreet angle to obscure the view.

The university celebrates **Eights Week** at the end of May, when all the colleges enter crews in bumping races and beautiful people gather on the banks to nibble strawberries and sip champagne. In early September, **St. Giles Fair** invades one of Oxford's main streets with an old-fashioned carnival, complete with Victorian roundabout and whirligigs. Daybreak on May 1 brings one of Oxford's loveliest moments: the Magdalen College Choir greets the summer by singing madrigals from the top of the tower to a crowd below, and the town indulges in morris dancing, beating the bounds, and other age-old rituals of merrymaking—pubs open at 7am.

■■■ STRATFORD-UPON-AVON

It is something, I thought, to have seen the dust of Shakespeare.
—*Washington Irving*

Many have craved Stratford's cachet ever since David Garrick's 1769 Stratford jubilee. England and this town have made an industry of the Bard, emblazoning him on £20 notes and casting him in beer advertisements. Crowds regularly flock to Stratford to pay homage.

Stratford's sights are most pleasant before 11am or after 4pm—the crowds peak at 2pm. Five **official Shakespeare properties** grace the town: Shakespeare's Birthplace and BBC Costume Exhibition, Anne Hathaway's cottage, Mary Arden's House and Countryside Museum, Hall's Croft, and New Place or Nash House. Diehard Bard fans should purchase the **combination ticket** (£7.50, students £7, children £3.50), a savings of £3.50 if you make it to every shrine. If you don't want to visit them all, buy a **Shakespeare's Town Heritage Trail ticket,** which covers only the three in-town sights (the Birthplace, Hall's Croft, and New Place) for £5 (students £4.50, children £2.30). The least crowded way to pay homage to Shakespeare himself is to visit his grave in **Holy Trinity Church,** Trinity St. (50p, students 30p).

In town, begin your walking tour at **Shakespeare's Birthplace** on Henley St. (tel. 269 890; enter through the adjoining museum). The Birthplace is half period recreation and half Shakespeare life-and-work exhibition. The adjacent **BBC Costume**

STRATFORD-UPON-AVON

Exhibition features costumes used in the BBC productions of Shakespeare's plays, complete with photo stills (both open Mon.-Sat. 9am-5:30pm; Sun. 10am-5:30pm; Nov.-Feb. Mon.-Sat. 9:30am-4pm; Sun. 10:30am-4pm; £2.60, children £1.20). Shakespeare bought **New Place,** Chapel St., in 1597. Also visit the **Great Garden** at the back (open Mon.-Sat. 9:30am-5pm, Sun. 10:30am-5:30pm; Nov.-Feb. Mon.-Sat. 10am-4pm, Sun. 1:30-4pm; house admission £1.80, children 80p; garden free).

Shakespeare learned his "small Latin and less Greek" at the **Grammar School,** on Church St. To visit, write in advance to the headmaster, N.W.R. Mellon, King Edward VI School, Church St., Stratford-upon-Avon, England CV37 6HB (tel. (01789) 293 351). The **guild chapel,** next door, is open daily. Shakespeare's eldest daughter once lived in **Hall's Croft,** Old Town Rd., an impressively furnished building with a beautiful garden (hours and admission same as New Place).

Stroll through the **theatre gardens** of the Royal Shakespeare Theatre. You can fiddle with RSC props and costumes at their **RSC Collection** museum (gallery open Mon.-Sat. 9:15am-8pm, Sun. noon-5pm; £2, students and seniors £1.50). Backstage tours, including a review of the RSC Collection, give new perspective on this drama mecca (tel. 296 655 for advanced booking; daily 1:30 and 5:30pm; £4, students £3). The **RST Summer House** in the gardens contains a **brass-rubbing studio** (free, but frottage materials cost 95p-£9, average £2.50; open April-Sept. daily 10am-6pm; Oct. daily 11am-4pm).

The well-respected **Shakespeare Centre,** Henley St., has a library and a bookshop (across the street) and archives open to students and scholars. The center exhibits 16th-century books, holds madrigal concerts, and hosts a fine poetry festival in July and August (concerts £1-1.50; festival tel. 204 016; poetry readings Sun. 8pm; tickets £3.50-5.50).

Anne Hathaway's Cottage, the birthplace of Shakespeare's wife, lies about 1 mi. from Stratford in Shottery; take the footpath north from Evesham Place or the bus from Bridge St. The cottage exhibits portray the Tudor rural lifestyle. View from outside if you've already seen the birthplace (open Mon.-Sat. 9am-5:30pm, Sun. 10am-5:30pm; Nov.-Feb. Mon.-Sat. 9:30am-4pm, Sun. 6:30am-4pm; £2.20, children £1). **Mary Arden's House,** the farmhouse restored in a style that a 19th-century entrepreneur determined to be that of Shakespeare's mother, stands 4 mi. from Stratford in Wilmcote; a footpath connects it to Anne Hathaway's Cottage (open Mon.-Sat. 9:30am-5pm, Sun. 10:30am-5pm; Nov.-Feb. Mon.-Sat. 10am-4pm, Sun. 1:30-4pm; £3, children £1.30, family £7).

ORIENTATION AND PRACTICAL INFORMATION

The corner of Waterside and Bridge St., at the Crystal Shop, is as close to a bus station as Stratford gets; National Express and Midland Red South buses stop here. Local Stratford Blue service also stops on Wood St. You can buy tickets for National Express buses at the tourist office.

Getting There: Stratford is 2¼ hr. from London by Intercity **rail** or by the bus/rail **Shakespeare Connection** (departs London Euston Mon.-Sat. 4 per day, Sun. 2 per day; 2 hr.; £22.50, day return £21; only Shakespeare Connection operates at night after plays; tel. 294 466). **National Express buses** run to and from London's Victoria Station (3 per day; 3 hr.; day return £13.75, period return £17).

Tourist Office: Bridgefoot (tel. 293 127). Cross Warwick Rd. at Bridge St. towards the waterside park. Books accommodations. Open Mon.-Sat. 9am-6pm, Sun. 11am-5pm; Oct.-March Mon.-Sat. 9am-5pm.

Tours: Mad Max Tours (tel. (01926) 842 999) caters to the "independent traveler" looking for a cheap, informative, and entertaining way to see the Cotswolds. Tours (£10) run Thurs. 9am-5pm, departing from the HI youth hostel. Book there or call. **Guide Friday** runs tours of Stratford Town Center daily every 15 min., from their office at 14 Rother St. (tel. 294 466). Tickets £6, seniors £4, children under 12 £1.50, under 5 free. They also offer tours of the Cotswolds. Book at their office. Tickets £12, seniors £11, children £6.

Royal Shakespeare Theatre Box Office, Waterside (tel. 295 623). Standby tickets may appear just before the show at the RST, the Swan, and The Other Place (tel. 292 965) for students and seniors (£8-13). **24hr. ticket information:** tel. 269 191. Open Mon.-Sat. 9:30am-8pm, or until 6pm when the theater's closed.
Postal Code: CV37 6AA. **Telephone Code:** 01789.
Train Station: off Alcester Rd. (train info tel. (01203) 555 211 or (0121) 643 4444). Call **Guide Friday, Ltd.** (tel. 294 466) in advance if you plan travel on the late-night Shakespeare Connection. Discount rail fares can be had by purchasing rail and theater tickets from **Theatre and Concert Travel** (tel. (01727) 411 15).
Bike Rental: Clarke's Gas Station, Guild St. (tel. 205 057), at Union St. Look for the Esso sign. £5.75/day, £25/week; deposit £50. Open daily 7am-9pm.
Hospital: Stratford-upon-Avon Hospital, Arden St. off Alcester Rd., tel. 205 831.
Emergency: Dial 999; no coins required. **Police:** Rother St. (tel. 414 111).

ACCOMMODATIONS

To B&B or not to B&B? Guest houses (£14-18) line **Grove Road, Evesham Place,** and **Evesham Road.** (From the train station, walk down Alcester Rd., take a right on Grove Rd., and continue to Evesham Place, which becomes Evesham Rd.) If these fail you, try **Shipston** and **Banbury Road** across the river.

HI Youth Hostel, Hemmingford House, Wellesbourne Rd., Alveston (tel. 297 093). 2 mi. from Stratford. Follow the B4086; take bus #518 or 18 from Wood St. (west of the tourist office), or walk. Large, attractive grounds and a 200-year-old building. 154 beds in rooms of 2-14. Reception open 7am-midnight, night guard on duty. Curfew midnight. Many rooms feature superb views. £12, under 18, £8.80. Breakfast included. Vegetarian food available.
The Hollies, 16 Evesham Pl. (tel. 266 857). Warm and attentive proprietors for whom the guest house has become a labor of love. All private facilities. TV and tea-making facilities in every room. Spacious doubles; no singles. £15.
Nando's, 18 Evesham Pl. (tel. 204 907; fax to the same number). Delightful owners, homey rooms. TVs in each room. Private facilities. £16.50-20.50 per person.
Ashley Court, 55 Shipston Rd. (tel. 297 278). Proprietors welcome you into their spacious, immaculate guest house. All rooms with private facilities, remote control TV, radio, tea/coffee pots. Half-acre garden in back. Only a 5min. walk to all the sights. Doubles £38-40. £15 deposit per room required upon booking.
Field View Guest House, 35 Banbury Rd. (tel. 292 694). Peaceful and refreshing accommodations. Only an 8min. walk to town, but less convenient to the train station. Tea and coffee-making facilities in each room. Singles £14. Doubles £28.
Greensleeves, 46 Alcester Rd. (tel. 292 131), on the way to the train station. Mrs. Graham will dote on you in her cheerful home. TV in every room. £14.
Bradbourne Guest House, 44 Shipston Rd. (tel. 204 178). Easygoing proprietors offer peace and quiet in charming rooms only ¾ mi. from the center of town. TV and tea set in every room. Singles £14-18. Doubles £25-40. Rates lower Oct.-April.
Moonraker House, 40 Alcester Rd. (tel. 267 115 or 299 346; fax 295 504). 5-10min. from town center. Luxury rooms with near-opulent facilities. No singles. All private facilities, from £19.50 per person.

FOOD

Café Natural, 10 Greenhill St. Behind a health food store, this popular café serves elaborate vegetarian foods. Tues. discount (10%) for students and seniors. Entrees £2.50-3.15. Open Tues.-Sat. 9am-4:30pm. Lunch served noon-2:30pm.
Kingfisher, 13 Ely St. A take-away that serves chips with everything. Cheap, greasy, and very popular; lines form outside. Meals £1.60-3.50. Open Mon. 11:30am-1:45pm and 5-9:30pm, Tues.-Thurs. 11:30am-1:45pm and 5-10:45pm, Fri.-Sat. 11:30am-1:45pm and 5-11pm.
Hussain's Indian Cuisine, 6a Chapel St. Probably Stratford's best Indian cuisine. 3-course lunch for £5.95. Open Mon.-Thurs. noon-2pm and 5:15-11:45pm, Fri.-Sat. noon-2pm and 5pm-midnight, Sun. 12:30-2:30pm and 5:30-11:45pm.
Vintner Bistro and Cafe Bar, 5 Sheep St. (tel. 297 259). Satisfying salads (£4.75-4.95) and uncommon desserts. Open Mon.-Sun. 10:30am-11pm.

Elizabeth the Chef/The Shakespeare Coffee House, Henley St., opposite the Birthplace. Perk up over a pot of tea surrounded by pink. Baked potatoes and sandwiches galore for a cafeteria-style lunch (£1.40-3.30). Open Mon.-Sat. 9:30am-5pm, Sun. 10am-5pm.

ENTERTAINMENT

Setttle into a plush chair in the recently redone theater at the **Royal Shakespeare Company** and let a sublime performance wash over you. To reserve seats (£4.50-41), call the box office (tel. 295 623 or 269 191 for 24hr. recorded information); they hold tickets for three days only. The box office opens at 9:30am. Good matinee seats are often available after 10:30am on the day of a performance. A limited number of tickets get set aside for same-day sale (apply in person; £4.50-10, limit 2 per person) and some customer returns and standing-room tickets may turn up later in the day for evening shows (line up 1-2 hr. before curtain). Student standbys for £8-13 exist in principle (available just before curtain—be ready to pounce). The company does not perform in Stratford during February or until the ides of March.

The **Swan Theatre** has been specially designed for RSC productions of plays written by Shakespeare's contemporaries. The theatre is located down Waterside, in back of the Royal Shakespeare Theatre, on the grounds of the old Memorial Theatre (tickets £8-25, standing room £4.50). The Swan also sets aside a few same-day sale tickets (£4.50-£13); standbys are most rare. **The Other Place** is the RSC's newest branch, producing modern dramas and avant-garde premieres (reserved seats £14, unnumbered seats and same-days £12, standbys £8).

The **Stratford Festival** (2nd fortnight in July) typically features world-class artists from all arenas of performance. Tickets (when required) can be purchased from the Civil Hall box office (tel. 414 513), on Rother St. Stratford also hosts an annual **Poetry Festival** held throughout July and August with readings and/or lectures every Sunday evening (tickets £4.50-13; tel. 295 623).

■■■ CAMBRIDGE

The town of Cambridge has been around for over 2000 years, but the University got its start 785 years ago when rebels "defected" from nearby Oxford to this settlement on the River Cam. Each term, battalions of bicycle-riding students invade this quintessential university town. In recent years, Cambridge has ceased to be the exclusive preserve of upper-class sons, although roughly half of its students still come from independent schools and only 35% are women.

The University itself exists mainly as a bureaucracy that handles the formalities of lectures, degrees, and real estate, leaving to individual colleges the small tutorials and seminars that form a Cambridge education. Since third-year finals shape many students' futures, most colleges close to visitors during the official quiet periods of May and early June. But at exams' end, Cambridge explodes with gin-soaked glee, and May Week (in mid-June) launches a dizzying schedule of cocktail parties.

Cambridge is an architect's dream, packing some of the most breathtaking monuments of English architecture over the last 700 years into less than one square mile. Most of the historic university buildings line the east side of the River Cam between Magdalene Bridge and Silver St. On both sides of the river, the gardens, meadows, and cows of the **Backs** bring a pastoral air to Cambridge.

The University of Cambridge has three eight-week terms: Michaelmas (Oct.-Dec.), Lent (Jan.-March), and Easter (April-June). Visitors can gain access to most of the college grounds daily from 9am to 5:30pm, though many close to sightseers during the Easter term, and virtually all are closed during exam period (mid-May to mid-June). Look and act like a student and you should be able to wander freely through most college grounds even after hours. Some university buildings close during vacations.

King's College, on King's Parade, possesses the university's most famous chapel, a spectacular Gothic monument. In 1441, Henry VI cleared away most of the center of medieval Cambridge for the foundation of King's College, and he intended this

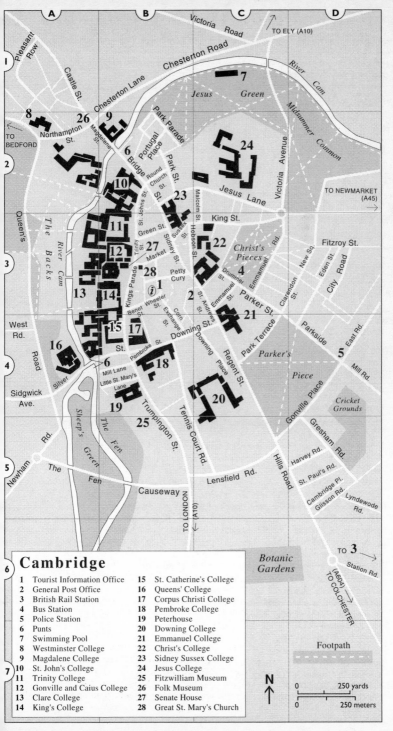

CAMBRIDGE

Cambridge

1	Tourist Information Office
2	General Post Office
3	British Rail Station
4	Bus Station
5	Police Station
6	Punts
7	Swimming Pool
8	Westminster College
9	Magdalene College
10	St. John's College
11	Trinity College
12	Gonville and Caius College
13	Clare College
14	King's College
15	St. Catherine's College
16	Queens' College
17	Corpus Christi College
18	Pembroke College
19	Peterhouse
20	Downing College
21	Emmanuel College
22	Christ's College
23	Sidney Sussex College
24	Jesus College
25	Fitzwilliam Museum
26	Folk Museum
27	Senate House
28	Great St. Mary's Church

Footpath

N

0   250 yards
0   250 meters

chapel to be England's finest. Although Henry wanted the inside to remain unadorned, his successors ignored this wish and spent nearly £5000 carving an elaborate interior. In fact, if you stand at the southwest corner of the courtyard, you can see where Henry VI's master mason John Wastell left off and where work under the Tudors began. The interior of the chapel consists of one huge chamber cleft by a carved wooden choir screen, one of the purest examples of the early Renaissance style in England. Wordsworth described the fan-vault ceiling as a "branching roof self-poised, and scooped into ten thousand cells where light and shade repose." Stained glass windows depicting the life of Jesus were preserved from the iconoclasm of the English Civil War, allegedly because John Milton, then Cromwell's secretary, groveled on their behalf. Behind the altar hangs Rubens' magnificent *Adoration of the Magi* (1639). Free music recitals often play at the chapel—pick up a schedule at the entrance (college open June-Oct. Mon.-Fri. 9:30am-4:30pm; Sun. 9am-5pm; £2, students and children £1, under 12 free with adults; chapel open term-time Mon.-Sat. 9:30am-3:30pm, Sun. 1:15-2:15pm and 4:45-5:15pm; free). The chapel and exhibition open during college vacations from 10am-5pm.

In early June the university posts the names and final grades of every student in the Georgian **Senate House** opposite the King's College chapel, designed by Gibbs and built in the 1720s; about a week later, degree ceremonies are held there.

Trinity College, on Trinity St., holds the largest purse at the University. The college's status as the wealthiest at Cambridge has become legendary—myth-mongers claim that it was once possible to walk from Cambridge to Oxford without stepping off Trinity land. Founded in 1546 by Henry VIII, Trinity once specialized in literature (alums include George Herbert, John Dryden, Lord Byron, and Lord Tennyson), but in this century has instead spat forth scientists and philosophers (Ernest Rutherford, Ludwig Wittgenstein, G.E. Moore, and Bertrand Russell). Byron used to bathe nude in a fountain (built in 1602) in the middle of the courtyard. The eccentric young poet lived in Nevile's Court and shared his rooms with a pet bear, whom he claimed would take his fellowship exams for him. Generations later, Prince Charles was an average student in anthropology.

The expanse of Trinity's **Great Court** encompasses an area so huge that you can almost fail to notice its utter lack of straight lines and symmetry. The great courtyard race in *Chariots of Fire* is set here. What William Wordsworth called the "loquacious clock that speaks with male and female voice" still strikes 24 times each noon. Sir Isaac Newton, who lived on the first floor of E-entry for 30 years, first measured the speed of sound by stamping his foot in the cloister along the north side of the court. Underneath the courtyards lie the well-hidden, well-stocked Trinity wine cellars. Recently the college purchased over £20,000 worth of port that won't be drinkable until 2020.

Amble through the college toward the river to reach the reddish stone walls of the stunning **Wren Library.** Notable treasures in this naturally lit building include A.A. Milne's handwritten manuscript of *Winnie the Pooh* and John Milton's *Lycidas.* The collection also contains works by Byron, Tennyson, and Thackeray. German-speakers might look for Wittgenstein's journals. His *Philosophical Investigations* was conceived here during years of intense discussion with G.E. Moore and students in his top-floor K-entry rooms (library open Mon.-Fri. noon-2pm; free; Trinity's courtyards close at 6pm; college and library closed during exams).

Established in 1511 by Lady Margaret Beaufort, mother of Henry VIII, **St. John's College** is one of seven Cambridge colleges founded by women. St. John's centers around a paved plaza rather than a grassy courtyard, and its two best buildings stand across the river from the other colleges. A copy of Venice's Bridge of Sighs connects the older part of the college to the towering neo-Gothic extravagance of New Court (chapel open during term Tues.-Fri. 9am-noon and 2-4pm; Sat. and Mon. 9am-noon; college open daily during vacation; £1, children and seniors 50p, families £2). Next door, you can see the modern **Cripps Building,** with clever bends that create three distinct courts under the shade of a noble willow.

The **School of Pythagoras,** a 12th-century pile of wood and stone rumored to be the oldest complete building in Cambridge, hides in St. John's Gardens (courtyard and some buildings open until 6pm; closed during exams).

Queens' College was founded not once, but twice—by Margaret of Anjou in 1448 and again by Elizabeth Woodville in 1465. It possesses the only unaltered Tudor courtyard in Cambridge, containing the half-timbered President's Gallery. The **Mathematical Bridge,** just past Cloister Court, was built in 1749 without a single bolt or nail, relying only on mathematical principle. A meddling Victorian took the bridge apart to see how it worked and couldn't put it back together without using a steel rivet every two inches (college open daily 1:45-4:30pm; during summer vacation also 10:30am-12:45pm; closed during exams; £1, under 14 free).

Clare College, founded in 1326 by the thrice-widowed, 29-year-old Lady Elizabeth de Clare, has preserved an appropriate coat of arms: golden teardrops on a black border. Across Clare Bridge lie the **Clare Gardens** (open Mon.-Fri. 2-4:45pm; during summer vacation also 10am-4:30pm). Walk through Clare's **Old Court** (open during exams after 4:45pm to groups of fewer than 3) for a view of the University Library, where 82 mi. of shelves hold books arranged according to size rather than subject (college open daily 10am-5pm; £1.50, under 10 free).

Christ's College, founded as "God's-house" in 1448 and renamed in 1505, has won fame for its gardens (open Mon.-Fri. 10:30am-12:30pm and 2-4pm; in summer Mon.-Fri. 9:30am-noon) and its association with the poet John Milton—a mulberry tree reputedly planted by the "Lady of Christ's" still thrives here. To reach the gardens, walk under the lovely neoclassical Fellows Building dubiously accredited to Inigo Jones. Charles Darwin dilly-dallied through Christ's. His rooms (unmarked and closed to visitors) were on G staircase in First Court. **New Court,** on King St., is one of the most stunning modern structures in Cambridge; its symmetrical gray concrete walls and black-curtained windows look like the whelp of an Egyptian pyramid. The college closes during exams, save for access to the chapel during services and concerts (inquire at the porter's desk.).

Cloistered on a secluded site, **Jesus College** has preserved an enormous amount of unaltered medieval work, dating from 1496. Beyond the long, high-walled walk called the "Chimny" lies a three-sided court fringed with colorful gardens. Through the archway on the right lie the remains of a medieval nunnery. The Pre-Raphaelite stained glass of Burne-Jones and ceiling decorations by William Morris festoon the chapel (courtyard open until 6pm; closed during exams).

Once the recipient of buildings from a 15th-century Benedictine hostel, **Magdalene College** (MAUD-lin), founded in 1524, has more recently acquired an aristocratic reputation. Don't forget to take a peek at the **Pepys Library** (labeled **Bibliotheca Pepysiana**) in the second court; the library displays the prolific diarist's collection in their original cases. The college dining hall hovers to the left as you walk to the second court (library open Mon.-Sat. 2:30-5:30pm; also Easter-Aug. 11:30am-12:30pm; free; courtyards closed during exams).

Thomas Gray wrote his *Elegy in a Country Churchyard* while staying in **Peterhouse,** on Trumpington St., the oldest and smallest college, founded in 1294. In contrast, **Robinson College,** across the river on Grange Rd., distinguishes itself by being the college's newest. Founded in 1977, this mod-medieval brick pastiche sits just behind the university library. Bronze plants writhe about the door of the college chapel, which features some fascinating stained glass.

Corpus Christi College, founded in 1352 by the common people, contains a dreary but extremely old courtyard forthrightly called Old Court, unaltered since its 1352 enclosure. The library maintains the snazziest collection of Anglo-Saxon manuscripts in England, including the Parker Manuscript of the *Anglo-Saxon Chronicle.* The 1347 **Pembroke College** next door harbors the earliest architectural effort of Sir Christopher Wren (courtyards open until 6pm; closed during exams).

A chapel designed by Sir Christopher Wren dominates the front court of **Emmanuel College.** Emmanuel, founded in 1584, on St. Andrew's St. at Downing St., and **Downing College,** founded in 1807, just to the south along Regent St., are both pleasantly isolated (courtyards open until 6pm; chapel open when not in use). Downing's austere neoclassical buildings open onto an immense lawn (open daily until 6pm; dining hall open when not in use; closed during exams). John Harvard, alleged founder of a certain New England university, attended Emmanuel; a stained glass panel depicting Harvard graces the college chapel.

The **Round Church (Holy Sepulchre),** Bridge St. and St. John's St., one of five circular churches surviving in England, was built in 1130 (and later rebuilt) on the pattern of the Church of the Holy Sepulchre in Jerusalem. The pattern merits comparison with **St. Benet's Church,** a rough Saxon church on Benet St. The tower of St. Benet's, built in 1050, is the oldest structure in Cambridge.

The **Fitzwilliam Museum,** Trumpington St. (tel. 332 900), a 10min. walk down the road from King's College, dwells within an immense Roman-style building. Inside, a cavernous marble foyer leads to a collection that includes paintings by Leonardo da Vinci, Michelangelo, Dürer, Corot, Monet, and Seurat. A goulash of Egyptian, Chinese, and Greek antiquities bides its time downstairs, coupled with an extensive collection of 16th-century German armor. Check out the illuminated manuscripts under their protective cloths. The drawing room displays William Blake's books and woodcuts (open Tues.-Fri. ground floor 10am-2pm, upper floor 2-5pm, Sat. both floors 10am-5pm; Sun. both floors 2:15-5pm; free; call to inquire about lunchtime and evening concerts; guided tours Sat.-Sun. at 2:30pm, £1.50).

The **Museum of Zoology** (tel. 336 650), off Downing St., houses a fine collection of wildlife specimens in a modern, well-lit building (open Mon.-Fri. 2:15-4:45pm; free; wheelchair accessible). Across the road, opposite Corn Exchange St., the **Museum of Archaeology and Anthropology,** Downing St. (tel. 333 516), contains prehistoric artifacts from American, African, Pacific, and Asian cultures, as well as exhibits from Cambridge through the ages (open Mon.-Fri. 2-4pm, Sat. 10am-12:30pm; free; wheelchair accessible, but call ahead). If you're near Magdalene College, stop by the **Folk Museum,** 2-3 Castle St. (tel. 355 159), by Northampton St., an appealing collection dating from the 17th century (open Mon.-Sat. 10:30am-5pm, Sun. 2-5pm; £1, student, seniors, and children 50p). **Kettle's Yard,** at the corner of Castle and Northampton St. (tel. 352 124), houses early 20th-century art (house open Tues.-Sun. 2-4pm; gallery open Tues.-Sat. 12:30-5:30pm, Sun. 2-5pm; free).

The **Botanic Gardens** (tel. 336 265; enter from Hill Rd. or Bateman St.) were ingeniously laid out by Henslow, Sir Joseph Hooker's father-in-law, circa 1846. When the wind gets rolling, the scented garden turns into a perfume factory (open daily 10am-4 or 6pm, depending on the season; Wed. free; Mon.-Fri. in Nov.-Feb. free; otherwise £1.50, under 18 £1). Guided tours available.

ORIENTATION AND PRACTICAL INFORMATION

Cambridge (pop. 100,000), about 60 mi. north of London, has two main avenues. The main shopping street starts at Magdalene Bridge and becomes Bridge St., Sidney St., St. Andrew's St., Regent St., and finally Hills Rd. The other—alternately St. John's St., Trinity St., King's Parade, Trumpington St., and Trumpington Rd.—is the academic thoroughfare, with several colleges lying between it and the River Cam.

Getting There: Trains to Cambridge run frequently from both London's King's Cross and Liverpool Street stations (every ½hr.; 1hr.; single £11.70, day return £11.80, period return £15.40). **National Express** coaches travel hourly between London's Victoria Station and Drummer St. Station in Cambridge (2hr.; single or day return £8.50). **Cambus,** the town's bus service, also runs numerous local and regional routes from Drummer St. (fares vary).

Tourist Office: Wheeler St. (tel. 322 640), a block south of the marketplace. Maps of the town 10p. Open Mon.-Tues. and Thurs.-Fri. 9am-6pm, Wed. 9:30am-6pm, Sat. 9am-5pm; Nov.-March closes at 5:30pm. Also open Easter-Sept. Sun. 10:30am-3:30pm. Info on Cambridge events also available at **Corn Exchange box office,** Corn Exchange St. (tel. 357 851), opposite the tourist office.

Tours: Walking tours (2hrs.) of the city and some colleges leave the main tourist office: April-June daily 11am and 2pm; July-Aug. every hr. 11am-3pm; Sept. every

hr. 11am-3pm. Special "Drama Tour" Tues. and Fri. at 6:30pm, led by guides in
period dress. Tours less frequent during the rest of the year. Sun. and bank holidays, first tour at 11:15am. £3.50-5.00.
Postal Code: CB2 3AA. **Telephone Code:** 01223.
Train Station: Station Rd. (tel. 311 999; recorded London timetable Mon.-Fri. tel.
359 602, Sat. tel. 467 098, Sun. tel. 353 465). Open daily 5am-11pm to purchase
tickets. Travel Centre open Mon.-Sat. 4:30am-11pm, Sun. 6am-11pm. To get to
Market Square in the city center from the train station, take a Citral Link bus
(Mon.-Sat. daytime every 8min., Sun. and evenings every 15min.; 60p) or walk
down Hills Road (25min.).
Bus Station: Drummer St. Station. **National Express** (tel. 460 711). **Cambus** (tel.
423 554) handles city and area service (40p-£1). Some local routes serviced by
Miller's or **Premier** coaches. Travel Centre open Mon.-Sat. 8:15am-5:30pm.
Taxi: Cabco (24-hr.; tel. 312 444). Or hail one at St. Andrew's St. and Market Sq.
Bike Rental: University Cycle, 9 Victoria Ave. (tel. 355 517). £7 per day, £15 per
week; cash deposit £25. Open Mon.-Sat. 9am-5:45pm. **C. Frost,** 118 New Market
Rd. (tel. 356464). £5/day, £10/week; deposit £20. Open Mon.-Fri. 9am-1pm and 2-
6pm, Sat. 9:30am-1pm and 2-5pm.
Hospital: Addenbrookes, Hills Rd. (tel. 245 151).
Emergency: Dial 999; no coins required. **Police:** Parkside (tel. 358 966).

ACCOMMODATIONS

Many of the cheap B&Bs around Portugal St. and Tenison Rd. house students during
the academic year and are open to visitors only during the summer. Check the comprehensive list in the tourist office window, or pick up their guide to lodgings (50p).

HI Youth Hostel, 97 Tenison Rd. (tel. 354 601; fax 312 780), entrance on Devonshire Rd. Relaxed, welcoming atmosphere. Well-equipped kitchen, laundry room,
TV lounge. 126 beds, mostly in 3-4-bed rooms; a few doubles. Couples may share
a room, space permitting. £12, under 18 £8.80. Breakfast and sleepsack included.
Packed lunch £2.10-2.80; evening meal £3.70. Small lockers to store valuables
available in some rooms. Crowded March-Oct.—call a few days in advance and
arrive by 6pm.
Home from Home B&B, Mrs. Flora Miles, 39 Milton Rd. (tel. 323 555). Mrs. Miles
welcomes guests into her sparkling, well-decorated home, located 15min. from
the bus station and city center. 2 doubles and 1 single with TV, washbasins, wonderful showers, and tea and coffee-making facilities. Singles £20. Doubles £32.
Full English breakfast included. Call a few days ahead for reservations.
Warkworth Guest House, Warkworth Terrace (tel. 63682). Charming and gracious hostess has 16 pastel rooms near the bus station. Use of kitchen, laundry
facilities, telephone. Singles £17. Doubles £30. Family £45. Breakfast included.
Tenison Towers, Mr. and Mrs. Madeira, 148 Tenison Rd. (tel. 566 511). Clean,
comfy rooms near train station. Singles in summer £18, in winter £14; doubles
£24, £28; triples £35, £39; quads £44, £52. Reductions for long-term stays.
Mrs. McCann, 40 Warkworth St. (tel. 314 098). A jolly hostess with comfortable
twin rooms in a quiet neighborhood near the bus station. Rates go down after two
nights. Singles £15, double £24, breakfast included.
YMCA, Queen Anne House, Gonville Pl. (tel. 356 998). 136 clean, bright dorm-
style rooms in a buzzing center which includes fitness facilities and a restaurant.
Ideal location. Singles £19.13 with breakfast. Doubles £31. Call a week ahead.

FOOD

Market Square has bright pyramids of fruit and vegetables for the hungry budgetar-
ian (open Mon.-Sat. approx. 8am-5:30pm). For vegetarian and wholefood groceries,
try **Arjuna,** 12 Mill Rd. (tel. 64845; Mon.-Fri. 9:30am-6pm, Sat. 9am-5:30pm). Both
Hills Rd. and Mill Rd., south of town, brim with good, cheap restaurants just becoming trendy with student crowds.

Nadia's, 11 St. John's St. The best bakery in town, and one of the cheapest. Wonderful flapjacks and quiches 55p-£1.30. Take-away only. Open Mon.-Sat. 7:30am-5:30pm, Sun. 7:30am-5pm.

Rajbelash, 36-38 Hills Rd. A spicy array of curries, *tandooris,* and *biryanis* £2.60-6.40. Open daily noon-2:30pm and 6pm-midnight. Sunday buffet noon-2:30pm £6.50, children £4.50.

Tatties, 26-28 Regent St. Delectable baked potatoes. With roof garden over Downing College. Vegetarians will delight. Hot potato with butter, £1.70. Open Mon.-Fri. 8am-9pm, 10am-9pm.

Clown's, 54 King St. A meeting place for foreigners. Practice your Esperanto over a mean cappuccino (£1), quiche (£1.50), or cake (£1). Open daily 9am-11pm.

Hobbs' Pavillion, Parker's Piece, off Park Terrace. Renowned for imaginative, rectangular pancakes. Mars Bar and cream pancake £3.50. Open Tues.-Sat. noon-2:15pm and 7pm-9:45pm.

The Little Tea Room, 1 All Saints' Passage, off St. John's St. Tip-top teas served in a teeny basement room. Scone, jam, and cream with pot of tea £2.50. Open March-Dec. Mon.-Sat. 9:30am-5:30pm, Sun. noon-6pm.

PUBS

Cantabrigian hangouts offer good pub-crawling year-round, though they lose some of their character and their best customers in summer. Most pubs stay open from 11am to 11pm, noon to 10:30pm on Sundays. A few close from 3 to 7pm, especially on Sundays. Students drink at the **Anchor,** Silver St. (by the river), on rainy days, and **The Mill,** Mill Lane off Silver St. Bridge, on sunny ones. The Anchor boasts live jazz bands on Tuesdays and Thursdays (tel. 353 554), and at the neighboring Mill you can partake of a pint along the banks of the Cam while punt-and-people watching. The **Pickerel** on Bridge St. holds the grand distinction of being Cambridge's oldest pub. **The Maypole,** on Portugal Pl. between Bridge St. and New Park St., conjures up cocktails more often than beer; the pub sports a billiards table. The **Burleigh Arms,** 9-11 Newmarket Rd., serves up beer and lager to its primarily gay, lesbian, and bisexual clientele. Amble down to the **Bird in Hand** (next to the roundabout), where gay men are welcome, and have a pint in the beer garden.

Those who prefer live music can take their choice of pubs. **Flambard's Wine Bar,** 4 Rose Crescent (tel. 358 108), has live blues and jazz on weekends, and to the east, **The Geldart,** 1 Ainsworth St. (tel. 355 983), features Irish folk, rock and R&B. **The Junction,** Clifton Rd. (tel. 412 600), off Cherry Hinton Rd. south of the town, proves a popular alternative dance venue on Friday nights and hosts top local bands.

ENTERTAINMENT

On a sunny afternoon, bodies sprawl on the lush banks of the Cam and the river fills with narrow, flat-bottomed **punts.** Punting is the sometimes stately, sometimes soggy pastime of propelling a flat little boat by pushing a long pole into the river bottom. Punters seeking calm and charm can take two routes—one from Magdalene Bridge to Silver St., and the other from Silver St. along the River Granta to Grantchester. On the first route—the shorter, busier, and more interesting of the two—you'll pass the colleges and the Backs. You can rent a punt from **Scudamore's Boatyards,** at Magdalene Bridge or Silver St. (tel. 359 750); hourly rates £6-8 for punts, rowboats, and canoes, plus a £40 cash deposit (open daily 9am-6pm). **Tyrell's,** Magdalene Bridge (tel. 352 847), has punts, rowboats, and a canoe for £8 per hour, plus a £30 deposit. Tyrell's offers chauffeured rides (45min.) from £15 per group. You can expect long lines for punts on weekends, particularly on Sundays. Guided tours, punted by students, are also available—inquire at the tourist office.

During the first two weeks of June, students celebrate the end of the term with **May Week,** crammed with concerts, plays, and elaborate balls that feature everything from hot air balloon rides to sleeping face-down drunk in the street. Along the Cam, the college boat clubs compete in an eyebrow-raising series of races known as the **bumps.** Crews line up along the river rather than across it and attempt to ram the boat in front before being bumped from behind. May Week's artistic repertoire stars the famous **Footlights Revue,** a collection of comedy skits; alumni include John Cleese, Eric Idle, and Graham Chapman.

The **Cambridge Festival** brightens the last two weeks of July with a series of concerts and special exhibits culminating in a huge folk festival. Tickets for the weekend (about £32) include camping on the grounds. (For the main festival, call the Corn Exchange box office, tel. 357 851.)

The **Arts Cinema,** Market Passage (tel. 352 001), screens comedy classics and undubbed foreign films and holds a film festival during the Festival (tickets £2.90-3.80; box office open Mon.-Sat. 10am-9:15pm, Sun. 1-9:15pm). The Cinema box office also handles **ADC Theatre** (Amateur Dramatic Club) ticket sales. The ADC, Park St., offers lively performances and movies during the term and the Cambridge Festival. You can get an earful of concerts at the **Cambridge Corn Exchange,** at the corner of Wheeler St. and Corn Exchange, a venue for band, jazz, and classical concerts (box office tel. 357 851; tickets £7.50-16; 50% off for student standby day of performance for certain concerts; box office open Mon.-Sat. 10am-6pm).

■ ■ ■ BRIGHTON

> *In Lydia's imagination, a visit to Brighton comprised every possibility of earthly happiness.*
>
> —Jane Austen, Pride and Prejudice

The undisputed home of the "dirty weekend," garish Brighton sparkles with a tawdry luster all its own. According to legend, the soon-to-be King George sidled into Brighton for some hanky panky around 1784. Having staged a fake wedding with a certain "Mrs. Jones" (Fitzherbert), he headed off to the farmhouse known today as the Royal Pavilion and the Royal rumpus began. Today, holiday-goers and locals alike peel it all off at England's first official clothing-optional beach. Kemp Town and its environs thrive with one of the biggest gay and lesbian populations in Britain.

Brighton's transformation from the sleepy village of Brighthelmstone to England's "center of fame and fashion" was catalyzed by the scientific efforts of one man. In 1750, Dr. Richard Russell wrote a Latin treatise on the merits of drinking and bathing in sea water for the treatment of glandular disease. Before that time, sea-swimming had been considered nearly suicidal. The treatment received universal acclaim, and seaside towns like Brighton began to prosper. Brighton's still-dignified rowhouses recall the days when Victorian holiday-goers paid to strut along certain stretches of grass and beach.

A visit to the city necessitates a visit to the wildly eclectic (and thrice-incarnated) **Royal Pavilion** (tel. 603 005) on Pavilion Parade, next to Old Steine, a locus of incandescent excess. Architect John Nash conjured up the Pavilion's current style during 1815-1822, embellishing Henry Holland's classically-inspired villa. It was at the request of George, prince of Wales, that the Pavilion underwent its third round of cosmetic surgery: George's reign as king (1820-1830) saw the complete transformation of his beloved Pavilion. Inside, not a surface has gone unadorned. Chinoiserie clutters every inch of floor and wallspace, with the exception of the King's apartments, which contain Regency furniture. A full 9 yd. high, the chandelier in the opulent Banquetting room sports a silver dragon on top. Serpents and dragons cover the Music Room. Queen Victoria sold the Pavilion to the city of Brighton in 1850 for next to nothing (open daily 10am-6pm; Oct.-May 10am-5pm; £3.75, seniors and students £2.75, children £2.10; partial wheelchair access).

Around the corner from the Pavilion stands the **Brighton Museum and Art Gallery** on Church St. (tel. 603 005), featuring paintings, English pottery, and an Art Deco collection which recalls the glamour of the inter-war years. The collection includes a sofa by Salavador Dalí entitled *Mae West's Lips*.

Before heading to the seafront, stroll through the **Lanes** where small fishing cottages once thrived. A hodge-podge of 17th-century streets—some no wider than three feet—cover the precincts south of North Street and constitute the heart of Old Brighton. Walking tours leave from the tourist office (June-Aug. Sun. 2:30pm; £3).

Few people actually swim along the pebbly beaches of Brighton—most spend their time wilting in deck chairs or padding along the stately promenade. The **Palace Pier**, 100 years old and recently painted, offers a host of amusements including a museum of slot machines between the piers under King's Road Arches. **Volk's Railway,** Britain's first three-foot-gauge electric train, shuttles back and forth along the waterfront (runs April-Sept. daily 10am-dusk; fare 85p, children 35p).

Although England's largest aquarium, **Brighton Sea Life Centre** (tel. 604 233) recently freed its dolphins, many other sea creatures remain enclosed in glass tanks for your viewing pleasure (open daily 10am-6pm; £4.50, children £3.25; wheelchair accessible). The **Grand Hotel,** on the front on King's Rd., has been substantially rebuilt since a 1984 IRA bombing that killed five but left then-Prime Minister Margaret Thatcher unscathed.

ORIENTATION AND PRACTICAL INFORMATION

The train station stands at least 10min. from the town center and seafront. To reach the tourist office in Bartholomew Square opposite the town hall, walk south along Queens Rd. towards the water. Turn left onto North St. and continue until you reach Ship St.; then turn right onto Ship and proceed along to Prince Albert St.

Trains travel regularly from London to Brighton (at least 2 per hr.; 1¼hr.; £11, day return £17.10). **National Express buses** from London to Brighton, also (8/day, 2hr., from £6.75 return).

Tourist Office: 10 Bartholomew Sq. (tel. 326 450). Book-a-bed ahead service £2.50 plus deposit; London booking fee slightly higher. Free basic street map available. Open June-mid July Mon.-Fri. 9am-6pm, Sat. 10am-5pm, Sun. 10am-4pm; mid-July-late Aug. Mon.-Fri. 9am-6pm, Sat. 10am-5:30pm, Sun. 10am-5:30pm; Sept.-May Mon.-Fri. 9am-5pm, Sat. 10am-5pm, Sun. 10am-4pm.

Postal Code: BN1 1BA.

Telephone Code: 01273.

Train Station: (tel. 206 755), at the end of Queen's Rd. away from the front. London timetable tel. 278 23.

Bus Station: National Express services stop at Pool Valley bus station at southern angle of Old Steine. Ticket and info booth at south tip of Old Steine green. Open Mon.-Sat. 8:30am-5:30pm, Sun. 9:30am-4pm. For info call 674 881. Get **Local bus** info from **One Stop Travel**, 16 Old Steine at St. James St. Open Mon.-Fri. 8:30am-5:45pm, Sat. 9am-5pm, Sun. 10am-4pm. For info, call 672 156 (Brighton and Hove Bus and Coach Co.).

Bike Rental: Harmon Leisure Hire, 21-24 Montpelier Rd. (tel. 205 206). £6.15 per day, £20 per week; deposit £50. Open Mon.-Fri. 8am-5pm, Sat. 8am-2pm.

Hospital: Royal Sussex County, Eastern Rd., parallel to Marine Rd. east of town (tel. 696 955).

Emergency: Dial 999; no coins required. **Police:** John St. (tel. 606 744).

ACCOMMODATIONS

Brighton's best bets for budget lodgings are the two independent hostels and the one operated by YHA. B&Bs and their larger equivalent, the cheap hotel, cost around £17 per person here. Cheaper and shabbier B&Bs and hotels nest west of West Pier and east of Palace Pier. A number of places to stay can be found in **Kemp Town,** the area which runs perpendicular to the sea past Palace Pier. Inquire at the tourist office for a list of gay and lesbian owned and operated guest houses.

Brighton Backpackers Hostel, 75-76 Middle St. (tel. 777 717). An independent hostel with attitude. Great location). No curfew. Mixed and/or single sex dorms, 4-8 per room. £9. Weekly rates negotiable, usually £40 per week. Sheets £1. Inexpensive breakfast and dinner. Laundry facilities available. £5 key deposit. Rodger and Tim also recently acquired a hotel on King's Rd. around the corner from the hostel. Doubles, twins, and triples at £12.50 per person.

Moonrider's Rest, 33 Oriental Place, near West Pier (tel. 733 740). The basement entry to the Rest leads into a cool bar with a blue mosaic floor. No curfew, no lockout. Mixed and single sex dorms as well as an odd assortment of doubles. £8 per person, £45 per week. Doubles £20. Duvets £1. Ask about the "pay for three nights, get one free" promotion. Laundry facilities.

HI Youth Hostel, Patcham Pl. (tel. 556 196), 4mi. north on the main London road (the A23). Take Patcham bus #773 or 5A (from stop E) from Old Steine to the Black Lion Hotel. Big country house with rooms that look new, though they're 400 years old. £7.50, 16-20 £6.30. Breakfast £2.30. Sleep sack hire 75p.

Catnaps, 21 Atlingworth St. (tel. 685193). A kindly, if absent-minded professor type, the proprietor keeps seven immaculate rooms with high ceilings and a pair of spaniels. Mostly gay men, but women welcomed. Singles up to £17; doubles £35. Full English breakfast. Will cater to vegetarians; vegans should phone requests ahead. TV lounge. Credit cards accepted with 5% surcharge.

Cavalaire Guest House, 34 Upper Rock Gdns. (tel. 696 899). Cheering good value, with TV, tea-making facilities, and assorted electrical appliances in each room. Singles £16-17. Doubles £26-40.

FOOD AND PUBS

The cheapest restaurants can be found up the hill between Western and Dyke Rd. American-style burger and pizza houses line up along Prince Albert St. The café scene doesn't suffer in Brighton; tourists and locals gather around tables inside and out for conversation, coffee, reading, or writing at **Sanctuary,** 51-55 Brunswick St. East, Hove (tel. 770 002), the **Dorset Bar** at the corner of North St. and Gardener St., and **Brown's,** 3 Duke St. (tel. 323 501).

Food for Friends, 17a Prince Albert St. (tel. 202 316). Well-seasoned vegetarian food in a hip and breezy atmosphere. The salads (in small, medium, and large portions) send the taste buds straight to heaven. Meals £2.50-4. Open Mon.-Sat. 9am-10pm, Sun. 9:30am-10pm. Also try their patisserie around the corner at 41 Market St., where *al fresco* dining's the norm.

The Coffee Company, corner of Meeting House Lane and Prince Albert S. (tel. 220 222). Large cappucino £1.10. Fresh cakes and baguettes every day. Brie baguette £1.95. Pasta salads from £1.10. Open daily 8am-10pm.

Noori's, 70-71 Ship St. (tel. 329 405 or 747 109). Spices up tandoori and curry dishes. Tandoori chicken £4.45. Vegetarians will take a hankering to Noori's *dal* (£3.45). Open Mon.-Sat. for lunch noon-2:15pm; Mon.-Thurs. 6pm-11:30pm; Fri.-Sat. 6pm-midnight; Sun. 11am-11pm.

Donatello, 3 Brighton Pl (tel. 775 477). Open-air Italian restaurant in the heart of the Lanes. Sumptuous salads £3.20, pizza £3.75-5. Open daily 11:30am-11:30pm.

ENTERTAINMENT

Brighton brims with nightlife options, earning it the nickname "London-by-the-Sea." Consult the local monthly, *The Punter,* which details evening events and is available at pubs, news agents, and record stores (70p). *What's On,* a poster-sized flysheet, offers information on happening scenes. **Gay and lesbian** venues can be found by perusing the latest issues of *Gay Times* or *Capital Gay*.

Numerous night clubs cater to all sensibilities. Most clubs open from 10pm-2am every day except Sunday. Trendier types dance at **The Escape Club** (tel. 606 906) near the pier at 10 Marine Parade. The multi-leveled **Zap Club,** at King's Rd. (tel. 821 588), pounds out hardcore rave and house music, and hosts frequent gay nights. **Zanzibar,** St. James St. (tel. 622 100), is a happening gay spot. **Paradox** (tel. 321 628) and **Event** (tel. 732627), both on West. St., admit the masses nightly onto their glitzy dance floors. Indie rock scenesters will feel at home in the **Underground** at 77 West St. (tel. 327 701). **Casablanca** on Middle St. (tel. 321 817) delivers live jazz to a largely student crowd.

The **Queen's Arms,** 8 George St. (tel. 696 873) packs an enthusiastic gay and lesbian crowd into its Sunday night cabaret. On Wednesday and Saturday nights the disco ball spins. Bedstands and vodka bottle chandeliers make **Smugglers** on Ship

CANTERBURY

St. an entertaining place to drink. Have a jazz lunch (Wed., Thurs., or Sun.) at **The King and Queen,** Marlborough Pl. (tel. 607 207).

Brighton Centre, King's Rd., and the **Dome,** #29 New Rd., host Brighton's mammoth rock and jazz concerts. Tickets can be acquired at the Brighton Centre **booking office** on Russell Rd. (tel. 202 881; open Mon.-Sat. 10am-5:30pm) and at the Dome booking office at 29 New Rd. (tel. 674 357; open Mon.-Sat. 10am-5:30pm). Tickets are also available at the tourist office.

Plays and touring London productions take the stage at the **Theatre Royal,** New Rd., a Victorian beauty with the requisite red plush interior (gallery tickets £4.50-8, circles and stalls £7-18.50; student standbys from 10am on day of performance except Sat. evenings £8-8.50; box office tel. 328 488; open Mon.-Sat. 10am-8pm). A café bar, theater, and cabaret coexist under one roof at **Komedia,** 14-17 Manchester St. between Marine Parade and St. James St. (box office tel. 670 030). A wide variety of dramatic events grace the Komedia's stage. Tickets range from £4-7.50. Senior and student discounts available. Stand-by tickets are subject to availability 15 minutes before a performance (all seats £4; box office open 12:30-2pm and 5-9pm daily; café bar open daily 10:30am-11pm).

Just west of Brighton Marina are **nude bathing** areas. Be sure to stay within the limits. **Telescombe beach,** nearly 4½ mi. to the east of Palace Pier, is frequented for the most part by a gay crowd. Look for a sign marked "Telescombe Cliffs."

■■■ CANTERBURY

> Whan Zephyrus eek with his sweete breeth
> Inspired hath in every holt and heeth
> The tendre croppes, and the yonge sonne
> Hath in the Ram his halve cours yronne...
> Thanne longen folk to goon on pilgrimages...
> Geoffrey Chaucer, Prologue to The Canterbury Tales

"There is no lovelier place in the world than Canterbury," wrote the much-traveled Virginia Woolf. There are those who would disagree, most notably Thomas à Becket, who clashed with Henry II over the clergy's freedom from state jurisdiction. Henry cried in exasperation, "Who will deliver me from this turbulent priest?" In December 1170 four loyal knights answered their king's query and murdered Becket in the Canterbury cathedral. Becket died a martyr and a saint, Henry a mere mortal. In the Middle Ages, the road from London to Canterbury became England's busiest, lined with pilgrims wending their way to Becket's shrine. Chaucer's winking satire of materialism on the pilgrimage trail remains ever-relevant.

Canterbury Cathedral overwhelms the tiny town from all vantage points. To observe every detail of this soaring 537-ft. building, amble through the grounds of King's School off Palace St. Inside the cathedral, pass through the nave to the left where the dramatic **Altar of the Sword's Point,** the site of the murder, has been restored. Explore the vast Norman **crypt,** the oldest part of the cathedral, and emerge into Trinity Chapel, where Becket's body lay enshrined until Henry VIII destroyed the memorial in 1538. (Open Easter-Oct. Mon.-Sat. 8:45am-7pm; Nov.-Easter 8:45am-5pm. Choral evensong Mon. 5:15pm, Sat.-Sun. 3:15pm; 45 min. Donation £2. Check nave pulpit for times of guided tours: tickets £2.40, students £1.20. 25-min. walkman tour £1.70. Services Sun. 11am and 6:30pm.)

After making the pilgrimage to the famed cathedral, see Chaucer's equally famous verses brought to life at **The Canterbury Tales** visitor attraction, St. Margaret's St. (tel. 454 888). A walkman-like gadget leads you through a virtual Canterbury pilgrimage complete with wax figures, moving sets, and the smells of sweat, hay, and grime. A waxen, black-cloaked Chaucer guides you along. (Open daily 9am-6pm; £4.75, seniors and students £3.95, children £3.50, family £15).

The remainder of medieval Canterbury crowds around the branches of the River Stour on the way to the **Westgate,** the only one of the city's seven medieval gates to survive the wartime blitz. A small museum in **Westgate Tower** (tel. 452 747) houses collections of old armor and prison relics (open Mon.-Sat. 11am-12:30pm and 1:30-3:30pm; 60p). Several rickety monastic houses perch precariously along the banks of the River Stour. For a quiet break, walk over to Stour St. and visit the riverside gardens of the **Greyfriars,** the first Franciscan friary in England, built over the river in 1267. A small museum and a chapel can be found inside the simple building (open in summer Mon.-Fri. 2-4pm; free).

The lovely medieval **Poor Priests' Hospital,** also on Stour St., now houses the **Museum of Canterbury Heritage** (tel. 452 747; open Mon.-Sat. 10:30am-5pm; June-Oct. Sun. 1:30-5pm; £1.30, students £1, children 65p).

On St. Peter's Street, across from Stour St., stand the **Weaver's Houses,** where Huguenots lived during the 16th century. Walk into the garden to see an authentic ducking stool (a medieval test for suspected witches) swinging over the river. **Weaver's River Tours** runs cruises from here several times daily (£3.50; row-it-yourself £2.50, children £1.50).

Near the medieval city wall across from East Station, lie the **Dane John Mound and Gardens** and the massive, solemn remnants of the Norman **Canterbury Castle.** If you fail to encounter the ghost of Canterbury's own Christopher Marlowe "rolling down the streets a-singing" you can at least find a statue of his muse in the garden. Not much remains of **St. Augustine's Abbey** (598 AD), but older Roman ruins and the site of St. Augustine's first tomb (605 AD) can be viewed outside the city wall near the cathedral (tel. 767 345; open Mon.-Sat. 9:30am-6pm, Sun. 2-6pm; off-season Mon.-Sat. 9:30am-4pm; £1, students 75p).

ORIENTATION AND PRACTICAL INFORMATION

Canterbury is roughly circular, enclosed by a ring road around a city wall that has been slowly eroding over the centuries. The circle is crossed from west to east by an unbroken street that is named, in different sections, **St. Peter's Street, High Street,** and **St. George's Street.** The cathedral rises from the northeast quadrant. To reach the tourist office from East Station, cross the footbridge, take a left down the hill, and turn right onto Castle St., which becomes St. Margaret's St. From West Station, walk southwest along Station Rd. West, turn left onto St. Dunstan's St., and walk through Westgate Tower onto St. Peter's St. (which becomes High St.), and then right onto St. Margaret's St.

Getting There: Trains run hourly from London's Victoria Station to Canterbury East Station, the stop nearest the youth hostel, and from Charing Cross and Waterloo stations to Canterbury West Station (1½hr., £11.70, day return £11.90). **Buses** to Canterbury leave London's Victoria Bus Station twice daily (1¾hr., £6.75-11.50).

Tourist Office: 34 St. Margaret's St. CT1 2TG (tel. 766 567). Book-a-bed ahead for £3 or 10% deposit of first night's stay. *City of Canterbury Guide* (£1.99). Open daily 9:30am-5:30pm; Nov.-March daily 9:30am-5pm.

Tours: Guided tours of the city depart from the tourist office April-Nov. daily 2pm; additional morning tour at 11am late May-early Sept. Mon.-Sat. On Friday evenings mid-July-late Aug. tours leave from the Buttermarket at 8pm. Tickets available at the tourist center. £2.50, seniors, students, and children £1.80, under 12 free when accompanied by parent.

Postal Code: CT1 2BA. **Telephone Code:** 01227.

Train Stations: East Station, Station Rd. East, off Castle St., southeast of town. **West Station,** Station Rd. West, off St. Dunstan's St. (tel. (01732) 770 111). Open Mon.-Fri. 6:15am-7:40pm, Sat. 6:30am-7:40pm, Sun. 9:15am-5:30pm.

Bus Station: St. George's Lane (tel. 472 082). Open Mon.-Sat. 8:15am-5:30pm. Get there by 5pm to book National Express tickets. **Luggage storage** until 5pm (£1).

Hospital: Kent and Canterbury Hospital: off Ethelbert Rd. (tel. 766 877).

Emergency: Dial 999; no coins required. **Police:** Old Dover Rd. (tel. 762 055).

ACCOMMODATIONS AND FOOD

The summer months see many pilgrims in Canterbury; book ahead. B&Bs bunch by both train stations and on London and Whitstable Rd., just beyond West Station.

HI Youth Hostel, 54 New Dover Rd. (tel. 462 911), ¾ mi. from East Station and ½ mi. southeast of the bus station. Turn right as you leave station and continue up the main artery, which becomes Upper Bridge St.; at second rotary, turn right onto St. George's Pl., which becomes New Dover Rd. 91 beds. Victorian villa with good facilities, washers, and hot showers. Doors open 7-10am and 1-11pm. £8.70, under 18 £5.80. Call for off-season openings.

The Tudor House, 6 Best Lane (tel. 765 650), off High St. Clean, bright rooms in a 450-year-old house full of warmth and character with TV and tea/coffeemakers. Agreeable owners and a central location. Bikes and boats for hire to guests. £16.

London Guest House, 14 London Rd. (tel. 765 860). Run by Shirley and Peter Harris, their mutt Bo, and their ginger kitten Tigger. Spacious Victorian house in immaculate condition. Nicely decorated rooms. £16.

Milton House, 9 South Canterbury Rd. (tel. 765 531). 20-min. walk from town center. Two tidy rooms and a warm welcome on a quiet street. Doubles £30.

York House, 22 Old Dover Rd. (tel. 765 743), close to East Station, just outside the city wall. Spacious B&B, all rooms with TV. 1 shower for every 3 rooms. £14.

Canterbury's only vegetarian restaurant, **Fungus Mungus,** 34 St. Peter's St., cooks great fresh food despite the unfortunate name (main dishes £4.95, starters £2.10; 0pen daily 10am-11pm). **Marlowe's,** 55 St. Peter's St., is an extremely friendly place with theatrical decor and an eclectic mix of vegetarian and beefy English, American, and Mexican food. They serve seven kinds of 6-oz. burgers for £5.75 (open daily 11am-11pm). Close to East Station on a small street within the city walls, **The White Hart,** Worthgate Pl., is a congenial pub with homemade luncheon specials for £3-6. Ask to eat in the rose garden (open for lunch Mon.-Sat. noon-2:30pm).

ENTERTAINMENT

The tourist center carries a number of leaflets pertaining to entertainment in the region. *Around Canterbury* provides an up-to-date listing of events; *Fifteen Days,* published biweekly, lists entertainment in all its various permutations in the city. Call 767 744 for the recorded "Leisure Line."

Young bands of players ramble from corner to corner, acting out the most absurd of Chaucer's scenes. But it's the pubs that keep Canterbury awake after dark. The **Miller's Arms,** Mill Lane off Radigund St., offers six draught beers. **Alberry's,** 38 St. Margaret's St., a snazzy wine bar, has live music Mondays and Thursdays from 9pm to 1am. The bar opens Monday through Saturday from noon to midnight.

The new **Marlowe Theatre,** The Friars (tel. 787 787), stages London productions and variety shows (tickets £4-17.50). The **Gulbenkian Theatre,** at the University of Kent, University Rd. (tel. 769 075), west of town out St. Dunstan's St., past St. Thomas' Hill, stages a series of amateur and professional productions. (Box office open Sept.-Dec. Mon. noon-4pm, Tues.-Fri. 10:30am-6pm (until 8pm performance evenings). Tickets £6-10; ask about student and senior discounts.

For information on summer arts events and the **Canterbury Festival**—two full October weeks of drama, opera, cabaret, chamber music, dance, and exhibitions—call 452 853, or write to Canterbury Festival, Christ Church Gate, The Precincts, Canterbury, Kent CT1 2EE.

■■■ BATH

Immortalized by Fielding, Smollet, Austen, and Dickens, the elegant Georgian town of Bath (pop. 83,000) was at one time the second social capital of England. Queen Anne's visit to the natural hot springs here in 1701 established Bath as one of the great meeting places for British artists and intellectuals of the 18th century.

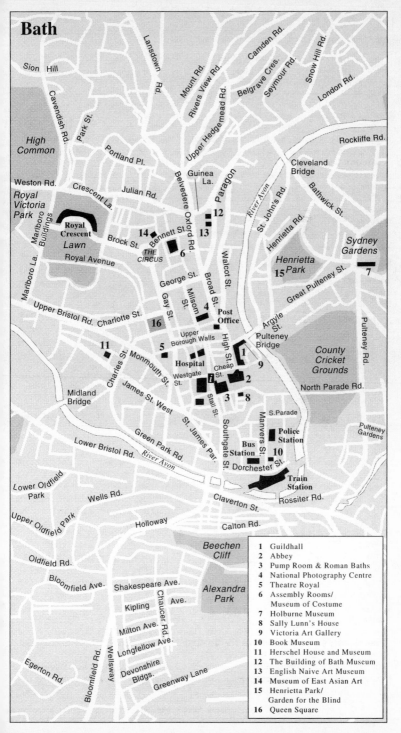

Bath

Sion Hill
Lansdown Rd.
Mount Rd.
Rivers View Rd.
Camden Rd.
Belgrave Cres.
Seymour Rd.
Snow Hill Rd.
London Rd.
Cavendish Rd.
Park St.
High Common
Portland Pl.
Rockliffe Rd.
Cleveland Bridge
Weston Rd.
Crescent La.
Julian Rd.
Guinea La.
Paragon
River Avon
St. John's Rd.
Bathwick St.
Royal Victoria Park
Belvedere Oxford Rd.
Henrietta Rd.
Sydney Gardens
Marlboro Buildings
Royal Crescent
Lawn
Brock St.
Bennett St.
14
6
THE CIRCUS
12
13
Henrietta Park
15
7
Marlboro La.
Royal Avenue
George St.
Walcot St.
Great Pulteney St.
Upper Bristol Rd.
Charlotte St.
Gay St.
Milsom St.
Broad St.
4
Post Office
Argyle St.
Pulteney Bridge
County Cricket Grounds
Pulteney Rd.
16
Upper Borough Walls
High St.
1
Pulteney Gardens
11
5
Hospital
Cheap St.
2
9
North Parade Rd.
Charles St.
Monmouth St.
Westgate St.
ℹ
3
8
Midland Bridge
James St. West
Stall St.
S.Parade
Manvers St.
Police Station
Green Park Rd.
St. James Par.
Southgate St.
10
Lower Bristol Rd.
River Avon
Bus Station
Dorchester St.
Lower Oldfield Park
Wells Rd.
Claverton St.
Train Station
Rossiter Rd.
Upper Oldfield Park
Oldfield Rd.
Holloway
Calton Rd.
Beechen Cliff
Bloomfield Ave.
Shakespeare Ave.
Alexandra Park
Kipling Ave.
Chaucer Rd.
Milton Ave.
Longfellow Ave.
Egerton Rd.
Bloomfield Rd.
Wellsway
Devonshire Bldgs.
Greenway Lane

1   Guildhall
2   Abbey
3   Pump Room & Roman Baths
4   National Photography Centre
5   Theatre Royal
6   Assembly Rooms/
    Museum of Costume
7   Holburne Museum
8   Sally Lunn's House
9   Victoria Art Gallery
10 Book Museum
11 Herschel House and Museum
12 The Building of Bath Museum
13 English Naive Art Museum
14 Museum of East Asian Art
15 Henrietta Park/
    Garden for the Blind
16 Queen Square

Legend ascribes the founding of Bath to King Lear's leper father Bladud, who wandered the countryside bemoaning his banishment from court. He took work as a swineherd, but his pigs soon caught "the affliction." The devoted and decomposing swine led their king to a therapeutic spring; out of gratitude, Bladud founded a city on the site.

Long before the age of Hanoverian refinement, Bath flourished for nearly 400 years as the Roman spa city of Aquae Sulis. **The Roman Baths** (tel. 461 111) retain their prominence in the town center. Sewer diggers first uncovered the site inadvertently in 1880, and recent deliberate excavation has yielded a splendid model of advanced Roman engineering. Also on display within the corridors are a gilded bronze head of Minerva and a heap of Roman pennies tossed into the baths for good luck (open daily March-July and Sept. 9am-6pm; Aug. 9am-6pm and 8-10pm; Nov.-Feb. Mon.-Sat. 9am-5pm, Sun. 10am-5pm; last tickets ½hr. before closing; partially wheelchair accessible; £5, children £3, family rate £13). Excellent guided tours of the baths leave twice per hour from beside the main pool.

Situated next door to the Baths, the 15th-century **Bath Abbey** towers over its neighbors; the tower beckons to visitors across the Bath skyline. The abbey saw the crowning of King Edgar, "first king of all England," in 973 AD. A stone just inside the entrance commemorates Reverend Dr. Thomas Malthus (1766-1834), founder of modern demographics and inspiration to family planners everywhere. Note the 56 stained-glass scenes of Jesus' life at the east end (open daily 9am-6pm; donation £1).

A short jaunt up Broad St., away from the tourist-trafficked abbey and baths, rests the **National Centre of Photography,** where visitors can purchase picture-perfect postcards, catch contemporary exhibits, and follow the history and growth of the camera (open daily 9:30am-5:30pm; £3, seniors and students £1.75).

Ever northward of the city center, the **Assembly Rooms,** Bennett St. (tel. 461 111), staged fashionable social events in the late 18th century. Although the ravages of World War II bombing decimated the rooms, renovations duplicate the originals in fine detail. The fascinating **Museum of Costume** dresses up several of the rooms, tracing the vagaries of fashion over 400 years. (Open daily 10am-5pm; £3.20, 18 and under £2, age 8 and below free; group rates available. Joint ticket with Roman Baths £6.60, children £3.50.)

In the city's residential northwest corner, Nash's contemporaries John Wood, *père et fils,* transformed the Georgian rowhouse into a design to be reckoned with. Walk up Gay St. to **The Circus,** which has attracted illustrious residents for two centuries. Blue plaques mark the houses of Thomas Gainsborough, William Pitt, and David Livingstone. Proceed from there up Brock St. to **Royal Crescent** and its great up-ended saucer of a lawn. The interior of **No. 1 Royal Crescent** (tel. 428 126) has been painstakingly restored by the Bath Preservation Trust to a near-perfect replica of a 1770 townhouse (open Tues.-Sun. 10:30am-5pm, Nov.-Dec. 10:30am-4pm; admission £3, children, students, and seniors £2.50). **Royal Victoria Park,** next to Royal Crescent, contains one of the finest collections of trees in the country, and its botanical gardens nurture 5000 species of plants from all over the globe. For bird aficionados, there's an aviary. (open Mon.-Sat. 9am-dusk, Sun. 10am-dusk; free).

Amble back down the hill to **Beckford's Tower,** Lansdown Rd. (tel. 338 727) for stupendous views to reward the 156 steps to the top (open April-late Oct. Sat., Sun., and bank holidays 2-5pm). If the climb makes you sing the blues, dally in the denim-swathed **History of Jeans Museum** (Britain's first and only) at Scallywag next to the Baths (tel. 445 040; open daily 9:30am-5:30pm; free).

Those with a more pretentious tastes might consider visiting the **Victoria Art Gallery**, Bridge St. (tel. 461 111 ext. 2772). Host to a collection of diverse works including Old Masters and contemporary British art, the museum stands next to the Pulteney Bridge (open Mon.-Fri. 10am-5:30pm, Sat. 10am-5pm; wheelchair accessible; free).

Homesick Yankees and others wanting to visit the United States vicariously should stop by the **American Museum** (tel. 460 503), perched high above the city at Claverton Manor. Inside is a fascinating series of furnished rooms transplanted from historically significant homes in the United States. Among the most impressive are a 17th-century Puritan Keeping Room, a Shaker Meeting House, and a cozy Revolutionary-War era tavern kitchen complete with a working beehive oven. (Climb Bathwick Hill to reach the manor. Museum open late-March-early Nov. Tues.-Sat. 2-5pm; Sun. and Mon. on bank holiday weekends 11am-5pm; gardens open Tues.-Fri. 1-6pm, Sat.-Sun. noon-6pm; admission to house, grounds, and galleries £5, seniors and students £4.50, children £2.50; grounds, Folk Art, and New Galleries only £2, children £1.) The #18 bus (£1.20) can save you a steep 2-mi. trudge up Bathwick Hill.

ORIENTATION AND PRACTICAL INFORMATION

The Pulteney Bridge and North Parade Bridge span the **River Avon,** which runs through the city from the east. The Roman Baths, the Abbey, and the Pump Room are all in the city center. The Royal Crescent and the Circus lie to the northwest. The train and bus stations are near the south end of Manvers St., at the bend in the river. From either terminal, walk up Manvers St. to the Orange Grove roundabout and turn left to the tourist office in the Abbey Churchyard.

Getting There: Bath is served by direct Intercity **rail** service from London's Paddington Station (every hr., 1½hr., single £26). **National Express** operates **buses** from London's Victoria coach station (9/day, 3hr., return £12.25).

Tourist Office: The Colonnades, (tel. 462 831 for information and accommodations). Map and mini-guide 25p. Pick up a free copy of *This Month in Bath*. Open Mon.-Sat. 9:30am-6pm, Sun. 10am-4pm; ,Sept.-mid-June Mon.-Sat. 9:30am-5pm.

Tours: Excellent free 2hr. guided **walking tours** leave from the Abbey Churchyard Sun.-Fri. at 10:30am and Mon., Wed., Thurs. at 2pm, Sun. 2:30pm; evening tours Tues., Fri., Sat. 7pm. City **tour bus tours** (every 15 min., 1hr, 9:30am-5pm) cost £3. **Mad Max Tours** (tel. (01926) 842 999; Mon.-Fri. 9am-5:30pm or call Maddy at (01836) 742 857 Mon.-Fri. 6-8pm) cater to young hordes eager for day-away bus treks to Wiltshire (Stonehenge, Avebury). 4-person min. is required for this day-long (8:45am-5pm) escapade (£12). Tours leave from "the statue" on Cheap St. by the Abbey.

Postal Code: BA1 1AA. **Telephone Code:** 01225.

Train Station: Railway Pl., at the south end of Manvers St. (tel. 463 075). Booking office open daily 6am-9:30pm. Travel Centre open Mon.-Fri. 8am-7pm, Sat. 9am-6pm, Sun. 10:30am-6pm. Lockers available.

Bus Station: Manvers St. (tel. 464 446). Lockers available.

Taxis: Ranks near stations. **Abbey Radio:** tel. 465 843. **Rainbow:** tel. 460 606.

Bike Rental: Avon Valley Bike Hire, Railway Pl. (tel. 461 880), behind train station. £4.50-6.50/hr., £10.50-22.50/day; deposit £20-75. Open daily 9am-6pm. Credit cards accepted.

Hospital: Royal United Hospital (tel. 428 331).

Emergency: Dial 999; no coins required. **Police:** Manvers St. (tel. 444 343).

ACCOMMODATIONS

Bath's well-to-do visitors drive up the prices of the B&Bs; expect to pay £14-17. B&Bs cluster on **Pulteney Road** and **Pulteney Gardens.** From the stations, walk up Manvers St., which becomes Pierrepont St., right on to N. Parade Rd. and past the cricket ground to Pulteney Rd. For a more relaxed (and more costly) setting continue past Pulteney Gdns. (or take the footpath from behind the rail station) to **Widcombe Hill.**

HI Youth Hostel, Bathwick Hill (tel. 465 674). From N. Parade Rd., turn left onto Pulteney Rd., then right onto Bathwick Hill. A footpath takes the hardy up the steep hill to the hostel (20min. walk). Badgerline "University" bus #18 (5 per hr. until 11pm, return 75p) runs from the bus station or the Orange Grove roundabout. Gracious, clean Italianate mansion overlooking the city. No lockout. 119 beds, shower, TV, laundry. £8.70; Sept.-May £7.50.

YMCA International House, Broad St. Place (tel. 460 471). Walk under the arch and up the steps from Walcot St. across from Beaufort Hotel. More central than HI hostel (3min. from tourist office). Laundry facilities. Singles £12. Doubles £22. Triples available as well. Dorm rooms with continental breakfast £9.50 per person. Key deposit £5.

Mrs. Guy, 14 Raby Pl. (tel. 465 120). From N. Parade, turn left onto Pulteney Rd., then right up Bathwick Hill. Georgian house with light, cool interiors, a modern art collection and views of the city. Seasonal fruits, homemade jams, and yogurts make a generous English breakfast. Singles £16. Doubles £32. No smoking.

The Shearns, Prior House, 3 Marlborough Lane (tel. 313 587). Great location on posh west side of town beside Royal Victoria Park. Take bus #14 or 15 from bus station (every 15min.). Doubles with full English breakfast £26. No smoking.

Mrs. Rowe, 7 Widcombe Crescent (tel. 422 726). Up the hill from the stations. The height of elegance. Blissfully quiet neighborhood. Full bath and TV. Singles £16-20. Doubles £30-36.

Avon Guest House, 1 Pulteney Gdns. (tel. 313 009), at Pulteney Rd. Large rooms, with full bath, color TV, and tea-making facilities. Friendly owners. Doubles with full English breakfast £34.

Hunter's Moon Inn, 10 Widcombe Parade (tel. 335 454). A variety of rooms above a pub and restaurant. Kindly owner will negotiate price and occupancy. £16 per person. No smoking.

FOOD AND PUBS

Harvest Natural Foods, 27 Walcot St., stocks a tremendous selection of organic produce (open Mon.-Sat. 9:30am-5:30pm). **Seasons,** 10 George St. (tel. 697 30), has a small deli and also offers a good selection of natural foods (open Mon.-Sat. 9am-5:30pm). Many pubs offer Sunday roast three-course lunches at bargain prices. Gossip over an elegant cream tea (£4.50) in the **Pump Room,** Abbey Churchyard, a palatial Victorian restaurant (open Mon.-Sat. 10am-5pm).

Scoff's, corner of Monmouth and Westgate St. Don't scoff at the freshly baked wholefood pastries and filling lunches served in a woody dining room with high ceilings. Big *tandoori* burger and salad £1.95. Open Mon.-Sat. 9am-5pm.

The Walrus and The Carpenter, 28 Barton St. (tel. 314 684), uphill from the Theatre Royal. Basic bistro foodstuffs. Good burgers with creative toppings £5-7. Vegetarian entrees £5-8. Open Mon.-Sat. noon-2:30pm and 6-11pm, Sun. 6-11pm.

The Canary, 3 Queen St. (tel. 424 846). Airy tea house serving light meals. Somerset rabbit from 18th-century recipe £4.50. Open Mon.-Fri. 9am-10pm, Sat. 9am-7pm, Sun. 11am-5:30pm.

The Crystal Palace, 11 Abbey Green, behind Marks and Sparks. A sprawling, 18th-century pub/restaurant with an outdoor patio. Ploughman's lunch 6 different ways (£3-4.50). Open for meals daily noon-2:30pm and 6pm-8:30pm.

Café Retro, at Orange Grobe (tel. 339 347). Let Ole Blue Eyes croon to you over pastries or burgers. Cool atmosphere. Smoked chicken and orange salad £3.90. Open Mon.-Sat. 10am-10:30p, Sun. 10am-6pm.

Pubs sit along Walcot St.; locals favor **The Bell,** where the best local bands (from rock to jazz) perform live nightly, and the trendy **Hat and Feather,** with two levels of indie and rave as well as mind-expanding light decorations. Those in search of powerful cider might venture up Broad St. to Belvedere St. and the **Beehive**. Next to the Theatre Royal, the Green Room at **The Garricks Head** is a pleasant gay pub.

ENTERTAINMENT

Classical and jazz concerts enliven the **Pump Room** (see Food and Pubs above) during morning coffee (Mon.-Sat. 10:30am-noon) and afternoon tea (2:30-5pm). In summer, buskers (street musicians) perform in the Abbey Churchyard, and a brass band often graces the Parade Gardens. Beau Nash's old pad, the magnificent **Theatre Royal,** Sawclose (tel. 448 844), at the south end of Barton St., sponsors a diverse dramatic program (tickets £7-30, matinees £7-14; student discounts available for all

DEAL

shows except Wed. matinees and evening performances on Sat. and Sun.; box office open Mon.-Sat. 10am-8pm, Sun. 1hr. before show).

Before a pub-and-club crawl, gather at the Huntsman Inn at North Parade Passage nightly at 8pm for the **Bizarre Bath Walking Tour** (tel. 335 124; no advance booking required). Punsters lead locals and tourists alike around Bath pulling pranks for about 1¼hrs (£3, students £2.50). Bath nights wake up at **The Bell**, 103 Walcot St. (tel. 460 426), an artsy pub featuring live jazz and blues. The Bell's partner in crime, **The Hub** (also on Walcot St.; tel. 446 288), starts up late and keeps going with reggae and funk vibes (open Wed.-Sat. 9pm-2am; cover £3-6). High-energy dance tracks draw a young crowd to the **Players Club,** on the corner of Pierrepont and North Parade (open nightly 9pm-2am; cover £5).

The renowned **Bath International Festival of the Arts,** over two weeks of concerts and exhibits, produces merriment all over town from late May to early June. The **Contemporary Art Fair** opens the festival by bringing together the work of over 700 British artists. Musical offerings range from major symphony orchestras and choruses to chamber music, solo recitals, and jazz. For a festival brochure and reservations, write to the Bath Festival Office, Linley House, 1 Pierrepont Pl., Bath BA1 1JY. The concurrent **Fringe Festival** (which also occurs city-wide) celebrates music, dance, and liberal politics.

■■■ DEAL

Deal Castle (tel. 372 762) warded off Catholic invaders from the Continent during the reign of Henry VIII. An indomitable fortress, rather than an elegant home, Deal Castle was done in the "Tudor Rose" style; it boasts six petals. Deal Castle stands south of town along the beach at the corner of Deal Castle Rd. and Victoria Rd. (open April-late Oct. daily 10am-6pm; Nov.-late March Wed.-Sun. 10am-4pm; £2, seniors and students £1.50, children £1; limited wheelchair accessibility; free tape tour available).

Walmer Castle (tel. 364 288), rests south of Deal on the A258 to Dover (around ½ mi. from town). The best preserved and most elegant of Henry VIII's coastal edifices, Walmer has since been transformed into a country estate. Since the 18th century, it has been the official residence of the Lords Warden of the Cinque Ports, a defensive system of coastal towns. Notable Lords Warden include the Duke of Wellington (whose precious "Wellies" are on display) and Winston Churchill. The post is currently filled by the Queen Mum. (Open April-Sept. daily 10am-6pm; Nov.-Dec. and March Weds.-Sun. 10am-4pm. Closed when Lord Warden is in residence. £2.70, students £1.90, children £1.30. Wheelchair access to courtyard and gardens.)

If you walk along the Coast to Deal Pier, you'll pass the **Timeball Tower,** a fascinating contraption connected by electric current to Greenwich Observatory. When ships used the Downs as a makeshift port before crossing the Channel, the ball on top of the tower was lowered at precisely 1pm each day to indicate the time to the sailors. Today, the ball drops every hour on the hour. Climb to the top for a panoramic view of town and sea (open late spring-early Sept. Tues.-Sun. 10am-5pm; in winter tours offered by arrangement; £1.10, seniors and children 70p). The **Maritime and Local History Museum,** 22 St. George's Rd. (tel. 369 576; inquiries directed to tourist office), located right behind the tourist office, delves into Deal's seafaring past with such unusual relics as figureheads, stern boards, and both real and model boats (open late May-late Sept. 2-5pm; 50p, seniors and students 40p, children 20p).

Deal's newest theatrical attraction is the **Trail of Blood,** the town's smuggling history brought to life by players on the city streets. This street theater performance and tour lasts 1½ hr. and includes a bit of pub-crawling through old Deal (reserve tickets at the tourist office; £3, children £2.50). If you're in Deal in late July or early August, the **Deal Summer Music Festival** hosts scores of musical performances. Call the box office at the Astor Theatre for details (tel. 366 077; tickets £7-12).

GETTING THERE

Deal lies 8 mi. north of Dover and 12 mi. southeast of Canterbury; trains and buses from London stop in Deal on their way to these cities. **Trains** run at least every hour to London (£15, cheap day return £15.10) via Dover and Sandwich. **National Express buses** run to Deal from London Victoria Station (£10.50-13.50).

ORIENTATION AND PRACTICAL INFORMATION

The town extends from north to south along the coast. Beach St., High St., and West St.—the major arteries—parallel the coast. Deal's **tourist office,** Town Hall, High St. (tel. 369 576), offers leaflets including *Deal Walks,* which details 10 3-8½ mi. walks around the area. For £3 or 10% of the first night's stay, they'll book a room (open Mon.-Fri. 9am-12:30pm and 1:30-5pm, Sat. 10am-3pm; Sept.-mid-May Mon.-Fri. 9am-12:30pm and 1:30-5pm). The **train station** (tel. 852 360) stands just west of town off Queen St., which becomes Broad St. as it runs toward the sea. To reach the center, turn left onto Queen St. and follow it until you reach the pedestrian precinct of High St. The **bus station** (tel. 374 088) idles on South St., which runs between High St. and Beach St., one block south of Broad St. (office open Mon.-Wed. and Fri. 8:45am-12:30pm and 1:30-5pm, Thurs. 8:45am-12:30pm, Sat. 8:45am-12:30pm). Bicycles can be rented at **Park Cycles,** rear of 42 High St. (tel. 366 080; £5-8.50 per day, £21.50-35 per week; deposit minimum £30; open Mon.-Sat. 8:30am-5:30). Deal's **postal code** is CT14 6ET. The **phone code** is 01304.

ACCOMMODATIONS AND FOOD

The nearest youth hostels are in Dover and Canterbury. Overlooking Deal Castle, **The Gables,** 10 Gilford Rd. (tel. 347 957) promises cleverly decorated rooms (single £13.50, doubles £25). **Cannongate,** 26 Gilford Rd. (tel. 375 238), resides on a placid street (singles £13.15, doubles £26 with full English breakfast). From the station turn right, away from town down Blenheim Rd.; Gilford Rd. is 10min. down on the left.

Enjoy the Channel view, photos of motley locals with their catch, and '78 flood scenes at the **Lobster Pot** (full English breakfast all day; take-away fish and chips £2.70; open daily 7:30am-10pm). Relax in a plush chair in **Ronnie's,** a beautifully appointed tea room just off High St. at #1B Stanhope Rd. (tel. 374 300).

■■■ DOVER

The grating roar of the English Channel has been drowned out by the puttering of ferries, the hum of hovercraft, and the squabbling of French families *en vacances.* Yet Dover has retained its identity despite the hum of tourist traffic.

The view from Castle Hill Rd., on the east side of town, reveals why **Dover Castle** is famed both for its magnificent setting and for its impregnability. (Take bus D77, 90 or 90A from Priory Station; minibus from town center April-Sept. weekends.) Many have launched assaults on it by land, sea, and air: the French tried in 1216, the English during the English Civil Wars in the mid-17th century, and the Germans in World Wars I and II. The **castle keep** exhibits an assortment of trivia and relics from the 12th century to the present. The top of the castle, accessible by several staircases, affords an arresting view of the battlements and countryside. Rumor has it that Boulogne can be seen on clear days; it was from that coast that the Germans launched V-1 and V-2 rocket bombs in World War II.

These rockets destroyed the **Church of St. James,** the ruins of which crumble at the base of Castle Hill. The empty **Pharos,** built in 43 BC, sits alongside **St. Mary's,** a Saxon church. The Pharos once served as a beacon for Caesar's galleys. The only Roman lighthouse still in existence, the Pharos' gaping keyhole windows testify to its original purpose.

Hell Fire Corner is a labyrinth of secret tunnels only recently declassified, totaling 3½ mi. The **tunnels,** originally built in the late 18th-century to defend Britain from attack by Napoleon, were the base for the evacuation of Allied troops from Dunkirk in World War II (Operation Dynamo). The tunnels served various functions for the county government of Kent until the 1980s, when operation costs became prohibitive. Graffiti covers most of the passageways. Though most date from the 1940s, a few inscriptions from the 19th-century are apparent. Convince the guides to show you the Napoleonic double helix staircase (open daily 10am-6pm; Nov.-March daily 10am-4pm; £5.25, seniors and students £3.95, children £2.60, family £15; partially wheelchair accessible).

Recent excavation has unearthed a remarkably well-preserved **Roman painted house** (tel. 203 279), New St., off Cannon St. near Market Sq., the oldest Roman house in Britain, complete with wall paintings and under-floor central heating system. (Open April and Sept.-Oct. Tues.-Sun. 10am-5pm, May-Aug. 10am-6pm. Open Mon. in July and August, too. £1.50, seniors and children 50p.)

The **Dover Museum,** Market Sq. (tel. 201 066), displays a permanent collection of curious bits of Victoriana, ship models, and clocks (open daily 10am-6pm; mid-Nov.-Feb. 10am-5:30pm; £1.20, seniors, students, and children 75p; wheelchair accessible).

A few miles west of Dover (25 min. by foot along Snargate St.) sprawls the whitest, steepest, most famous, and most unaccommodating of the white cliffs. Known as **Shakespeare Cliff** (look for the signs), it is traditionally identified with the cliff scene in *King Lear.* Closer to town on Snargate St. is the **Grand Shaft** (tel. 201 200), a 140-ft. triple spiral staircase shot through the rock in Napoleonic times to link the army stationed on the Western Heights and the city center. (Ascend May-Sept. Wed.-Sun. 2-5pm, on bank holidays 10am-5pm; £1, children 40p.)

ORIENTATION AND PRACTICAL INFORMATION

To reach the tourist office from the railway station, turn left onto Folkestone Rd. Continue along until you come to York St., turn right onto York and follow it to its end. Turn left onto Townwall St.; the tourist office will be on the left. From the bus station, turn left from Pencester onto Cannon St. Proceed through the pedestrianized city to Townwall St. and turn left. York St., which becomes High St. and eventually London Rd., borders the center of town. Maison Dieu Rd. borders the town on the other side.

Getting There: Trains chug to Dover's Priory Station from London's Victoria, Waterloo, Cannon St., London Bridge, and Charing Cross stations approximately every 45 minutes (2hr., £15.60, return £18.60). Beware when you board at London that trains branch off en route. From Victoria, express lines continue to the Western Docks Station. **Buses** run regularly (2 per hr.) from London's Victoria Coach Station; they continue to the Eastern Docks after stopping at the bus station on Pencester Rd. (2¾hr., £10).

Tourist Office: Townwall St. (tel. 205 108), 1 block from the shore. The staff posts a list of accommodations after hours. They also supply ferry tickets, hoverport tickets, and rental cars. Open daily 9am-6pm.

Postal Code: CT16 1BA. **Telephone Code:** 01304.

Train Station: Priory Station (tel. (01732) 770 111), off Folkestone Rd.

Bus Station: Pencester Rd., which runs between York St. and Maison Dieu Rd. (tel. 240 024; information (01813) 581 333). Purchase tickets on the bus or in the ticket office. Open Mon.-Fri. 8:30am-5:30pm, Sat. 8:30am-2pm.

Hospital: Buckland Hospital (tel. 201 624), on Coomb Valley Rd. northwest of town. Take local bus D9 or D5 from outside the post office.

Police: Ladywell St., right off High St. (tel. 240 055).

ACCOMMODATIONS

Several of the hundreds of B&Bs on **Folkestone Road** (by the train station) receive guests at all hours; if the lights are on, ring the bell. For daytime arrival, also try the B&Bs near the center of town on **Castle Street.**

Charlton House Youth Hostel (HI), 306 London Rd. (tel. 201 314), with overflow at **14 Goodwyne Rd.** (closer to town center). Hostel is a ½ mi. walk from the train station: turn left onto Folkestone Rd., left onto Effingham St., past the gas station onto Saxon St, and left at the bottom of the street onto High St., which becomes London Rd. Lockout 10am-1pm. Curfew 11pm. 70 beds. Goodwyne Rd. has 60 beds with bathrooms in each room. Both hostels £8.80, under 18 £5.95. Breakfast £2.70. Lockers available. Kitchen and lounge area.

Elmo Guest House, 120 Folkestone Rd. (tel. 206 236). A proprietor with a calming presence has airy rooms near the train station. £12-16 per person.

Amanda Guest House, 4 Harold St. (tel. 201 711). Well-located house built by a former mayor of Dover. £15 per person, children half-price.

Gordon Guest House, 23 Castle St. (tel. 201 894). The management is quite cordial. Comfortable rooms, all with showers (4 with full bathrooms). From £12-19 per person.

Victoria Guest House, 1 Laureston Pl. (tel. 205 140). The Hamblins extend a family welcome to their international guests. TV, tea/coffee-making facilities. Doubles £26-40. Family rooms £48-54. 5-day rates available.

YMCA, 4 Leyburne Rd. (tel. 206 138). Turn right off Goodwyne Rd. Rough it with a pallet on the floor. Co-ed. No curfew. Showers. Reception open daily 9am-noon and 5-10pm. £5 per person, bed and breakfast.

FOOD

Cheap food fries from dawn to dusk in the fish-and-chip shops and grocery stores on London Rd. and Biggin St. Vegetarians in Dover might check out **The Cabin,** 91 High St. (tel. 206 118), and **Topo Gigio,** 1-2 King St. (tel. 201 048), which offer both veggie and meaty dishes.

Chaplin's, 2 Church St. (tel. 204 870). A floral restaurant sprinkled with Chaplin ephemera. Sandwiches come cheap at £1.50 and cheeseburgers with fries cost £2.80. Open Mon.-Sat. 8:30am-9pm, Sun. 11:30am-5pm.

Jermain's Café, 18 Leighton Rd., on a quiet street off London Rd., just past the hostel; turn onto Beaconsfield Rd., then left into Jermain's. Menu on chalkboards outside. Roast beef, potatoes, and veggies £3.20. Open daily 11:30am-2pm.

Pizza Pronto, 7 Ladywell (tel. 214234). Medium-sized pizzas made while you wait. Good and hot. The plain Margherita rings in at £3.50. Open daily 5pm-midnight.

■ ■ ■ RYE

Settled before the Roman invasion, Rye's port flourished until the waterways choked with silt. Through the 18th century, the town was best known for its gangs of smugglers, who darted past royal authorities to stash contraband in an elaborate network of massive cellars, secret passageways, and attics.

A handful of cobbled streets recall the days when smugglers stole through a sleepy Rye. Extraordinarily well-preserved half-timber homes cover the hill on which much of the town sits. **Lamb House** stands on West St. (at the corner of West and Mermaid Sts.). Henry James wrote his later novels while living in the brick home, including *The Wings of the Dove* and *The Golden Bowl,* a novel to which some have ascribed excess agency (open April-Oct. Wed. and Sat. 2-5:30pm; £2).

Before descending the hill, contemplate **St. Mary's Church,** the huge medieval parish church at the top of Lion St., which houses one of the oldest functioning clocks in the country. The clock's gold-plated "quarter boys,"—they tolled every quarter hour—were forced into early retirement by upstart fiberglass models. A climb up the tower steps (£1.50, children 75p) reveals the inner-workings of the clock and the best view of the river valley £1.50 can buy.

Around the corner from the church lurks the **Ypres Tower** which shelters the **Rye Museum.** Originally built to fortify the town against invaders from the sea (c. 1250), the tower has served as a jail and currently contains a haphazard display on reform politics, military paraphernalia, domestic life, and Rye pottery (open April-Oct. daily 10:30am-5pm; £1.50, seniors and students £1, children 50p).

ORIENTATION AND PRACTICAL INFORMATION

Surrounded by waterways, Rye resides at the mouth of the River Rother. To reach the oldest and prettiest part of town, hike up Market Rd. to High St., Lion St., and Mermaid St. **Trains** roll from the station off Cinque Port St. (tel. (01424) 429 325) to London's Charing Cross and Cannon St. stations (1½hr.; £13.30, return £13.40). **National Express buses** run from London to Rye's train station (£11; for bus info call (01797) 223 343). The **tourist office** rests at the Rye Heritage Centre, The Strand Quay (tel. (01797) 226 696), sells *Adam's Historical Guide to Rye Royal* (£1.85) and the *Color Guide to Rye* (£1.50). The free *Rye: 1066 Country* guide lists points of interest, lodgings, and eating establishments (office open daily 9am-5:30pm; Nov.-March Mon.-Fri. 11am-1pm, Sat.-Sun. 10am-4pm). Rye's **postal code** is TN31 7AA. The folks at 8/9 Ropewalk Arcade (tel. (01797) 223 121) rent **bikes** for £7.50 per day. Rye's **police station** is on Cinque Port St. (tel. (01424) 425 000).

ACCOMMODATIONS

HI Youth Hostel, Guestling, Rye Rd., Hastings (tel. (01424) 812 373), 5 mi. down the A259 past Winchelsea on west side of main Hastings-Rye Rd. Take bus #11 or 12 from Rye to the White Hart in Guestling, 200 yd. downhill on left from the White Hart. (Mon.-Sat. roughly every hr., summer Sun. every 2hr.; £1.60; last bus around 5pm). You can also take the train to Three Oaks (£1.90) and walk 1¼ mi. 58 beds. Some family rooms available, but book early. £6.90, under 18 £4.60. Open July-Aug. daily; Sept.-Oct. and Feb. 12-March Tues.-Sat.; Nov. Fri.-Sat.; April 11-June Mon.-Sat.

Mrs. Jones, 2 The Grove (tel. (01797) 223 447), a 3min. walk from the train station. Turn left through the car park and left again onto Rope Walk, which becomes The Grove just past the train tracks. Well-read landlady pipes classical music through the house. Plush rooms accompanied by an equally extravagant breakfast. £14.

Mrs. Clifton, 4 Love Lane (tel. (01797) 222 979). Gorgeous flowers line the walk up to this brick home with large rooms quite near the train station. £14 per night.

Riverhaven Guest House, 60 New Winchelsea Rd. (tel. (01797) 223267). Clean guest house. All rooms with washbasins. Friendly proprietors will pick you up from train station if your luggage is cumbersome. £10-15 per person.

Amberley Bed and Breakfast, 5 New Rd. (tel. (01797) 225 693). Richard and Jane McGowan run a spotless family B&B. Beautifully furnished, with views of the water. £14-18 per person.

Tillingham Bed and Breakfast, 13 Winchelsea Rd. (tel. (01797) 224 807). Second generation B&Bers welcome you into their tidy, comfortable home. Big screen TV and VCR in lounge. £15, winter £12.50.

FOOD

Full-service eateries, take-away joints, and teashops riddle Rye. **Ye Olde Tuck Shoppe** on Market St. and **Simon the Pieman** on Lion St. peddle baked goods.

Union Inn, East St., offers a wide selection of foods (£1.70-5.45) in a building erected around the 15th century (open Mon.-Sat. 11am-3pm and 6-11pm; Sun. noon-3pm and 7-10:30pm.

Fletcher's House, Lion St. (tel. (01797) 223 101), in front of the church. Dramatist John Fletcher was born here in 1579. Open for morning coffee, lunch, and tea. After a meal, wander upstairs to the 15th-century oak room filled with antiques. Filling lunches £3-5; cream tea £3.40. Open daily 10am-5:15pm.

Jempson's Coffee House and Bakery, Cinque Port St. and Market Rd. Mouthwatering assortment of pastries, and cream teas for £2.25. Open Mon.-Sat. 8am-6pm.

Fu Wing Chinese Restaurant, 2 High St. (tel. (01797) 223 360). Though too dear at dinnertime, Fu Wing offers an abbreviated menu of cheaper lunch options: curry mixed vegetables £3.20, beef with green peppers in black bean sauce

£3.60. Open Sun.-Mon. and Thurs. noon-2pm and 5:30-10:30pm, Fri.-Sat. noon-2pm and 5:30-11pm, Wed. 5:30-10:30pm.

■■■ ARUNDEL

Built in the shadow of a Norman castle and a Catholic cathedral, Arundel (pop. 3200) is filled with wealthy Brits on holiday and white-vested cricketeers.

Arundel Castle (tel. (01903) 882 173) commands the eye of anyone entering the wee town. Ravaged during the Civil War, the castle was repeatedly restored by the various dukes who called it home in the 1700s and 1800s. The seat of the Duke of Norfolk, Earl Marshal of England, the castle holds the distinction of being the third oldest in all of England. Portraits by Van Dyck and Gainsborough people the **baron's hall** (open April-Oct. Sun.-Fri. 11am-5pm; last entry 4pm; £4.50, students and seniors £4, children £3.50). In late August, the castle hosts the **Arundel Festival,** ten days of concerts, jousting, and outdoor theater. For information call 883 690.

The quite steep and aptly named High St. leads to the **Cathedral of Our Lady and St. Philip Howard.** Decidedly more impressive from the outside, the French Gothic cathedral peers over Arundel from its perch up top. Joseph Hansom, inventer of the Hansom Cab, designed the Church. Despite being executed for cheering on the Spanish Armada in 1588, St. Philip occupies an honored place in the north transept (cathedral open daily 9am-6pm, in winter 9am-dusk).

Concealed observation enclosures at the **Wildfowl and Wetlands Trust Centre** on Mill Rd., ¾ mi. past the entrance to the castle (tel. (01903) 883 355), enable visitors to "come nose to beak with nature." Over 12,000 birds roost within the reserve's 55 acres (open daily 9:30am-5:30pm, winter daily 9:30am-4:30pm; last admission 1 hour prior to closing; £3.75, seniors and students £2.80, children £1.90; wheelchair accessible; 20% discount available with coupon from tourist office).

ORIENTATION AND PRACTICAL INFORMATION

To reach the center of town from the rail station, turn left onto the A27; it becomes the Causeway, Queen St., and then, as it crosses the river, High St. **Trains** leave London's Victoria Station for Arundel hourly (1¼hr., day return £12.30-14.10). At the **tourist office** at 61 High St. (tel. 882 268), pick up a free *Town Guide,* which lists attractions and a small street plan (open Mon.-Fri. 9am-5pm, Sat.-Sun. 10am-5pm; off-season Mon.-Fri. 9am-3pm, Sat.-Sun. 10am-3:30pm). Arundel's **postal code** is BN18 9AD, its **telephone code** 01903.

ACCOMMODATIONS AND FOOD

Expect to pay at least £14 for a B&B along the River Arun.

Warningcamp Youth Hostel (HI) (tel. 882 204), 1½ mi. out of town. From the train station, turn right onto the A27 and take the first left; after a mile, turn left at the sign and then follow the other signs (two right turns). When the reasonable B&Bs in town fill up, it's the best value. Lockout 10am-5pm. Curfew 11pm. £7.15, under 18 £5. Sheets included. Breakfast £2.60. Kitchen. Open April-Aug. daily; Sept.-Oct. and March Tues.-Sat.

Arden House, 4 Queens Lane (tel. 882 544). Just off Queen St. Plush facilities. Doubles £31-35.

The Bridge House and Cottage, 18 Queen St. (tel. 882 142 or 882 779). Many perks. Singles £18-24. Doubles £34-40. Laundry facilities.

Castle View, 63 High St. (tel. 883 029). Lets rooms for a pittance compared to other B&Bs in town. All rooms come with bath and cost £14-16.

Arundel's pubs and tea shops usually fall on the wrong side of reasonable. Locals frequent **Belinda's,** 13 Tarrant St., (tel. 882 977) off High St., a 16th-century tea room with a chirping, bird-filled garden. Diners consume plentiful steak and kidney pie (£4.50) and cream teas (£2.95; open Tues.-Sat. 9am-5:30pm, Sun. 11am-5:30pm).

Scrumptious baked goods are cooked on the premises. **The Castle View,** 63 High St. (tel. 883 029), produces both a meaty and a veggie homemade lasagna for around £3.80 (open in summer daily 10am-5:30pm; winter 10:30am-5pm). For pub grup try the **White Hart,** 12 Queen St. (tel. 882 374) which serves food daily noon-2:30pm and 7-9pm. For picnics or late-night snacks, try the rather incongruous **Circle K,** 17 Queen St. (open daily 6am-10pm). Clearly strange things are afoot in Arundel.

■■■ PORTSMOUTH

> *Don't talk to me about the naval tradition. It's nothing but rum, sodomy, and the lash.*
>
> —*Winston Churchill*

Set Victorian prudery against a lot of bloody cursing sailors and Portsmouth emerges. Overlord of British maritime history, the city (pop. 180,000) served as the base of the D-Day armada. 1994 marked the 50th anniversary of D-Day and the 900th anniversary of Portsmouth itself.

Portsmouth overflows with magnificent ships and seafaring relics; the bulk of sights worth seeing anchor near the Hard. Plunge head first into the unparalleled **Naval Heritage Centre** (tel. 839 766) in the Naval Base (entrance right next to the Hard tourist office; follow the brown signs to Portsmouth Historic Ships). Henry VIII's best-loved ship, the **Mary Rose** (tel. 750 521 or 812 931), set sail from Portsmouth in July 1545 only to keel over and sink before the monarch's eyes. Not until 1982 was she raised from her watery grave. Not yet entirely restored, the *Mary Rose* offers a glimpse at a work in progress. An enthralling collection of Tudor artifacts, salvaged along with the wreck is displayed in a separate exhibition hall (open daily 10am-5:30pm; Nov.-Feb. 10am-5pm; see below for rates; wheelchair accessible).

Two 100-ft. masts lead the way to Admiral Horatio Nelson's flagship **HMS Victory** (tel. 839 766 or 822 357), the oldest surviving Ship of the Line in the world. The ship won the decisive Battle of Trafalgar against the French and Spanish in 1805 (open daily 10am-4:50pm; Nov.-Feb. 10:30am-4:20pm).

HMS Warrior (tel. 822 351) provides an intriguing companion to the *Victory.* The pride and joy of Queen Victoria's navy and the first iron-clad battleship in the world, *Warrior* has never seen battle (open daily 10am-5:30pm; Jul.-Aug. 10am-6:45pm; Nov.-Feb. 10am-5pm; last entry 1hr. before close). The five galleries of the **Royal Naval Museum** (tel. 733060) fill in the historical gaps between the three ships (open daily 10:30am-4:30pm; museum £2.50, students and children £1.75, family £7).

Entrance to the **Historic Dockyard** is free (open 10am-7pm; March-June and Sept.-Oct. 10am-6pm; Nov.-Feb. 10am-5:30pm). But the ships are worth the admission expense: tickets to see one ship are £4.75, seniors £4.25, students and children £3.50, family £15. A combined ticket to explore two ships is £9, seniors £8, students and children £6.50, family £27.50. A Supersaver ticket for all three ships is £13, seniors £11.50, students and children £9.25, family £33.75. Admission to ships includes the fee for the Royal Naval Museum. Admission to the Museum is £2.65, seniors £2.10, students and children £1.85, family £7.50. The cost of other sights can be tacked onto your combined ticket. (All open 10am-6:45pm; March-June and Sept.-Oct. 10am-5:30pm; Nov.-Feb. 10am-5pm. Last admission 1hr. before closing.)

Show up at the jetty by *Warrior* for a 45 minute guided ride (harbor tour only £3.50, seniors £2.75, students and children 32, family £10). Vessels frequent **Spitbank Fort,** which has protected Portsmouth for well over a century. Boats depart from the Historic Dockyard (open Easter-Oct., weather permitting; crossing 25 min.; departures 10:45am, noon, 1:15pm, and 2:30pm; fort trip £5.75, seniors £4.75, students and children £4, family £17). While at The Hard, consider taking **Portsmouth Harbour Tours** (tel. 822 584), a more scenic way to make the trek to Southsea Esplanade (tours run Easter-Oct. 11am-5pm; 50min.; return £2.20, children £1.50).

Continue along the water's edge to Clarence Esplanade, the other side of Portsmouth's seaside attractions. In the **D-Day Museum** (tel. 827 261), along Clarence Esplanade, the Overlord Embroidery recounts the invasion of France (open daily 9:30am-5:30pm; £3.50, children and students £2, family £9; wheelchair accessible). Next door, the **Sea Life Centre** (tel. 734 461) displays aquatic exhibits with a finful of verve (open daily 10am-5pm, until 6-9pm in summer; £4.25, seniors £3.50, students and children £3.25).

Also at Clarence Esplanade is **Southsea Castle,** (tel. 827 261) yet another coastal fortification built by Henry VIII in 1544 (open daily 10am-5:30pm; Nov.-March. Sat.-Sun. 11am-5pm; partially wheelchair accessible; 31.50, seniors £1.20, students and children 90p, under 13 free).

The **Portsmouth City Museum,** Museum Rd., conjures up the area's history with multi-media exhibits (open Mon.-Fri. noon-5:30pm, Sat.-Sun. 11am-5:30pm; £1, seniors 75p, students and children 60p, family £2.60; wholly wheelchair accessible).

Charles Dickens spent his early years here; he was born in 1812 at 395 Old Commercial Rd., ¾ mi. north of the town station. The house has been done up in the Regency style. Morbidly enough, the only authentic Dickens artifacts are the couch on which he died and a lock of his hair (open April-Sept. daily 10:30am-5:30pm; £1, seniors 75p, students and children 60p).

ORIENTATION AND PRACTICAL INFORMATION

The city of Portsmouth is widely dispersed along the coast stretching from The Hard down to Eastney Esplanade. Major sights cluster at **The Hard, Old Portsmouth** (near the town station), and **Southsea Esplanade.** A relatively reliable and comprehensive bus system runs between these various regions of the city. Three tourist offices are open year-round on the Hard and in town on Commercial Rd.; one more opens during the high season.

> **Getting There:** Portsmouth lies on the south coast 75 mi. southwest of London. **Trains** from London Waterloo stop at both Portsmouth and Southsea station ("town station") and Portsmouth harbor station (2/hr.; 1½hr.; cheap day return £15.70). **National Express buses** run from London every 2 hours (2½hr.; single £12.25, return £13-15.50).
>
> **Tourist Office:** The Hard (tel. 826 722), right by the entrance to historic ships; or 102 Commercial Rd. (tel. 838 382), by the town station. *Bureau de Change.* Room booking service. The Hard open daily 9:30am-5:45pm; Commercial Rd. open Mon.-Sat. 9:30am-5:45pm. **Seasonal offices** at the Continental Ferry Port (tel. 838 635; open daily noon-2pm and 6:30-10:30pm) and at the Pyramids Resort Centre, Clarence Esplanade, Southsea (tel. 832 464; open daily 9:30am-5:45pm).
>
> **Postal Code:** PO1 1AB. **Telephone Code:** 01705.
>
> **Train Station: Portsmouth and Southsea Station,** Commercial Rd. Travel center open Mon.-Sat. 9am-4:30pm. **Portsmouth Harbour Station,** The Hard, ¾ mi. away at the end of the line. Luggage lockers £1-2. To Cosham, for the hostel, every 20min.; £1.30, day return from £1.50. Trips between town and harbor cost 80p, day return £1. Call (01703) 229 393 for information about all 3 stations.
>
> **Bus Station:** The Hard Interchange, The Hard, next to the Harbour station. Local routes (enquiries tel. 738 570 or 815 452) and National Express services (tel. (01329) 230 023). National Express tickets sold at Wight Link office (open July-Aug. daily 8am-5pm; Oct.-June Mon.-Sat. 8am-5pm).
>
> **Taxi: Streamline Taxis,** tel. 811 111. **Mainline Taxis,** tel. 751 111.
>
> **Hospital: Queen Alexandra Hospital,** Southwick Hill Rd., Cosham (tel. 379 451).
>
> **Emergency:** Dial 999; no coins required. **Police:** Winston Churchill Ave., Cosham (tel. 321 111).

ACCOMMODATIONS AND FOOD

Moderately priced B&Bs clutter Southsea, Portsmouth's contiguous resort town 1½ mi. east along the coast from the Hard. Many are located along Waverly Rd., Clarendon Rd., and South Parade. Take Southdown Portsmouth bus #6, 43, or 44 to South

Parade. Cheaper lodgings lie two or three blocks inland—Whitwell, Granada, St. Roman's, and Malvern Rd. all have a fair sprinkling.

YMCA, Penny St. (tel. 864 341), 10min. from the Hard. Very basic rooms; those on higher floors afford a truly amazing view. With sleeping bag £6.20. Twin B&B £11.15. Single B&B £12.35. Dinner £3.75, lunch £3.75. Confirmation deposit £10, key deposit £1. Most space fills up with students after July-Sept.

University of Portsmouth Halls of Residence, booking office at Nuffield Centre, St. Michaels Road (tel. 843 178), overlooking Southsea common, 15min. from the Hard. Halls are scattered within 3mi. Single and twin rooms available July 10-Sept. 27. **Burrell House** has small modern rooms with puritanically narrow beds; older **Rees Hall** shows more signs of age and character. £13.50.

HI Youth Hostel, Wymering Manor, Old Wymering Lane, Medina Rd., Cosham (tel. 375 661). Take bus #1, 12, or 22 from the Hard or #40, 42, 43, or 44 from Commercial Rd. by Abbey National Bank at Stand D, to Cosham police station and walk left on Medina Rd., or take the train to Cosham, then right out of the station to the police station. T 58 beds. Lockout 10am-5pm. £7.75, under 18 £5.20. Open July-Aug. and Jan.1-4 daily; March-June Mon.-Sat.; Sept.-Nov. Tues.-Sat.; mid-Jan. to Feb. open Fri.-Sat.

Testudo House, 19 Whitwell Rd., Southsea (tel. 824 324). Consolingly quiet residential area. Mrs. Parkes fluffs up the pillows in her spick-and-span home, adorned with a TV, tea/coffee kettle, and washbasin for all rooms. £16. doubles £30. Ask about the room with bath and family quarters.

Decent restaurants with bunch along Osborne, Palmerston, and Clarendon Rd. in the Southsea shopping district (buses #6, 43, and 44 all stop at Palmerston Rd.). Standard fast-food joints abound near Commercial Rd. and the town station. **Country Kitchen,** at 59A Marmion Rd., offers savory veggie specials for about £3 and quiche from £1.60 in a fine hardwood wholefood restaurant (open Mon.-Sat. 9:30am-5pm, last order at 4:45pm). You'll find solid English food in relaxed low-key surroundings at **Brown's,** 9 Clarendon Rd. Gulp down the daily roast £5.50, or omelettes from £2.95-3.50 (open Mon. 9:30am-6:30pm, Tues.-Sat. 9:30am-9:30pm).

■■■ SALISBURY

Salisbury's small grid of streets (five running north to south and six east to west) was carefully charted by Bishop Moore in the early 13th century. Clean and congenial to the many travelers stopping off before heading to Stonehenge, Salisbury (pop. 38,000) shouldn't be given short shrift.

Salisbury Cathedral (tel. 328 726) rises from its grassy close (the biggest in England) to a height of 404 ft.The bases of the marble pillars buckle under the strain of 6400 tons of limestone. Nearly 700 years of use and weathering have left the cathedral in need of structural repair. Scaffolding will shroud the spire, tower, and west front of the cathedral for years to come. A tiny stone figure rests in the nave; legend has it that either a boy bishop is entombed on the spot or that it covers the heart of Richard Poore, bishop and founder of the cathedral. Tours of the tower begin at 11:30am and 2:30pm (£2). Bursars also lead adventuring souls to the roof area at 11am, 2, 3, and 6pm (£1).

One of four surviving copies of the *Magna Carta* rests in the **Chapter House.** Detailed medieval friezes around the perimeter of the Chapter House narrate stories from Genesis and Exodus (open Mon.-Sat. 9:30am-4:45pm, Sun. 1-4:45pm; Nov.-Feb. Mon.-Sat. 11am-3pm, Sun. 1-3:15pm; 30p, students and seniors 20p). The **cloisters** adjoining the cathedral somehow grew to be the largest in England, though the cathedral never housed any monks. (Cathedral open daily 8am-6:30pm; July 8am-8:15pm. Virtually mandatory donation £2.50, seniors and students £1, children 50p. Evensong Mon.-Sat. 5:30pm, Sun. 3pm.)

The open lawns of the **cathedral close** flank some beautifully preserved old homes, including **Malmesbury House,** where Handel once lived. Tours available on the hour and half-hour (open April-Oct. Tues.-Thurs., Bank Holiday Mon. noon-5pm; admission £3, children and seniors £2.50). **Mompesson House,** another sumptuous residence, holds fine plasterwork, a Queen Anne interior, and an inspiring collection of 18th-century drinking glasses (tel. 335 659; open April-Oct. Sat.-Wed. noon-5:30pm; £3, children £1.50, seniors £1.30).

ORIENTATION AND PRACTICAL INFORMATION

You'll find the Salisbury bus station in the center of town; the train station is a 10-min. walk. To reach the tourist office from the train station, turn left out of the station onto South Western Rd., bear right onto Fisherton St. (which becomes Bridge St.), pass over the bridge, and cross High St. Walk straight ahead onto Silver St., which becomes Butcher Row and then Fish Row.

Getting There: Trains depart Salisbury station to London (every hr.; £16.90-18.40). **National Express buses** run from Victoria (2 per day; 2hr. 30min.; £12.25).

Tourist Office: Fish Row (tel. 334 956), in the Guildhall in Market Sq. National Express ticket service. Books rooms. Guided tours May-late Sept. 11am and 6pm, £1.50. Open July-Aug. Mon.-Sat. 9:30am-7pm, Sun. 11am-5pm; June and Sept. 9:30am-6pm, Sun. 11am-4pm; Oct.-April Mon.-Sat. 9:30am-5pm; May Mon.-Sat. 9:30am-5pm, Sun. 11am-4pm.

Postal Code: SP1 1AB. **Telephone Code:** 01722.

Train Station: South Western Rd. (tel. Southampton (01703) 229393), west of town across the river. Lockers for **luggage storage** on train station concourse (50p-£1). Information office open Mon.-Fri. 9:30am-4:45pm, Sat. 8:15am-2:45pm.

Bus Station: 8 Endless St. (tel. 336 855). Booking office open Mon.-Fri. 8:15am-5:45pm, Sat. 8:15am-5:15pm.

Taxis: tel. 334 343. Taxi stands at train station and New Canal (near the cinema).

Bike Rental: Hayball and Co., 26-30 Winchester St. just beyond McDonalds (tel. 411 378). £9 per day; deposit £25. Open Mon.-Sat. 9am-5:30pm.

Hospital: Salisbury District Hospital, Odstock (tel. 336 212).

Emergency: Dial 999; no coins required. **Police:** Wilton Rd. (tel. 411 444).

ACCOMMODATIONS, FOOD, AND PUBS

Guesthouses grace Castle Rd., a short hike north of the town center up Castle St.

Ron and Jenny Coats, 51 Salt Lane (tel. 327 443), just up from the bus station. A welcoming and clean 400-year-old house with warped floors and ceiling beams. Hostel-style 2-, 3- and 6-bed rooms. Centrally located. Mrs. C will lodge you on her floor or at her friends' £11 B&B (tel. 328 905) if her beds fill up. £7.50, with breakfast £9-9.50 (depending on how much you eat). Sheets 80p.

HI Youth Hostel, Milford Hill House, Milford Hill (tel. 327 572). From the tourist office, turn left on Fish Row, right on Queen St., left on Milford St., and walk ahead a few blocks under the overpass; the hostel will be on the left. A beautiful old house outside with the usual stark hostel interior (bunkbeds). Lockout 10am-1pm. Curfew 11:30pm. 74 beds. £11.30, under-18 £8.40. Breakfast included. Surrounded by 2 acres of garden.

Mrs. Spiller, Nuholme, Ashfield Rd. (tel. 336 592), 10min. from the train station. Bear right out of station, cross the car park straight ahead, turn right onto Churchfields Rd., then turn right again onto Ashfield—a white house on the right. Very friendly place run by an elderly woman. £11, students £10.

Reeve the Baker (main branch next to the tourist office, between the town square and Fish Row) stocks all the strolling sightseer could crave, from Cornish pasties to caterpillar meringues. **Salisbury Health Foods,** 15 Queen St., vends life-inducing edibles and frozen yogurt (open Mon.-Sat. 9am-5:30pm). **Mo's,** 62 Milford St. (tel. 331 377), on the way to the youth hostel, offers carnivores cheeseburgers (£4.75) or ribs (£5.95) while vegans ruminate over "lentil creation" (£4.55) or veggie burgers (£4.15). Mo's milkshake (£1.75) is magnificent (open Mon.-Sat. noon-2pm and 6-

10:30pm, Sun. 5:30-10:30pm). At **La Gondola,** 155 Fisherton St. (tel 324 856), pastas line the windows and phenomenal Italian specialties fill your plate. Open daily noon-2:30pm and 6pm-midnight.

Even the most jaded pub dweller will find a pleasing venue among Salisbury's 67-odd watering holes. **The Pheasant,** Salt Lane (tel. 320 675), serves lunch, and stages new music on Thursday nights. **Wig & Quill,** One New St. (tel. 335 665), offers a traditional interior backed up by a garden with a view and an original cathedral wall section (bar meals £3-4). **The Old Mill,** atop the river at the end of a ten-minute stroll along Town Path, is *the* setting for an outdoor drink on a summer evening.

■■■ STONEHENGE

Stonehenge is a potent reminder that England seemed ancient even to the Saxons and Normans. The much-touted stones, only 22 ft. high, are surrounded by imperturbable cows and swirled by winds exceeding 50mph. The stones fascinate in part because they were lifted by a simple but infinitely tedious process of rope-and-log leverage. Buffeted by sensationalistic theories and outlandish fantasies, Stonehenge has yielded none of its ageless mystery.

The most famous Stonehenge legend holds that the circle was built by Merlin, who magically transported the stones from Ireland. (Actually, the seven-ton Blue Stones are made of rock quarried in Wales.) Other stories attribute the monument to giants, Romans, Danes, Phoenicians, Druids, Mycenaean Greeks, and aliens. In any case, whether they traveled by land, water, or spaceship, the Bronze Age builders would seem to have possessed more technology than anthropologists can explain. Archeologists now date construction from approximately 2800 to 1500 BC, dividing the complex into three successive incarnations of the monument. The relics of the oldest are the Aubrey Holes (white patches in the earth) and the Heel Stone (the isolated, rough block standing outside the circle). This first Stonehenge may have been a worship and burial site for seven centuries. The next monument consisted of about 60 stones imported from Wales around 2100 BC to mark astronomical directions. The present shape was formed by 1500 BC; it may once have been composed of two concentric circles and two horseshoes of megaliths, enclosed by substantial earthworks.

Many different peoples have worshiped at Stonehenge, from late Neolithic and Early Bronze Age chieftains to contemporary mystics. In 300 BC the Druids arrived from the Continent and claimed Stonehenge as their shrine. The true Druids have died out, but the Druid Society of London still honors the sun's rising over the Heel Stone on Midsummer's Day. The summer of 1988 saw an acrid confrontation between hippie-pagan celebrants and police amid spotlights, a haze of tear gas, and barbed wire. Recently, officials have felt obliged to close access to Stonehenge on the summer solstice, outraging the devout Druid and inconveniencing the romantic tourist. These ongoing conflicts were documented by the Scottish band Oi Polloi! in their seminal protest song, "Free The Stones, " which decries attempts to regulate and commercialize similarly mystical monuments in Scotland.

Savvy travelers will do well to photograph the stones from the roadside vantage, thereby avoding the entry fee and the crush of people waiting to be admitted. The finest view of the monument can be captured from Amesbury Hill, 1.5 mi. up the A303. On some winter Tuesdays and Fridays, in clear weather, the ropes around the monument are taken down to allow a closer view (Stonehenge open daily 10am-6pm; Nov.-late March10am-4pm; £2.85, students and seniors £2.15, children £1.40).

Getting to Stonehenge takes little effort. **Wilts & Dorset** (tel. (01722) 336 855) runs several **buses** daily from Salisbury center and from the train station (return £3.75). The first bus leaves Salisbury at 8:45am (Sat. 8:50am, Sun. 10:45am), and the last leaves Stonehenge at 4:20pm (Sun. 3:50pm; 30min.). Some private operators run **tours** to Stonehenge and Avebury for £9 to £10.

Appendices

■ BLUE PLAQUE HOUSES

Matthew Arnold (1822-1888)	poet and essayist	2 Chester Sq., SW1
John L. Baird (1888-1946)	TV pioneer	22 Frith St., W1
Sir James Barrie (1860-1937)	novelist, playwright	100 Bayswater Rd., W2
Aubrey Beardsley (1872-1898)	illustrator	114 Cambridge St., SW1
David Ben-Gurion (1886-1973)	Israeli statesman	75 Warrington Crescent, W9
Hector Berlioz (1803-1869)	composer	58 Queen Anne St., W1
James Boswell (1740-1795)	author	8 Russell St., WC2
Elizabeth Barrett Browning (1806-1861)	poet	99 Gloucester Pl., W1
Beau Brummell (1778-1840)	dandy	4 Chesterfield St., W1
Sir Edward Burne-Jones (1833-1898)	painter	17 Red Lion Sq., WC1
Thomas Carlyle (1795-1881)	essayist and historian	24 Cheyne Walk, SW3
Frederic Chopin (1810-1849)	composer	4 St. James's Pl., SW1
Sir Winston Churchill (1874-1965)	statesman, soldier, author	28 Hyde Park Gate, SW7
Samuel Clemens (Mark Twain) (1835-1910)	writer	23 Tedworth Sq., SW3
Muzio Clementi (1752-1832)	composer	128 Kensington Church St., W8
Joseph Conrad (1857-1924)	novelist	17 Gillingham St., SW1
Charles Darwin (1809-1882)	naturalist	University College, Science Building, WC1
General Charles de Gaulle (1890-1970)	French president	4 Carlton Gdns., SW1
Charles Dickens (1812-1870)	novelist	48 Doughty St., WC1
Benjamin Disraeli (1804-1881)	prime minister 1868, 1874-80	19 Curzon St., W1
General Dwight D. Eisenhower (1890-1969)	U.S. president	31 St. James's Sq., SW1
T.S. Eliot (1888-1965)	poet and critic	3 Kensington Ct., W8
Mary Ann Evans (George Eliot) (1819-1880)	novelist	4 Cheyne Walk, SW3
Benjamin Franklin (1706-1790)	statesman and inventor	36 Craven St., WC2

Thomas Gainsborough (1727-1788)	portrait artist	82 Pall Mall, SW1
John Galsworthy (1867-1933)	novelist and playwright	1-3 Robert St., WC2
Edward Gibbon (1737-1792)	historian	7 Bentinck St., W1
George Frederick Händel (1685-1759)	composer	25 Brook St., W1
Washington Irving (1783-1859)	author and diplomat	Argyll St., W1
Henry James (1843-1916)	writer	34 De Vere Gdns., W8
Samuel Johnson (1709-1784)	author and lexicographer	17 Gough Sq., EC4
Rudyard Kipling (1865-1936)	poet and writer	43 Villiers St., WC2
Lillie Langtry (1852-1929)	actress	Pont St., SW1
T.E. Lawrence (1888-1935)	soldier and writer	14 Barton St., SW1
Gugliemo Marconi (1874-1937)	inventor of the wireless	71 Hereford Rd., W2
Karl Marx (1818-1883)	economist and philosopher	28 Dean St., W1
Somerset Maugham (1874-1965)	novelist and playwright	6 Chesterfield St., W1
Samuel Mors (1791-1872)	inventor and painter	141 Cleveland St., W1
Wolfgang A. Mozart (1756-1791)	composer	180 Ebury St., SW1
Sir Isaac Newton (1642-1727)	physicist and mathematician	87 Jermyn St., SW1
Florence Nightingale (1820-1910)	founder of modern nursing	10 South St., W1
Samuel Pepys (1633-1703)	diarist	14 Buckingham St., WC2
Sir Joshua Reynolds (1723-1792)	portrait painter	Leicester Sq., WC2
Dante Gabriel Rossetti (1828-1882)	poet and painter	16 Cheyne Walk, SW3
George Bernard Shaw (1856-1950)	playwright and critic	29 Fitzroy Sq., W1
Percy Bysshe Shelley (1792-1882)	Romantic poet	15 Poland St., W1
William Makepeace Thackeray (1811-1863)	novelist	36 Onslow Sq., SW7
Anthony Trollope (1815-1882)	novelist	39 Montagu Sq., W1
Vincent Van Gogh (1853-1890)	impressionist painter	87 Hackford Rd., SW9
Ralph Vaughan Williams (1872-1925)	composer	10 Hanover Terrace, NW1
James A. McNeil Whistler (1834-1903)	painter and etcher	96 Cheyne Walk, SW10
Oscar Wilde (1854-1900)	wit and dramatist	34 Tite St., SW3

PLACE NAME PRONUNCIATION

■ PLACE NAME PRONUNCIATION

Berkeley	BARK-lee
Beauchamps	BEECH-am
Buckingham	BUCK-ing-um
Dulwich	DULL-idge
Ely	EEL-ee
Gloucester	GLOS-ter
Greenwich	GREN-idge
Holborn	HO-burn
Leicester	LES-ter
Marylebone	MAR-lee-bun
Magdalene	MAUD-lin
Norwich	NOR-idge
Peterborough	PETER-brer
quay	KEY
Salisbury	SAULS-bree
Southwark	SUTH-uk
Woolwich	WOOL-idge

■ BANK HOLIDAYS

January 1	New Year's
April 14	Good Friday
April 17	Easter Monday
first Monday in May	May Day Holiday
last Monday in May	Spring or Whitsun Holiday
last Monday in August	Late Summer Holiday
December 25	Christmas
December 26	Boxing Day

Index

★ FREE T-SHIRT ★

JUST ANSWER THE QUESTIONS ON THE FOLLOWING PAGES AND MAIL THEM TO:

Attn: Let's Go Survey
St. Martin's Press
175 Fifth Avenue
New York, NY 10010

WE'LL SEND THE FIRST 1,500 RESPONDENTS A LET'S GO T-SHIRT!

(Make sure we can read your address.)

■ LET'S GO 1995 READER ■ QUESTIONNAIRE

1) Name _____

2) Address _____

3) Are you: female   male

4) How old are you?   under 17   17-23   24-30   31-40   41-55   over 55

5) Are you (circle all that apply):   in high school   in college   in grad school
                                       employed   retired   between jobs

6) What is your personal yearly income?
Under $15,000 $15,000 - $25,000 $26,000 - $35,000 $36,000 - $50,000
$51,000 - $75,000 $76,000 - $100,000   over $100,000   not applicable

7) How often do you normally travel with a guidebook?
This is my first trip
Less than once a year
Once a year
Twice a year
Three times a year or more

8) Which *Let's Go* guide(s) did you buy for your trip?
_____
_____

9) Have you used *Let's Go* before?
Yes   No

10) How did you first hear about *Let's Go*? (Choose one)
Friend or fellow traveler
Recommended by store clerk
Display in bookstore
Ad in newspaper/magazine
Review or article in newspaper/magazine
Radio

11) Why did you choose *Let's Go*? (Choose up to three)
Updated every year
Reputation
Easier to find in stores
Better price
"Budget" focus
Writing style
Attitude
Better organization
More comprehensive
Reliability
Better Design/Layout
Candor
Other _____
_____
_____

12) Which of the following guides have you used, if any?
Frommer's $-a-Day
Fodor's Affordable Guides
Rough Guides/Real Guides
Berkeley Guides/On the Loose
Lonely Planet
None of the above

13) Is *Let's Go* the best guidebook?
Yes
No (which is?) _____
Haven't used other guides

14) When did you buy this book?
Jan   Feb   Mar   Apr   May   Jun
Jul   Aug   Sep   Oct   Nov   Dec

15) When did you travel with this book? (Circle all that apply)
Jan   Feb   Mar   Apr   May   Jun
Jul   Aug   Sep   Oct   Nov   Dec

16) How long was your stay in London?
less than 1 week   1-3 weeks
1-3 months   4-12 months

17) How many travel companions did you have?   0 1 2 3 4 over 4

18) Roughly how much did you spend per day in London?
$0-15 $51-70
$16-30 $71-100
$31-50 $101-150
             over $150

LONDON

19) What was the purpose of your trip?
(Circle all that apply)

Pleasure   Business
Work/internship   Volunteer
Study

20) What were the main attractions of your trip? (Circle top three)
Sightseeing
New culture
Learning Language
Meeting locals
Camping/Hiking
Sports/Recreation
Nightlife/Entertainment
Meeting other travelers
Hanging Out
Food
Shopping
Adventure/Getting off the beaten path

21) How reliable/useful are the following features of *Let's Go*?
v = very, u = usually, s = sometimes
n = never, ? = didn't use

Accommodations	v u s n ?
Camping	v u s n ?
Food	v u s n ?
Entertainment	v u s n ?
Sights	v u s n ?
Maps	v u s n ?
Practical Info	v u s n ?
Directions	v u s n ?
"Essentials"	v u s n ?
Cultural Intros	v u s n ?

22) On the list above, please circle the top 3 features you used the most.

23) Would you use *Let's Go* again?
Yes
No (why not?) _____
_____

24) Do you generally buy a phrasebook when you visit a foreign destination?
Yes   No

25) Do you generally buy a separate map when you visit a foreign city?
Yes   No

26) Which of the following destinations are you planning to visit as a tourist in the next five years?
(Circle all that apply)

Australasia

Australia	Japan
New Zealand	China
Indonesia	Hong Kong
Vietnam	India
Malaysia	Nepal
Singapore	

Europe And Middle East

Middle East	Switzerland
Israel	Austria
Egypt	Berlin
Africa	Russia
Turkey	Poland
Greece	Czech/Slovak
Scandinavia	Rep.
Portugal	Hungary
Spain	Baltic States

The Americas

Caribbean	The Midwest
Central America	Chicago
Costa Rica	The Southwest
South America	Texas
Ecuador	Arizona
Brazil	Colorado
Venezuela	Los Angeles
Colombia	San Francisco
U.S. Nat'l Parks	Seattle
Rocky Mtns.	Hawaii
The South	Alaska
New Orleans	Canada
Florida	British Columbia
Mid-Atlantic	Montreal/
States	Quebec
Boston/New	Maritime
England	Provinces

27) Where did you stay in London?

Hostel	Hotel
Apartment	Friend's home
Student housing	Campground

28) What other countries did you visit on your trip? _____
_____

29) Which of these do you own?
(Circle all that apply)

Computer	CD-Rom
Modem	On-line Service

Mail this to:
Attn: Let's Go Survey
St. Martin's Press
175 Fifth Avenue
New York, NY 10010

Thanks For Your Help!

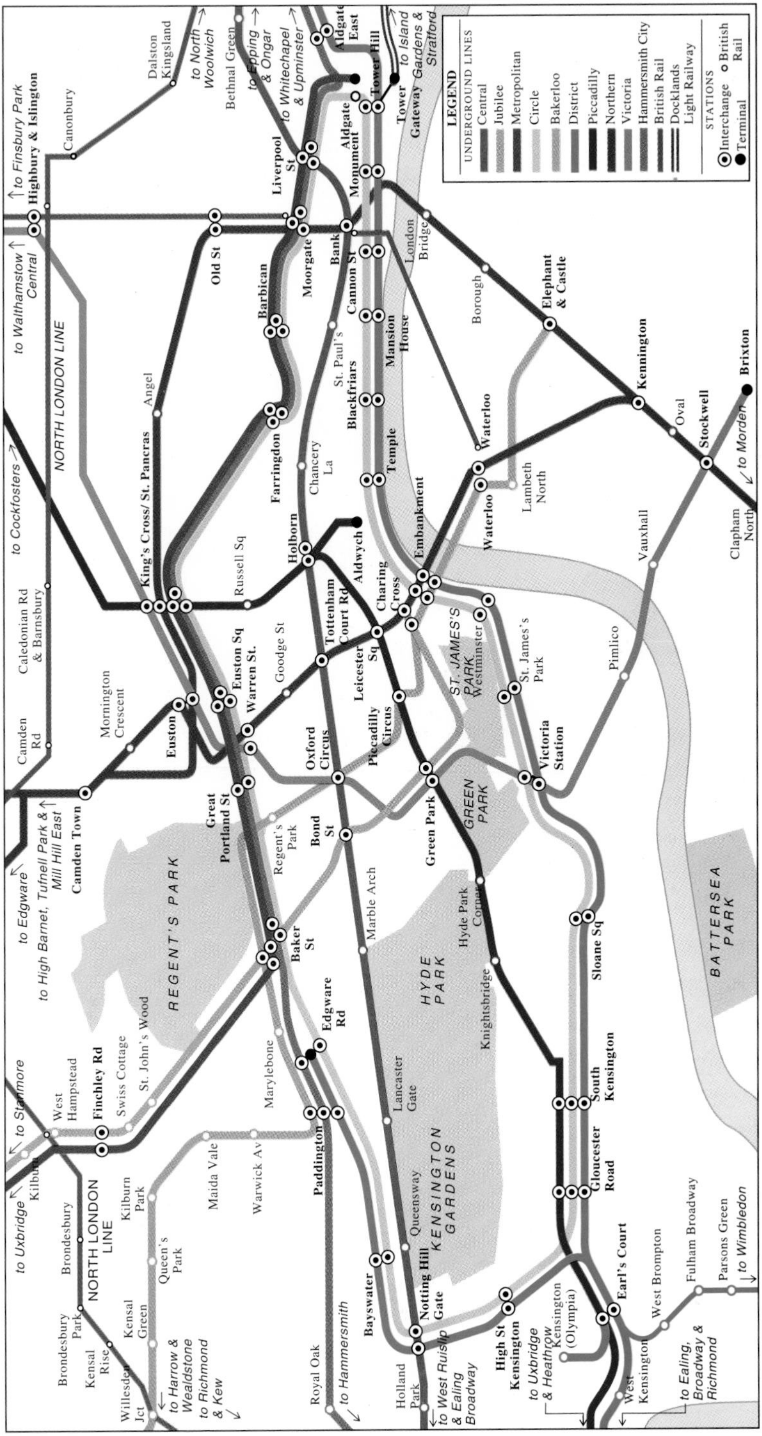
LEGEND
UNDERGROUND LINES
Central
Jubilee
Metropolitan
Circle
Bakerloo
District
Piccadilly
Northern
Victoria
Hammersmith City
British Rail
Docklands Light Railway
STATIONS
Interchange
British Rail
Terminal
NORTH LONDON LINE
REGENT'S PARK
HYDE PARK
KENSINGTON GARDENS
GREEN PARK
ST. JAMES'S PARK
BATTERSEA PARK
to Finsbury Park
Highbury & Islington
Canonbury
Dalston Kingsland
to North Woolwich
Bethnal Green
to Epping & Ongar
to Whitechapel & Upminster
Aldgate East
Aldgate
Tower Hill
Tower Gateway
to Island Gardens & Stratford
Liverpool St
Monument
Old St
Moorgate
Bank
Cannon St
London Bridge
Borough
Elephant & Castle
Kennington
Brixton
Oval
Stockwell
to Morden
Clapham North
Vauxhall
Pimlico
Barbican
St. Paul's
Mansion House
Blackfriars
Temple
Waterloo
Lambeth North
Farringdon
Chancery La
Embankment
Holborn
Aldwych
Charing Cross
Tottenham Court Rd
Leicester Sq
Westminster
St. James's Park
Victoria Station
Piccadilly Circus
Oxford Circus
Green Park
Hyde Park Corner
Knightsbridge
Sloane Sq
South Kensington
Gloucester Road
Earl's Court
West Brompton
Fulham Broadway
Parsons Green
to Wimbledon
to Walthamstow Central
to Cockfosters
Angel
King's Cross/ St. Pancras
Russell Sq
Goodge St
Euston Sq
Warren St.
Euston
Caledonian Rd & Barnsbury
Mornington Crescent
Camden Rd
Camden Town
to Edgware
to High Barnet, Tufnell Park & Mill Hill East
Great Portland St
Regent's Park
Bond St
Marble Arch
Baker St
Edgware Rd
Marylebone
Lancaster Gate
Queensway
Paddington
Bayswater
Notting Hill Gate
Holland Park
to West Ruislip & Ealing Broadway
High St Kensington
Kensington (Olympia)
to Uxbridge & Heathrow
West Kensington
to Ealing, Broadway & Richmond
to Stanmore
West Hampstead
Finchley Rd
Swiss Cottage
St. John's Wood
Kilburn
to Uxbridge
Brondesbury
Kilburn Park
Maida Vale
Warwick Av
Queen's Park
Brondesbury Park
Kensal Rise
Kensal Green
Willesden Jct
to Harrow & Wealdstone
to Richmond & Kew
Royal Oak
to Hammersmith

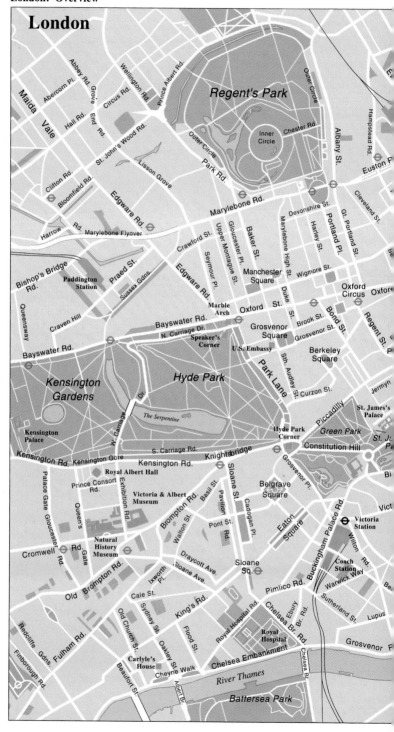

London

King's Cross Station
Pancras ation
Pentonville Rd.
City Rd.
East Road
Hoxton St.
Kingsland Rd.

King's Cross Rd.
Gray's Inn Rd.
Judd St.
Rosebery Ave.
St. John's St.
Goswell Rd.
Lever St.
Bath St.
Old St.
Gt. Eastern St.
Shoreditch High
Commercial St.

Coram's Fields
Guilford St.
Farringdon Rd.
Clerkenwell Rd.
Aldersgate
City Rd.

Barbican Centre

Theobalds Rd.
Southampton Row
Charterhouse St.
Smithfield Market
London Wall
Moorgate
Liverpool St. Station

Holborn
ew rd St.
High
Kingsway
Chancery La.
Fetter La.
Holborn Viaduct
Old Bailey
Newgate St.
St. Paul's
Bank of England
Cheapside
Cornhill
Leadenhall St.
Bishopsgate
Houndsditch
Fenchurch St.

Drury La.
Aldwych
Law Courts
Fleet St.
Strand
Queen Victoria St.
Cannon St.
Gracechurch St.
Eastcheap
The Tower
Tower Hill

National Gallery
Charing Cross Stn.
Victoria Embankment
Waterloo Br.
National Theatre
Blackfriars Br.
Blackfriars Station
Southwark Br.
Cannon St. Station
London Br.
Upper Thames St.
Tower Br.

Royal Festival Hall
Stamford St.
Southwark St.
River Thames
Tooley St.

Whitehall
York Rd.
Waterloo Rd.
The Cut
Union St.
Blackfriars Rd.
Borough High St.
St. Thomas St.
London Bridge Station
Bridge Rd.
Abbey St.

Houses of Parliament
Westminster Br.
Westminster Br. Rd.
Waterloo Station
Borough Rd.
London Rd.
Long La.
Tabard St.
Great Dover St.
Harper Rd.
Tower Bridge Rd.

Millbank
Lambeth Palace Rd.
Lambeth Rd.
Kennington Rd.
Imperial War Museum
New Kent Rd.
Willow Walk

ry Rd.
Lambeth Br.
Black Prince Rd.
Albert Embankment
Crampton St.
Rodney Pl.
Flint St.
East St.
Old Kent Rd.

Kennington La.
Kennington Park Rd.
Manor Pl.
Walworth Rd.
Portland St.
Thurlow St.

uxhall Br.
Vauxhall Station
Kennington Oval
Braganza St.
Albany Rd.

N

| 0 | 1/2 mile |
| 0 | 1/2 kilometer |

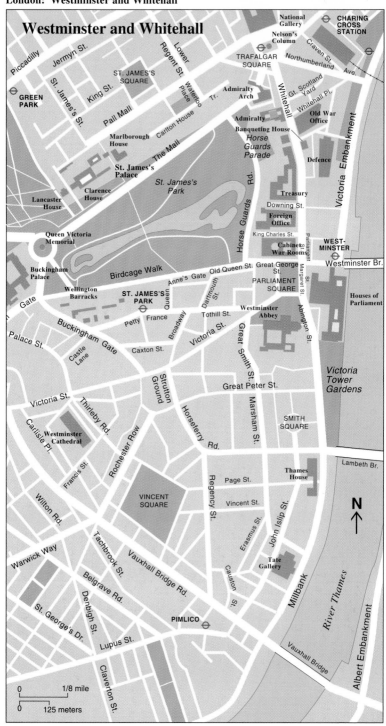

Westminster and Whitehall

NATIONAL GALLERY
Nelson's Column
CHARING CROSS STATION
TRAFALGAR SQUARE
Craven St.
Northumberland Ave.
Piccadilly
Jermyn St.
ST. JAMES'S SQUARE
Lower Regent St.
Waterloo Place
Tr.
Admiralty Arch
Whitehall
Gt. Scotland Yard
Whitehall Pl.
GREEN PARK
St. James's St.
King St.
Pall Mall
Carlton House
Admiralty
Banqueting House
Old War Office
Marlborough House
The Mall
Horse Guards Parade
Defence
St. James's Palace
Lancaster House
Clarence House
St. James's Park
Treasury
Downing St.
Foreign Office
King Charles St.
Victoria Embankment
Queen Victoria Memorial
Horse Guards Rd.
Cabinet War Rooms
WEST-MINSTER
Buckingham Palace
Birdcage Walk
Anne's Gate
Old Queen St.
Great George St.
PARLIAMENT SQUARE
Westminster Br.
Gate
Wellington Barracks
ST. JAMES'S PARK
Queen
Dartmouth St.
Margaret St.
Parliament St.
Houses of Parliament
Palace St.
Buckingham Gate
Petty France
Broadway
Tothill St.
Westminster Abbey
Abingdon St.
Castle Lane
Caxton St.
Victoria St.
Great Smith St.
Victoria Tower Gardens
Victoria St.
Thirleby Rd.
Strutton Ground
Great Peter St.
Carlisle Pl.
Westminster Cathedral
Francis St.
Rochester Row
Horseferry Rd.
Marsham St.
SMITH SQUARE
Lambeth Br.
Page St.
Thames House
VINCENT SQUARE
Regency St.
Vincent St.
John Islip St.
Wilton Rd.
Tachbrook St.
Vauxhall Bridge Rd.
Erasmus St.
Millbank
River Thames
Warwick Way
Belgrave Rd.
Tate Gallery
St. George's Dr.
Denbigh St.
Causton St.
PIMLICO
Albert Embankment
Lupus St.
Vauxhall Bridge
Claverton St.

0   1/8 mile
0   125 meters

N

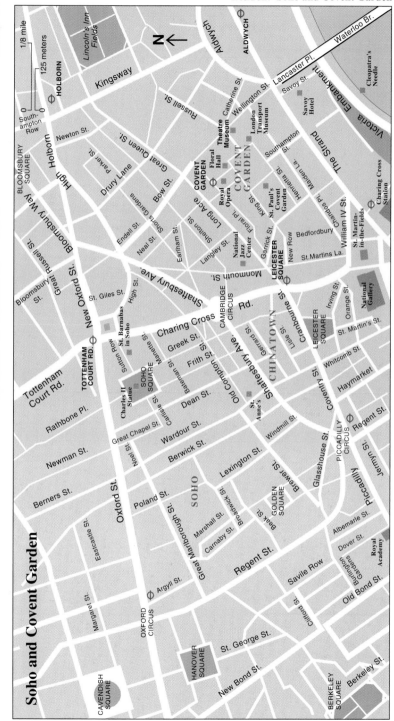

London: Soho and Covent Garden

Soho and Covent Garden

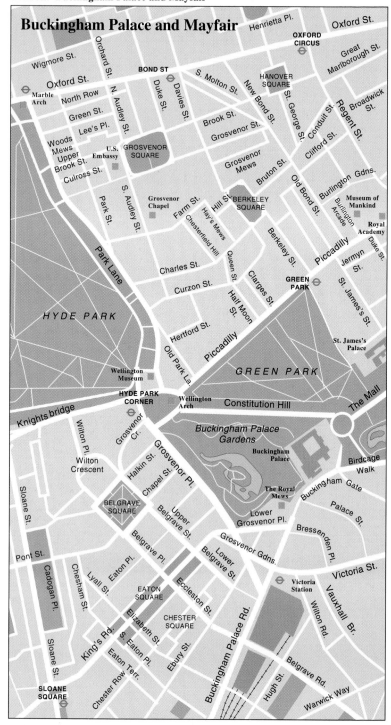

Buckingham Palace and Mayfair

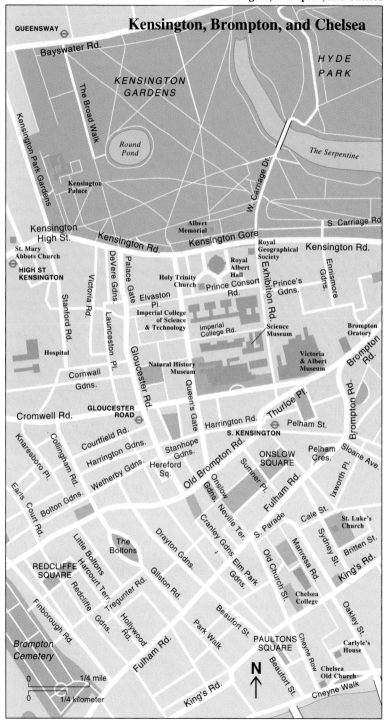

Kensington, Brompton, and Chelsea

QUEENSWAY

Bayswater Rd.

KENSINGTON GARDENS

The Broad Walk

Kensington Park Gardens

HYDE PARK

Round Pond

The Serpentine

W. Carriage Dr.

Kensington Palace

Kensington High St.

St. Mary Abbots Church

HIGH ST KENSINGTON

Albert Memorial

Kensington Rd.

Kensington Gore

S. Carriage Rd

Royal Geographical Society

Kensington Rd.

DeVere Gdns.

Palace Gate

Victoria Rd.

Stanford Rd.

Launceston Pl.

Holy Trinity Church

Royal Albert Hall

Prince Consort Rd.

Exhibition Rd.

Prince's Gdns.

Ennismore Gdns.

Elvaston Pl.

Imperial College of Science & Technology

Imperial College Rd.

Science Museum

Brompton Oratory

Hospital

Gloucester Rd.

Natural History Museum

Victoria & Albert Museum

Brompton Rd.

Cornwall Gdns.

Queen's Gate

Thurloe Pl.

Cromwell Rd.

GLOUCESTER ROAD

Harrington Rd.

Pelham St.

S. KENSINGTON

Knaresboro Pl.

Collingham Rd.

Courtfield Rd.

Stanhope Gdns.

ONSLOW SQUARE

Pelham Cres.

Sloane Ave.

Harrington Gdns.

Hereford Sq.

Old Brompton Rd.

Fulham Rd.

Ixworth Pl.

Earls Court Rd.

Bolton Gdns.

Wetherby Gdns.

Onslow Gdns.

Summer Pl.

S. Parade

Cale St.

St. Luke's Church

Neville Ter.

Sydney St.

Britten St.

Little Boltons

The Boltons

Drayton Gdns.

Cranley Gdns.

Elm Park Gdns.

Manresa Rd.

King's Rd.

REDCLIFFE SQUARE

Harcourt Terr.

Tregunter Rd.

Gilston Rd.

Old Church St.

Oakley St.

Redcliffe Gdns.

Chelsea College

Finborough Rd.

Hollywood Rd.

Beaufort St.

Park Walk

PAULTONS SQUARE

Cheyne Row

Carlyle's House

Brompton Cemetery

Fulham Rd.

Beaufort St.

Chelsea Old Church

0 ____ 1/4 mile

0 ____ 1/4 kilometer

King's Rd.

N

Cheyne Walk

London: City of London

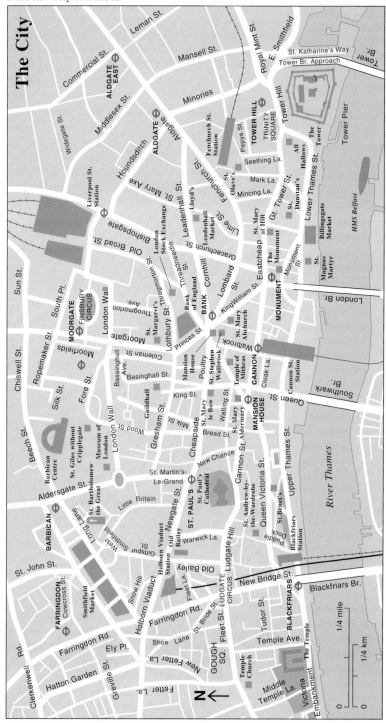

The City

ALDGATE EAST
Commercial St.
Leman St.
Middlesex St.
Mansell St.
Royal Mint St.
E. Smithfield
St. Katharine's Way
Tower Br. Approach
Tower Br.
Widegate St.
Minories
Houndsditch
ALDGATE
Fenchurch St. Station
Pepys St.
TOWER HILL
TRINITY SQUARE
Tower Hill
The Tower
Tower Pier
Liverpool St. Station
St. Mary Axe
Seething La.
All Hallows
Old Broad St.
Bishopsgate
London Stock Exchange
Leadenhall St.
Fenchurch St.
St. Olave's
Mark La.
Mincing La.
St. Dunstan's
Lower Thames St.
Sun St.
Threadneedle St.
Leadenhall Market
Lime St.
Gracechurch St.
St. Mary at Hill
Gt. Tower St.
HMS Belfast
Billingsgate Market
South Pl.
Throgmorton Ave.
St. Margaret's
Bank of England
Cornhill
Lombard St.
Eastcheap
The Monument
Monument St.
MONUMENT
St. Magnus Martyr
London Br.
MOORGATE
FINSBURY CIRCUS
London Wall
Moorgate
Lothbury St.
BANK
Princes St.
King William St.
St. Mary Abchurch
Ropemaker St.
Moorfields
Coleman St.
Mansion House
Poultry
St. Stephen Walbrook
Temple of Mithras
Walbrook
CANNON
Cloak La.
Cannon St. Station
Southwark Br.
Chiswell St.
Silk St.
Fore St.
Basinghall Ave.
Basinghall St.
Guildhall
King St.
Gresham St.
Milk St.
St. Mary le Bow
Watling St.
St. Mary Aldermary
MANSION HOUSE
Cannon St.
Queen St.
Beech St.
Barbican Centre
St. Giles without Cripplegate
Museum of London
Wood St.
Cheapside
Bread St.
River Thames
Aldersgate St.
BARBICAN
Long Lane
St. Bartholomew the Great
Little Britain
St. Martin's-Le-Grand
New Chance
Cannon St.
St. Andrew-by-the-Wardrobe
Queen Victoria St.
St. Benet's
Upper Thames St.
St. John St.
West Smithfield
Giltspur St.
ST. PAUL'S
St. Paul's Cathedral
Old Bailey
Warwick La.
Ludgate Hill
Puddle Dock
Blackfriars Station
FARRINGDON
Cowcross St.
Smithfield Market
Snow Hill
Holborn Viaduct
Holborn Viaduct Station
Old Bailey
Fleet St.
Farringdon Rd.
New Bridge St.
LUDGATE CIRCUS
BLACKFRIARS
Blackfriars Br.
Clerkenwell Rd.
Farringdon Rd.
Ely Pl.
Hatton Garden
Greville St.
Fetter La.
New Fetter La.
Shoe Lane
St. Bride St.
GOUGH SQ.
Fleet St.
Tudor St.
Temple Ave.
Temple Church
The Temple
Victoria Embankment
Middle Temple La.

N

1/4 mile
1/4 km
0